G000292442

STREET ATLAS

Suffolk

Bury St Edmunds, Felixstowe, Ipswich, Lowestoft, Newmarket

First published in 2003 by

Philip's, a division of
Octopus Publishing Group Ltd
2-4 Heron Quays, London E14 4JP

Second edition 2007
First impression 2007
SUFBA

ISBN-10   0-540-08996-6 (spiral)
ISBN-13   978-0-540-08996-3 (spiral)

© Philip's 2007

Ordnance Survey®

This product includes mapping data licensed
from Ordnance Survey® with the permission of
the Controller of Her Majesty's Stationery Office.
© Crown copyright 2007. All rights reserved.
Licence number 100011710.

Ordnance Survey and the OS Symbol are
registered trademarks of Ordnance Survey, the
national mapping agency of Great Britain.

Post Office is a trade mark of Post Office Ltd in
the UK and other countries.

Printed by Toppan, China

Contents

II	**Key to map pages**
IV	**Route planning**
VIII	**Administrative and Postcode boundaries**
1	**Key to map symbols**
2	**Street maps** at 1¾ inches to 1 mile
109	**Street maps** at 3½ inches to 1 mile
154	**Street maps of centres of Bury St Edmunds and Ipswich** at 7 inches to 1 mile
156	**Index** of towns and villages
159	**Index** of streets, hospitals, industrial estates, railway stations, schools, shopping centres, universities and places of interest

Digital Data

The exceptionally high-quality mapping found in this atlas is available as digital data in TIFF format, which is easily convertible to other bitmapped (raster) image formats.

The index is also available in digital form as a standard database table. It contains all the details found in the printed index together with the National Grid reference for the map square in which each entry is named.

For further information and to discuss your requirements, please contact Philip's on 020 7644 6932 or james.mann@philips-maps.co.uk

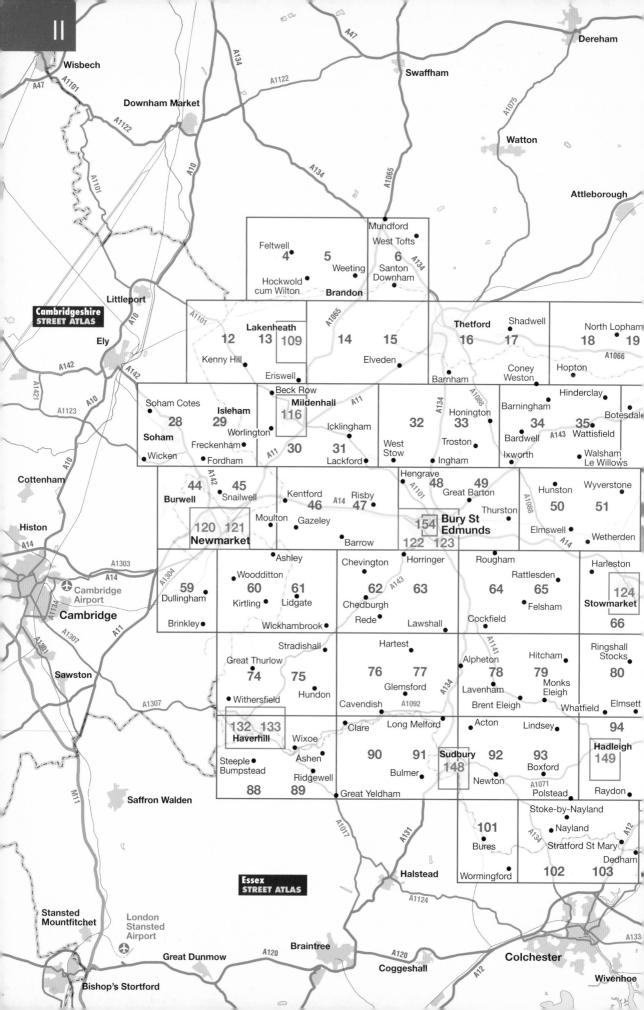

Wisbech

Downham Market

Swaffham

Watton

Dereham

Attleborough

Cambridgeshire STREET ATLAS

Littleport

Ely

Mundford
West Tofts
4 Feltwell
5
Weeting
Santon Downham
6
Brandon
Hockwold cum Wilton

Lakenheath
12 13 109
14 15
Thetford
16 17
Shadwell
North Lopham
18 19
Kenny Hill
Elveden
Hopton
Coney Weston
Eriswell
Barnham
Beck Row
Hinderclay
Mildenhall
Soham Cotes
28 Isleham 29
116
Icklingham
32 33
Honington
Barningham
34 35
Botesdale
Wattisfield
Worlington
Soham
Freckenham
30 31
West Stow
Troston
Bardwell
Ixworth
Walsham Le Willows
Wicken
Fordham
Lackford
Ingham

Cottenham

Histon

Hengrave
44 45
48 49
Hunston
Wyverstone
Burwell
Snailwell
Kentford
Risby
Great Barton
50 51
46 47
Moulton
Gazeley
Thurston
Elmswell
Wetherden
120 121
Newmarket
154 Bury St Edmunds
Barrow
122 123

Cambridge Airport

Cambridge

Ashley
Horringer
Rougham
Harleston
59 60 61
WooddITTon
Chevington
62 63
64 65
Rattlesden
124 Stowmarket
Dullingham
Kirtling
Lidgate
Chedburgh
Cockfield
Felsham
Brinkley
Wickhambrook
Rede
Lawshall
66

Sawston

Ringshall Stocks
Stradishall
Hartest
Alpheton
Hitcham
74 75
76 77
78 79
80
Great Thurlow
Glemsford
Lavenham
Monks Eleigh
Withersfield
Hundon
Cavendish
Brent Eleigh
Whatfield
Elmsett

Acton
Lindsey
94
132 133
Clare
Long Melford
92 93
Hadleigh
Haverhill
Wixoe
90 91
Sudbury 148
Boxford
149
Steeple Bumpstead
Ashen
Bulmer
Newton
Polstead
Raydon
Ridgewell
88 89
Great Yeldham

Saffron Walden

Stoke-by-Nayland
101
Nayland
Bures
Stratford St Mary
Dedham
Wormingford
102 103

Halstead

Essex STREET ATLAS

Stansted Mountfitchet

London Stansted Airport

Braintree

Colchester

Great Dunmow

Coggeshall

Wivenhoe

Bishop's Stortford

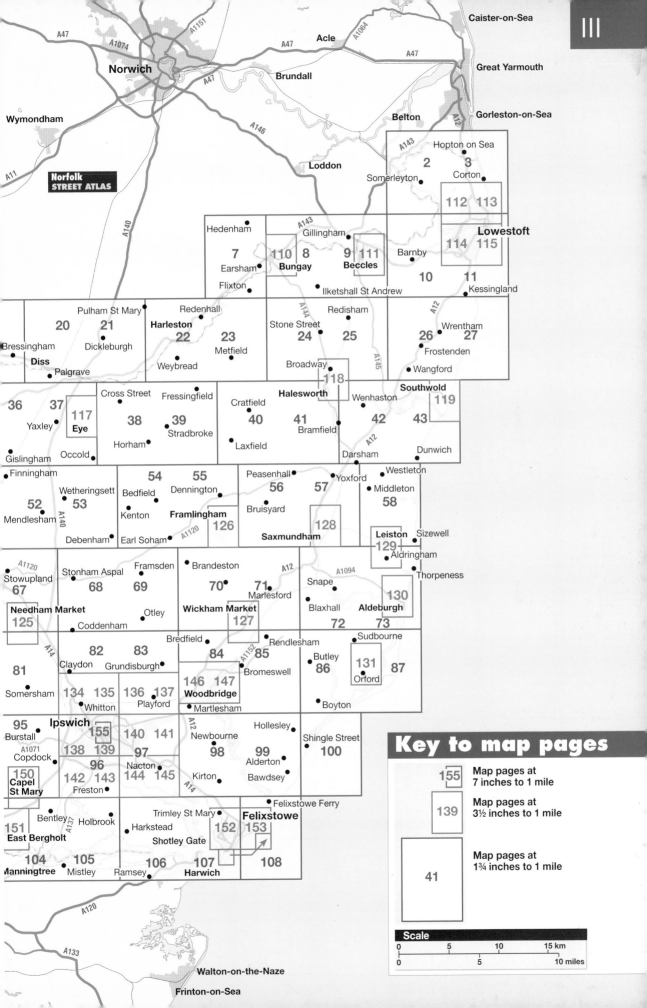

Norfolk
STREET ATLAS

Key to map pages

155	Map pages at 7 inches to 1 mile
139	Map pages at 3½ inches to 1 mile
41	Map pages at 1¾ inches to 1 mile

Scale

0 ———— 5 ———— 10 ———— 15 km

0 ———— 5 ———— 10 miles

Route planning

Scale

0   5   10 km
0   1   2   3   4   5   6 miles

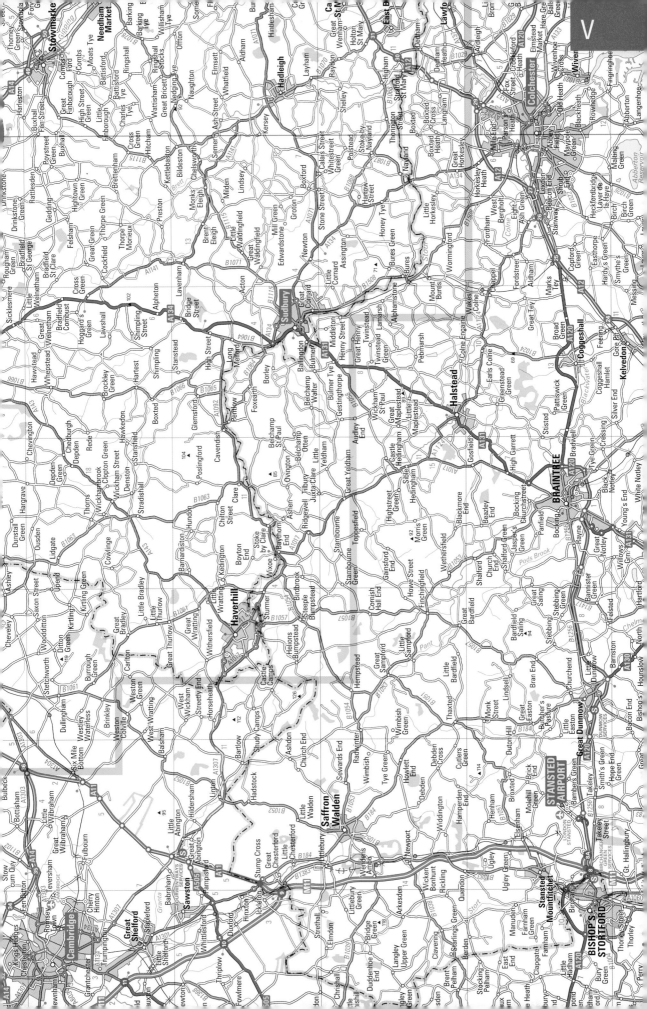

Scale

0   5   10 km

0   1   2   3   4   5   6 miles

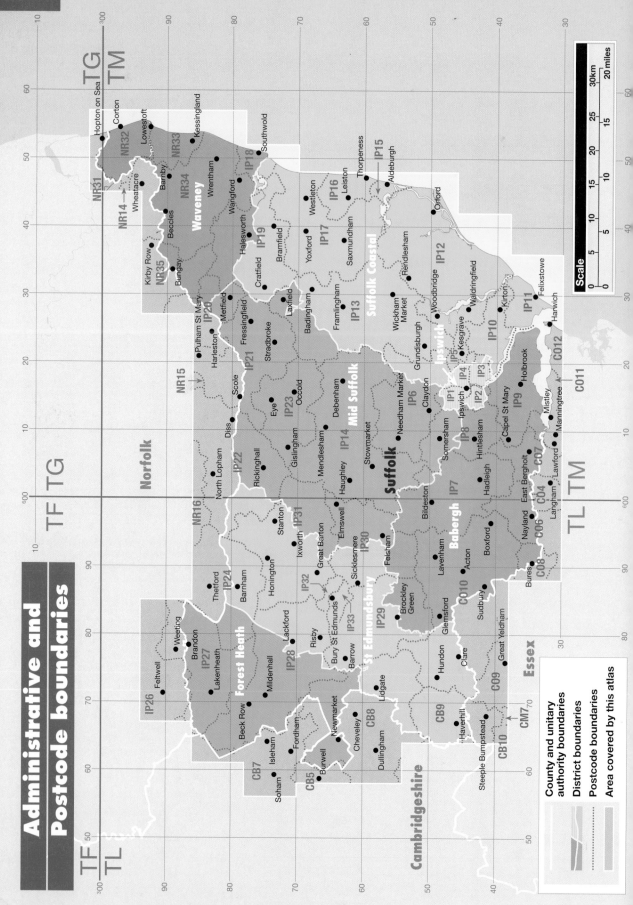

Administrative and Postcode boundaries

Scale

0 5 10 15 20 25 30km
0 5 10 15 20 miles

County and unitary authority boundaries
District boundaries
Postcode boundaries
Area covered by this atlas

Motorway with junction number	
Primary route – dual/single carriageway	
A road – dual/single carriageway	
B road – dual/single carriageway	
Minor road – dual/single carriageway	
Other minor road – dual/single carriageway	
Road under construction	
Tunnel, covered road	
Rural track, private road or narrow road in urban area	
Gate or obstruction to traffic (restrictions may not apply at all times or to all vehicles)	
Path, bridleway, byway open to all traffic, road used as a public path	
Pedestrianised area	
Postcode boundaries	
County and unitary authority boundaries	
Railway, tunnel, railway under construction	
Tramway, tramway under construction	
Miniature railway	
Railway station	
Private railway station	
Metro station	
Tram stop, tram stop under construction	
Bus, coach station	

Walsall

South Shields

◆	Ambulance station
◆	Coastguard station
◆	Fire station
◆	Police station
✚	Accident and Emergency entrance to hospital
Ⓗ	Hospital
+	Place of worship
𝒊	Information Centre (open all year)
🛒	Shopping Centre
P P&R	Parking, Park and Ride
PO	Post Office
⅄ ⏚	Camping site, caravan site
✕	Picnic site
▶	Golf course
Prim Sch	Important buildings, schools, colleges, universities and hospitals
	Built up area
	Woods
River Ouse	Tidal water, water name
	Non-tidal water – lake, river, canal or stream
	Lock, weir, tunnel
Church	Non-Roman antiquity
ROMAN FORT	Roman antiquity
87	Adjoining page indicators and overlap bands
237	The colour of the arrow and the band indicates the scale of the adjoining or overlapping page (see scales below)

Enlarged mapping only

	Railway or bus station building
	Place of interest
	Parkland

Acad	Academy	Inst	Institute	Recn Gd	Recreation Ground
Allot Gdns	Allotments	Ct	Law Court		
Cemy	Cemetery	L Ctr	Leisure Centre	Resr	Reservoir
C Ctr	Civic Centre	LC	Level Crossing	Ret Pk	Retail Park
CH	Club House	Liby	Library	Sch	School
Coll	College	Mkt	Market	Sh Ctr	Shopping Centre
Crem	Crematorium	Meml	Memorial	TH	Town Hall/House
Ent	Enterprise	Mon	Monument	Trad Est	Trading Estate
Ex H	Exhibition Hall	Mus	Museum	Univ	University
Ind Est	Industrial Estate	Obsy	Observatory	W Twr	Water Tower
IRB Sta	Inshore Rescue Boat Station	Pal	Royal Palace	Wks	Works
		PH	Public House	YH	Youth Hostel

■ The small numbers around the edges of the maps identify the 1 kilometre National Grid lines ■ The dark grey border on the inside edge of some pages indicates that the mapping does not continue onto the adjacent page

The scale of the maps on the pages numbered in blue is 5.52 cm to 1 km • 3½ inches to 1 mile • 1: 18103

0	¼	½	¾	1 mile
0	250m	500m	750m	1 kilometre

The scale of the maps on pages numbered in green is 2.76 cm to 1 km • 1¾ inches to 1 mile • 1: 36206

0	¼	½	¾	1 mile
0	250m	500m	750m	1 kilometre

The scale of the maps on pages numbered in red is 11.04 cm to 1 km • 7 inches to 1 mile • 1: 9051

0	220 yards	440 yards	660 yards	½ mile
0	125m	250m	375m	½ kilometre

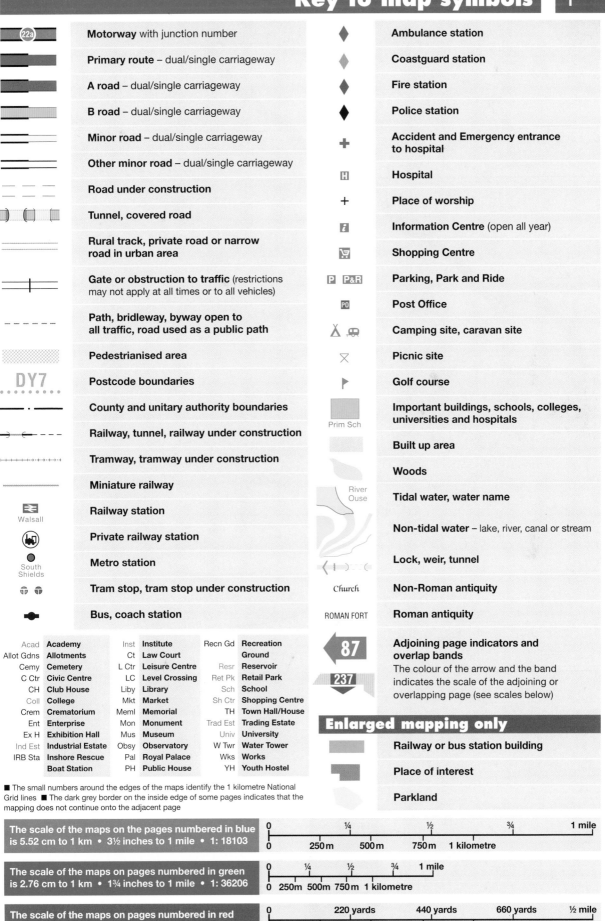

Scale: 1¾ inches to 1 mile

0   ¼   ½ mile
0   250m 500m 750m 1 km

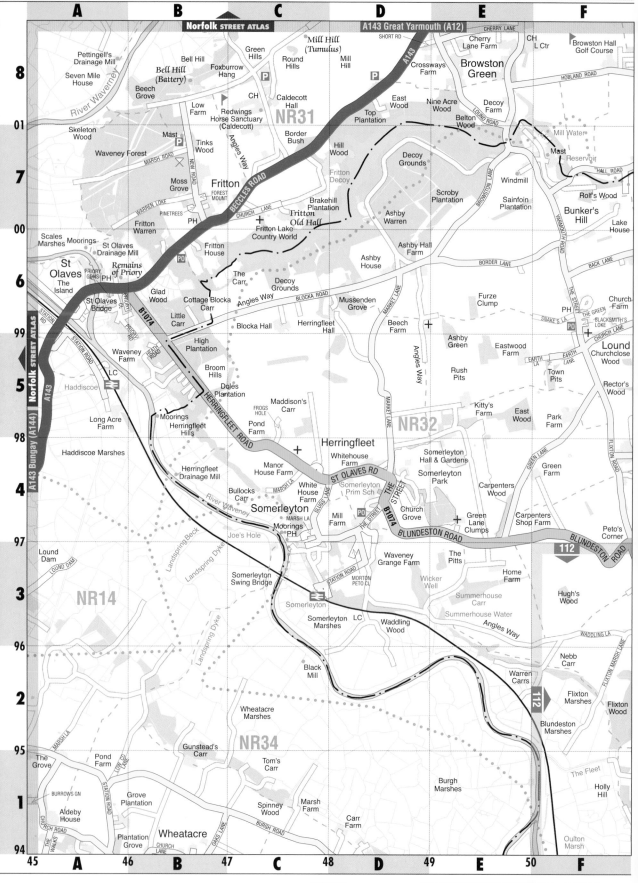

For full street detail of the highlighted area see pages 112 and 113

10

112

Norfolk STREET ATLAS

Scale: 1¾ inches to 1 mile

0   ¼   ½   mile

0 250m 500m 750m 1 km

B7
1 RACKHAM CL
2 RANDALL CL
3 ST MARGARET'S WAY
4 FLOWERDAY CL
5 GROOMES CL
6 HOPTON GDNS

7 HALL RD
8 THE LAURELS
9 WALTERS CL
10 BISHOPS WK
11 MARINERS PK CL
12 JULIAN WY
13 ST CLEMENT MEWS

14 ST VINCENT WK
15 ST CLARE CT

B8
1 THE FAIRWAY
2 MARINER'S CL
3 MARINE CL
4 MEADOW CT
5 JOSHUA CT

B6
1 OLD CHURCH RD
2 CULLEY WY
3 SEAFIELDS DR

C6
1 CADIZ WAY
2 TURIN WAY
3 ZURICH CL
4 GENEVA GDNS
5 NAPLES CL
6 MISBURGH WAY
7 MANOR GD
8 PEBBLE VW WK
9 SANDS CL

A4
1 MEADOWLANDS
2 ORCHARD CL
3 ORCHARD LA
4 MICAWBER MEWS
5 PICKWICK DR
6 DICKENS CT

D4
1 BAKER'S SCORE
2 FOWLER'S CR
3 WIGG'S WY
4 COLMAN RD
5 CORNFIELD CR
6 TIBBENHAM'S SCORE
7 THE CLOSE
8 STATION RD
9 RUBY CL
10 MILLS DR
11 LINDA CL

A12 Great Yarmouth

Hopton on Sea

Hopton
1 ST ANDREW CL
2 BARN CL
3 WATSONS CL

Gorleston Golf Course

Blundeston

Corton

Gunton

Normanston

LOWESTOFT

Lowestoft
North Roads

NR31

NR32

For full street detail of the
highlighted area see pages
112 and 113

112   113   11

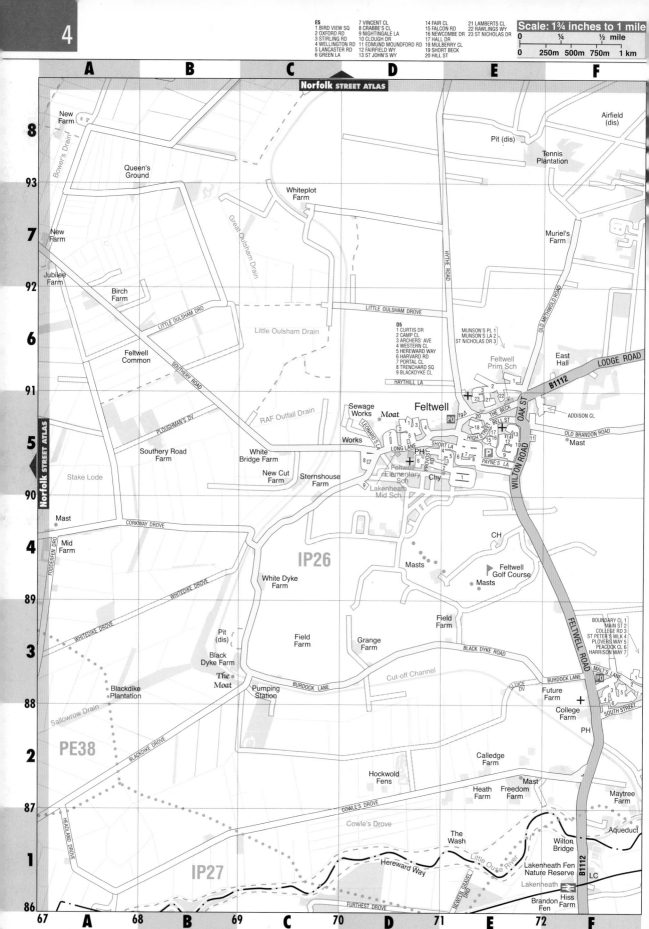

E5
1 BIRD VIEW SQ
2 OXFORD RD
3 STIRLING RD
4 WELLINGTON RD
5 LANCASTER RD
6 GREEN LA

7 VINCENT CL
8 CRABBE'S CL
9 NIGHTINGALE LA
10 CLOUGH DR
11 EDMUND MOUNDFORD RD
12 FAIRFIELD WY
13 ST JOHN'S WY

14 FAIR CL
15 FALCON RD
16 NEWCOMBE DR
17 HALL DR
18 MULBERRY CL
19 SHORT BECK
20 HILL ST

21 LAMBERTS CL
22 RAWLINGS WY
23 ST NICHOLAS DR

Scale: 1¾ inches to 1 mile

0   ¼   ½   mile

0   250m   500m   750m   1 km

Norfolk STREET ATLAS

D5
1 CURTIS DR
2 CAMP CL
3 ARCHERS' AVE
4 WESTERN CL
5 HEREWARD WAY
6 HARVARD RD
7 PORTAL CL
8 TRENCHARD SQ
9 BLACKDYKE CL

MUNSON'S PL 1
MUNSON'S LA 2
ST NICHOLAS DR 3

Feltwell

IP26

PE38

IP27

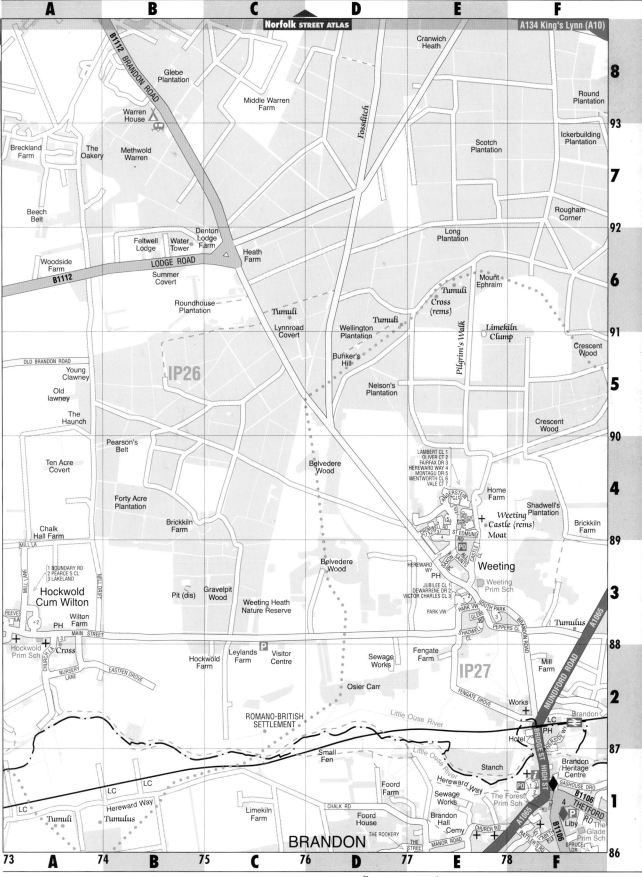

Scale: 1¾ inches to 1 mile
0 ¼ ½ mile
0 250m 500m 750m 1 km

6

5

A B C D E F

Norfolk STREET ATLAS

A134 King's Lynn (A10)

8
93
7
92
6
91
5
90
4
89
3
88
2
87
1
86

Cranwich Heath

Round Plantation

Ickerbuilding Plantation

Breckland Farm

The Oakery

Methwold Warren

Glebe Plantation

Middle Warren Farm

Fossditch

Scotch Plantation

Rougham Corner

Warren House

Beech Belt

Feltwell Lodge

Water Tower

Denton Lodge Farm

Heath Farm

Long Plantation

Woodside Farm

B1112

LODGE ROAD

Summer Covert

Roundhouse Plantation

Mount Ephraim

Tumuli Cross (rems)

Tumuli

Limekiln Clump

Crescent Wood

Young Clawney

OLD BRANDON ROAD

IP26

Tumuli

Lynnroad Covert

Wellington Plantation

Tumuli

Bunker's Hill

Pilgrim's Walk

Old lawney

The Haunch

Nelson's Plantation

Crescent Wood

Pearson's Belt

Belvedere Wood

LAMBERT CL 1
OLIVER CT 2
FAIRFAX DR 3
HEREWARD WAY 4
MONTAGU DR 5
WENTWORTH CL 6
VALE CT 7

Ten Acre Covert

Forty Acre Plantation

Home Farm

Shadwell's Plantation

Weeting Castle (rems) Moat

Brickkiln Farm

Chalk Hall Farm

Brickkiln Farm

ARGERSTEIN CL

CROMWELL RD

ST EDMUND RD

Belvedere Wood

HEREWARD WY PH

SAXON CL

ALL SAINTS

CASTLE CL

Weeting

1 BOUNDARY RD
2 PEARCE'S CL
3 LAKELAND

Hockwold Cum Wilton

MILL LANE

MILL DRIFT

Pit (dis)

Gravelpit Wood

Weeting Heath Nature Reserve

JUBILEE CL 1
DEWARRENE DR 2
VICTOR CHARLES CL 3

Weeting Prim Sch

REEVES LA

Wilton Farm

PH

MAIN STREET

Park VW

SOUTH PARK

Park VW

GLEBE RD

BRANDON ROAD

PEPPERS CL

Tumulus

A1065

Hockwold Prim Sch

Cross

CHURCH LA

NURSERY LANE

EASTFEN DROVE

Hockwold Farm

Leylands Farm

Visitor Centre

Sewage Works

Fengate Farm

SHADWELL CL

IP27

Mill Farm

Osier Carr

FENGATE DROVE

Works

MUNDFORD ROAD

Brandon

LC

ROMANO-BRITISH SETTLEMENT

Little Ouse River

Hotel

BRIDGE ST

PH

RIVERSIDE WY

Small Fen

Little Ouse River

Stanch

HIGH ST

PO

Brandon Heritage Centre

GASHOUSE DRO

LC

Hereward Way

Tumuli

Tumulus

Hereward Way

CHALK RD

Foord Farm

Sewage Works

Brandon Hall Cemy

The Forest Prim Sch

A1065

B1106

THETFORD RD

Liby

Limekiln Farm

Foord House

CHURCH RD

RATTLER'S RD

B1106

The Glade Prim Sch

SPRUCE DR

BRANDON

THE ROOKERY

MANOR ROAD

THE STREET

F1
1 COULSON LA
2 SUFFOLK CT
3 GENTLE CT
4 GEORGE ST

For full street detail of Brandon see
Philip's STREET ATLAS of Norfolk

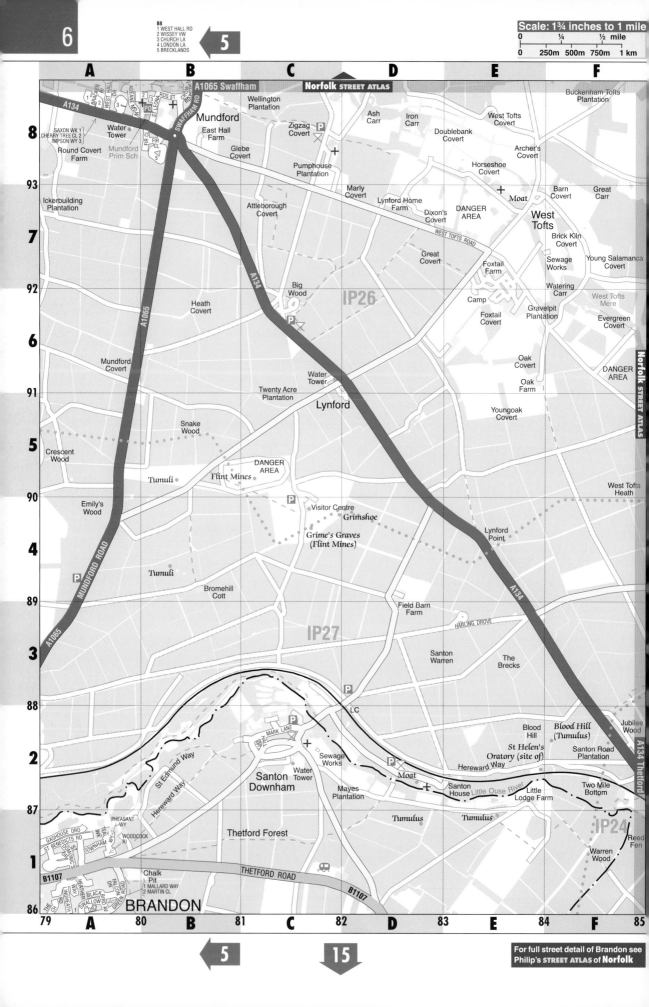

B8
1 WEST HALL RD
2 WISSEY VW
3 CHURCH LA
4 LONDON LA
5 BRECKLANDS
5

A   B   C   D   E   F

A1065 Swaffham

Norfolk STREET ATLAS

8

SAXON WK 1
CHERRY TREE CL 2
IMPSON WY 3

Round Covert
Farm

Water
Tower

Mundford
Prim Sch

Mundford

East Hall
Farm

Glebe
Covert

Wellington
Plantation

Zigzag
Covert

Pumphouse
Plantation

Ash
Carr

Iron
Carr

Doublebank
Covert

West Tofts
Covert

Buckenham Tofts
Plantation

Archer's
Covert

Horseshoe
Covert

93

Ickerbuilding
Plantation

Attleborough
Covert

Marly
Covert

Lynford Home
Farm

Dixon's
Covert

DANGER
AREA

Moat

Barn
Covert

Great
Carr

West
Tofts

7

WEST TOFTS ROAD

Brick Kiln
Covert

Young Salamanca
Covert

92

Heath
Covert

Big
Wood

Great
Covert

Foxtail
Farm

Camp

Sewage
Works

Watering
Carr

Gravelpit
Plantation

West Tofts
Mere

Evergreen
Covert

IP26

6

Mundford
Covert

Water
Tower

Foxtail
Covert

Oak
Covert

DANGER
AREA

91

Twenty Acre
Plantation

Lynford

Oak
Farm

Youngoak
Covert

5

Crescent
Wood

Snake
Wood

Tumuli

Flint Mines

DANGER
AREA

West Tofts
Heath

90

Emily's
Wood

Visitor Centre

Grimshoe

Grime's Graves
(Flint Mines)

Lynford
Point

4

Tumuli

Bromehill
Cott

Field Barn
Farm

HARLING DROVE

89

IP27

3

Santon
Warren

The
Brecks

88

LC

Blood
Hill

Blood Hill
(Tumulus)

Jubilee
Wood

2

St Edmund Way

Hereward Way

Santon
Downham

Water
Tower

Sewage
Works

Mayes
Plantation

Moat

Santon
House

Hereward Way

St Helen's
Oratory (site of)

Little Ouse River

Santon Road
Plantation

Little
Lodge Farm

Two Mile
Bottom

87

PHEASANT
WY

WOODCOCK
RI

Hereward Way

Thetford Forest

Tumulus

Tumulus

IP24

Warren
Wood

Reed
Fen

1

GASHOUSE DRO

ST BENEDICTS RD

Chalk
Pit

1 MALLARD WAY
2 MARTIN CL

THETFORD ROAD

B1107

B1107

86

B1107

BRANDON

79   80   81   82   83   84   85

A   B   C   D   E   F

5

15

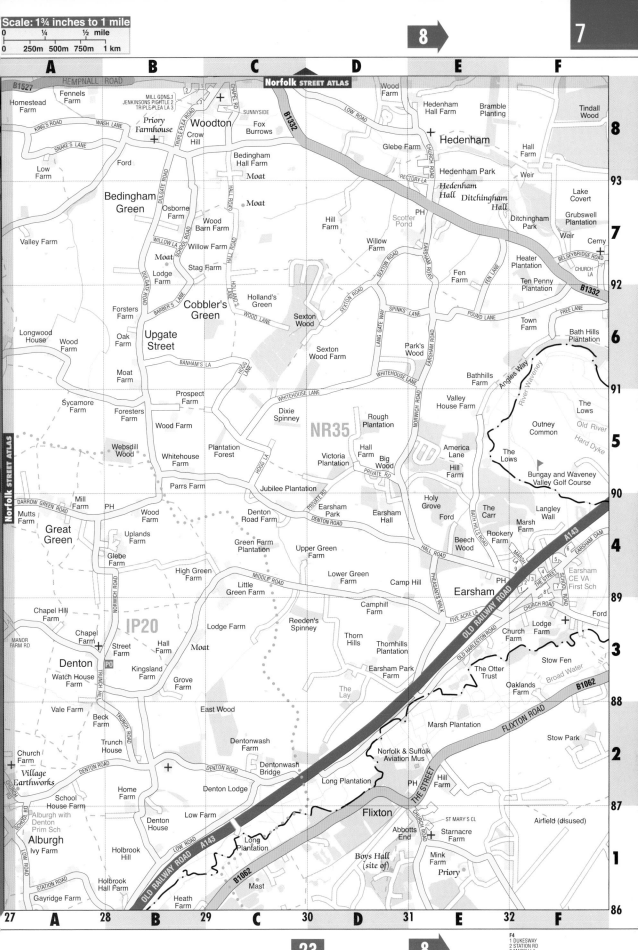

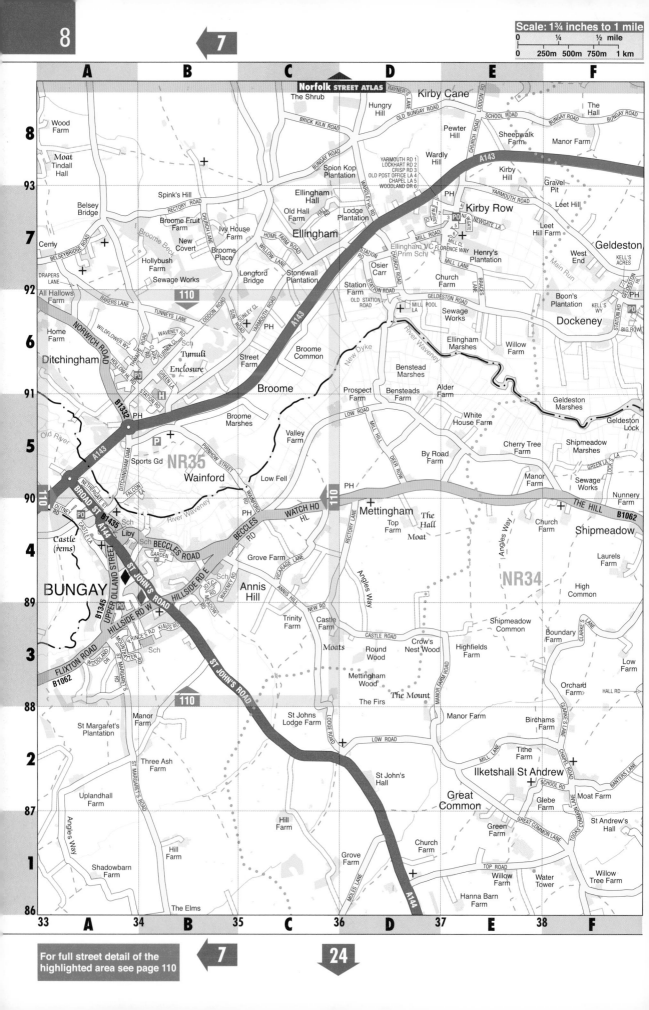

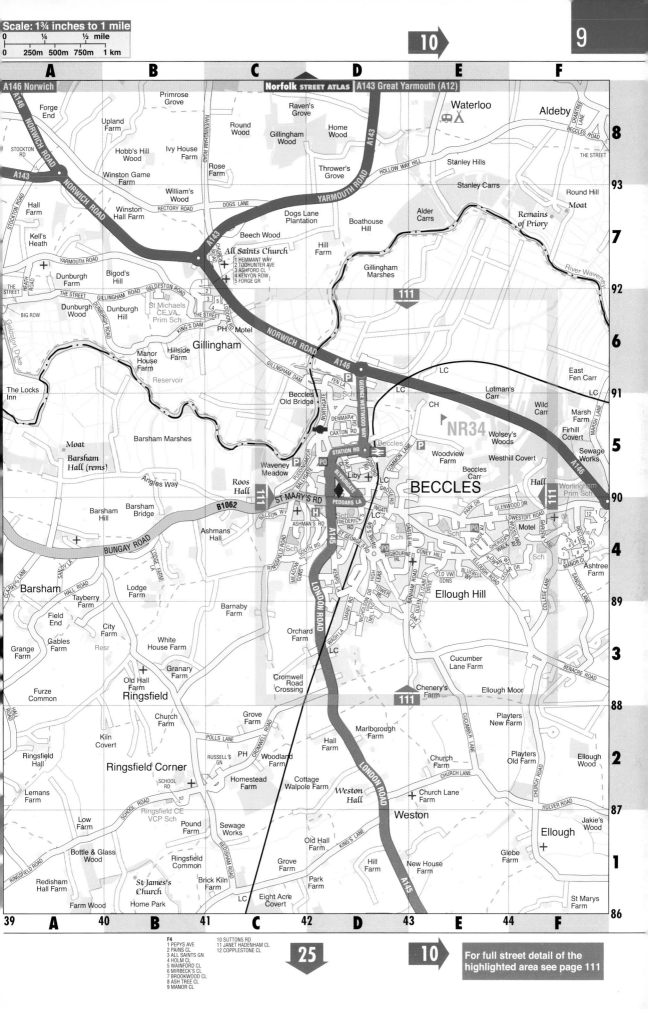

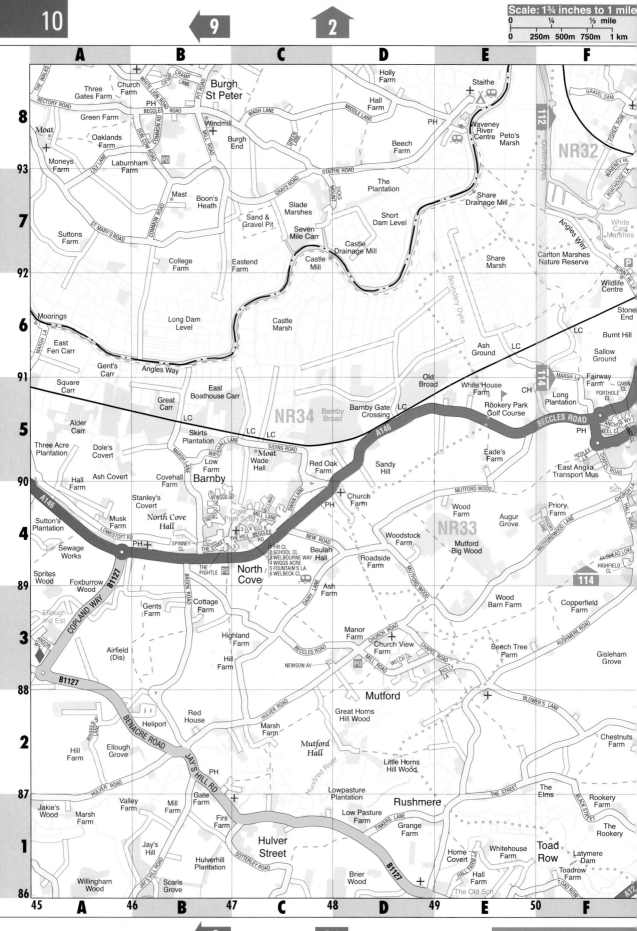

9
2

Scale: 1¾ inches to 1 mile

0   ¼   ½   mile
0   250m   500m   750m   1 km

Row 8

THE WALKS
RECTORY ROAD
Three Gates Farm
Church Farm
WHITE LION ROAD
PIT LANE
CRAMP LANE
Burgh St Peter
Holly Farm
Staithe
NR32
GRAVEL DAM
FISHER ROW

Green Farm
BECCLES ROAD
Hall Farm
MIDDLE LANE
PH
Waveney River Centre
Peto's Marsh
112
Outton Dyke
WAVENEY HILL
BOATHOUSE LA
WAVENEY LA

Moat
Oaklands Farm
DUN COW ROAD
COMMON ROAD
Burgh End
Windmill
WASH LANE
Beech Farm

Row 93

Moneys Farm
Laburnham Farm
LILY LANE
PO
Mast
Boon's Heath
GRAYS ROAD
Slade Marshes
STAITHE ROAD
DUCKS MOUNT
The Plantation
Share Drainage Mill
Carlton Marshes Nature Reserve
Angles Way
White Cast Marshes
BURNT HILL

Row 7

Suttons Farm
ST MARY'S ROAD
COMMON ROAD
College Farm
Eastend Farm
Sand & Gravel Pit
Seven Mile Carr
Castle Mill
Castle Drainage Mill
Short Dam Level
Share Marsh
Wildlife Centre
Stone End
Burnt Hill
Sallow Ground

Row 92

Fairway Farm
114
MARSH LA
CABIN LA
PORTHOLE CL

Row 6

Moorings
East Fen Carr
MARSH LA
Gent's Carr
Angles Way
Long Dam Level
Castle Marsh
Boundary Dyke
Ash Ground
LC
LC
Long Plantation
ANCHOR WY
KEEL CL
MAST CL

Row 91

Square Carr
Great Carr
East Boathouse Carr
Old Broad
White House Farm
CH
Rookery Park Golf Course
BECCLES ROAD
PH

Row 5

Alder Carr
Three Acre Plantation
Dole's Covert
Skirts Plantation
MARSH LANE
WADEHALL LANE
SIDING ROAD
LC
LC
LC
NR34
Barnby Broad
Barnby Gate Crossing
LC
A146
Eade's Farm
East Anglia Transport Mus
HEDLEY
CHAPEL ROAD
Sch
CHURCH ROAD

Row 90

Hall Farm
Ash Covert
Covehall Farm
Barnby
Low Farm
Moat
Wade Hall
Red Oak Farm
Church Farm
MUTFORD WOOD
Wood Farm
Priory Farm
A146
Stanley's Covert
North Cove Hall
PINEWOOD RD
Cove Prim Sch
MILL LANE
SWAN LANE
Sandy Hill
Augur Grove

Row 4

Sutton's Plantation
Sewage Works
Musk Farm
LOWESTOFT RD
PH
SPINNEY CL
THE STREET
THE HILL
BECCLES RD
1 FIR CL
2 SCHOOL CL
3 WELBOURNE WAY
4 WIGGS ACRE
5 FOUNTAIN'S LA
6 WELBECK CL
Beulah Hall
NEW ROAD
Woodstock Farm
Roadside Farm
NR33
Mutford Big Wood
Wood Barn Farm
MUTFORDWOOD LANE
FAIRHEAD LOKE
HIGHFIELD CL
Copperfield Farm

Row 89

Sprites Wood
Foxburrow Wood
B1127
COPLAND WAY
Gents Farm
Cottage Farm
BROOK ROAD
THE PIGHTLE
PO
North Cove
DAIRY LANE
Ash Farm
CHURCH ROAD
MUTFORD WOOD
Wood Barn Farm
RUSHMERE ROAD
114

Row 3

Ellough Ind Est
ANSON WY
Airfield (Dis)
Highland Farm
Hill Farm
BECCLES ROAD
NEWSON AV
Manor Farm
Church View Farm
MILL ROAD
WELCH CL
CHAPEL ROAD
HOLLY LA
Beech Tree Farm
Gisleham Grove

Row 88

B1127
Heliport
Red House
Marsh Farm
HULVER ROAD
Mutford
Great Horns Hill Wood
Mutford Hall
BLOWER'S LANE
Chestnuts Farm

Row 2

WARREN LANE
Hill Farm
Ellough Grove
BENACRE ROAD
JAY'S HILL RD
PH
Little Horns Hill Wood
Hundred River

Row 87

HULVER ROAD
Valley Farm
Mill Farm
Gate Farm
Firs Farm
Lowpasture Plantation
Low Pasture Farm
TINKERS LANE
Grange Farm
Rushmere
THE STREET
The Elms
BLACK STREET
Rookery Farm
The Rookery

Row 1

Jakie's Wood
Marsh Farm
Jay's Hill
JAY'S HILL ROAD
Hulverhill Plantation
SOTTERLEY ROAD
Hulver Street
B1127
Brier Wood
Home Covert
HALL FARM LA
Whitehouse Farm
Hall Farm
Toad Row
Latymere Dam
Toadrow Farm
TOAD ROW

Row 86

Willingham Wood
Scarls Grove
The Old Sch
A12

Bottom grid labels: 45 A 46 B 47 C 48 D 49 E 50 F

9
26

For full street detail of the highlighted area see page 114

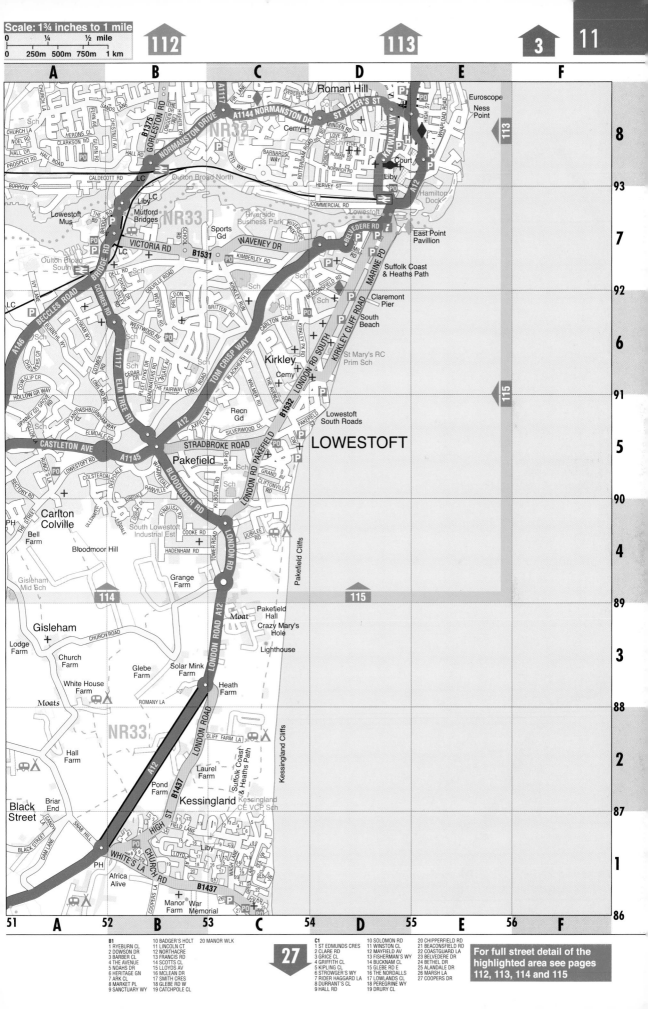

Scale: 1¾ inches to 1 mile

| 0 | ¼ | ½ mile |

| 0 | 250m | 500m | 750m | 1 km |

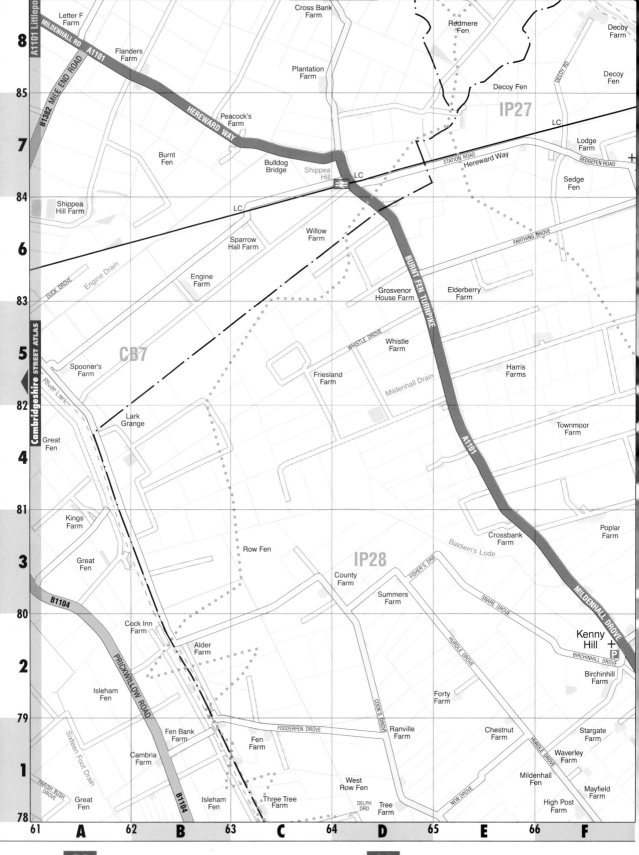

Norfolk STREET ATLAS

A1101 Littleport

B1382 MILE END ROAD

MILDENHALL RD

A1101

Letter F Farm

Flanders Farm

HEREWARD WAY

Peacock's Farm

Burnt Fen

Bulldog Bridge

Shippea Hill

Shippea Hill Farm

LC

Sparrow Hall Farm

Willow Farm

Cross Bank Farm

Plantation Farm

Redmere Fen

Decoy Farm

Decoy Fen

IP27

Decoy Fen

DECOY RD

LC

Lodge Farm

SEDGEFEN ROAD

STATION ROAD

Hereward Way

LC

Sedge Fen

FARTHING DROVE

DUCK DROVE

Engine Drain

Engine Farm

Grosvenor House Farm

Elderberry Farm

BURNT FEN TURNPIKE

CB7

Spooner's Farm

River Lark

Lark Grange

Great Fen

Whistle Farm

WHISTLE DROVE

Friesland Farm

Mildenhall Drain

Harris Farms

A1101

Townmoor Farm

Kings Farm

Great Fen

Row Fen

IP28

County Farm

Baldwin's Lode

FISHER'S DRO

Crossbank Farm

Poplar Farm

B1104

Cock Inn Farm

Alder Farm

PRICKWILLOW ROAD

Summers Farm

SNARE DROVE

HURDLE DROVE

Kenny Hill

MILDENHALL DROVE

BIRCHINHILL DROVE

Birchinhill Farm

Isleham Fen

Sixteen Foot Drain

Fen Bank Farm

FODDERFEN DROVE

Fen Farm

COOK'S DRIVE

Ranville Farm

Forty Farm

Chestnut Farm

HURDLE DROVE

Stargate Farm

Waverley Farm

Cambria Farm

PARISH BUSH DROVE

Great Fen

B1104

Isleham Fen

Three Tree Farm

DELPH DRO

West Row Fen

Tree Farm

NEW DROVE

Mildenhall Fen

High Post Farm

Mayfield Farm

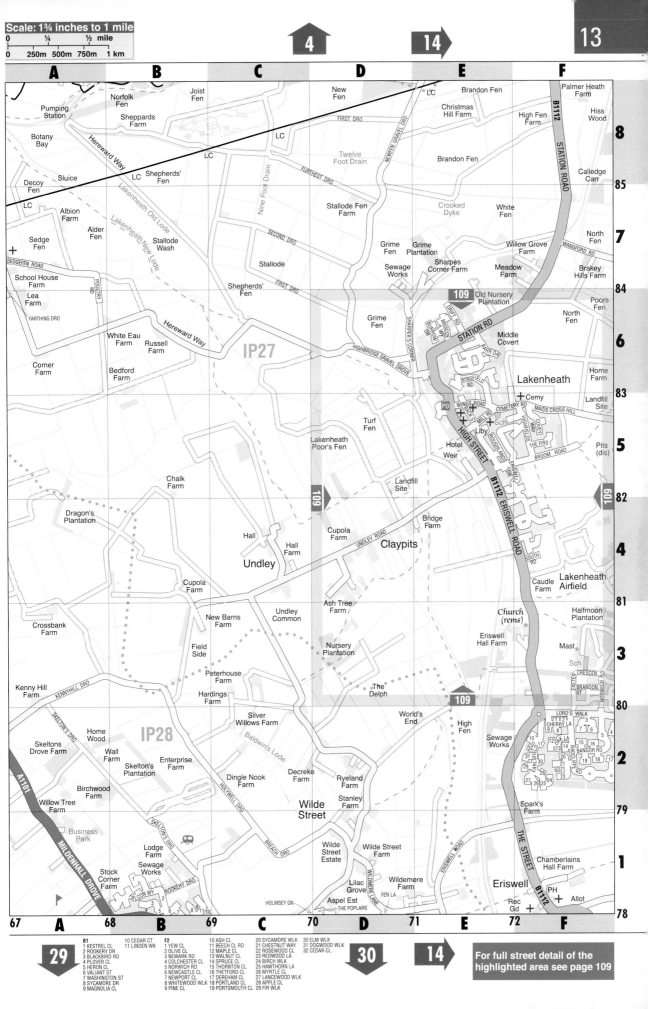

A   B   C   D   E   F

8
85
7
84
6
83
5
82
4
81
3
80
2
79
1
78

Pumping Station

Norfolk Fen

Joist Fen

New Fen

Brandon Fen

Palmer Heath Farm

Botany Bay

Sheppards Farm

Christmas Hill Farm

High Fen Farm

Hiss Wood

Hereward Way

FIRST DRO

LC

Decoy Fen

Sluice

Shepherds' Fen

LC

Twelve Foot Drain

FURTHEST DRO

Brandon Fen

Calledge Carr

Albion Farm

Alder Fen

Stallode Wash

Lakenheath Old Lode

Lakenheath New Lode

NINE FOOT DRAIN

SECOND DRO

Stallode

Stallode Fen Farm

Crooked Dyke

White Fen

North Fen

WANGFORD RD

Sedge Fen

SEDGEFEN ROAD

School House Farm

Lea Farm

POULTRY RD

Shepherds' Fen

FIRST DRO

Grime Fen

Grime Plantation

Sharpes Corner Farm

Willow Grove Farm

Meadow Farm

Brakey Hills Farm

Sewage Works

DRIFT RD

BRISCOE BURRW

STATION RD

109 Old Nursery Plantation

Poors Fen

FARTHING DRO

White Eau Farm

Russell Farm

Hereward Way

Grime Fen

HIGHBRIDGE GRAVEL DROVE

SHARPER'S CORNER

PARR DR

Station Rd

Middle Covert

North Fen

Corner Farm

Bedford Farm

IP27

WINGFIELD RD

Lakenheath

Home Farm

PO

Cemy

Landfill Site

Chalk Farm

Turf Fen

Lakenheath Poor's Fen

HIGH STREET

WINGS ROAD

Liby

MILL RD

CEMETERY RD

Sch

HIGHELDS

MAIDS CROSS HILL

Pits (dis)

Dragon's Plantation

109

Hotel Weir

Landfill Site

BROOM ROAD

THE FIRS

B1112 ERISWELL ROAD

109

Hall

Hall Farm

Cupola Farm

Cupola Farm

Bridge Farm

SOUTH DR

Caudle Farm

Lakenheath Airfield

Undley

Claypits

UNDLEY ROAD

Crossbank Farm

New Barns Farm

Undley Common

Ash Tree Farm

Church (rems)

Halfmoon Plantation

Field Side

Nursery Plantation

Eriswell Hall Farm

Mast

Sch

CRESCEN

EXETER ST

NORWICH CL

Kenny Hill Farm

KENNYHILL DRO

Peterhouse Farm

Hardings Farm

The Delph

109

World's End

High Fen

BRANDON ST

LORD'S WALK

CHERRY LA

A1101

SKELTON'S DRO

Home Wood

Wall Farm

Skelton's Plantation

Enterprise Farm

Silver Willows Farm

Baldwin's Lode

Decreke Farm

Ryeland Farm

Sewage Works

Spark's Farm

BANGOR RD

CARLSFIELD

RADCLIFF

Skeltons Drove Farm

IP28

DINGLE NOOK DRO

HOLWELL DRO

Stanley Farm

Birchwood Farm

MILDENHALL DROVE

Willow Tree Farm

Business Park

SKELTON'S DRO

BREACH DRO

Lodge Farm

Sewage Works

Wilde Street

Wilde Street Estate

Wilde Street Farm

Wilde Street Farm

Chamberlains Hall Farm

THE STREET

B1112

PH

Stock Corner Farm

ROOKERY DRO

Lilac Grove

WILDMERE LANE

FEN LA

Eriswell

Rec Gd

Allot

HOLMSEY GN

Aspel Est THE POPLARS

Wildemere Farm

ERISWELL ROAD

67   A   68   B   69   C   70   D   71   E   72   F

B1
1 KESTREL CL
2 ROOKERY DR
3 BLACKBIRD RD
4 PLOVER CL
5 HERON CL
6 VALIANT ST
7 WASHINGTON ST
8 SYCAMORE DR
9 MAGNOLIA CL
10 CEDAR CT
11 LINDEN WK

F2
1 YEW CL
2 OLIVE CL
3 NEWARK RD
4 COLCHESTER CL
5 NORWICH RD
6 NEWCASTLE CL
7 NEWPORT CL
8 WHITEWOOD WLK
9 PINE CL
10 ASH CL
11 BEECH CL RD
12 MAPLE CL
13 WALNUT CL
14 SPRUCE CL
15 THORNTON CL
16 THETFORD CL
17 DEREHAM CL
18 PORTLAND CL
19 PORTSMOUTH CL
20 SYCAMORE WLK
21 CHESTNUT WAY
22 ROSEWOOD LA
23 REDWOOD LA
24 BIRCH WLK
25 HAWTHORN LA
26 MYRTLE CL
27 LANCEWOOD WLK
28 APPLE CL
29 FIR WLK
30 ELM WLK
31 DOGWOOD WLK
32 CEDAR CL

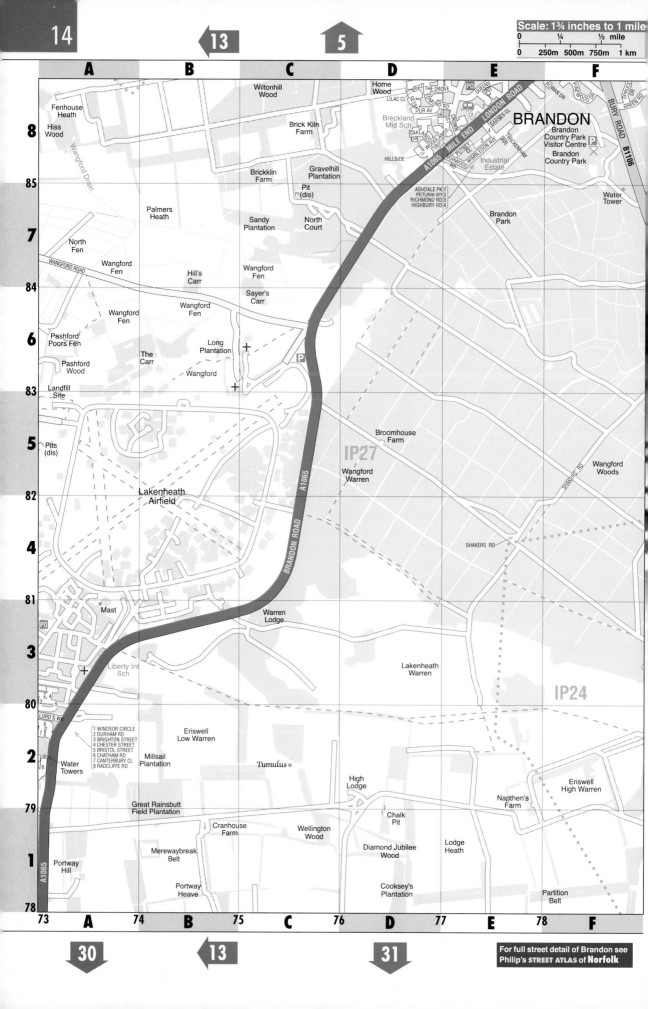

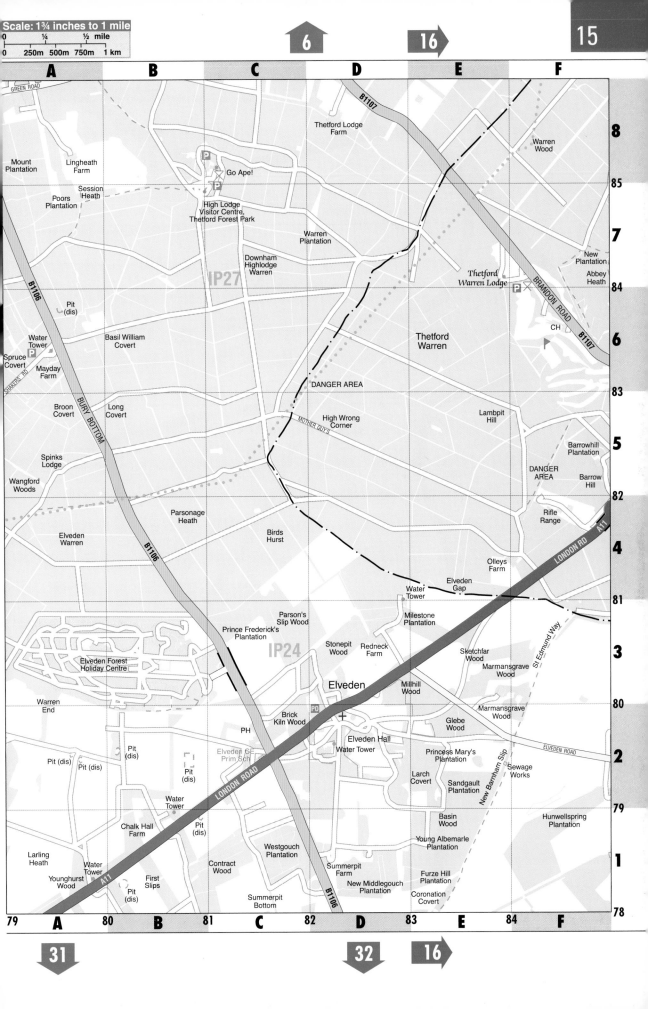

16

A5
1 MONTPELIER DR
2 NEW ENGLAND WAY
3 PORTLAND PL
4 MAINE ST
5 NEW HAMPSHIRE WAY
6 BOSTON END

15

B6
1 ABBEY FARM JUN SCH
2 CANTERBURY INF SCH

C7
1 RALEIGH INF SCH
2 ADMIRALS JUN SCH
3 DRAKE INF SCH

Scale: 1¾ inches to 1 mile
0   ¼   ½ mile
0   250m 500m 750m   1 km

Norfolk STREET ATLAS

A134 King's Lynn (A10)   A1075 Watton   A11 Norwich

8

Little Ouse River
St Edmund Way
Chisley Vale
New Plantation
Breck Plantation
Box Covert
Dreadnought
Ladyship Wood
Hockham Belt
Milestone Plantation

85

Lodge Farm
Gallows Hill
Blakeney Farm
Jane's Wood
Landfill Site
LC
Tollgate Wood
Waterloo Wood
Diamond Plantation

7

Abbey Heath
WYATT WY
LODGE
BRUNEL WY
FISON WY
HOWLETT WY
ST HELENS WY
ANNE BARTHOLOMEW
CROXTON ROAD
Rosemary Musker County High Sch
BETJEMAN
TENNYSON WY
SHELLEY WY
WOODLANDS DR
THE GLADE
Field Barn Farm
Spruce Covert
War Memorial
D7
1 ETHELREDA DR
2 LAWRENCE RD
3 PETER DRIVE
4 PENNYCRESS DR
5 CHARLOCK RD

Depot
STURSTON CL
RICHARD EASTER RD
FAIRFIELDS
CHURCHILL RD
HARWOOD RD
Superstore
Kilverstone Hall

84

Croxton End
Thetford
Sewage Works
EXETER WY
CANTERBURY WY
MOMGATE
STATION RD
VICARAGE RD
Norwich Road Sch
Norwich Road
MALLOW RD
CORIANDER
BIRCH COVERT
Broom Covert
Mount Plantation
Snarehill Hall
Church (rems)

6

B1107 BRANDON RD
Weir
HALING CL
CONEY CL
CANTERBURY
LONDON ROAD
Mus
Thetford Cottage
Thetford Grammar Sch
NORWICH ROAD
GROVE LA
NORFOLK SQ
CARAWAY
PO
H
HURTH WY
Thetford
Weir
Limekiln Plantation
Square Covert

83

BRANDON ROAD
BRIDGE
MACKENZIE RD
ST JOHN'S
ST MARTINS
SPENCER WY
STEPHEN RD
Church
Mag Ct
Liby
Castle Street
RAMPART
Motte and Bailey
Church
A1066
THETFORD
IP24
Snarehill Wood

5

A11
Ind Est
Cemy
Queensway Inf Sch
ICKNIELD WY
NUNS BRIDGES RD
Church
Nuns Bridges
ARLINGTON WY
D6
1 MALLOW RD
2 CUTHBERT CL
3 GEORGE RD
4 HAZEL COVERT
5 COVERT SYCAMORE
6 ALDER COVERT
7 VALERIAN RISE
8 CHERVIL WALK
The Slough
Oak Wood

Superstore
Forest Retail Park
BURRELL WY
KINGS BELT
NAPIER PL
FILMERSTON RD
Queensway
Charles Burrell High Sch
Playing Field
KESTREL CL
Snarehill Farm

82

Forest Retail Park
LONDON ROAD
STEPHENSON WY
ELM ROAD
ASH
ALMOND GR
FRI ROAD
PO
A134
Nunnery Stud
Tutt Hill
Tutt Hill (Tumulus)
Seven Hills Plantation

B5
1 SAXON PL
2 NELSON CR
3 ST MARGARET'S CR
4 JUBILEE CL
5 Thetford Adult Ed Ctr
6 Redcastle Furze Prim Sch
7 Queensway Com Jun Sch

KELVIN PL
Barnhamcross Common
BURY ROAD
Nature Reserve
Seven Hills (Barrow Cemetery)
Seven Hills

4

St Edmund Way
Boundary Belt
Aughton Spinney
Barnham Camp
Barnham Cross (rems)
Great Snare Hill
Elder Hill
County Hole
Weir
Ashfen Carr

3

Gorse Industrial Estate
Pit (dis)
Warren Plantation
Black Carr
Gravelpit Plantation

80

Water Tower
Thetford Heath National Nature Reserve
Pig Farm
PH
Pit (dis)
Barnham Heath
Warren Cott
Rushfordroad Belts

2

ELVEDEN ROAD
St Martin's (rems)
Low Wood
WATER LA
Pit (dis)
Tumulus
Barnham Carr
Severals Plantation
THETFORD ROAD
RUSHFORD ROAD
Long Spinney
Long Spinney

79

North Farm
STATION ROAD
Works
Tumulus
THE STREET
CHURCH LA
THE STREET
Barnham
Quarry
BARNHAM ROAD
Decoy Covert
Euston

Barnham CE Prim Sch
East Farm
Gravelhill Plantation
Barnham Spinney
Icknield Way Path
Icewell Plantation
Euston Hall

1

Triangle Plantation
ST MARTIN'S LA 1
BLACKSMITH LA 2
Blackbird Spinney
Home Farm
A1088
Euston Hall
The Basin
The Temple
Broad Water

78

85   A   86   B   87   C   88   D   89   E   90   F

32

15

C2
1 ELLINGTON RD
2 NEWALL RD
3 TEDDER CL
4 PORTAL CL
5 SALMOND DR
6 EDINBURGH CL
7 WINDSOR CL

33

For full street detail of Thetford see
Philip's STREET ATLAS of Norfolk

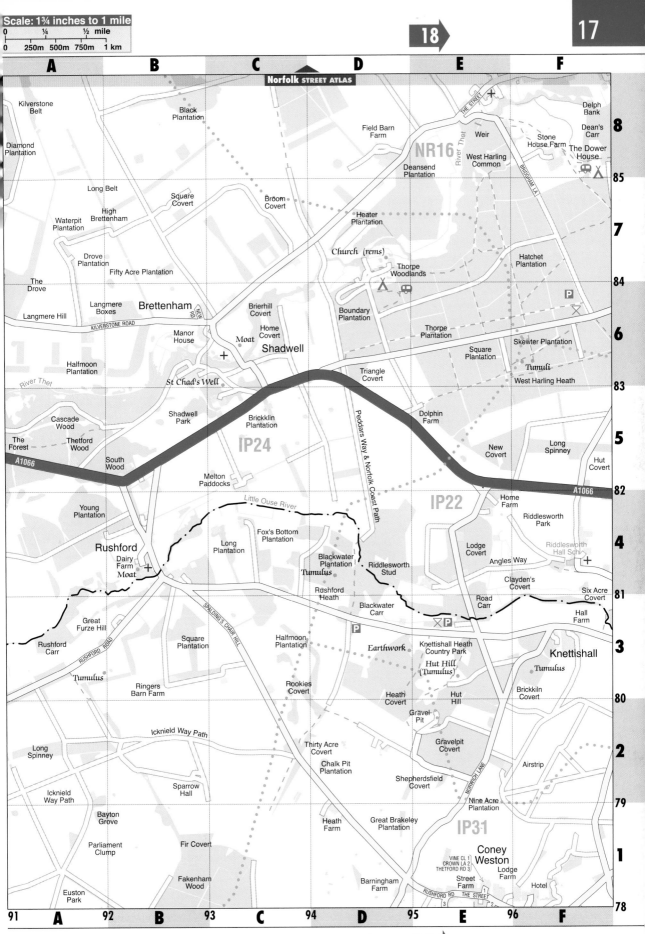

Scale: 1¾ inches to 1 mile

0 ¼ ½ mile
0 250m 500m 750m 1 km

Norfolk STREET ATLAS

Kilverstone Belt
Diamond Plantation
Long Belt
Waterpit Plantation
High Brettenham
Drove Plantation
Fifty Acre Plantation
The Drove
Langmere Hill
Langmere Boxes
Brettenham
Halfmoon Plantation
River Thet
Cascade Wood
The Forest
Thetford Wood
South Wood
A1066
Young Plantation
Rushford
Dairy Farm
Moat
Great Furze Hill
Rushford Carr
Tumulus
Ringers Barn Farm
Long Spinney
Icknield Way Path
Bayton Grove
Parliament Clump
Euston Park

Black Plantation
Square Covert
Broom Covert
Manor House
Moat
Home Covert
Shadwell
St Chad's Well
Shadwell Park
Brickklin Plantation
IP24
Melton Paddocks
Little Ouse River
Long Plantation
Fox's Bottom Plantation
Square Plantation
Spalding's Chair Hill
Rushford Road
Halfmoon Plantation
Square Plantation
Sparrow Hall
Fir Covert
Fakenham Wood
Icknield Way Path
Thirty Acre Covert
Chalk Pit Plantation
Rookies Covert
Heath Farm

Field Barn Farm
Deansend Plantation
Heater Plantation
Church (rems)
Thorpe Woodlands
Boundary Plantation
Triangle Covert
Peddars Way & Norfolk Coast Path
Blackwater Plantation
Tumulus
Rushford Heath
Blackwater Carr
Earthwork
Heath Covert
Great Brakeley Plantation
Barningham Farm

NR16
The Street
Weir
West Harling Common
River Thet
Thorpe Plantation
Square Plantation
West Harling Heath
Dolphin Farm
IP22
Riddlesworth Stud
Riddlesworth Park
Lodge Covert
Angles Way
Home Farm
New Covert
Clayden's Covert
Road Carr
Knettishall Heath Country Park
Hut Hill (Tumulus)
Hut Hill
Gravel Pit
Gravelpit Covert
Shepherdsfield Covert
Nine Acre Plantation
IP31
Coney Weston
VINE CL 1
CROWN LA 2
THETFORD RD 3
Street Farm
Rushford Rd
The Street
Norwich Lane

Delph Bank
Dean's Carr
Stone House Farm
The Dower House
Hatchet Plantation
Bridgham La.
Skewter Plantation
Tumuli
Long Spinney
Hut Covert
A1066
Riddlesworth Hall Sch
Six Acre Covert
Hall Farm
Knettishall
Tumulus
Brickkiln Covert
Airstrip
Lodge Farm
Hotel

Micklemoor Hill
Settlement
Black Carr
Berdewell Hall Farm
West Harling
Middle Harling
West Harling Rd
Mauleys Farm
Middle Harling Farm
Allot
Cemy
Town Farm
Mauleys Farm
Herridges
Hamblings Piece
Hill Harling Farm
Hill Harling
Grove Farm
East Harling Road

8

NR16

85

Big Wood
Lodge Plantation
Privet Plantation

Garboldisham Road

Lopham Road

Guiltcross Farm

7

Tumulus
Triangle Covert

Flint Hall Farm

Garboldisham Road

84

Ten Acre Plantation
East Harling Heath
Tumulus

Harling Road

Uphall Farm

Dairy Farm

6

Twenty Acre Plantation
West Harlinghill Plantation

Old Sheep Pen Plantation
Hall Farm
Sandy Betty's Plantation

Cranespond Plantation

Finchams Farm
Dickersons Farm

83

Garboldisham Heath
Georgiana Plantation

IP22

Garboldisham Manor
Stubbings's Farm

Fir Tree Farm
Whitebreads Farm

5

Hut Covert
Fir Covert

Wilderness Plantation

Ling Farm

Orchard Farm

Lyng La

Devil's Ditch

Seventeen Acre Plantation
Twelve Acre Plantation

Long Furlong Plantation
Home Covert

The Hall
Water La
Back St

B1111

Garboldisham
Garboldisham VC Prim Sch

Allotments Farm

Gables Farm

High Common Road

82
A1066

Tumulus

Hill Plantation
Oldoak Plantation

THETFORD ROAD

PO
Forge Rd
Ely La
Harbour Lane
DISS ROAD

Church Rd
Smallworth La

Mill Pond Farm

THETFORD ROAD A1066

4

St John's Covert

Church Farm
Chapel Cl
Thomas Bole Cl

Smallworth Farm

81

Gasthorpe
St Nicholas's Church (rems of)
Lodge La
Lodge Farm

Hopton Road

Fen Farm
Old Fen
Fen La
Rec Gd
Smallworth

Three Wells Farm

Six Acre Covert
The Street
Alder Carr
Angles Way

Garboldisham Common
Windmill

Boundary Farm
Broomscot Common

Willow Farm

White House Farm
Lodge Farm

Blo' Norton La

3

Wall Covert

Hopton Fen
Common Farm

Hotel
Mill La

Fir Covert

The Street

Selfs La

All Saints Church
Wall Covert

Common Road

Hall Farm
Moat
Hilldrop Farm

Church Farm
MEADOWSIDE
Middle Road

Manor Farm
Ash Tree Farm

80

2

Dairy Farm
SHICKLE PL 1
LEWIS CL 2
HOLME CL 3
PINE TREE CT 4
Nethergate Street
High Street
Manor Farm
Raydon Common
Angles Way
Spring Farm

Church Rd

Blo' Norton

Fen Farm
Willow Farm
The Banks

Fen Street
Hopton
PH
Thelnetham Windmill
Buggs Hole La

79

Broom Covert
Robsons Farm
PO
Greyhound La
Walnut Cl
Thelnetham Road

Kays Farm

Thelnetham
Mill Rd
Fen Lane
(Nature Reserve) Thelnetham Fen

Little Ouse River
Blo Norton Fen
Hinderclay Fen

IP31

Weston Fen
Hillside Farm
Church Farm

Hopton CE VC Prim Sch

Water La
Loggers La
School La
Church La
Hinderclay La
Fen Street

Holiday Farm

1

HOLLOW LA
Bury Road
Church Road
B1111
Cinque Farm
Hopton End Farm

Cross Green Farm

Hopton Road
Moat
PH
St Mary's Well (Spring)

78

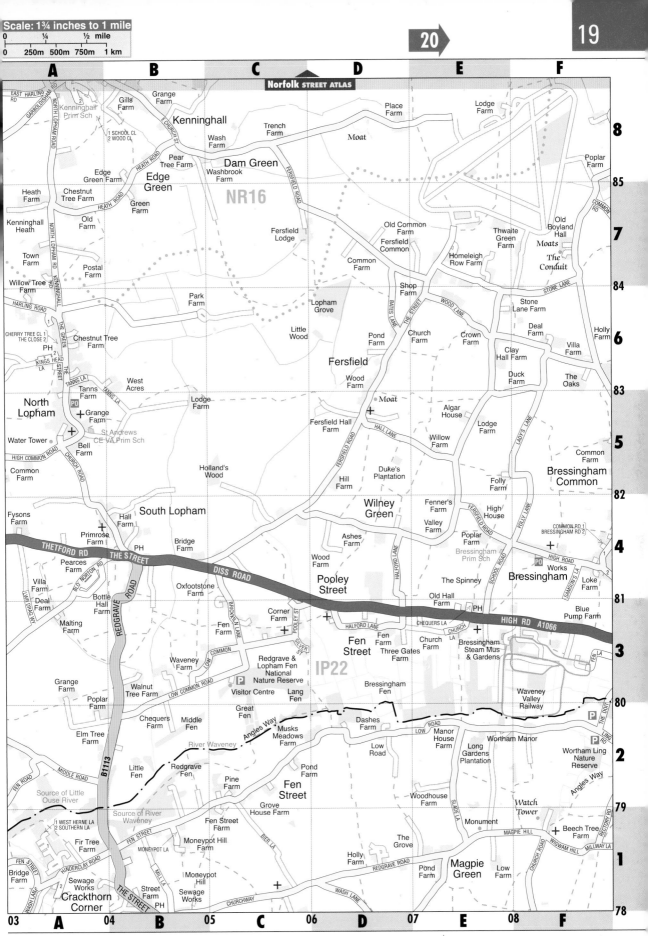

A   B   C   D   E   F

8

Winfarthing

Holly Farm
PH
Church Farm
All Saints CE VA Prim Sch
Messuage Farm
Bridge Farm
Marlers Plantation
Water Tower
Home Wood
Gissing
PH
Hotel
Moats
Old Hall
Elm Tree Farm

High London Farm

85

Mill Farm
Green Dragon Farm
Hill House Farm
Hamilton House
Holly Farm
HEYWOOD RD
Top Wood
New Plantation
Market Field Plantation
Wood Cottage Farm

Moats
Fiddler's Dykes

7

Boyland Common

Manor Farm
Eaton Farm
Vine Farm
Oak Farm
Old Hall Farm
Moat
Laurel Farm
Mill Green
Grove Farm
Bridge Green
Bridge Green Farm

West Hall Farm
Limetree Farm

COMMON ROAD
DRUIDS LANE

84

Street Farm
Shelfanger
Moat
The Heywood
Culpher Farm
Home Farm
Lime Grove
Far End
Manor House Farm
LC

Church Farm
Shelfanger Grove
HEYWOOD ROAD

6

Osierbed Plantation
Shelfanger Hall
Green Farm
St Martins Farm
Moat
Burston
P
Burston Prim Sch
Moat
Hall Farm
Spa Farm
Hall La
Moat

Home Farm
Recn Gd
PH
CROWN GREEN

83

Hazel Farm
Lodge Farm
Dairy Farm
IP22
Hill Farm
Market Farm
Audley End
LC
Valley Farm
Station Road
IP21

LODGE LANE

5

Farrows Farm
Prospect Farm
Homeway Farm
Lark Farm

Misty Wood
Darrow Wood Farm
DARROW WOOD LANE

82

Jubilee Farm
Willow Farm
Darrow Farm
Chestnut Tree Farm
Wolsey Bridge Farm
Three Corner Plantation
Gravel Pit Plantation
Bridge Farm

Westbrook Green

4

Gables Farm
Snow Street
Glebe Farm
Stollerie's Farm
Wolsey Farm
Westbrook Green Farm
Bow Bridge
Walcot Green Farm
Walcot Wood
Blackthorn Farm
Coursing Barn Plantation
The Grange

Lime Tree Farm
Fir Tree Farm
Boundary Farm

81

Home Farm
Moat
Brewers Green
Manor Farm
DISS
Cemy
Walcot Green
Algars Farm
Moat
Grove Farm
Pretoria Plantation

White House Farm
Poplar Farm

3

HIGH ROAD   A1066
Roydon
PH
HIGH RD
OLD HIGH RD
ROYDON RD
B1132
Diss Church Jun Sch
Diss High Sch
Home Farm
Alder Carr
Frenze
Scole Common
Pettits Farm
Scole Common

80

Moat
Grove Farm
Roydon Fen
STANLEY RD
DENMARK RD
The Mere
PARK RD
VICTORIA RD
Diss Inf Sch
Clynt Plantation
Long House
IP21

2

Wortham Ling
Oak Farm
Angles Way
Denmark Bridge
Cock Street Fen
Swimming Pool
Windmill Sewage Works
Frenze Bridge
Angles   Way
Waterloo

79

Pollard Tree Farm
Cemy
Longs Farm
Elm Vale Farm
Stuston Bridge
Flax Farm
River Waveney
Stuston Common
Scole Bridge

Palgrave VC Prim Sch
MILLWAY LANE

1

Millway Farm
The Priory
Palgrave
Priory Farm
LC
Orchard End
Willow Farm
Stuston
A143
Hall Farm
Moat
Scole Plantation

78

09   A   10   B   11   C   12   D   13   E   14   F

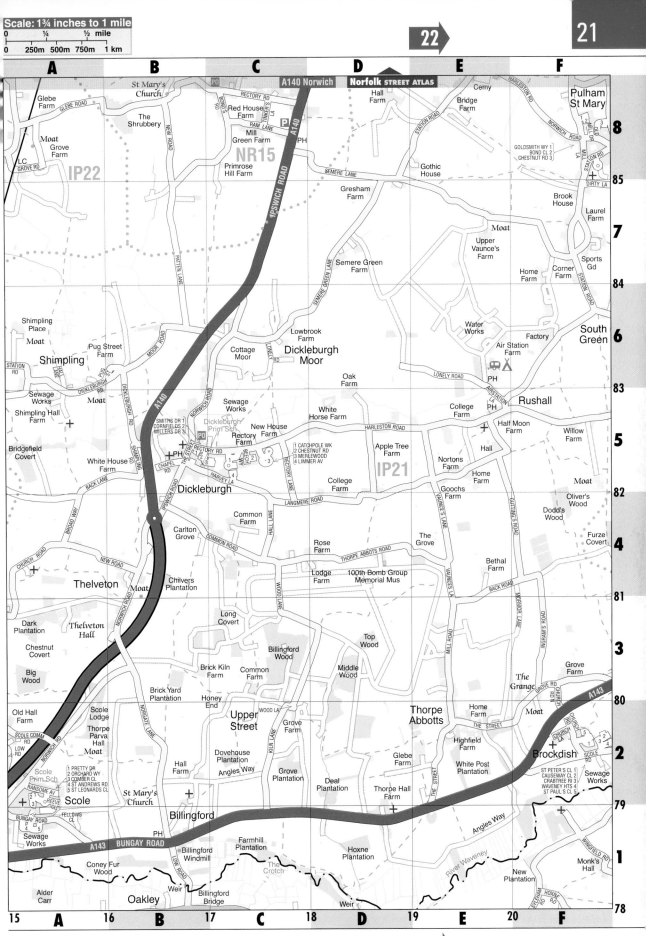

Scale: 1¾ inches to 1 mile

0   ¼   ½ mile
0   250m 500m 750m 1 km

Norfolk STREET ATLAS

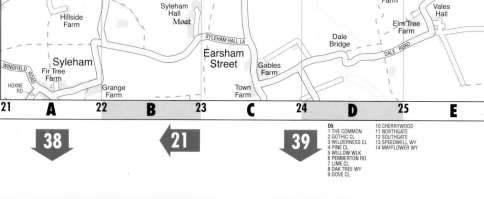

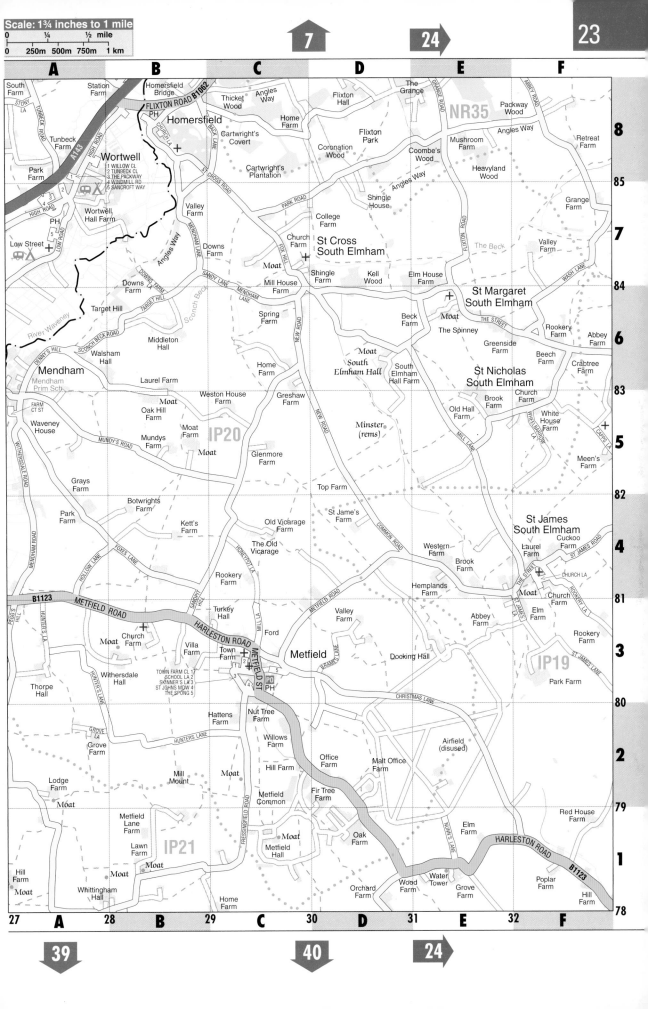

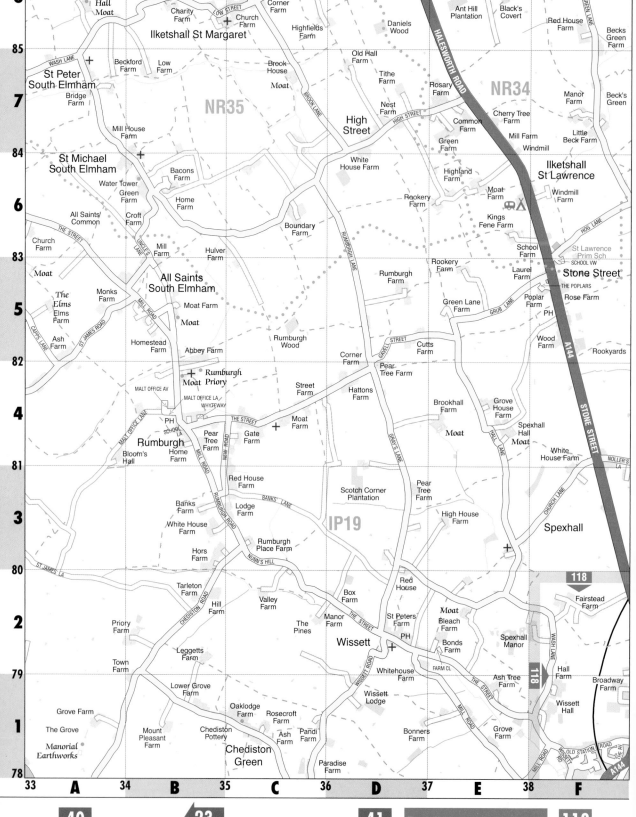

A   B   C   D   E   F

8

85

7

84

6

83

5

82

4

81

3

80

2

79

1

78

St Peter's Brewery & Visitor Centre
St Peter's Hall
Moat
St Peter South Elmham
Bridge Farm
WASH LANE
Beckford Farm
Low Farm
Elms Farm
School Farm
Charity Farm
Ilketshall St Margaret
LOW STREET
SNOE DEVIL LANE
Ropers Farm
Church Farm
Corner Farm
Highfields Farm
Brook House
Moat
Tithe Farm
Daniels Wood
Old Hall Farm
Tithe Farm
Rec Gd
Ilketshall Hall
Moat
Ant Hill Plantation
Black's Covert
Red House Farm
BECKS GREEN LANE
Becks Green Farm

NR35
NR34

St Michael South Elmham
Mill House Farm
Bacons Farm
BROOK LANE
High Street
HIGH STREET
Nest Farm
Rosary Farm
Common Farm
Cherry Tree Farm
Mill Farm
Windmill
Manor Farm
Beck's Green
Little Beck Farm
Ilketshall St Lawrence
Windmill Farm

Water Tower
Green Farm
Croft Farm
Home Farm
UNGLE'S LANE
Mill Farm
Hulver Farm
White House Farm
Boundary Farm
RUMBURGH LANE
Green Farm
Highland Farm
Rookery Farm
Moat Farm
Kings Fene Farm
HOG LANE
St Lawrence Prim Sch
SCHOOL VW
School Farm
Laurel Farm
Stone Street
A144

All Saints' Common
THE STREET
Church Farm
Moat
The Elms
Elms Farm
Ash Farm
CAPS LANE
Monks Farm
MILL ROAD
ST JAMES ROAD
All Saints South Elmham
Moat Farm
Moat
Homestead Farm
Abbey Farm
Rumburgh Wood
Street Farm
Corner Farm
Rumburgh Farm
GAVEL STREET
Cutts Farm
Pear Tree Farm
Rookery Farm
Green Lane Farm
GRUB LANE
Poplar Farm
PH
THE POPLARS
Rose Farm
Wood Farm
Rookyards

Rumburgh Priory
Moat
MALT OFFICE AV
MALT OFFICE LA
WHYTEWAY
PH
Rumburgh
MALT OFFICE LANE
SCHOOL LA
Bloom's Hall
Home Farm
Pear Tree Farm
Gate Farm
THE STREET
Moat Farm
Hattons Farm
GRAY'S LANE
Brookhall Farm
Moat
HALL LANE
Grove House Farm
Spexhall Hall
Moat
White House Farm
STONE STREET
NOLLER'S LA

MILL ROAD
NEW ROAD
RUMBURGH ROAD
Red House Farm
BANKS LANE
Banks Farm
Lodge Farm
White House Farm
Scotch Corner Plantation
IP19
Pear Tree Farm
High House Farm
Spexhall
118
Fairstead Farm

St James La
CHEDISTON ROAD
Hors Farm
Rumburgh Place Farm
NUNN'S HILL
Tarleton Farm
Hill Farm
Valley Farm
The Pines
Box Farm
THE STREET
Manor Farm
Red House
St Peters Farm
PH
Moat
Bleach Farm
Bonds Farm
FARM CL
Spexhall Manor
WASH LANE
118
Hall Farm
Broadway Farm

Priory Farm
Leggetts Farm
Town Farm
Lower Grove Farm
Oaklodge Farm
Rosecroft Farm
WISSETT ROAD
Wissett
Whitehouse Farm
Wissett Lodge
THE STREET
MILL ROAD
Ash Tree Farm
Wissett Hall

Grove Farm
The Grove
Manorial Earthworks
Mount Pleasant Farm
Chediston Pottery
Chediston Green
Ash Farm
Pandi Farm
Paradise Farm
Bonners Farm
Grove Farm
OLD STATION ROAD
MILL ROAD
A144

33   A   34   B   35   C   36   D   37   E   38   F

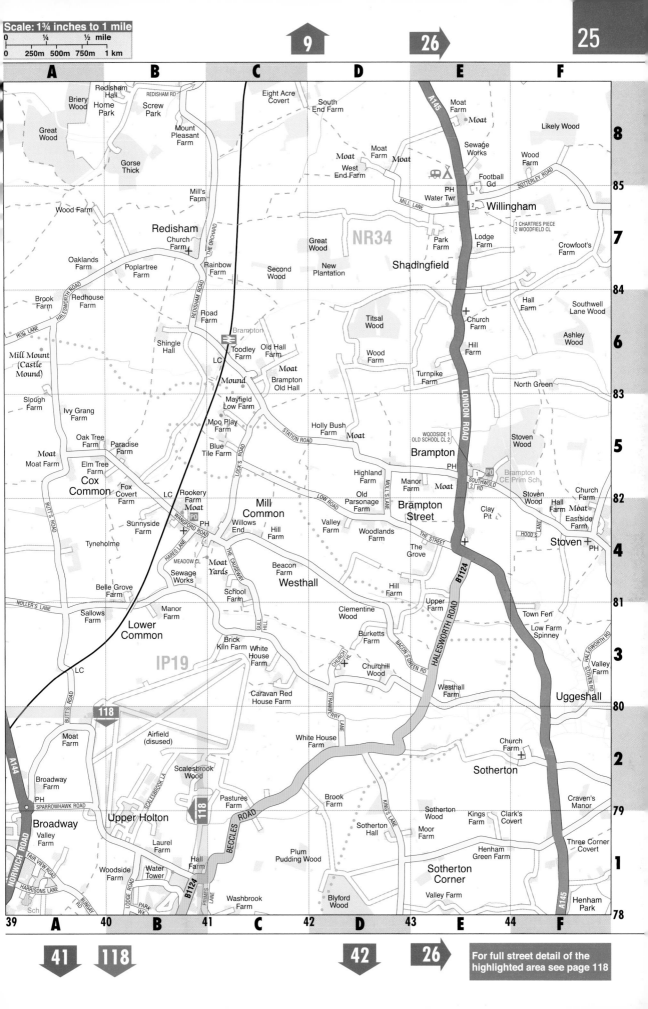

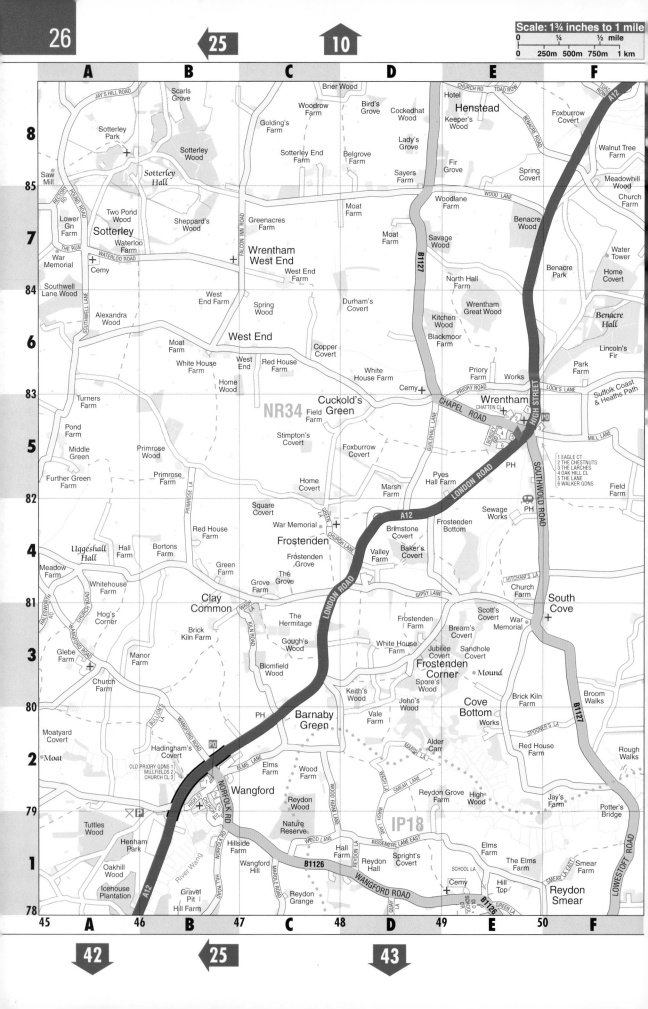

¼   ½   mile
250m   500m   750m   1 km

A   B   C   D   E   F

Kessingland Beach

NR33

PH CHURCH RD

COOPERS LA

MARSH LA

BEACH RD

Blackcap Wood

Sewage Works

HOLLY GRANGE ROAD

Churchfarm Marshes

Suffolk Coast & Heaths Path

8

85

Benacre

Kessingland Level

+ War Memorial

Church Covert

Beachfarm Marshes

Pumping Station

7

THE STREET

Northwalk Plantation

The Denes

84

Hall Farm

Blackwater Covert

Beach Farm

Alder Carr

6

Wood Farm

Coney Hill

Boathouse Covert

Craft Plantation

Benacre National Nature Reserve

83

Holly Hang

NR34

Benacre Broad

Holly Grove

North Common Wood

Chancel Covert

Long Covert

5

St Andrew's Church

82

Ausgates

Covehithe

Church Farm

4

Covehithe Cliffs

Porter's Farm

Green Heath

81

Covehithe Broad

Warren House

Suffolk Coast & Heaths Path

The Warren

3

Easton Wood

80

Benacre National Nature Reserve

Easton Home Covert

2

Easton Broad

Pottersbridge Marshes

Easton Marshes

79

IP18

1

Easton Bavents

Easton Cliffs

EASTON LA

78

51   A   52   B   53   C   54   D   55   E   56   F

Cambridgeshire STREET ATLAS

D5		
1 NORTH DR	7 FOX WOOD N
2 ST FELIX CL	8 MARTIN CL
3 CALFE FEN CL	9 POPPY FIELDS
4 OLD SCHOOL CL	10 PRIMROSE LA
5 HOLMES LA	11 FOX WOOD S
6 SNOWBERRY WY	

Scale: 1¾ inches to 1 mile

0   ¼   ½   mile
0   250m 500m 750m 1 km

Cambridgeshire STREET ATLAS

CB7

CB5

44

D3	D4		
1 LODE CL	1 ROSEBAY GDNS	10 TEN BELL LA	20 WHITE HART LA
2 COLLEGE RD	2 BLUEBELL WK	11 BERRYCROFT	21 GARDENERS LA
3 REGENT PL	3 HERBERT HUMAN CL	12 GUNTONS CL	22 BROOK DAM LA
4 FRANK BRIDGES CL	4 HONEYSUCKLE CL	13 BELL GDNS	
5 REDHOUSE GDNS	5 NIGHTALL CL	14 FREDERICK TALBOT CL	
6 THE CRESCENT	6 CHESTNUT DR	15 CHURCHGATE ST	
7 FORDHAM RD	7 GIMBERT RD	16 MARKET ST	
8 MEADOW CL	8 QUEENSWAY	17 ADELAIDE CL	
9 MILL CFT	9 WEATHERALLS CL	18 EASTERN AV	
		19 BREWHOUSE LA	

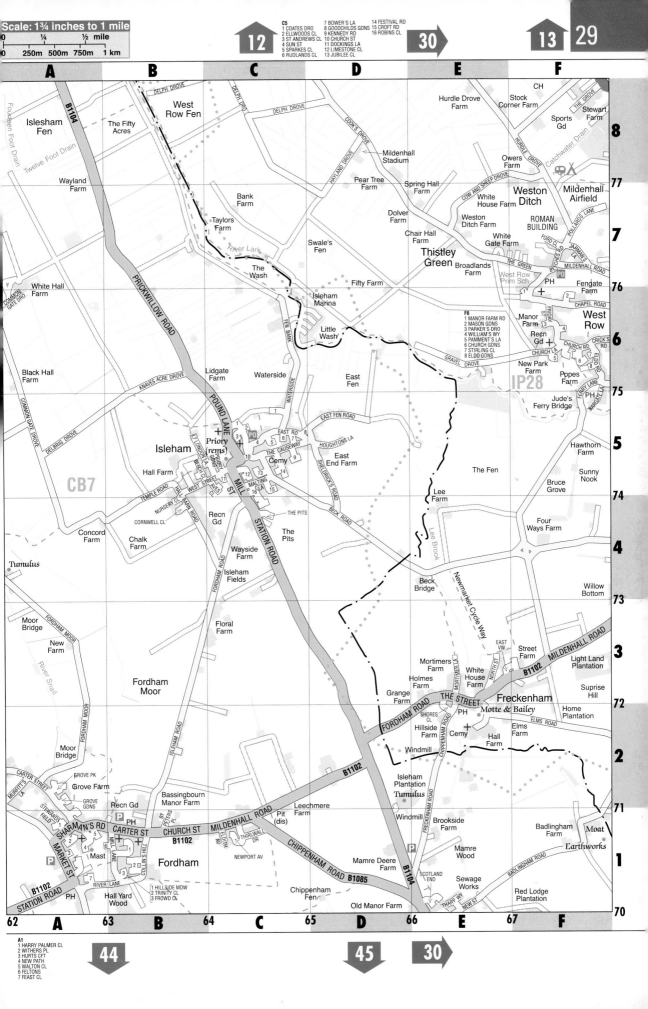

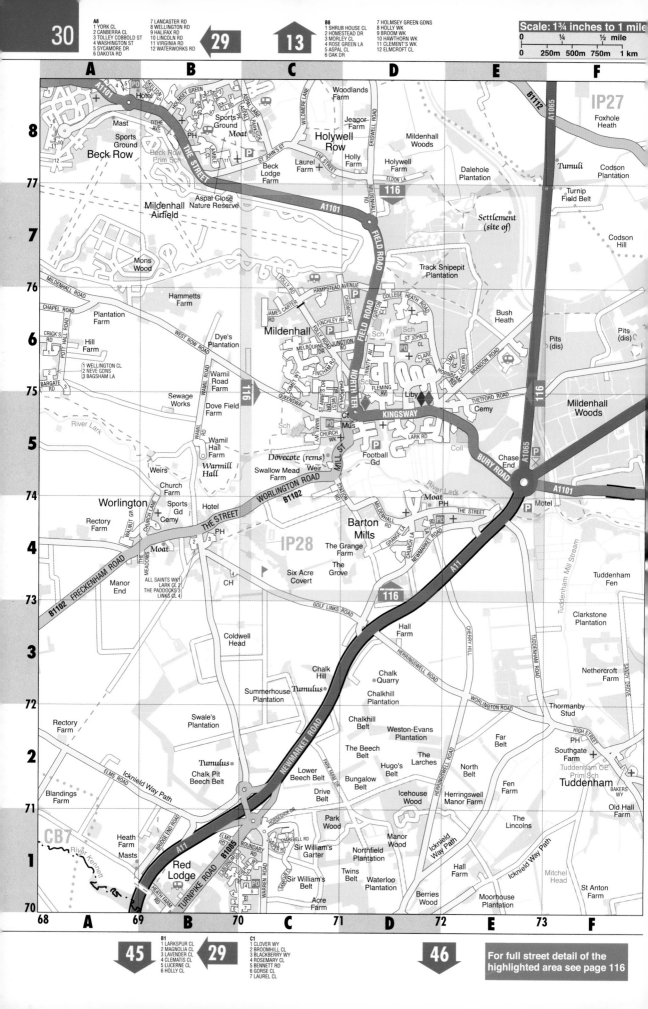

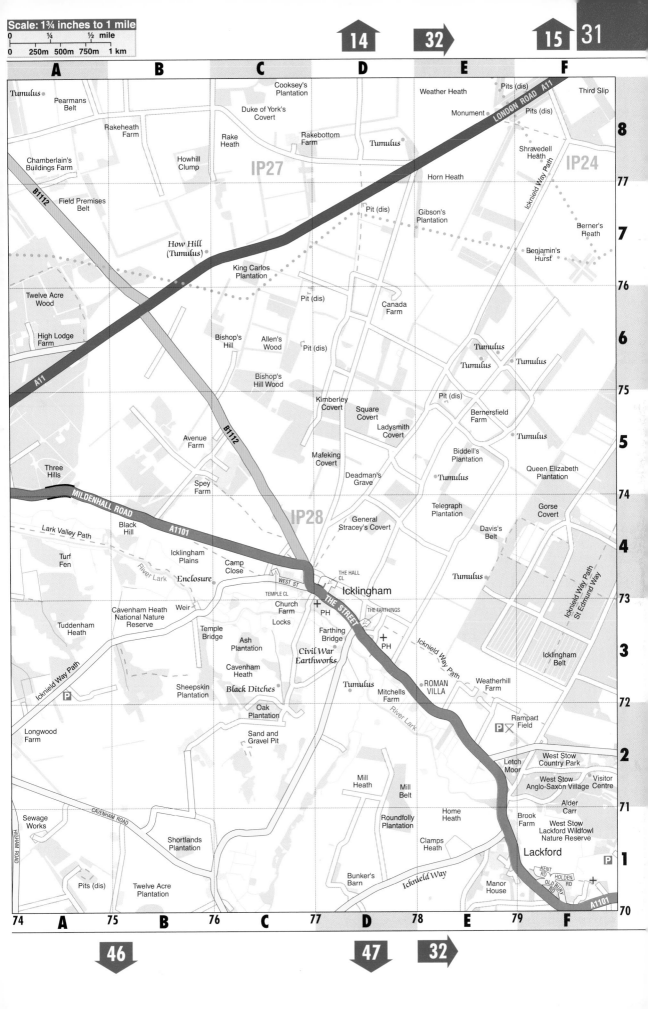

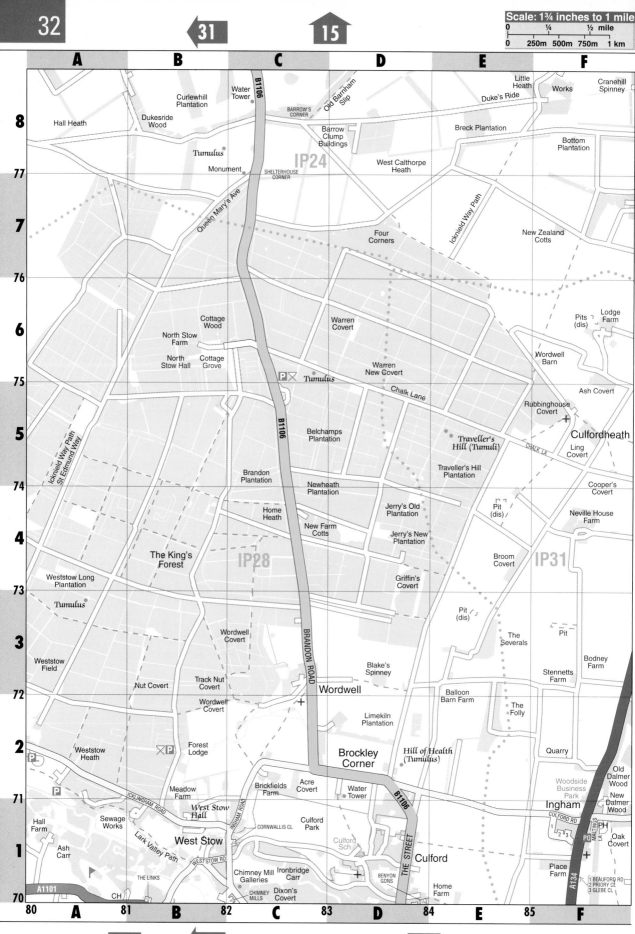

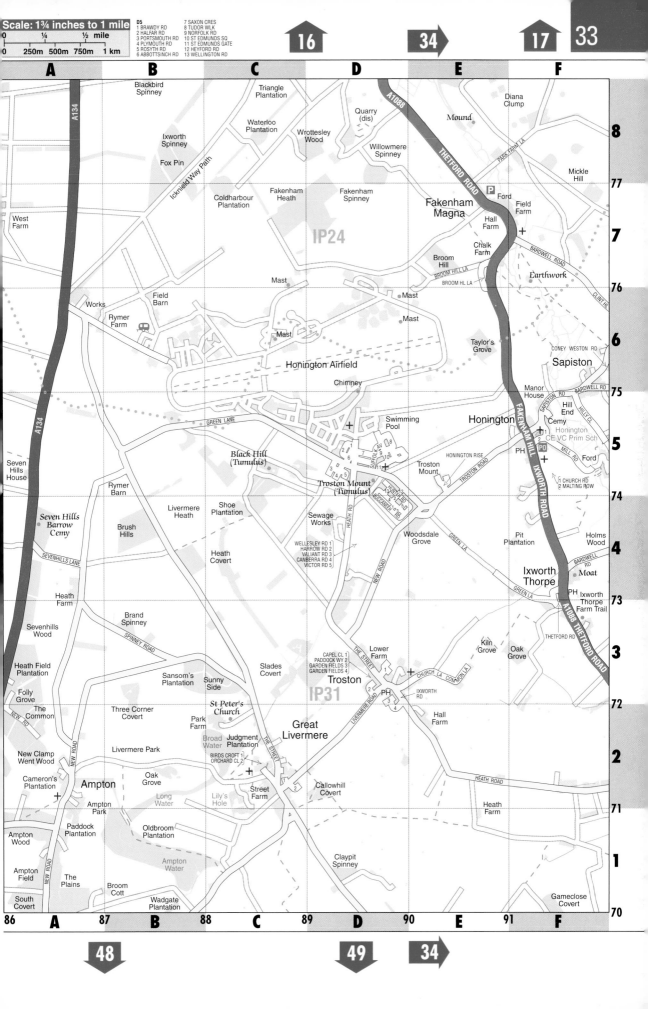

33
17

Scale: 1¾ inches to 1 mile
0 ¼ ½ mile
0 250m 500m 750m 1 km

A B C D E F
8
77
7
76
6
75
5
74
4
73
3
72
2
71
1
70
92 93 94 95 96 97
Fakenham Wood
Barningham Park
NORWICH LANE
SWAN LA 1
PADDOCK FARM 2
THETFORD ROAD
Willowtree Farm
Meadow Farm
Coney Weston
THE STREET
Square Plantation
HOLLOW LANE
Hollow Lane Farm
PH
Pinnocks Farm
CROW ST
CONEY WESTON ROAD
DAY'S LA
Moat Plantation
SANDY LA
SANDY LANE
B1111
HOPTON ROAD
Barningham
Lych Gate Cemy
CHURCH GDNS 1
ST ANDREWS CL 2
CHURCH RD
MILL RD
Barningham CE VC Prim Sch
PO
1 JARROLD CL
2 MILLFIELD RD
HEPWORTH ROAD
Triangle Plantation
Wellmere Grove
Pilgrim Shed
Park Grove
Heath Cottages
HEATH ROAD
White House Farm
DROUT'S LA
Lodge Farm
BARDWELL ROAD
STANTON ROAD
Home Farm
Great Grove
Upper Grove
North Common
IP22
Meadow Farm
CLINT HILL
CONEY WESTON RD
Grove Farm
Water Tower
Bowbeck
Stanton Road Farm
Ringers Farm
Lanket's Grove
B1111
Dale Farm
BARNINGHAM ROAD
BARDWELL ROAD
Little Dale Farm
Chapel Farm
DALE RD
Stanton Chare
Black Bridge
IP31
HILLTOP
Hill Farm
HILL TOP
Mill Farm
Blackwater Farm
Lower Chare Farm
CHARE ROAD
Little Hill Farm
Pit (dis)
Ford
SPRING ROAD
Manor Farm
ROMAN VILLA
Little Chare Farm
Bardwell VC Prim Sch
Chare Farm
Church
The Black Bourn
Thorpe Carr
LAMMAS CL
Beech Farm
STANTON ROAD
BARDWELL ROAD
GEORGE HL
DUKE ST
Ford
Bardwell Windmill
SCHOOL LA
Dexters Farm
BARDWELL ROAD
UPPER ST
A143
BURY ROAD
CHURCH RD
QUAKER LA
PH
Stanton
Holms Wood
Place Farm
Bardwell
QUAKER LA
Stanton Com Prim Sch
OLD BURY RD
HEPWORTH ROAD
High Wood
DAVEY'S LANE
GLASSFIELD ROAD
Stanton Post Mill
Hall Farm
THE STREET
POTTERS LA
PH
Recn Gd
Little Carr
KNOX LANE
Blackbourne CE VC Mid Sch
GROVE LANE
Great Carr
LOW STREET
UPTHORPE ROAD
Upthorpe
BURY LA
Paddock End
PARK FARM DR
Cottage Farm
Mount Farm
New Grove
Half Grove
Bromptons Farm
The Grundle
Vicarage Farm
WASH LA
The Black Bourn
Home Covert
WYKEN ROAD
Pond Farm
BARDWELL ROAD
Alecock's Grave
Hockhouse Grove
WYKEN ROAD
Park Farm
Kiln Wood
Sleights Wood
St John's Wood
Bangrove Wood
Bardwell Manor
Shepherd's Grove
THETFORD ROAD
Dovehouse Wood
WYKEN ROAD
Abbey Farm
Great Carr
Wyken Vineyard & Gardens
Long Grove
STANTON ROAD
Wyken Hall
WOOLPIT ROAD
HEATH ROAD
A1088
Ixworth
THISTLEDOWN DR
Rushgreen Grove
Burntfirs Plantation
Ash Grove
Water Twr
Wyken Wood
Mulley's Grove
CLAY LA
DAIRY LA
THE LANGRIDGE
BARDWELL RD
Potter's Plantation
WALSHAM ROAD
Long Carr
Ixworth Mid Sch
A143
Rabbit Plantation
Hillwatering Farm
WOOLPIT RD
KILN LANE
Moat
HIGH ST
CROWN LA
Cemy
Priory (rems)
Ixworth Abbey
PO
Ixworth CE Prim Sch
Woodstreet Farm
Hall & Liby
CROWN LA
CROWN LA
STOW ROAD
Sandyways Farm
Sunny Side
Priory Waterfowl Farm
Bridge Farm
A1088

49
33
50

B1
1 PEDDARS CL
2 CHALK LA
3 PEASECROFT RD
4 STREET FARM LA
5 ST EDMUND CL
6 WALSHAM RD
7 COLTSFOOT CL
8 CODDINGTON WY
9 GOUGH PL
10 ABBEY CL
11 BEECHES CL
12 GARRARD PL
13 SCOTT RD
14 COMMISTER LA
15 CROWN CRES
16 THE PADDOCK
17 SADDLERS YARD
18 PEACOCK RISE
19 NEW RD
20 THOMAS CL
21 KETTLEBORROW CL
22 PLUMMER CL
23 MICKLESMERE DR
24 FORDHAM PL

E4
1 OLD BARNINGHAM RD
2 CAPELL WLK
3 PARKSIDE
4 CULVERS MDW
5 THE CHASE
6 GRUNDLE CL
7 DUKE ST
8 BUCKLES FIELD
9 NORTH CL
10 CATCHPOLE WY
11 LOFFT CL
12 MICHAELHOUSE WY
13 SHETLANDS
14 JACOBS CL
15 CHURCH CL
16 MEADOW CT
17 THE KNOWLE
18 FIELD WY
19 WINDMILL GN
20 SCHOOL CL
21 FORDHAMS CL
22 STURGEON WY
23 HONEYMEADE CL

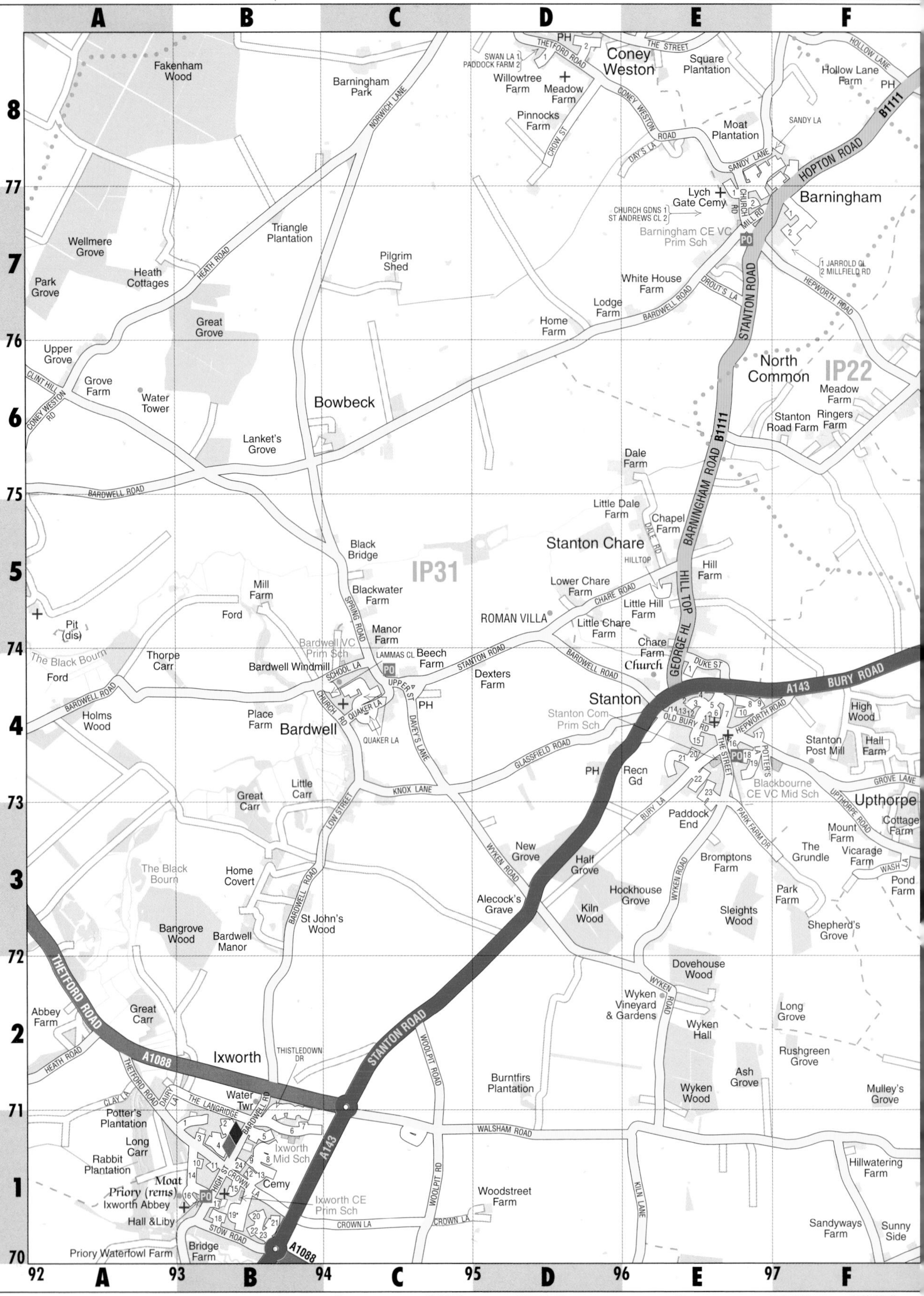

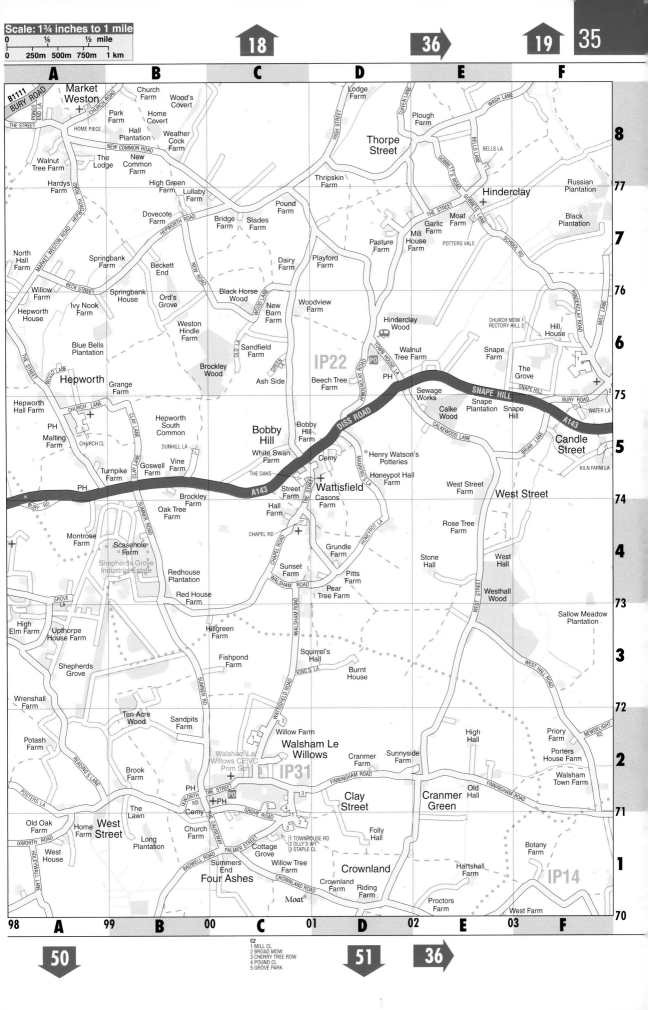

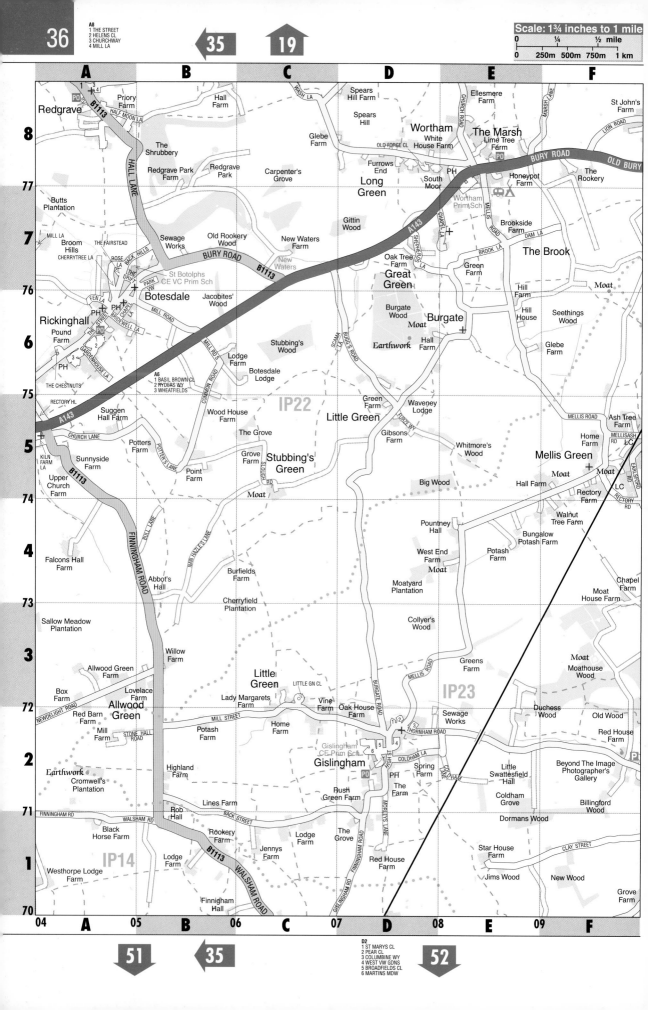

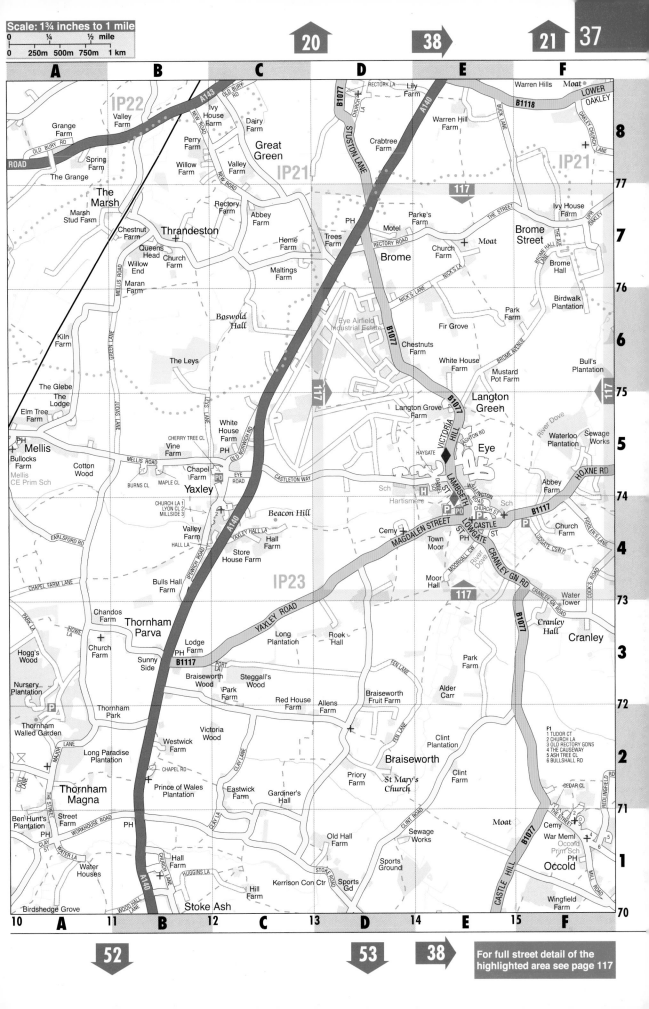

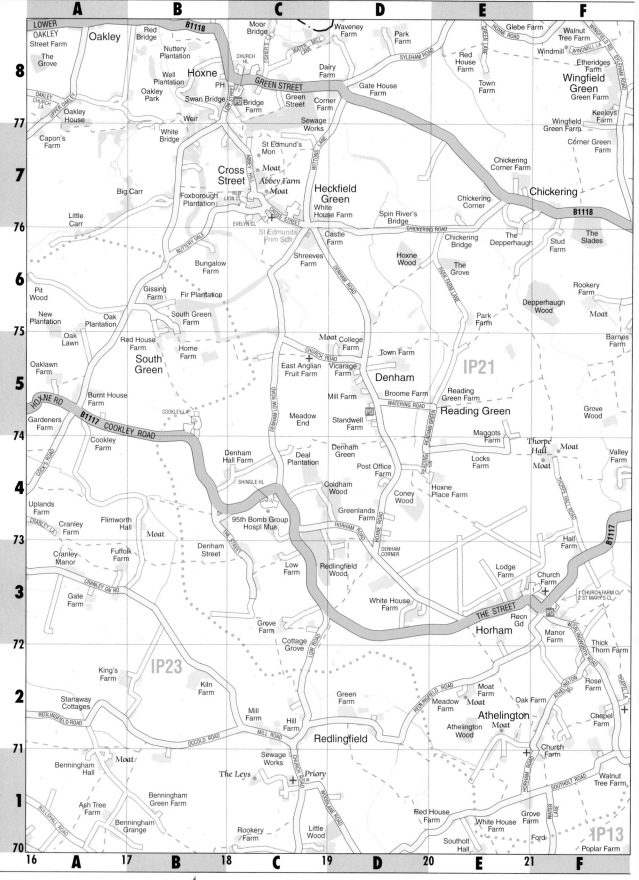

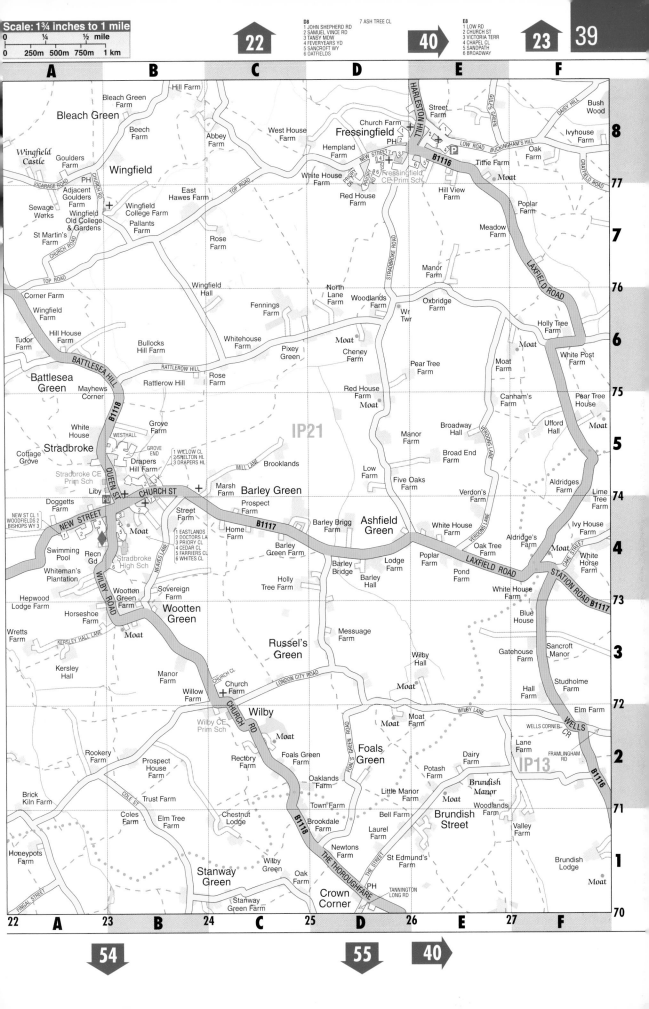

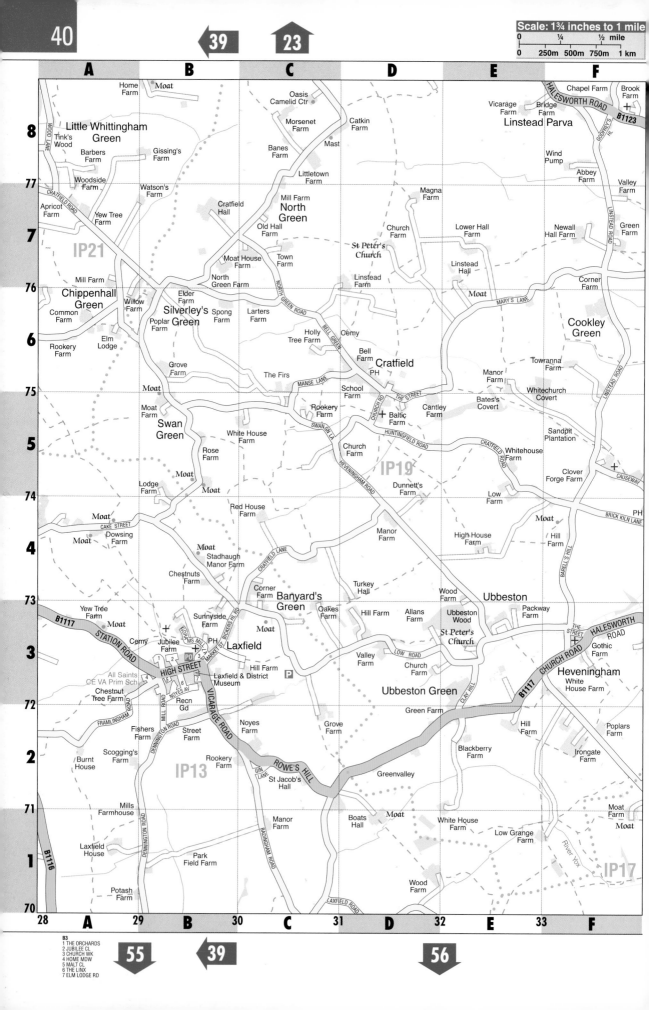

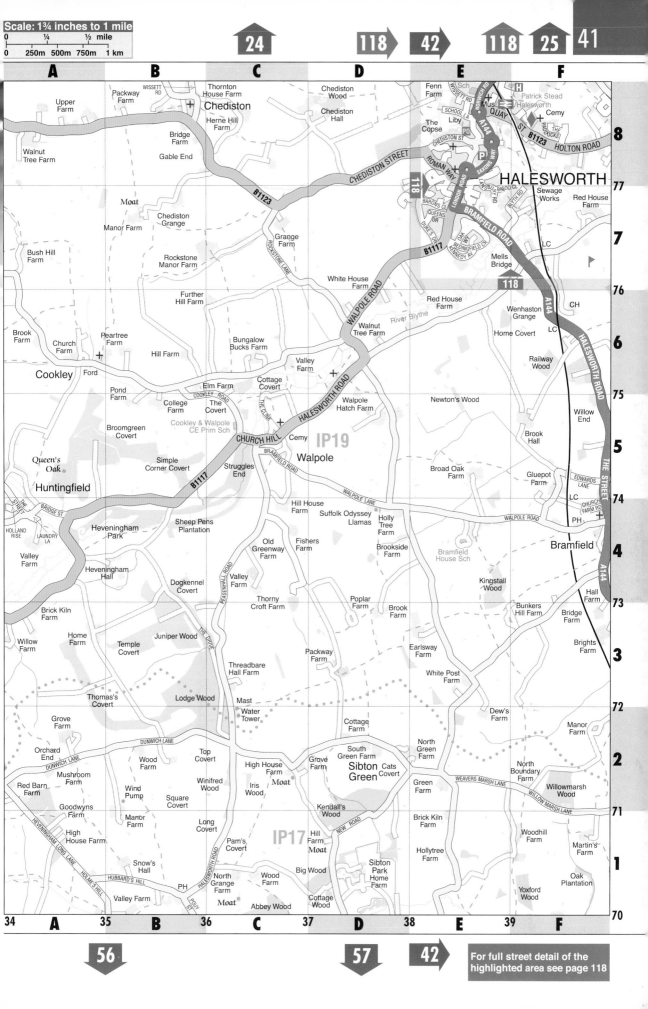

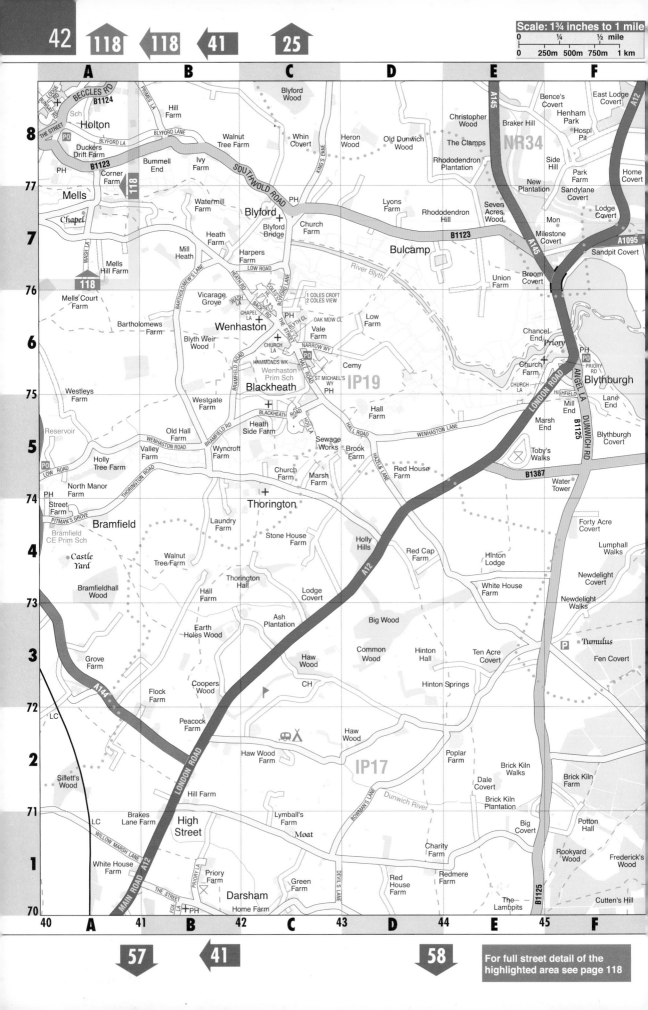

44

A6
1 CHESTNUT RISE
2 APPLETREE GR
3 WESTHORPE
4 ORCHARD WY
5 NEW RD
6 KINGFISHER DR
7 HATLEY DR
8 CHANDLERS CT
9 HYTHE CL
10 MURTON CL
11 LABURNUM LA
12 PANTILE LA
13 CASBURN LA
14 NEWNHAM LA
15 BUNTINGS CR
16 MARTIN RD

28

29

Scale: 1¾ inches to 1 mile
0   ¼   ½   mile
0   250m 500m 750m   1 km

New River
Hundred Acre Farm
Burwell Poors' Fen
Chestnut Tree Farm
The Broads
COCKPEN RD
Tollgate Farm
STATION ROAD
B1102
LC
CB7
Abbey Wood
Brackland Rough
Fordham Abbey
Underdown Plantation

Broads Farm
Ness Farm
West Fen
A142
Fordham House
Water Tower
Limekiln Plantation

Goosehall Farm
Little Fen
Sewage Works
Klondyke Farm
High Ness Farm
Lark Hall Farm
Crow Hall Farm
Snailwell Fen

FIRST DROVE
Catch Water Drain
BROADS ROAD
NEWMARKET ROAD
Wadebridge Farm
River Snail
SNAILWELL ROAD
FORDHAM ROAD

Broads Road Business Park
NESS ROAD
Breach Farm
Landwade Farm
Earthworks
Moat
Lynx Business Park
The Pines Industrial Estate

Ashbridge Farm
Little Fen
ANCHOR LA
GRANTCHESTER RI 1
MASON RD 2
LITTLE FEN DROVE
DYSON'S DRO
Townsend Farm
B1102
LANDWADE RD
The Hall
Landwade
LANDWADE ROAD
Glebe Farm
Bloomfield Farm
Four Ponds

Rec Gd
TOYSE LANE
MONTFORD CL
B6
1 TOYSE CL
2 GARDEN CT
3 THE AVENUE
4 BAKER DR
5 OLD SCHOOL CL
Cemy
Slade Farm
COTTON END ROAD
Sewage Works
Plantation Stud

Burwell
Sports Ctr
Libry
B5
1 HOLKHAM MEAD
2 MELFORD CL
3 KENTWELL PL
4 BAYFIELD DR
5 BURGHLEY RISE
6 MILL CL
7 MILL LA
8 BLOOMFIELD
9 BARKWAYS
10 BEWICKS MD
11 COPPERFIELD WAY
CB8
A142

CB5
Parsonage Farm
PO
Burwell Mus
NEWMARKET RD
Northmore Farm
NORTH END
MILL LA
120
37
SNAILWELL SHORT RD
WINDMILL HL

Burwell Castle (site of)
HIGH ST
ISAACSON RD
B1103
BURWELL ROAD
Hill Farm
Eleanor Terrace
THE DRIFT
OXFORD ST
CHURCH ST
120
FORDHAM RD

REACH ROAD
SCOTRED CL
RAILWAY
B1102
STATION GATE
A5
1 POPLARS CL
2 BOLTON CL
3 ROMAN CL
4 TUNBRIDGE CL
5 PARSONAGE CL
6 GUYATT CT
7 PRIORY CL
8 POUND CL
9 SAXON DR
10 ABBEY CL
11 MEADOWLANDS
12 THE PADDOCKS
13 WILD ACRES
14 MANDEVILLE
15 CHURCH LA
16 SCHOOL LA
17 ASH GR
Sch
PO
Hotel
Exning
Football Gd
LACEY'S LANE
Dovecote
Cemy
HYPERION WY
PARKERS WK
BRICKFIELDS AV
STUDLANDS PK AVE
OAKS RD
Oaks Business Park

Crownall Farm
SWAFFHAM ROAD
Lower Portland Farm
Industrial Estate
EXNING ROAD
B1103
Sch
Sch
H

P
Devil's Ditch
Devils Dyke Nature Reserve
Ditch Farm
Gravel Pit Farm
Warbraham Wood
The Marsh
St Wendred's Well
HAMILTON RD
Hamilton Stud
Sch
PO
Sch
GEORGE LAMBTON AVE
Colf
Leisure Centre
Sch

Plantation Farm
Springhead Farm
HEATH ROAD
120
Warbraham Mains Farm
Southfields Farm
ELIZABETH AVE
MANDERSTON ROAD
ST PHILIPS
EDINBURGH ROAD
WINDSOR RD
HAMILTON ROAD
ROWLEY DRIVE

Vicarage Farm
HEATH ROAD
A14
Newmarket Heath
Exercise Track
Newmarket Lawn Tennis Club
BIRDCAGE WK
HIGH ST
B1061

Gravelpit Farm
Beacon (Cesarewitch) Course
July Course
Sand Gallop
Rowley Mile Course
Newmarket Race Course
Millennium Grandstand
Cambridge Hill
A1304
BARBARA STRADBROKE AVENUE
Stour Valley Path
Cemy
DULLINGHAM RD
Wyck Hall Stud

Devil's Ditch
120

For full street detail of the highlighted area see page 120

Cambridgeshire Street Atlas

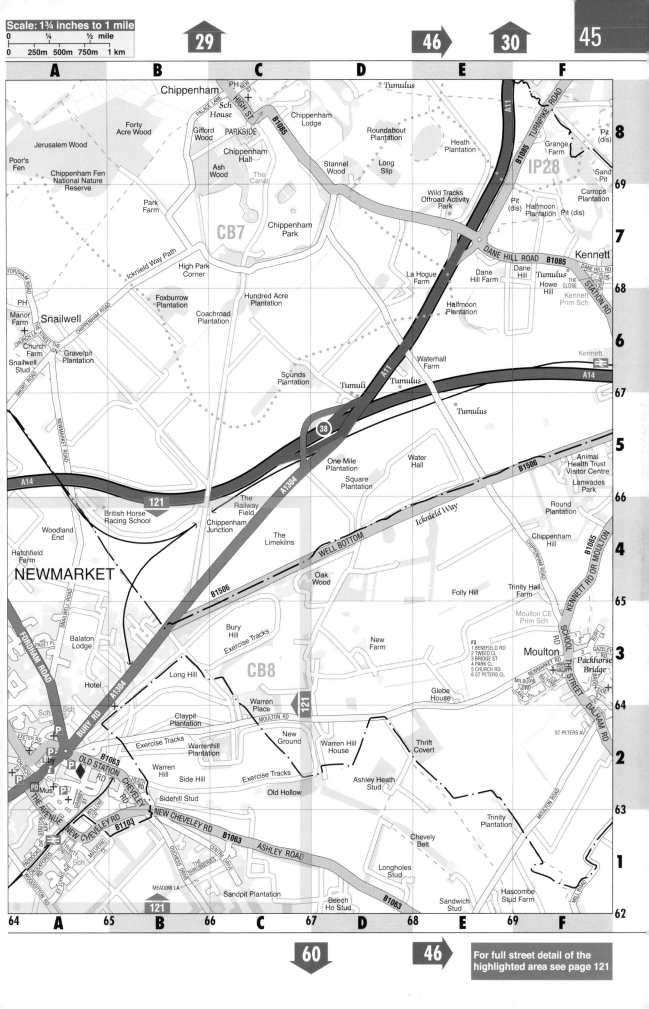

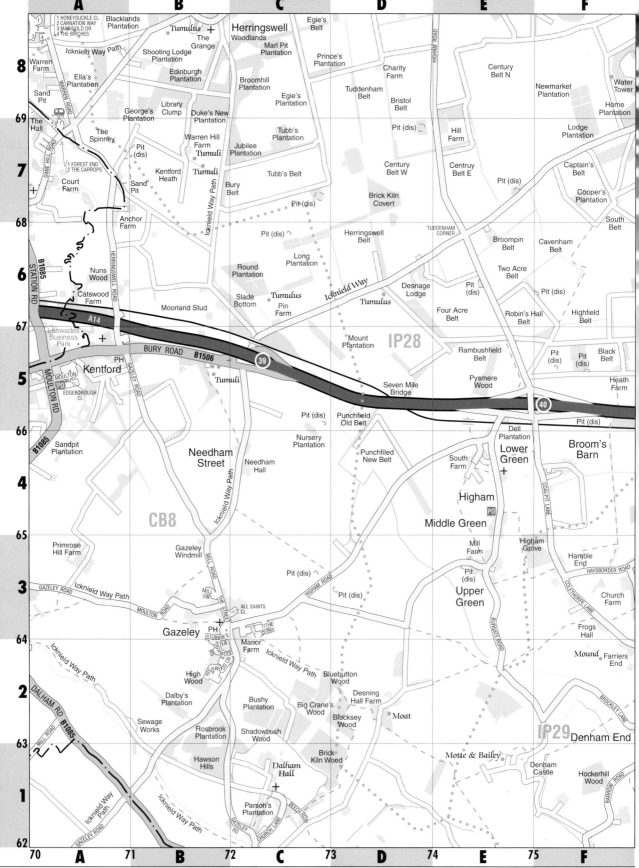

Scale: 1¾ inches to 1 mile
0   ¼   ½ mile
0   250m 500m 750m 1 km

1 HONEYSUCKLE CL
2 CARNATION WAY
3 MARIGOLD DR
4 THE BIRCHES

Blacklands Plantation

Tumulus

The Grange

Herringswell
Woodlands

Egie's Belt

Water Tower

Warren Farm

Ella's Plantation

Shooting Lodge Plantation

Marl Pit Plantation

Prince's Plantation

Charity Farm

Century Belt N

Newmarket Plantation

Sand Pit

Edinburgh Plantation

Broomhill Plantation

Tuddenham Belt

Bristol Belt

Home Plantation

Icknield Way Path

George's Plantation

Library Clump

Egie's Plantation

The Hall

Duke's New Plantation

Pit (dis)

Hill Farm

Lodge Plantation

The Spinney

Warren Hill Farm Tumuli

Jubilee Plantation

Tubb's Plantation

Century Belt W

Centruy Belt E

Pit (dis)

Captain's Belt

Court Farm

Pit (dis)

Kentford Heath

Tumuli

Tubb's Belt

Cooper's Plantation

Sand Pit

Bury Belt

Pit (dis)

Brick Kiln Covert

South Belt

Anchor Farm

Pit (dis)

Herringswell Belt

TUDDENHAM CORNER

Broompin Belt

Cavenham Belt

Nuns Wood

Round Plantation

Long Plantation

Icknield Way

Two Acre Belt

Pit (dis)

Catswood Farm

Moorland Stud

Slade Bottom

Tumulus

Pin Farm

Tumulus

Desnage Lodge

Pit (dis)

Robin's Hall Belt

Highfield Belt

B1085
STATION RD

A14

Lanwades Business Park

Four Acre Belt

IP28

Rambushfield Belt

Pit (dis)

Pit (dis)

Black Belt

PH

BURY ROAD   B1506

39

Mount Plantation

Pysmere Wood

Heath Farm

Kentford

Tumuli

Seven Mile Bridge

40

Pit (dis)

MOULTON AVE
Edgeborough CL

Pit (dis)

Punchfield Old Belt

Dell Plantation

Pit (dis)

MOULTON RD

B1085

Sandpit Plantation

Needham Street

Nursery Plantation

Punchfiled New Belt

Lower Green

Broom's Barn

Needham Hall

South Farm

CB8

Icknield Way Path

MILL ROAD

Higham

Middle Green

Mill Farm

Higham Grove

Hamble End

Primrose Hill Farm

Gazeley Windmill

Pit (dis)

HIGHAM ROAD

Pit (dis)

Upper Green

HAYSBORDER ROAD

COLETHORPE LANE

Church Farm

GAZELEY ROAD

Icknield Way Path

MOULTON ROAD

MILL VW

THE STREET

Pit (dis)

BURGATE ROAD

COAL PIT LANE

Frogs Hall

ALL SAINTS CL

Gazeley

PH

TITHE CLOSE

Manor Farm

Icknield Way Path

Bluebutton Wood

Mound

Farriers End

DALHAM RD
B1085

STUBBIN'S LA

HIGHWOOD RD

HIGHWOOD CL

High Wood

Dalby's Plantation

Bushy Plantation

Big Crane's Wood

Desning Hall Farm

Moat

IP29 Denham End

Sewage Works

Rosbrook Plantation

Shadowbush Wood

Blocksey Wood

Motte & Bailey

Denham Castle

Hockerhill Wood

MILL ROAD

Icknield Way Path

Hawson Hills

Dalham Hall

Brick Kiln Wood

BROCKLEY ROAD

BARROW ROAD

Icknield Way Path

Parson's Plantation

GAZELEY RD

CHURCH LANE

BEECH ROW

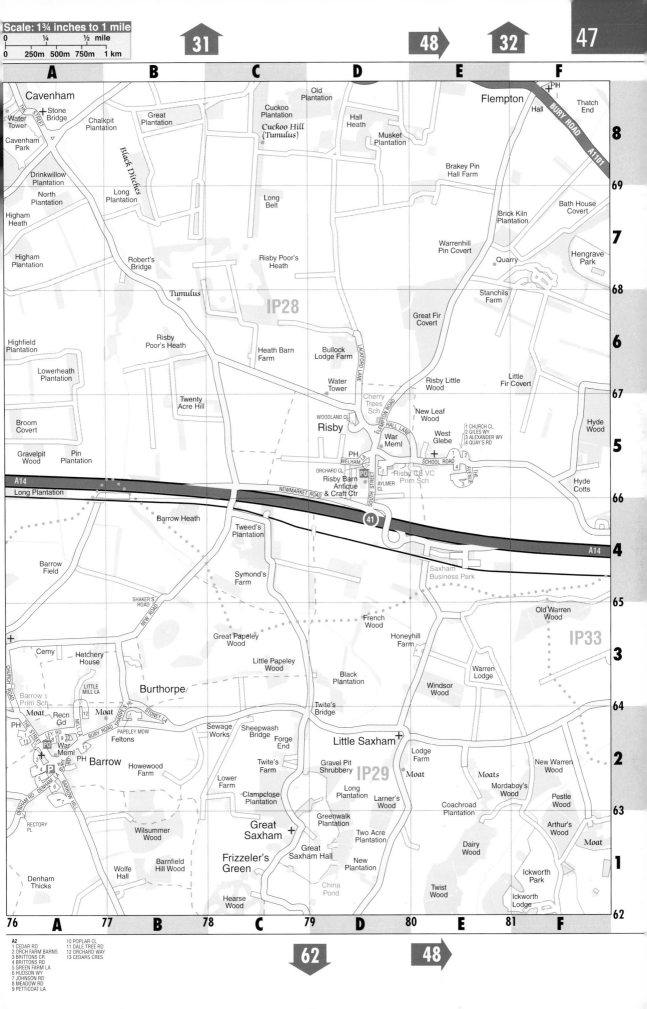

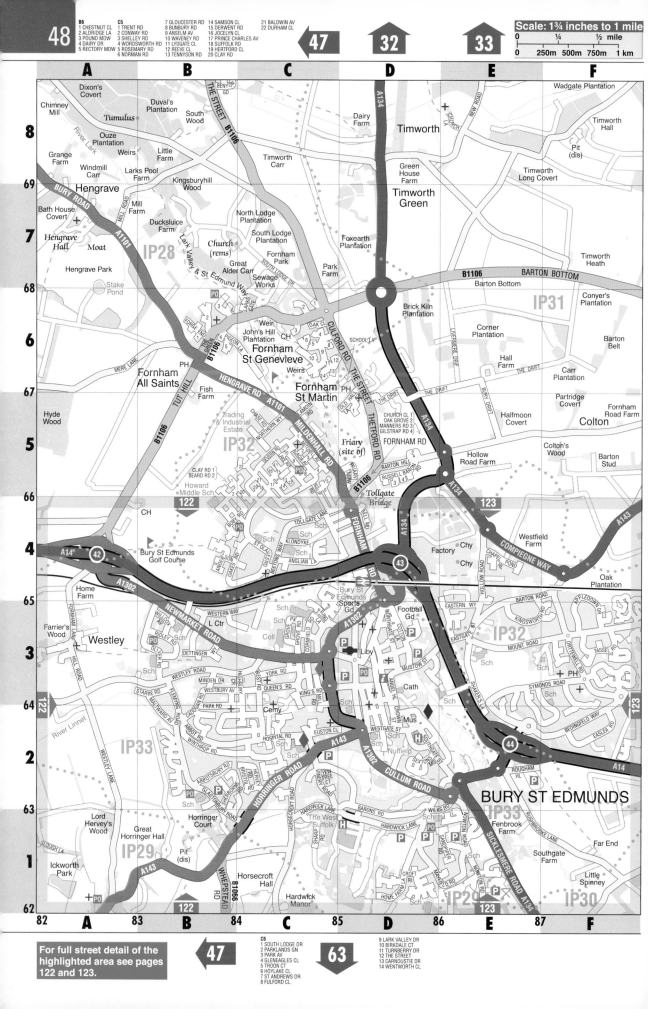

48

B6
1 CHESTNUT CL
2 ALDRIDGE LA
3 POUND MDW
4 DAIRY DR
5 RECTORY MDW

C5
1 TRENT RD
2 CONWAY RD
3 SHELLEY RD
4 WORDSWORTH RD
5 ROSEMARY RD
6 NORMAN RD

7 GLOUCESTER RD
8 BUNBURY RD
9 ANSELM AV
10 WAVENEY RD
11 LYDGATE CL
12 REEVE CL
13 TENNYSON RD

14 SAMSON CL
15 DERWENT RD
16 JOCELYN CL
17 PRINCE CHARLES AV
18 SUFFOLK RD
19 HERTFORD CL
20 CLAY RD

21 BALDWIN AV
22 DURHAM CL

47 32 33

Scale: 1¾ inches to 1 mile

0   ¼   ½ mile
0 250m 500m 750m 1 km

Dixon's Covert
Chimney Mill
Tumulus
Duval's Plantation
South Wood
Wadgate Plantation

River Lark
Ouze Plantation
Weirs
Little Farm
Kingsburyhill Wood
Timworth
Timworth Hall
Pit (dis)
Timworth Hall

Grange Farm
Windmill Carr
THE STREET
B1106
North Lodge Plantation
Timworth Carr
Dairy Farm
Timworth
Green House Farm
Timworth Long Covert
Timworth Heath

Hengrave
BURY ROAD
Mill Farm
Ducksluice Farm
South Lodge Plantation
Fornham Park
Foxearth Plantation
Timworth Green
B1106 BARTON BOTTOM

Bath House Covert
Hengrave Hall
Moat
IP28
A1101
MILL ROAD
Church (rems)
Great Alder Carr
Sewage Works
Park Farm
Barton Bottom
IP31
Conyer's Plantation

Hengrave Park
Stake Pond
FORGE END
PO
Weir
John's Hill Plantation
CH
OAK LA
Weirs
Brick Kiln Plantation
Corner Plantation
Barton Belt

Mere Lane
B1106
GREEN
PIGEON LA
Fornham St Genevieve
CULFORD RD
SCHOOL LA
Hall Farm
THE DRIFT
Carr Plantation

Hyde Wood
Fornham All Saints
TUT HILL
Fish Farm
HENGRAVE RD A1101
Weirs
PH
Fornham St Martin
THE STREET
OLD HALL LA
THE DRIFT
BURY DRIFT
Halfmoon Covert
Partridge Covert
Fornham Road Farm
Colton

Trading & Industrial Estate
CHASE LA
NORTHERN WY
Friary (site of)
THETFORD RD
CHURCH 1 OAK GROVE 2 MANNERS RD 3 GILSTRAP RD 4
A134
Colton's Wood
Barton Stud

B1106
IP32
CLAY RD 1 BEARD RD 2
MILDENHALL RD
SEVERN RD
FORNHAM RD
BARTON HILL
FRIARY LA MONK
RUSSELL BARON
A134
Hollow Road Farm
Westfield Farm
A1143

Howard Middle Sch
122
Tollgate Bridge
FORNHAM
B1106
123
Compiegne Way

CH
BURY RD
PO
TOLLGATE LANE
Sch
BELL RD
A134
Factory
Chy
Chy
CHAPEL POND
Westfield Farm
Oak Plantation

A14 42
KLONDYKE
ST OLAVES RD
BEETONS WAY
Sch
ANGLIAN LA
RD
43
Barton Road
APPLEDOWN DR

Bury St Edmunds Golf Course
A1302
NEWMARKET ROAD
WESTERN WY
L Ctr
Bury St Edmunds Sports Gd
Football Gd
EASTERN WY
KINGSWORTH RD
IP32
ORTTEWELL RD
TASSEL RD

Home Farm
FORNHAM LANE
RIDLEY RD
WILLCOX AV
Sch
DETTINGEN WY
Coll
A1302
GROVE PK GROVE RD
COTTON LA
MUSTOW ST
MOUNT ROAD
Sch
PH

Farrier's Wood
Westley
HILL ROAD
OLIVER RD
WESTLEY ROAD
HIGHBURY
WESTBURY AV
York RD
QUEEN'S RD
King's RD
MILL RD
ANGEL HL CROWN ST
Cath
Mus
SHAKERS LA
SYMONDS ROAD
Sch

STARRE RD
MALTWARD AV
MINDEN DR
CADOGAN RD
PARK RD
Cemy
i
PO
Cath
H
BEDINGFIELD WAY
EASLEA RD
123

River Linnet
IP33
WINTHROP RD
ABBOT RD
Sch
Hospital RD
EUSTON CL
WESTGATE ST
Nuffield
SEXTONS MDW
44
A14

Lord Hervey's Wood
Great Horringer Hall
HORRINGER ROAD
ABBOTSBURY RD
GLASTONBURY ROAD
SHERBORN
BRISTOL RD
HERVEY
A143
A1302
CULLUM ROAD
BARONS RD
WILKS RD
NOWTON ROAD
ROUGHAM HL
PO
BURY ST EDMUNDS
IP33
Fenbrook Farm
Far End

Ickworth Park
SLOUGH LA
IP29
Pit (dis)
A143
WHEPSTEAD RD
B1066
Horsecroft Hall
HORSECROFT ROAD
HARDWICK LANE
The West Suffolk
H
Hardwick Lane
SHARP RD
SANDPIPER
CROFT RI
HOME FARM LA
MANNERS RD
SICKLESMERE ROAD
A134
Southgate Farm
Little Spinney

Hardwick Manor
IP29
123
IP30

For full street detail of the highlighted area see pages 122 and 123.

47 63

C6
1 SOUTH LODGE DR
2 PARKLANDS GN
3 PARK AV
4 GLENEAGLES CL
5 TROON CT
6 HOYLAKE CL
7 ST ANDREWS DR
8 FULFORD CL
9 LARK VALLEY DR
10 BIRKDALE CT
11 TURNBERRY DR
12 THE STREET
13 CARNOUSTIE DR
14 WENTWORTH CL

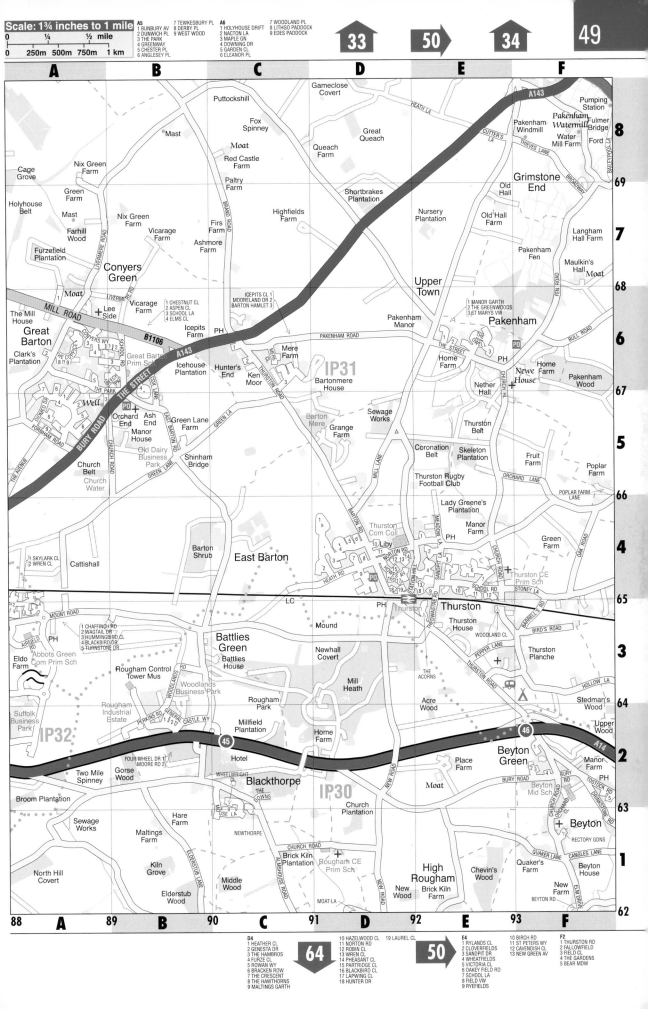

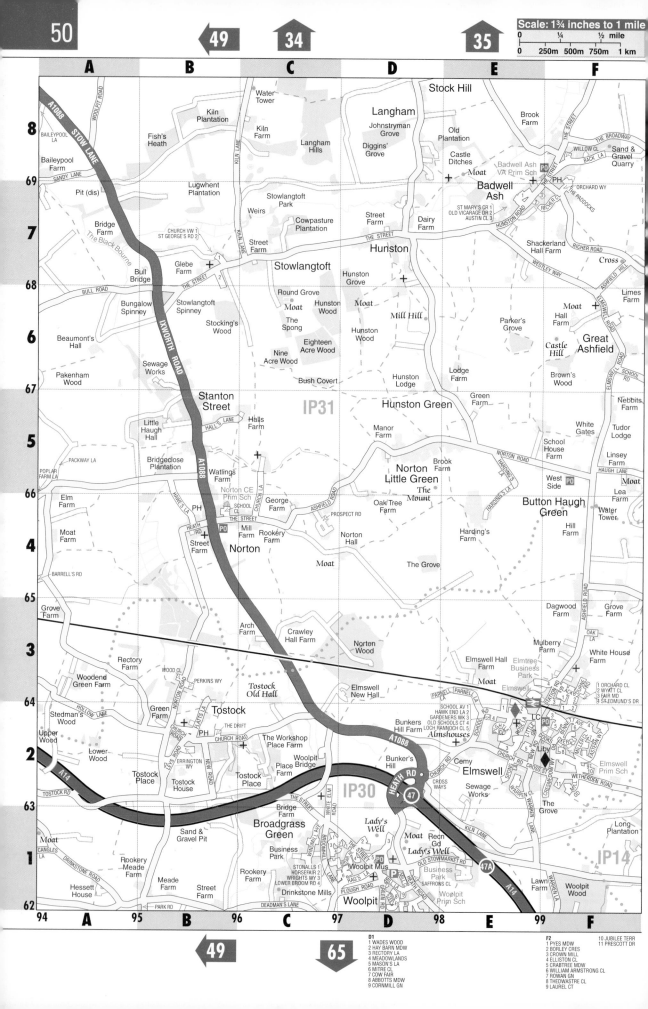

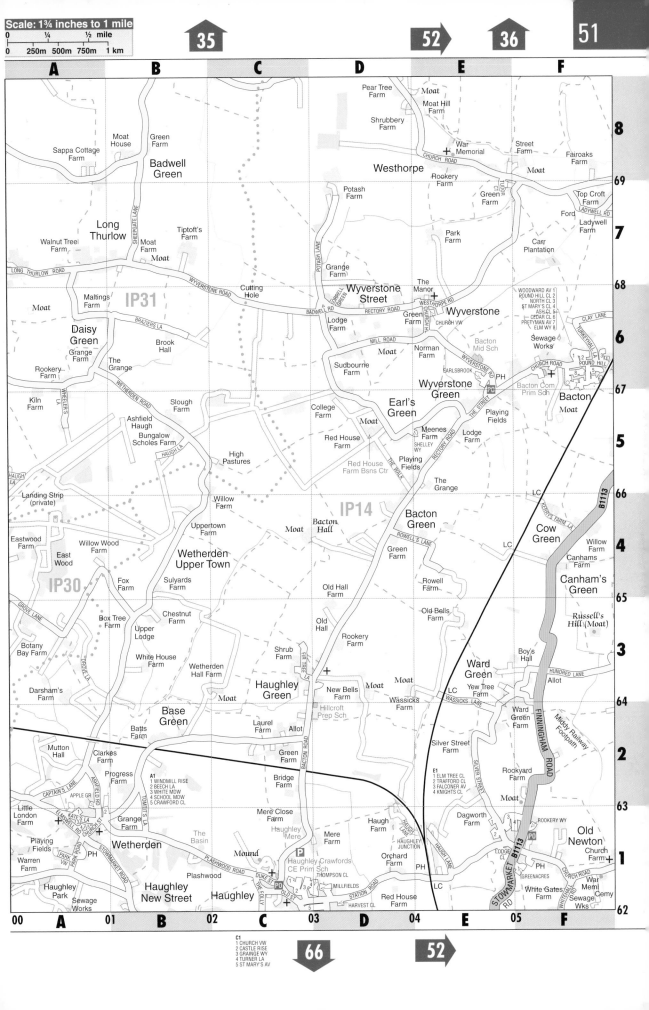

Scale: 1¾ inches to 1 mile
0   ¼   ½ mile
0   250m   500m   750m   1 km

Row 8 / 69:
Eastlands Farm, Drivers Farm, Wickham Street, Ford, Birdshedge Grove, Moat, Stanwell Farm, Street Farm, The Place, Wood Hall, Stoke Ash, Church Farm, Wickham Green, Place Farm, Hall, Stoke Ash Prim Sch, Lime Tree Farm, Green Farm, Finningham, Knoll Farm, Wickham Skeith, Colsey Wood, Lime Tree Farm, Mill Farm, Hollybank Farm, Allfield Farm, IP23, Walnut Tree Farm, Daisy Green, St Andrews Cl, Low Meadow Plantation, Wickham Abbey Farm, Great Oak Farm, White House Farm, Millhill Farm, Lodge Farm, Moat, Thwaite, Water Twr, Middlegate Farm, Surwood Farm, Elm Farm, Wickham Rd, Buck's Head

Row 6 / 67:
Bramble End, Pheasant Farm, Sewage Works, Park Farm, Hempnalls Hall, Cottage Abbot's Wood, Hill House, Mechanical Music Mus & Bygones, Dandy Corner, Poplar Farm, Moat, Granary Farm, Pine Vw, Pound Hill, Oakfield Rd, Mile & Pddck, Willow La, Cotton, Willow Farm, Cock Rd, Parker's Road, Gable End, Church Rd, Boundry Farm, Batt's Farm, Moat, White House Farm, Brockford Street, Low Road Farm, Moat, Willow End, Mendlesham Road, Mid Suffolk Footpath, River Dove

Row 5 / 66:
Lime Tree Farm, Elm Tree Farm, Hill Farm, Potters Farm, Lodge Farm, Poplar Farm, Church Farm, Buces Farm, Swilltub Lane, Hayes Farm, Moat, Lodge Farm, Moat, Allot, Moat, Mayfield Way, Mead Way, Mendlesham, Moat, Ravens Farm, Moat, Moat, Eldens Lane Farm, Moat, Chapel Rd, Walnut Tree Farm, Whicks Farm, Bendalls Farm, Mendlesham Prim Sch, PH, Glebe Wy, Ropers Farm, Sewage Works, Cotton Hall, Red House Farm, Vicarage Farm, Ducksen Road, Old Market St, Horsefair Cl, Mill Road, Freelands, Mills Farm

Row 3 / 2 / 1:
Hundred Lane, Wimble, Maltings, Denters Hill Farm, Denters Hill, Wash Lane, Tower Farm, Tollgate Farm, Yew Tree Farm, Gipping Lone, Martins Farm, IP14, Hoggars Road, Grove Farm, White Oak Farm, Brown Place Farm, Stonham Road, Lambert's Lane, Kerseys Farm, Whitings Farm, Ashes Farm, Oak Farm, Brown Street Farm, Grange Farm, Red House Farm, Hawkins Farm, Willow Farm, Tan Office Farm, War Memorial, Mayhews Farm, Shop Plantation, Cay Hill, The Green, Recreation Gd, Memorial Hall, Middy Railway Footpath, Chapel Farm, Deal Plantation, Old Hundred Lane Farm, Green Farm, Fir Tree Farm, Duncans Farm, Mid Suffolk Footpath, Tan Office, Brown Street, Gipping, Ash Plantation, Hill Farm, Mendlesham Green, Cherry Tree Farm, Woods Barn, Perkins Farm, Ash Tree Farm, Netherhall Cl, Guidepost Plantation, Gipping Little Wood, Rookery Farm, Palgrave Farm, Tan Office Lane, Old Newton CE Prim Sch, Gipping Great Wood, Wood Farm, Lapwings, Poplar Farm, Westwood Hall, Waltham Hall, Hill Farm, Bushes Grove

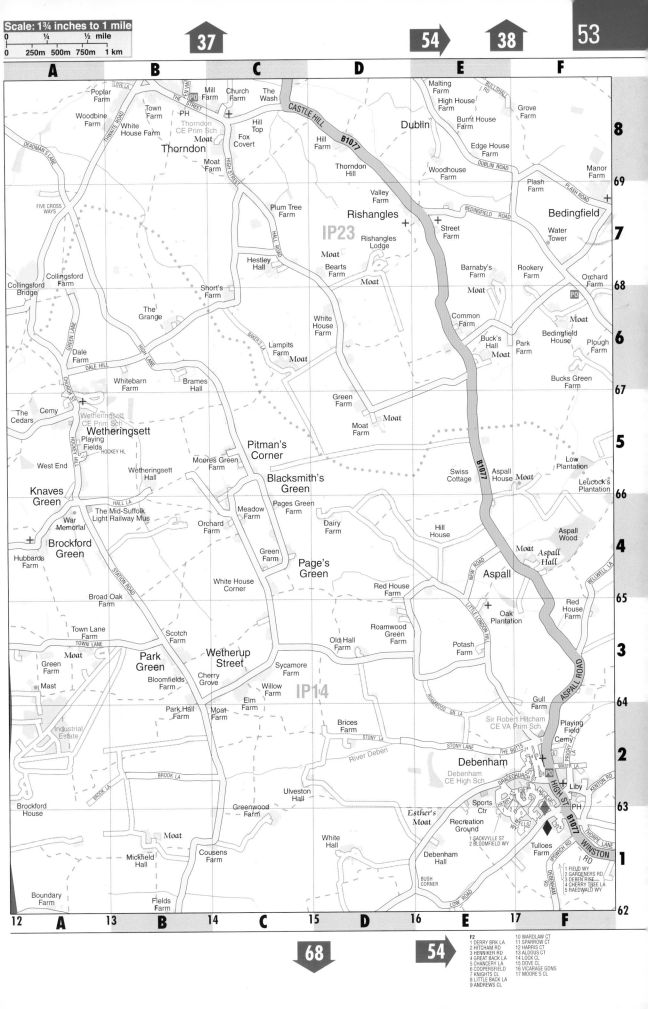

A **B** **C** **D** **E** **F**

The Rookery

Oaklands Farm

Carters Farm

Poplar Farm

Potash Farm

Lodge Farm

Park Farm

Yew Tree Farm

Town Farm

Oak Tree Farm

Pond Farm

Redhouse Farm

Valley Farm

Worlingworth

White Hall Farm

Home Farm

Newtown

1 PIPERS MDW
2 OLD STORES CL
3 WILLOW GN
4 LABURNUM CL
5 CHURCH RD
6 SMITHS CL

Bedingfield

IP23

Moat

Southolt

The Street

Willow Farm

Sycamore Farm

Patrick Lane Farm

Mill Farm

Paradise Farm

Red House

Sewage Works

Maisie's MD

Worlingworth CE Prim Sch

Beecrofts Farm

Oak Farm

Hall Road

Moat Fleming's Hall

Charity Farm

Bond's Farm

Grove Farm

PH Willow Farm

Grange Farm

Spring Farm

Fleming's Hall Farm

Bedingfield Hall

Moat

Bedingfield Plantation

Sewage Works

Poplar Farm

Chandos Farm

Moss Farm

Boxbush Farm

Lodge Farm

Bull's Hall

Wood Farm

Low Farm

Low Farm

Green Farm

Broadway Farm

Trust Farm

Bulls Hall Farm

Oak Farm

Kenton Plantation

Green Farm

IP13

The Firs

Bedfield

Ivy House Farm

Bedfield Hall Moat

Potash Farm

Moat

Monk Soham Green

Moat

Cottage Glebe

PH

Church Road

Sycamore Farm

Oakwood Farm

Grants Farm

Boltons Farm

White House Farm

Mill Farm

Crown Farm

Church La

Low Farm

Messuage Farm

Moat Farm

Moat Farm

White House Farm

Kenton

Suddon Hall

Moat

Bedfield CE Prim Sch

Leucock's Plantation

Church Cl

Moat Hill Farm

Abbey House

Glebe Farm

Hungers Green

The Grove

Bellwell Plantation

Bellwell Lane

Church Lane

Kenton Corner

Primrose Farm

Mole End

Tavern Farm

White House Farm

Bedfield Little Green

Monk Soham

School Road

Home Farm

Green Farm

Red-House Farm

Moat

Kenton Hall

Cottage Glebe

Earl Farm

Church Farm

Red House

Moat

Blood Hall

Oak Tree Farm

Kenton Lodge

Low Road

Grove Farm

Soham Town Corner

Pages Farm

Woodcroft Hall

White House Farm

Waddlegoose Lane

Hill Farm

Waddlegoose La

IP14

Grove Farm

Page's Wood

Driver's Farm

Clowes's Corner

Windwhistle Farm

Kenton Rd

Crowborough Farm

Grove Lane

Timber Top Farm

Ashfield Lodge

Low Road

Moat

The Causeway

Cemy

Camp Green Farm

Peartree Farm

Earl Soham

Earl Soham Prim Sch

PH

Great Wood

Heater Plantation

Ashfield

Earl Soham Lodge

PD

The Street

Rookery Farm

Church Farm

Moat

The Ashes

Hill Farm

PH

Street Farm

Little Green

Crows Hall

Nuttery Belt

Warners End

Stone House Farm

Mill Hill

Sewage Works

Fen Street

Vicarage Road

B1077

Winston Grange

Thorpe Lane

Ashfield Cum Thorpe

Thorpe Hall

High Row Farm

The Street

Whitepost Corner

A1120

Cretingham Lodge

Swan Lane

Boundry Farm

Brandeston Road

King's Hill

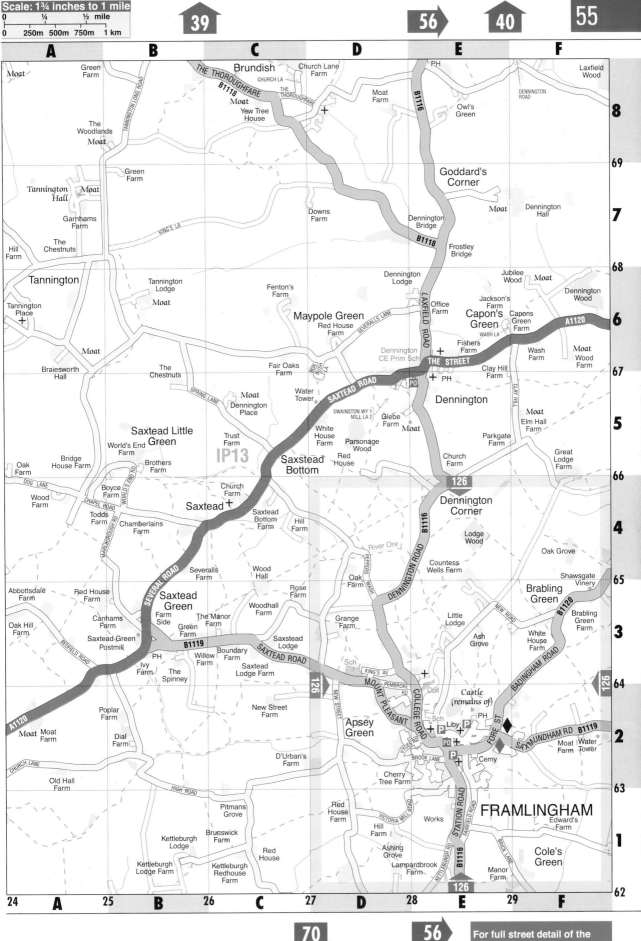

A   B   C   D   E   F

8
Moat
Green Farm
Brundish
Church Lane
Church Farm
PH
Laxfield Wood
THE THOROUGHFARE
B1118
Church La
THE THOROUGHFARE
Moat Farm
B1116
DENNINGTON ROAD
Moat
Yew Tree House
The Woodlands
Moat

69
Owl's Green
Goddard's Corner

7
Tannington Hall
Moat
Green Farm
Downs Farm
Dennington Bridge
B1118
Frostley Bridge
Moat
Dennington Hall
Garnhams Farm
KING'S LA

68
Hill Farm
The Chestnuts
Dennington Lodge
Jubilee Wood
Moat
Dennington Wood

6
Tannington
Tannington Lodge
Fenton's Farm
Maypole Green
Red House Farm
SEVERALLS LANE
LAXFIELD ROAD
Office Farm
Jackson's Farm
Capon's Green
Capons Green Farm
A1120
Tannington Place
Moat
Dennington CE Prim Sch
WASH LA
Fishers Farm
Wash Farm
Moat Wood Farm

67
Moat
The Chestnuts
Fair Oaks Farm
BOK BUSH LA
SAXTEAD ROAD
THE STREET
PO
PH
Clay Hill Farm
Braiesworth Hall
SPRING LANE
Moat
Water Tower
SWAINSTON WY 1
MILL LA 2
Glebe Farm
Dennington
CLAY HILL

5
Dennington Place
White House Farm
Parsonage Wood
Moat
Moat
Elm Hall Farm
Saxstead Bottom
Trust Farm
Red House
Church Farm
Parkgate Farm
Great Lodge Farm
IP13
Saxtead Little Green
World's End Farm

66
Oak Farm
Bridge House Farm
Brothers Farm
Saxtead
Church Farm
Saxtead Bottom Farm
126
Dennington Corner
DOG LANE
WORLD'S END RD
Boyce Farm
Hill Farm
Wood Farm
CHAPEL ROAD
Todds Farm

4
Chamberlains Farm
River Ore
Lodge Wood
Oak Grove
NARBROUGH RD
DENNINGTON ROAD
B1116

65
Abbottsdale Farm
Red House Farm
Severalls Farm
Wood Hall
Oak Farm
Countess Wells Farm
Shawsgate Vinery
Saxtead Green
PEPPERS WASH
Brabling Green
B1120

3
Oak Hill Farm
Canhams Farm
SEVERAL ROAD
The Manor Farm
Rose Farm
Woodhall Farm
Grange Farm
Little Lodge
Brabling Green Farm
Farm Side
Green Farm
Ash Grove
White House Farm
Saxtead Green Postmill
B1119
Boundary Farm
Saxtead Lodge
BADINGHAM ROAD

64
BEDFIELD ROAD
PH
Willow Farm
SAXTEAD ROAD
NEW ROAD
Sch
Coll
126
Ivy Farm
The Spinney
Saxtead Lodge Farm
126
KING'S AV
Castle (remains of)
Sch
PH
A1120
NEW STREET
MOUNT PLEASANT
PEMBROKE RD
Liby
P
FORE ST
SAXMUNDHAM RD
B1119

2
Moat Moat Farm
Poplar Farm
New Street Farm
Apsey Green
COLLEGE ROAD
PO
P
Cemy
Moat Farm
Water Tower
Dial Farm
D'Urban's Farm
VICE RD
BROOK LANE

63
Old Hall Farm
CHURCH LANE
HIGH ROAD
Cherry Tree Farm
VICTORIA MILL RD
STATION ROAD
FRAMLINGHAM
Red House Farm
Hill Farm
Works
Edward's Farm

1
Kettleburgh Lodge
Brunswick Farm
Pitmans Grove
Red House
Ashing Grove
Lampardbrook Farm
KETTLEBURGH RD
FAIRFIELD RD
BRICK LANE
Cole's Green
Manor Farm
Kettleburgh Lodge Farm
Kettleburgh Redhouse Farm
B1116
126

62

24   A   25   B   26   C   27   D   28   E   29   F

A   B   C   D   E   F

Laxfield Wood
Valley Farm
Sunflower Farm
BADINGHAM RD
Cherry Tree Farm
NEW ROAD
Walnut Tree Farm
Wind Pump
Red House Farm
REDHOUSE ROAD
Manor House Farm
OLD HALL ROAD
Bungalow Farm
Lodge Farm
MILL ROAD
Vale Farm
Aylesbury Farm
Valley Farm Spinney
Sibton Abbey
THE MOUNTS
POST ST

8

White House Farm
LAXFIELD ROAD
TWIN OAK DR
POUND GREEN ROAD
Bowling Green Farm
Hill Farm
Segmore Farm
Trust Farm
Spring Wood
Peasenhall
Peasenhall Prim Sch
HACKNEY RD THE STREET CHAPEL ST
PO

69

Castle Farm
Church Farm
ORCHARD RISE
Twin Oak Farm
Plains Farm
High House Farm
Lime Tree Farm
A1120
Boundary Farm
BADINGHAM ROAD
High Ash Farm
BADINGHAM RD
Hiltons Farm
Orchard Farm
Clare Farm
Wood Farm
Streetgrove Farm
Cemy
Cottage West End
Boundary Farm
RENDHAM ROAD

7

Low Street
MILL ROAD
Low Farm
Brick Kiln Farm
Chapel Farm
Pikes Farm
Bears Farm
HOLLOW LANE
Hollow Lane Farm
Broad Oak Farm
Apple Tree Farm
Shelleys Farm
Woodlands Farm
BRUISYARD ROAD
The Gull
Gales Farm

68

Badingham
The Old Rectory
OLD RECTORY ROAD
HIGH ROAD
Trust Farm
Shrublands Farm
BRUISYARD ROAD
Wood Farm
Hernsey Wood

6

A1120
Badingham House
PH
Hill Farm
CARRS HILL
WOOD ROAD
Colston Hall
Colston Hall Wood
Risings Farm
Bruisyard Wood
Hernsey Wood Farm
Upper Grove Farm

67

River Alde
Hill Top Farm
High House Farm
College Farm
IP17
The White House Farm

White House
Oakenhill Hall
Bruisyard Vineyard
Home Farm
CHURCH ROAD
Church Farm
Moat
Bruisyard Hall
THE STREET
Hill Farm
Rendham Hall Farm

5

B1120
Oak Barn Farm
White House Farm
Bruisyard
HILL FARM ROAD
Hill Farm Farm

66

BADINGHAM ROAD
Fisk's Farm
IP13
Hill Farm
Sandpit Farm
MILL LANE
LOW ROAD
RENDHAM ROAD
Grange Farm
Hill Farm Road
RENDHAM ROAD
PIPNEY HILL

4

The Moat Farm
BANNOCKS LANE
Cransford Hall
Yew Tree Farm
BRUISYARD ROAD
Manor Farm
Gables Farm
SANDY LANE
Rookery Farm

65

Poplar Farm
Red House Farm
Cransford
Cottage Glebe
High House Farm
Swefling Hall Farm
BRUISYARD ROAD
Pound Farm
CHAPEL LA
PH
SANDY LANE
Rendham Barnes

3

Culpho Farm
Church Moat Farm
Sewage Works
PH
LOW ROAD
Rendham
Church Farm
Rendham Bridge
Broadmeadow Covert

64

Boundary Farm
Fiddler's Hall
Moat
Little Lonely Farm
West Farm
B1119
Gull Covert
MILL ROAD
The Gull
Poplar Farm
Bridge Farm
King Edward's Coronation Wood

B1119 SAXMUNDHAM ROAD
Hatherleigh Farm
Kilderbee's Grove
Queen Mary's Covert
Broom Covert
Gold Medal Wood
Hill Farm
HOLDANS LANE
HOLDANS MDW
Swefling
GLEMHAM ROAD
Burrows Hill Farm

2

Rookery Farm
Oak Farm
Queen Mary's Plantation
Pound Farm Nature Reserve
Hall Farm
Valley Meadow Wood
Friar's Grove
White House Farm
Blackamoor Covert
Calaveras Grove
Dodd's Wood

63

Home Farm
Elm Tree Farm
North Green
Stone Farm
LOW ROAD
High Grove
SIMPERS DRIFT
Low Grove
Street Farm
CHAPEL LANE
THE GROVE
Haw Wood
Sewage Works
White House Farm
River Alde
Shingle Farm

1

62

30   A   31   B   32   C   33   D   34   E   35   F

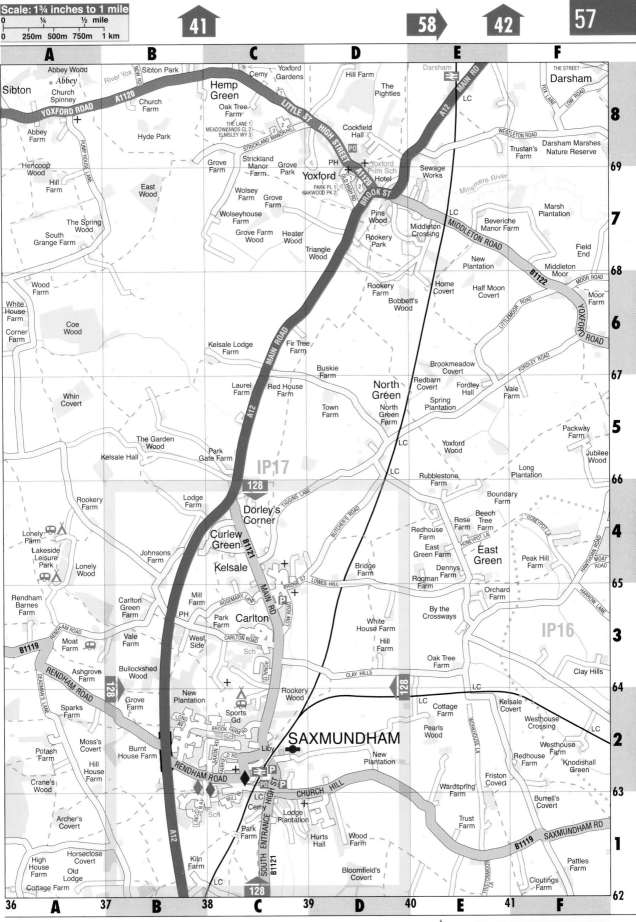

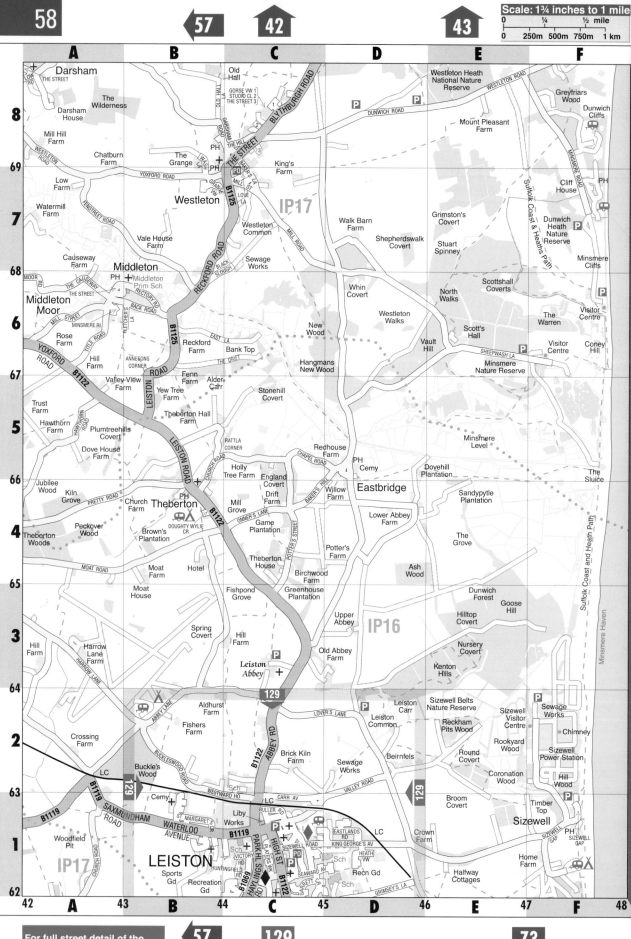

Scale: 1¾ inches to 1 mile
0   ¼   ½ mile
0 250m 500m 750m 1 km

A   B   C   D   E   F

Darsham
THE STREET
LOW RD
Darsham House
Mill Hill Farm
Chatburn Farm
The Wilderness
Old Hall
GORSE VW 1
STUDIO CL 2
THE STREET 3
BLYTHBURGH ROAD
Westleton Heath National Nature Reserve
WESTLETON ROAD
Greyfriars Wood
Dunwich Cliffs

Westleton Road
Low Farm
Yoxford Road
The Grange
PH
PH
THE HILL
THE STREET 3
WASH
GRANGE VW
MILL ST
PO
King's Farm
Dunwich Road
Mount Pleasant Farm
Suffolk Coast & Heaths Path
MINSMERE ROAD
Cliff House
PH

Watermill Farm
FENSTREET ROAD
Westleton
B1125
Westleton Common
IP17
Walk Barn Farm
Shepherdswalk Covert
Grimston's Covert
Stuart Spinney
Dunwich Heath Nature Reserve
Minsmere Cliffs

Causeway Farm
MOOR RD
Middleton
THE CAUSEWAY
THE STREET
PH
Middleton Prim Sch
RECKFORD ROAD
MILL ROAD
Sewage Works
Whin Covert
Westleton Walks
North Walks
Scottshall Coverts
The Warren
Visitor Centre

Middleton Moor
MINSMERE RI
TITLE ROAD
BACK ROAD
B1125
Reckford Farm
East La
Bank Top
New Wood
Westleton Walks
Vault Hill
Scott's Hall
SHEEPWASH LA
Visitor Centre
Coney Hill

Rose Farm
Hill Farm
Yoxford Road
B1122
ANNESONS CORNER
Fenn Farm
THE DRIFT
Hangmans New Wood
Minsmere Nature Reserve
Minsmere Level

Trust Farm
HAWTHORN ROAD
Valley View Farm
Yew Tree Farm
LEISTON ROAD
Theberton Hall Farm
Stonehill Covert
Redhouse Farm
PH Cemy
Dovehill Plantation
The Sluice

Hawthorn Farm
Plumtreehills Covert
Dove House Farm
RATTLA CORNER
CHURCH ROAD
Holly Tree Farm
England Covert
CHAPEL ROAD
Willow Farm
Eastbridge
Sandypytle Plantation

Jubilee Wood
Kiln Grove
PRETTY ROAD
Church Farm
Theberton
PH
Mill Grove
Drift Farm
BAKER'S HILL
Lower Abbey Farm
The Grove

Theberton Woods
Peckover Wood
Brown's Plantation
DOUGHTY WYLIE CR
B1122
ONNER'S LANE
Game Plantation
Potter's Farm
Ash Wood

MOAT ROAD
Moat Farm
Hotel
Theberton House
POTTER'S STREET
Birchwood Farm
Dunwich Forest
Goose Hill

Moat House
Fishpond Grove
Greenhouse Plantation
Hilltop Covert

Hill Farm
HARROW LANE
Spring Covert
Hill Farm
Upper Abbey
IP16
Nursery Covert
Kenton Hills

Harrow Lane Farm
ABBEY LANE
Aldhurst Farm
Fishers Farm
Leiston Abbey
129
LOVER'S LANE
Leiston Carr
Leiston Common
Sizewell Belts Nature Reserve
Reckham Pits Wood
Sizewell Visitor Centre
Sewage Works
Chimney

Crossing Farm
LC
129
Buckle's Wood
BUCKLESWOOD ROAD
WESTWARD HO
B1122
ABBEY RD
Brick Kiln Farm
Sewage Works
Beirnfels
Round Covert
Coronation Wood
Rookyard Wood
Sizewell Power Station
Hill Wood

B1119
SAXMUNDHAM ROAD
WATERLOO AVENUE
Cemy
ST MARGARET'S
CARR AV
VALLEY ROAD
LC
129
Broom Covert
Timber Top
Sizewell
PH
SIZEWELL GAP

Woodfield Pit
IP17
CHURCH ROAD
LEISTON
Sports Gd
Recreation Gd
Liby Works
B1119
PARK HL
HIGH ST
VICTORY RD
HUNTINGFIELD RD
PLAYERS WK
B1069
SIZEWELL RD
PO
B1122
GARRETT RD
BULLER RD
EASTLANDS RD
KING GEORGE'S AV
Sch
HEATH VW
SEAWARD AV
Recn Gd
Sch
GRIMSEY'S LA
LC
Crown Farm
Halfway Cottages
Home Farm
SIZEWELL GAP

42   43   44   45   46   47   48

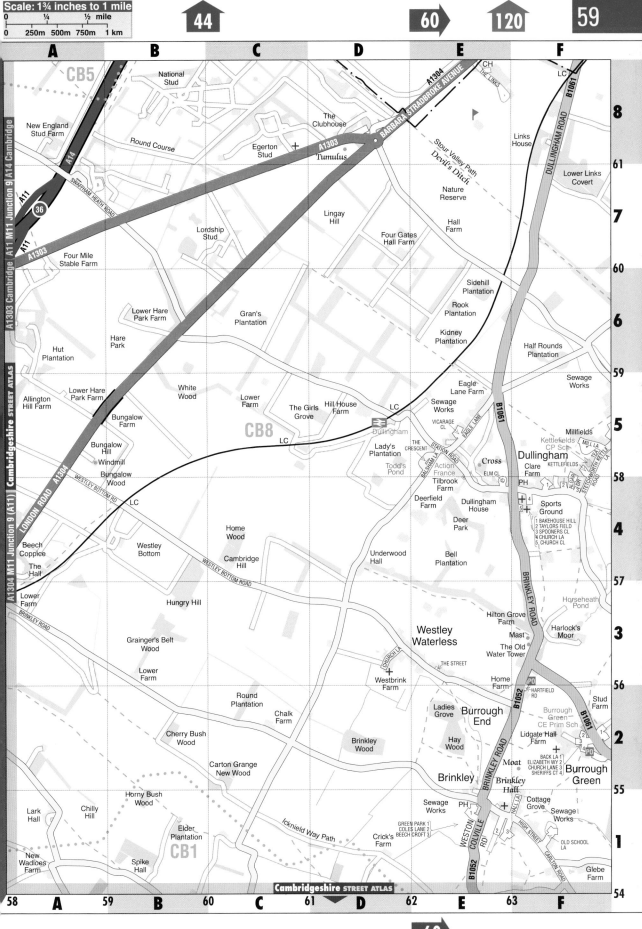

Cambridgeshire STREET ATLAS
A1303 Cambridge | A11 M11 Junction 9 | A14 Cambridge
A1304 M11 Junction 9 (A11)

CB5

National Stud
The Clubhouse
Egerton Stud
Tumulus
A1303
A1304
A1304
Stour Valley Path
Devil's Ditch
CH
THE LINKS
B1061
Links House
Lower Links Covert
DULLINGHAM ROAD

New England Stud Farm
A14
SWAFFHAM HEATH ROAD
36
A11
A1303
Round Course
Nature Reserve
Hall Farm

Four Mile Stable Farm
Lordship Stud
Lingay Hill
Four Gates Hall Farm
Sidehill Plantation
Rook Plantation
Kidney Plantation
Half Rounds Plantation
Sewage Works

Lower Hare Park Farm
Gran's Plantation
Hare Park
Hut Plantation
Eagle Lane Farm
B1061
Millfields
MILL LA
Kettlefields CP Sch
Dullingham
KETTLEFIELDS

Allington Hill Farm
Lower Hare Park Farm
White Wood
Lower Farm
The Girls Grove
Hill House Farm
LC
Sewage Works
VICARAGE CL
CB8
Dullingham
LC
Lady's Plantation
Todd's Pond
THE CRESCENT
Action France
ELM CL
Cross
Clare Farm
PH
Bungalow Farm
Bungalow Hill
Windmill
Bungalow Wood
LC
WESTLEY BOTTOM RD
Home Wood
Cambridge Hill
Tilbrook Farm
Deerfield Farm
Dullingham House
Deer Park
Sports Ground
LONDON ROAD A1304

Beech Coppice
The Hall
Westley Bottom
WESTLEY BOTTOM ROAD
Underwood Hall
Bell Plantation
BRINKLEY ROAD

Lower Farm
Hungry Hill
Hilton Grove Farm
Mast
Harlock's Moor
Horseheath Pond
BRINKLEY ROAD

Grainger's Belt Wood
Lower Farm
Westley Waterless
The Old Water Tower
Home Farm
B1052
HARTFIELD RD
Stud Farm
B1061

Round Plantation
Chalk Farm
CHURCH LA
THE STREET
Westbrink Farm
Ladies Grove
Hay Wood
Burrough End
Burrough Green CE Prim Sch
Lidgate Hall Farm
Burrough Green

Cherry Bush Wood
Brinkley Wood
Moat
Brinkley
Brinkley Hall
BACK LA
CHURCH LANE
HALL LA
WESTON COLVILLE RD
Cottage Grove
CARLTON ROAD
High Street
Sewage Works

Horny Bush Wood
Carton Grange New Wood
Icknield Way Path
Crick's Farm
GREEN PARK
COLES LANE
BEECH CROFT
PH
Sewage Works
OLD SCHOOL LA

Lark Hall
Chilly Hill
Elder Plantation
CB1
Spike Hall
New Wadloes Farm
B1052
Glebe Farm

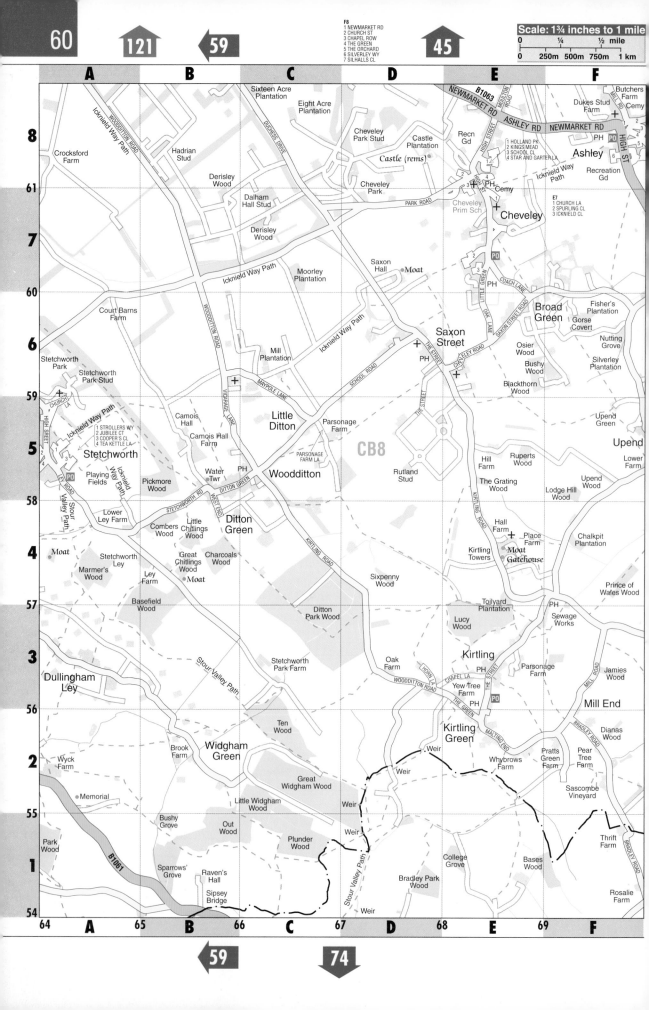

60

121

59

45

F8
1 NEWMARKET RD
2 CHURCH ST
3 CHAPEL ROW
4 THE GREEN
5 THE ORCHARD
6 SILVERLEY WY
7 SILHALLS CL

Scale: 1¾ inches to 1 mile
0   ¼   ½   mile
0   250m 500m 750m   1 km

A   B   C   D   E   F

8

Crocksford Farm

Sixteen Acre Plantation

Eight Acre Plantation

Cheveley Park Stud

Castle Plantation

Castle (rems)

Recn Gd

NEWMARKET RD

B1063

ASHLEY RD

NEWMARKET RD

Butchers Farm

Dukes Stud Farm

PH

Ashley

1 HOLLAND PK
2 KINGS MEAD
3 SCHOOL CL
4 STAR AND GARTER LA

PO

Recreation Gd

Hadrian Stud

Derisley Wood

61

Dalham Hall Stud

Derisley Wood

Cheveley Park

Cheveley Prim Sch

Cheveley

Cemy

F7
1 CHURCH LA
2 SPURLING CL
3 ICKNIELD CL

Icknield Way Path

7

Icknield Way Path

Moorley Plantation

Saxon Hall

Moat

Coach Lane

PH

Broad Green

Fisher's Plantation

Gorse Covert

60

Court Barns Farm

Icknield Way Path

Mill Plantation

Woodditton Road

Icknield Way Path

Saxon Street

The Street

PH

Saxon Street Road

Little Green

Oak Lane

Osier Wood

Bushy Wood

Nutting Grove

Silverley Plantation

6

Stetchworth Park

Stetchworth Park Stud

Church La

Maypole Lane

Vicarage Lane

Camois Hall

Little Ditton

Parsonage Farm

School Road

Blackthorn Wood

Upend Green

Upend

59

High Street

Icknield Way Path

1 STROLLERS WY
2 JUBILEE CT
3 COOPER'S CL
4 TEA KETTLE LA

Camois Hall Farm

CB8

Greeley Road

Hill Farm

Ruperts Wood

Lower Farm

5

Stetchworth

PO

Playing Fields

Icknield Way Path

Pickmore Wood

Water Twr

PH

Parsonage Farm La

Woodditton

Rutland Stud

The Grating Wood

Lodge Hill Wood

Upend Wood

Stour Valley Path

Ley Road

Stetchworth Rd

West End

Ditton Green

Ditton Green

Kirtling Road

Hall Farm

Place Farm

Chalkpit Plantation

4

Moat

Stetchworth Ley

Combers Wood

Little Chitlings Wood

Charcoals Wood

Kirtling Towers

Moat

Gatehouse

Marmer's Wood

Ley Farm

Great Chitlings Wood

Moat

57

Basefield Wood

Ditton Park Wood

Toilyard Plantation

PH

Sewage Works

Prince of Wales Wood

3

Dullingham Ley

Stour Valley Path

Stetchworth Park Farm

Oak Farm

Lucy Wood

Kirtling

The Street

Parsonage Farm

Mill Road

Jamies Wood

56

Woodditton Road

Horn La

Chapel La

Yew Tree Farm

PO

PH

Mill End

Dianas Wood

2

Wyck Farm

Brook Farm

Widgham Green

Ten Wood

Weir

Kirtling Green

Weir

Whybrows Farm

Malting End

Pratts Green Farm

Pear Tree Farm

Bradley Road

Sascombe Vineyard

55

Memorial

Bushy Grove

Out Wood

Little Widgham Wood

Great Widgham Wood

Plunder Wood

Weir

Weir

Thrift Farm

1

Park Wood

B1061

Sparrows' Grove

Raven's Hall

Sipsey Bridge

Stour Valley Path

Weir

College Grove

Bradley Park Wood

Bases Wood

Rosalie Farm

54

64   A   65   B   66   C   67   D   68   E   69   F

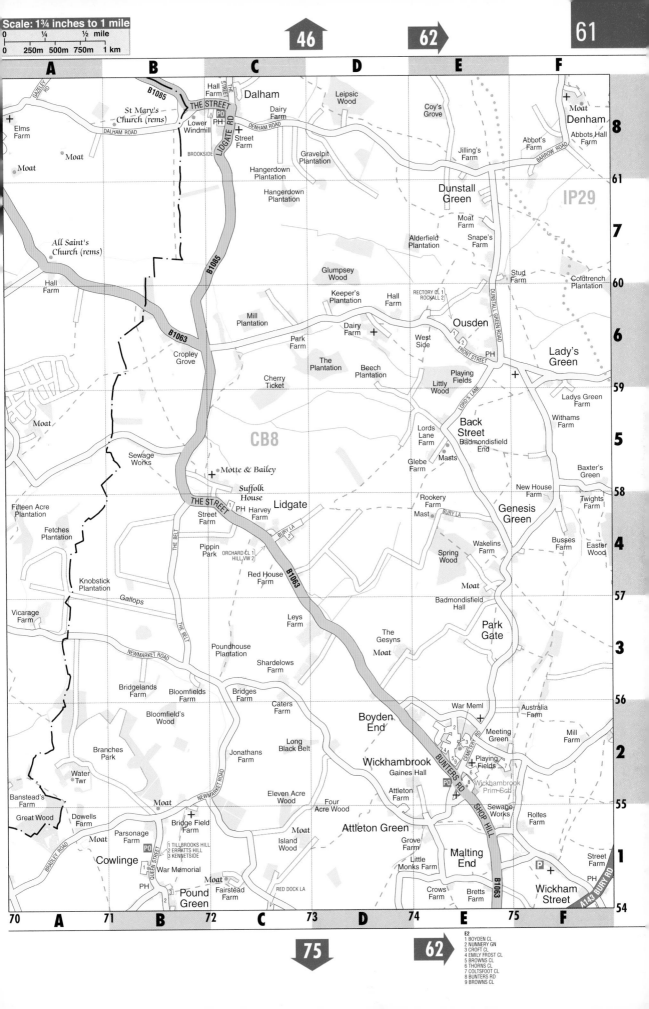

Scale: 1¾ inches to 1 mile

0 ¼ ½ mile
0 250m 500m 750m 1 km

A B C D E F

B1085

GAZELEY RD

Elms Farm

Moat

Moat

DALHAM ROAD

St Mary's Church (rems)

Lower Windmill

BROOKSIDE

Hall Farm

PO
PH

Dalham

THE STREET

LIDGATE RD

Street Farm

Dairy Farm

DENHAM ROAD

Leipsic Wood

Hangerdown Plantation

Gravelpit Plantation

Hangerdown Plantation

Coy's Grove

Jilling's Farm

Moat Denham

Abbot's Farm

Abbots Hall Farm

BARROW ROAD

Dunstall Green

IP29

All Saint's Church (rems)

Hall Farm

B1085

B1063

Cropley Grove

Mill Plantation

Park Farm

Glumpsey Wood

Keeper's Plantation

Dairy Farm

The Plantation

Hall Farm

West Side

Alderfield Plantation

Snape's Farm

RECTORY CL 1
ROCKALL 2

Ousden

FRONT STREET

PH

Moat Farm

Stud Farm

Coldtrench Plantation

DUNSTALL GREEN ROAD

Lady's Green

Ladys Green Farm

Withams Farm

Moat

Sewage Works

CB8

Cherry Ticket

Beech Plantation

Littly Wood

Playing Fields

Back Street

Badmondisfield End

LORD'S LANE

Lords Lane Farm

Glebe Farm

Masts

New House Farm

Baxter's Green

Twights Farm

Fifteen Acre Plantation

Fetches Plantation

Motte & Bailey

THE STREET

Suffolk House

PH Harvey Farm

Street Farm

Lidgate

BURY LA

Rookery Farm

Mast

BURY LA

Genesis Green

Busses Farm

Easter Wood

Knobstick Plantation

THE BELT

Gallops

Pippin Park

ORCHARD CL 1
HILL VW 2

Red House Farm

B1063

Spring Wood

Wakelins Farm

Moat

Badmondisfield Hall

Park Gate

Vicarage Farm

NEWMARKET ROAD

Poundhouse Plantation

Leys Farm

The Gesyns

Moat

Bridgelands Farm

Bloomfields Farm

Bridges Farm

Shardelows Farm

Caters Farm

War Meml

Australia Farm

Mill Farm

Branches Park

Bloomfield's Wood

Jonathans Farm

Long Black Belt

Boyden End

Wickhambrook

Gaines Hall

Meeting Green

Playing Fields

Wickhambrook Prim Sch

PO

BUNTERS RD

Water Twr

NEWMARKET ROAD

Eleven Acre Wood

Four Acre Wood

Attleton Farm

Sewage Works

Rolfes Farm

Banstead's Farm

Great Wood

Dowells Farm

Moat

Parsonage Farm

PO

Bridge Field Farm

Moat

Island Wood

RED DOCK LA

Attleton Green

Grove Farm

SHOP HILL

Malting End

Street Farm

P

PH

BRADLEY ROAD

QUEEN STREET

Cowlinge

War Memorial

PH

Pound Green

1 TILLBROOKS HILL
2 ERRATTS HILL
3 KENNETSIDE

Moat

Fairstead Farm

Little Monks Farm

Crows Farm

Bretts Farm

B1063

Wickham Street

A143 BURY RD

8
61
7
60
6
59
5
58
4
57
3
56
2
55
1
54

E2
1 BOYDEN CL
2 NUNNERY GN
3 CROFT CL
4 EMILY FROST CL
5 BROWNS CL
6 THORNS CL
7 COLTSFOOT CL
8 BUNTERS RD
9 BROWNS CL

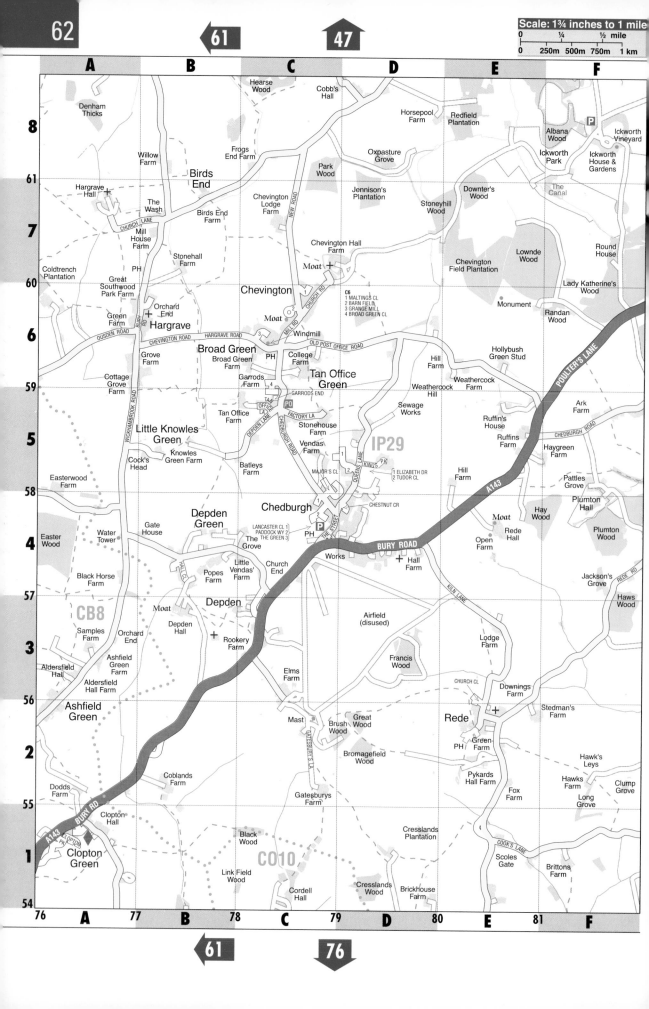

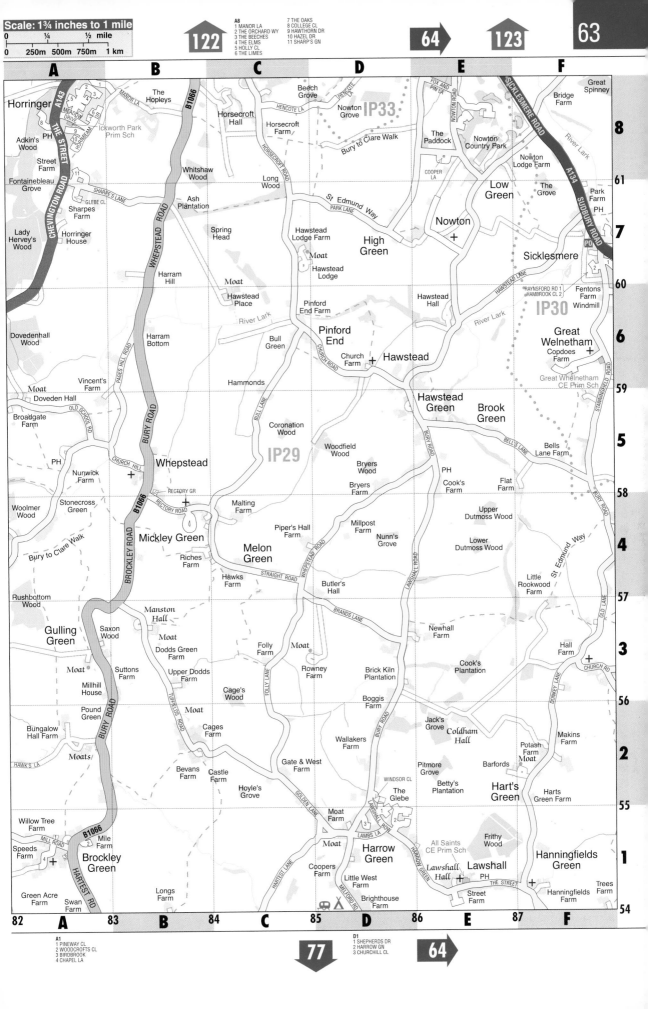

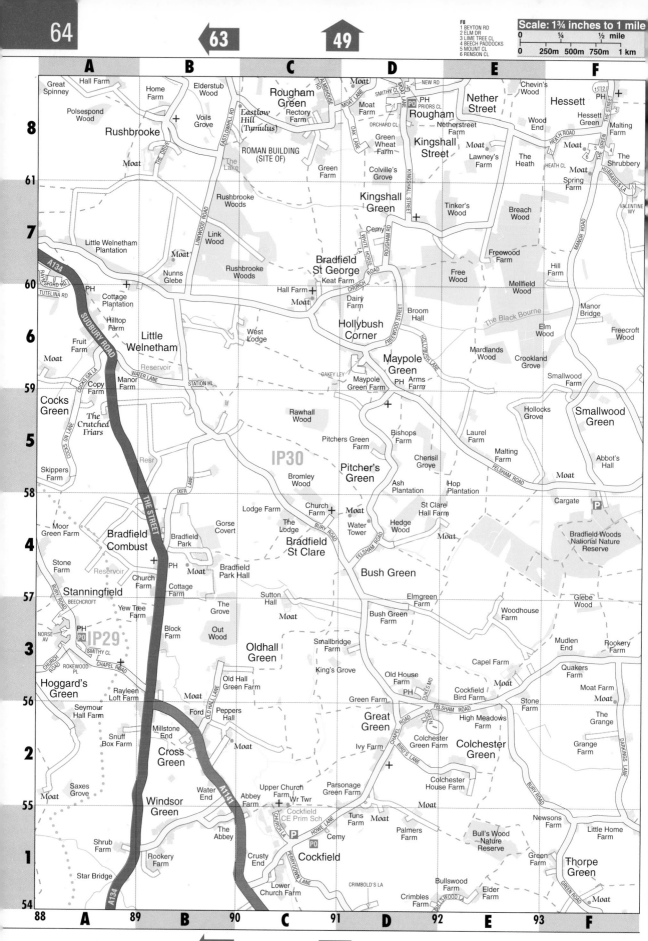

F8
1 BEYTON RD
2 ELM DR
3 LIME TREE CL
4 BEECH PADDOCKS
5 MOUNT CL
6 RENSON CL

Scale: 1¾ inches to 1 mile

0   ¼   ½   mile
0   250m 500m 750m 1 km

8

Great Spinney
Hall Farm
Home Farm
Elderstub Wood
Rougham Green
Moat
NEW RD
Chevin's Wood
Hessett
SMITHY CL
PH PRIORS CL
Rougham
Nether Street
Polsespond Wood
Eastlow Hill (Tumulus)
Voils Grove
Rectory Farm
Moat Farm
ORCHARD CL
Netherstreet Farm
Hessett Green
Malting Farm
Rushbrooke
ROMAN BUILDING (SITE OF)
Green Wheat Farm
OAK LANE
Kingshall Street
Wood End
HEATH ROAD
Moat
The Shrubbery
Moat
Green Farm
Colville's Grove
Lawney's Farm
The Heath
HEATH CL
Spring Farm

61

The Lake
Kingshall Green
Moat
Breach Wood
Hill Farm

7
Little Welnetham Plantation
Link Wood
Rushbrooke Woods
Moat
Cemy
Tinker's Wood
Freewood Farm
Free Wood
Mellfield Wood
Manor Bridge
Freecroft Wood

60
A134
RAYS FORD RD
PH
TUTELINA RD
Cottage Plantation
Hilltop Farm
Nunns Glebe
Rushbrooke Woods
West Lodge
Hall Farm
Keat Farm
Dairy Farm
Moat
CHURCH
Broom Hall
Elm Wood
The Black Bourne
Manor Bridge

6
Moat
Fruit Farm
SUDBURY ROAD
Little Welnetham
Reservoir
WATER LANE
Manor Farm
STATION HL
Bradfield St George
Hollybush Corner
FREEWOOD STREET
HOLLYBUSH LANE
Mardlands Wood
Crookland Grove
Smallwood Farm
Freecroft Wood

59
COCKS GN LA
Copy Farm
Oakey Ley
Maypole Green
Maypole Green Farm
PH Arms Farm
Smallwood Green

5
Cocks Green
The Crutched Friars
Resr
IXER LANE
Rawhall Wood
IP30
Pitchers Green Farm
Bishops Farm
Chensil Grove
Laurel Farm
Hollocks Grove
Smallwood Green
Abbot's Hall

58
Skippers Farm
Bromley Wood
Pitcher's Green
Ash Plantation
Hop Plantation
Malting Farm
Moat
Cargate
P

4
Moor Green Farm
Bradfield Combust
Bradfield Park
Gorse Covert
The Lodge
Bradfield St Clare
Lodge Farm
Church Farm
Moat
Water Tower
FELSHAM ROAD
Hedge Wood
Moat
St Clare Hall Farm
Bradfield Woods National Nature Reserve

57
Stone Farm
Stanningfield
BEECHCROFT
Yew Tree Farm
Bradfield Park Hall
Cottage Farm
Sutton Hall
Moat
Bush Green
Elmgreen Farm
Woodhouse Farm
Glebe Wood

3
NORSE AV
PH PO
IP29
SMITHY CL
CHURCH ROAD
ROKEWOOD PL
CHAPEL ROAD
Block Farm
Out Wood
The Grove
Oldhall Green
Smallbridge Farm
King's Grove
Old House Farm
Capel Farm
Cockfield Bird Farm
PH
Moat
Mudlen End
Rookery Farm
Quakers Farm
Moat Farm

56
Hoggard's Green
Rayleen Loft Farm
Ford
Peppers Hall
Old Hall Green Farm
OLD HALL LANE
Moat
Green Farm
FELSHAM ROAD
DUKES MD
GREEN LA
High Meadows Farm
Stone Farm
Moat
The Grange

2
Seymour Hall Farm
Snuff Box Farm
Millstone End
Cross Green
Moat
Great Green
Ivy Farm
CHAPEL ROAD
BIRD'S LANE
Colchester Green Farm
Colchester Green
Grange Farm
BURY ROAD
DARKINGS LANE

55
Saxes Grove
Moat
Windsor Green
Water End
A134
A1141
Upper Church Farm
Wr Twr
Abbey Farm
Cockfield CE Prim Sch
Parsonage Green Farm
Colchester House Farm
Moat
Bull's Wood Nature Reserve
Newsons Farm
Little Home Farm

1
Shrub Farm
Rookery Farm
The Abbey
Crusty End
CHURCH LANE
PERRYDOWN LANE
HOWE LANE
Cemy
PO
Cockfield
Tuns Farm
Moat
Palmers Farm
Green Farm
Thorpe Green
Star Bridge
A134
Lower Church Farm
CRIMBOLD'S LA
Crimbles Farm
Bullswood Farm
BULLSWOOD LA
Elder Farm
Moat

54

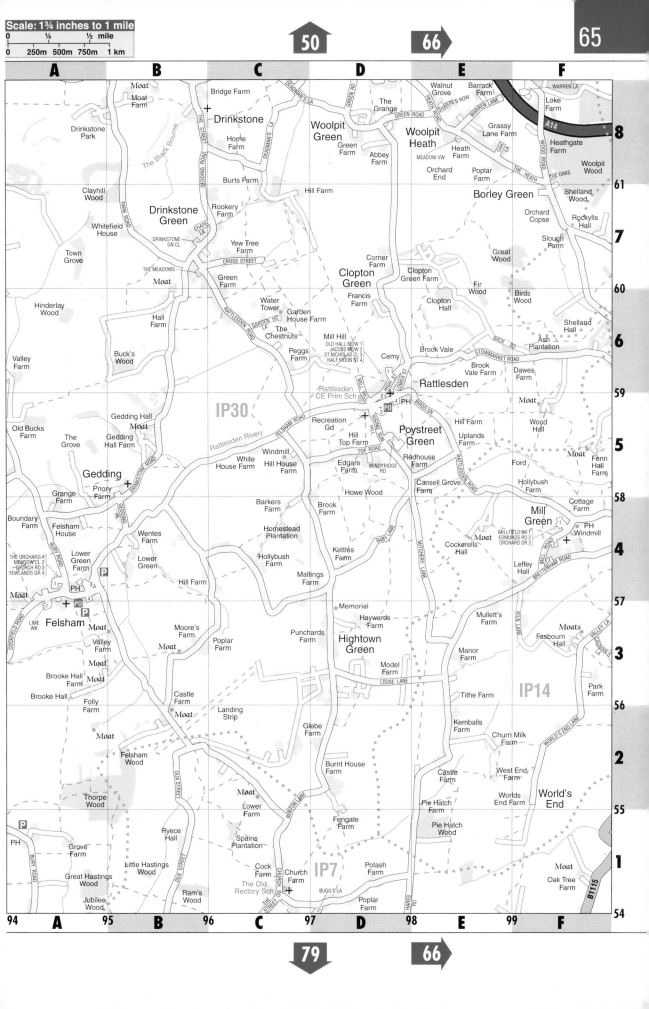

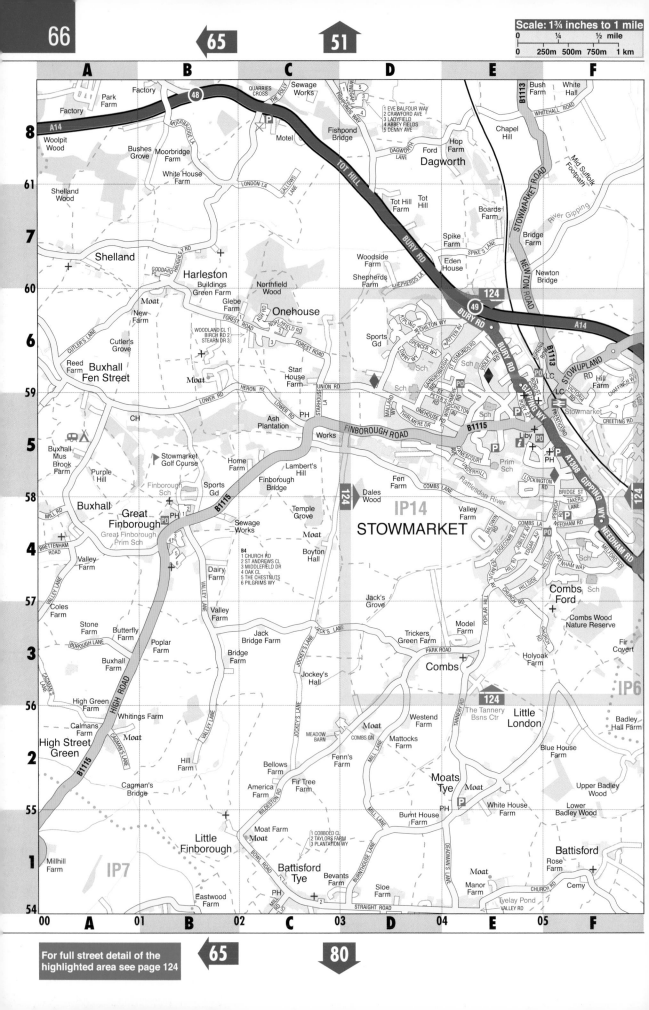

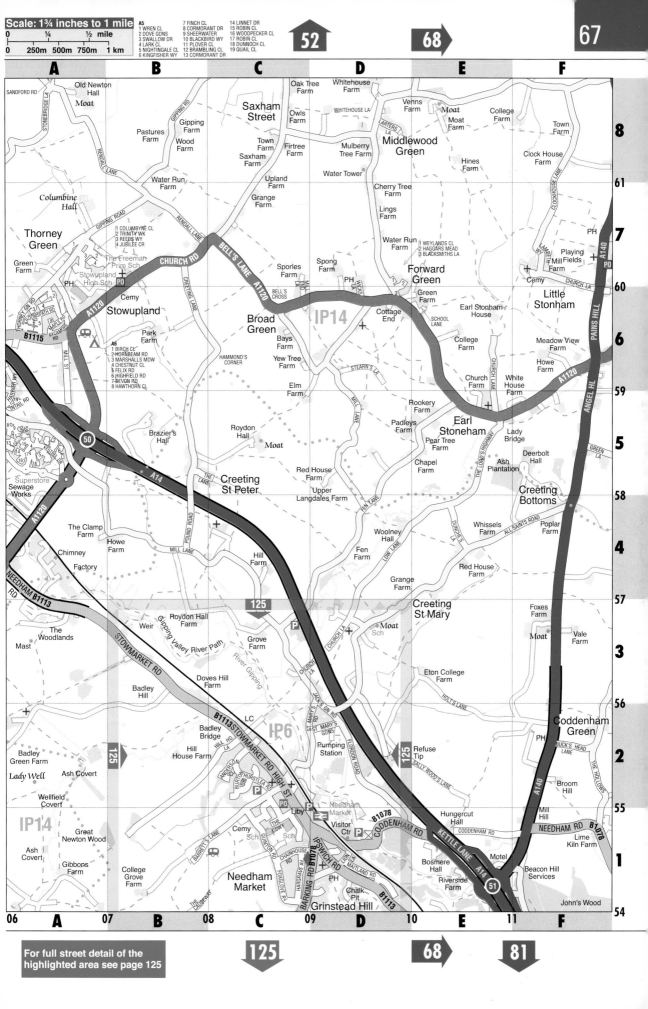

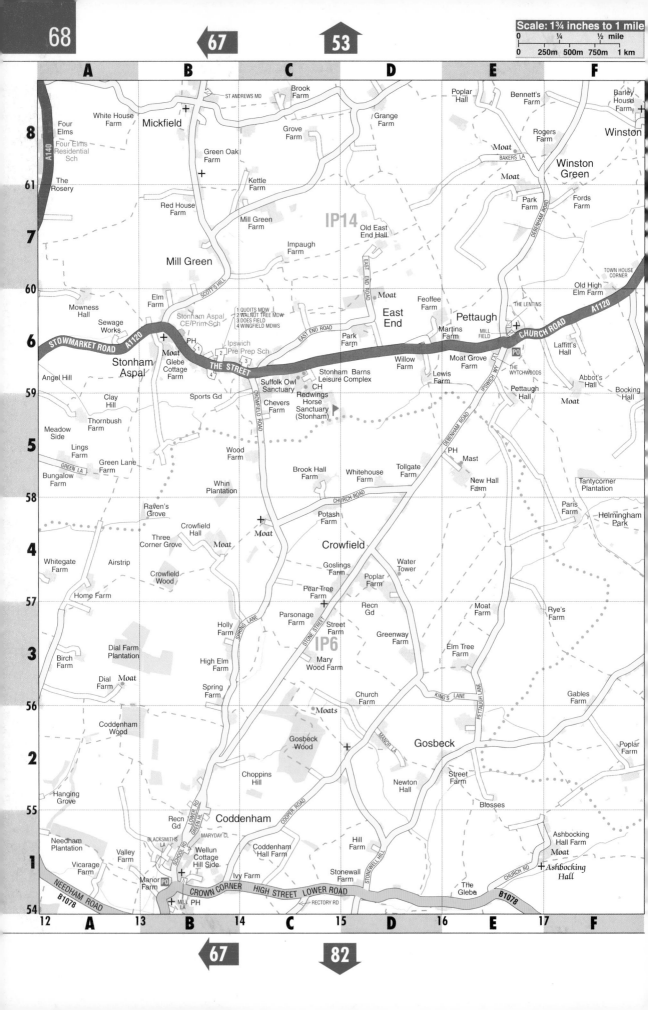

A **B** **C** **D** **E** **F**

Four Elms
White House Farm
Mickfield
Four Elms Residential Sch
St Andrews MD
Brook Farm
Grove Farm
Grange Farm
Poplar Hall
Bennett's Farm
Barley House Farm
Winston

8

The Rosery
Green Oak Farm
Rogers Farm
Moat
Winston Green

61

Red House Farm
Kettle Farm
Moat
Park Farm
Fords Farm

BAKERS LA
DEBENHAM ROAD

7

Mill Green Farm
IP14
Impaugh Farm
Old East End Hall
TOWN HOUSE CORNER

Mowness Hall
Elm Farm
SCOTT'S HILL
Old East End Hall
Moat
Feoffee Farm
Pettaugh
Old High Elm Farm
A1120

60

Sewage Works
Stonham Aspal CE/Prim Sch
1 QUOITS MDW
2 WALNUT TREE MDW
3 DOES FIELD
4 WINGFIELD MDWS
East End
Martins Farm
MILL FIELD
The Lentins
A1120
CHURCH ROAD

6

STOWMARKET ROAD A1120
Moat
Glebe Cottage Farm
PH
Ipswich Pre Prep Sch
EAST END ROAD
Park Farm
Willow Farm
Moat Grove Farm
PO
Laffitt's Hall

Angel Hill
Stonham Aspal
THE STREET
Suffolk Owl Sanctuary
Stonham Barns Leisure Complex
CH
Lewis Farm
Pettaugh Hall
THE WYTCHWOODS
Abbot's Hall
Bocking Hall

59

Clay Hill
Sports Gd
Chevers Farm
Redwings Horse Sanctuary (Stonham)
Moat

Thornbush Farm
CROWFIELD ROAD

Meadow Side
Lings Farm
Wood Farm
Brook Hall Farm
Whitehouse Farm
Tollgate Farm
PH
Mast
New Hall Farm
Tantycorner Plantation

5

Green Lane Farm
GREEN LA
DEBENHAM ROAD

58

Bungalow Farm
Whin Plantation
CHURCH ROAD
Paris Farm
Helmingham Park

Raven's Grove
Crowfield Hall
Moat
Potash Farm

4

Whitegate Farm
Airstrip
Three Corner Grove
Crowfield Wood
Moat
Crowfield
Goslings Farm
Water Tower
Moat Farm
Rye's Farm

Home Farm
Pear Tree Farm
Poplar Farm

57

Birch Farm
Dial Farm Plantation
Holly Farm
SPRING LANE
Parsonage Farm
STONE STREET
Street Farm
Recn Gd
Greenway Farm
Elm Tree Farm

3

Dial Farm
Moat
High Elm Farm
IP6
Mary Wood Farm
KING'S LANE
PETTAUGH LANE
Gables Farm

Spring Farm
Church Farm

56

Coddenham Wood
Moats
Gosbeck Wood
MANOR LA
Gosbeck

2

Hanging Grove
Choppins Hill
Newton Hall
Street Farm
Poplar Farm

55

Recn Gd
LOWER RD
GREEN HL
Coddenham
MARYDAY CL
Coddenham Hall Farm
COOPER ROAD
Hill Farm
Blosses
Ashbocking Hall Farm

Needham Plantation
BLACKSMITHS LA
Wellun Cottage Hill Side
STONEWELL HILL
Moat

1

Vicarage Farm
Valley Farm
SCHOOL RD
Ivy Farm
Stonewall Farm
Ashbocking Hall
CHURCH RD

NEEDHAM ROAD
Manor Farm
PO
PH
MILL LA
CROWN CORNER
HIGH STREET
LOWER ROAD
RECTORY RD
The Gleba
B1078

54

B1078

12 **A** **13** **B** **14** **C** **15** **D** **16** **E** **17** **F**

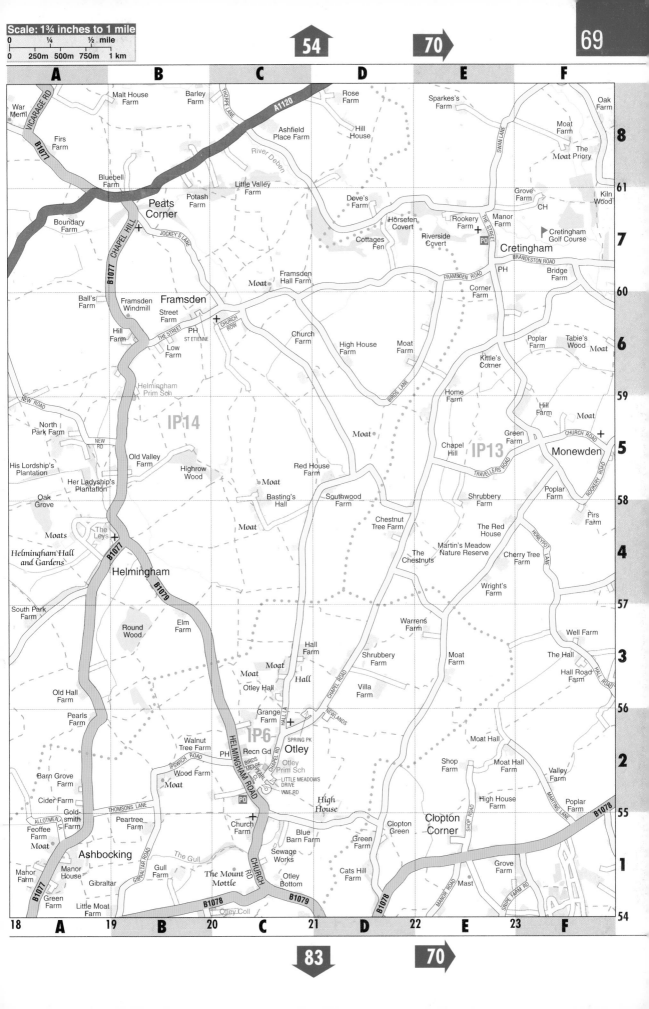

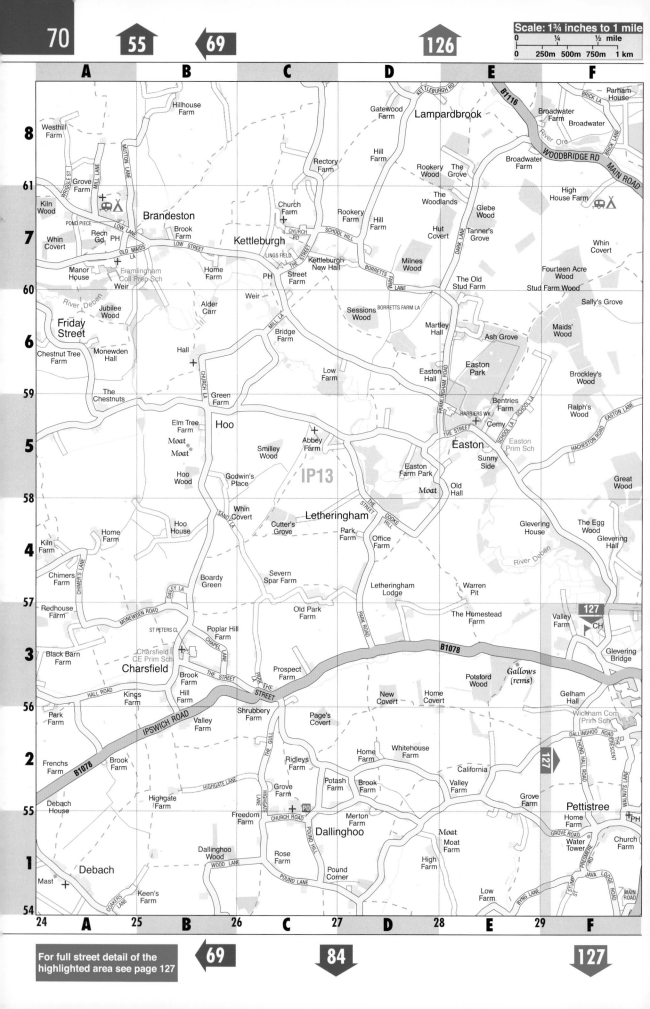

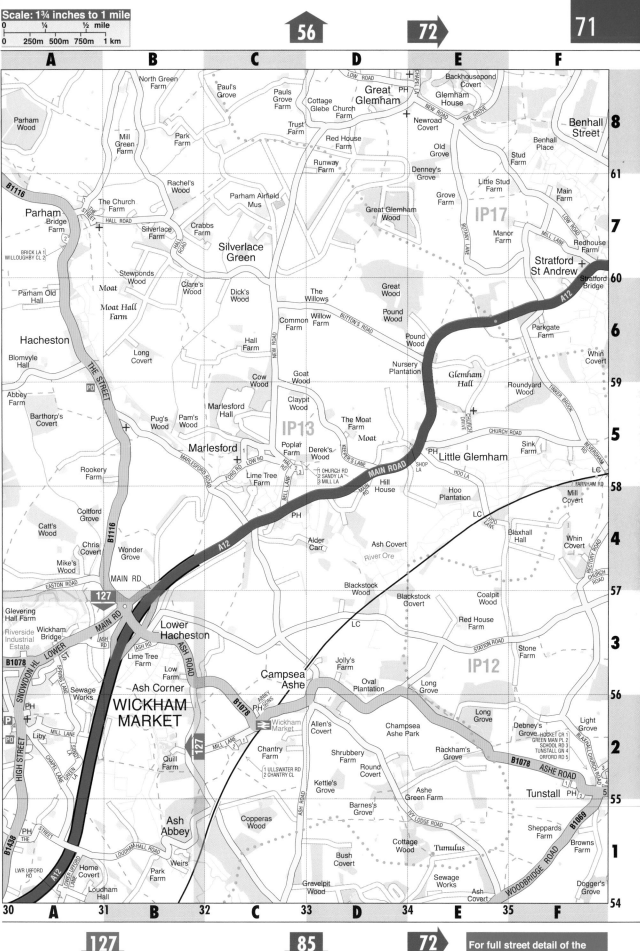

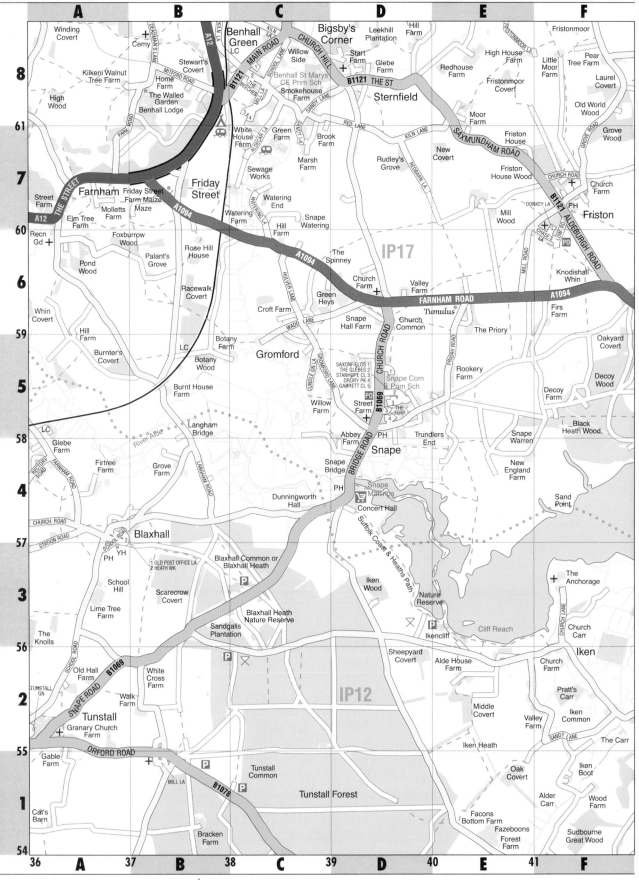

71
128
57

C8
1 CHALFONT DR
2 FORGE CL
3 MEADOW WK
4 FESTIVAL CL

Winding Covert
Cemy
Kilkeni Walnut Tree Farm
Stewart's Covert
Benhall Green LC
Bigsby's Corner
Leekhill Plantation
Hill Farm
Fristonmoor
High House Farm
Little Moor Farm
Pear Tree Farm

High Wood
Home Farm
The Walled Garden
Benhall Lodge
The Beeches
THE MILL
Willow Side
Benhall St Marys CE Prim Sch
Smokehouse Farm
Start Farm
Glebe Farm
Redhouse Farm
Fristonmoor Covert
Laurel Covert
Old World Wood

White House Farm
Green Farm
Sternfield
Moor Farm
Friston House
Grove Wood

Sewage Works
Marsh Farm
Brook Farm
Red Lane
New Covert
SAXMUNDHAM ROAD
Church Road
Church Farm

Farnham
Friday Street Farm Maize Maze
Friday Street
Watering End
Snape Watering
Rudley's Grove
Friston House Wood
Mill Wood
Friston
DONKEY LA
PH

Street Farm
Elm Tree Farm
Molletts Farm
Watering Farm
Hill Farm
The Spinney
IP17
Valley Farm
CHASE'S LOW RD LA
PO

Recn Gd
Foxburrow Wood
Palant's Grove
Rose Hill House
Church Farm
FARNHAM ROAD
Tumulus
Firs Farm
Knodishall Whin

Pond Wood
Racewalk Covert
Croft Farm
Green Heys
Snape Hall Farm
Church Common
The Priory
Oakyard Covert

Whin Covert
Hill Farm
Burnter's Covert
LC
Botany Farm
Botany Wood
Gromford
WADD LANE
Willow Farm
SAXONFIELDS 1
THE GLEBES 2
STANHOPE CL 3
DRURY PK 4
GARRETT CL 5
Snape Com & Prim Sch
Rookery Farm
Decoy Farm
Decoy Wood

LC
Burnt House Farm
Langham Bridge
Street Farm
THE TERR
Snape Warren
Black Heath Wood

LC
Glebe Farm
Firtree Farm
Grove Farm
LANGHAM ROAD
Abbey Farm
PH
Snape
Trundlers End
New England Farm

Blaxhall
PH YH
Dunningworth Hall
Snape Bridge
BRIDGE ROAD
PH
Snape Maltings
Concert Hall
Iken Wood
Nature Reserve
Sand Point

School Hill
1 OLD POST OFFICE LA
2 HEATH WK
Scarecrow Covert
Blaxhall Common or Blaxhall Heath
P
Suffolk Coast & Heaths Path
Ikencliff
P
Cliff Reach
The Anchorage
Church Carr
Iken

Lime Tree Farm
Blaxhall Heath Nature Reserve
Sandgalls Plantation
Sheepyard Covert
Alde House Farm
Church Farm

The Knolls
Old Hall Farm
B1069
White Cross Farm
P
IP12
Middle Covert
Pratt's Carr
Iken Common

Tunstall GN
SNAPE ROAD
Walk Farm
Tunstall
Granary Church Farm
Valley Farm
SANDY LANE
The Carr

Gable Farm
ORFORD ROAD
P
Tunstall Common
Iken Heath
Oak Covert
Iken Boot

MILL LA
B1078
Tunstall Forest
Facons Bottom Farm
Alder Carr
Wood Farm

Cat's Barn
Bracken Farm
Fazeboons Forest Farm
Sudbourne Great Wood

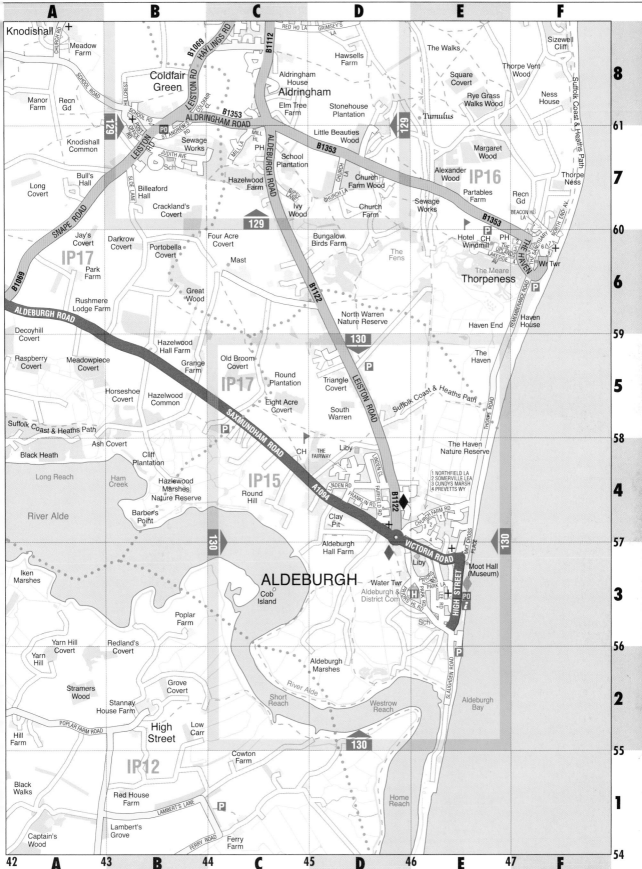

Scale: 1¾ inches to 1 mile

0 | ¼ | ½ mile
0 | 250m | 500m | 750m | 1 km

A **B** **C** **D** **E** **F**

Carlton

River Stour

Ford

Weir

East Green

East Green Farm

BRADLEY RD

BRINKLEY RD

CHURCH RD

Hall Farm

Moat

ACRE ROAD

B1061

THE STREET

Waterfield Barn Farm

Mill Farm

WATER LA

FOX GN

CB8

Doley Wood

8

Handy Bar Grove

Matthews Farm

Moat

Stour Valley Path

53

Church Farm

Carlton Wood

MATTHEWS LA

EVERGREEN LA

Great Bradley

Fox Farm

THURLOW ROAD

Little Bradley

CARLTON GREEN RD

Ever Green

CLARENDALE EST

7

Hart Wood

Broad Road

52

Lopham's Hall Farm

Mill Mound

Almshouses

Little Thurlow Green

Wadgell's Wood

Carlton Green

Lopham's Wood

Moat

CHURCH RD

Thurlow CE Prim Sch

Little Thurlow

6

Finchley Farm

Girton Farm

Sewage Works

Grove Wood

51

Gover's Grove

Temple End Plantation

Temple End

Temple End Stream

PH

School House

Bury Road

CB1

Temple End Farm

TEMPLE END

THE STREET

Manor Farm

Drift Side

Great Thurlow

Foxburrow Wood

5

The New Plantation

Wasteland Plantation

Goldings Farm

PH

PO

Great Thurlow Hall

Playing Fields

Trundley Wood

50

Cadge's Wood

Dowsett Wood

Moat

Windmill

WRATTING ROAD

Ganwick Wood

West End Lane

Smoothies Plantation

Glebe Plantation

Willow Hall Plantation

B1061

4

North Wood

Tuffill's Plantation

Hunts Park Farm

CB9

Gravel Pit Plantation

WITHERSFIELD ROAD

High Noon Plantation

Hungry Hill Plantation

Nursery Plantation

Stour Valley Path

49

Exhibition Farm

Littley Wood

The Spinney

Abbacy Wood

Hill Wood

Pelican House Farm

Greenfields Farm

THE STREET

Maltings Farm

High Noon Farm

Moor Pasture Plantation

Jarvis Hill

THURLOW RD

Hall Farm

Ford

3

Stour Brook

Lawn Farm

SNIPPER'S LANE

Charity Farm

Moat

Bittons Farm

Moor Pasture Farm

Paradise Farm

WITHERSFIELD ROAD

Rook Tree Farm

PH

Wash Farm

BURTON HL

ROSE HL

48

Lawn Wood

Recreation Gd

PH

Lilley Farm

Sports Ground

Great Wratting

Church End

SCHOOL RD

P

Chimney

Factory

HORSEHEATH RD

TURNPIKE HL

Withersfield

CHURCH ST

Burton Ley Plantation

Old Haverhill Rd

2

Silver Street Farm

SILVER ST

HOLLOW HL

PH

HOMESTALL CR

Church Farm

Hall Farm

Sewage Works

QUEENS ST

Water Twr

Reservoir

Norney Plantation

Little Wratting

B1061 HAVERHILL RD

Sports Gd

Howe Wood

47

A1307 Cambridge

Spring Grove Farm

Hanchet End

Bridge End

132

HAWTHORN RD

WITHERSFIELD RD

Boyton Hall

Boyton Hall Farm

PH

HAVERHILL RD

A143

Hilltop Farm

133

Kedington

A1307

A1077

Hanchett Hall Farm

HANCHET END

132

BAINES CONEY

WOODS RD

PARK RD

Howe RD

ARREMORE RD

WRATTING RD

ANN SUCKLING ROAD

ABBOTTS RD

CHAPPLE DR

BLACKSMITH WY

CHALKSTONE WY

Samuel Ward Upper Sch & Tech Coll

Great Wilsey Farm

Great Field Plantation

Moat

1

MELLIS CL 1
LANGHAM WY 2
NOTLEY DR 3
HOPTON RI 4

CHIMSWELL WY

SPRINGE RD

CAMBR DR

ASH GR

A1307

Sch

46

64 **A** **65** **B** **66** **C** **67** **D** **68** **E** **69** **F**

For full street detail of the highlighted area see pages 132 and 133

Cambridgeshire STREET ATLAS

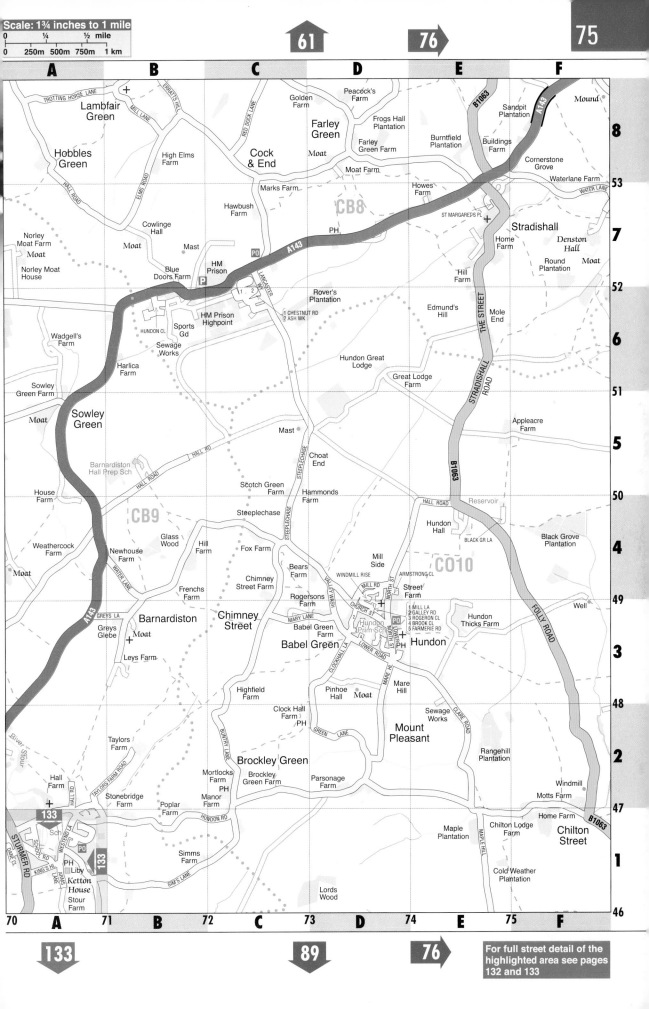

A   **B**   **C**   **D**   **E**   **F**

8

Deersleys Farm
Moat Plantation
Moat
Moat Gifford's Hall
Wickham House
Purton Green Farm
Windolphs Farm
Hawkedon House
Manor Farm
Francis Farm
Manor Farm

CB8
Garbs Grove
Sewage Works
Moat
Brick House Farm
CRESSLANDS LA
Church Farm

53
Elm Grove
Purton Green
War Memorial
PO
PH
Somerton

Denston Bridge
Redfield Grove
Hawkedon
Brook's Wood
Cross (rems)

7
Denston
Glebe Farm
Windmill
Ford
Ford

River Glem
Stansfield
THURSTON LANE
HALL LANE
Bury to Clare Walk
Gallowgate Farm
Somerton Hall

52
Elm Farm
PIPPIN POST CL
Lower Street
Thurlston Hall
Ford
Moat
IP29
Ford
Lodge Farm
River Glem

6
Hollybud Wood
Laurel Bank Farm
HIGH STREET
PH
Bayments Farm
Stansfield Hall
Hungriff Hall
Browns Farm

Assington Green
UPPER STREET
Upper Street
Thurston End
Swan's Hall
Moat

51
Price Wood
Fenstead End
Asgood Wood
Lownage Wood

5
Gosland Green
Shadowbush Farm
Shadowbush Wood
Houghton Grove
Hooks Hall
Fishers
Longley Wood
Truckett's Hall

Northey Wood
Moat
Moor's Farm
Sparrow's Wood

50
Clopton Hall
Poslingford House
Long Wood

Chipley Abbey
Flax Farm
King's Wood
Wales End

4
Wales End Farm

49
Easty Wood
New Street Farm

3
THE STREET
Brynbank Farm
JONES RD
CO10
Robb's Farm

Poslingford
Haven Farm
NEW HOUSE LANE
New House Farm

48
Bury to Clare Walk
Ducks Hall

2
CLARE ROAD
Colt's Hall
CAVENDISH LANE

Nether Hall Mus & Gall
Moat
Blacklands Hall
1 THE COLUMBINES
2 PENTLOW DR
3 CLUANIE ORCHARD

47
Wentford Farm
Peacocks Road
Sports Gd

Chilton Stream
B1063
SNOW HILL
Wentford
Houghton Hall
Stour Valley
Path
Cavendish
A1092
MELFORD ROAD

1
Chapel (rems)
Hermitage Farm
Moat
Alder Carr
Scotts Farm
Cavendish CE Prim Sch
Cemy
HIGH STREET
LOWER STREET
Sue Ryder Foundation Museum
River Stour
Moat
B1064

46
HERMITAGE MDWS
POOLE ST
Green End
Pentlow

A   **B**   **C**   **D**   **E**   **F**

A1
1 WENTFORD VW
2 MARCH PL
3 MORTIMER PL
4 GLOUCESTER PL
5 HERTFORD RD
6 DE BURGH PL
7 CLARENCE RD

E1
1 PEACOCKS CL
2 NETHER RD
3 MANOR CL
4 CHURCH CL
5 GREYS CL

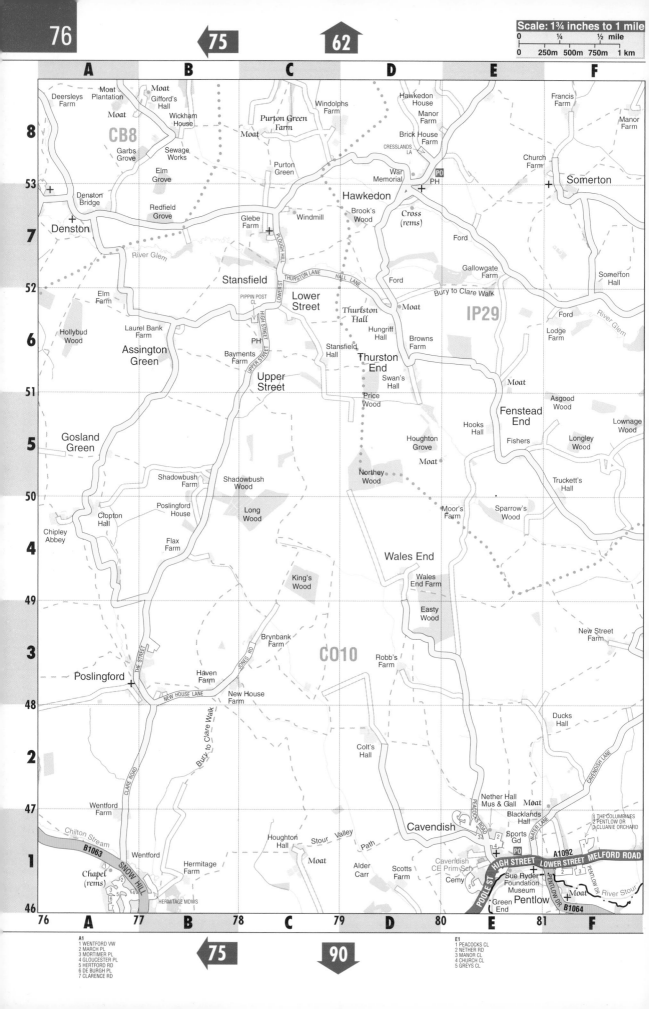

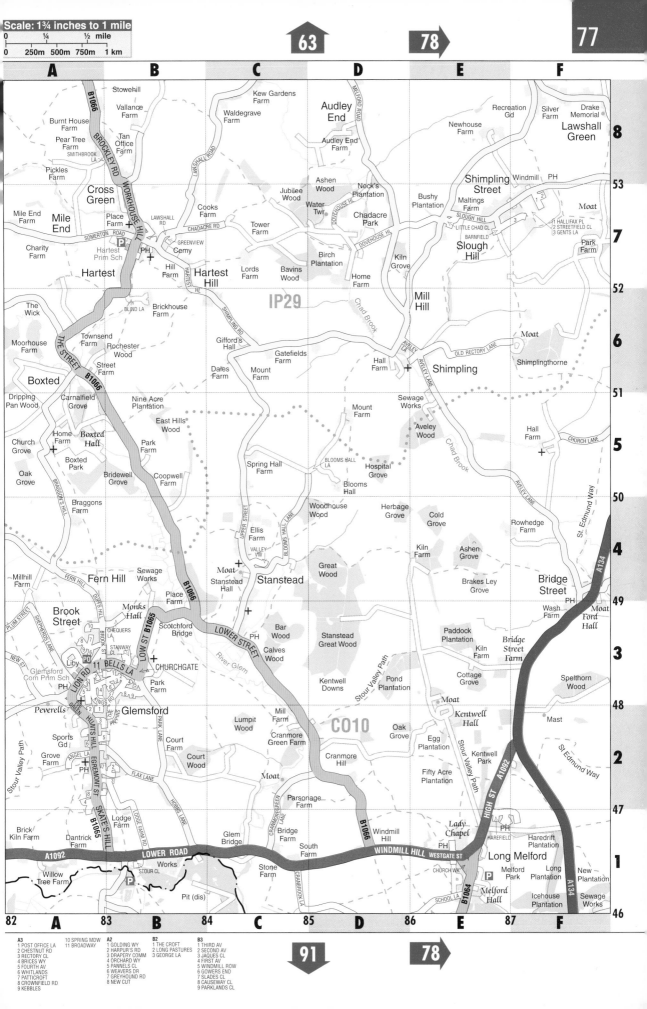

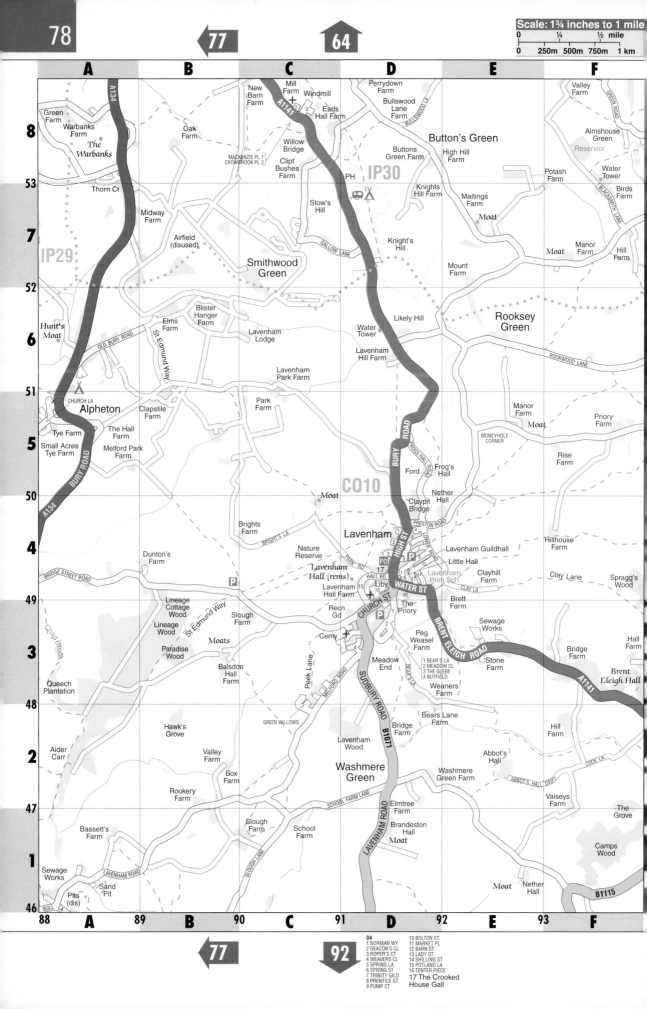

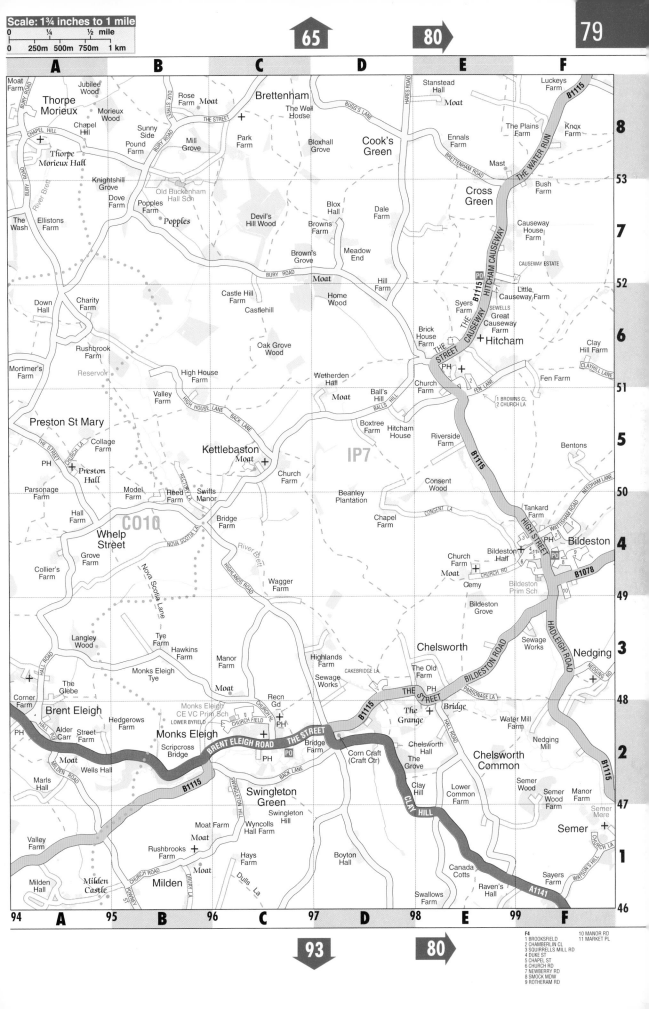

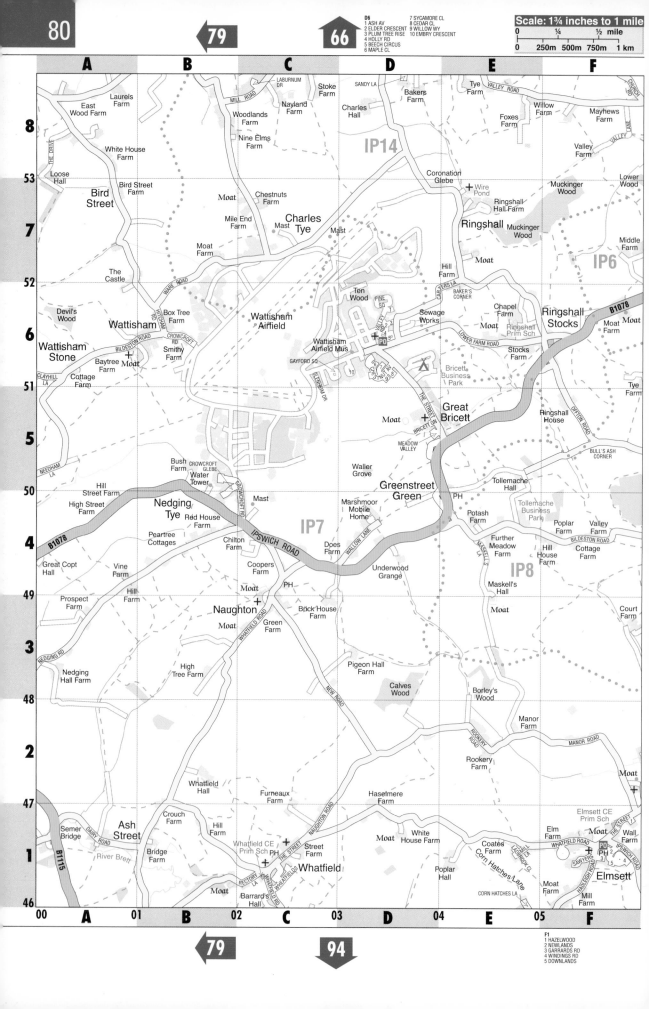

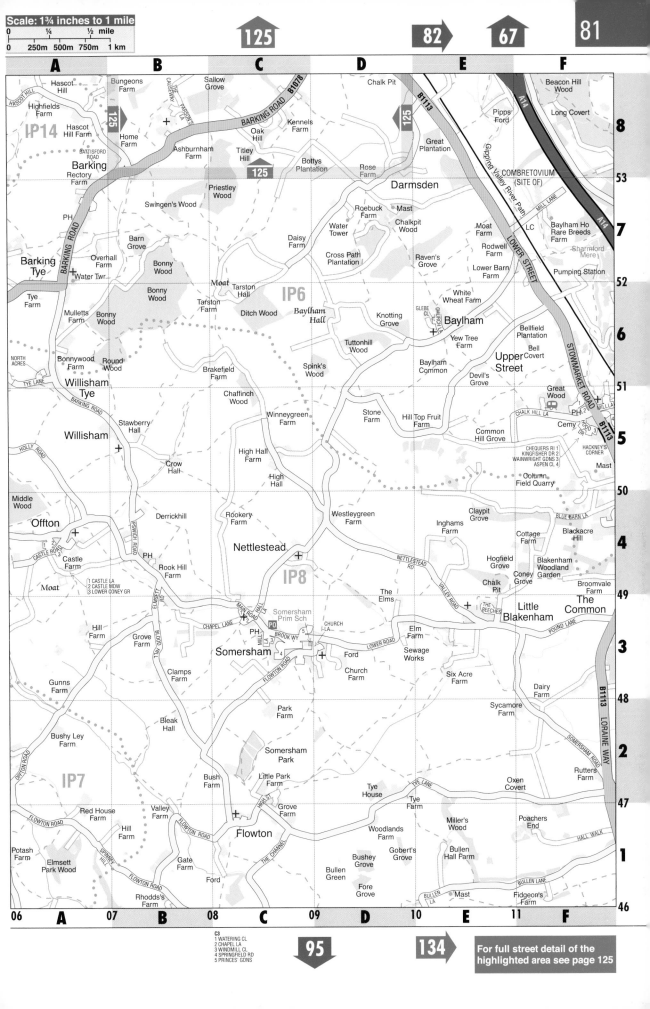

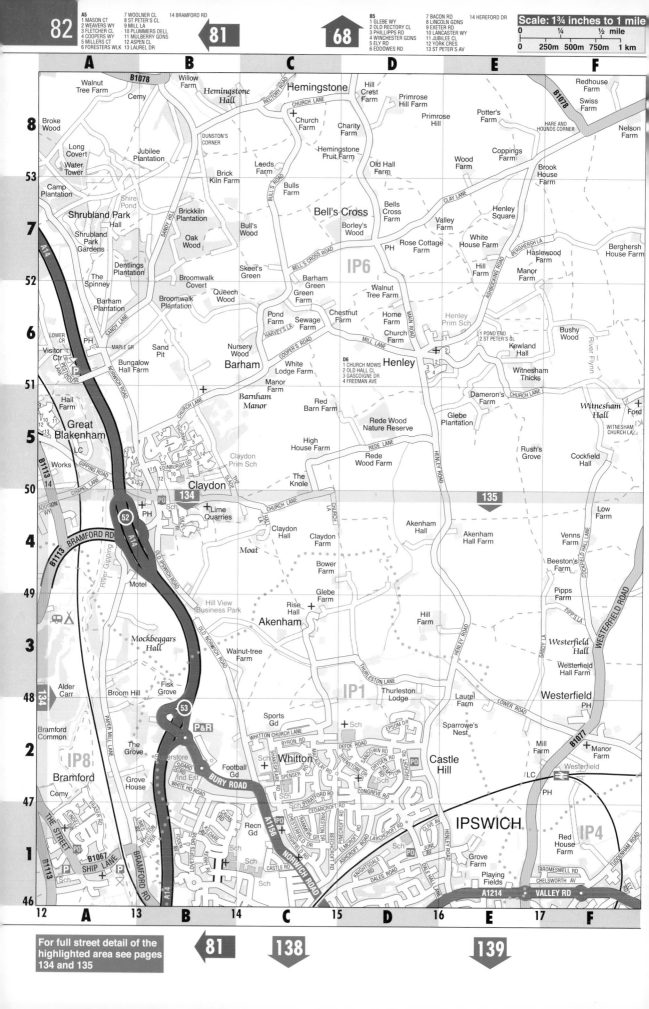

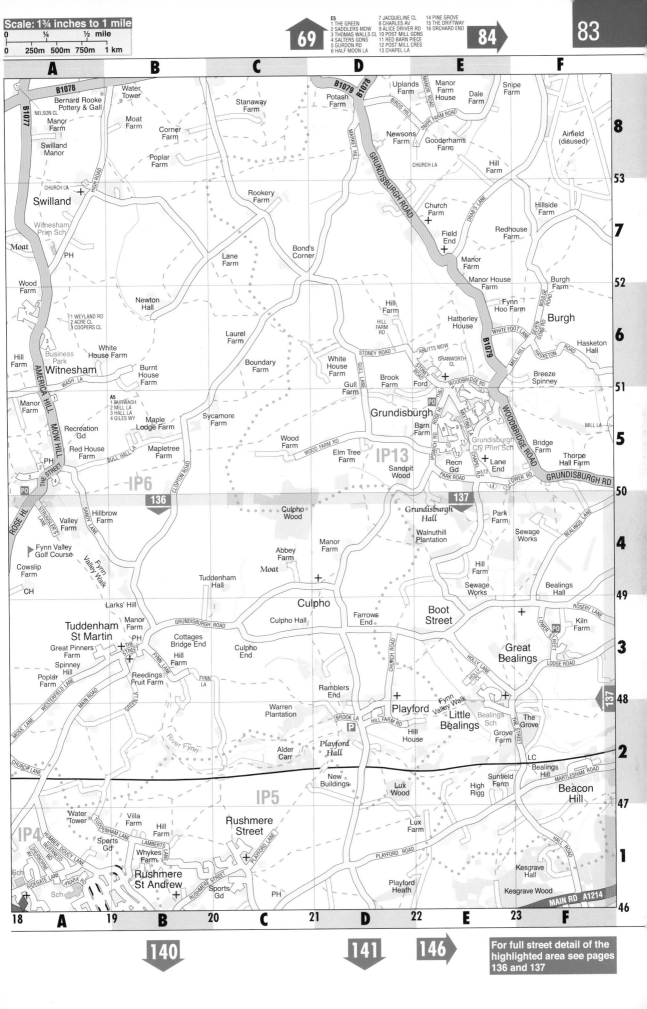

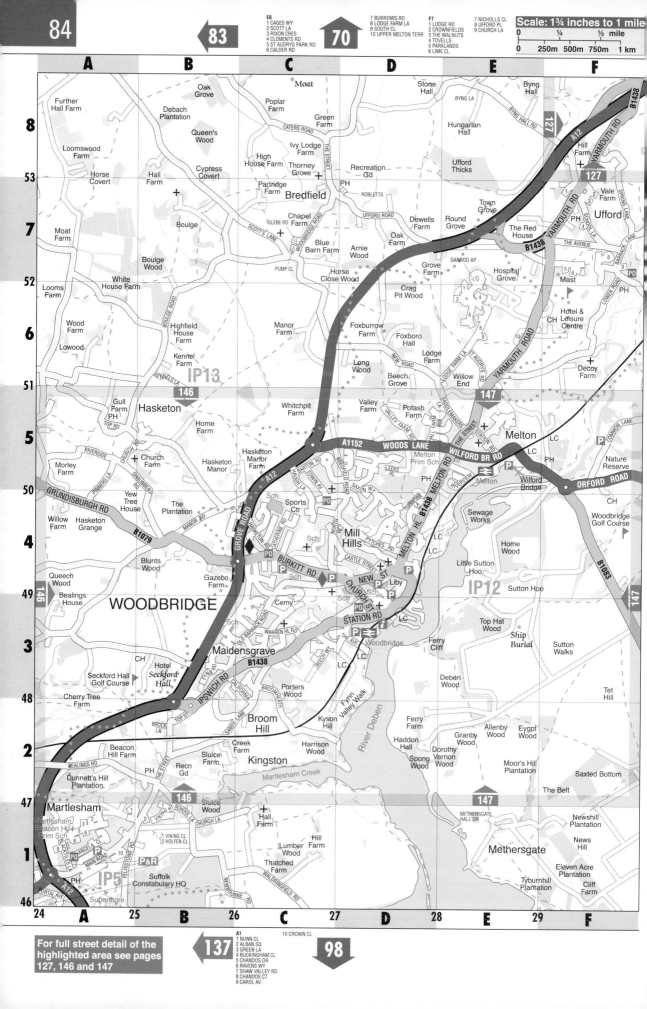

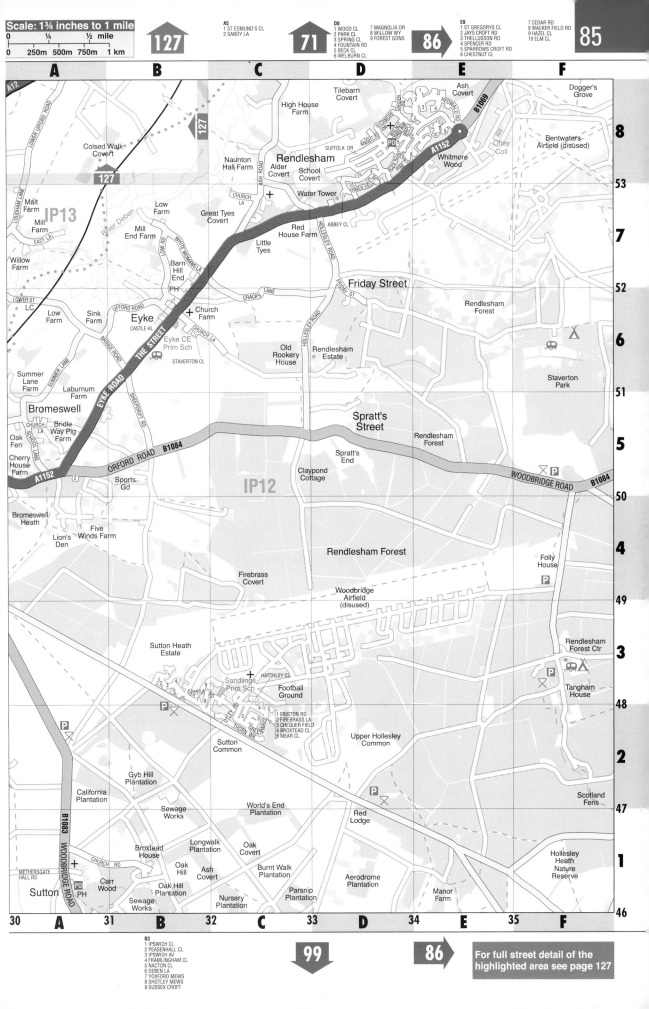

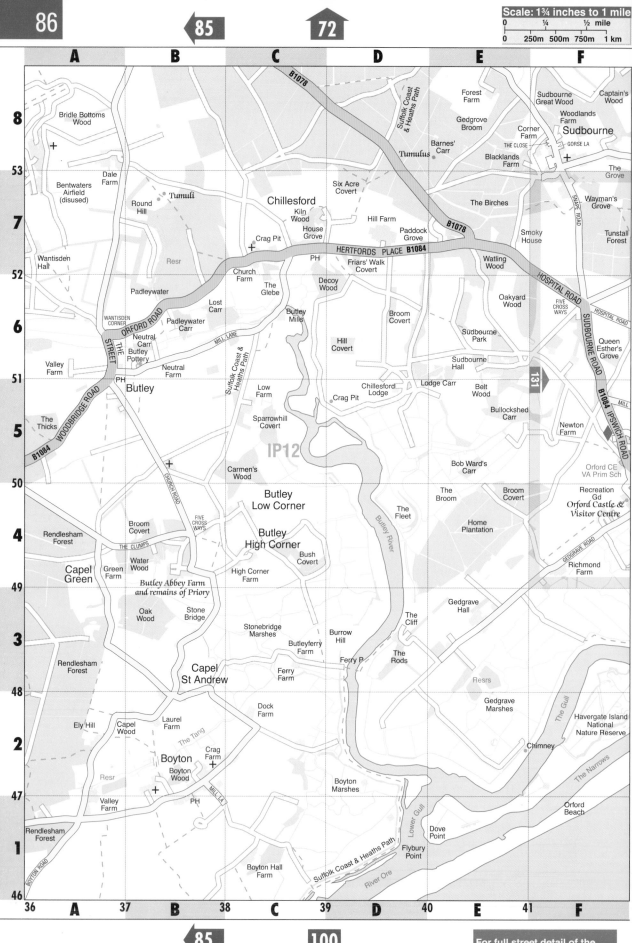

A   B   C   D   E   F

8

B1078

Suffolk Coast & Heaths Path

Forest Farm

Sudbourne Great Wood

Captain's Wood

Bridle Bottoms Wood

Gedgrove Broom

Woodlands Farm

Corner Farm

Sudbourne

THE CLOSE

GORSE LA

Tumulus

Barnes' Carr

Bentwaters Airfield (disused)

Dale Farm

Blacklands Farm

The Grove

53

Round Hill

Tumuli

Chillesford

Six Acre Covert

The Birches

Wayman's Grove

7

Kiln Wood

Hill Farm

Paddock Grove

Smoky House

B1078

Tunstall Forest

Crag Pit

House Grove

HERTFORDS PLACE B1084

Wantisden Hall

Resr

PH

Friars' Walk Covert

Watling Wood

52

Church Farm

Decoy Wood

Oakyard Wood

FIVE CROSS WAYS

Padleywater

The Glebe

Broom Covert

HOSPITAL ROAD

6

WANTISDEN CORNER

Lost Carr

Butley Mills

Sudbourne Park

Padleywater Carr

MILL LANE

ORFORD ROAD

Neutral Carr Butley Pottery

Hill Covert

Sudbourne Hall

SUDBOURNE ROAD

131

Valley Farm

THE STREET

Neutral Farm

Suffolk Coast & Heaths Path

Chillesford Lodge

Lodge Carr

Belt Wood

51

PH

Butley

Low Farm

Crag Pit

Bullockshed Carr

Newton Farm

B1084 IPSWICH ROAD

MILL

The Thicks

Sparrowhill Covert

Carmen's Wood

Bob Ward's Carr

Orford CE VA Prim Sch

5

B1084

WOODBRIDGE ROAD

CHURCH ROAD

Butley River

The Broom

Broom Covert

Recreation Gd

Orford Castle & Visitor Centre

50

Rendlesham Forest

Broom Covert

FIVE CROSS WAYS

Butley Low Corner

The Fleet

Home Plantation

GEDGRAVE ROAD

Richmond Farm

THE CLUMPS

Water Wood

Butley High Corner

Bush Covert

4

Capel Green

Green Farm

High Corner Farm

Gedgrave Hall

Oak Wood

Stone Bridge

Butley Abbey Farm and remains of Priory

49

Stonebridge Marshes

The Cliff

Gedgrave Marshes

The Gull

Havergate Island National Nature Reserve

Rendlesham Forest

Butleyferry Farm

Burrow Hill

The Rods

3

Ferry P

Ely Hill

Capel Wood

Laurel Farm

Ferry Farm

Chimney

The Tang

Capel St Andrew

48

Dock Farm

Resrs

The Narrows

2

Crag Farm

MILL LA

Boyton

Orford Beach

Boyton Wood

Lower Gull

47

Valley Farm

PH

Boyton Marshes

Dove Point

Rendlesham Forest

BOYTON ROAD

Resr

Flybury Point

1

Boyton Hall Farm

Suffolk Coast & Heaths Path

River Ore

46

36   A   37   B   38   C   39   D   40   E   41   F

IP12

A   B   C   D   E   F

Aldeburgh Bay

IP15

Firs Farm

Longdrift Carr

Sudbourne Marshes

The Firs

River Alde

Sudbourne Beach

8

The White House

SCHOOL ROAD

Valley Farm

53

131

High House Farm

HIGH HOUSE FARM ROAD

Elm Covert

Crag Farm

7

Crag Pit

FERRY ROAD

CRAG FARM ROAD

Chaplin's Carr

Blackstakes Reach

52

Church Farm

Moss' Carr

Ox Carr

Lantern Marshes

6

Masts

FERRY ROAD

Prettyman's Whin

IP12

131

Lodge Farm

Cobbins Farm

Masts

51

Bullockshed Grove

BROADWAY

BULLOCKSHED LA

Ash Carr

Raydon Hall

Wireless Station

5

Orford

RAYDON LANE

Town Marshes

Pig Pail Bridge

RECTORY RD

PH

HIGH ST

DAPPLING RD

King's Marshes

50

Town Hall

BROAD ST

FRONT ST

QUAY ST

P   PH   P   P

River Ore

4

Chantry Farm

Orfordness

Orford Ness

Sewage Works

131

Orford Ness

49

Chantry Point

Orford Ness National Nature Reserve

Orfordness Lighthouse

3

Stony Ditch

Stonyditch Point

Cuckold's Point

48

Orford Beach

2

47

1

46

For full street detail of the highlighted area see page 131

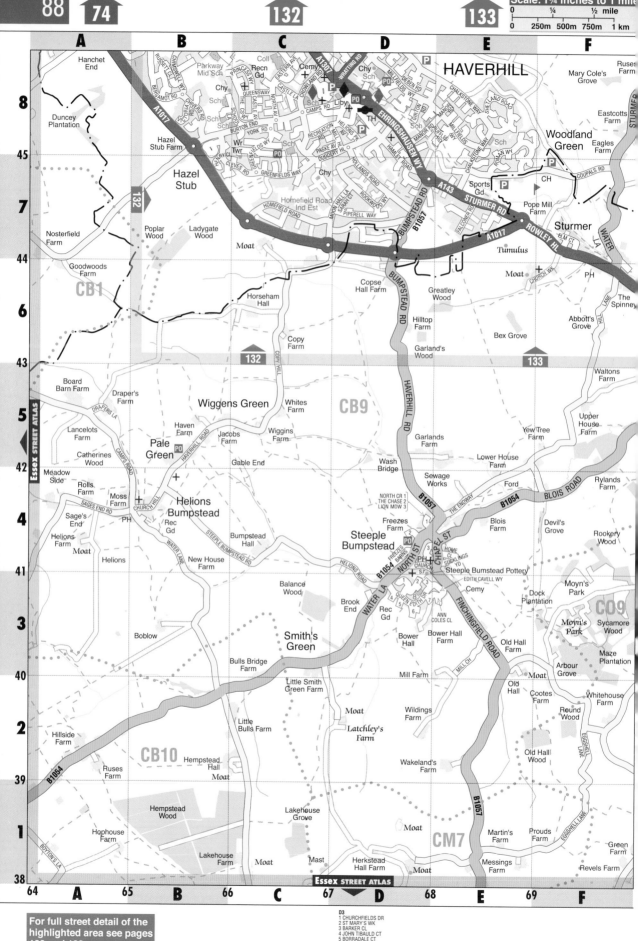

Scale: 1¾ inches to 1 mile

HAVERHILL

D3
1 CHURCHFIELDS DR
2 ST MARY'S WK
3 BARKER CL
4 JOHN TIBAULD CT
5 BORRADALE CT
6 WOOLNOUGH CL
7 GEORGE GENT CL
8 Stanley Drapkin Prim Sch

Essex STREET ATLAS

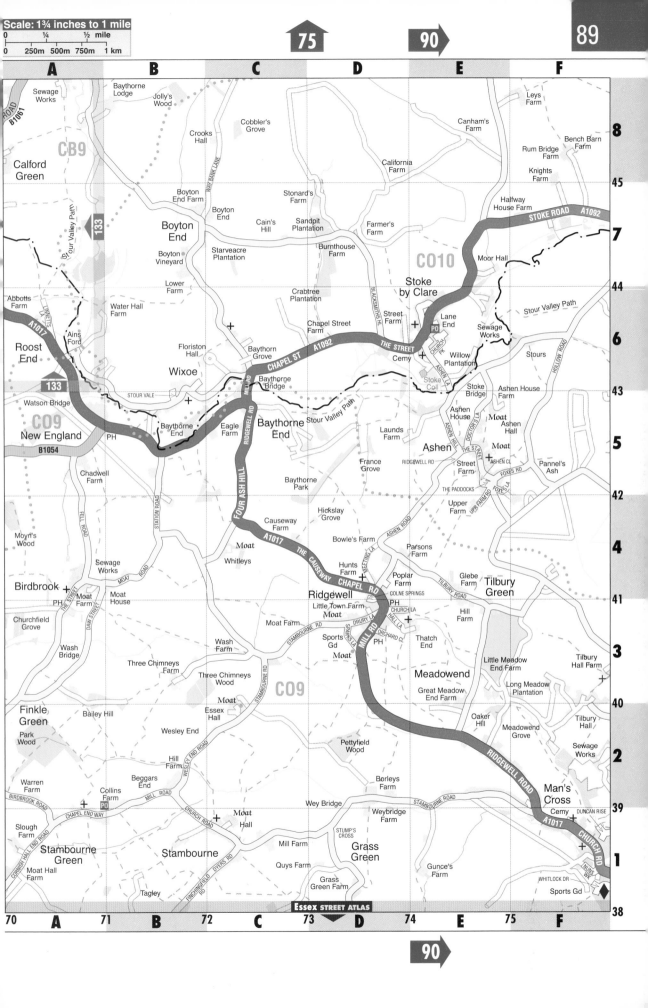

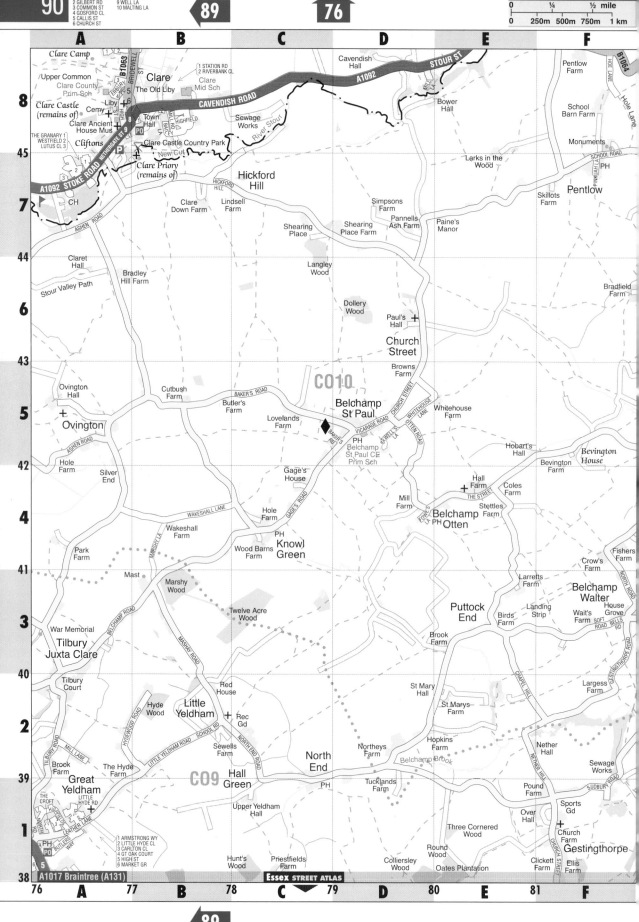

90

A8
1 CLARENCE RD
2 GILBERT RD
3 COMMON ST
4 GOSFORD CL
5 CALLIS ST
6 CHURCH ST
7 BUCKS LA
8 MARKET HL
9 WELL LA
10 MALTING LA

89

76

Scale: 1¾ inches to 1 mile

0   ¼   ½   mile
0 250m 500m 750m 1 km

A B C D E F

Clare Camp
Upper Common
Clare County Prim Sch
Clare Castle (remains of)
Clare Ancient House Mus
THE GRANARY 1
WESTFIELD 2
LUTUS CL 3
Cliftons
CH

B1063
BRIDEWELL ST
Clare
The Old Liby
Clare Mid Sch
Cemy
Highfield
Town Hall
PO
Clare Castle Country Park
New Cut
Clare Priory (remains of)
ASHEN ROAD
A1092 STOKE ROAD
NETHERGATE ST
HIGH ST
BAILEY

1 STATION RD
2 RIVERBANK CL
CAVENDISH ROAD
Sewage Works
River Stour
Hickford Hill
HICKFORD HILL

Cavendish Hall
A1092
STOUR ST
MILL
Bower Hall
Larks in the Wood

B1064
Pentlow Farm
HOLE LANE
School Barn Farm
Monuments
PINNUCK'S LA
PH
SCHOOL ROAD
Pentlow
Skillots Farm

Clare Down Farm
Lindsell Farm
Shearing Place
Shearing Place Farm

Simpsons Farm
Pannells Ash Farm
Paine's Manor

Claret Hall
Stour Valley Path
Bradley Hill Farm

Langley Wood
Dollery Wood

Paul's Hall
Church Street
Browns Farm

Bradfield Farm

Ovington Hall
Ovington
Hole Farm
ASHEN ROAD
Silver End

Cutbush Farm
Butler's Farm
Lovelands Farm
BAKER'S ROAD
BAKER'S RD

CO10
Belchamp St Paul
VICARAGE ROAD
PH
Belchamp St Paul CE Prim Sch
CHURCH STREET
S WELL'S LA
WHITEHOUSE LANE
OTTEN ROAD

Whitehouse Farm

Hobart's Hall
Bevington Farm
Bevington House

Gage's House
Wakeshall Lane
Hole Farm
GAGE'S ROAD
PH
Knowl Green
Wood Barns Farm

Mill Farm
Belchamp Otten
PH
Hall Farm
THE STREET
Coles Farm
Stettles Farm

Fishers Farm

Park Farm
MARSHY LA
Wakeshall Farm
Mast
Marshy Wood

Twelve Acre Wood

Larretts Farm
Crow's Farm
Belchamp Walter
House Grove
Wait's Farm
SOFT ROAD
BELLS RD
NORTH ROAD
GESTINGTHORPE ROAD

Puttock End
Birds Farm
Landing Strip

Brook Farm

War Memorial
Tilbury Juxta Clare
BELCHAMP ROAD
Tilbury Court

Red House
Hyde Wood
Little Yeldham
Rec Gd

St Mary Hall
St Marys Farm
Hopkins Farm

Largess Farm
CHAPEL HILL
Nether Hall
NETHER HILL
SUDBURY ROAD
Sewage Works

Brook Farm
THE CROFT
Great Yeldham
LITTLE HYDE RD
The Hyde Farm
HYDEWOOD ROAD
MILL LANE
LITTLE YELDHAM ROAD
SCHOOL RD
NORTH END ROAD
Sewells Farm
CO9
Hall Green
PH
Upper Yeldham Hall

North End
Belchamp Brook
Northeys Farm
Tucklands Farm

Pound Farm
Over Hall
Sports Gd
Church Farm
Gestingthorpe
CHURCH STREET
Ellis Farm
Clickett Farm

PH
PO
LEATHER LANE
BUTLER'S WAY
1 ARMSTRONG WY
2 LITTLE HYDE CL
3 CARLTON CL
4 GT OAK COURT
5 HIGH ST
6 MARKET GR
Hunt's Wood
Priestfields Wood
Colliersley Wood
Round Wood
Oates Plantation
Three Cornered Wood

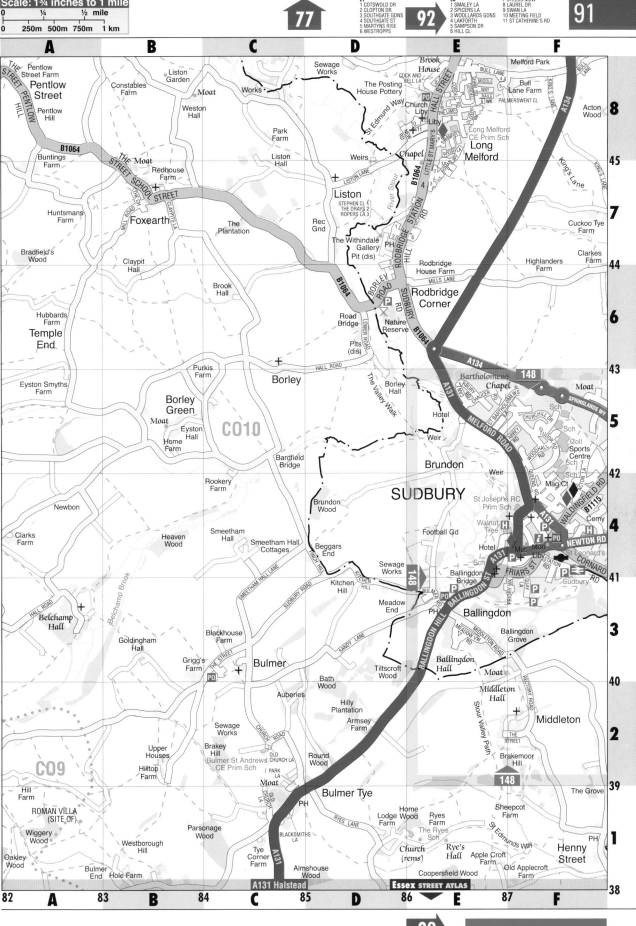

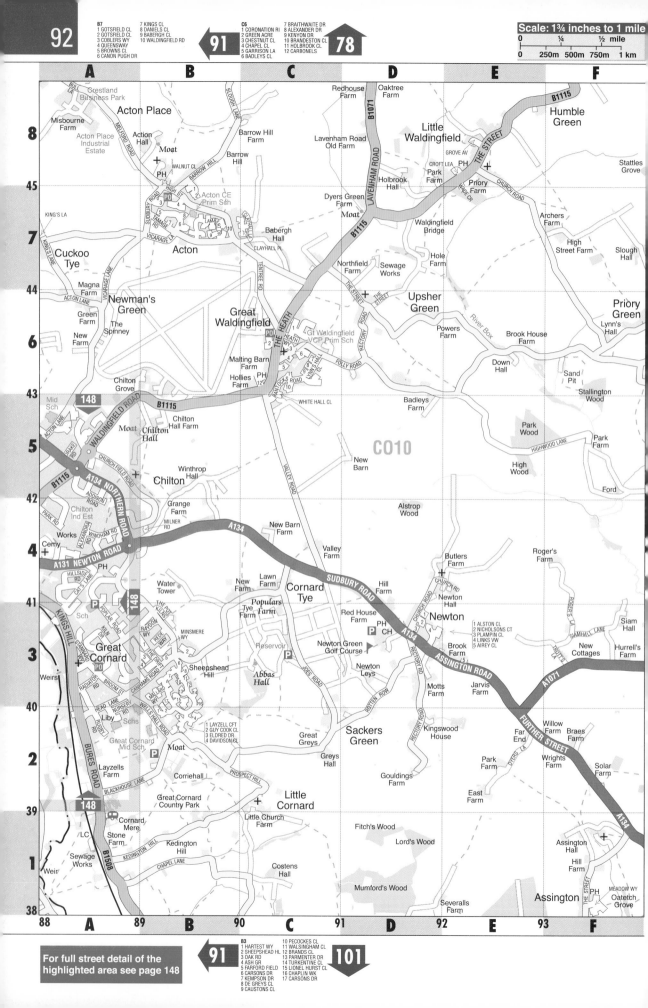

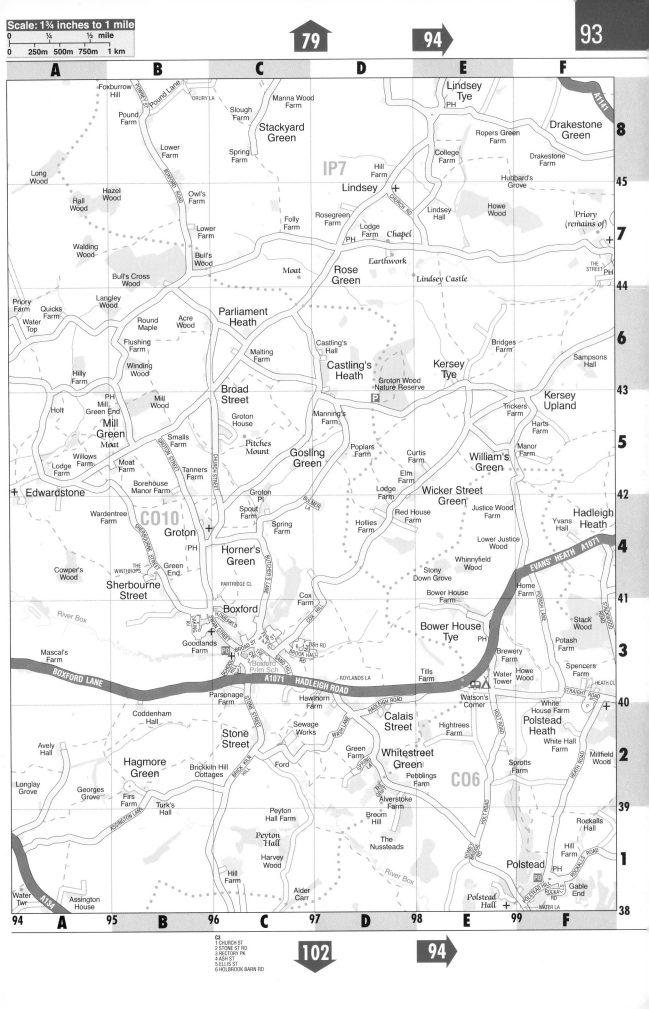

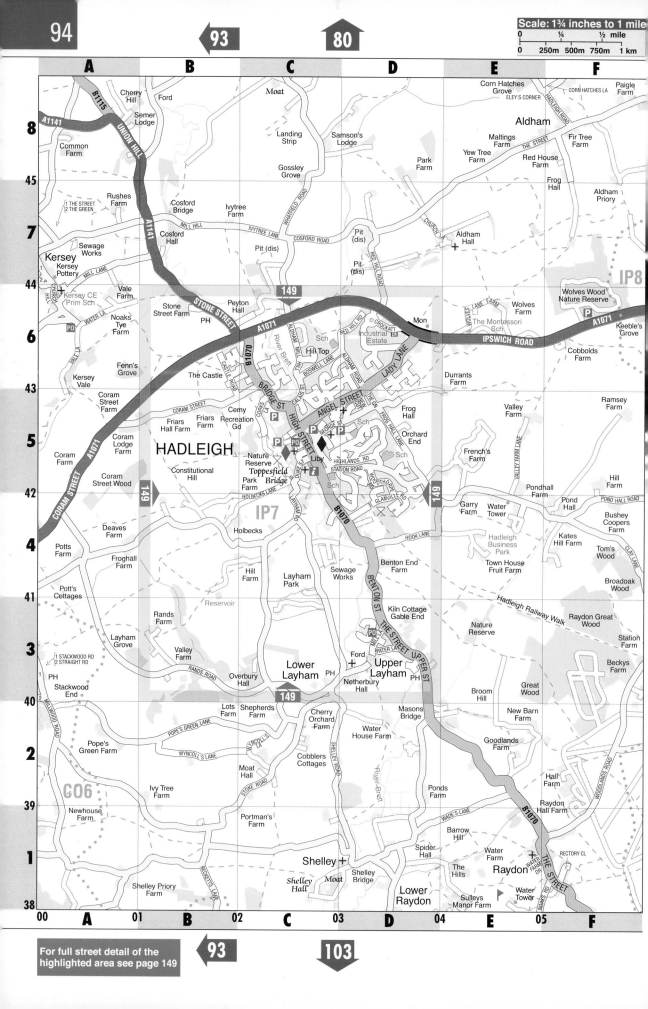

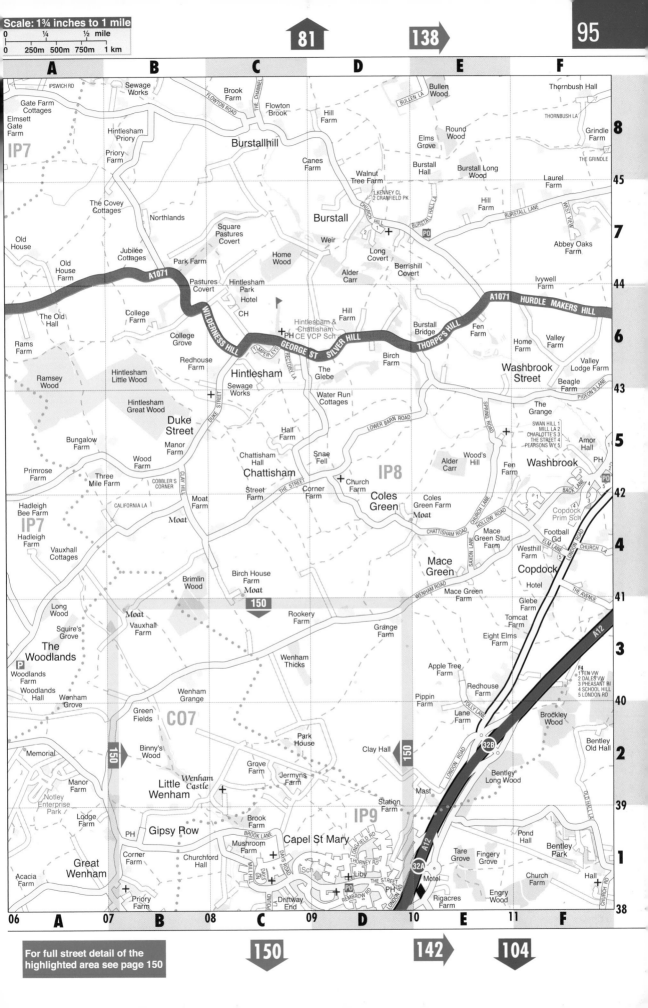

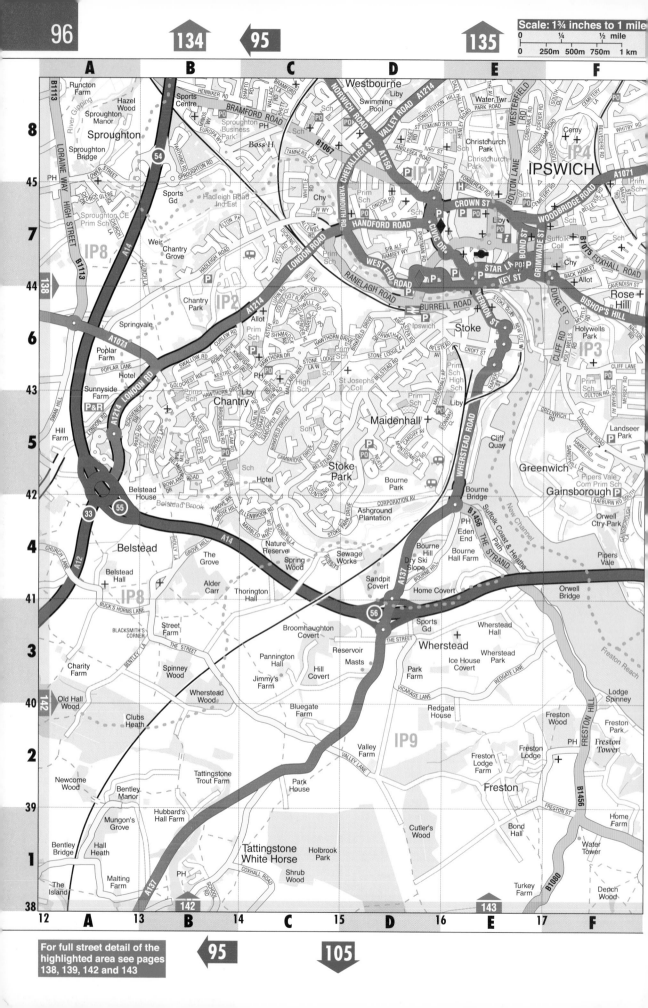

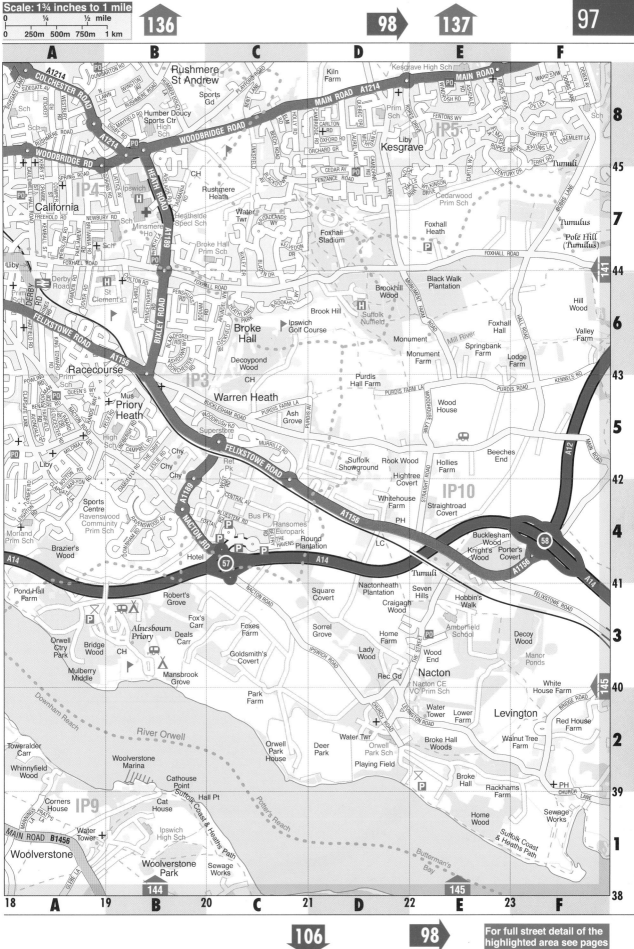

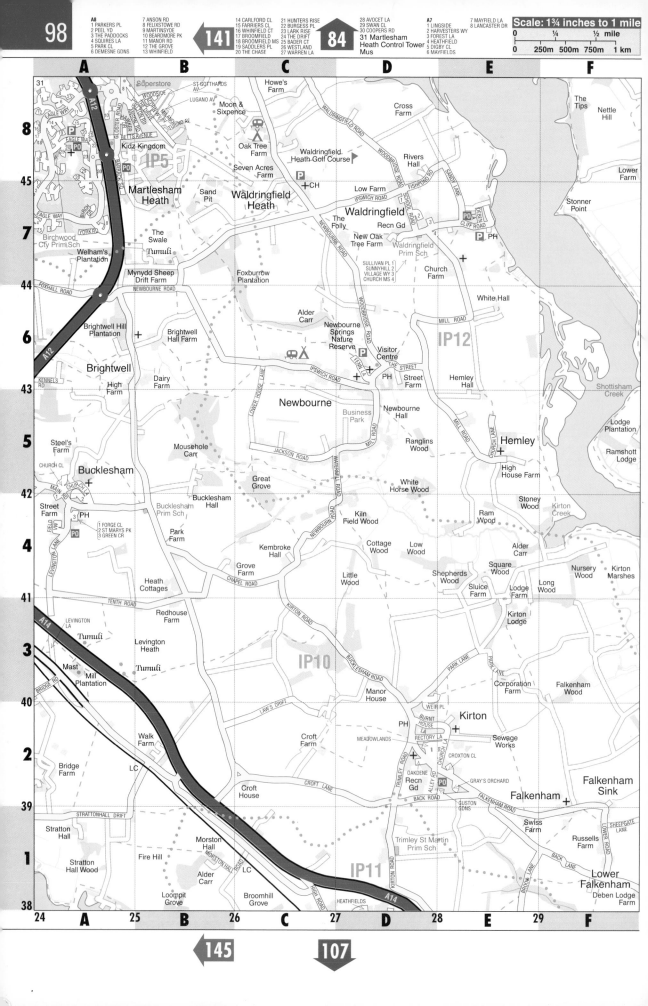

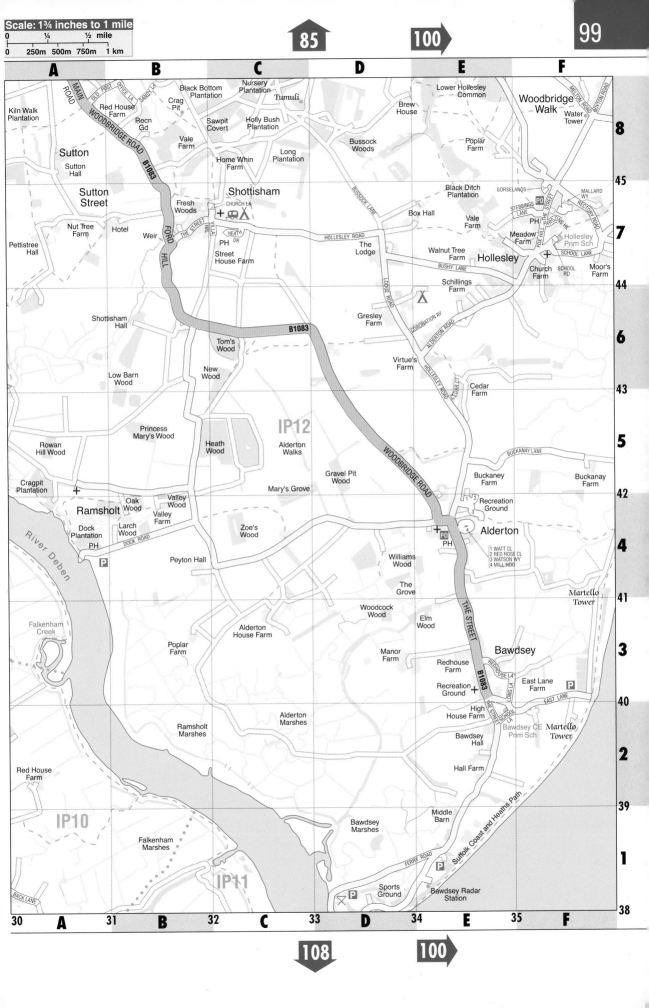

Oak Hill

HM Prison

Sports Ground

Grove House

The Grove

IP12

River Ore

Hollesley Bay Colony
(HM Young Offender
Institution)

Hollesley Bay

Orford Haven

Sewage Works

Oxley Dairy

Oxley Marshes

North Weir Point

P

Shingle Street

Martello Tower

Suffolk Coast & Heaths Path

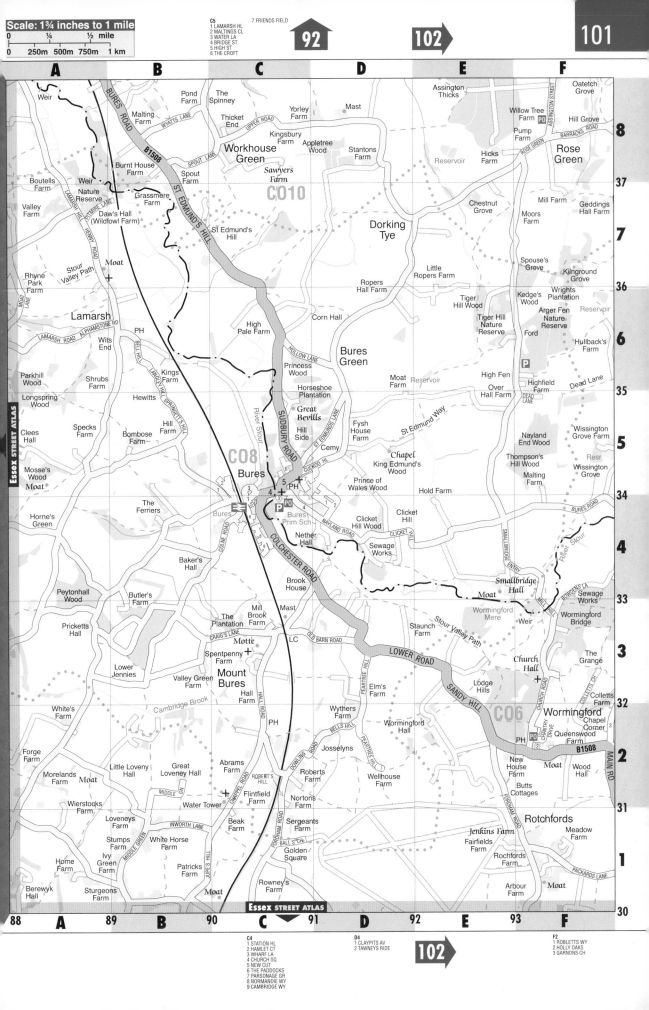

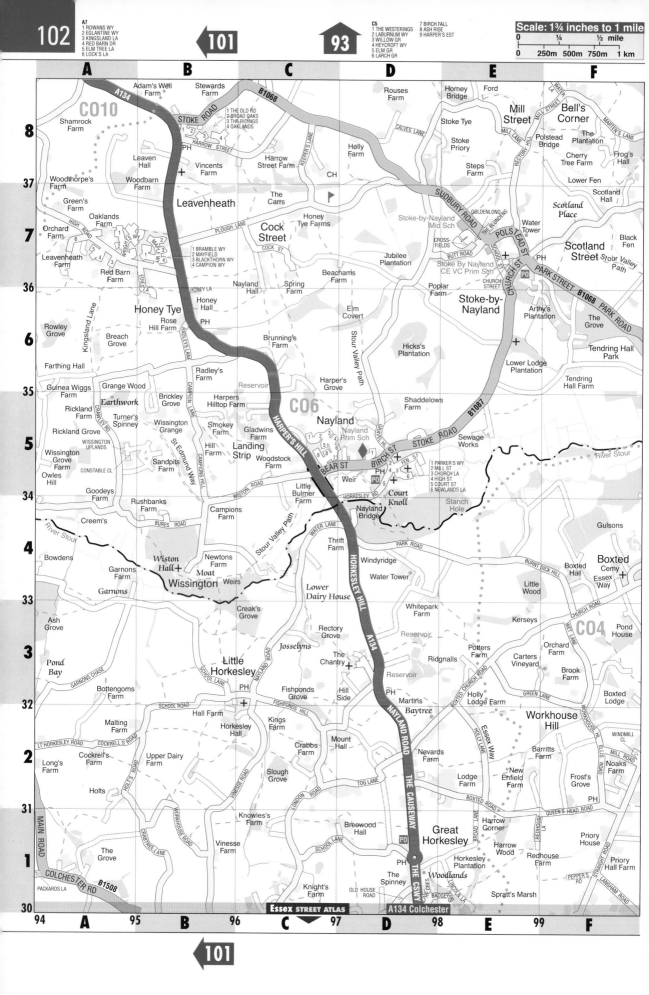

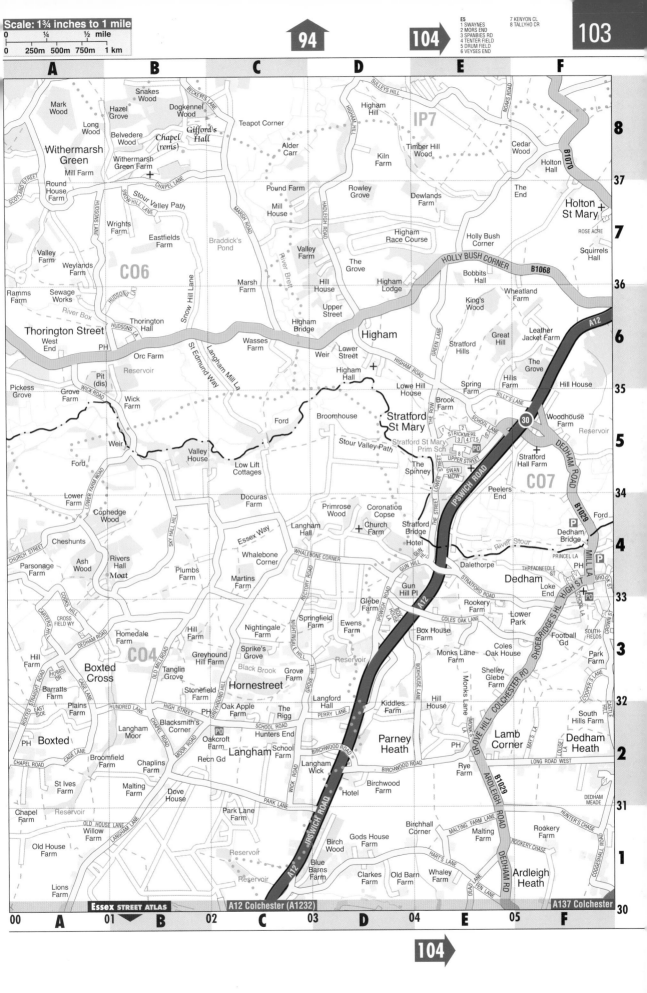

E4
1 PINE CL
2 GROVE RD
3 ASH GROUND CL
4 PATTERN BUSH CL
5 MERRIAM CL
6 WESTERN'S END

7 ROWLEY CL
8 HARDY CL
9 GRIMWADE CL
10 BROWNING RD
11 TEMPLE PATTLE
12 CATTAWADE ST

E5
1 BROOM KNOLL
2 THE DRIFT
3 THE POPLARS
4 VALLEY CL
5 SCHOOL LA
6 ELM CL

7 CEDAR CL
8 BIRCH DR
9 QUINCE CL
10 BLENHEIM CL

Map labels

Sewage Works, Springhill, Capelgrove, Capelgrove Farm, Wenham Place, Wenham Hill, Lattinford Bridge, Boydland Farm, Manor House, Hill Farm, Great Gilberts Farm, White Horse Farm, Windy Farm, Berry Farm, Grove Farm, Potash, Potash Lan, Potash Farm, Falslaff Manor, Bentley, Bentley Prim Sch

Lattinford Hill, Oaks Farm, Four Sisters Farm, B1070, IPSWICH ROAD A12, Four Sisters, Hughes Corner, Road Covert, East Bergholt, Woodgates Farm, Sports Centre, Rookery Farm, Chaplain's Farm, Hustlers Grove, Ford, Great Martin's Hill Wood, IP9, Holly Wood, Martins Hill Farm, Willow End, Bentley Grove, Coppey Farm, Dodnash Coppey Farm

Lodge Plantation, Allen's Farm, Ackworth House, Vale Farm, Fishpond Wood, CO7, Whistler's Wood, Highlands, Willowtree Farm, Sports Gd, Gardens, Home Farm, Smart's Wood, Park House, Warren Wood, Touchey's Lane, Meadow Farm, Elm Farm, Laurel Grove, Woodlands Farm, Park Farm, East End, Church Barn Farm, Keeble's Grove, Willow Spinney, Mower's Spinney, Martins Glen, Dodnash Wood, Little Martin's Hill Wood, Augustinian Priory, Little Charles New Plantation, Dodnash Priory Farm, Church Farm, Brantham Glebe

St Edmund Way, Fen Bridge, Gossnalls Farm, Old Hall, Clapper Farm, Sewage Works, Orvis Farm, Baker's End, Spooner's Wood, Braham Wood, Braham Hall, Brookland Farm, Orchard End, Brantham, Sewage Works, Rare Breeds Farm, Flatford Lane, Lock, Flatford Mill, Valley Farm, Mus, Stour Valley Path, B7070, BERGHOLT RD, BRANTHAM HILL, Decoy Pond, Factory Lane, Cattawade, Wks

Pound Farm, Lower Barn Farm, Weirs, St Edmund Way, Manningtree, Causeway End, Nash Cl, Munnings Wy, White Bridge, A137, LC, Nature Reserve, Hopping Bridge, Mistley Towers, Craft Centre, F2 1 KILN LA 2 THE GREEN 3 THE LANE 4 SCHOOL LA

East House, Castle House, PH, Stour House, Tumulus, Lawford Hall, Lawford Hall, Hill Farm, Jupes Hill Farm, Mill Hill, CO11, Sports Ctr, Dale Hall, Manningtree High Sch, Lawford, B1352, STATION RD, THE WALLS, Mistley Place Park, HIGH STREET, Manningtree, Superstore, Mus, Liby, Recreation Ground, Mistley Wood, Long Plantation, Furze Hill

Keepers End, Heath Farm, Bargate Farm, Birchetts Wood, Foxwood Cl, Great Hickle Farm, ESSEX WAY, LONG RD WEST, LONG RD EAST, HARWICH ROAD, WIGNALL ST, LONG RD, Recreation Ground, Bromley Corner, COXS HILL, COLCHESTER RD, LONG ROAD B1352, B1035, CLACTON ROAD, Mistley Hall, Laundry Wood, Dairy Wood

Cherry Tree Farm, A137, Foxash Estate, Lower Farm, Glanfields, Grange Road, Lawford House, Grange Farm, Lawfordhouse Farm, Aldhams, Dead Lane, Aldhams Farm, Stacies Farm, Ford Farm, Bricklin Grove, Beech Plantation

D2
1 TURNER AVE
2 KEATING CL
3 CONSTABLE CL
4 FITZGERALD CL
5 BURROWS CL
6 BARKER CL
7 BLAKE CL
8 COTMAN AV
9 STUBBS CL

10 STANTON HUGHES WY
11 DIXON CL
12 SITWELL CL
13 CORNFORD WY
14 LYDGATE CL
15 EDGEFIELD AV
16 SPRINGBANK AV
17 MERRIAM CL
18 SEATON CL
19 HUNTER DR

20 LINDEN CL
21 CAVENDISH DR
22 MEADWAY
23 WALDEGRAVE CL
24 NICHOLS CL
25 CORNWALL CL
26 PARRINGTON WY
27 STOURDALE CL

E2
1 KINGS CL
2 VICTORIA CL
3 QUEENSWAY
4 THE ROOKERY
5 LUSHINGTON RD
6 KNIGHTS CL
7 HARVEY CL
8 TAYLOR DR
9 SKELTON CL

10 COLCHESTER RD
11 NORTH ST
12 SOUTH ST
13 QUAY ST
14 ERSKINE RD
15 HILTON CL
16 ST MICHAELS CT
17 STOUR ST
18 MILL LA
19 RAILWAY ST

20 REGENT ST
21 FALKLANDS DR
22 MALTHOUSE RD
23 NORMAN RD
24 PARSONS YD
25 OXFORD RD
26 BARNFIELD
27 THE CHASE
28 TRINITY CL
29 ELMDALE DR

30 CEDAR CR
31 THE BEECHES

E3
1 SOUTH STRAND
2 GREENSMILL
3 COMMERCE WY
4 RIVERSIDE AVENUE W
5 JUBILEE END
6 RIVERSIDE AVENUE E

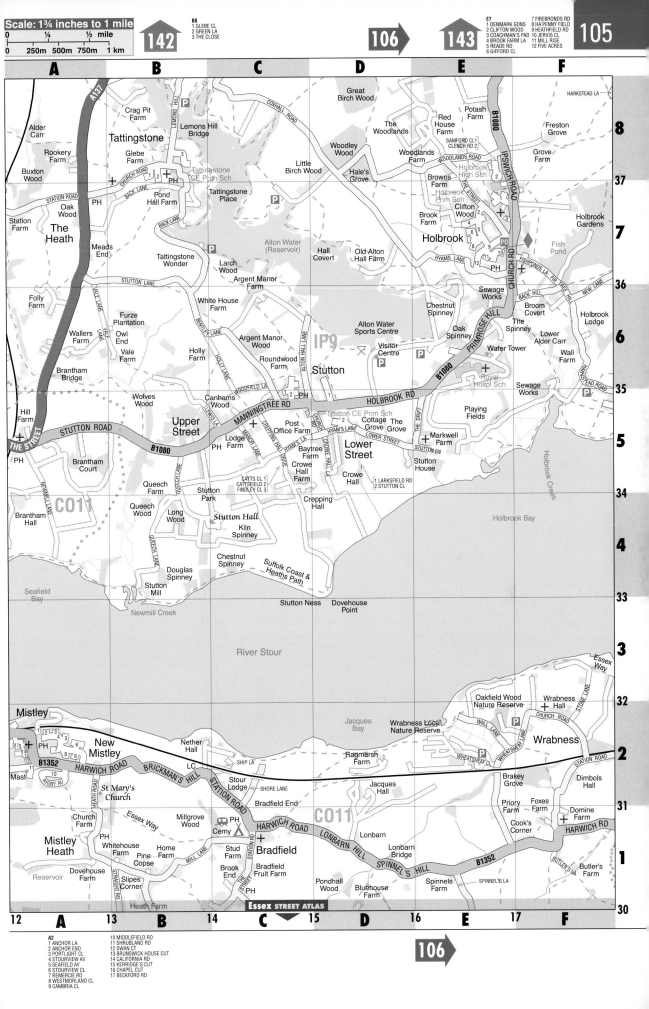

Scale: 1¾ inches to 1 mile

0   ¼   ½ mile
0   250m 500m 750m 1 km

142

106 ▶

143

105

A137

Great Birch Wood

HARKSTEAD LA

Crag Pit Farm

Alder Carr

Lemons Hill Bridge

Lemons Hill

Rookery Farm

Tattingstone

Glebe Farm

Lemons Hill

The Woodlands

Red House Farm

Potash Farm

Freston Grove

B1080

Buxton Wood

Church Road

Back Lane

PH

Tattingstone CE Prim Sch

Little Birch Wood

Woodley Wood

Woodlands Farm

Hale's Grove

Browns Farm

Holbrook High Sch

SAMFORD CL1
CLENCH RD 2

Grove Farm

Woodlands Road

8

Station Road

Oak Wood

Station Farm

The Heath

PH

Meads End

Pond Hall Farm

Tattingstone Place

Holbrook Prim Sch

Clifton Wood

Holbrook

Brook Farm

37

Back Lane

Church Road

Tattingstone Wonder

Larch Wood

Alton Water (Reservoir)

Hall Covert

Old Alton Hall Farm

Holbrook Gardens

Fish Pond

7

Ipswich Road

Church Rd

Folly Farm

Stutton Lane

Argent Manor Farm

Hyams Lane

PH

Sewage Works

Back Hill

Fishponds La

Fir Tree Hill

New Lane

36

White House Farm

Bentley Lane

Vale Lane

Wallers Farm

Furze Plantation

Owl End

Vale Farm

Argent Manor Wood

Holly Farm

Roundwood Farm

IP9

Alton Water Sports Centre

Visitor Centre

P

Chestnut Spinney

Oak Spinney

Water Tower

Primrose Hill

Broom Covert

The Spinney

Lower Alder Carr

Holbrook Lodge

6

Brantham Bridge

Holly Lane

Woodfield La

Canhams Wood

MANNINGTREE RD

Stutton

B1080

Water Tower

Royal Hospl Sch

Wall Farm

Sewage Works

35

Hill Farm

The Street

Stutton Road

Upper Street

B1080

Lewis La

Manor Lane

Lodge Farm

PH

Crepping Hall Drive

Hyam's La

Post Office Farm

Church La

Stutton CE Prim Sch

Cottage Grove

The Grove

Lower Street

The Drift

Playing Fields

Markwell Farm

Stutton Gn

Holbrook Creek

5

PH

Brantham Court

Queech Farm

Oueech Lane

Stutton Park

CATTS CL 1
CATTSFIELD 2
FINDLEY CL 3

Baytree Farm

Crowe Hall Farm

Lower Street

Lower Street

Crowe Hall La

Crowe Hall

Stutton House

1 LARKSFIELD RD
2 STUTTON CL

CO11

34

Brantham Hall

Queech Wood

Long Wood

Stutton Hall

Kiln Spinney

Crepping Hall

Holbrook Bay

4

Oueech Lane

Douglas Spinney

Stutton Mill

Chestnut Spinney

Suffolk Coast & Heaths Path

Seafield Bay

Newmill Creek

Stutton Ness

Dovehouse Point

33

River Stour

3

Essex Way

Oakfield Wood Nature Reserve

Wrabness Hall

Stone Lane

32

Mistley

Jacques Bay

Wrabness Local Nature Reserve

Wall Lane

P

Church Road

Wrabness

PH

New Mistley

Nether Hall

SHIP LA

Ragmarsh Farm

Wheatsheaf La

P

Wheatsheaf Cl

Station Road

B1352

HARWICH ROAD

Heath Road

BRICKMAN'S HILL

Station Road

LC

Stour Lodge

SHORE LANE

Jacques Hall

Brakey Grove

2

Mast

RIGBY AV

St Mary's Church

Bradfield End

CO11

Priory Farm

Cook's Corner

Foxes Farm

Domine Farm

31

Church Farm

Essex Way

Millgrove Wood

PH

Cemy

Harwich Road

Lonbarn

Lonbarn Bridge

HARWICH RD

Mistley Heath

PH

Whitehouse Farm

Pine Copse

Home Farm

Mill Lane

Stud Farm

Bradfield

Lonbarn Hill

Spinnels Hill

B1352

Butler's La

Butler's Farm

1

Reservoir

Dovehouse Farm

Slipes Corner

Straight Rd

Brook End

The Street

Bradfield Fruit Farm

Pondhall Wood

Bluehouse Farm

PH

Spinnels Farm

SPINNEL'S LA

Spinnels Farm

Heath Farm

Grid labels: A B C D E F (top and bottom), 8 37 7 36 6 35 5 34 4 33 3 32 2 31 1 30 (right side)
Bottom grid numbers: 12 13 14 15 16 17

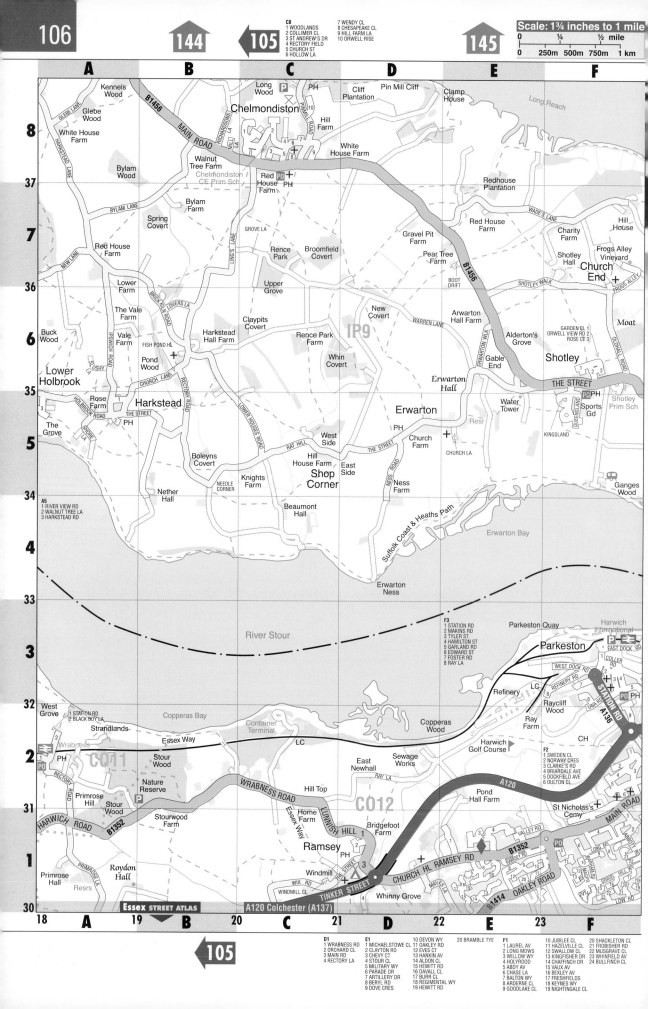

Scale: 1¾ inches to 1 mile

0   ¼   ½   mile
0 250m 500m 750m 1 km

A5
1 CHILDERS CL
2 GATE FARM RD
3 TUDOR CL
4 BLAKE AV
5 KITCHENER WY
6 HERVEY CL

7 LINK RD

D8
1 MILL CL
2 HIGH HALL CL
3 RED HOUSE CL
4 CAPEL CL
5 SANDY CL
6 CROSWELL CT

7 CRAIG CL
8 MEADOW CL
9 JASMINE CL
10 ASH GROUND CL
11 JUBILEE CL
12 HEATH CT
13 BLUE BARN CL

14 ST MARTINS GN
15 BRICK KILN CL

98   108

For full street detail of the
highlighted area see page 152

107

FELIXSTOWE

Trimley
St Martin

Trimley
St Mary

Walton

HARWICH

Dovercourt

Shotley
Gate

The Port of Felixstowe

107
99

IP10

Walton Marshes

King's Fleet

Felixstowe Marshes

Ferry P

Visitor Centre

Sports Gd

Alexanders International Sch

Bawdsey Manor Workshops

IP12

Rosier Marshes

Felixstowe Ferry

PH

153

Rue's Farm

MARSH LA

Martello Tower

Woodbridge Haven

Felixstowe Ferry Golf Course

Gulpher Farm

Laurel Farm

Fleet House

Marsh End

Martello Tower

GULPHER ROAD

IP11

The Grove

Old Felixstowe

Park Farm

HYEM'S LANE

Prim Sch

BRINKLEY WY

WESTMORLAND RD

CH

P

UPPERFIELD DR

WESTERN AVE

FERRY ROAD

LINKS AVE

COLNEIS ROAD

Sch

GUNNINGDALE RD

GOSSOD

ST GEORGES RD

WESTERN AV

ROMAN WY

NORMAN CL

Sports Gd

ROSEMARY RD

SUDBURY RD

LOOE

PO

CHURCH RD

CLIFF RD

153

DELLWOOD AV

LYNWOOD AV

HIGH RD E

PARK RD

PICKETTS

MAYBUSH LANE

FOXGROVE LA

EGLE RD RD

Cobbolds Point

GT ENFIELD AVE

Sch

BEATRICE AV

HAMILTON RD

ANDREW'S RD

QUILTER RD

BROOK LA

BATH RD

St Felixstowe

153

P

PO

A1021

P

PO

i

PO

B1082

A1021

P

COBBOLD RD

H Bartlet

UNDERCLIFF RD E

HAMILTON GDNS

Spa Pavilion

107

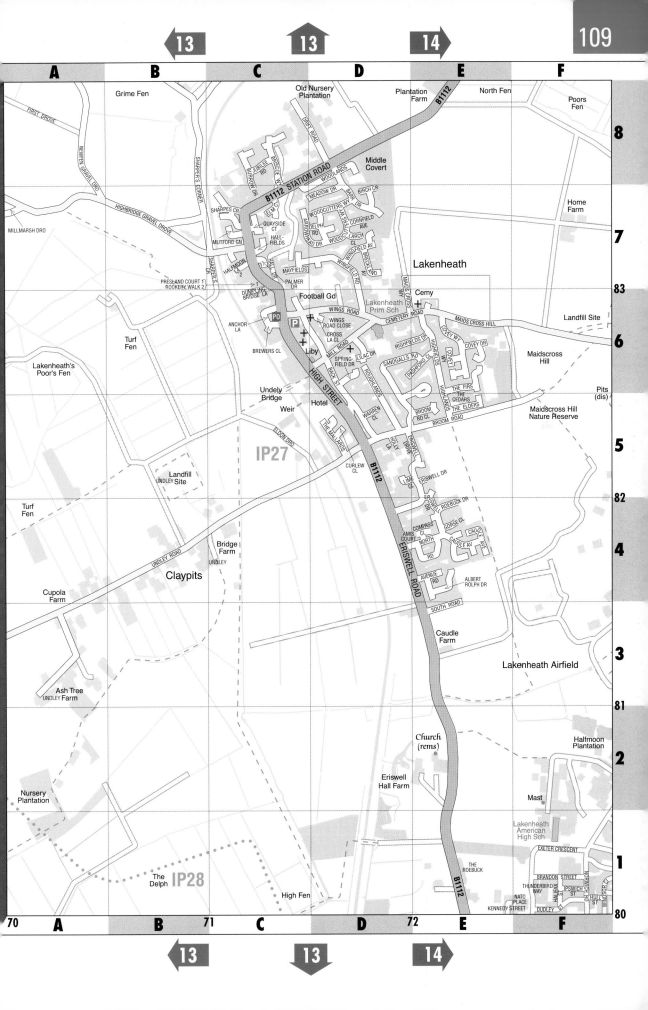

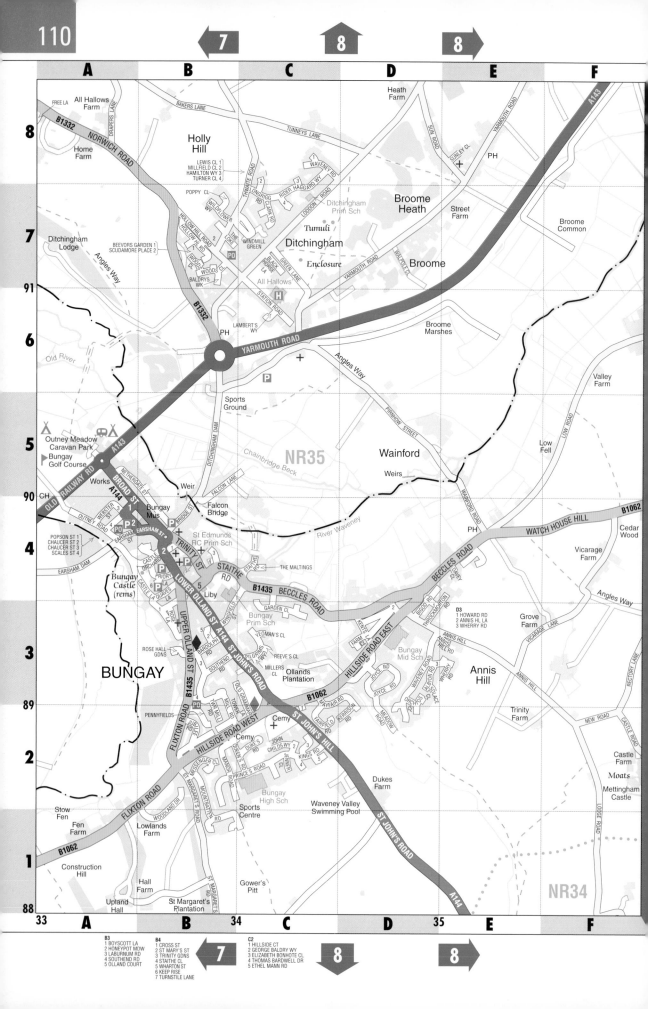

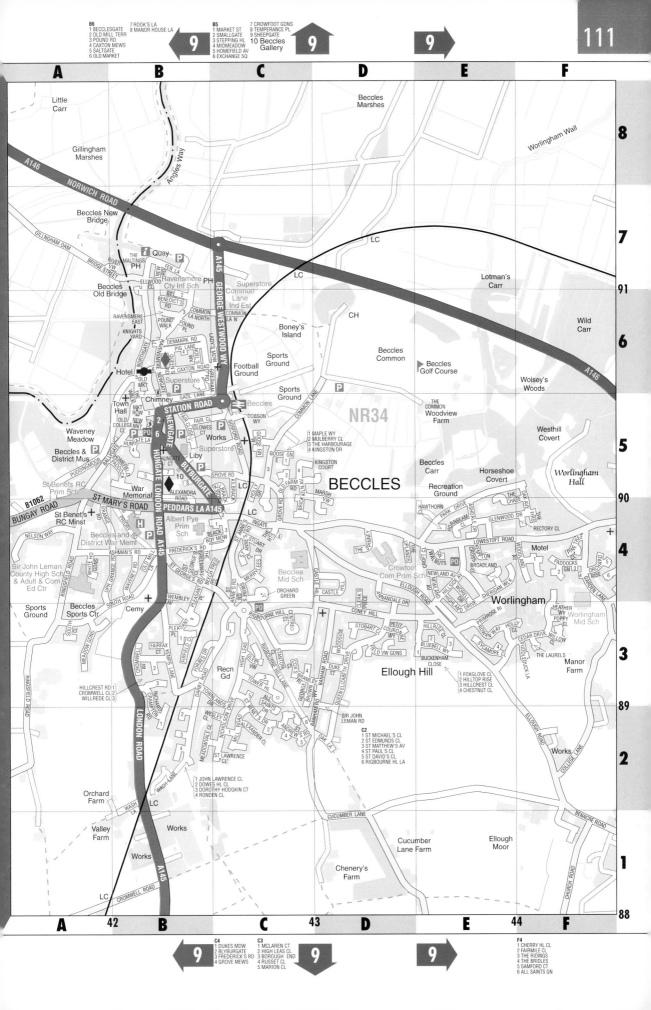

B6
1 BECCLESGATE
2 OLD MILL TERR
3 POUND RD
4 CAXTON MEWS
5 SALTGATE
6 OLD MARKET

7 ROOK'S LA
8 MANOR HOUSE LA

B5
1 MARKET ST
2 SMALLGATE
3 STEPPING HL
4 MIDMEADOW
5 HOMEFIELD AV
6 EXCHANGE SQ

7 CROWFOOT GDNS
8 TEMPERANCE PL
9 SHEEPGATE
10 Beccles Gallery

9 ← 9 ← 9 →

Little
Carr

Beccles
Marshes

Worlingham Wall

Gillingham
Marshes

A146

NORWICH ROAD

Angles Way

Beccles New
Bridge

GILLINGHAM DAM

Lotman's
Carr

LC

LC

Wild
Carr

Quay

THE MALTINGS PH

River

BRIDGE STREET

Beccles
Old Bridge

RAVENSMERE EAST

KNIGHTS YARD

Ravensmere Cty Inf Sch PH

Superstore

Common
Lane
Ind Est

COMMON LA NORTH

COMMON LA N

CH

Boney's
Island

Beccles
Common

Beccles
Golf Course

A146

Wolsey's
Woods

Hotel

POUND WALK

DENMARK RD

PIG LANE

CAXTON ROAD

Football
Ground

Sports
Ground

Sports
Ground

COMMON LANE

THE COMMON
Woodview
Farm

Westhill
Covert

Chimney

Superstore

Beccles

STATION ROAD

DOBSON WY

NR34

1 MAPLE WY
2 MULBERRY CL
3 THE HARBOURAGE
4 KINGSTON DR

Beccles
Carr

Horseshoe
Covert

Worlingham
Hall

Town
Hall

Waveney
Meadow

Beccles &
District Mus

HUNGATE LA

Liby

Works
Superstore

GOOSE GN

GOOSE GN E

KINGSTON
COURT

Recreation
Ground

BECCLES

Beccles
Carr

THE CHASE

OAK AVE

THE FIRS

War
Memorial

St Benets RC
Prim Sch

BUNGAY ROAD

B1062

St Benet's
RC Minst

ST MARY'S ROAD

PEDDARS LA A145

Albert Pye
Prim Sch

ALEXANDRA
ROAD

GROVE RD

KILBRACK

LC

LOLLY RD

OLD FARM LN

MARSH VW

BRICK KILN LN

Hawthorn

PARK DRIVE

HORNBEAM

GLENWOOD DR

RECTORY CL

Motel

PINE TREE

Sir John Leman
County High Sch
& Adult & Com
Ed Ctr

WHITE HO GDNS

UPR GRANGE RD

FREDERICK'S RD

BLACK BOY MDW

ST ANN'S

INGATE

STUART DR

MERRYLEES

THE UPLANDS

THE NUTS

CROWFOOT RD

Crowfoot
Com Prim Sch

NEWLAND AV

LOWESTOFT ROAD

CREMPTON CL

BROADLAND CL

HIGHLAND DRIVE

SHERIDAN WLK

Worlingham

Worlingham
Mid Sch

Sports
Ground

Beccles
Sports Ctr

Cemy

Beccles
Mid Sch

ORCHARD
GREEN

Castle Hill

CASTLE
HILL

CLERK'S
PIECE

ANNANDALE DR

ELLOUGH ROAD

Coney Hill

STOBART CT

Hillrise

PRIMROSE CL

HEATHER WY

POPPY CL

WILLOW

THE LAURELS

Manor
Farm

HILLCREST RD
CROMWELL CL
WILLREDE CL

Recn
Gd

TOWER HL

ALL
SAINTS

PETIT
COURONNE
WY

BUCKENHAM
CLOSE

CEDAR DRIVE

PUDDLEDUCK LA

Ellough Hill

1 FOXGLOVE CL
2 HILLTOP RISE
3 HILLCREST CL
4 CHESTNUT CL

LONDON ROAD

A145

FAIRFAX CT

KEMPS LANE

RIGBOURNE HILL

HIGH LEAS

GLEBE VW

RIGBOURNE HILL LANE

BANHAM ROAD

DUKE RD

OAK LA

SIR JOHN
LEMAN RD

Works

C2
1 ST MICHAEL'S CL
2 ST EDMUNDS CL
3 ST MATTHEW'S AV
4 ST PAUL'S CL
5 ST DAVID'S CL
6 RIGBOURNE HL LA

Orchard
Farm

WASH LANE

LC

1 JOHN LAWRENCE CL
2 DOWES HL CL
3 DOROTHY HODGKIN CT
4 RONDEN CL

Valley
Farm

WASH LA

Works

CUCUMBER LANE

Cucumber
Lane Farm

Ellough
Moor

BENACRE ROAD

Works

Chenery's
Farm

CHURCH ROAD

C4
1 DUKES MDW
2 BLYBURGATE
3 FREDERICK'S RD
4 GROVE MEWS

C3
1 MCLAREN CT
2 HIGH LEAS CL
3 BOROUGH END
4 RUSSET CL
5 MARION CL

F4
1 CHERRY HL CL
2 FAIRMILE CL
3 THE RIDINGS
4 THE BRIDLES
5 SAMFORD CT
6 ALL SAINTS GN

9 ← 9 ← 9 →

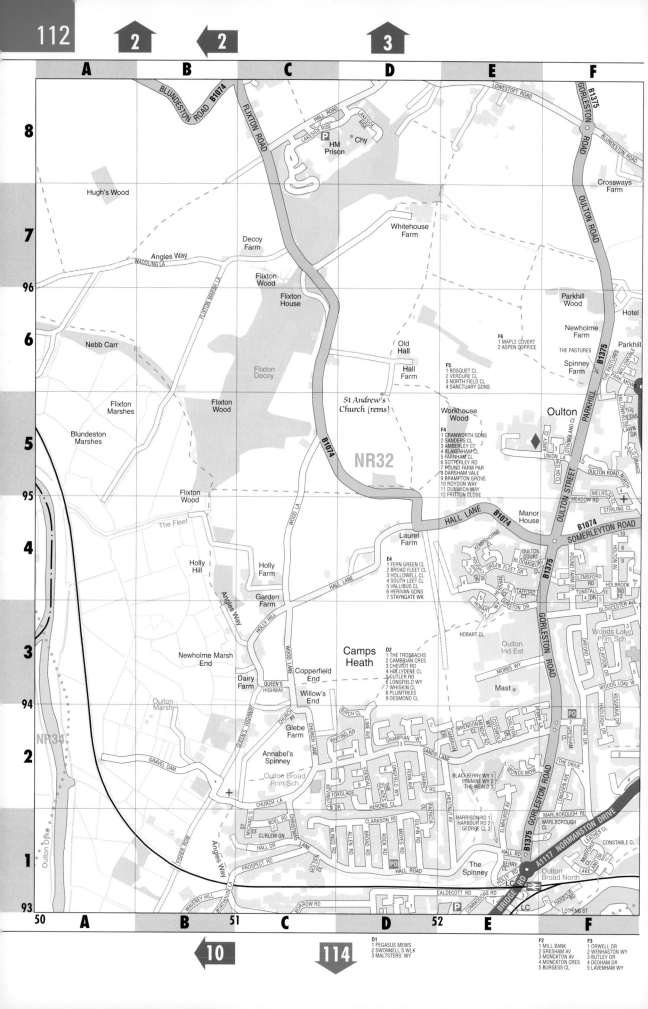

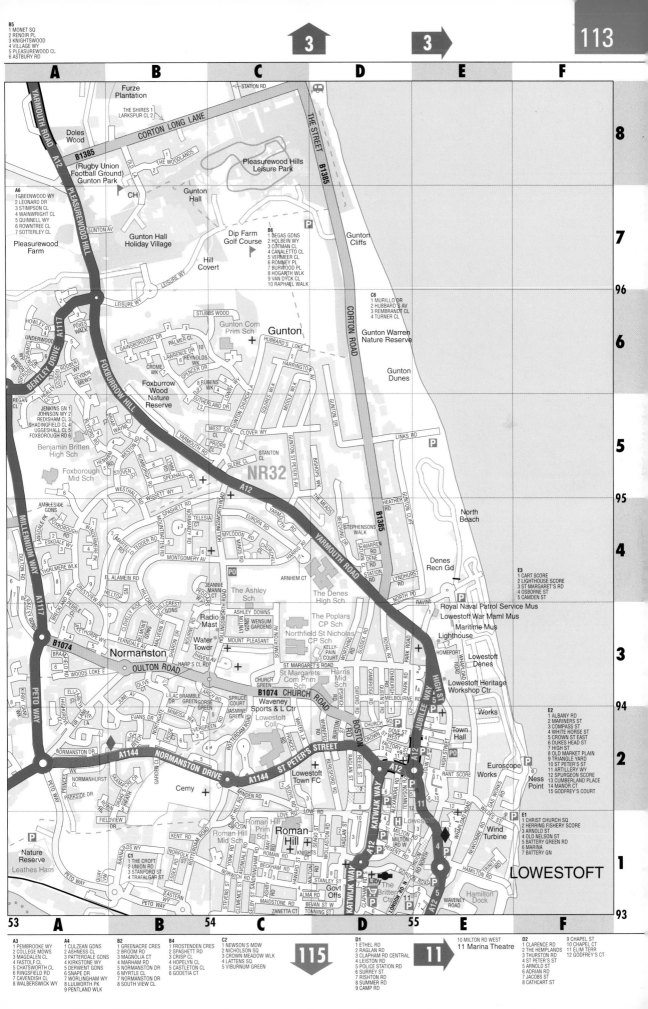

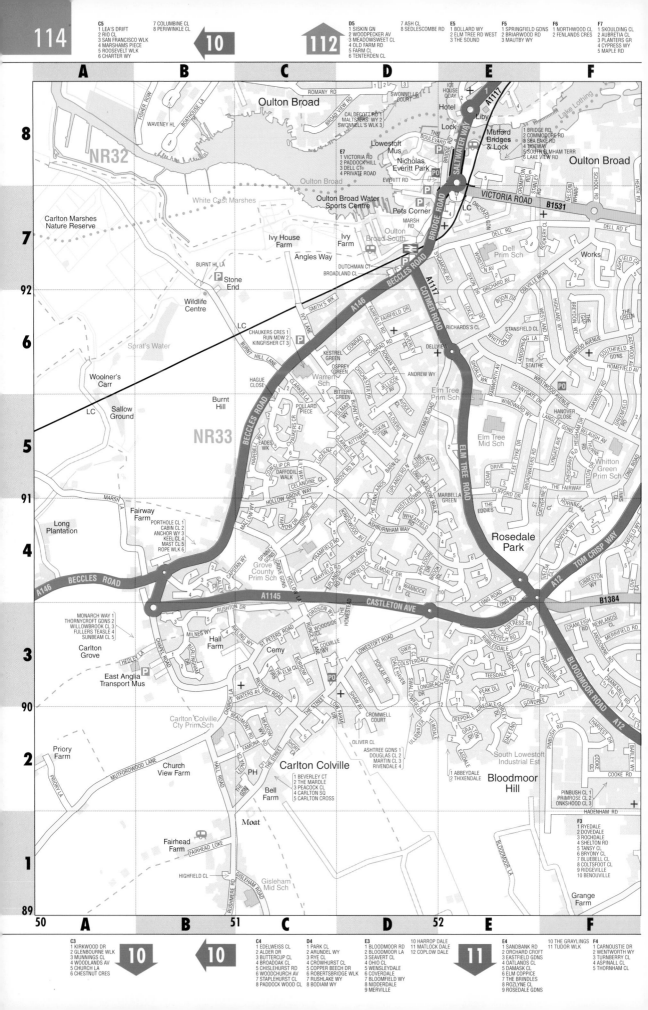

10   112

10   10   11

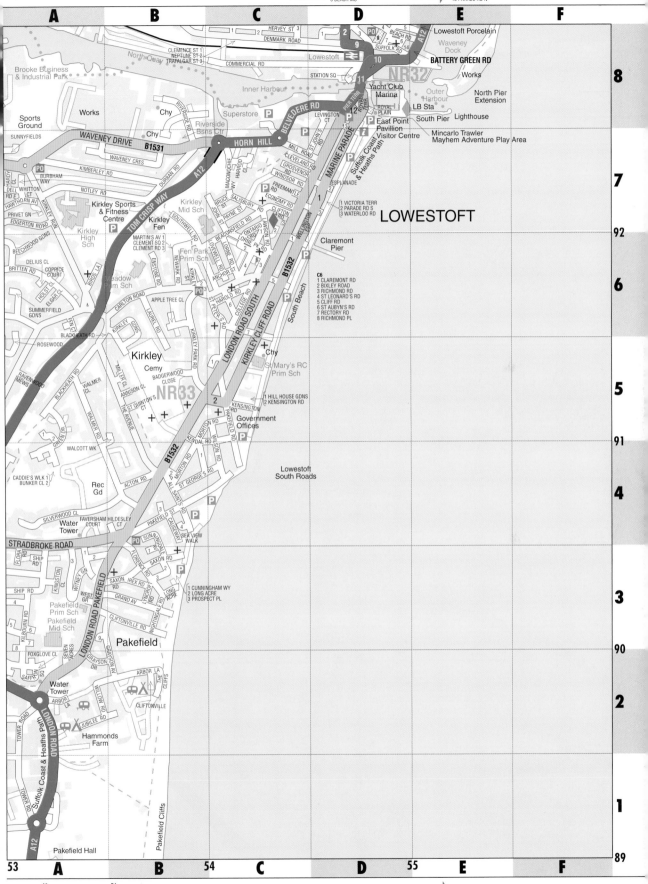

C7
1 ST LEONARD'S RD
2 LAWSON CT
3 UNION PL
4 ORCHARD TERR

113

D8
1 FLENSBURGH ST
2 KATWIJK WY
3 BEVAN ST E
4 SURREY ST
5 GROVE RD
6 BEACH MS

11

7 BON MARCHE
8 LONDON RD N
9 DENMARK RD
10 WAVENEY RD
11 STATION SQ
12 FYFFE WY
13 PARADE RD N

14 HERRING MARKET

A3
1 NELSON RD
2 WELLINGTON RD
3 WITNEY RD
4 CRANFIELD CL
5 MARSDEN CL
6 KILBOURN RD
7 SPEEDWELL CL
8 HONEYSUCKLE CL

B4
1 ROCHESTER RD
2 SHORT ST
3 DOLPHIN CL
4 KIRKDALE CT

 11

 11

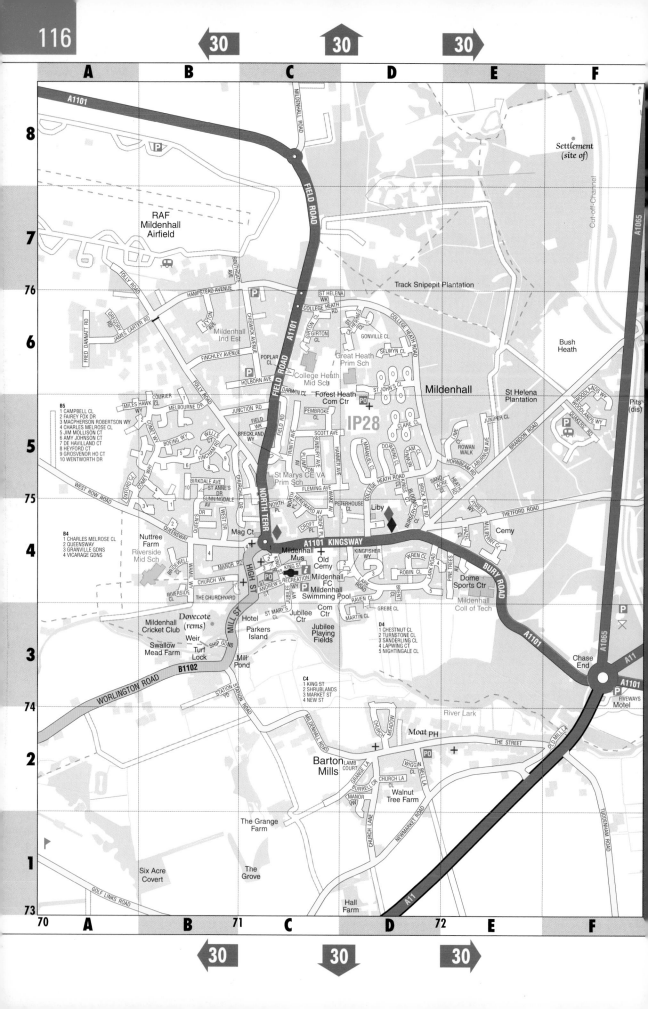

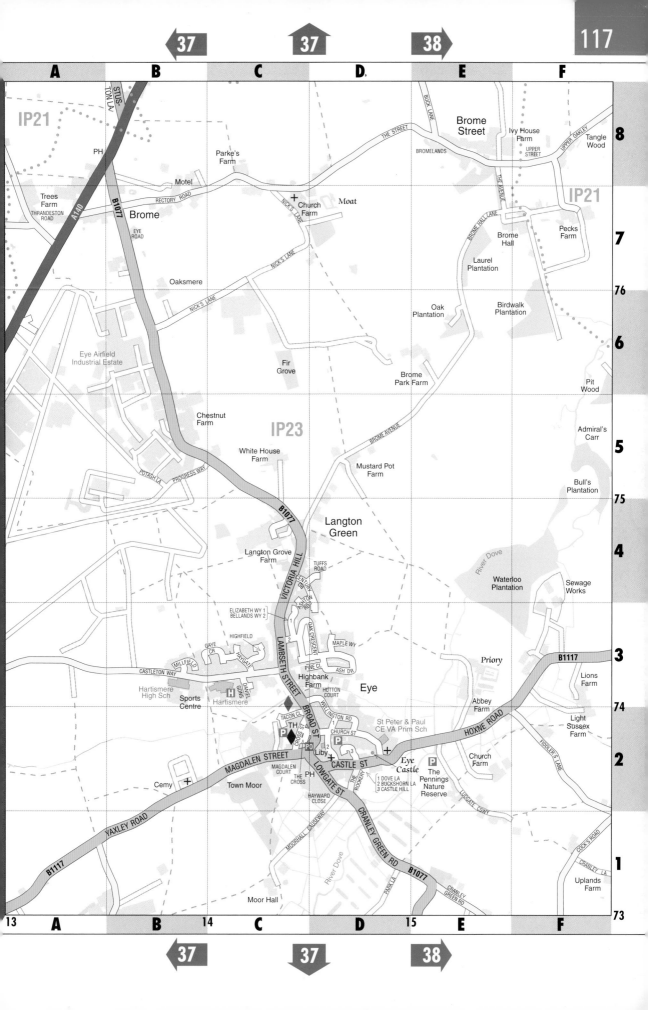

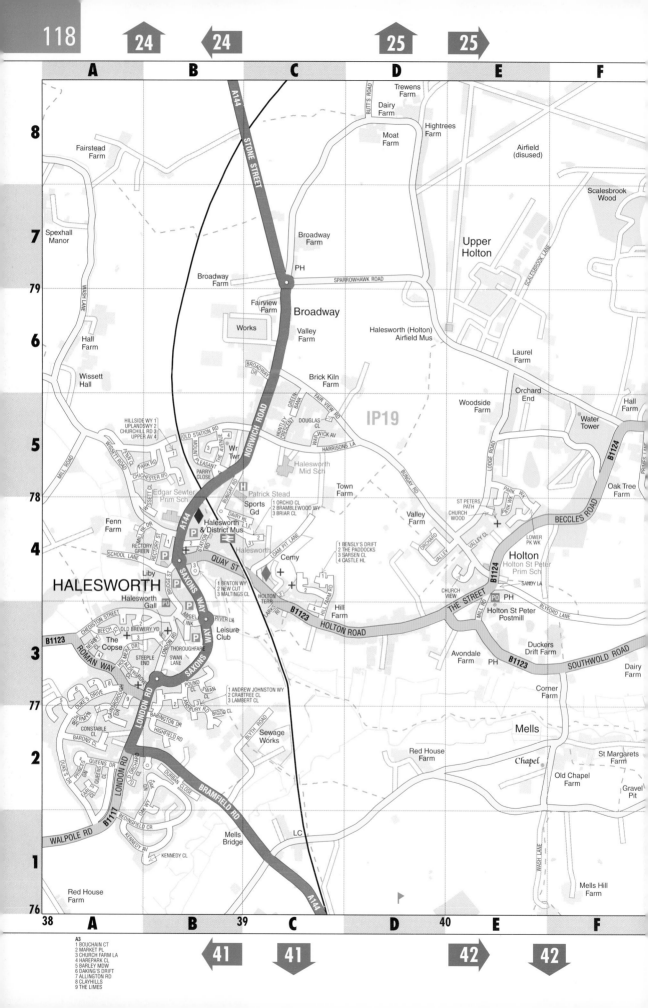

A B C D E F

8

7

79

6

5

78

4

3

77

2

1

76

Fairstead
Farm

Spexhall
Manor

Hall
Farm

Wissett
Hall

Fenn
Farm

HALESWORTH

Halesworth
Gall

The Copse

Red House
Farm

WASH LANE

MILL ROAD

WISSETT ROAD

FENN CL

PARK RD

CHICHESTER RD

WISSETT RD

MILL HE DR

RECTORY
GREEN

SCHOOL LANE

CHEDISTON STREET

NEWRY

BEECH

Liby

ANGEL
LINK

Old Brewery Yd

THOROUGHFARE

SWAN
LANE

STEEPLE
END

HOLMES DR

LONDON RD

GAINSBOROUGH DR

VOLUNTEER

ALDERGROVE

DUKES DRIVE

JERMYN
WY

CONSTABLE
CL

BARONS CL

PRINCES CL

QUEENS DR

DUKES DR

CARL CL

GN

OLD ORCHARD

OAK WY

B1117

WALPOLE RD

LONDON RD

BEDINGFIELD CR

KENNEDY AV

KENNEDY CL

DURBAN CLOSE

BRAMFIELD RD

B1123

ROMAN WAY

SAXONS WAY

SAXONS WAY

BRIDGE ST

RECTORY ST

MOUNT
PLEASANT

PARRY
CLOSE

Edgar Sewter
Prim Sch

HILLSIDE WY 1
UPLANDS WY 2
CHURCHILL RD 3
UPPER AV 4

OLD STATION RD

THE AVENUE

BUNGAY RD

Wr
Twr

DAIRY HL

H

Patrick Stead

Sports
Gd

Halesworth
& District Mus

Halesworth

QUAY ST

STATION RD

LOAM PIT LANE

RIVER LA

Leisure
Club

POUND
RD

LANSBURY RD

BABINGTON DR

HIGHFIELD RD

BIGOD CL

BLYTH ROAD

Sewage
Works

SWAN
CL

1 ANDREW JOHNSTON WY
2 CRABTREE CL
3 LAMBERT CL

Mells
Bridge

LC

A144

STONE STREET

A144

NORWICH ROAD

A144

Broadway
Farm

Fairview
Farm

Works

Valley
Farm

Broadway

BROADWAY
DR

GREEN
BANK

FAIR VIEW RD

HUNTLEY
CRESENT

DOUGLAS
CL

WARWICK AV

HARRISONS LA

Brick Kiln
Farm

Halesworth
Mid Sch

1 ORCHID CL
2 BRAMBLEWOOD WY
3 BRIAR CL

Town
Farm

Cemy

1 BENSLY'S DRIFT
2 THE PADDOCKS
3 SARSEN CL
4 CASTLE HL

HOLTON
TERR

LARKS RD

HILL FARM RD

1 BENTON WY
2 NEW CUT
3 MALTINGS CL

B1123

HOLTON ROAD

Hill
Farm

PH

Broadway
Farm

SPARROWHAWK ROAD

Halesworth (Holton)
Airfield Mus

IP19

BUNGAY RD

Valley
Farm

ORCHARD

VALLEY

Red House
Farm

Trewens
Farm

Dairy
Farm

Moat
Farm

Hightrees
Farm

Woodside
Farm

ST PETERS
PATH

CHURCH
WOOD

Valley

CHURCH
VIEW

THE STREET

Avondale
Farm

PH

B1123

SOUTHWOLD ROAD

Corner
Farm

Mells

Chapel

Upper
Holton

Airfield
(disused)

SCALESBROOK LANE

Laurel
Farm

Orchard
End

LODGE ROAD

PARK WK

LOWER
PK WK

B1124

Holton

Holton St Peter
Prim Sch

MILL RD

SANDY LA

BLYFORD LANE

PO PH

Holton St Peter
Postmill

Ducker's
Drift Farm

B1123

Old Chapel
Farm

Scalesbrook
Wood

Water
Tower

Hall
Farm

B1124

Oak Tree
Farm

BECCLES ROAD

PRIMES LANE

St Margarets
Farm

Gravel
Pit

Mells Hill
Farm

Dairy
Farm

A3
1 BOUCHAIN CT
2 MARKET PL
3 CHURCH FARM LA
4 HAREPARK CL
5 BARLEY MDW
6 DAKING'S DRIFT
7 ALLINGTON RD
8 CLAYHILLS
9 THE LIMES

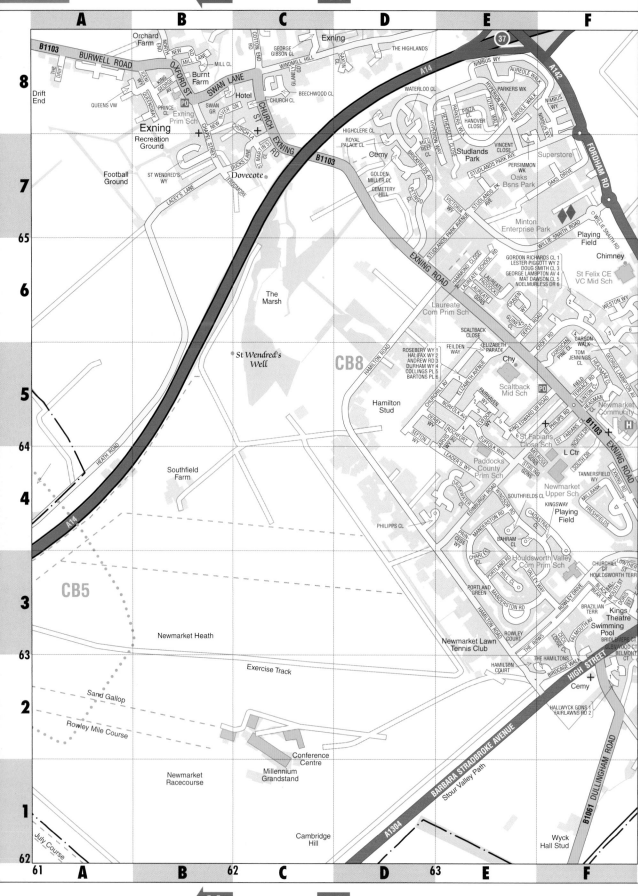

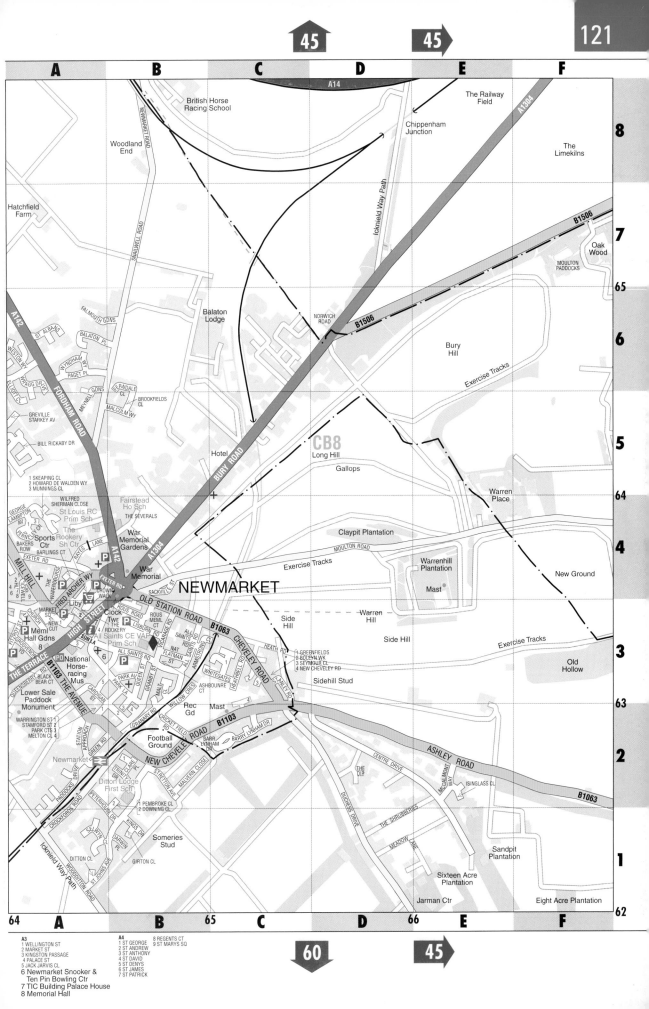

A B C D E F

8 7 65 6 5 64 4 3 63 2 1 62

A14
British Horse Racing School
The Railway Field
Chippenham Junction
Woodland End
The Limekilns
Icknield Way Path
A1304
B1506
Hatchfield Farm
Oak Wood
MOULTON PADDOCKS
NEWMARKET ROAD
SNAILWELL ROAD
Balaton Lodge
Norwich Road
B1506
Bury Hill
A42
FALMOUTH GDNS
ST ALBANS
WESTON WY
WYGG DRIVE
ELLIOTT CT
WYNDHAM WY
PAGET PL
BALATON PL
MC NEILL GDNS
MALCOLM WY
FERNDALE CL
BROOKFIELDS CL
FORDHAM ROAD
Exercise Tracks
GREVILLE STARKEY AV
BILL RICKABY DR
Hotel
BURY ROAD
CB8
Long Hill
Gallops
Warren Place
1 SKEAPING CL
2 HOWARD DE WALDEN WY
3 MUNNINGS CL
WILFRED SHERMAN CLOSE
Fairstead Ho Sch
THE SEVERALS
GEORGE LAMPTON AV
St Louis RC Prim Sch
FERNS
BAKERS ROW
BARLINGS CT
The Rookery Sh Ctr
RATES LANE
A42
A1304
War Memorial Gardens
Claypit Plantation
Exercise Tracks
Warrenhill Plantation
MOULTON ROAD
New Ground
MILL HILL
EXETER RD
Sports Ctr
War Memorial
Exercise Tracks
NEWMARKET
Mast
CROWN WALK
FRED ARCHER WY
Liby
Warren Hill
Side Hill
Mast
THE WATERHOUSE
CHURCH
MARKET SQ
Clock Twr
OLD STATION ROAD
B1063
Side Hill
1 GREENFIELDS
2 BOLEYN WK
3 SEYMOUR CL
4 NEW CHEVELEY RD
Meml Hall Gdns
ROUS MEML CT
LISBURN RD
ALL SAINTS RD
HEATH RD
HEATHBELL RD
CAVELEY RD
CHEVELEY ROAD
Sidehill Stud
Old Hollow
THE TERRACE
National Horse-racing Mus
PO
Black Bear Ct
B1103
All Saints CE VA Prim Sch
SUN LA
THE ROOKERY
VICARAGE RD
NAT FLATMAN ST
ARMSTRONG
WHITEGATES
ASHBOURNE CT
Lower Sale Paddock Monument
QUEENSBERRY RD
STAMFORD ST
PARK CTS
MELTON CL
PARK AV
GRANBY RD
MALL
WILLOW CRES
Rec Gd
Mast
CRICKET FIELD RD
B1103
WARRINGTON ST
Newmarket
STATION APPROACH
GREEN RD
CARRIGAN
PADDOCKS DRIVE
PETERHOUSE DR
Football Ground
BARR. LYNHAM DR
Barry Lynham Dr
ASHLEY ROAD
THE DIP
CENTRE DRIVE
MC CALMONT WAY
ISINGLASS CL
B1063
Ditton Lodge First Sch
NEW CHEVELEY ROAD
STRETTON AVE
MALVERN CLOSE
TRINITY CL
CROCKFORDS ROAD
KINGS DR
DARWIN CL
SELWYN CL
ST JOHNS AVE
WOODDITTON ROAD
DITTON CL
1 PEMBROKE CL
2 DOWNING CL
Someries Stud
GIRTON CL
DUCHESS DRIVE
MEADOW LANE
THE SHRUBBERIES
Sandpit Plantation
Sixteen Acre Plantation
Jarman Ctr
Eight Acre Plantation
Icknield Way Path

A3
1 WELLINGTON ST
2 MARKET ST
3 KINGSTON PASSAGE
4 PALACE ST
5 JACK JARVIS CL
6 Newmarket Snooker &
   Ten Pin Bowling Ctr
7 TIC Building Palace House
8 Memorial Hall

A4
1 ST GEORGE
2 ST ANDREW
3 ST ANTHONY
4 ST DAVID
5 ST DENYS
6 ST JAMES
7 ST PATRICK
8 REGENTS CT
9 ST MARYS SQ

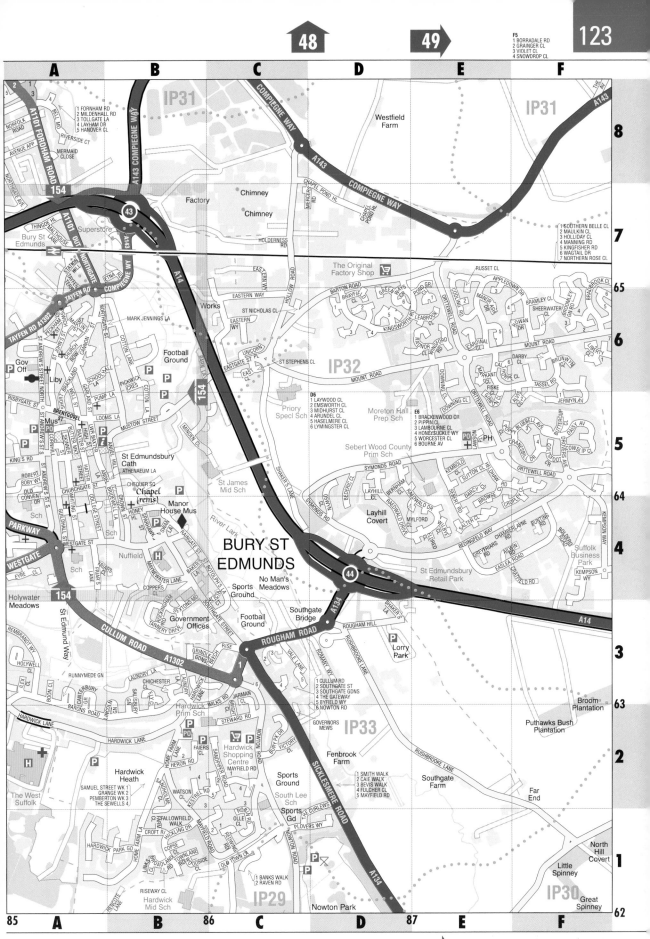

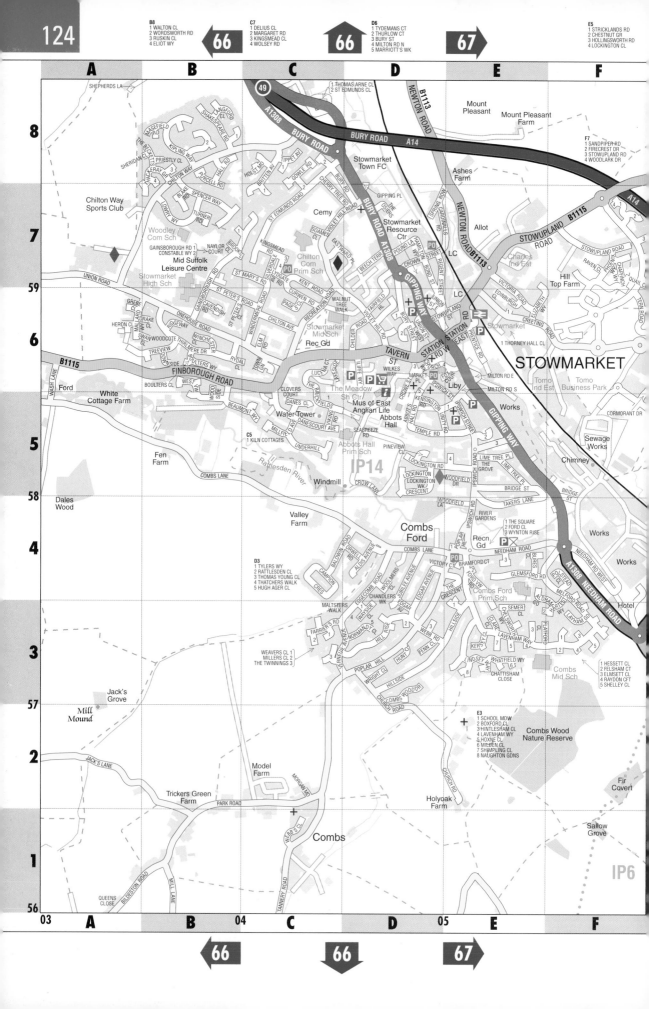

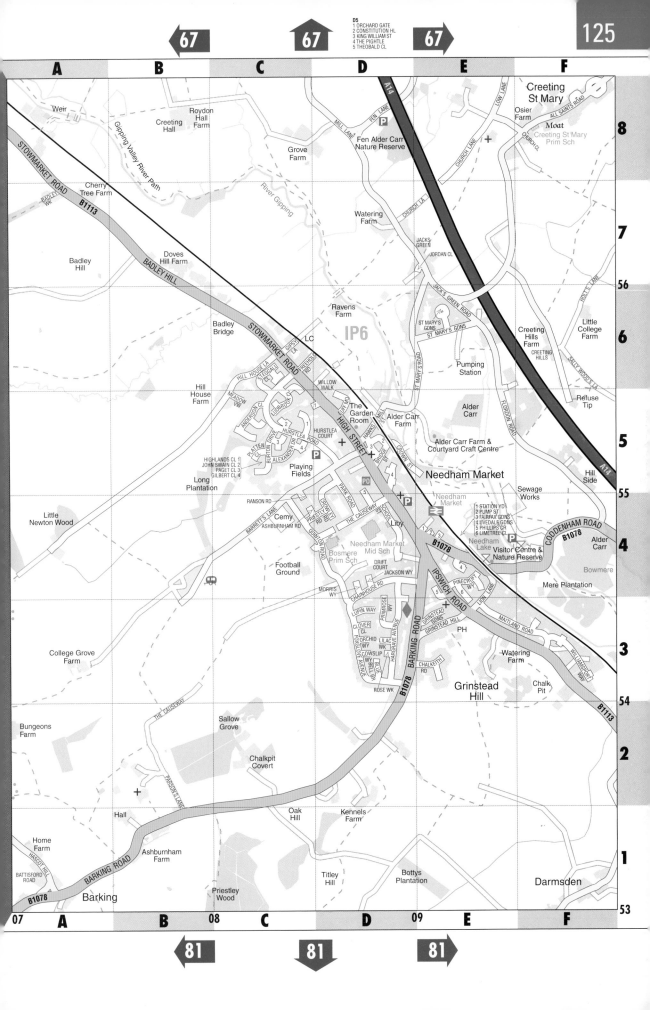

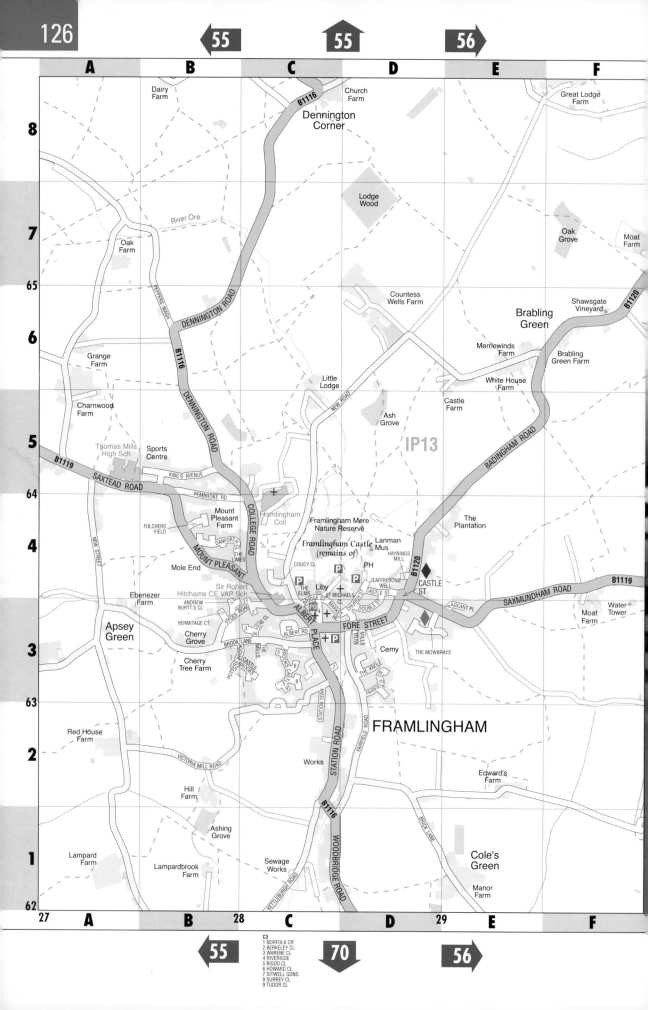

55
55
56

A B C D E F

8

7

65

6

5

64

4

63

2

1

62

27 A B 28 C D 29 E F

Dairy Farm
Church Farm
B1116
Dennington Corner
Great Lodge Farm

River Ore
Lodge Wood
Oak Grove
Moat Farm

Oak Farm
Countess Wells Farm
Shawsgate Vineyard
B1120

Peppers Wash
Dennington Road
B1116
Brabling Green

Grange Farm
Merrlewinds Farm
Brabling Green Farm

Charnwood Farm
Little Lodge
New Road
White House Farm
Castle Farm

Thomas Mills High Sch
Sports Centre
Ash Grove
IP13
Badingham Road

B1119
Saxtead Road
King's Avenue
Framlingham Coll
The Plantation

Pembroke Rd
Framlingham Mere Nature Reserve
Lanman Mus
Haynings Mill

New Street
Mount Pleasant Farm
Framlingham Castle (remains of)
PH
B1120
CASTLE ST

Fulchers Field
Danforth Cl
The Limes
Coucy Cl
P
Jeaffresons Well
B1119
Saxmundham Road

Mole End
Castle St
Double St

Ebenezer Farm
Sir Robert Hitchams CE VAP Sch
Andrew Burtt's Cl
The Elms
Liby
St Michaels
Pageant Pl
Moat Farm
Water Tower

Apsey Green
Hermitage Ct
Vyces Road
De Vere Cl
PO
Fore Street

Cherry Grove
Brook Lane
The Mills
Albert Rd
Cemy

Cherry Tree Farm
Potters Brooks
Brooks Cas Rd
The Mowbrays

Red House Farm
Station Terr
The Knoll
Fairfield Cr

Victoria Mill Road
63
FRAMLINGHAM

Hill Farm
Station Road
Fairfield Road
Edward's Farm

Works
B1116

Ashing Grove
Brick Lane
Cole's Green

Lampard Farm
Lampardbrook Farm
Sewage Works
Kettleburgh Road
Woodbridge Road
Manor Farm

55
70
56

C3
1 NORFOLK CR
2 BERKELEY CL
3 WARENE CL
4 RIVERSIDE
5 BIGOD CL
6 HOWARD CL
7 SITWELL GDNS
8 SURREY CL
9 TUDOR CL

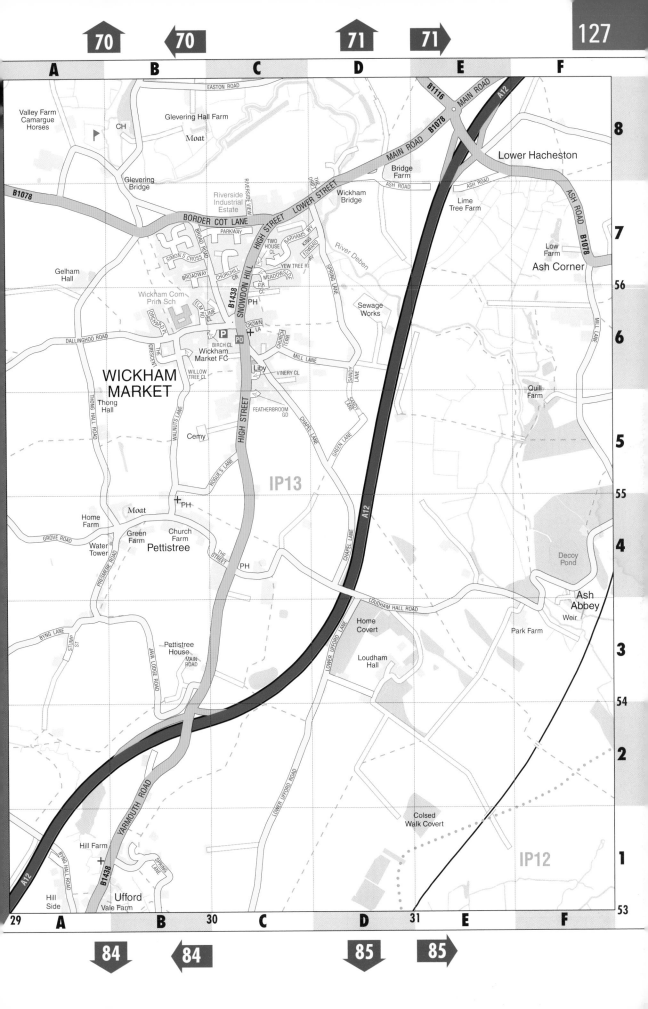

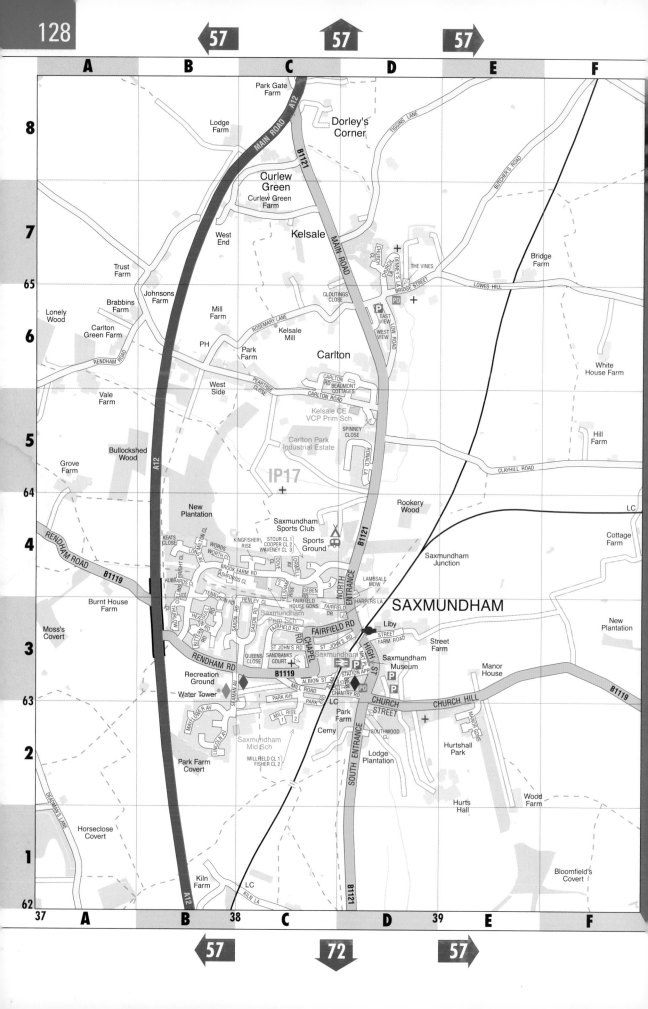

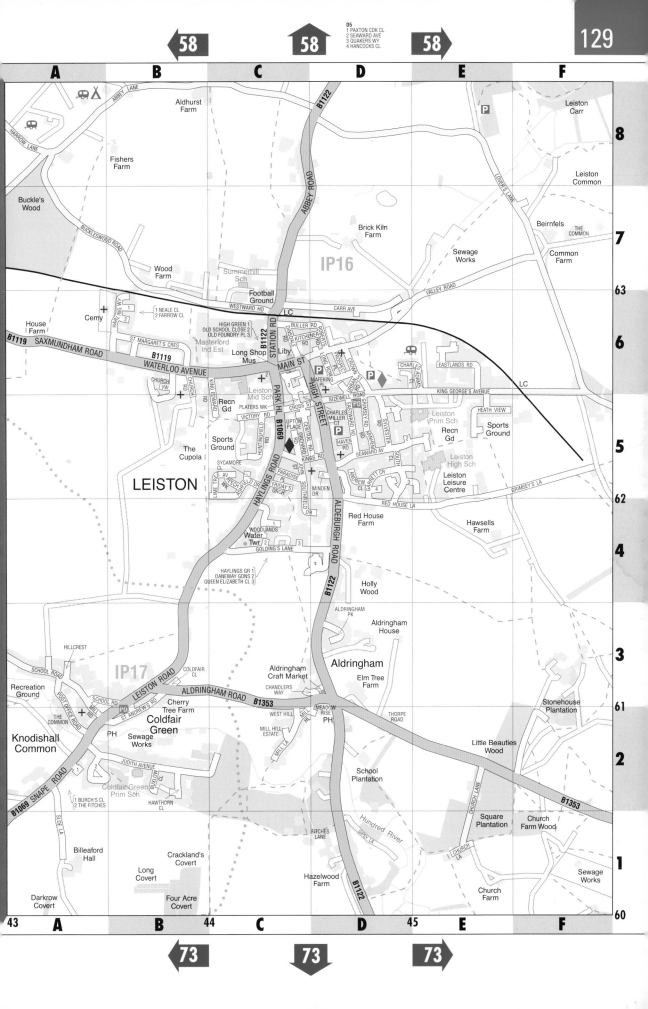

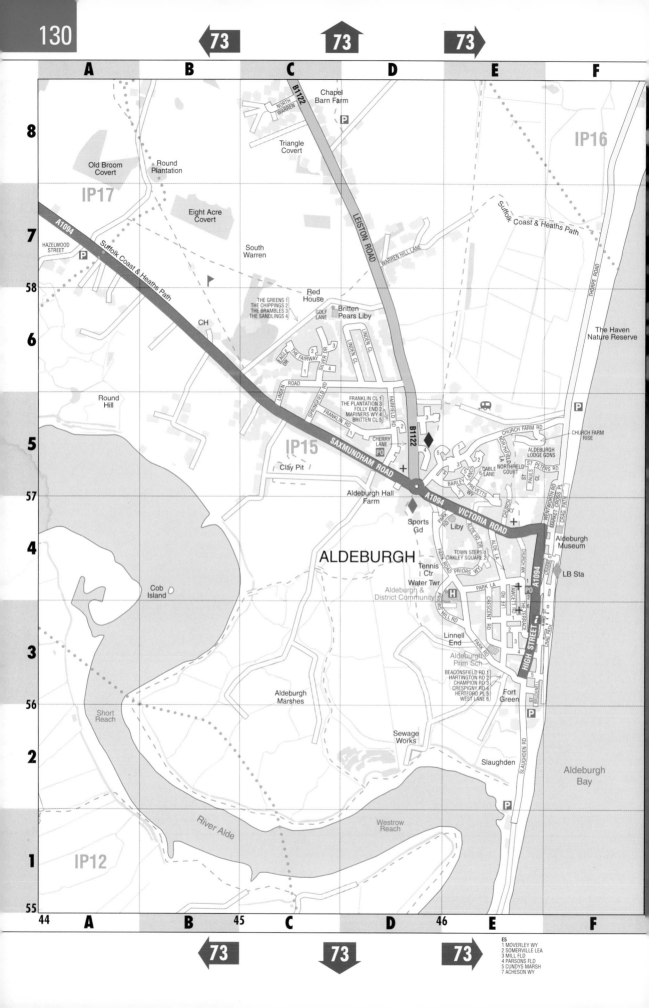

73 73 73

A B C D E F

8

IP16

Chapel
Barn Farm

P

NORTH
WARREN

Triangle
Covert

B1122

Old Broom
Covert

Round
Plantation

IP17

Eight Acre
Covert

7

A1094

HAZELWOOD
STREET

P

Suffolk Coast & Heaths Path

South
Warren

LEISTON ROAD

WARREN HILL LANE

Suffolk Coast & Heaths Path

THORPE ROAD

58

CH

Red
House

The Greens 1
The Chippings 2
The Brambles 3
The Sandlings 4

Golf Lane

Britten
Pears Liby

The Haven
Nature Reserve

6

Round
Hill

LINDEN ROAD

EAGLE DR

THE FAIRWAY

SILVER DR

LINDEN CL

SPRINGFIELD RD

FRANKLIN RD

FAIRFIELD RD

FRANKLIN CL 1
THE PLANTATION 3
FOLLY END 2
MARINERS WY 4
BRITTEN CL 5

CHURCH FARM RD

CHURCH FARM
RISE

ALDEBURGH
LODGE GDNS

NORTHFIELD RD

ST PETERS RD

IP15

Clay Pit

SAXMUNDHAM ROAD

CHERRY
LANE

PO

B1122

P

CABLE
LANE

NORTHFIELD
COURT

ST PAULS
CL

5

57

Aldeburgh Hall
Farm

BARLEY LN

PREVETTS
WY

CHURCH
CL

WENTWORTH RD

MARKET CROSS PL

CRAG PATH

A1094

VICTORIA ROAD

Aldeburgh
Museum

Sports
Gd

PARK RD

Liby

ALDE RD DR

ALDE LA

P

4

ALDEBURGH

Tennis
Ctr

Water Twr

Aldeburgh &
District Community

TOWN STEPS 1
OAKLEY SQUARE 2

PARK ROAD

PRIORS WY

H

PARK LA

CRESCENT RD

FAWCETT RD

CHURCH WY

PO

CORBIE ST

A1094

LB Sta

Cob
Island

3

PRIORS HILL RD

Linnell
End

Aldeburgh
Prim Sch

BEACONSFIELD RD 1
HARTINGTON RD 2
CHAMPION RD 3
CRESPIGNY RD 4
HERTFORD PL 5
WEST LANE 6

PARK RD

Fort
Green

HIGH STREET

ST BRUDENELL

CRAG PATH

56

Short
Reach

Aldeburgh
Marshes

Sewage
Works

P

2

Slaughden

SLAUGHDEN RD

Aldeburgh
Bay

River Alde

Westrow
Reach

P

1

IP12

55

44 A B 45 C D 46 E F

73 73 73

E5
1 MOVERLEY WY
2 SOMERVILLE LEA
3 MILL FLD
4 PARSONS FLD
5 CUNDYS MARSH
7 ACHESON WY

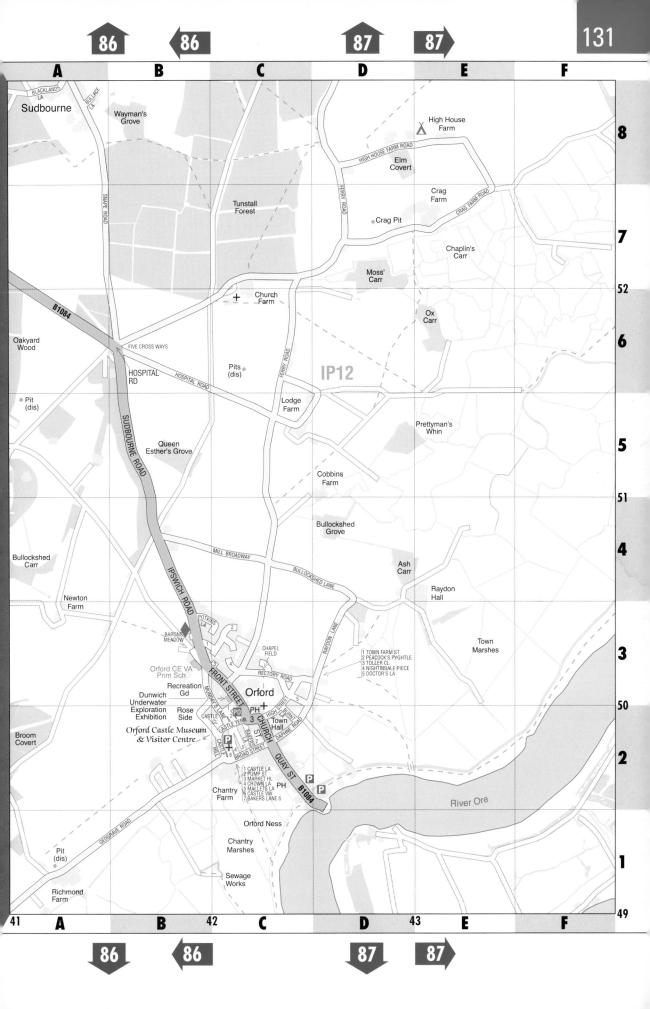

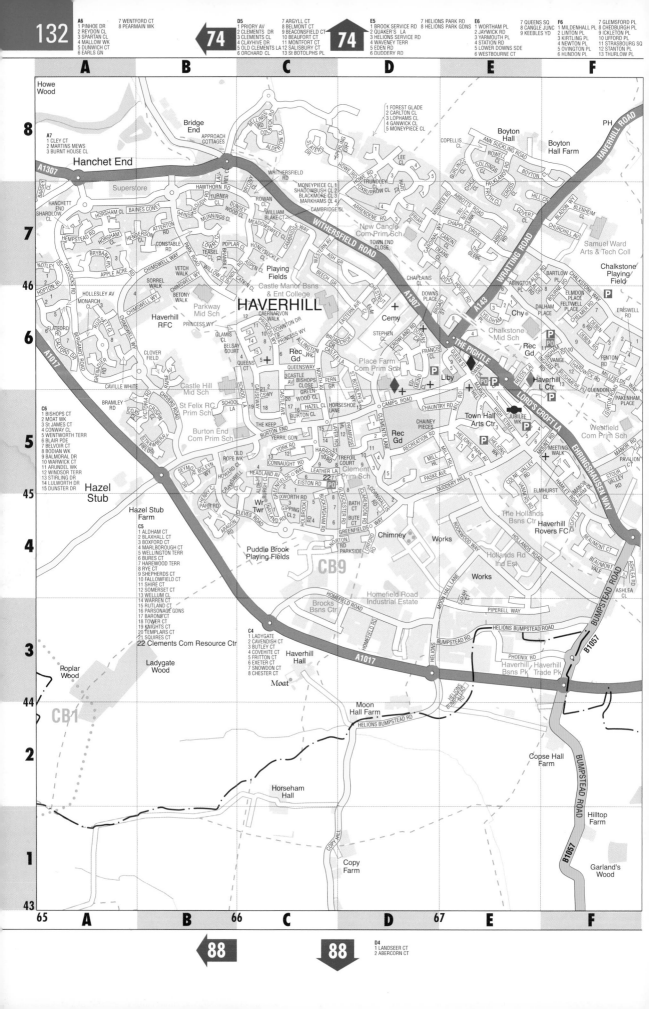

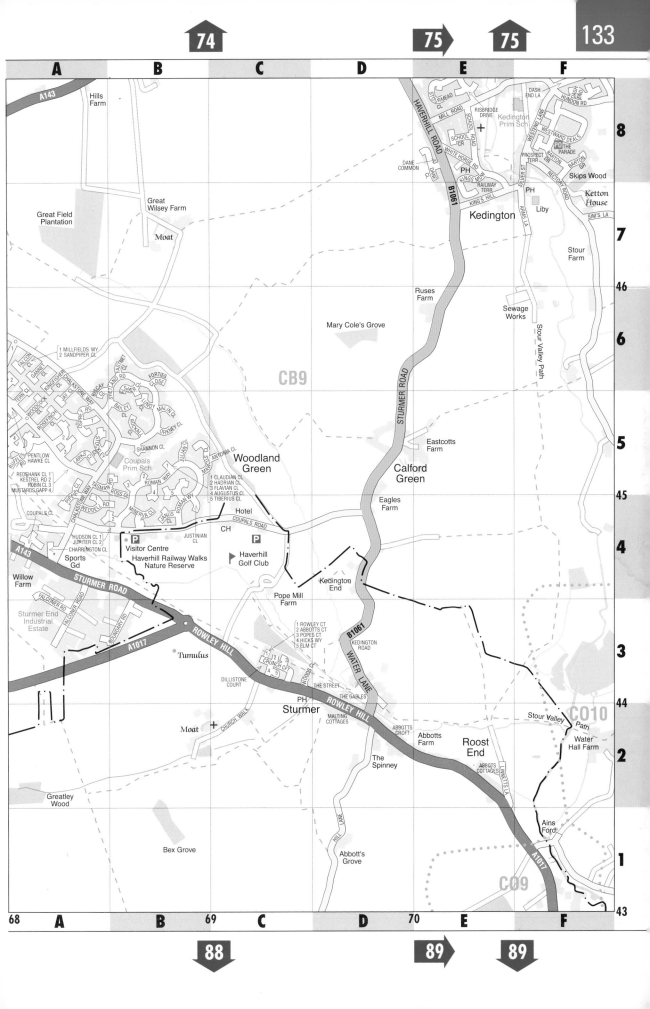

A   B   C   D   E   F

A143   Hills Farm

Great Field Plantation

Great Wilsey Farm

Moat

8

HAVERHILL ROAD

STORMEAD CL   MILL ROAD   SCHOOL LANE   RISBRIDGE DRIVE   Kedington Prim Sch   DASH END LA   HUNDON RD   WESTEND LANE   WESTWARD DEALS

SCHOOL CR   SCHOOL ROAD   WHITE HORSE RD   THE PARADE   BARTON   RECTORY ROAD   BARTON GR

DANE COMMON   DANE CL   PH   KINGS MDW   RAILWAY TERR   KING'S HILL   PROSPECT TERR   PO   SILVER ST

PH   Liby   Skips Wood   Ketton House

Kedington   ARMS LA   SIM'S LA

B1061   Stour Farm

46

Ruses Farm

Mary Cole's Grove   Sewage Works   Stour Valley Path

7

6

CB9

STURMER ROAD

1 MILLFIELDS WY   2 SANDPIPER CL

FALCON CL   GANNET CL   TERN CL   KINGFISHER CL   CHALKSTONE WAY   BISCAY   SHETLAND RD   ASTNET   FORTIES CLOSE

WOODCOCK RD   JAY RD   FISHER CL   BAILEY   LUNDY CL   MALIN CL   ORKNEY CL

ROSEFINCH   OSPREY RD   LARK CL   SHANNON CL   JULIAN CL   ANTONIA CL

Coupals Prim Sch

Eastcotts Farm

5

PENTLOW HAWKE CL   REDSHANK CL 1   KESTREL RD 2   ROBIN CL 3   MUSTARDS GAPP 4

PIPER CL   CHALKSTONE WAY   TASMAN CL   ROSS GL   ROMAN WAY   MINERVA CL   JANUS CL   ROMAN WY   MARY

Woodland Green

Calford Green

1 CLAUDIAN CL   2 HADRIAN CL   3 FLAVIAN CL   4 AUGUSTUS CL   5 TIBERIUS CL

Eagles Farm

45

COUPALS CL

WEDDELL RD

Hotel   COUPALS ROAD   CH   JUSTINIAN CL

A143   HUDSON CL 1   JUPITER CL 2   CHARRINGTON CL

P   Visitor Centre   Haverhill Railway Walks Nature Reserve

P   Haverhill Golf Club

Kedington End

4

Sports Gd

Willow Farm   STURMER ROAD

FALCONER RD   FALCONER ROAD   BOUNDARY RD

Pope Mill Farm

B1061   KEDINGTON ROAD

Sturmer End Industrial Estate

A1017   ROWLEY HILL

Tumulus

1 ROWLEY CT   2 ABBOTTS CT   3 POPES CT   4 HICKS WY   5 ELM CT

WATER LANE

3

44

DILLISTONE COURT

CRUNCH CFT   1 2 3   4 5   HINDOS CL

THE STREET   THE GABLES

PH   Sturmer   ROWLEY HILL

THE GABLES

Stour Valley Path   CO10

Moat   CHURCH WALK   MALTING COTTAGES   ABBOTTS CROFT   Abbotts Farm

Roost End   Water Hall Farm

2

Greatley Wood

The Spinney

ABBOTTS COTTAGES   LINNETTS LA

Ains Ford

Bex Grove

HILL LANE

Abbott's Grove

A1017   CO9

1

68   A   B   69   C   D   70   E   F   43

81
82

C8
1 ST PETER'S AV
2 QUOITS FIELD
3 MORGAN CT
4 POPLAR CL
5 LAUREL WY
6 WILLOW CL
7 LIMEKILN CL
8 OLD PAPER MILL LA
9 ALASDAIR PL

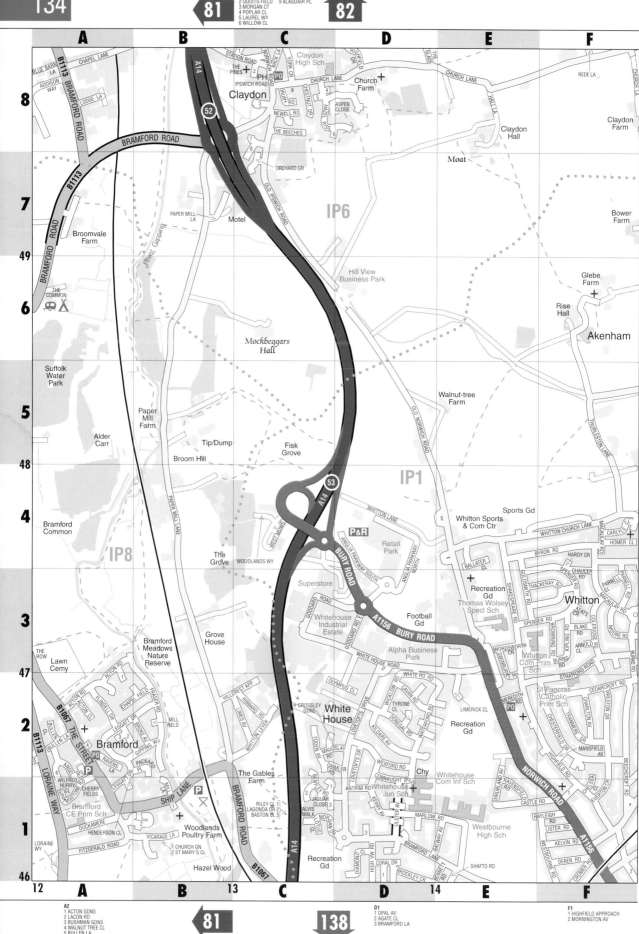

81
138

A2
1 ACTON GDNS
2 LACON RD
3 BUSHMAN GDNS
4 WALNUT TREE CL
5 BULLEN LA
6 ORCHARD RD

D1
1 OPAL AV
2 AGATE CL
3 BRAMFORD LA

F1
1 HIGHFIELD APPROACH
2 MORNINGTON AV

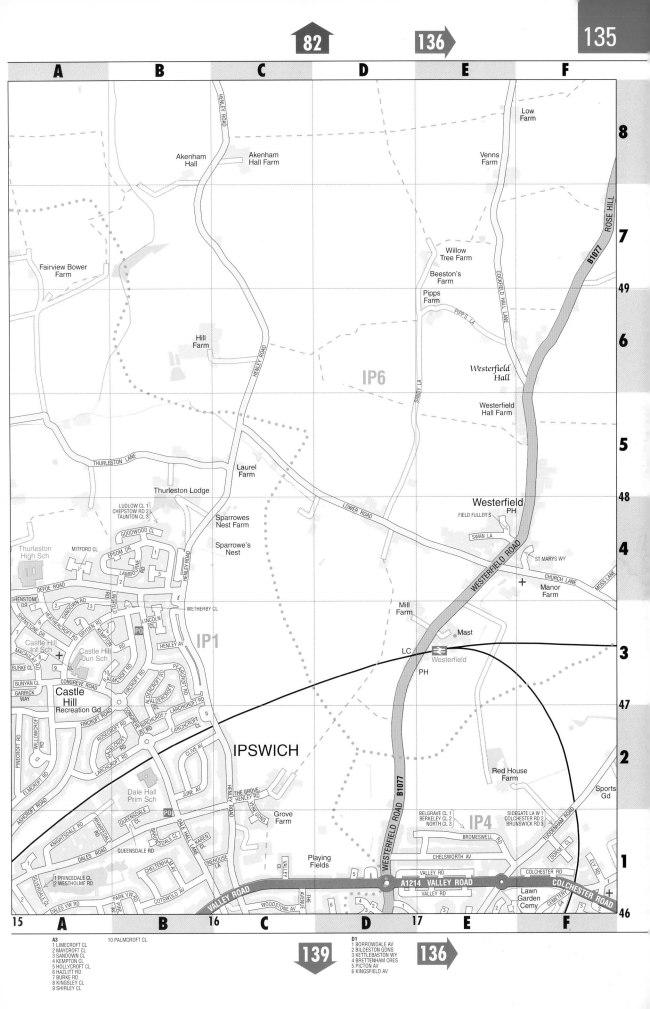

A   B   C   D   E   F

Low
Farm

Akenham
Hall

Akenham
Hall Farm

Venns
Farm

HENLEY ROAD

ROSE HILL

B1077

Willow
Tree Farm

Fairview Bower
Farm

Beeston's
Farm

Pipps
Farm

COCKFIELD HALL LANE

PIPP'S LA

Hill
Farm

IP6

Westerfield
Hall

HENLEY ROAD

SANDY LA

Westerfield
Hall Farm

THURLESTON LANE

Laurel
Farm

LOWER ROAD

Westerfield
PH

FIELD FULLER'S

Thurleston Lodge

SWAN LA

WESTERFIELD ROAD

LUDLOW CL 1
CHEPSTOW RD 2
TAUNTON CL 3

Sparrowes
Nest Farm

Sparrowe's
Nest

ST MARYS WY

CHURCH LANE

MOSS LANE

Thurleston
High Sch

GOODWOOD CL

MITFORD CL

EPSOM DR

LAMBOURNE RD

Manor
Farm

DEFOE ROAD

SHENSTONE DR

SANDOWN RD

HEATHERCROFT RD

DRYDEN RD

KEMPTON RD

LINGFIELD RD

WETHERBY CL

LINCOLN CL

IP1

Mill
Farm

SHENSTONE DR

Castle Hill
Inf Sch

Castle Hill
Jun Sch

HENLEY AV

Mast

BURKE CL

MACAULAY RD

PALMCROFT RD

FIRCROFT RD

PEARCROFT RD

LC

Westerfield

BUNYAN CL

CONGREVE ROAD

ALDERCROFT RD

BIRCHCROFT RD

LARCHCROFT RD

PH

GARRICK WAY

Castle
Hill
Recreation Gd

FIRCROFT ROAD

ROSECROFT RD

CONGREVE RD

LARCHCROFT CL

PINECROFT RD

WILLOWCROFT

IPSWICH

Red House
Farm

Sports
Gd

ELMCROFT RD

LARCHCROFT RD

CLIVE AV

HENLEY ROAD

THE GROVE
HENLEY RD

JUNE AV

WESTERFIELD ROAD B1077

BELGRAVE CL 1
BERKELEY CL 2
NORTH CL 3

SIDEGATE LA W 1
COLCHESTER RD 2
BRUNSWICK RD 3

TUDDENHAM RD

IP4

ASHCROFT ROAD

KNIGHTSDALE RD

VINDALE RD

Dale Hall
Prim Sch

QUEENSDALE CL

BARNSDALE CL

DALE HALL LANE

KAREN CL

VERE GDNS

Grove
Farm

ONEHOUSE LA

BROMESWELL

CHELSWORTH AV

DORSET CL

ELY RD

DALES ROAD

QUEENSDALE RD

CHELTENHAM AV

VALLEY CL

Playing
Fields

VALLEY RD

COLCHESTER RD

SILVERDALE RD

1 PRINCEDALE CL
2 WESTHOLME RD

DALES VW RD

PARK VW RD

PINE

COTSWOLD AV

WOODSTONE AV

THE AVENUE

VALLEY ROAD

A1214 VALLEY ROAD

VALLEY RD

Lawn
Garden
Cemy

COLCHESTER ROAD

CEMETERY LA

15   A   B   16   C   D   17   E   F   46

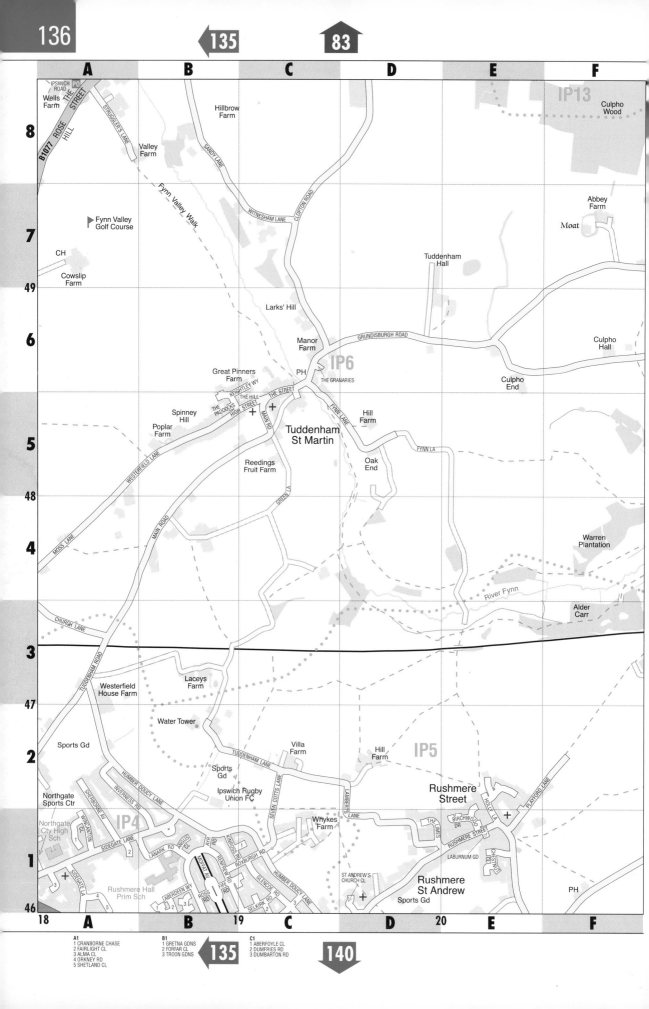

A

8

7

49

6

5

48

4

3

47

2

1

46

B

C

D

E

F

18

19

20

IP13

Culpho
Wood

Abbey
Farm

Moat

Culpho
Hall

Culpho
End

Tuddenham
Hall

Wells
Farm

IPSWICH
ROAD

PO

THE STREET

ROSE HILL

B1077

STRUGGLER'S LANE

Hillbrow
Farm

Valley
Farm

SANDY LANE

WITNESHAM LANE

CLOPTON ROAD

Fynn Valley Walk

Fynn Valley
Golf Course

CH

Cowslip
Farm

Larks' Hill

Manor
Farm

GRUNDISBURGH ROAD

IP6

PH

THE GRANARIES

Great Pinners
Farm

KEIGHTLEY WY

THE HILL

HIGH STREET

THE PADDOCKS

THE STREET

MAIN RD

Spinney
Hill

Poplar
Farm

Tuddenham
St Martin

Hill
Farm

FYNN LANE

FYNN LA

Oak
End

WESTERFIELD LANE

Reedings
Fruit Farm

GREEN LA

Warren
Plantation

MOSS LANE

MAIN ROAD

River Fynn

Alder
Carr

CHURCH LANE

TUDDENHAM ROAD

Westerfield
House Farm

Laceys
Farm

Water Tower

Sports Gd

TUDDENHAM LANE

Villa
Farm

Hill
Farm

IP5

Rushmere
Street

Sports
Gd

Ipswich Rugby
Union FC

SEVEN COTTS LANE

LAMBERTS LANE

HOLLY LA

PLAYFORD LANE

Northgate
Sports Ctr

HUMBER DOUCY LANE

INVERNESS RD

SHERBORNE AV

IP4

Whykes
Farm

THE LIMES

BIRCHWOOD DR

RUSHMERE STREET

CHESTNUT CL

LABURNUM GD

Northgate
Cty High
Sch

WINCANTON CL

SIDEGATE LANE

LANARK RD

ANGUS CL

AYR RD

KINROSS CL

ROXBURGH RD

HUMBER DOUCY LANE

ST ANDREW'S CHURCH CL

Rushmere
St Andrew

Sports Gd

PH

Rushmere Hall
Prim Sch

SIDEGATE LA

ABERDEEN WY

MORFEN AV

ROSS RD

FIFE RD

RENFREW RD

GLENCOE RD

SELKIRK RD

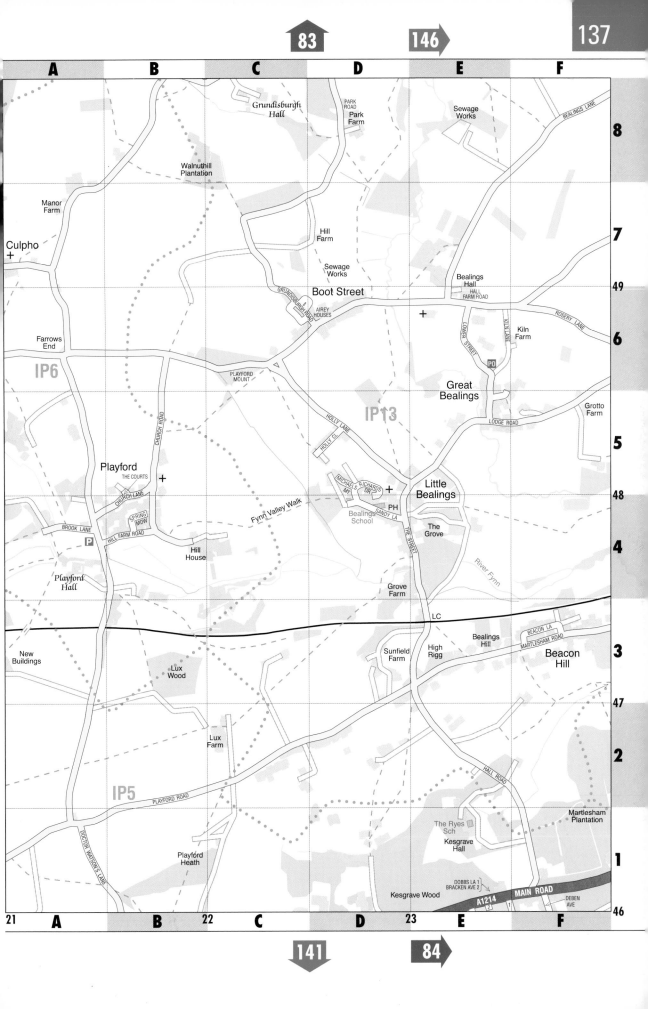

A   B   C   D   E   F

8

7

45

6

5

44

4

3

43

2

1

42

12   A   13   B   C   13   D   14   E   F

Grid reference labels: IP1, IP2, IP8

Place names and features:

Thornbush La, B1113, Thornbush La, Loraine Way, Runcton Farm, River Gipping, Hazel Wood, Sproughton Manor, Recn Gd, River Hill, Sports Centre, B1067, Pearl Rd, Opal, Coral, Westbourne Rd, Bramford Rd, Cromer Rd, Brookfield Rd, Thompson Rd, Springfield La, Springfield Jun Sch, Springfield Inf Sch, Kitchener Rd, Windsor, B1067, The Grindle, Hope Farm, Sproughton, Farthing Rd, Farthing Road Ind Est, Sproughton Business Park, Sproughton Road, IP1, PH, Boss Hall Ind Est, Boss Hall, Westbourne, Hadleigh Rd Ind Est, Brookhouse Business Park, Lower Street, Sproughton Bridge, Beech Cl, Church Cres, Glebe Cl, Broomfield, Comm, Gipping Way, Sproughton Court, Samford Pl, Church Lane, Sproughton CE Prim Sch, Monks Gate, A14, Sports Ground, Factory, Chimney, Superstore, Crompton Rd, Hadleigh Rd Ind Est, Brunel, Dunlop Rd, New Way, Chimney, High Street, Bungalow Farm, IP8, Weir, Chantry Grove, Woodward Cl, Larchwood Cl, Orchard Gate, Red House, Elton Park, Elton Pk, Hadleigh Road, Nine Acres, Collinson's, Hyntle Cl, Anita Close West, Anita Close East, Milden Rd, Lavenham Rd, Kelly Rd, Copperfield, Ombey Rd, Pickworth Rd, Diggens Rd, Ranelagh Prim Sch, A1214, London Road, B1075, Springvale, Hadleigh Road, Chantry Park, IP2, Crane Hill, Gippeswyk Park, Columbine Gdns, Iris Close, Waller's Gr, Poppy Cl, Cotswold Rd, Cotsmip, A1071, B1113, Hotel, Linnet Rd, A1214, Curlew Rd, Archangel Gdns, Pennyroyal Gdns, Honeysuckle Gdns, Buddleia Cl, Orchid Cl, Cornflower Cl, Aster Cl, Bluebell, Shamrock Av, Crocus Cl, Thistle Cl, Lavender, Primrose Cl, Clover, Campion Road, Violet Cl, Speedwell, Harebell Rd, Poplar Farm, Poplar Lane, Hotel, Peewit Rd, Lapwing Rd, Oaks Community Prim Sch, Marigold Rd, Pimpernel Rd, Larkspur, Hawthorn Drive, St Marks RC Prim Sch, Jasmine Cl, Stone Lodge Lane W, Water Tower, Pigeon's Lane, Swallow Rd, Wren Ave, Robin Drive, Partridge, Pheasant Rd, Kingfisher Avenue, Hawthorn Drive, Heron Rd, Pelican, Widgeon, Chantry High Sch, Birkfield Drive, Beacon Hill Specl Sch, Merlin Rd, Greenwich Av, Chaffinch, Kestrel Rd, Redwing, Kittiwake, Bittern, Chantry, Goldcrest Rd, Stonechat Rd, Woodpecker Rd, Hawthorn Drive, Whitworth, Royston Dr, Middleton Cl, Liby, Birkfield Drive, Downing Prim Sch, Sunnyside Farm, Hotel, Cherry Blossom Cl, Scrivener Dr, Shepherd Dr, Sprites La, Sprites Prim Sch, Denton, Lakeside Road, Manchester Road, Woodcock, Peterhouse, Sandringham, Copdock Interchange, P&R, Bishop Mews, Chamberlain Wy, Sky Lark La, Ash Ton Cl, Wilmslow Dr, Clifton Wy, Monton Rise, Dunlin Rd, Magdalene Cl, Cambridge Drive, Sandpiper Rd, Downing, Hill Farm, Chapel Lane, Whights Corner, Mill La, The Barvens, A14, Superstore, Green Spire Gr, Cottingham Rd, Belstead Sch, Butterbury, Belmont, Acer Cl, Mill, Pendleton, Bramhall, Ellenbrook Green, Gusford Prim Sch, Lynnbrook Close, Carolbrook Rd, Woodlark Cl, Leicester, Stoke Park, A1214, Southgate Rd, Belstead House, Belstead Brook Park, Bowland Dr, Curtis Ford, Quilter Dr, Dashwood Cl, Short Lands, Wardley, Swinton, Ellenbrook Rd, Skipper Rd, Brookview, Hotel, Newark Cl, A55 (roundabout)

Index (C2):
1 BRAMBLEWOOD
2 BROAD MDW
3 LABURNUM CL
4 INNES END
5 PEACOCK CL
6 HALFORD CT
7 WENTWORTH DR
8 MAGPIE CL
9 ACORN CL
10 MILNROW
11 THE CHESTNUTS
12 MERRION CL
13 MATLOCK CL
14 MOTTRAM CL

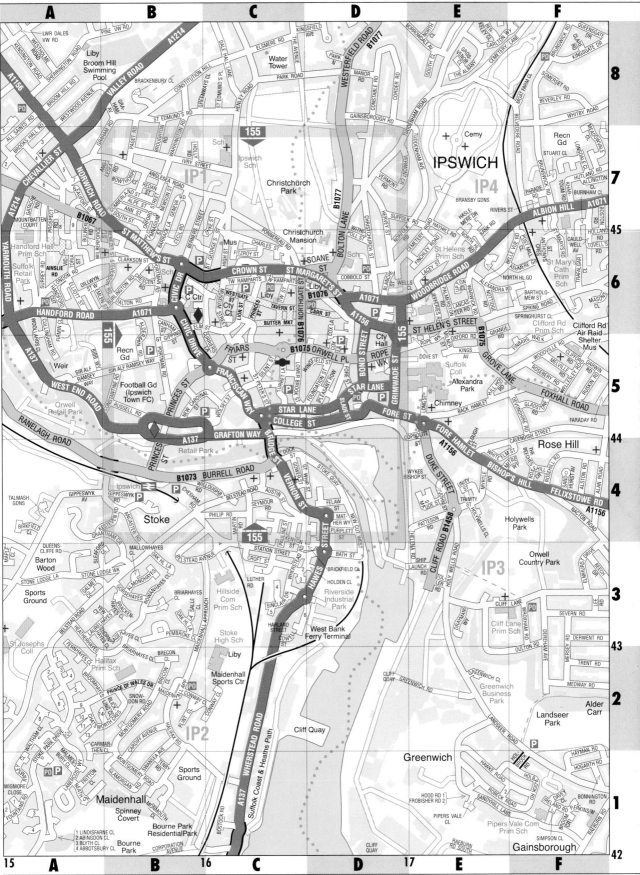

For full street detail of the highlighted area see page 155

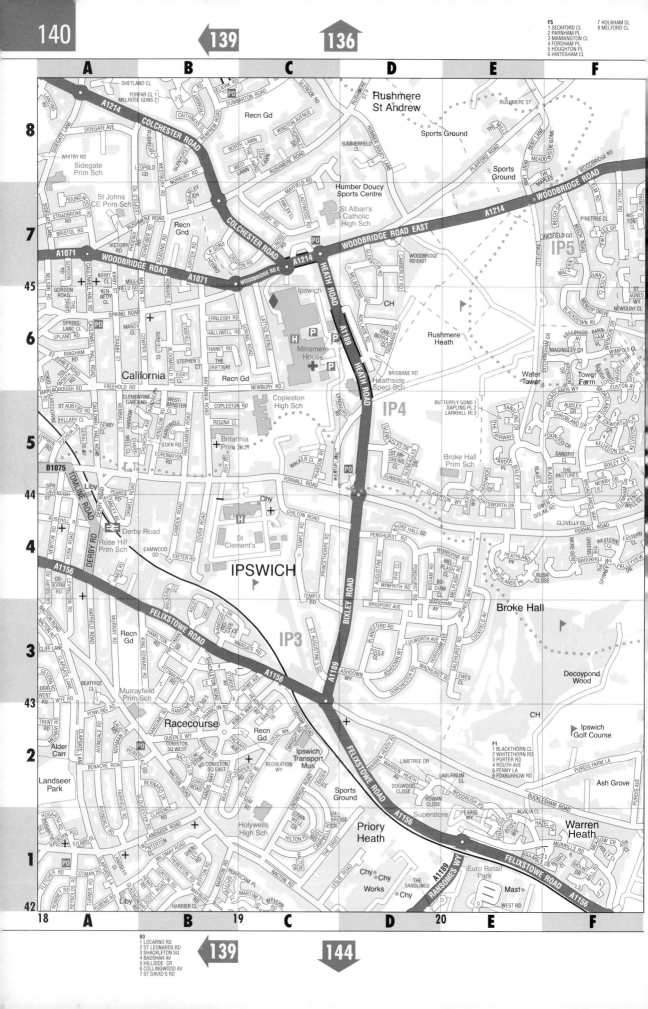

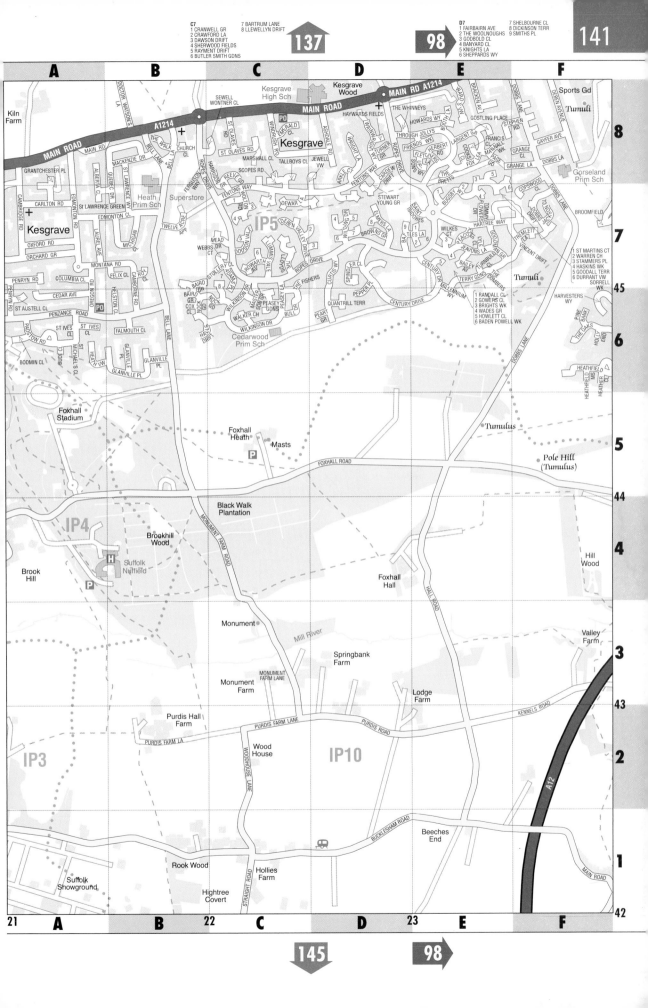

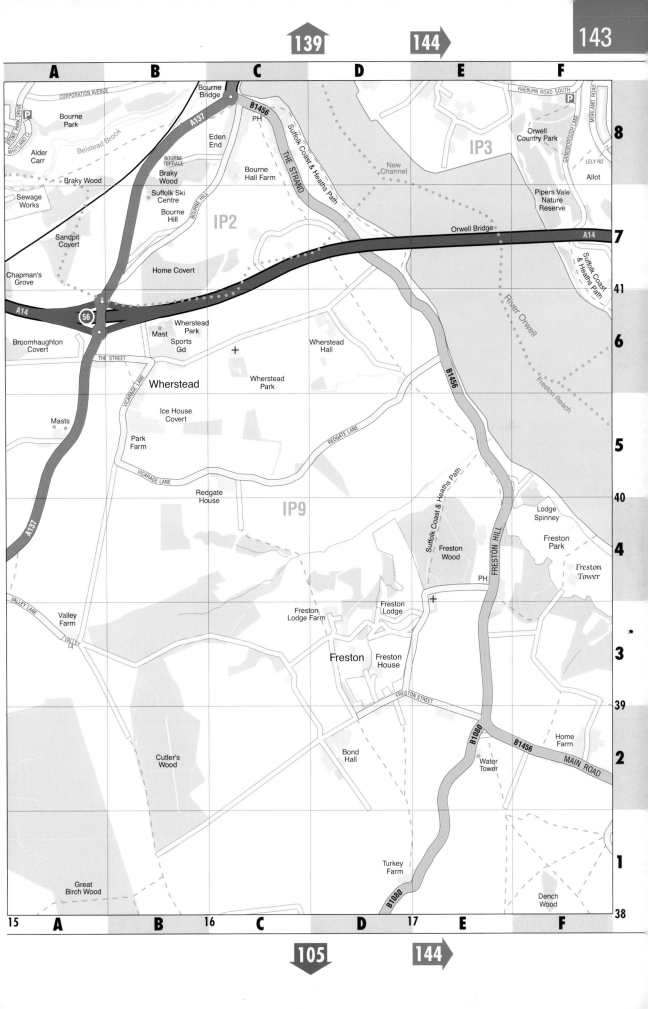

A B C D E F

15 A B 16 C D 17 E F 38

CORPORATION AVENUE

STOKE PARK DRIVE
WHITLANDS
P
Bourne Park
Belstead Brook
Alder Carr
Braky Wood
Sewage Works
Sandpit Covert
Chapman's Grove

A137
BOURNE TERRACE
Eden End
Bourne Bridge
PH
B1456
THE STRAND
Bourne Hall Farm

Braky Wood
Suffolk Ski Centre
Bourne Hill
BOURNE HILL
IP2

Home Covert

A14
56

Broomhaughton Covert
THE STREET
VICARAGE LANE
Wherstead
Masts

Mast
Wherstead Park Sports Gd

Wherstead Park

Wherstead Hall

Ice House Covert

Park Farm
VICARAGE LANE

Redgate House

REDGATE LANE

IP9

Suffolk Coast & Heaths Path

New Channel

IP3

RAEBURN ROAD SOUTH
P
Orwell Country Park
GAINSBOROUGH LANE
MORLAND ROAD
LELY RD
Allot

Pipers Vale Nature Reserve

Orwell Bridge
A14
41

River Orwell
Freston Reach

Suffolk Coast & Heaths Path

B1456

6

5

40

4

Freston Wood
FRESTON HILL
PH
Freston Lodge

Lodge Spinney
Freston Park
Freston Tower

Freston Lodge Farm

Freston
Freston House
FRESTON STREET

3

39

VALLEY LANE
Valley Farm
VALLEY LA

Cutler's Wood

Bond Hall

B1080
B1456
Water Tower
Home Farm
MAIN ROAD

2

A137

Great Birch Wood

Turkey Farm
B1080

Dench Wood

1

38

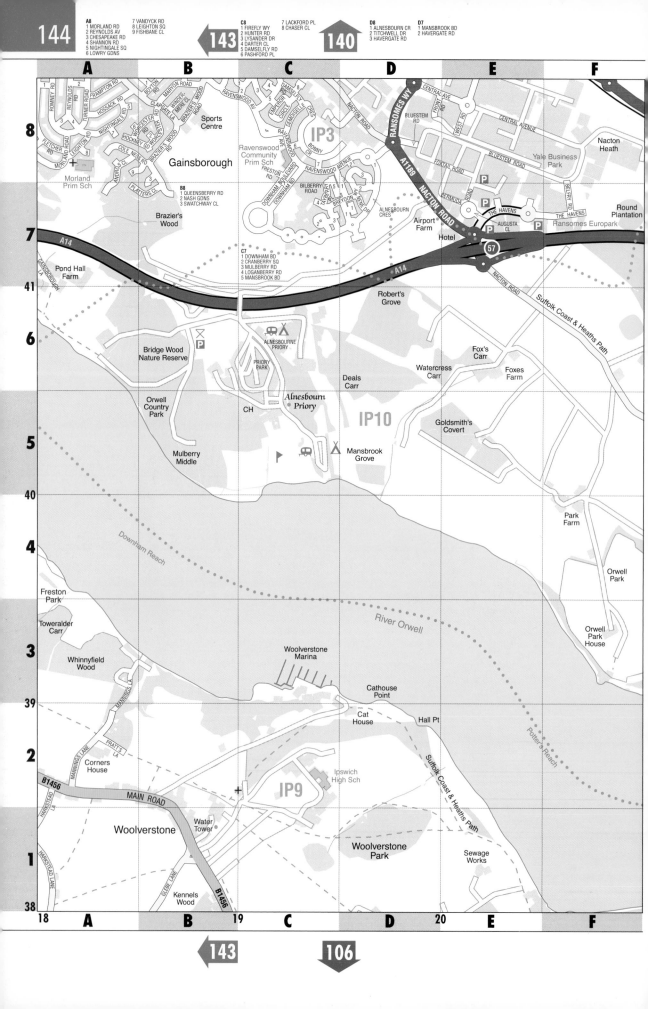

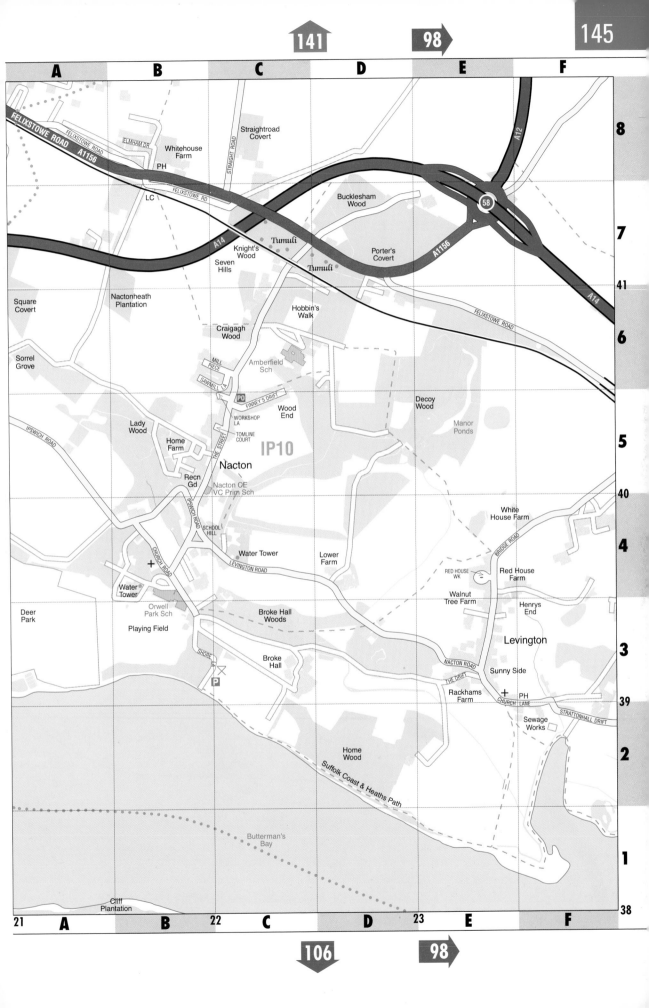

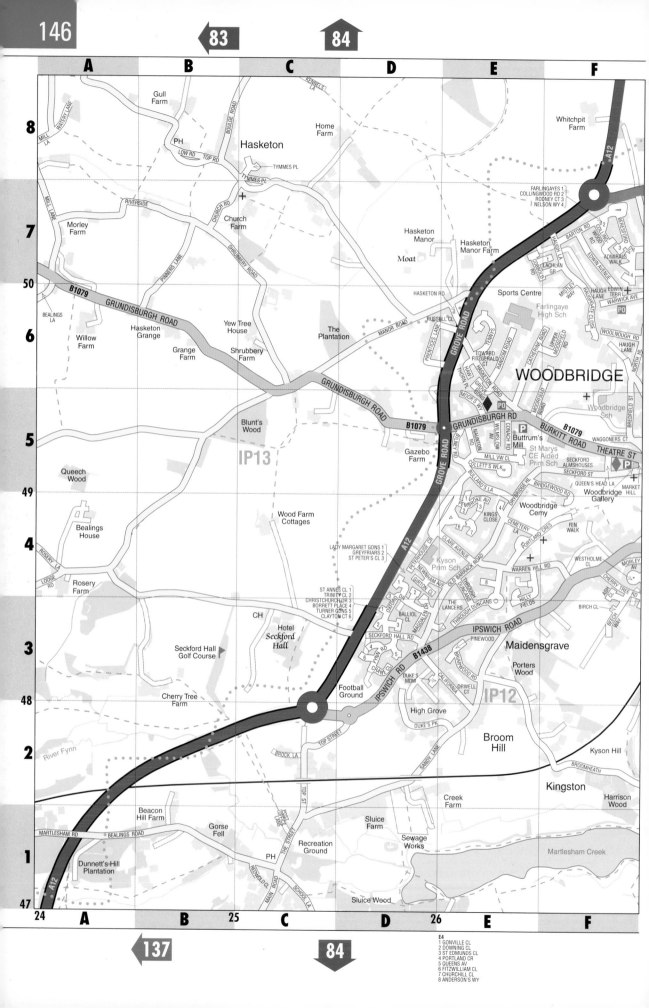
E4
1 GONVILLE CL
2 DOWNING CL
3 ST EDMUNDS CL
4 PORTLAND CR
5 QUEENS AV
6 FITZWILLIAM CL
7 CHURCHILL CL
8 ANDERSON'S WY

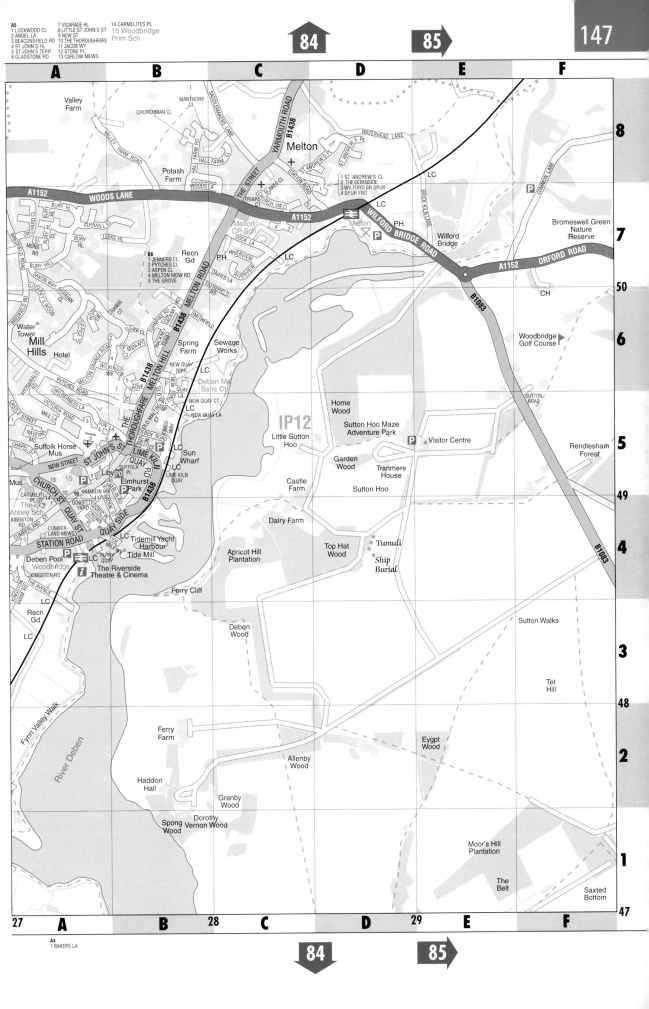

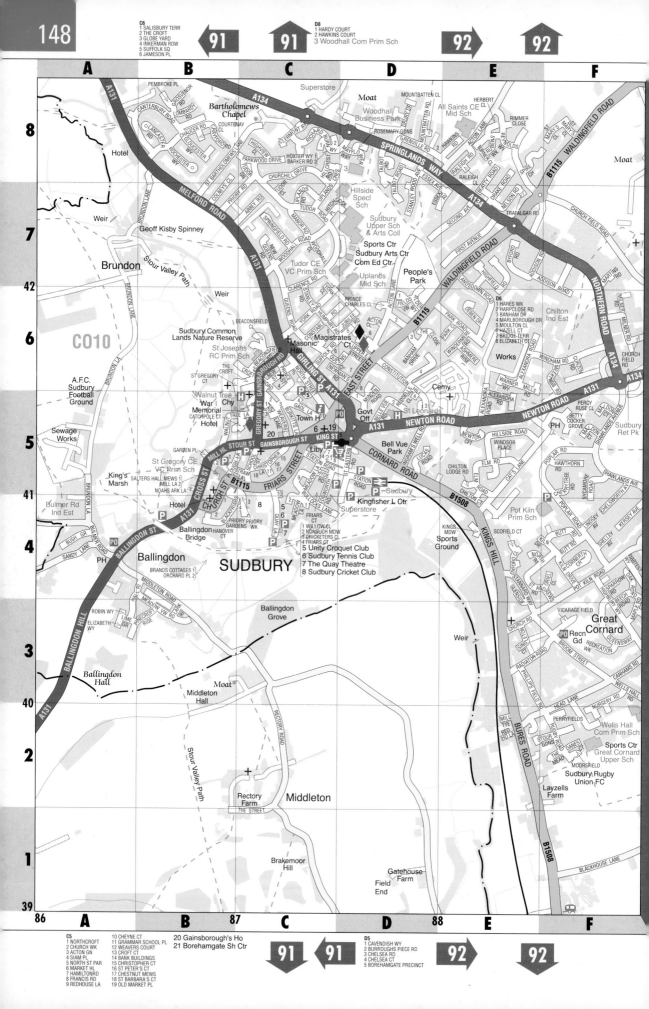

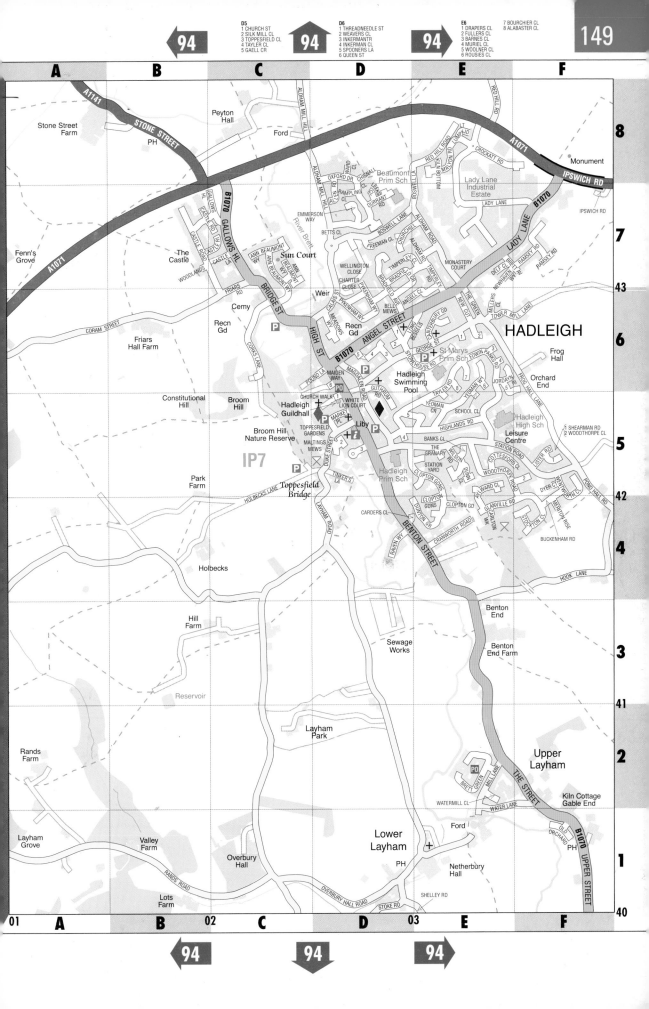

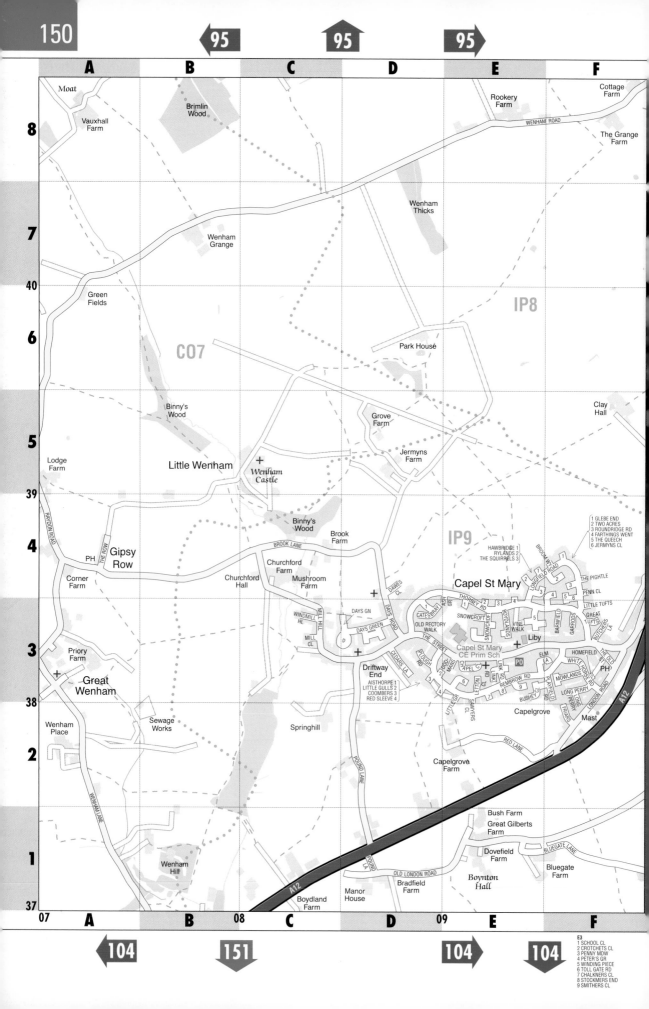

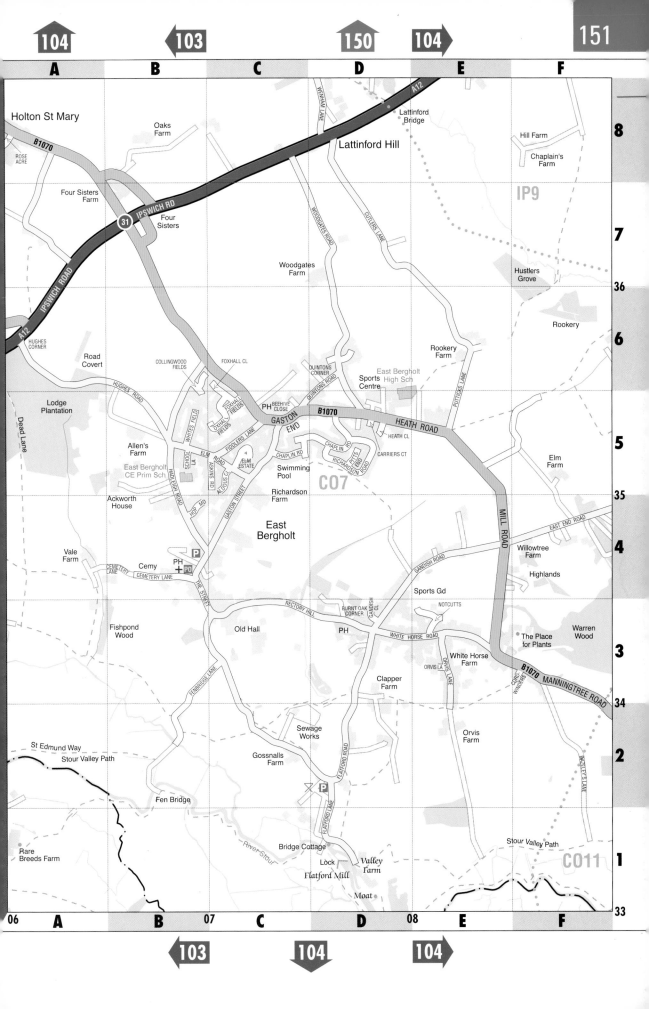

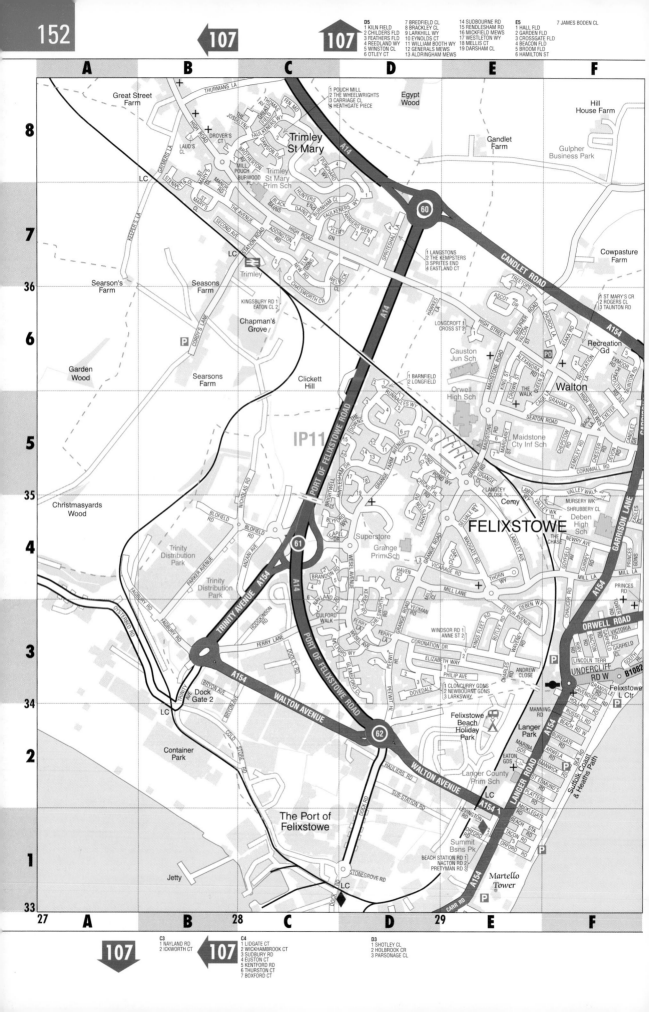

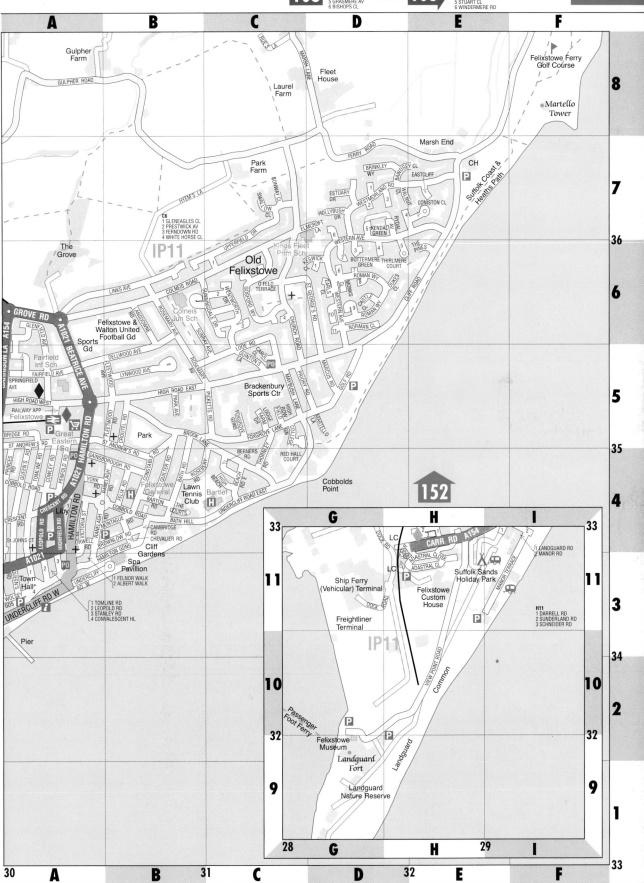

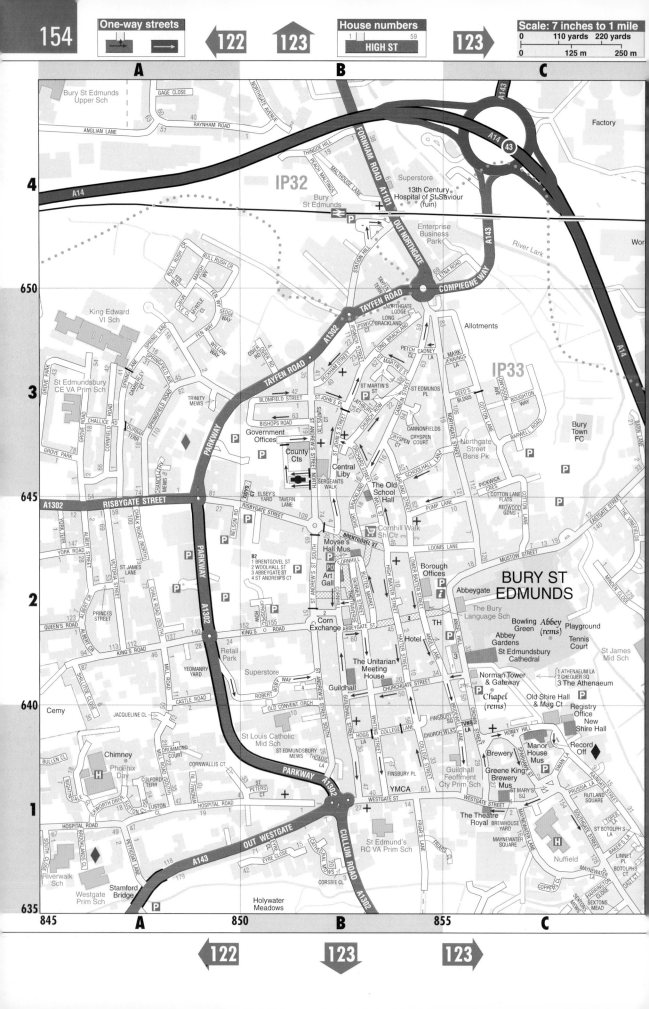

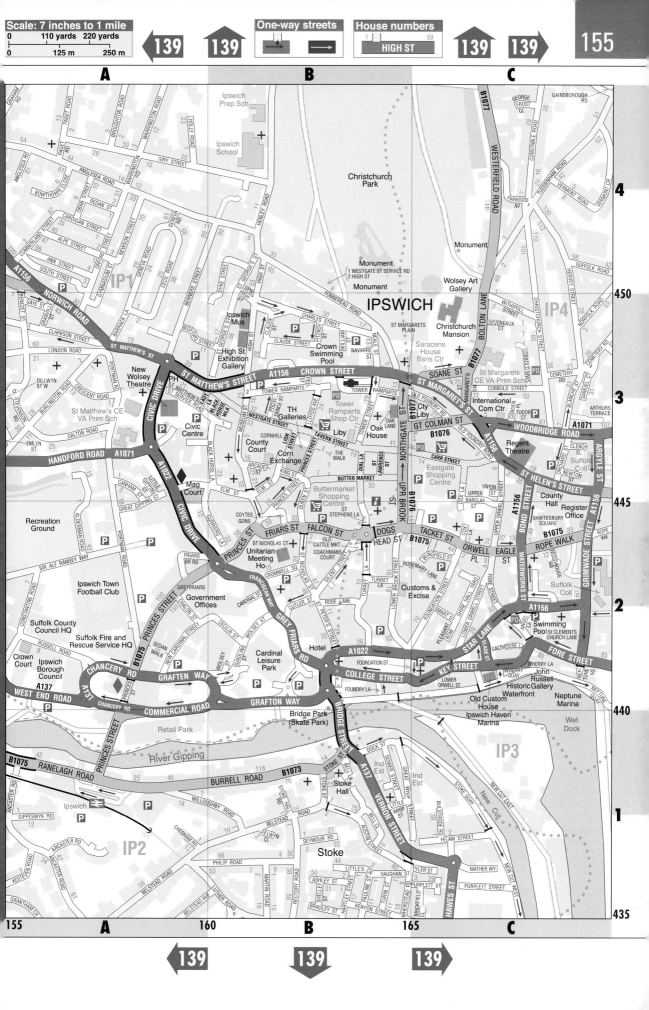

Index

Place name May be abbreviated on the map

Location number Present when a number indicates the place's position in a crowded area of mapping

Locality, town or village Shown when more than one place has the same name

Postcode district District for the indexed place

Page and grid square Page number and grid reference for the standard mapping

→ **Church Rd** **6** Beckenham BR2.........**53** C6

Public and commercial buildings are highlighted in magenta **Places of interest** are highlighted in blue with a star*

Abbreviations used in the index

Acad	**Academy**	Comm	**Common**	Gd	**Ground**	L	**Leisure**	Prom	**Promenade**
App	**Approach**	Cott	**Cottage**	Gdn	**Garden**	La	**Lane**	Rd	**Road**
Arc	**Arcade**	Cres	**Crescent**	Gn	**Green**	Liby	**Library**	Recn	**Recreation**
Ave	**Avenue**	Cswy	**Causeway**	Gr	**Grove**	Mdw	**Meadow**	Ret	**Retail**
Bglw	**Bungalow**	Ct	**Court**	H	**Hall**	Meml	**Memorial**	Sh	**Shopping**
Bldg	**Building**	Ctr	**Centre**	Ho	**House**	Mkt	**Market**	Sq	**Square**
Bsns, Bus	**Business**	Ctry	**Country**	Hospl	**Hospital**	Mus	**Museum**	St	**Street**
Bvd	**Boulevard**	Cty	**County**	HQ	**Headquarters**	Orch	**Orchard**	Sta	**Station**
Cath	**Cathedral**	Dr	**Drive**	Hts	**Heights**	Pal	**Palace**	Terr	**Terrace**
Cir	**Circus**	Dro	**Drove**	Ind	**Industrial**	Par	**Parade**	TH	**Town Hall**
Cl	**Close**	Ed	**Education**	Inst	**Institute**	Pas	**Passage**	Univ	**University**
Cnr	**Corner**	Emb	**Embankment**	Int	**International**	Pk	**Park**	Wk, Wlk	**Walk**
Coll	**College**	Est	**Estate**	Intc	**Interchange**	Pl	**Place**	Wr	**Water**
Com	**Community**	Ex	**Exhibition**	Junc	**Junction**	Prec	**Precinct**	Yd	**Yard**

Index of localities, towns and villages

A

Acton 92 B7
Acton Place 92 B8
Akenham 134 F6
Alburgh 7 A1
Aldeburgh 130 D4
Aldeby 9 F8
Alderton 99 E4
Aldham 94 E8
Aldringham 129 D3
All Saints South Elmham 24 B5
Allwood Green 36 A2
Alpheton 78 A5
Ampton 33 A2
Annis Hill 110 E3
Apsey Green 126 A3
Ardleigh Heath 103 F1
Ash Abbey 127 F3
Ashbocking 69 A1
Ash Corner 127 F7
Ashen 89 E5
Ashfield 54 D2
Ashfield Cum Thorpe.... 54 C1
Ashfield Green
  Stradbroke 39 D4
  Wickhambrook 62 A2
Ashley 60 F8
Ash Street 80 A1
Aspall 53 E4
Assington 92 F1
Assington Green 76 B6
Athelington 38 E2
Attleton Green 61 D1
Audley End
  Burston and Shimpling 20 E5
  Lawshall 77 D8

B

Babel Green 75 D3
Back Street 61 E5
Bacton 51 F5
Bacton Green 51 E4
Badingham 56 A6
Badwell Ash 50 E7
Badwell Green 51 B8
Ballingdon 148 B4
Banyard's Green 40 C4
Bardwell 34 C4
Barham 82 C6
Barking 125 A1
Barking Tye 81 A7
Barley Green 39 C5
Barnaby Green 26 C2

Barnardiston 75 B3
Barnby 10 B5
Barnham 16 C2
Barningham 34 F7
Barrow 47 A2
Barsham 9 A4
Barton Mills 116 D2
Base Green 51 B2
Bath Side 107 B3
Battisford 66 F1
Battisford Tye 66 C1
Battlesea Green 39 A6
Battlies Green 49 C3
Bawdsey 99 E3
Baylham 81 E6
Baythorne End 89 C5
Beacon Hill 137 F3
Beccles 111 D5
Beck Row 30 A8
Bedfield 54 E5
Bedingfield 53 F7
Bedingham Green....... 7 B7
Belchamp Otten 90 E4
Belchamp St Paul ... 90 D5
Belchamp Walter 90 F3
Bell's Corner 102 F8
Bell's Cross 82 D7
Belstead 142 C7
Benacre 27 A7
Benhall Green 72 C8
Benhall Street 71 F8
Bentley 104 F8
Beyton 49 F1
Beyton Green 49 F2
Bigsby's Corner 72 D8
Bildeston 79 F4
Billingford 21 B1
Birdbrook 89 A4
Birds End 62 B7
Bird Street 80 A7
Blackheath 42 C5
Blacksmith's Green . 53 C5
Black Street 11 A2
Blackthorpe 49 C2
Blaxhall 72 B4
Bleach Green 39 A8
Blo' Norton 18 E2
Bloodman's Corner .. 3 A6
Bloodmoor Hill 114 A2
Blundeston 3 A4
Blyford 42 C7
Blythburgh 42 F6
Bobby Hill 35 C5
Boot Street 137 D6
Borley 91 C5
Borley Green
  Borley 91 B5

Woolpit 65 E7
Botesdale 36 B6
Bowbeck 34 C6
Bower House Tye 93 E3
Boxford 93 C3
Boxted
  Colchester 77 A6
  Glemsford 102 F4
Boxted Cross 103 A3
Boyden End 61 D2
Boyland Common 20 A7
Boyton 86 B2
Boyton End 89 B7
Brabling Green 126 E6
Bradfield 105 C1
Bradfield Combust .. 64 A4
Bradfield St Clare . 64 C4
Bradfield St George 64 D7
Braiseworth 37 D2
Bramfield 41 F4
Bramford 134 A2
Brampton 25 E5
Brampton Street ... 25 E4
Brandeston 70 B7
Brandon 6 A1
Brantham 104 F4
Bredfield 84 C7
Brent Eleigh 79 A2
Bressingham 19 F4
Bressingham Common . 19 F5
Brettenham
  Stowmarket 79 C8
  Thetford 17 B6
Brewers Green 20 B3
Bridge Green 20 F6
Bridge Street 77 F4
Brightwell 98 A6
Brinkley 59 E2
Broadgrass Green .. 50 C1
Broad Green
  Cheveley 60 F6
  Chevington 62 B6
  Creeting St Peter or West
    Creeting 67 C6
Broad Street 93 C5
Broadway 118 C6
Brockdish 21 F2
Brockford Green ... 53 A4
Brockford Street .. 52 F5
Brockley Corner ... 32 D2
Brockley Green
  Hartest 63 A1
  Hundon 75 C2
Broke Hall 140 E3
Brome 117 B7
Brome Street 117 E8
Bromeswell 85 A5

Brook Green 63 E5
Brook Street 77 A3
Broome 110 D7
Broome Heath 110 D7
Broom Hill 146 E2
Broom's Barn 46 F4
Brown Street 52 A2
Browston Green 2 E8
Bruisyard 56 C5
Brundish 55 C8
Brundish Street ... 39 E1
Brundon 148 A7
Bucklesham 98 A5
Bulcamp 42 D7
Bulmer 91 C3
Bulmer Tye 91 D1
Bungay 110 B3
Bures 101 C5
Bures Green 101 D6
Burgate 36 E6
Burgh 83 F6
Burgh St Peter 10 B8
Burrough End 59 E2
Burrough Green 59 F2
Burstall 95 D7
Burstallhill 95 C8
Burston 20 E6
Burthorpe 47 B3
Burwell 44 A5
Bury St Edmunds.... 154 C2
Bush Green 64 D4
Butley 86 B5
Butley High Corner. 86 C4
Butley Low Corner . 86 C4
Button Haugh Green. 50 F4
Button's Green 78 E8
Buxhall 66 A4
Buxhall Fen Street. 66 A6

C

Calais Street 93 D2
Calford Green 133 D5
California 140 B6
Camps Heath 112 D3
Canham's Green 51 F4
Capel Green 86 A4
Capel St Andrew ... 86 B3
Capel St Mary 150 E4
Capon's Green 55 E6
Carlton
  Carlton 74 A8
  Kelsale cum Carlton 128 C6
Carlton Colville .. 114 C2
Carlton Green 74 A6

Castle Hill 135 A3
Castling's Heath .. 93 D6
Cattawade 104 E4
Cavendish 76 D1
Cavenham 47 A8
Cay Hill 52 C2
Chantry 138 D2
Charles Tye 80 C7
Charsfield 70 B3
Chattisham 95 C5
Chedburgh 62 C4
Chediston 41 C8
Chediston Green ... 24 C1
Chelmondiston 106 C8
Chelsworth 79 E3
Chelsworth Common . 79 E2
Cheveley 60 E7
Chevington 62 C6
Chickering 38 F7
Chillesford 86 C7
Chilton 92 B5
Chilton Street 75 F1
Chimney Street 75 C3
Chippenhall Green . 40 A6
Chippenham 45 C8
Church End 106 F7
Church Street 90 D6
Clare 90 B8
Clay Common 26 B4
Claydon 134 C8
Claypits 109 B4
Clay Street 35 D2
Clopton Corner 69 C1
Clopton Green
  Wickhambrook 62 A1
  Woolpit 65 D7
Cobbler's Green 7 C6
Cock & End 75 C8
Cockfield 64 C1
Cocks Green 64 A5
Cock Street 102 C7
Coddenham 68 C1
Coddenham Green ... 67 F2
Colchester Green .. 64 E2
Coldfair Green ... 129 B2
Coles Green 95 D4
Cole's Green 126 E1
Colton 48 F5
Combs 124 C1
Combs Ford 124 D4
Coney Weston 17 E1
Conyers Green 49 B7
Cookley 41 A6
Cookley Green 40 F6
Cook's Green 79 D8
Copdock 95 F4
Cornard Tye 92 C4

Corton ... 3 C4
Cotton ... 52 B6
Cove Bottom ... 26 E3
Covehithe ... 27 B4
Cow Green ... 51 F4
Cowlinge ... 61 B1
Cox Common ... 25 A5
Crackthorn Corner ... 19 A1
Cranley ... 37 F3
Cranmer Green ... 35 E2
Cransford ... 56 B3
Cratfield ... 40 D6
Creeting Bottoms ... 67 F5
Creeting St Mary ... 125 F8
Creeting St Peter ... 67 C5
Cretingham ... 69 F7
Cross Green
  Cockfield ... 64 B2
  Hartest ... 77 A7
  Hitcham ... 79 E7
Cross Street ... 38 C7
Crowfield ... 68 D4
Crown Corner ... 39 D1
Crownland ... 35 D1
Cuckold's Green ... 26 C5
Cuckoo Green ... 3 A6
Cuckoo Tye ... 92 A7
Culford ... 32 D1
Culfordheath ... 32 F5
Culpho ... 137 A7
Curlew Green ... 128 C7

D
Dagworth ... 66 E8
Daisy Green
  Great Ashfield ... 51 A6
  Wickham Skeith ... 52 D7
Dalham ... 61 C8
Dallinghoo ... 70 D1
Dam Green ... 19 C8
Dandy Corner ... 52 B6
Darmsden ... 125 F1
Darsham ... 42 C1
Debach ... 70 A1
Debenham ... 53 E2
Dedham ... 103 F4
Dedham Heath ... 103 F2
Denham
  Denham ... 61 F8
  Hoxne ... 38 D5
Denham End ... 46 F2
Dennington ... 55 E5
Dennington Corner ... 126 C8
Denston ... 76 A7
Denton ... 7 A3
Depden ... 62 B3
Depden Green ... 62 B4
Dickleburgh ... 21 B5
Dickleburgh Moor ... 21 D6
Diss ... 20 C4
Ditchingham ... 110 C2
Ditton Green ... 60 B4
Dockeney ... 8 F6
Dorking Tye ... 101 D7
Dorley's Corner ... 128 D8
Dovercourt ... 107 B2
Down Field ... 28 F2
Drakestone Green ... 93 F8
Drinkstone ... 65 C8
Drinkstone Green ... 65 B7
Dublin ... 53 E8
Duke Street ... 95 B5
Dullingham ... 59 F5
Dullingham Ley ... 60 A3
Dunstall Green ... 61 E7
Dunwich ... 43 B1

E
Earl's Green ... 51 D5
Earl Soham ... 54 E2
Earl Stoneham ... 67 E5
Earsham ... 7 E4
Earsham Street ... 22 C1
East Barton ... 49 C4
East Bergholt ... 151 D4
Eastbridge ... 58 D4
East End
  East Bergholt ... 104 E6
  Stonham Aspal ... 68 D6
East Green
  Great Bradley ... 74 E8
  Kelsale cum Carlton ... 57 E4
Easton ... 70 E5
Edge Green ... 19 B8
Edwardstone ... 93 A5
Ellingham ... 8 D7
Ellough ... 9 F1
Ellough Hill ... 111 D3
Elmsett ... 80 F1
Elmswell ... 50 E1
Elveden ... 15 D3
Eriswell ... 13 F1
Erwarton ... 106 D5
Euston ... 16 F1
Exning ... 120 B8
Eye ... 117 D3
Eyke ... 85 B6

F
Fakenham Magna ... 33 E7
Falkenham ... 98 E2
Falkenham Sink ... 98 F2

Farley Green ... 75 D8
Farnham ... 72 A7
Felixstowe ... 152 E4
Felixstowe Ferry ... 108 C8
Felsham ... 65 A3
Feltwell ... 4 D5
Fenstead End ... 76 E5
Fen Street
  Hopton ... 18 B2
  Redgrave ... 19 C2
Fern Hill ... 77 B4
Fersfield ... 19 D6
Finkle Green ... 89 A2
Finningham ... 52 B8
Flempton ... 47 F8
Flixton ... 7 D1
Flowton ... 81 C1
Foals Green ... 39 D2
Fordham ... 29 B1
Fornham All Saints ... 48 B6
Fornham St Genevieve ... 48 C6
Fornham St Martin ... 48 C6
Forward Green ... 67 E7
Four Ashes ... 35 C1
Foxash Estate ... 104 B1
Foxearth ... 91 B7
Framlingham ... 126 D2
Framsden ... 69 B6
Freckenham ... 29 F3
Frenze ... 20 F3
Fressingfield ... 39 D8
Freston ... 143 D3
Friday Street
  Benhall ... 72 B7
  Brandeston ... 70 A6
  Rendlesham ... 85 D7
Friston ... 72 F7
Fritton ... 2 B7
Frizzeler's Green ... 47 C1
Frostenden ... 26 C4
Frostenden Corner ... 26 D3

G
Gainsborough
  Ipswich ... 139 F1
  Ipswich ... 144 B8
Garboldisham ... 18 D4
Garlic Street ... 22 A6
Gasthorpe ... 18 A4
Gazeley ... 46 B3
Gedding ... 65 A5
Geldeston ... 8 F7
Genesis Green ... 61 F4
Gestingthorpe ... 90 F1
Gillingham ... 9 C6
Gipping ... 52 B2
Gipsy Row ... 150 A4
Gisleham ... 11 A3
Gislingham ... 36 D2
Gissing ... 20 F8
Glemsford ... 77 B2
Goddard's Corner ... 55 E7
Gosbeck ... 68 D2
Gosland Green ... 76 A5
Gosling Green ... 93 C5
Grass Green ... 89 D1
Great Ashfield ... 50 F6
Great Barton ... 49 A6
Great Bealings ... 137 E6
Great Blakenham ... 82 A5
Great Bradley ... 74 C7
Great Bricett ... 80 E5
Great Common ... 8 E2
Great Cornard ... 148 F3
Great Finborough ... 66 B4
Great Glemham ... 71 D8
Great Green
  Burgate ... 36 D7
  Cockfield ... 64 D2
  Denton ... 7 A4
  Thrandeston ... 37 C8
Great Horkesley ... 102 E1
Great Livermere ... 33 C2
Great Saxham ... 47 C1
Great Thurlow ... 74 E5
Great Waldingfield ... 92 C6
Great Welnetham ... 63 F6
Great Wenham ... 150 A3
Great Wratting ... 74 E3
Great Yeldham ... 90 A1
Greenstreet Green ... 80 D5
Greenwich ... 139 E1
Grimstone End ... 49 F8
Grinstead Hill ... 125 E3
Gromford ... 72 C5
Groton ... 93 B4
Grundisburgh ... 83 D5
Gulling Green ... 63 A3
Gunton ... 113 C6

H
Hacheston ... 71 A6
Hadleigh ... 149 F6
Hadleigh Heath ... 93 F4
Hagmore Green ... 93 B2
Halesworth ... 118 A4
Hall Green ... 90 C2
Hanchet End ... 132 A8
Hanningfields Green ... 63 F1
Hargrave ... 62 B6
Harkstead ... 106 B5
Harleston
  Harleston ... 66 B7
  Redenhall with Harleston ... 22 E5

Harrow Green ... 63 D1
Hartest ... 77 A7
Hartest Hill ... 77 C7
Hart's Green ... 63 E2
Harwich ... 107 A3
Hasketon ... 146 E5
Haughley ... 51 C1
Haughley Green ... 51 C3
Haughley New Street ... 51 B1
Haverhill ... 132 C6
Hawkedon ... 76 D7
Hawstead ... 63 D6
Hawstead Green ... 63 E3
Hazel Stub ... 132 A5
Heckfield Green ... 38 D7
Hedenham ... 7 E8
Helions Bumpstead ... 88 B4
Helmingham ... 69 B4
Hemingstone ... 82 C8
Hemley ... 98 E5
Hemp Green ... 57 C8
Hengrave ... 48 A3
Henley ... 82 D6
Henny Street ... 91 F1
Henstead ... 26 E8
Hepworth ... 35 A6
Herringfleet ... 2 D4
Herringswell ... 46 C8
Hessett ... 64 F3
Heveningham ... 40 F3
Hickford Hill ... 90 C7
Higham
  Bury St Edmunds ... 46 E4
  Stratford St Mary ... 103 D6
High Green ... 63 D7
High Rougham ... 49 E1
High Street
  Darsham ... 42 B1
  Iken ... 73 B2
  St Margaret, Ilketshall ... 24 D7
High Street Green ... 66 A2
Hightown Green ... 65 D3
Hinderclay ... 35 E7
Hintlesham ... 95 C6
Hitcham ... 79 E6
Hobbles Green ... 75 A8
Hockwold cum Wilton ... 5 A3
Hoggard's Green ... 64 A3
Holbrook ... 105 E7
Hollesley ... 99 E7
Hollybush Corner ... 64 D6
Holly Hill ... 110 B8
Holton ... 118 E4
Holton St Mary ... 151 A8
Holywell Row ... 30 C8
Homersfield ... 23 B8
Honey Tye ... 102 B6
Honington ... 33 E5
Hoo ... 70 B5
Hopton ... 18 C2
Hopton on Sea ... 3 C7
Horham ... 38 E3
Horner's Green ... 93 C4
Hornestreet ... 103 C3
Horringer ... 63 A8
Hoxne ... 38 B8
Hulver Street ... 10 C1
Humble Green ... 92 F8
Hundon ... 75 E3
Hunston ... 50 D7
Hunston Green ... 50 D5
Huntingfield ... 41 A5

I
Icklingham ... 31 D4
Iken ... 72 F2
Ilketshall St Andrew ... 8 E2
Ilketshall St Lawrence ... 24 F6
Ilketshall St Margaret ... 24 B8
Ingham ... 32 F1
Ipswich ... 155 B3
Isleham ... 29 B5
Ixworth ... 34 B2
Ixworth Thorpe ... 33 F4

K
Kedington ... 133 E7
Kelsale ... 128 C7
Kennett ... 45 F7
Kenninghall ... 19 B8
Kenny Hill ... 12 F2
Kentford ... 46 A5
Kenton ... 54 B5
Kenton Corner ... 54 C4
Kersey ... 94 A7
Kersey Tye ... 93 E6
Kersey Upland ... 93 F5
Kesgrave ... 141 C8
Kessingland ... 11 C2
Kessingland Beach ... 27 C8
Kettlebaston ... 79 C5
Kettleburgh ... 70 C7
Kingshall Green ... 64 D7
Kingshall Street ... 64 D8
Kingston ... 146 F2
Kirby Cane ... 8 E8
Kirby Row ... 8 E7
Kirkley ... 115 B5
Kirtling ... 60 E3
Kirtling Green ... 60 E2
Kirton ... 98 E2
Knaves Green ... 53 A5
Knettishall ... 17 F3
Knodishall ... 73 A8

Knodishall Common ... 129 A2
Knowl Green ... 90 C4

L
Lackford ... 31 F1
Lady's Green ... 61 F6
Lakenheath ... 109 E7
Lamarsh ... 101 A6
Lamb Corner ... 103 E2
Lambfair Green ... 75 A8
Lampardbrook ... 70 E8
Landwade ... 44 D6
Langham
  Bury St Edmunds ... 50 B8
  Stratford St Mary ... 103 C2
Langton Green ... 117 D4
Lattinford Hill ... 151 D8
Lavenham ... 78 D4
Lawford ... 104 E2
Lawshall ... 63 E1
Lawshall Green ... 77 F8
Laxfield ... 40 C3
Leavenheath ... 102 B7
Leiston ... 129 B5
Letheringham ... 70 C4
Levington ... 145 E3
Lidgate ... 61 C4
Lindsey ... 93 D7
Lindsey Tye ... 93 E8
Linstead Parva ... 40 E8
Liston ... 91 D7
Little Bealings ... 137 E5
Little Blakenham ... 81 F3
Little Bradley ... 74 E6
Little Cornard ... 92 C2
Little Ditton ... 60 C5
Little Finborough ... 66 B1
Little Glemham ... 71 E5
Little Green
  Burgate ... 36 D5
  Gislingham ... 36 C3
Little Horkesley ... 102 B3
Little Knowles Green ... 62 B5
Little London ... 66 E2
Little Saxham ... 47 D2
Little Stonham ... 67 F6
Little Thurlow ... 74 E5
Little Thurlow Green ... 74 E6
Little Waldingfield ... 92 D8
Little Welnetham ... 64 B6
Little Wenham ... 150 B5
Little Whittingham
  Green ... 40 A8
Little Wratting ... 74 E2
Little Yeldham ... 90 B2
Long Green ... 36 D8
Long Melford
  Long Melford ... 77 F1
  Long Melford ... 91 E8
Long Thurlow ... 51 B7
Lound ... 2 F5
Lower Common ... 25 B3
Lower Falkenham ... 98 F1
Lower Green ... 46 E4
Lower Hacheston ... 127 F8
Lower Holbrook ... 106 A6
Lower Layham ... 149 D1
Lower Raydon ... 94 D1
Lower Street
  Stansfield ... 76 C6
  Stutton ... 105 D5
Lowestoft ... 113 F1
Low Green ... 63 E7
Lynford ... 6 C5

M
Mace Green ... 95 E4
Magpie Green ... 19 E1
Maidenhall ... 139 B1
Maidensgrave ... 146 E3
Malting End ... 61 E1
Manningtree ... 104 F2
Man's Cross ... 89 F2
Market Weston ... 35 A8
Marlesford ... 71 C5
Martlesham ... 84 A1
Martlesham Heath ... 98 B7
Maypole Green
  Bradfield St George ... 64 D6
  Dennington ... 55 D6
Meadowend ... 89 E3
Mellis ... 37 A5
Mellis Green ... 36 F5
Mells ... 118 E2
Melon Green ... 63 C4
Melton ... 147 C8
Mendham ... 23 A6
Mendlesham ... 52 E4
Mendlesham Green ... 52 D2
Metfield ... 23 C3
Methersgate ... 84 E1
Mettingham ... 8 D4
Mickfield ... 68 B8
Mickley Green ... 63 B4
Middle Green ... 46 E4
Middle Harling ... 18 B8
Middleton
  Leiston ... 58 B6
  Sudbury ... 148 C2
Middleton Moor ... 58 A6
Middlewood Green ... 67 D8
Milden ... 79 B1
Mildenhall ... 116 D6
Mile End ... 77 A7

Mill Common ... 25 C4
Mill End ... 60 F3
Mill Green
  Burston and Shimpling ... 20 E7
  Buxhall ... 65 F4
  Edwardstone ... 93 B5
  Stonham Aspal ... 68 B7
Mill Hill ... 77 E6
Mill Hills ... 147 A6
Mill Street ... 102 E8
Mistley ... 105 A2
Mistley Heath ... 105 A1
Moats Tye ... 66 E2
Monewden ... 69 F5
Monks Eleigh ... 79 B2
Monk Soham ... 54 D4
Moulton ... 45 F3
Mount Bures ... 101 C3
Mount Pleasant ... 75 D2
Mundford ... 6 B8
Mutford ... 10 D2

N
Nacton ... 145 C5
Naughton ... 80 C3
Nayland ... 102 C5
Nedging ... 79 F3
Nedging Tye ... 80 B4
Needham ... 22 B4
Needham Market ... 125 E5
Needham Street ... 46 B4
Nether Street ... 64 E8
Nettlestead ... 81 C4
Newbourne ... 98 C5
New England ... 89 A5
Newman's Green ... 92 A6
Newmarket ... 121 B4
New Mistley ... 105 A2
Newton ... 92 D3
Newtown ... 54 D7
Normanston ... 113 B3
North Common ... 34 F6
North Cove ... 10 C4
North End ... 90 C2
North Green
  Cratfield ... 40 C7
  Kelsale cum Carlton ... 57 D5
  Parham ... 56 B1
North Lopham ... 19 A5
Norton ... 50 B4
Norton Little Green ... 50 D5
Nowton ... 63 E7

O
Oak Hill ... 100 A8
Oakley ... 38 A8
Occold ... 37 F1
Offton ... 81 A4
Old Felixstowe ... 153 C6
Oldhall Green ... 64 C3
Old Newton ... 51 F1
Onehouse ... 66 C6
Orford ... 131 C3
Otley ... 69 C2
Oulton ... 112 F5
Oulton Broad ... 114 C8
Ousden ... 61 E6
Ovington ... 90 A5

P
Page's Green ... 53 C4
Pakefield ... 115 B3
Pakenham ... 49 E6
Pale Green ... 88 B5
Palgrave ... 20 C1
Parham ... 71 A7
Parkeston ... 106 F3
Park Gate ... 61 E3
Park Green ... 53 B3
Parliament Heath ... 93 C6
Parney Heath ... 103 D2
Peasenhall ... 56 B8
Peats Corner ... 69 B7
Pentlow
  Pentlow ... 76 E1
  Pentlow ... 90 F7
Pentlow Street ... 91 A8
Pettaugh ... 68 E6
Pettistree ... 127 B4
Pinford End ... 63 D6
Pitcher's Green ... 64 D5
Pitman's Corner ... 53 C5
Playford ... 137 B5
Polstead ... 93 F1
Polstead Heath ... 93 F2
Pooley Street ... 19 D4
Poslingford ... 76 A3
Potash ... 104 F8
Pound Green ... 61 B1
Poystreet Green ... 65 E5
Preston St Mary ... 79 A5
Priory Green ... 92 F6
Priory Heath ... 140 D1
Pulham St Mary ... 21 F8
Puttock End ... 90 E3

R
Racecourse ... 140 B2
Ramsey ... 106 C1
Ramsholt ... 99 A4

Rattlesden.............. 65 E6
Raydon................. 94 E1
Reading Green.......... 38 E5
Rede 62 E2
Redenhall.............. 22 E7
Redgrave............... 36 A8
Redisham............... 25 B7
Redlingfield............ 38 D2
Red Lodge.............. 30 B1
Rendham............... 56 E3
Rendlesham............ 85 C8
Reydon................ 119 C7
Reydon Smear.......... 26 F1
Rickinghall............. 36 A6
Ridgewell.............. 89 D4
Ringsfield..............9 B3
Ringsfield Corner........9 B2
Ringshall.............. 80 E7
Ringshall Stocks 80 F6
Risby.................. 47 D5
Rishangles............. 53 D7
Rodbridge Corner....... 91 E6
Roman Hill............ 113 C1
Rooksey Green.......... 78 E6
Roost End 133 E2
Rosedale Park 114 E4
Rose Green
    Assington............ 101 F8
    Lindsey 93 D7
Rose Hill 139 F4
Rotchfords............ 101 F1
Rougham............... 64 D8
Rougham Green 64 C8
Roydon................ 20 A3
Rumburgh.............. 24 B4
Rushall................ 21 F5
Rushbrooke............ 64 B8
Rushford............... 17 B4
Rushmere 10 D1
Rushmere St Andrew... 136 E1
Rushmere Street....... 136 E2
Russel's Green.......... 39 C3

S

Sackers Green 92 D2
St Cross South Elmham.. 23 D7
St James South Elmham.. 23 F4
St Margaret South
Elmham............... 23 E6
St Michael South
Elmham............... 24 A6
St Nicholas South
Elmham............... 23 E6
St Olaves 2 A6
St Peter South Elmham.. 24 A7
Santon Downham 6 C2
Sapiston............... 33 F6
Saxham Street......... 67 C8
Saxmundham........... 128 D3
Saxon Street........... 60 D6
Saxstead Bottom 55 C5
Saxstead.............. 55 C4
Saxstead Green 55 B3
Saxstead Little Green ... 55 B5
Scole.................. 21 A2
Scole Common 20 F3
Scotland Street 102 F7
Semer................. 79 F1
Shadingfield........... 25 E7
Shadwell 17 C6
Shelfanger 20 C6

Shelland............... 66 A7
Shelley................. 94 C1
Sherbourne Street 93 B4
Shimpling
    Burston and Shimpling ... 21 A6
    Shimpling................ 77 E6
Shimpling Street........ 77 E8
Shingle Street 100 A5
Shipmeadow.............8 F4
Shop Corner........... 106 C5
Shotford Heath 22 D4
Shotley................ 106 F6
Shotley Gate.......... 107 A4
Shottisham............ 99 C7
Sibton................. 57 A8
Sibton Green 41 D2
Sicklesmere 63 F7
Silverlace Green 71 C7
Silverley's Green 40 B6
Sizewell............... 58 F1
Slough Hill 77 E7
Smallwood Green....... 64 F5
Smallworth............. 18 D3
Smith's Green 88 C3
Smithwood Green...... 78 C7
Snailwell 45 A6
Snape 72 D4
Snow Street 20 A4
Soham 28 D4
Soham Cotes 28 B6
Somersham............ 81 C3
Somerton.............. 76 F8
Sotherton.............. 25 E2
Sotherton Corner 25 E1
Sotterley.............. 26 A7
South Cove 26 F4
South Green
    Hoxne 38 B5
    Pulham St Mary 21 F6
South Lopham 19 B4
Southolt 54 B7
Southwold............ 119 C5
Sowley Green 75 A5
Spexhall 24 F3
Spratt's Street 85 D5
Sproughton............ 138 A7
Stackyard Green 93 C8
Stambourne............ 89 B1
Stambourne Green..... 89 A1
Stanningfield.......... 64 A4
Stansfield.............. 76 C7
Stanstead............. 77 C4
Stanton 34 D4
Stanton Chare 34 D5
Stanton Street........ 50 B5
Stanway Green 39 C1
Starston............... 22 C7
Steeple Bumpstead 88 D4
Sternfield 72 D8
Stetchworth 60 A5
Stock Hill............. 50 E8
Stoke................. 155 B1
Stoke Ash 37 B1
Stoke by Clare 89 E6
Stoke-by-Nayland 102 E6
Stoke Park 138 F1
Stone Street
    Boxford 93 C2
    Spexhall 24 F5
Stonham Aspal........ 68 A6
Stoven 25 F4
Stowlangtoft.......... 50 C7
Stowmarket 124 E6

Stowupland............ 67 B6
Stradbroke 39 A5
Stradishall............. 75 F7
Stratford St Andrew.... 71 F7
Stratford St Mary 103 D5
Stubbing's Green 36 C5
Sturmer................ 133 C2
Stuston................. 20 E1
Stutton................ 105 D6
Sudbourne 86 F8
Sudbury............... 148 C4
Sutton.................. 85 A1
Sutton Street 99 A7
Swan Green 40 B5
Sweffling.............. 56 E2
Swilland............... 83 A7
Swingleton Green...... 79 C2
Syleham............... 22 A1

T

Tannington 55 A6
Tan Office 52 F2
Tan Office Green....... 62 C6
Tattingstone 105 B8
Tattingstone White
    Horse.............. 142 D1
Temple End
    Foxearth 91 A6
    Little Thurlow 74 C5
Theberton 58 B4
The Brook 36 F7
The Common 81 F3
The Heath 105 A7
Thelnetham 18 D1
Thelveton 21 A4
The Marsh 36 E8
The Port of Felixstowe . 152 C1
Thetford.............. 16 D5
The Woodlands 95 A3
Thistley Green 29 E7
Thorington 42 C4
Thorington Street..... 103 A6
Thorndon............. 53 B8
Thorney Green........ 67 A7
Thornham Magna 37 A2
Thornham Parva 37 B3
Thorpe Abbotts 21 E2
Thorpe Common 107 C8
Thorpe Green......... 64 F1
Thorpe Morieux 79 B4
Thorpeness........... 73 E6
Thorpe Street......... 35 D8
Thrandeston 37 B7
Thurston.............. 49 E3
Thurston End 76 D6
Thwaite 52 F7
Tilbury Green 89 E4
Tilbury Juxta Clare.... 90 A3
Timworth............. 48 D8
Timworth Green 48 D7
Toad Row 10 F1
Tostock 50 B2
Tower Hill............ 107 C3
Trimley Lower Street .. 107 D7
Trimley St Martin 107 D8
Trimley St Mary 152 C8
Troston............... 33 D3
Tuddenham........... 30 F2
Tuddenham St Martin . 136 C5
Tunstall 71 F2

U

Ubbeston............. 40 E4
Ubbeston Green 40 D3
Ufford................ 84 F7
Uggeshall 25 F3
Undley 13 C4
Upend................ 60 F5
Upgate Street..........7 B6
Upper Green.......... 46 E3
Upper Holton 118 E7
Upper Layham 149 F2
Upper Street
    Baylham.............. 81 E6
    Dickleburgh and Rushall . 21 C2
    Stansfield............. 76 C6
    Stutton............. 105 B5
Upper Town 49 E7
Upper Weybread 22 B2
Upsher Green 92 D6
Upthorpe 34 F3

W

Wainford 110 D5
Walberswick.......... 119 A2
Walcot Green 20 D4
Waldringfield........ 98 D7
Waldringfield Heath..... 98 C7
Wales End 76 D4
Walpole 41 C5
Walsham Le Willows .. 35 C2
Walton 152 F6
Wangford 26 B2
Ward Green 51 E3
Warren Heath........ 140 F1
Washbrook 95 F5
Washbrook Street..... 95 F6
Washmere Green 78 D2
Waterloo
    Aldeby 9 E8
    Dickleburgh and Rushall . 20 F2
Wattisfield 35 D5
Wattisham............ 80 B6
Wattisham Stone..... 80 A6
Weeting 5 E3
Wenhaston 42 C6
Westbourne 138 F7
Westbrook Green 20 C4
West End 26 B6
Westerfield 135 E4
Westhall.............. 25 C4
West Harling 18 A8
Westhorpe........... 51 D8
Westleton 58 B7
Westley 122 A6
Westley Waterless 59 E3
Weston 9 D1
Weston Ditch 29 F7
West Row 29 F6
West Stow 32 B1
West Street
    Rickinghall Inferior 35 E5
    Walsham-le-willows 35 A1
West Tofts 6 E7
Wetherden 51 B1
Wetherden Upper Town . 51 B4
Wetheringsett 53 A5
Wetherup Street 53 C3
Weybread 22 D3
Whatfield............. 80 C1

Wheatacre.............2 B1
Whelp Street 79 B4
Whepstead 63 B5
Wherstead........... 143 B6
Whitestreet Green 93 D2
Whitton 134 F3
Wicken 28 B1
Wicker Street Green ... 93 E5
Wickhambrook 61 E2
Wickham Green 52 C8
Wickham Market 127 B6
Wickham Skeith 52 E8
Wickham Street
    Wickhambrook........ 61 F1
    Wickham Skeith....... 52 C8
Widgham Green 60 B2
Wiggens Green 88 C5
Wilby................. 39 C2
Wilde Street 13 D2
William's Green 93 E5
Willingham 25 E7
Willisham 81 A5
Willisham Tye 81 A6
Wilney Green 19 D4
Windsor Green 64 B2
Winfarthing 20 B8
Wingfield 39 B8
Wingfield Green 38 F8
Winston 68 F8
Wissett 24 D2
Withermarsh Green ... 103 A8
Withersdale Street ... 22 F4
Withersfield 74 B2
Witnesham 83 A6
Wixoe 89 B6
Woodbridge 146 F6
Woodbridge Walk 99 F8
Woodditton 60 C5
Woodland Green 133 C5
Woodton 7 C8
Woolpit 50 D1
Woolpit Green 65 D8
Woolpit Heath 65 E8
Woolverstone 144 B1
Wootten Green 39 B3
Wordwell 32 D3
Workhouse Green 101 C8
Workhouse Hill 102 F2
World's End 65 F2
Worlingham 111 F3
Worlington 30 A4
Worlingworth 54 F8
Wormingford 101 F2
Wortham 36 D8
Wortwell 23 B8
Wrabness............ 105 F2
Wrentham 26 E5
Wrentham West End .. 26 C7
Wyverstone 51 E6
Wyverstone Green ... 51 E6
Wyverstone Street 51 D6

Y

Yaxley................ 37 B5
Yoxford 57 D7

1

13th Century Hospl of St Saviour★ IP32 ......154 B4
100th Bomb Group Meml Mus★ IP21 ....21 D4

9

95th Bomb Group Hospl Musuem★ IP21 ....38 C4

A

Abbey Cl 10 Burwell CB5 ..44 A5
10 Ixworth IP31 ....34 B1
Rendlesham IP12 ....85 D7
Abbey Farm Jun Sch 1 IP24 ......16 B6
Abbey Fields IP14 ......66 D8
Abbey Gdns IP13 ....71 C2
Abbey Hill IP21 ....38 C7
Abbey La IP16 ....129 B8
Abbey Rd Flixton NR35 ..23 F8
Leiston IP16 ....129 C7
Sudbury CO10 ....148 C7
Abbey Sch The IP12 ...147 A4
Abbeydale NR32 ......114 E2
Abbeygate St 3 IP33 ..154 B2
Abbot Cl IP33 ....122 D4
Abbot Rd IP33 ....122 D4
Abbot's Hall Drift CO10 .78 E2
Abbot's Hall Rd IP14 ..124 D5
Abbots Cotts CB9 .....133 E2
Abbots Hall★ IP14 ....124 D5
Abbots Hall Prim Sch IP14 ......124 C5
Abbotsbury Cl IP2 ....139 A1
Abbotsbury Rd IP33 ...122 D3
Abbott Rd CO12 ....106 F1
Abbotts Croft CB9 .....133 D2
Abbotts Ct CB9 ....133 C3
Abbotts Gn Com Prim Sch IP32 ....49 A3
Abbotts Meadow 8 IP30 50 D1
Abbotts Rd CB9 ......132 E7
Abbottsinch Rd 6 IP31 .33 D5
Abdy Ave 5 CO12 ....106 F1
Abercorn Ct 2 CB9 ...132 D4
Aberdeen Way IP4 ....136 B1
Aberfoyle Cl 1 IP4 ...136 C1
Abingdon Cl IP2 .....139 A1
Abington Pl CB9 .....132 E7
Ablitts Meadow IP13 ...83 E6
Acacia Ave IP32 ......48 C5
Acacia Cl IP3 ....140 E1
Acer Gr IP8 ....138 C1
Acer Rd IP12 ....85 D8
Acheson Way 7 IP15 ..130 E5
Acorn Cl 9 IP8 ......138 C2
Acorn Way IP5 ....98 B8
Acorns The IP30 ......49 E3
Acre Cl IP6 ....83 A6
Acre Rd CB8 ....74 B8
Action France CB8 ....59 E5
Acton CE Prim Sch CO10 ......92 B7
Acton Cl Bramford IP8 ..134 A2
Sudbury CO10 ....148 D6
Acton Gdns 1 IP8 .....134 A2
Acton Gn 3 CO10 .....148 C5
Acton La Acton CO10 ...92 A6
Sudbury CO10 ....148 D6
Acton Pl Ind Est CO10 ..92 A8
Acton Rd Bramford IP8 .134 A2
Lowestoft NR33 ....115 B4
Adair Rd IP1 ....138 D8
Adam's La IP18 ....43 C5
Adams Pl IP5 ....141 C7
Adamson Rd IP18 .....119 B8
Adastral Cl
Felixstowe IP11 ......153 H11
Newmarket CB8 ....120 E4
Addington Rd IP11 ....152 C7
Addison Cl IP26 ....4 F5
Addison Rd CO10 .....148 E7
Addison Way IP8 .....134 A8
Adeane Meadow IP26 ...6 A8
Adelaide Cl 17 CB7 ....28 D4
Adelaide Rd IP4 ......140 D6
Admiral Rd IP8 ....142 E8
Admirals Jun Sch 2 IP24 ......16 C7
Admirals Wlk IP12 ....146 F7
Adrian Rd 6 NR32 ....113 D2
Africa Alive★ NR33 ....11 A1
Agate Cl 2 IP1 ....134 D1
Ailwin Rd IP32 ....123 E4
Ainslie Rd IP1 ....139 A6
Airedale NR33 ....114 E2
Airey Cl Lowestoft NR32 .112 F5
Newton CO10 ....92 E3
Airey Houses IP13 ....137 D6
Airfield Rd IP32 ....49 A3
Airstation La IP21 .....21 E6
Aisthorpe IP9 ....150 D3
Akethorpe Way NR32 ..113 A3
Alabaster Cl 8 IP7 ....149 E6
Alan Rd IP3 ....139 F4
Alandale Dr 25 NR33 ...11 C1
Alasdair Pl 9 IP6 .....134 C8
Alban Sq 2 IP12 ....84 A1
Albany Rd 1 NR32 ....113 E2
Albany The IP4 ....139 E8
Albemarle Rd IP33 ....122 D4
Albemarle St 6 CO12 ..107 B3
Albert Cres IP33 .....154 A2
Albert Pl IP13 ....126 C3
Albert Pye Prim Sch NR34 ....111 B4
Albert Rd IP13 ....126 C3
Albert Rolph Dr IP27 ..109 E4
Albert St IP33 ....154 A2
Albert Wlk IP11 ....153 B3
Alberta Cl IP5 ....141 A8
Albion Hill IP4 ....139 F7
Albion Rd NR35 ....110 D3
Albion St IP17 ....128 C3
Alburgh with Denton Prim Sch IP20 ....7 A1
Alde House Dr IP15 ...130 E4
Alde La IP15 ....130 E4
Alde Rd CB9 ....132 E7
Aldeburgh & District Com Hospl IP15 ....130 D4
Aldeburgh Cl CB9 .....132 C5
Aldeburgh Lodge Gdns IP15 ......130 E5
Aldeburgh Mus★ IP15 ....130 F4
Aldeburgh Prim Sch IP15 ....130 E3
Aldeburgh Rd
Friston IP17 ....72 F7
Leiston IP16 ....129 D4
Aldecar La IP17 ....72 C7
Alder Carr Farm & Ctyd Craft Ctr★ IP6 ......125 E5
Alder Covert 6 IP24 ....16 D6
Alder Dr 2 NR33 ......114 C4
Alder Way CO10 ......148 D6
Aldercroft Cl IP1 .....135 B3
Aldercroft Rd IP1 .....135 B3
Aldergrove Cl IP19 ....118 A3
Alderlee IP2 ....142 F8
Alderman Rd IP1 .....155 A2
Alderton Cl CB9 ......132 C8
Alderton Rd IP12 ......99 E6
Aldham Ct 1 CB9 .....132 C5
Aldham Gdns IP14 ....124 E4
Aldham Mill Hill IP7 ..149 C8
Aldham Rd IP7 ....149 E7
Aldis Ave IP14 ....124 D4
Aldon Cl 14 CO12 .....106 E1
Aldous Cl CO7 ....151 C5
Aldous Ct 13 IP14 .....53 F2
Aldridge La 2 IP28 ....48 B6
Aldringham Craft Mkt★ IP16 ....129 C3
Aldringham Mews 13 IP11 ......152 D5
Aldringham Pk IP16 ...129 D3
Aldringham Rd IP17 ...129 B3
Aldwyck Way NR33 ....114 F4
Alexander Cl NR34 ....111 C2
Alexander Dr
8 Great Waldingfield CO10 92 C6
Needham Market IP6 ....125 C5
Alexander Way IP28 ....47 E5
Alexanders Int Sch IP12 ......108 D8
Alexandra Rd
Beccles NR34 ....111 B5
Felixstowe IP11 ....152 E6
Ipswich IP4 ....139 E6
Lowestoft NR32 ....113 D1
Sudbury CO10 ....148 E5
Alexandra St 3 CO12 ..107 B3
Alfred Corry Mus★ IP18 .....119 C2
Algar Dr CB8 ....59 F4
Alice Driver Rd 9 IP13 ..83 E5
Alicia Ct IP33 ....123 C3
All Hallows' Hospl NR35 ......110 C7
All Saints IP27 ....5 E3
All Saints CE Mid Sch CO10 ......148 E8
All Saints CE Prim Sch IP29 .....63 E1
All Saints CE VA Prim Sch
Laxfield IP13 ....40 A3
Newmarket CB8 ....121 B3
Winfarthing IP22 ....20 C8
All Saints Cl CB8 ......46 C3
All Saints Ct IP33 .....154 B3
All Saints Dr NR34 ....111 C3
All Saints Gn 6 NR34 ..111 F4
All Saints Rd IP6 .....125 F8
All Saints' Rd
Ipswich IP1 ....139 A7
Lowestoft NR33 ....115 B4
All Saints Rd CB8 .....121 B3
All Saints Wlk IP28 ....30 B4
Allen Rd Hadleigh IP7 ..149 D7
Lowestoft NR32 ....112 D1
Allenby Rd IP2 ....138 F6
Alley Rd IP10 ....98 D2
Allfields 3 CO12 .....107 A1
Allington Cl IP4 ......139 F7
Allington Rd 7 IP19 ...118 A3
Allington Wlk CB9 ....132 C6
Allotment La IP6 ......69 A1
Allthorpe Rd 12 IP20 ...22 D6
Alma Cl 3 IP4 ....136 A1
Alma Pl IP17 ....128 D3
Alma Rd NR32 ....113 C1
Almond Gr IP24 ....16 A4
Almondhayes IP2 .....139 B3
Almshouse Rd IP30 ....49 C1
Alnesbourn Cres
1 Gainsborough IP2 ....144 D8
Ipswich IP3 ....144 D7
Alnesbourne Priory IP10 ....144 C6
Alpe St IP1 ....155 A4
Alpha Bsns Pk IP1 ....134 D3
Alphamstone Rd CO8 ..101 A6
Alston Cl CO10 ....92 D3
Alston Rd IP3 ....139 F4
Alton Hall La IP9 .....105 C6
Alton Wr Sports Ctr IP9 ......105 D6
Alvis Cl IP32 ....123 F5
Alvis Wlk IP1 ....134 C1
Amber Mus The★ IP18 .....119 D5
Amberfield Sch IP10 ..145 C6
Amberley Ct 3 NR32 ...112 F4
Ambleside Gdns NR32 .113 A4
America Hill IP6 ....83 A6
Amis Ct IP27 ....109 D4
Amy Johnson Ct 6 IP28 ......116 B5
Ancaster Rd IP2 ......155 A1
Anchor End 2 CO11 ....105 A2
Anchor La Burwell CB5 ..44 A6
Dedham CO7 ....104 A2
Lakenheath IP27 ......109 C6
1 Mistley CO11 ....105 A2
Anchor St NR33 ....115 C6
Anchor Way NR33 .....114 B4
Anderson Cl IP6 ......125 C5
Anderson Wlk IP32 ...122 D7
Anderson's Way 8 IP12 146 E4
Andrew Burtt's Cl IP13 ......126 B3
Andrew Cl
Felixstowe IP11 ......152 E3
Leiston IP16 ....129 D5
Andrew Johnston Way IP19 .....118 B3
Andrew Rd CB8 ....120 E5
Andrew Way NR33 ....114 D6
Andrews Cl 9 IP14 .....53 F2
Andrews Wlk IP32 ....122 D8
Andros Cl IP3 ....144 A7
Angel Hill
Bury St Edmunds IP33 ..154 C2
Stonham Earl IP14 ......67 F5
Angel La Blythburgh IP19 .42 F6
Bury St Edmunds IP33 ..154 B2
Glemsford CO10 ....77 A2
Ipswich IP4 ....155 C2
2 Woodbridge IP12 ....147 A5
Angel Link IP19 ....118 B3
Angel Rd IP8 ....134 A2
Angel St IP7 ....149 D6
Angela Cl IP12 ....84 A1
Angelgate Espl 4 CO12 107 C3
Angerstein Cl IP27 .....5 E4
Anglesea Rd IP1 ......155 A4
Anglesey Pl 6 IP31 ....49 A5
Anglia Parkway N IP1 .134 D4
Anglia Parkway S IP1 .134 D3
Anglian La IP32 ....154 A4
Anglian Way NR31 ....3 B7
Angus Cl IP4 ....136 B1
Animal Health Trust Visitor Ctr★ CB8 ....45 F5
Anita Cl E IP2 ....138 E5
Anita Cl W IP2 ....138 E5
Ann Beaumont Way IP7 ....149 C7
Ann Coles Cl CB9 ......88 E3
Ann St IP1 ....155 A4
Ann Suckling Rd CB9 ..132 E8
Annandale Dr NR34 ...111 D4
Annbrook Rd IP2 .....138 E1
Anne Bartholomew Rd IP24 ......16 C7
Anne St IP11 ....152 E3
Annesons Cnr IP17 ....58 B6
Annis Hill NR35 ....110 E3
Annis Hill La 2 NR35 ..110 D3
Annis Hill Rd NR35 ....110 D3
Annison Cl NR33 .....115 B5
Ansell Cl IP7 ....149 D6
Anselm Ave 9 IP32 ....48 C5
Anson Rd 7 IP5 ....98 A8
Anson Way NR34 ....10 A3
Antonia Cl CB9 ....133 C5
Antrim Rd IP1 ....134 D1
Anzani Ave IP11 ......152 C4
Apple Acre Rd CB9 ....132 A7
Apple Cl 28 IP27 ....13 F2
Apple Gr IP14 ....51 A2
Apple Tree Cl NR33 ...115 B6
Appleby Cl IP8 ....138 C1
Appledore Dr NR33 ...114 D4
Appledown Dr IP30 ...123 E7
Appletree Gr 2 CB5 ....44 A6
Appletree La IP22 ......20 C3
Approach Cotts CB9 ...132 B8
Aragon Rd CB9 ....132 B4
Arbor La NR33 ....115 A2
Arcade St IP1 ....155 B3
Archangel Gdns IP2 ...138 E4
Archbishop Sancroft High Sch IP20 ....22 C6
Archers' Ave 3 IP26 .....4 D5
Arderne Cl 8 CO12 ....106 F1
Ardleigh Rd CO7 ......103 E2
Arger Fen Nature Reserve★ CO10 ......101 F6
Argyle St IP4 ....155 C3
Argyll Ct 7 CB9 ....132 D5
Ark Cl 7 NR33 ....11 B1
Arkle Ct IP5 ....141 D7
Arkwright Rd IP2 .....138 E6
Arlington Way IP24 ....16 C5
Arms La CB9 ....133 F7
Armstrong Cl
Hundon CO10 ....75 D4
Newmarket CB8 ....121 B3
Armstrong Way CO9 ....90 A1
Arnhem Ct NR32 ......113 C4
Arnhem Rd IP16 ......129 D5
Arnold Cl IP1 ....134 F3
Arnold St 3 NR32 .....113 E1
Arras Rd IP33 ....122 D5
Arrendene Rd CB9 ....132 D7
Arrowhead Dr IP27 ....109 C7
Arthurs Terr IP4 .....155 C3
Artillery Dr 7 CO12 ...106 E1
Artillery Way 11 NR32 ..113 E2
Arundel Cl 4 IP32 ....123 D6
Arundel Way
Ipswich IP3 ....140 E3
2 Lowestoft NR33 .....114 D4
Arundel Wlk 11 CB9 ...132 C6
Arwela Rd IP11 ....152 F2
Ascot Dr
Felixstowe IP11 ....152 E6
Ipswich IP3 ....140 B3
Ash Ave 1 IP7 ....80 D6
Ash Cl Bacton IP14 .....51 F6
10 Lakenheath IP27 .....13 F2
7 Lowestoft NR33 .....114 D5
Thetford IP24 ....16 A4
Warren Heath IP3 .....140 F1
Woodbridge IP12 .....146 F4
Ash Dr IP23 ....117 D3
Ash Gd Cl
3 Brantham CO11 .....104 E4
10 Felixstowe IP11 ....107 D8
Ash Gr 17 Burwell CB5 ...44 A5
Capel St Mary IP9 .....150 E3
Haverhill CB9 ....132 C7
4 Sudbury CO10 ....92 B3
Ash Rd
Campsey Ash IP12 ......71 C1
Hacheston IP13 ....127 F7
Onehouse IP14 ....66 C6
Rendlesham IP12 ....85 C7
Ash Rise 8 CO6 ....102 C5
Ash St 4 CO10 ....93 C3
Ash Tree Cl
8 Beccles NR34 ....9 F4
7 Fessingfield IP21 .....39 D8
5 Occold IP23 ....37 F1
Ash Wlk CB8 ....75 C6
Ashbocking Rd IP6 .....82 E6
Ashbourne Ct CB8 .....121 B3
Ashburnham Rd IP6 ....125 C4
Ashburnham Way NR33 ....114 D4
Ashby Rd NR32 ....113 C1
Ashcroft Rd IP1 ......135 A1
Ashdale Dr NR34 .....111 E4
Ashdale Pk IP27 ....14 E8
Ashdale Rd IP5 ....141 D8
Ashdown Way IP3 ....140 D3
Ashe Rd IP12 ....71 F2
Ashen Cl CO10 ....89 E5
Ashen Hill CO10 ....89 E5
Ashen La CO10 ....89 E6
Ashen Rd Ashen CO10 ...90 A7
Ridgewell CO9 ....89 D4
Ashes The IP14 ....54 D1
Ashfield Cres NR33 ....114 F7
Ashfield Dr IP16 ......129 C5
Ashfield Hill IP31 ....50 F6
Ashfield Rd
Elmswell IP30 ....50 F3
Norton IP31 ....50 C4
Wetherden IP14 ....51 A2
Ashford Cl NR34 ....9 B6
Ashfords Cl IP17 ......128 B4
Ashlea Cl CB9 ....132 F4
Ashlea Rd CB9 ....132 F4
Ashley Downs NR32 ...113 C3
Ashley Rd Cheveley CB8 ..60 E8
Harwich CO12 ....107 A2
Newmarket CB8 ....121 E2
Ashley Sch The NR32 ..113 C4
Ashley St IP2 ....155 B1
Ashman's Rd NR34 ....111 A4
Ashmere Gr IP4 ....139 F6
Ashmere Rise CO10 ...148 E6
Ashness Cl 2 NR32 ....113 A4
Ashton Cl IP2 ....138 C2
Ashton Rd IP23 ....117 C3
Ashtree Gdns NR33 ...114 D3
Ashwell Rd IP33 ......122 D4
Askins Rd CO7 ....151 C5
Aspal Cl 5 IP28 ....30 B8
Aspal Close Nature Reserve★ IP28 ....30 B7
Aspal Hall Rd IP28 .....30 B8
Aspal La IP28 ....30 C8
Aspal Pk IP28 ....30 B8
Aspall Rd IP14 ....53 F3
Aspel Est IP28 ....13 D1
Aspen Cl Claydon IP6 ..134 D8
Great Barton IP31 ......49 B6
Haverhill CB9 ....132 C7
3 Woodbridge IP12 ....147 B6
Aspen Coppice 6 NR32 112 F5
Aspinall Cl 4 NR33 ....114 F4
Assington La CO6 ......93 A1
Assington Rd CO10 ....92 D3
Assington St CO10 ....101 F8
Astbury Rd 6 NR32 ...113 B5
Aster Rd IP2 ....138 E4
Aston Cl IP1 ....134 C1
Ataka Rd IP11 ....152 F6
Athelington Rd IP21 ...38 F2
Athenaeum La IP33 ...154 C2
Athenaeum The★ IP33 ......154 C2
Atherton Rd IP2 ......138 D2
Atterton Rd CB9 ......132 B7
Aubretia Cl 2 NR33 ....114 F7
Audley End IP21 ....20 F5
Audley Gr IP4 ....140 F5
Augusta Cl IP10 ......144 E7
Augustus Cl CB9 .....133 B5
Aureole Wlk CB8 .....120 E8
Austin Cl IP31 ....50 E7
Austin St IP2 ....155 B1
Aveley La IP29 ....77 D6
Aveling Way NR33 ....114 B3
Avenue App IP32 .....123 A8
Avenue Rd IP27 ......109 E4
Avenue The
Brome & Oakley IP23 ..117 E8
3 Burwell CB5 ....44 B6
Copdock & Washbrook IP8 ......95 F4
Felixstowe IP11 ......152 B7
Great Barton IP31 .....123 F8
Halesworth IP19 ......118 B5
Ipswich IP1 ....135 C1
4 Kessingland NR33 ....11 B1
Lowestoft NR33 ....115 B5
Newmarket CB8 ....121 A3
Risby IP28 ....47 E5
Ufford IP13 ....84 F7
Woodbridge IP12 ......147 A4
Aves Cl CB7 ....29 C5
Avocet Cl NR33 ....114 D5
Avocet Gr 12 CB7 ......28 D5
Avocet La 28 IP5 ....98 A8
Avondale Rd
Ipswich IP3 ....140 A2
Lowestoft NR32 ....113 C1
Aylmer Cl IP28 ....47 D5
Aylward Cl IP7 ....149 E4
Ayr Rd IP4 ....136 B1

B

Babb's La IP14 ....52 F2
Babergh Cl 9 CO10 ....92 B7
Babington Dr IP19 ....118 B2
Baby La IP30 ....65 D4
Back Hamlet IP3 .....139 E5
Back Hill IP9 ....105 F6
Back Hills IP22 ....36 A7
Back La
Badwell Ash IP31 ......50 F8
Burrough Green CB8 ....59 F2
Claydon IP6 ....134 C8
Copdock & Washbrook IP8 .....95 F5
Diss IP22 ....20 D7
Falkenham IP10 ....98 F1
Felixstowe IP11 ......152 F5
Kettlebaston IP7 ....79 C5
Lound NR32 ....2 F6
Monks Eleigh IP7 ......79 C2
St Mary, South Elmham otherwise Homersfield IP20 ....23 C8
Scole IP21 ....21 A5
Tattingstone IP9 ......105 B7
Wicken CB7 ....28 A1
Back Rd Brockdish IP21 ..21 E4
Middleton IP17 ....58 B6
Rattlesden IP30 ....65 E6
Trimley St Martin IP10 ...98 D2
Wenhaston with Mells Hamlet IP19 ......42 C6
Back St
Garboldisham IP22 .....18 D5
Gislingham IP23 ....36 B1
Lakenheath IP27 ......109 D6
Bacon Rd 7 IP6 ....82 B5
Bacon's Gn Rd IP19 ....25 D3
Bacton Com Prim Sch IP14 ......51 F6
Bacton Mid Sch IP14 ...51 E6
Bacton Rd
Felixstowe IP11 ......152 F3
Haughley IP14 ....51 C2
Baden Powell Wlk IP5 ....141 E7
Bader Cl IP3 ....140 C2
Bader Ct 25 IP5 ....98 A8
Badger's Holt 10 NR33 ..11 B1
Badgers Bank IP2 .....138 E1
Badgers Gr CO6 ....102 D1
Badgerwood Cl NR33 ..115 B5
Badingham Rd
Badingham IP13 ....56 A4
Framlingham IP13 .....126 E5
Laxfield IP13 ....40 C1
Peasenhall IP17 ....56 D7
Badley Hill IP6 ....125 B7
Badley Wlk IP6 ....125 A7
Badleys Cl 6 CO10 ....92 C6
Badlingham Rd CB7 ....29 E1
Badshah Ave 4 IP3 ....140 B3
Badwell Ash VA Prim Sch IP31 ......50 E8
Badwell Rd
Walsham le Willows IP31 ..35 B1
Wyverstone IP14 ....51 C6
Bagsham La IP28 ......30 A6
Bahram Cl CB8 ....120 E4
Bailey Ave IP5 ....141 E7
Bailey Cl Haverhill CB9 ..133 B5

Bailey Cl *continued*
Ipswich IP2 . . . .**138** E6
Bailey La CO10 . . . .**90** B8
Baileypool La IP31 . . . .**49** F8
Baines Coney CB9 . . . .**132** A7
Baird Cl IP2 . . . .**138** F7
Baird Gr IP5 . . . .**141** B6
Bakehouse Hill CB8 . . . .**59** F4
Baker Dr 4 CB5 . . . .**44** B6
Baker Rd 2 IP9 . . . .**107** A4
Baker's Cnr IP14 . . . .**80** E6
Baker's Hill IP16 . . . .**58** C4
Baker's La
Bury St Edmunds IP33 . . .**154** C1
Thorndon IP23 . . . .**53** C6
Westleton IP17 . . . .**58** C8
Baker's Rd CO10 . . . .**90** D5
Baker's Score 1 NR32 . . .**3** C2
Bakers La
Ditchingham NR35 . . . . . .**110** B8
Orford IP12 . . . .**131** C2
Winston IP14 . . . .**68** E8
1 Woodbridge IP12 . . . .**147** A4
Bakers La S IP12 . . . . . .**131** C2
Bakers Row CB8 . . . .**121** A4
Bakers Way IP28 . . . .**30** F2
Balaton Pl CB8 . . . .**121** A6
Baldry Cl IP8 . . . .**138** C1
Baldrys Wlk NR35 . . . . . .**110** B7
Baldwin Ave IP32 . . . . . .**122** E8
Baldwin Rd IP14 . . . .**124** C4
Ball's Chace CO6 . . . .**101** C1
Ballater Cl IP7 . . . .**134** E4
Ballingdon Hill CO10 . . .**148** A3
Ballingdon St CO10 . . . .**148** A4
Balliol Cl IP7 . . . .**146** D3
Balls Hill IP7 . . . .**79** D5
Ballygate NR34 . . . .**111** A5
Balmoral Cl IP2 . . . .**138** F1
Balmoral Dr 9 CB9 . . . .**132** C6
Balton Way 7 CO12 . . . .**106** F1
Bancroft La CB7 . . . .**28** D5
Bangor Rd IP27 . . . .**13** F2
Banham Dr 3 CO10 . . . .**148** D6
Banham Rd NR34 . . . . . .**111** C2
Banham's La NR35 . . . . . .**7** B6
Bank Alley 8 IP18 . . . . . .**119** D5
Bank Bldgs 14 CO10 . . . .**148** C5
Bank Rd IP4 . . . .**139** E6
Banks Cl IP7 . . . .**149** E5
Banks' La IP19 . . . .**24** C3
Banks Wlk IP33 . . . .**123** C1
Bannocks La IP13 . . . .**56** B4
Banters La NR34 . . . .**8** F2
Bantocks Rd CO10 . . . . . .**92** C5
Bantoft Terr IP3 . . . .**140** C2
Banyard Cl 4 IP5 . . . . . .**141** D7
Barbara Stradbroke Ave
CB8 . . . .**120** D1
Barber Cl 3 NR33 . . . . . .**11** B1
Barber's La NR35 . . . .**7** B6
Barcham Rd CB7 . . . .**28** C7
Bardolph Rd NR35 . . . . .**110** B3
Bardwell Rd IP31 . . . .**33** F5
Bardwell VC Prim Sch
IP31 . . . .**34** C5
Bardwell Windmill★
IP31 . . . .**34** B4
Barell's Hill IP19 . . . .**40** F4
Bargate La
Beck Row, Holywell Row
& Kenny Hill IP28 . . . .**29** F5
Dedham CO7 . . . .**104** A2
Bargate Rd IP12 . . . .**30** A6
Barham Picnic Site Visitor
Ctr★ IP6 . . . .**82** A6
Barhams Way IP13 . . . . .**127** C2
Barker Cl Ipswich IP2 . . .**138** D5
6 Manningtree CO11 . . . .**104** D2
3 Steeple Bumpstead CB9 . .**88** D3
Barker Rd CO10 . . . .**148** C8
Barking Rd
Barking IP6 . . . .**125** A1
Willisham IP8 . . . .**81** A5
Barkis Meadow NR32 . . . .**3** A4
Barkways 9 CB5 . . . .**44** B5
Barley Lands IP15 . . . . . .**130** E5
Barley Meadow 5 IP19 .**118** A3
Barley Way IP14 . . . .**114** F2
Barlings Ct CB8 . . . .**121** A4
Barn Cl
2 Hopton on Sea NR31 . . .**3** C7
Lowestoft NR33 . . . .**114** D8
Southwold IP18 . . . .**119** B8
Barn Field 2 IP29 . . . . . .**62** C6
Barn La IP33 . . . .**154** C3
Barn St 12 CO10 . . . .**78** D4
Barnaby Gn IP18 . . . .**119** C5
Barnardiston Hall Prep Sch
CB9 . . . .**75** A5
Barnards Way NR32 . . . .**113** A5
Barnby & N Cove Prim Sch
NR34 . . . .**10** C4
Barnes Cl Brandon IP27 . . .**14** E8
3 Hadleigh IP7 . . . .**149** E6
Barnfield
Capel St Mary IP9 . . . . . .**150** F3
Felixstowe IP11 . . . .**152** D6
26 Manningtree CO11 . . . .**104** E2
Barnham CE Prim Sch
IP24 . . . .**16** B1
Barnham Pl IP5 . . . .**140** F6
Barnham Rd IP24 . . . .**16** B2
Barningham CE VC Prim Sch
IP31 . . . .**34** E7

Barningham Rd IP31 . . . .**34** E5
Barons Cl
9 Felixstowe IP11 . . . . . .**153** D6
Halesworth IP19 . . . .**118** A2
Barons Ct 17 CB9 . . . . . .**132** C5
Barons Meadow IP12 . . .**131** B3
Baronsdale Cl IP1 . . . . . .**135** B1
Barr Dr IP27 . . . .**109** D7
Barrack La
Harwich CO12 . . . .**107** C2
Ipswich IP1 . . . .**155** A3
Ufford IP13 . . . .**84** F7
Barrack Sq IP5 . . . .**98** A8
Barracks Rd CO10 . . . . . .**101** F8
Barrell's Rd IP31 . . . .**49** F3
Barrett's La IP6 . . . .**125** C4
Barrow Hill Acton CO10 . .**92** B8
Barrow IP29 . . . .**47** A3
Barrow Prim Sch IP29 . . .**47** A3
Barrow Rd IP29 . . . .**46** F1
Barrow's Cnr IP24 . . . .**32** C8
Barry Lynham Dr CB8 . . .**121** B2
Barsey Cl CB9 . . . .**132** A7
Bartholomew Gn
IP18 . . . .**119** D5
Bartholomew St IP4 . . . .**139** F6
Bartholomew's La IP19 . .**42** B6
Bartlow Rd CB9 . . . .**132** F7
Barton Bottom IP31 . . . .**48** E7
Barton Dr CB9 . . . .**133** F8
Barton Gr CB9 . . . .**133** F8
Barton Hamlet IP31 . . . . .**49** C6
Barton Hill IP31 . . . .**48** D5
Barton Rd
Bury St Edmunds IP32 . . .**123** D6
Felixstowe IP11 . . . .**153** B4
Thurston IP31 . . . .**49** D4
Woodbridge IP12 . . . .**146** F7
Bartons Pl CB8 . . . .**120** E5
Bartrum La 7 IP5 . . . . . .**141** C7
Barvens The **138** A1
Barway Rd CB7 . . . .**28** A6
Barwell Rd IP33 . . . .**154** C3
Basil Brown Cl 1 IP22 . . .**36** A6
Bates La **19** D6
Bath Ct CB9 . . . .**132** D4
Bath Hill IP11 . . . .**153** B4
Bath Hills Rd NR35 . . . . . .**7** E4
Bath Rd IP11 . . . .**153** B4
Bath St IP2 . . . .**139** D3
Battery Gn 7 NR32 . . . . .**113** E1
Battery Gn Rd 5 NR32 . .**113** E1
Battery La 10 IP9 . . . . . .**107** A4
Battisford Rd IP6 . . . . . .**125** A1
Battles La IP5 . . . .**141** D7
Battlesea Hill IP21 . . . . . .**39** A6
Bawdsey CE Prim Sch
IP12 . . . .**99** E2
Bawdsey Cl IP3 . . . .**153** D7
Bawdsey Manor Workshops★
IP12 . . . .**108** D8
Bawdsey Radar Sta★
IP12 . . . .**99** E1
Bay Rd 11 CO12 . . . .**107** B2
Bayfield Dr 4 CB5 . . . . . .**44** B5
Baylham House Rare Breeds
Farm★ IP6 . . . .**81** F7
Baynard's La IP22 . . . . . .**20** A3
Bays The 4 IP16 . . . .**73** F6
Beach Mews 6 NR32 . . .**113** E1
Beach Rd Dunwich IP17 . .**43** B1
1 Harwich CO12 . . . .**107** B1
Hopton on Sea NR31 . . . . .**3** C8
Kessingland NR33 . . . .**27** C8
Lowestoft NR32 . . . .**115** D8
Beach Rd E IP11 . . . .**153** C4
Beach Rd W IP11 . . . .**152** F2
Beach Sta Rd IP11 . . . . .**152** E1
Beacon Field 4 IP11 . . .**152** E5
Beacon Hill Ave CO10 . .**107** C2
Beacon Hill La IP16 . . . . .**73** F7
Beacon Hill Specl Sch
IP2 . . . .**138** F2
Beacon La IP13 . . . .**137** F3
Beaconsfield Cl CO10 . . .**148** C6
Beaconsfield Ct 9 CB9 .**132** D5
Beaconsfield Rd
Aldeburgh IP15 . . . .**130** E3
Ipswich IP1 . . . .**138** F7
21 Kessingland NR33 . . . .**11** C1
Lowestoft NR33 . . . .**115** C6
Sudbury CO10 . . . .**148** C6
3 Woodbridge IP12 . . . .**147** A5
Bealings La IP13 . . . .**137** F8
Bealings Rd IP12 . . . .**146** A1
Bealings Sch IP13 . . . .**137** D4
Bear Meadow 5 IP30 . . . .**49** F2
Bear St CO6 . . . .**102** C5
Beard Rd IP32 . . . .**122** D8
Beardmore Pk 10 IP5 . . .**98** A8
Bear's La CO10 . . . .**78** D3
Beatrice Ave IP11 . . . . . .**153** A5
Beatrice Cl IP3 . . . .**140** A3
Beatty Rd Ipswich IP3 . . .**140** B2
Sudbury CO10 . . . .**148** E7
Beauford Rd IP31 . . . .**32** F1
Beaufort Ct 10 CB9 . . . .**132** D5
Beaufort St IP1 . . . .**139** A7
Beaumont Cl 3 IP33 . . . .**122** C4
Beaumont Cotts IP17 . . .**128** C6
Beaumont Cr CB9 . . . . . .**132** F4
Beaumont Prim Sch
IP7 . . . .**149** D8
Beaumont Rd NR34 . . . .**114** B2
Beaumont Vale CB9 . . . .**132** F4
Beaumont Way IP14 . . . .**124** B5

Beccles & District Mus★
NR34 . . . .**111** A5
Beccles & District War Meml
Hospl NR34 . . . .**111** B4
Beccles Gall★ q0 NR34 **111** B5
Beccles Mid Sch
NR34 . . . .**111** B4
Beccles Rd Aldeby NR34 . . .**9** F8
Aldeby/Wheatacre/Burgh
St Peter NR34 . . . .**10** B8
Blyford IP19 . . . .**25** C1
Bungay NR35 . . . .**110** C4
Carlton Colville NR33 . . . .**114** A4
Fritton & St Olaves NR31 . . .**2** C7
Holton IP19 . . . .**118** F4
Lowestoft NR33 . . . .**114** D7
Mutford NR34 . . . .**10** C3
Beccles Sports Ctr
NR34 . . . .**111** A3
Becclesgate 1 NR34 . . . .**111** B6
Beck Cl 5 IP12 . . . .**85** D8
Beck Rd CB7 . . . .**29** D4
Beck Row Prim Sch
IP28 . . . .**30** B8
Beck St IP22 . . . .**35** A7
Beck View 3 IP20 . . . .**22** D6
Beckett Cl IP33 . . . .**122** A6
Becketts La IP7 . . . .**94** B1
Becketts The IP14 . . . . . .**124** B8
Beckford Rd 17 CO11 . . .**105** A2
Beckham Rd NR31 . . . . . .**113** C1
Becks Gn La NR34 . . . .**24** F8
Bedell Cl IP33 . . . .**122** C3
Bederic Cl IP32 . . . .**123** D4
Bedfield CE Prim Sch
IP13 . . . .**54** D5
Bedfield Rd IP13 . . . .**55** A3
Bedford Rd 3 IP32 . . . . .**122** E8
Bedford St IP1 . . . .**155** A4
Bedingfield Way IP32 . . .**123** E4
Bedingfield Cres IP19 . . .**118** A1
Bedingfield Rd IP23 . . . . .**53** E7
Beech Circus 5 IP7 . . . . . .**80** D6
Beech Cl
Halesworth IP19 . . . .**118** A3
Isleham CB7 . . . .**29** B5
11 Lakenheath IP27 . . . .**13** F2
Sproughton IP8 . . . .**138** A6
Beech Croft CB8 . . . .**59** E1
Beech Gr Haverhill CB9 . .**132** C7
Ipswich IP3 . . . .**139** F3
Beech La 2 IP14 . . . .**51** A1
Beech Paddocks 4 IP30 . .**64** F8
Beech Pk IP31 . . . .**49** B6
Beech Rd Ipswich IP5 . . .**140** F7
Lowestoft NR33 . . . .**114** D3
Sudbury CO10 . . . .**148** F4
Beech Rise IP33 . . . .**123** C3
Beech Row CB8 . . . .**46** C1
Beech Terr IP14 . . . .**124** D7
Beech Tree Cl NR35 . . . . . .**7** F4
Beech Tree Way 9 NR35 . .**7** F4
Beech Way
Dickleburgh IP21 . . . .**21** C5
Woodbridge IP12 . . . .**146** C5
Beech Wlk IP16 . . . .**129** C5
Beechcroft IP29 . . . .**64** A3
Beechcroft Rd IP1 . . . . . .**134** F2
Beeches Cl 11 IP31 . . . . . .**34** B1
Beeches Rd IP28 . . . .**29** F7
Beeches The
Benhall Green IP17 . . . .**72** C8
Claydon IP6 . . . .**134** C8
Horringer IP29 . . . .**63** A8
Ipswich IP4 . . . .**139** F4
31 Lawford CO11 . . . . . .**104** E2
Little Blakenham IP8 . . . . .**81** E3
Beeching Dr NR32 . . . . . .**113** D4
Beechwood Cl CB8 . . . . .**120** C8
Beechwood Gdns
NR33 . . . .**115** A6
Beehive Cl CO7 . . . .**151** C5
Beetons Way IP32 . . . . . .**122** C6
Beevors Gdn NR35 . . . . .**110** B7
Belaugh Ave NR33 . . . . .**114** F5
Belchamp Hall★ CO10 . .**91** A3
Belchamp St Paul CE Prim
Sch CO10 . . . .**90** D5
Belcher Gn IP18 . . . .**119** C8
Belfry Rd IP13 . . . .**144** F7
Belgrave Cl IP4 . . . .**135** C1
Bell Cl IP2 . . . .**155** B1
Bell Gdns 13 CB7 . . . .**28** D4
Bell Gn IP19 . . . .**40** C6
Bell Hill CO8 . . . .**101** B6
Bell La
Barton Mills IP28 . . . .**116** D2
Ipswich IP2 . . . .**155** B1
Marlesford IP13 . . . .**71** C4
Bell Meadow IP32 . . . . . .**123** A8
Bell Mews IP7 . . . .**149** D6
Bell St IP20 . . . .**22** D5
Bellands Way IP23 . . . . . .**117** C5
Bell's Cross IP14 . . . .**67** C6
Bell's Cross Rd IP6 . . . . . .**82** C7
Bell's La Hawstead IP29 . . .**63** E5
Stowupland IP14 . . . .**67** C7
Belle Vue Rd
Ipswich IP4 . . . .**139** F6
Sudbury CO10 . . . .**148** D6
Bellings Rd CB9 . . . .**132** D4
Bells Hill CO8 . . . .**101** D2
Bells La Glemsford CO10 . .**77** A3
Hinderclay IP22 . . . .**35** E8
Bells Rd CO10 . . . .**90** F3

Bellwell La
Debenham IP14 . . . .**53** F4
Kenton IP14 . . . .**54** A4
Belmont Ct
8 Haverhill CB9 . . . .**132** D5
Newmarket CB8 . . . .**120** F3
Belmont Gdns NR32 . . . .**113** B3
Belmont Rd IP8 . . . .**138** C1
Belsay Ct CB9 . . . .**132** B6
Belseybridge Rd NR35 . . .**7** F7
Belstead Ave IP2 . . . .**155** A1
Belstead Rd IP2 . . . .**155** A1
Belstead Sch IP8 . . . .**138** C2
Belt The CB8 . . . .**61** B4
Belvedere Dr 23 NR33 . . .**11** C1
Belvedere Rd
Ipswich IP4 . . . .**139** F8
Lowestoft NR33 . . . .**115** C7
Belvoir Ct 7 CB9 . . . .**132** C6
Benacre National Nature
Reserve★ NR34 . . . .**27** B6
Benacre Rd
Ellough NR34 . . . .**111** F1
Henstead with Hulver Street
NR34 . . . .**26** E8
Benefield Rd 1 CB8 . . . . .**45** F3
Benezet St IP1 . . . .**155** A3
Benhall St Marys CE Prim
Sch IP17 . . . .**72** C8
Benjamin Britten High Sch
NR32 . . . .**113** A5
Bennett Ave
Bury St Edmunds IP33 . . .**122** C6
Elmswell IP30 . . . .**50** F2
Bennett Rd
Ipswich IP1 . . . .**134** E1
5 Red Lodge IP28 . . . . .**30** C1
Benouville 10 NR33 . . . .**114** F5
Bensly's Drift IP19 . . . . .**118** C4
Bent La IP4 . . . .**140** E8
Bentley Dr NR32 . . . .**113** A6
Bentley La
Belstead IP8 . . . .**142** C5
Stutton IP9 . . . .**105** B6
Bentley Prim Sch IP9 . . .**104** F8
Bentley Rd IP1 . . . .**134** C2
Benton Cl IP7 . . . .**65** C1
Benton St IP7 . . . .**149** D6
Benton Way IP19 . . . .**118** B4
Benyon Gdns IP28 . . . . . .**32** D1
Beresford Dr IP12 . . . . . .**146** F7
Beresford Rd NR32 . . . . .**113** D2
Bergamot Rd IP30 . . . . . .**132** A6
Berghersh La IP6 . . . .**82** E7
Bergholt Rd CO11 . . . . . .**104** D4
Berkeley Cl
2 Framlingham IP13 . . .**126** C3
Ipswich IP4 . . . .**135** E1
Berkeley Gdns
Bury St Edmunds IP33 . . .**122** E4
Lowestoft NR32 . . . .**113** A4
Bermuda Rd IP10 . . . .**144** D7
Bernard Rooke Pottery &
Gall★ IP6 . . . .**83** A8
Berners Rd IP11 . . . .**153** C4
Berners St IP1 . . . .**155** A3
Bernham Rd IP32 . . . .**123** D5
Berry Cl Ipswich IP3 . . . .**140** F1
Lowestoft NR33 . . . .**112** E1
Berrycroft 11 CB7 . . . .**28** D4
Beryl Rd 8 CO12 . . . .**106** E1
Bethel Dr 24 NR33 . . . . . .**11** C1
Betjeman Cl IP7 . . . .**149** D7
Betony Wlk CB9 . . . .**132** B6
Betts Ave IP5 . . . .**98** A8
Betts Cl IP7 . . . .**149** D7
Betty Cocker Gr CO10 . . .**148** F5
Bevan St E 3 NR32 . . . . .**113** D8
Bevan St W NR32 . . . . . .**113** C1
Beverley Ct NR33 . . . . . .**114** D6
Beverley Rd NR33 . . . . . .**114** C2
Beverley Rd IP4 . . . .**139** F8
Beversham Rd IP13 . . . . .**71** F5
Bevis Wlk IP33 . . . .**123** D2
Beyond the Image
Photographers Gall★
IP23 . . . .**36** F2
Beyton Rd IP30 . . . .**49** F1
Beyton Mid Sch IP30 . . . .**49** F1
Bibb Way IP1 . . . .**139** A5
Bickers Hill Rd IP13 . . . . .**40** B3
Bier La IP22 . . . .**19** C1
Big Row NR34 . . . .**8** F6
Bigod Cl
5 Framlingham IP13 . . .**126** C3
Halesworth IP19 . . . .**118** B2
Bigod Rd NR35 . . . .**110** D3
Bilberry Rd IP3 . . . .**144** C7
Bildeston Gdns 2 IP1 . . .**135** D1
Bildeston Prim Sch IP7 . .**79** E4
Bildeston Rd
Chelsworth IP7 . . . .**79** E3
Combs IP14 . . . .**124** A1
Offton IP7 . . . .**80** F4
Bill Rickaby Dr CB8 . . . .**121** A5
Billy's La CO7 . . . .**103** C5
Bilney Rd IP12 . . . .**146** E5
Birch Ave CO12 . . . .**107** A2
Birch Cl
Lowestoft NR32 . . . .**112** D2
1 Stowupland IP14 . . . . .**67** A6
Wickham Market IP13 . . . .**127** C6
Woodbridge IP12 . . . .**146** F3
Birch Covert IP24 . . . . . .**16** D6

Birch Cres IP27 . . . .**109** D7
Birch Dr 8 CO11 . . . .**104** E5
Birch Fall 7 CO6 . . . .**102** C5
Birch Gr IP5 . . . .**98** A7
Birch Rd Onehouse IP14 . .**66** C5
10 Thurstow IP31 . . . . . .**49** E4
Birch St CO6 . . . .**102** D5
Birch Wlk 24 IP27 . . . . . .**13** F2
Birchcroft Rd IP1 . . . . . .**135** B2
Birches The
Kennett IP28 . . . .**46** A8
Soham CB7 . . . .**28** C5
Birchgrove IP23 . . . .**52** F7
Birchinhill Dro IP28 . . . . .**12** F2
Birchwood Cty Prim Sch
IP5 . . . .**98** A8
Birchwood Dr IP5 . . . . . .**136** E1
Birchwood Rd CO7 . . . . .**103** D2
Bird View Sq 1 IP26 . . . . .**4** E5
Bird's La IP30 . . . .**64** D2
Bird's Rd IP31 . . . .**49** F3
Birdbrook 3 IP29 . . . .**63** A1
Birdbrook Rd CO9 . . . . . .**89** A2
Birdcage Wlk CB8 . . . . . .**120** F2
Birds Croft IP31 . . . .**33** C2
Birds Gn IP30 . . . .**65** E5
Birds Hill IP13 . . . .**83** D8
Birds La Framsden IP14 . .**69** C2
Lowestoft NR33 . . . .**115** B6
Birds Meare IP6 . . . .**69** C2
Birkdale Ave IP28 . . . . . .**116** B5
Birkdale Ct 10 IP28 . . . . .**48** C6
Birkfield Cl IP2 . . . .**139** A4
Birkfield Dr IP2 . . . .**138** E1
Biscay Cl CB9 . . . .**133** A5
Bishop Mews IP8 . . . .**138** B2
Bishop's Hill IP3 . . . .**139** E4
Bishops Cl
6 Felixstowe IP11 . . . . . .**153** D6
Haverhill CB9 . . . .**132** C6
Bishops Ct 1 CB9 . . . . . .**132** C6
Bishops Rd IP33 . . . .**154** B3
Bishops Way IP21 . . . .**39** A4
Bishops Wlk
10 Hopton on Sea NR31 . . .**3** B7
Lowestoft NR32 . . . .**113** D5
Bittern Cl IP27 . . . .**138** E3
Bittern Gn NR33 . . . .**114** C6
Bittern Rd IP17 . . . .**128** B3
Bixley Dr IP4 . . . .**140** E5
Bixley La IP4 . . . .**140** E5
Bixley Rd Ipswich IP3 . . .**140** D3
2 Lowestoft NR33 . . . . .**115** C6
Black Barns IP11 . . . .**152** C7
Black Bear Ct CB8 . . . . . .**121** A3
Black Bear La CB8 . . . . . .**120** F3
Black Boy La CO11 . . . . . .**106** A2
Black Boy Meadow
NR34 . . . .**111** B4
Black Dyke Rd IP26 . . . . . .**4** E3
Black Gr La CO10 . . . .**75** C4
Black Hill (Tumulus)★
IP31 . . . .**33** C5
Black Horse La
Ditchingham NR35 . . . . . .**110** C7
Ipswich IP1 . . . .**155** A3
Black Horse Wlk IP1 . . . .**155** B3
Black Mill Rd IP18 . . . . .**119** C5
Black Slough IP17 . . . .**58** B7
Black St NR33 . . . .**10** C1
Blackberry Way
Lowestoft NR32 . . . .**112** E2
3 Red Lodge IP28 . . . . .**30** C1
Blackbird Ave IP27 . . . . . .**6** A1
Blackbird Cl 16 IP31 . . . .**49** D4
Blackbird Dr IP32 . . . .**49** A3
Blackbird Rd 3 IP28 . . . . .**13** F2
Blackbird Way 10 IP14 . . .**67** A5
Blackbourne CE VC Mid Sch
IP31 . . . .**34** F4
Blackbourne Rd IP30 . . . .**50** F3
Blackdike Dro IP26 . . . . . .**4** A2
Blackdown Ave IP5 . . . . .**140** F6
Blackdyke Cl 9 IP26 . . . . .**4** D5
Blackfriars CO10 . . . .**148** B4
Blackheath Rd
Lowestoft NR33 . . . .**115** A5
Wenhaston with Mells Hamlet
IP19 . . . .**42** C5
Blackhouse La CO10 . . . .**148** F1
Blacklands La IP12 . . . . .**131** A8
Blackmore Cl CB9 . . . . . .**132** D7
Blacksmith La
Barnham IP24 . . . .**16** B2
Thorpe Morieux IP30 . . . .**78** F7
Blacksmiths Rd IP14 . . . . .**52** A6
Blacksmith's Cnr IP8 . . .**142** C6
Blacksmith's Loke NR32 . .**2** F6
Blacksmiths Hill CO10 . . .**89** D6
Blacksmiths La
Bulmer CO10 . . . .**91** C1
Coddenham IP6 . . . .**68** B1
Stonham Earl IP7 . . . .**67** D6
Blackthorn Cl IP3 . . . . . .**140** F1
Blackthorn Ct CB7 . . . . . .**28** C5
Blackthorn Way CO6 . . .**102** D7
Blackthorn Wlk IP32 . . .**122** D8
Blacktiles La IP12 . . . .**84** A1
Bladen Dr IP4 . . . .**140** F5
Bladon Way CB9 . . . .**132** F7
Blagge Cl IP33 . . . .**122** C4
Blair Cl IP4 . . . .**140** E5
Blair Par 6 CB9 . . . .**132** C6
Blake Ave 4 IP9 . . . .**107** A5
Blake Cl 3 CO11 . . . .**104** D2
Blake Rd Ipswich IP1 . . . .**134** F3
Stowmarket IP14 . . . .**124** B7
Blakenham 4 NR32 . . . . .**112** C4

Blakenham Woodland Gdn★ IP6 81 F4
Blakes Cl IP12 147 C7
Blanche St IP4 155 C3
Blandford Rd IP3 140 D3
Blaxhall Church Rd IP12 71 F2
Blaxhall Ct 2 CB9 132 C5
Blaxhall Heath Nature Reserve★ IP12 72 C3
Blenheim Cl
10 Brantham CO11 104 E5
Bury St Edmunds IP33 122 D5
Haverhill CB9 132 F7
Blenheim Dr IP7 80 C6
Blenheim Rd 3 IP1 139 A7
Blenheim Way 2 IP22 20 A3
Blickling Cl IP2 139 B2
Blinco Rd NR32 112 C1
Blind La IP29 77 B6
Blo' Norton Rd
Blo' Norton IP22 18 F3
South Lopham IP22 19 A4
Block Rd CB7 28 E1
Blocka Rd NR32 2 C6
Blockmoor Rd CB7 28 A6
Blofield Rd IP11 152 B4
Blois Rd CB9 88 F4
Blomfield St IP33 154 B3
Blood Hill IP8 81 B3
Bloodmoor La 2 NR33 114 E3
Bloodmoor Rd 1 NR33 114 E3
Bloomfield St IP4 140 B6
Bloomfield Way
Debenham IP14 53 E1
7 Lowestoft NR33 114 E3
Blooms Ct IP28 116 D5
Blooms Hall La CO10 77 D5
Bloomsbury Cl NR32 112 E4
Bloomsfield 8 CB5 44 B5
Blower's La NR33 10 E2
Blue Barn Cl 13 IP11 107 D8
Blue Barn La IP8 134 A8
Blue House La IP14 52 F3
Bluebell Ave IP32 123 F5
Bluebell Cl Ipswich IP2 138 E4
7 Lowestoft NR33 114 F3
Bluebell Gr IP6 125 D3
Bluebell Way NR34 111 E3
Bluebell Wlk 2 CB7 28 D4
Bluegate La IP9 150 F1
Bluestem Rd IP3 144 D8
Blundens The CO6 102 E7
Blundeston Rd
Corton NR32 112 F8
Somerleyton, Ashby & Herringfleet NR32 112 B8
Blyburgate 2 NR34 111 C4
Blyford La Blyford IP19 42 B8
Holton IP19 118 E3
Wenhaston with Mells Hamlet IP19 42 C6
Blyford Rd NR32 113 A5
Blyford Way IP11 152 C4
Blyth Cl Ipswich IP2 139 A1
Wenhaston IP19 42 C6
Blyth Rd
Halesworth IP19 118 C2
Southwold IP18 119 B5
Blythburgh Rd IP17 58 C8
Boathouse La
Carlton Colville NR32 114 B8
Lowestoft NR32 112 B1
Boatman Cl 16 IP8 142 E8
Bobbits La
Pinewood IP9 142 E8
Wherstead IP9 143 A7
Boby Rd IP32 122 D8
Bockhill Rd IP33 122 C5
Bodiam Cl IP3 140 D4
Bodiam Rd IP3 140 D4
Bodiam Way 8 NR33 114 D4
Bodian Wlk 8 CB9 132 C6
Bodmin Cl IP5 141 A6
Boeing Way IP28 116 B5
Boldero Rd IP32 123 F4
Boleyn Way CB9 132 B5
Boleyn Wlk CB8 121 C3
Bollard Way NR33 114 E5
Bolton Cl 2 CB5 44 A5
Bolton La IP1 155 C3
Bolton St 10 CO10 78 D4
Bon Marche 7 NR32 115 D8
Bond Cl IP21 21 F8
Bond St Ipswich IP4 155 C2
Stowmarket IP14 124 D7
Bond's Rd NR15 21 C8
Bonds Meadow NR32 112 E2
Bonnington Rd IP3 139 F1
Bonny Cres IP3 144 C8
Bonsey Gdns NR34 26 E5
Boon Cl IP33 123 A3
Boon Dr NR33 114 E6
Boot Drift IP9 106 E7
Booth La IP5 141 E8
Border Cot La IP13 127 B7
Border La NR32 2 E6
Borehamgate Prec 5 CO10 148 D5
Borehamgate Sh Ctr 21 CO10 148 C5
Borley Cres 2 IP30 50 F2
Borley Rd CO10 91 D6
Borough End 3 NR34 111 C3
Borough La IP14 66 A3
Borradale Ct 5 CB9 88 D3
Borradale Rd IP32 123 F5
Borrett Pl IP12 146 D3
Borretts Farm La IP13 70 D6
Borrow Cl NR33 114 C3
Borrow Rd NR32 112 C1
Borrowdale Ave 1 IP4 135 D1
Bosmere Prim Sch IP6 125 D4
Bosquet Cl 1 NR32 112 F5
Boss Hall Ind Est IP1 138 E7
Boss Hall Rd IP1 138 E7
Bostock Rd IP2 139 C1
Boston End 6 IP24 16 A5
Boston Rd Ipswich IP4 139 F7
Lowestoft NR32 113 D2
Boswell La IP7 149 D7
Botany La IP17 71 E7
Botolphs Ct IP33 154 C1
Bouchain Ct 1 IP19 118 A3
Boughton Way IP33 154 C3
Boulevard The NR32 114 D8
Boulge Rd Burgh IP13 83 F6
Hasketon IP13 146 B8
Boulters Cl IP14 124 B6
Boulters Way IP14 124 B6
Boundary Cl IP26 4 F3
Boundary Rd
Haverhill CB9 133 B3
1 Hockwold cum Wilton IP26 5 A3
Red Lodge IP28 30 C1
Bourchier Cl 7 IP7 149 E6
Bourne Ave 6 IP32 123 E6
Bourne Hill IP2 143 B7
Bourne Pk Residential Park IP2 139 B1
Bourne Rd
Haverhill CB9 132 F6
Lowestoft NR32 113 B3
Bourne Terr IP2 143 B8
Bowdens La CO6 101 F3
Bower's La 7 CB7 29 C5
Bowl Rd IP14 66 C1
Bowland Dr IP8 138 C1
Bowman's La IP17 42 D1
Bowthorpe Cl IP1 155 A4
Box Bush La IP13 55 D5
Boxford Cl 2 IP14 124 E3
Boxford Ct
7 Felixstowe IP11 152 C4
3 Haverhill CB9 132 C5
Boxford La CO10 93 A3
Boxford Prim Sch CO10 93 C3
Boxford Rd IP7 93 B8
Boxhouse La CO7 103 D3
Boxted Church Rd CO6 102 E2
Boxted Rd CO6 102 E2
Boxted Straight Rd CO4 103 A2
Boyden Cl 1 CB8 61 E2
Boydlands IP9 150 E3
Boyne Rd IP33 122 E4
Boyscott La 1 NR35 110 B3
Boyton Cl CB9 132 E8
Boyton Rd
Hollesley IP12 86 A1
Ipswich IP3 140 B1
Boyton Vineyard★ CO9 89 B7
Boyton's La CB10 88 A1
Braces La NR35 8 E7
Bracken Ave IP5 137 E1
Bracken Rise IP26 6 A8
Bracken Row 6 IP31 49 D4
Brackenbury Cl IP1 139 B8
Brackenbury Sports Ctr IP11 153 C5
Brackenhayes Cl IP2 139 B3
Brackenwood Cres 1 IP32 123 E6
Brackley Cl 8 IP11 152 D5
Bradbrook Cl IP32 123 F6
Braddock Sq IP32 122 E7
Bradfield Ave IP7 149 D7
Bradfield Cres IP7 149 D7
Bradfield Woods National Nature Reserve★ IP30 64 F4
Bradley Rd Cowlinge CB8 60 F1
Great Bradley CB8 74 F8
Kirtling CB8 60 F2
Bradley St IP2 155 B1
Braggon's Hill IP29 77 A5
Braithwaite Dr 7 CO10 92 C6
Bramble Cl CB9 132 B7
Bramble Dr IP3 140 E1
Bramble Gn NR32 113 B3
Bramble Tye 20 CO12 106 E1
Bramble Way CO6 102 B7
Brambles The IP15 130 C6
Bramblewood 1 IP8 138 C2
Bramblewood Way IP19 118 C4
Brambling Cl 12 IP14 67 A5
Brames La IP20 23 D3
Bramfield CE Prim Sch IP19 42 A4
Bramfield House Sch IP19 41 E4
Bramfield Rd
Halesworth IP19 118 B2
Lowestoft NR32 113 A3
Walpole IP19 41 C5
Wenhaston with Mells Hamlet IP19 42 B5
Bramford CE Prim Sch IP8 134 A1
Bramford Ct IP14 124 E4
Bramford La 6 IP1 139 A7
Bramford Meadows Nature Reserve★ IP1 134 B3
Bramford Rd
Bramford IP8 134 B1
Claydon IP8 134 A8
Great Blakenham IP6 134 A8
Ipswich IP1 138 E8
Bramhall Cl IP2 138 D1
Bramley Chase IP4 140 B7
Bramley Cl IP32 123 F6
Bramley Rd Diss IP22 20 B3
Haverhill CB9 132 A5
Bramley Rise NR34 111 C3
Brampton CE Prim Sch NR34 25 E5
Brampton Gr 9 NR32 112 F4
Brampton Sta NR34 25 C6
Brand Rd IP31 49 C7
Brandeston Cl 10 CO10 92 C6
Brandeston Rd
Cretingham IP13 69 E7
Earl Soham IP13 54 F1
Brandon Ctry Pk Visitor Ctr★ IP27 14 F8
Brandon Her Ctr★ IP27 5 F1
Brandon Rd
Felixstowe IP11 152 C4
Lakenheath IP27 14 C4
Methwold IP26 5 B8
Mildenhall IP28 116 E5
Thetford IP24 15 F6
Weeting IP27 5 F3
Wordwell IP28 32 C3
Brandon St IP27 109 F1
Brandon Sta IP27 5 F2
Brands Cl 12 CO10 92 B3
Brands La IP29 63 D3
Bransby Gdns IP4 139 E7
Brantham Hill CO11 104 E4
Brawdy Rd 1 IP31 33 D5
Brayfield Cl IP32 123 D6
Braziers La IP31 51 B6
Brazier's Wood Rd IP3 144 B8
Brazilian Terr CB8 120 F3
Breach Dro IP28 13 C1
Breckland Ave IP27 109 D7
Breckland Mid Sch IP27 14 D8
Breckland Way
Lowestoft NR32 113 A3
Mildenhall IP28 116 C5
Brecklands 5 IP26 6 B8
Brecon Cl IP2 139 B2
Bredfield Cl 7 IP11 152 D5
Bredfield Rd IP12 147 A7
Bredfield St IP12 146 F5
Brendon Cl NR32 112 E2
Brendon Dr IP5 140 F6
Brent Cl IP28 116 D4
Brent Eleigh Rd
Lavenham CO10 78 D3
Monks Eleigh IP7 79 B2
Brentgovel St 1 IP33 154 B2
Bressingham Prim Sch IP22 19 E4
Bressingham Rd IP22 19 F4
Bressingham Steam Mus & Gdns★ IP22 19 E3
Brett Ave IP7 149 E7
Brett Cl IP1 138 E8
Brett Gn IP7 149 E2
Brettenham Cres 4 IP1 135 D1
Brettenham Rd
Buxhall IP14 65 F4
Hitcham IP7 79 E8
Bretts The IP5 141 E8
Brewers Cl IP27 109 C6
Brewers Gn La IP22 20 B3
Brewhouse La 19 CB7 28 D4
Breydon Way
Gainsborough IP3 144 C7
Lowestoft NR33 114 F6
Briar Cl
Halesworth IP19 118 C4
Lowestoft NR32 113 B5
Briar Hill IP30 50 D1
Briar La IP22 35 F5
Briar Rd 39 IP20 22 D6
Briardale Ave 4 CO12 106 F2
Briarhayes Cl IP2 139 B3
Briarwood Ave IP33 122 D5
Briarwood Rd
Lowestoft NR33 114 F5
Woodbridge IP12 146 E3
Brices Way 4 CO10 77 A3
Bricett Bsns Pk IP7 80 E6
Bricett Gn IP7 80 D5
Brick Kiln Ave NR34 111 C4
Brick Kiln Cl 15 IP11 107 D8
Brick Kiln Hill CO6 93 C2
Brick Kiln La
Huntingfield IP19 40 F4
Melton IP12 147 E7
Brick Kiln Rd
Ellingham NR35 8 C8
Harkstead IP9 106 B6
Mildenhall IP28 116 D5
Brick La
Framlingham IP13 126 D1
Parham IP13 71 A7
Brickfield Cl IP2 155 C1
Brickfields Ave CB8 120 D7
Brickfields The IP14 124 C6
Brickkiln La IP22 19 C3
Brickman's Hill CO11 105 B2
Bridewell Cl IP28 116 B4
Bridewell La
Botesdale IP22 36 A6
Bury St Edmunds IP33 154 C2
Bridewell St CO10 90 B8
Bridge Cl 16 IP20 22 D6
Bridge Cottage★ CO7 151 D1
Bridge End Rd IP28 30 B1
Bridge Foot Cnr IP18 119 C7
Bridge Pk (Skate Park)★ IP1 155 B1
Bridge Rd
Bromeswell IP12 85 A6
Burston & Shimpling IP22 20 E7
Felixstowe IP11 153 A5
Levington IP10 145 E4
Lowestoft NR32 112 E1
Reydon IP18 119 C7
6 Scole IP21 20 F1
Snape IP17 72 D4
Bridge St Beccles NR34 111 A7
Brandon IP27 5 F2
Bungay NR35 110 B4
4 Bures Hamlet CO8 101 C5
Carlton IP17 128 D6
Framlingham IP13 126 C3
Hadleigh IP7 149 C7
Halesworth IP19 118 B4
Huntingfield IP19 41 A4
Ipswich IP1 155 B2
Moulton CB8 45 F3
Needham Market IP6 125 D5
Stowmarket IP14 124 F5
Thetford IP24 16 B5
Bridge St Rd CO10 78 A4
Bridge Terr 7 CO10 148 D6
Bridge Wood Nature Reserve★ IP3 144 B6
Bridgeman Wlk IP32 122 E7
Bridgewood Rd IP12 146 E5
Bridgham La NR16 17 F8
Bridgwater Rd IP2 138 D2
Bridlemere Ct CB8 120 F3
Bridles The 4 NR34 111 F4
Bridport Ave IP3 140 D3
Bright Cl
Bury St Edmunds IP33 123 C3
Saxmundham IP17 128 B4
Bright's La CO10 78 C4
Brighton St 3 IP27 14 A3
Brights Wlk IP5 141 E7
Brightwell Cl IP11 152 C4
Brimstone Rd IP8 142 E8
Brindles The 7 NR33 114 E4
Brinkley Rd Brinkley CB8 59 E1
Carlton CB8 74 A8
Dullingham CB8 59 F4
Brinkley Way IP11 153 D7
Brisbane Rd IP4 140 D6
Briscoe Way IP27 109 C8
Bristol Hill IP9 107 A4
Bristol Rd
Bury St Edmunds IP33 122 E3
Ipswich IP4 140 A7
Bristol St 5 IP27 14 A2
Britannia Prim Sch IP4 140 B5
Britannia Rd IP4 140 B6
Britten Ave IP14 124 C7
Britten Cl IP15 130 D5
Britten Ctr The NR32 113 D1
Britten Rd NR33 115 A6
Brittons Cres 3 IP29 47 A2
Brittons Rd 4 IP29 47 A2
Broad Fleet Cl 2 NR32 112 E4
Broad Gn Cl 4 IP29 62 C6
Broad La CO6 102 E1
Broad Meadow
2 Ipswich IP8 138 C2
2 Walsham le Willows IP31 35 C2
Broad Oaks CO6 102 B8
Broad Piece CB7 28 C5
Broad Rd Cotton IP14 52 A6
Little Thurlow CB9 74 F6
Lowestoft NR32 112 D1
Wickham Market IP13 127 B7
Broad St Boxford CO10 93 C3
Bungay NR35 110 A5
Eye IP23 117 C2
20 Harleston IP20 22 D6
Haverhill CB9 132 D6
Orford IP12 131 C2
Broad View Rd NR32 114 C8
Broad Way IP21 21 A4
Broadcroft Cres CB9 132 C6
Broadfields Rd 5 IP23 36 D2
Broadland Cl
Beccles NR34 111 E4
Lowestoft NR33 114 C7
Broadland Rd IP33 123 B1
Broadlands Way IP4 140 F5
Broadmere Rd IP1 138 E8
Broadoak Cl 4 NR33 114 C4
Broads Rd CB5 44 B8
Broads Rd Bsns Pk CB5 44 B7
Broadwater Gdns 6 IP9 107 A4
Broadwaters Rd NR33 114 E5
Broadway
6 Fressingfield IP21 39 E8
11 Glemsford CO10 77 A3
Pakenham IP31 49 F8
Wickham Market IP13 127 B7
Broadway Dr IP19 118 C6
Broadway The
Badwell Ash IP31 50 F8
Wickham Skeith IP23 52 D8
Brock La IP13 146 C2
Brockdish Prim Sch IP21 22 A2
Brockesby Wlk IP33 122 D4
Brockford Rd IP14 52 F4
Brockley Cres IP1 134 D1
Brockley La IP29 46 F2
Brockley Rd
Hartest IP29 77 A8
Whepstead IP29 63 B4
Brocks Bsns Ctr CB9 132 C3
Broke Ave IP8 134 B2
Broke Hall Gdns IP3 140 D4
Broke Hall Prim Sch IP4 140 E5
Brome Ave IP23 117 D5
Brome Hall La IP23 117 E7
Bromelands IP23 117 E8
Bromeswell Gn Nature Reserve★ IP12 147 F7
Bromeswell Rd IP4 135 E1
Bromley Cl 4 IP2 139 C3
Bromley Rd CO11 104 D1
Bronyon Cl IP33 122 C5
Brook Cl
Horringer IP29 122 B1
Hundon CO10 75 D3
Lowestoft NR33 114 D4
Stowmarket IP14 124 B7
Brook Dam La 22 CB7 28 D4
Brook Dr 3 IP17 56 F8
Brook Farm La 4 IP9 105 E7
Brook Farm Rd IP17 128 B4
Brook Hall Rd CO10 93 C3
Brook House Rd IP14 52 B6
Brook La Burgate IP22 36 E7
Capel St Mary IP9 150 C4
Felixstowe IP11 153 B5
Framlingham IP13 126 B3
Mickfield IP14 53 A2
Needham IP20 22 B4
Playford IP6 137 A4
St Margaret, Ilketshall NR35 24 C7
Trimley St Martin IP10 98 E1
Brook Rd NR34 10 B4
Brook Service Rd 1 CB9 132 E5
Brook St Dedham CO7 103 F4
Glemsford CO10 77 A3
Soham CB7 28 D3
Woodbridge IP12 147 A5
Yoxford IP17 57 D7
Brook Way IP8 81 C3
Brooke Bsns & Ind Pk NR33 115 A8
Brookfield Rd IP1 138 F8
Brookfields Cl CB8 121 B5
Brookhill Way IP4 140 F4
Brookhouse Bsns Pk IP2 138 F6
Brooklands Cl IP33 154 A1
Brooklands Rd CO11 104 E4
Brooklands Rise CO11 104 E4
Brooklyn Rd 14 CO12 107 B2
Brooks Castle IP13 126 C3
Brooks Hall Rd IP1 139 A7
Brooksfield 1 IP7 79 F4
Brookside Dalham CB8 61 C8
Moulton CB8 45 F3
Brookview Ipswich IP2 142 E8
Pinewood IP2 138 E1
Brookwood Cl 7 NR34 9 F4
Broom Cres IP3 139 F1
Broom Field 5 IP11 152 E5
Broom Hill La IP24 33 E7
Broom Hill Nature Reserve★ IP7 149 C5
Broom Hill Rd IP1 139 A8
Broom Hill Swimming Pool IP1 139 A8
Broom Knoll 1 CO11 104 E5
Broom Rd
Lakenheath IP27 109 E5
2 Lowestoft NR32 113 B2
Broom Rd Cl IP27 109 E5
Broom St CO10 148 F3
Broom Way IP9 150 E4
Broom Wlk 9 IP28 30 B8
Broomfield
Martlesham IP5 141 F7
17 Martlesham Heath IP5 98 A8
Broomfield Comm IP8 138 B6
Broomfield Mews 18 IP5 98 A8
Broomhayes IP2 139 A2
Broomheath IP12 146 F2
Broomhill Cl 2 IP28 30 C1
Broomhill La IP30 50 C1
Broomley Gn Rd IP32 123 F6
Broomspath Rd IP14 67 A6
Brotherton Ave IP11 152 B8
Broughton Rd IP1 155 A4
Brown St IP14 52 A3
Browning Rd
10 Brantham CO11 104 E4
Ipswich IP1 134 F3
Brownlow Rd IP11 153 A4
Browns Cl 5 Acton CO10 92 B7
Hitcham IP7 79 E6
5 Wickhambrook CB8 61 E2
Browns Gr IP5 141 D7
Browse Cl IP32 123 E4
Browston La NR32 2 E7
Broxtead Cl IP12 85 C2
Bruce St NR33 115 C7

Brudenell St IP15 ....130 E3
Bruges Cl **14** CO12 ......107 A1
Bruisyard Rd IP13 ....56 C3
Bruisyard Vineyard★
  IP17 ....56 C5
Brundon La CO10 ....148 A5
Brunel Rd IP2 ....138 E6
Brunel Way IP24 ....16 B7
Brunswick House Cut **18**
  CO11 ....105 A2
Brunswick Rd IP4 ....135 F1
Brunwyn Cl IP32 ....123 F6
Brussels Cl **15** CO12 ....107 A1
Brybank Rd CB9 ....132 A7
Bryon Ave IP11 ....152 B2
Bryony Cl Haverhill CB9 .132 C2
  6 Lowestoft NR33 ....114 F3
Buccaneer Rd IP31 ......17 D8
Buck La IP23 ....117 E8
Buckanay La IP12 ....99 E5
Buckenham Ct **17** IP18 .119 D5
Buckenham Rd IP7 ......149 F4
Buckfast Cl **4** IP2 .....139 A2
Buckingham Cl **4** IP12 ..84 A1
Buckingham Rd CB9 .....132 C4
Buckingham's Hill IP21 .39 E8
Buckles Field **8** IP31 ..34 E4
Bucklesham Prim Sch
  IP10 ....98 B4
Bucklesham Rd
  Ipswich IP3 ....140 E2
  Kirton IP10 ....98 D3
Buckleswood Rd IP16 ...129 A7
Bucknam Cl **14** NR33 ....11 C1
Buck's Head La IP6 .....67 F2
Buck's Horns La IP8 ....142 B6
Bucks La **7** CO10 ......90 A8
Buckshorn La IP23 .....117 D2
Buddleia Cl IP2 ....138 E4
Bude Cl IP5 ....141 A6
Bugg's La
  Brettenham IP7 ....65 D1
  Hitcham IP7 ....79 D8
Bugg's Rd IP22 ....36 D6
Buggs Hole La IP22 .....18 D2
Bugsby Way IP25 ....141 E7
Bulcamp Drift IP19 .....43 A7
Bull Dr IP5 ....141 C6
Bull Hall La IP6 ....83 A5
Bull La Acton CO10 .....78 A1
  Hawstead IP29 ....63 C5
  Long Melford CO10 .....91 E8
  Rickinghall Superior IP22 ..36 B4
Bull Rd IP31 ....49 F6
Bull Rush Cres IP33 ....154 A4
Bullace La IP12 ....131 A8
Bullard's La IP12 ......146 E5
Bull's Ash Cnr IP7 .....80 F5
Bull's Rd IP6 ....82 C7
Bullen Cl Bramford IP8 ..134 A2
  Bury St Edmunds IP33 ..154 A1
Bullen La **5** IP8 ......134 A2
Bullens Rd IP33 ....122 A5
Buller Rd IP16 ....129 C6
Bullfinch Cl **24** CO12 ..106 F1
Bullion's La NR34 ......26 B2
Bullock Fair Cl **14** IP20 ..22 D6
Bullocks La CO10 ....148 C5
Bullockshed La IP12 ....131 C4
Bull's Wood Nature Reserve★
  IP30 ....64 E1
Bullshall Rd **6** IP23 ..37 F1
Bullswood La IP30 ......64 D1
Bulmer La CO10 ....93 C4
Bulmer Rd CO10 ....148 A4
Bulmer Rd Ind Est
  CO10 ....148 A4
Bulmer St Andrews CE Prim
  Sch CO10 ....91 C2
Bulstrode Rd IP2 ......155 C1
Bulwer Rd IP4 ....139 A6
Bumpstead Rd CB9 .....132 F3
Bunbury Ave
  1 Great Barton IP31 ..49 A5
  Mildenhall IP28 ....116 C6
Bunbury Rd **8** IP32 ...48 C5
Bungay Ave
  1 Great Barton IP31 ..49 A5
Bungay Castle (rems)★
  NR35 ....110 A4
Bungay High Sch
  NR35 ....110 C2
Bungay Mid Sch NR35 ..110 D3
Bungay Mus★ NR35 ....110 D3
Bungay Prim Sch
  NR35 ....110 C3
Bungay Rd Barsham NR34 ..9 B4
  Beccles NR34 ....111 A4
  Dickleburgh & Rushall
  IP21 ....21 B1
  Ellingham NR35 ....8 C8
  Halesworth IP19 ......118 B4
  Scole IP21 ....21 A1
  Stockton NR34 ....8 F8
Bunker Cl NR33 ....115 A5
Bunn's La IP20 ....22 C6
Bunters Rd **8** CB8 ....61 E2
Buntry La CO10 ....75 C4
Bunting Rd
  Bury St Edmunds IP32 ..123 F4
  Ipswich IP2 ....138 D3
Buntings Cres **15** CB5 ..44 A6
Buntings Path CB5 .....44 A6
Bunyan Cl IP1 ....135 A3
Burch's Cl IP7 ....129 A2
Burdock La IP26 ....4 C3
Buregate Rd IP11 ......152 F2

Bures Cl IP14 ....124 E4
Bures Ct **6** CB9 ......132 C5
Bures Prim Sch CO8 ...101 C4
Bures Rd
  Little Cornard CO10 ...101 A8
  Nayland-with-Wissington
  CO6 ....101 A4
  Sudbury CO10 ....148 E2
Bures Sta CO8 ....101 C4
Burgate Rd
  Gislingham IP23 ......36 D3
  Higham IP28 ....46 E3
Burgess Cl **5** NR32 ...112 F2
Burgess Pl **22** IP5 ....98 A8
Burgh Rd NR34 ....2 C1
Burghley Cl **4** IP2 ....139 A2
Burghley Rise **14** CB5 ..44 B5
Burke Cl IP1 ....135 A3
Burke Rd **7** IP1 ......135 A3
Burkitt Rd IP12 ....146 E5
Burkitts La CO10 ......148 C5
Burlingham Dr NR33 ...114 B3
Burlington Rd IP1 .....155 A3
Burnet Cl IP8 ....142 D8
Burnham Cl
  Felixstowe IP11 ....152 C7
  Ipswich IP4 ....139 F7
Burnham Way NR33 ....115 A2
Burns Cl IP23 ....37 B5
Burns Rd IP1 ....134 E3
Burnt Dick Hill CO4 ...102 E4
Burnt Fen Turnpike
  IP28 ....12 D6
Burnt Hill La NR33 ....114 B7
Burnt Hill Way NR33 ...114 B7
Burnt House Cl **3** CB9 .132 A7
Burnt House La IP10 ...98 D2
Burnt La IP12 ....131 C2
Burnt Oak Cnr CO7 ....151 D3
Burnthouse La
  Battisford IP14 ....66 D1
  Needham IP20 ....22 B4
Burntoak La IP20 ......22 E8
Burr Cl **17** CO12 .....106 E1
Burrell Cres IP28 ......116 D2
Burrell Rd IP2 ....155 B1
Burrell Way IP2 ....16 A5
Burrell's Orch IP33 ....122 A6
Burroughs Gn CE Prim Sch
  CB8 ....59 F2
Burroughs Piece Rd **2**
  CO10 ....148 D5
Burrow Dr IP27 ....109 C8
Burrows Cl **5** CO11 ...104 D2
Burrows Gn NR34 ......2 A1
Burrows Rd **7** IP22 ...84 E6
Burstall Hall La IP8 ...95 E7
Burstall La IP8 ....95 E7
Burston Com Prim Sch
  IP22 ....20 E6
Burston Rd
  Dickleburgh & Rushall
  IP21 ....20 F4
  Diss IP22 ....20 D4
  Gissing IP22 ....20 F7
Burton Cl CB9 ....132 C5
Burton Dr IP28 ....125 C5
Burton End CB9 ....132 C5
Burton End Com Prim Sch
  CB9 ....132 B5
Burton Hill CB9 ....74 B3
Burton St NR32 ....113 D2
Burwash IP6 ....83 A5
Burwell Mus★ CB5 ...44 B5
Burwell Rd CB8 ....120 A8
Burwood Pl
  7 Lowestoft NR32 ...113 B6
  Trimley St Mary IP11 ..152 C8
Bury Bottom IP27 .....15 A5
Bury Hill IP12 ....147 A7
Bury Hill Cl IP12 .....147 A7
Bury La Lidgate CB8 ...61 C4
  Moulton CB8 ....45 F3
  Stanton IP31 ....34 E3
  Wickhambrook CB8 ....61 E4
Bury Language Sch The
  IP33 ....154 C2
Bury Pk Dr IP33 ......123 C2
Bury Rd Alpheton CO10 ..78 A5
  Barrow IP29 ....47 A2
  Beyton IP30 ....49 E2
  Botesdale IP22 ....36 B7
  Bradfield St Clare IP30 ..64 C4
  Brandon IP27 ....14 F8
  Brettenham IP7 ....79 C7
  Brockley IP29 ....63 A2
  Chedburgh IP29 ......62 D4
  Felsham IP30 ....65 A4
  Flempton IP28 ....47 F8
  Great Barton IP31 ....49 A5
  Great Thurlow CB9 ....74 F5
  Great Whelnetham IP30 ..63 F4
  Haughley IP14 ....66 D7
  Hengrave IP28 ....48 A7
  Hepworth IP22 ....35 A4
  Ipswich IP1 ....134 D4
  Kentford CB8 ....46 B5
  Lavenham CO10 ....78 D5
  Lawshall IP29 ....63 D2
  Market Weston IP22 ...18 B1
  Mildenhall IP28 ......116 E4
  Newmarket CB8 ......121 C5
  Rickinghall Inferior IP22 ..36 A5
  Stanton IP31 ....34 F4
  Stowmarket IP14 .....124 C4
  Thetford IP24 ....16 B3
  Thorpe Morieux IP30 ..64 E2

Bury Rd continued
  Wickhambrook CB8 ....61 F1
  Wortham IP22 ....36 E8
Bury St **3** IP14 ......124 D6
Bury St Edmunds Abbey★
  IP33 ....154 C2
Bury St Edmunds Abbey
  Gdns★ IP33 ....154 C2
Bury St Edmunds Art Gall★
  IP33 ....154 B2
Bury St Edmunds Leisure Ctr
  IP33 ....122 E6
Bury St Edmunds Sta
  IP32 ....154 B4
Bury St Edmunds Upper Sch
  IP32 ....154 A4
Bush Cnr IP14 ....53 E1
Bush Gr CO10 ....148 A4
Bushel La CB7 ....28 D4
Bushey Cl IP9 ....150 E3
Bushman Gdns **3** IP8 ..134 A2
Bushy La IP12 ....99 E7
Bussock La IP12 ......99 D7
Buston Rd **5** IP22 ...20 B2
Butcher's La CO10 ....93 C4
Butcher's Rd IP17 ....128 E2
Butchers La IP9 ......150 E3
Bute Cl CB9 ....132 D4
Butfield CO10 ....78 D3
Butler Smith Gdns **6**
  IP5 ....141 C7
Butler's La CO11 .....105 F1
Butlers Way CO9 .....90 A1
Butley Cl IP2 ....142 F8
Butley Ct **3** IP13 ....132 C3
Butley Dr **8** NR32 ...112 F3
Butley Pottery★ IP12 ..86 B6
Butley Rd IP11 ....152 E3
Butt Rd
  Stoke-by-Nayland CO6 ..102 E7
  Sudbury CO10 ....148 F4
Butt's Rd Holton IP19 ..118 D8
  Spexhall IP19 ....25 A4
Butter Mkt
  Bury St Edmunds IP33 ..154 B2
  Ipswich IP1 ....155 B3
Buttercup Cl
  Bury St Edmunds IP32 ..123 F5
  3 Lowestoft NR33 ...114 C4
Butterfly Gdns IP4 ...140 E5
Buttermarket Sh Ctr
  IP1 ....155 B3
Buttermere Cl IP11 ...153 D6
Button's Rd IP13 .....71 D6
Buttrum's Mill★ IP12 ..146 E5
Butts The
  Debenham IP14 ....53 E2
  Soham CB7 ....28 D3
Buxhall Museum★
  IP14 ....66 A5
Buxlow Cl IP17 ....129 B2
Byfield Way IP33 .....123 C3
Byford Rd CO10 ......148 E2
Bylam La IP9 ....106 A7
Byland Cl **6** IP2 .....139 A2
Byng Hall Rd
  Pettistree IP13 ....84 E8
  Ufford IP13 ....127 A1
Byng La IP13 ....127 A3
Byrd Cl IP33 ....122 A3
Byron Rd IP1 ....134 E4

C

Cabin Cl NR33 ....114 B4
Cable La IP15 ....130 E5
Caddie's Wlk IP33 ....115 A5
Cadiz Way **1** NR31 ...3 C6
Cadmus Rd IP1 ....138 D7
Cadney La IP33 ......154 B3
Cadogan Rd IP33 ....122 A3
Caernarvon Wlk CB9 ..132 C6
Cage La Boxted CO4 ..103 A3
  Felixstowe IP11 ....152 E5
Cages Way **1** IP12 ...84 E6
Cagman's La IP14 ....65 F3
Caie Wlk IP4 ....139 E8
Caithness Cl IP4 .....140 B8
Cake St IP13 ....39 F4
Cakebridge La IP7 ....79 D3
Calais St IP7 ....149 D6
Caldecott Rd NR32 ...112 D1
Calder Rd **6** IP12 ...84 E6
Caledonia Rd **8** IP9 ..107 A4
Calfe Fen Cl **3** CB7 ..28 D5
Calfe Fen Dro CB7 ...28 D5
Calford Dr CB9 ......132 A6
California IP12 ....146 D3
California La IP8 .....95 B4
California Rd **14** CO11 ..105 A2
Calkewood La IP22 ...35 E5
Callis St **5** CO10 ....90 A8
Calthorpe Cl IP32 ....123 E6
Calthorpe Cl CO6 ....102 D8
Calves La CO6 ....102 D8
Camberley Ct IP33 ...154 A3
Camberley Rd IP4 ....140 D7
Camborne Rd IP5 ....141 B7
Cambria Cl **9** CO11 ...105 A2
Cambrian Cres **2** NR32 ..112 D2
Cambridge Cl CB9 ...132 C7
Cambridge Dr IP2 ....138 F2
Cambridge Rd
  Felixstowe IP11 ......153 B4
  Ipswich IP5 ....141 A7
  Lowestoft NR32 ......113 D3

Cambridge Way
  9 Bures CO8 ....101 C4
  Mildenhall CB9 ......132 C7
Camden Rd IP3 ......140 B4
Camden St **5** NR32 ..113 C3
Camp Cl **2** IP26 ....4 D5
Camp Rd IP3 ....140 D1
Campbell Cl **1** IP28 ..116 B5
Campbell Rd IP3 .....140 C1
Campion Cl CB7 .....28 C5
Campion Cres IP14 ...124 C4
Campion La CO6 .....102 B6
Campion Rd IP2 .....138 C4
Campion Way CO6 ...102 B7
Campions Hill CO6 ...102 B5
Camps Rd
  Haverhill CB9 ....132 D5
  Helions Bumpstead CB9 ..88 A5
Camwood Gdns IP3 ..140 B4
Canaletto Cl **4** NR32 ..113 B6
Canberra Cl
  Ipswich IP4 ....140 D6
  2 Mildenhall IP28 ...30 A8
Canberra Rd IP31 ....33 D8
Candler's La **18** IP20 ..22 D6
Candlet Gr IP11 .....152 F5
Candlet Rd IP11 .....152 E7
Cangle Junc **8** CB9 ..132 E6
Cangles La IP30 .....49 F1
Canham St IP1 ......155 A3
Canhams Rd CO10 ...148 A5
Cannon St IP33 .....154 B3
Cannonfields IP33 ...154 B3
Canon Cl CB9 ....132 D7
Canon Pugh Dr **6** CO10 ..92 B7
Canterbury Cl
  Ipswich IP4 ....142 F8
  7 Lakenheath IP27 ..14 A2
Canterbury Gdns IP7 ..149 E6
Canterbury Gn IP23 ..123 A3
Canterbury Inf Sch **2**
  IP4 ....16 B6
Canterbury Rd CO10 ..148 B8
Canterbury Way IP24 ..16 B6
Capel Cl
  4 Felixstowe IP11 ...107 D8
  Troston IP31 ....33 D3
Capel Dr IP11 ....152 C4
Capel Hall La IP11 ...107 D8
Capel St Mary CE Prim Sch
  IP9 ....150 E3
Capell Wlk **2** IP31 ...34 E4
Capps La IP19 ....23 F5
Capstan Way NR33 ...114 B4
Captain's La CO11 ...51 A2
Caraway Rd IP24 ....16 D6
Carbonels **12** CO10 ..92 C6
Carders Cl IP7 ......149 D4
Cardew Drift IP5 ....141 D8
Cardiff Ave IP2 .....139 B1
Cardigan St
  Ipswich IP1 ....155 A4
  Newmarket CB8 ......121 A3
Cardinal Cl IP32 ....123 E6
Cardinal Pk IP1 .....155 B2
Cardinal St IP1 .....155 B2
Cardinal Way CB9 ...132 D7
Cardinalls Rd IP14 ...124 D7
Carlford Cl IP5 ......98 A8
Carlow Mews **13** IP14 ..147 A5
Carlton Cl
  Great Yeldham CO9 ...90 A1
  Haverhill CB9 ....132 D8
Carlton Colville Cty Prim Sch
  NR33 ....114 B4
Carlton Cross NR33 ..114 C2
Carlton Gn Rd CB8 ...74 A7
Carlton Marshes Nature
  Reserve★ NR33 ......114 A7
Carlton Pk Ind Est
  IP17 ....128 C5
Carlton Rd Brinkley CB8 ..59 F1
  Carlton IP17 ....128 C5
  Ipswich IP5 ....141 A7
  Lowestoft NR33 ......115 B6
Carlton Sq NR33 ....114 C2
Carlton Way IP4 .....139 E8
Carlton Wlk IP7 .....149 E4
Carlyle Cl IP1 ....134 F4
Carmarthen Cl IP2 ...139 A2
Carmelite Pl **14** IP12 ..147 A5
Carnation Way **2** IP28 ..46 B4
Carnoustie Dr
  13 Fornham St Martin IP28 ..48 C6
  1 Lowestoft NR33 ...114 F4
Carol Ave **9** IP12 ...84 A1
Caroli Cl IP11 ....153 C5
Carolbrook Rd IP2 ...138 E1
Carr Ave IP16 ....129 D6
Carr Rd IP11 ....152 E1
Carr St IP4 ....155 C3
Carriage Ct IP11 ....152 C8
Carriers Ct CO7 .....151 D5
Carrops The CB8 ....46 A7
Carrs Hill IP13 ......56 B6
Carson Wlk CB8 ....120 F6
Carsons Dr **6** CO10 ..92 B3
Carter Rd CB5 ......44 A6
Carter St CB7 ....29 B1
Carters Hill CO4 ....103 A3
Carters La IP14 .....80 E6
Carters Teapot Pottery★
  IP14 ....53 F1
Carters Vineyard★
  CO4 ....102 F3
Casburn La **18** CB5 ..44 A6

Case La IP9 ....104 E8
Castle Ave CB9 ......132 C6
Castle Brooks IP6 ...126 B3
Castle Cl
  Felixstowe IP11 ......153 D6
  Orford IP12 ....131 B2
  Weeting-with-Broomhill
  IP27 ....5 E3
Castle Hill
  Beccles NR34 ....111 C4
  Dedham CO7 ....103 F2
  Eye IP23 ....117 D2
  Eyke IP12 ....85 B6
  Halesworth IP19 .....118 C3
  Orford IP12 ....131 C2
  Thorndon IP23 ......37 E1
Castle Hill Inf Sch
  IP1 ....135 A3
Castle Hill Jun Sch
  IP1 ....135 A3
Castle Hill Mid Sch
  CB9 ....132 B6
Castle La Bungay NR35 ..110 A4
  Hadleigh IP7 ....149 C7
  Haverhill CB9 ....132 C6
  Offton IP8 ....81 A4
  Orford IP12 ....131 C2
  Thetford IP24 ....16 C5
Castle Manor Bsns &
  Enterprise Coll CB9 ..132 C6
Castle Meadow IP8 ...81 A4
Castle Orch NR35 ....110 B4
Castle Rd
  Bury St Edmunds IP33 ..154 A1
  Hadleigh IP7 ....149 B7
  Ipswich IP1 ....134 E1
  Mettingham NR35 ...110 F2
  Offton IP8 ....81 A4
Castle Rise
  Hadleigh IP7 ....149 B7
  2 Haughley IP14 ....51 C1
Castle St Eye IP23 ...117 D2
  Framlingham IP13 ...126 D4
  Thetford IP24 ......16 C5
  Woodbridge IP12 ...147 A5
Castle Terr IP12 .....131 C2
Castle View IP12 ....131 C2
Castleton Ave NR33 ..114 B4
Castleton Cl NR32 ...113 C4
Castleton Way
  Eye IP23 ....117 B3
  Yaxley IP23 ....37 C5
Catchpole Cl **19** NR33 ..11 B1
Catchpole Ct CO10 ..148 B5
Catchpole Way **10** IP31 ..34 E4
Catchpole Wlk IP21 ..21 C5
Caters Rd IP13 ......84 C8
Catesbray IP9 ....150 D3
Cathcart St **8** NR32 ..113 C2
Cathedral Meadows
  IP33 ....154 B1
Catherine Rd IP12 ...146 E6
Catkin Cl CB9 ....132 B7
Cat's La CO10 ....148 C5
Cattawade St **12** CO11 ..104 E4
Catts Cl IP9 ....105 C5
Cattsfield IP9 ....105 C5
Caudle Ave IP27 ....109 E4
Cauldwell Ave IP4 ...139 F6
Cauldwell Hall Rd IP4 ..140 A5
Caulfield Cl **2** IP33 ..122 F3
Causeway
  Haverhill CB9 ....132 C5
  Huntingfield IP19 ...40 F3
  Lowestoft NR33 .....115 B4
Causeway Cl
  Brockdish IP21 ......21 F2
  8 Glemsford CO10 ..77 B3
Causeway End CO11 ..104 D3
Causeway Est IP7 ...79 F7
Causeway The
  Barking IP6 ....125 B2
  Boxford CO10 ....93 C3
  Burwell CB5 ....44 A5
  Earl Soham IP13 ....54 F2
  Great Horkesley CO6 ..102 D1
  Hitcham IP7 ....79 E6
  Isleham CB7 ....29 C5
  Middleton IP17 .....58 A6
  Needham Market IP6 ..125 B2
  4 Occold IP23 .....37 F1
  Ridgewell CO9 ......89 C4
  Soham CB7 ....28 D3
  Walsham le Willows IP31 ..35 B2
  Westhall IP19 ......25 C4
Causton Jun Sch IP11 ..152 E6
Caustons Cl **9** CO10 ..92 B3
Cautley Rd IP18 .....119 D6
Cavan Rd IP1 ....134 D2
Cavendish CE Prim Sch
  CO10 ....76 E1
Cavendish Cl
  7 Lowestoft NR32 ...113 A3
  12 Thurston IP31 ....49 E4
Cavendish Ct **2** CB9 ..132 C4
Cavendish Dr **21** CO11 ..104 D2
Cavendish La CO10 ..76 F2
Cavendish Rd
  Bury St Edmunds IP33 ..122 C6
  Clare CO10 ....90 B8
  Felixstowe IP11 .....152 F3
  Stowmarket IP14 ...124 B6
Cavendish St IP3 ....139 F4
Cavendish Way **1** CO10 ..148 D5
Cavenham Heath National
  Nature Reserve★
  IP28 ....31 C3
Cavenham Rd IP28 ...31 A1

Caville White CB9 132 A6
Cawley Rd CO6 102 A5
Caxton Mews 4 NR34 111 B6
Caxton Rd NR34 111 B6
Cecil Lodge Cl CB8 120 F3
Cecil Rd IP1 155 A4
Cecilia St IP1 155 B2
Cedar Ave IP5 141 A6
Cedar Cl Bacton IP14 51 F6
7 Brantham CO11 104 E5
8 Great Bricett IP7 80 D6
32 Lakenheath IP27 13 F2
Occold IP23 37 F2
Stradbroke IP21 39 B4
Cedar Cres
13 Barrow IP29 47 A2
30 Manningtree CO11 104 E2
Cedar Ct Alderton IP12 99 E5
10 Beck Row, Holywell Row & Kenny Hill IP28 13 B1
Cedar Dr
Lowestoft NR33 114 E5
Worlingham NR34 111 F3
Cedar Rd 1 Barrow IP29 47 A2
7 Bentwaters Airfield IP12 85 E8
Cedarcroft Rd IP1 134 F2
Cedars La IP9 150 D3
Cedars The IP27 109 E5
Cedarwood Prim Sch IP5 141 C6
Celandine Cl NR33 114 C5
Cemetery Hill CB8 120 D7
Cemetery La
East Bergholt CO7 151 A4
Ipswich IP4 135 F1
Woodbridge IP12 146 E4
Cemetery Rd
Ipswich IP4 155 C3
Lakenheath IP27 109 D6
Wickhambrook CB8 61 E2
Central Ave IP3 144 D8
Central Rd IP16 129 C5
Centre Cl NR34 111 C3
Centre Cliff IP18 119 D5
Centre Dr CB8 121 D2
Centre Rd CB7 28 E2
Century Dr IP5 141 E7
Century Rd IP23 117 C4
Chadacre Rd IP29 77 B7
Chaffinch Dr 14 CO12 106 F1
Chaffinch Rd IP32 49 A3
Chaffinch Way IP14 124 F7
Chainey Pieces CB9 132 D5
Chainhouse Rd IP6 125 D3
Chalfont Dr 1 IP17 72 C8
Chalk Hill La IP6 81 F5
Chalk La Culford IP31 32 E5
2 Ixworth IP31 34 B1
Chalk Rd (North) IP33 154 A2
Chalk Rd (South) IP33 154 A2
Chalk Rd IP27 5 D1
Chalkeith Rd IP6 125 E3
Chalkners Cl 7 IP9 150 E3
Chalkstone Mid Sch CB9 132 E6
Chalkstone Way CB9 133 A6
Challice Rd IP33 154 A3
Chalon St IP1 155 A2
Chamberlain Way IP8 138 C2
Chamberlayne Rd IP32 123 E4
Chamberlin Cl 2 IP7 79 F4
Champion Rd IP15 130 E3
Chancellery Mews IP33 154 A3
Chancery La 5 IP14 53 F2
Chancery Rd IP1 155 A2
Chandlers Ct 8 CB5 44 A6
Chandlers Way IP16 129 C3
Chandlers Wlk IP14 124 D4
Chandos Ct 8 IP12 84 A1
Chandos Dr 5 IP12 84 A1
Channel The IP8 81 C1
Chantry Cl IP13 71 C2
Chantry Dr CO6 101 F2
Chantry Gn IP2 138 D3
Chantry High Sch IP2 138 F3
Chantry Rd IP17 128 C3
Chapel Cl
Capel St Mary IP9 150 E3
4 Fressingfield IP21 39 E8
Garboldisham IP22 18 D4
4 Great Waldingfield CO10 92 C6
Chapel Ct 10 NR32 113 D2
Chapel Cut 16 CO11 105 A2
Chapel End Way CO9 89 A1
Chapel Farm La IP23 37 A4
Chapel Field IP8 134 A2
Chapel Hill
Belchamp Walter CO10 90 E3
Framsden IP14 69 B7
Thorpe Morieux IP30 79 A8
Chapel La Belstead IP8 142 C7
Botesdale IP22 36 A6
4 Brockley IP29 63 A1
Claydon IP6 134 A8
Copdock & Washbrook IP8 138 A1
Drinkstone IP30 65 B7
Great Glemham IP17 56 D1
13 Grundisburgh IP13 83 E5
Horham IP21 38 F2
Kirby Row NR35 8 E7
Kirtling CB8 60 E3
Little Cornard CO10 92 B1
2 Somersham IP8 81 C3

Chapel La *continued*
Stoke-by-Nayland CO6 103 B7
Wenhaston with Mells Hamlet IP19 42 C6
Wicken CB7 28 A1
Wickham Market IP13 127 C5
Wortham IP22 36 D7
Chapel Pond Hill IP32 123 C8
Chapel Rd
Beck Row, Holywell Row & Kenny Hill IP28 29 F6
Bedingham NR35 7 C8
Boxted CO4 103 A2
Bradfield Combust with Stanningfield IP29 64 A3
Bucklesham IP10 98 B4
Cockfield IP30 64 D2
Grundisburgh IP13 83 E5
Langham CO4 103 B2
Lowestoft NR33 114 B3
Mendlesham IP14 52 E5
Mutford NR34 10 D3
Old Newton with Dagworth IP14 52 A1
Otley IP6 69 D3
Rendham IP17 56 E3
Ridgewell CO9 89 D4
St Andrew, Ilketshall NR34 8 F2
Saxmundham IP17 128 C3
Saxtead IP13 55 A4
Scole IP21 21 B5
Stoke Ash IP23 37 B2
Theberton IP16 58 C5
Wattisfield IP22 35 C4
Wrentham NR34 26 D5
Chapel Row 3 CB8 60 F8
Chapel St 5 Bildeston IP7 79 F4
Diss IP22 20 C2
Exning CB8 120 B8
9 Lowestoft NR32 113 D2
Peasenhall IP17 56 F8
Steeple Bumpstead CB9 88 E4
Stoke-by-Clare CO9 89 C6
Woodbridge IP12 147 A5
Chapelfield IP12 131 C3
Chaplains Cl CB9 132 D7
Chaplin Rd CO7 151 C5
Chaplin Wlk 16 CO10 92 B3
Chappel Rd CO6 101 C2
Chapple Dr CB9 132 E7
Chare Rd IP31 34 D5
Charity La IP13 54 D6
Charles Adams Cl IP16 129 D6
Charles Ave 8 IP13 83 E5
Charles Burrell High Sch IP24 16 B4
Charles Cl CB8 120 E3
Charles Ind Est IP14 124 E7
Charles Melrose Cl 1 IP28 116 B4
Charles Miller Ct IP16 129 D5
Charles Rd IP11 152 E3
Charles St IP1 155 B3
Charlock Rd 5 IP24 16 D7
Charlotte's IP8 95 F5
Charlton Ave IP1 134 F2
Charrington Cl CB9 133 A4
Charsfield CE Prim Sch IP13 70 B3
Charter Cl IP7 149 D7
Charter Way 6 NR33 114 C5
Chartres Piece NR34 25 E7
Chartwell Cl IP4 140 A5
Chase Cl CB9 132 E7
Chase La 6 CO12 106 F1
Chase Rd IP28 48 C5
Chase The
Beccles NR34 111 E5
Brandon IP27 6 A1
Brantham CO11 104 F5
Dedham CO7 104 A2
Felixstowe IP11 152 F4
Foxearth CO10 91 B7
27 Manningtree CO11 104 E2
20 Martlesham Heath IP5 98 A8
5 Stanton IP31 34 E4
Steeple Bumpstead CB9 88 D4
Chaser Cl 6 IP3 144 C8
Chase's La IP17 72 F6
Chatham Rd 6 IP27 14 A2
Chatsworth Cl 5 NR32 113 A3
Chatsworth Cres
Felixstowe IP11 152 C7
Ipswich IP2 139 A2
Chatsworth Dr IP4 140 E4
Chatten Cl NR34 26 E5
Chattisham Cl IP10 124 E3
Chattisham Rd IP8 95 E4
Chaucer Rd
Felixstowe IP11 152 F3
Ipswich IP1 134 F3
Sudbury CO10 148 B8
Chaucer St NR35 110 A4
Chaukers Cres NR33 114 C5
Chauntry Rd CB9 132 D5
Chedburgh Pl 8 CB9 132 F6
Chedburgh Rd
Chevington IP29 62 C5
Whepstead IP29 62 F5
Chedgrave Rd NR33 114 F5
Chediston Pottery★ IP19 24 B1
Chediston Rd IP19 24 B2
Chediston St
Chediston IP19 41 D8

Chediston St *continued*
Halesworth IP19 118 A3
Chelmer Rd CB9 132 F6
Chelmondiston CE Prim Sch IP9 106 B8
Chelsea Cl
Bury St Edmunds IP33 122 D5
Ipswich IP1 134 F1
Chelsea Ct 4 CO10 148 D5
Chelsea Rd 3 CO10 148 D5
Chelsworth Ave
Ipswich IP4 135 E1
Sudbury CO10 148 F4
Chelsworth Rd IP11 152 D3
Chelsworth Way IP14 124 E3
Cheltenham Ave IP1 135 B1
Chepstow Rd
Bury St Edmunds IP33 122 D3
Felixstowe IP11 152 F5
Ipswich IP1 135 B4
Chequer Field IP12 85 C2
Chequer Sq IP33 154 C2
Chequers La
Bressingham IP22 19 E3
Burston & Shimpling IP22 20 E8
Glemsford CO10 77 B3
Chequers Rd CO11 104 E1
Chequers Rise IP6 81 F5
Cherry Blossom Cl IP8 138 B2
Cherry Hill IP28 30 E3
Cherry Hill Cl 1 NR34 111 F4
Cherry La
Aldeburgh IP15 130 D5
Belton with Browston NR31 2 E8
Lakenheath IP27 13 F2
Cherry La Gdns IP4 140 B7
Cherry Tree Cl
Mundford IP26 6 A8
North Lopham IP22 19 A6
Yaxley IP23 37 B5
Cherry Tree La IP14 53 F1
Cherry Tree Rd
Stowmarket IP14 124 C8
Woodbridge IP12 146 F4
Cherry Tree Row 3 IP31 35 C2
Cherry Tress Sch IP28 47 D5
Cherryfields IP8 134 A1
Cherrytree La
Rickinghall Inferior IP22 36 A7
Soham CB7 28 D3
Cherrytree Rd CO10 148 F5
Cherrywood 10 IP20 22 D5
Chervil Wlk 8 IP24 16 D6
Chesapeake Cl 8 IP9 106 C8
Chesapeake Rd 3 IP3 144 A8
Chesham Rd IP2 155 A1
Chessington Gdns IP1 138 F8
Chester Ct 8 CB9 132 C4
Chester Pl 5 IP31 49 A5
Chester Rd
Felixstowe IP11 152 F5
6 Southwold IP18 119 D5
Chester St 4 IP27 14 A3
Chesterfield Dr IP1 134 F2
Chesterton Cl IP2 138 F1
Chestnut Ave
Great Bricett IP7 80 D6
Lowestoft NR32 112 E2
Chestnut Cl
4 Beccles NR34 111 E3
6 Bentwaters Airfield IP12 85 E8
1 Fornham All Saints IP28 48 B6
Great Barton IP31 49 B6
3 Great Waldingfield CO10 92 C6
Haverhill CB9 132 D6
1 Mildenhall IP28 116 D4
Rushmere St Andrew IP5 136 E1
4 Stowupland IP14 67 A6
Chestnut Cres
Chedburgh IP29 62 D4
6 Lowestoft NR33 114 C3
Chestnut Dr
Claydon IP6 134 C8
6 Soham CB7 28 D4
Chestnut Gr 2 IP14 124 E5
Chestnut Mews 17 CO10 148 C5
Chestnut Rd
Dickleburgh IP21 21 C5
Glemsford CO10 77 A3
Pulham St Mary IP21 21 F8
Stradishall CB8 75 C6
Chestnut Rise 1 CB5 44 A6
Chestnut Way 21 IP27 13 F2
Chestnuts The
5 Great Finborough IP14 66 B4
11 Ipswich IP2 138 C2
Rickinghall Superior IP22 36 A6
Wrentham NR34 26 E5
Chevalier Rd IP11 153 B4
Chevallier St IP1 139 A7
Cheveley Prim Sch CB8 60 E7
Cheveley Rd
Newmarket CB8 121 C3
Woodditton CB8 60 E6
Chevington Rd
Hargrave IP29 62 B6
Horringer IP29 63 A7
Cheviot Rd 3 NR32 112 D2
Chevy Ct 3 CO12 106 E1
Cheyne Ct 10 CO10 148 C5
Chichester Cl IP33 123 B3
Chichester Dr NR33 114 D6
Chichester Rd IP19 118 A5
Chickering Rd IP21 38 D6
Childer Rd IP14 124 D6

Childers Cl 1 IP9 107 A5
Childers Field 2 IP11 152 D5
Chiltern Cres NR32 112 E2
Chilton Ave IP14 124 C6
Chilton Com Prim Sch IP14 124 C7
Chilton Ct CO10 148 E5
Chilton Ind Est CO10 148 F6
Chilton Lodge Rd CO10 148 E5
Chilton Rd IP3 140 C4
Chilton Way IP14 124 B7
Chilton Way Sports Club IP14 124 A7
Chimer's La IP13 70 A4
Chimney Mill Galleries★ IP19 24 C1
Chimney Mills IP28 32 C1
Chimswell Way CB9 132 A6
Chippenham Fen National Nature Reserve★ CB7 45 A8
Chippenham Rd
Chippenham IP28 29 E2
Fordham CB7 29 C1
Moulton CB8 45 F3
Chipperfield Rd 20 NR33 11 C1
Chippings The IP15 130 C6
Chislehurst Rd 5 NR33 114 C4
Chisnall Cl IP7 149 D8
Chiswick Ave IP28 116 C6
Chivers Rd CB9 132 B5
Christ Church Sq NR32 113 E1
Christchurch Dr IP12 146 D3
Christchurch Mansion★ IP1 155 C3
Christchurch St IP4 155 C3
Christmas La
Lowestoft NR32 112 C1
Metfield IP20 23 D3
Christopher Ct 15 CO10 148 C5
Christopher La CO10 148 C5
Church Ave NR32 112 C2
Church Cl
Aldeburgh IP15 130 E4
Bucklesham IP10 98 A5
Carlton IP17 128 D7
4 Cavendish CO10 76 E1
Creeting St Mary IP6 125 F8
Dullingham CB8 59 F4
Exning CB8 120 C8
Fornham St Martin IP28 48 D5
Hepworth IP22 35 A5
Ipswich IP5 141 B8
Kenton IP14 54 B4
Pulham St Mary IP21 22 A8
Rede IP29 62 E3
Risby IP28 47 E5
1 Roydon IP22 20 A3
15 Stanton IP31 34 E4
Wangford NR34 26 B2
Wilby IP21 39 C3
Wortwell IP20 22 F7
Church Cres IP8 138 A6
Church Dr IP13 71 E5
Church Farm Cl IP21 38 F3
Church Farm La 3 IP19 118 A3
Church Farm Rd
Aldeburgh IP15 130 E5
Bramfield IP19 41 F4
Church Field
Monks Eleigh IP7 79 C2
Walberswick IP18 119 A2
Church Field Rd CO10 148 F7
Church Fm Rise IP15 130 F5
Church Gdns
1 Barningham IP31 34 E7
6 Beck Row, Holywell Row & Kenny Hill IP28 29 F6
Church Gn
Bramford IP8 134 B1
Normanston NR32 113 C3
Church Hill Benhall IP17 72 C8
Burstall IP8 95 D7
Cookley IP19 41 C5
Helions Bumpstead CB9 88 B4
Hoxne IP21 38 C8
Kersey IP7 94 A6
Lawford CO11 104 C2
Monks Eleigh IP7 79 C2
Pakenham IP31 49 E6
Ramsey & Parkeston CO12 106 D1
Saxmundham IP17 128 D2
Starston IP20 22 C7
Westhall IP19 25 D3
Whepstead IP29 63 B5
Wyverstone IP14 51 E6
Church La
Aldeby/Wheatacre/Burgh St Peter NR34 2 B1
Aldham IP7 94 D7
Aldringham cum Thorpe IP16 129 E1
Alpheton CO10 77 F5
Arwarton IP9 106 E5
Barnham IP24 16 C2
Barton Mills IP28 116 D1
Baylham IP6 81 E6
Beck Row, Holywell Row & Kenny Hill IP28 29 F6
Bedfield IP13 54 E5
Birds End IP29 62 A7
Blo' Norton IP22 18 E2
Blythburgh IP19 42 E6
Brantham CO11 104 F5
Bressingham IP22 19 E3

Church La *continued*
Brockdish IP21 21 F2
Bromeswell IP12 85 A5
Broome NR35 8 B7
Brundish IP13 55 C8
Bucklesham IP10 98 A5
Burrough Green CB8 59 F2
15 Burwell CB5 44 A5
Carlton IP17 128 D7
1 Cheveley CB8 60 E7
Claydon IP6 134 E8
Clopton IP13 83 E8
Cockfield IP30 64 C1
Copdock & Washbrook IP8 142 A7
Corton NR32 3 C4
Creeting St Mary IP6 125 D7
Dalham CB8 46 C1
Ditchingham NR35 7 F7
Dullingham CB8 59 F4
Earl Soham IP13 55 A2
Exning CB8 120 B8
Felixstowe IP11 152 E6
Finningham IP14 52 A8
Fritton & St Olaves NR31 2 C7
Frostenden NR34 26 C4
Harkstead IP9 106 B6
3 Harwich CO12 107 B3
Hemingstone IP6 82 C8
Hemley IP12 98 E5
Henley IP6 82 E5
Hepworth IP22 35 A5
Hitcham IP7 79 E6
Hockwold cum Wilton IP26 5 A2
Hoo IP13 70 B6
Iken IP12 72 F3
Kennett CB8 45 F6
Kenton IP14 54 A4
Kirton IP10 98 E2
Levington IP10 145 E3
Lowestoft NR33 114 B2
Martlesham IP12 84 B1
Mistley CO11 104 F2
3 Mundford IP26 6 B8
Nayland CO6 102 D5
Newmarket CB8 121 A3
Norton IP31 50 C4
2 Occold IP23 37 F1
Playford IP6 137 B4
Preston St Mary CO10 79 A5
Redenhall with Harleston IP20 22 E7
Rendlesham IP12 85 C7
Rickinghall Superior IP22 36 A5
Ridgewell CO9 89 D3
St James, South Elmham IP19 23 F4
St Mary, South Elmham otherwise Homersfield IP20 23 B8
Semer IP7 79 F1
Shottisham IP12 99 C7
Somersham IP8 81 D3
Spexhall IP19 24 F3
Sproughton IP8 138 B6
Stetchworth CB8 60 A5
Stoke Ash IP23 37 B1
Stonham Earl IP14 67 E6
Stuston IP21 37 D8
Swilland IP6 83 A7
Thelnetham IP22 18 E1
Thwaite IP23 52 F7
Timworth IP31 48 E8
Troston IP31 33 E3
9 Ufford IP13 84 F7
Walberswick IP18 43 C5
Wenhaston with Mells Hamlet IP19 42 C6
Westerfield IP6 135 F4
Westley Waterless CB8 59 D3
Weston NR34 9 E2
Winfarthing IP22 20 B8
Worlington IP28 30 B4
Yaxley IP23 37 C4
Church La Cl IP28 116 D2
Church Meadow
Barton Mills IP28 116 D2
Rickinghall Inferior IP22 35 F6
Church Meadows
1 Henley IP6 82 D6
Waldringfield IP12 98 D7
Church Pk CO10 89 E6
Church Rd Alburgh IP20 7 A2
Ashbocking IP6 68 E1
Bacton IP14 51 F6
Bardwell IP31 34 B4
Barningham IP31 34 E7
Barrow IP29 47 A3
Battisford IP14 66 E1
Bedfield IP13 54 E5
Bentley IP9 142 A1
Beyton IP30 49 F1
6 Bildeston IP7 79 F4
Blaxhall IP12 71 F4
Blundeston NR32 3 A4
Boxted CO4 102 F3
Bradfield Combust with Stanningfield IP29 63 F3
Bradfield St George IP30 64 D6
Brandon IP27 5 E1
Brettenham IP7 65 C1
Brockdish IP21 21 F2
Bruisyard IP17 56 C5
Bulmer CO10 91 C2
Butley IP12 86 B5

Church Rd continued
Carlton CB8 . . . .**74** A8
Chevington IP29 . . . .**62** C6
Combs IP14 . . . .**124** E2
Cotton IP14 . . . .**52** B5
Cratfield IP19 . . . .**40** D5
Crowfield IP6 . . . .**68** C4
Dallinghoo IP13 . . . .**70** C1
Denham IP21 . . . .**38** C5
Dickleburgh & Rushall
  IP21 . . . .**20** F3
Earsham NR35 . . . .**7** A3
Ellingham NR35 . . . .**8** D1
Ellough NR34 . . . .**111** F1
Elmswell IP30 . . . .**50** E2
Felixstowe IP11 . . . .**153** C6
Felsham IP30 . . . .**65** A4
Flixton NR35 . . . .**7** E1
Friston IP17 . . . .**72** F7
Garboldisham IP22 . . . . . .**18** D4
Gillingham NR34 . . . .**9** C7
Gisleham NR33 . . . .**11** A3
Great Barton IP31 . . . . . .**49** A5
1 Great Finborough IP14 . .**66** B4
Great Yeldham CO9 . . . . .**89** F1
Haacketon IP13 . . . .**146** B2
Hedenham NR35 . . . .**7** A8
Henstead with Hulver Street
  NR34 . . . .**26** E8
Heveningham IP19 . . . . . .**40** E3
Holbrook IP9 . . . .**105** F6
Honington IP31 . . . .**33** F5
Kessingland NR33 . . . . . .**11** B1
Kettleburgh IP13 . . . .**70** C7
Kirby Cane NR35 . . . .**8** E1
Knodishall IP17 . . . .**58** A1
Leiston IP16 . . . .**129** B6
Lindsey IP7 . . . .**93** D7
Little Glemham IP13 . . . . .**71** E5
Little Thurlow CB9 . . . . . .**74** D6
Little Waldingfield CO10 . . .**92** E8
Lowestoft NR32 . . . .**113** C3
Market Weston IP22 . . . . .**18** C1
Marlesford IP13 . . . .**71** C5
Mendlesham IP14 . . . .**52** E4
Milden IP7 . . . .**79** B1
Monewden IP13 . . . .**69** F5
5 Moulton CB8 . . . .**45** F3
Mutford NR34 . . . .**10** D3
Nacton IP10 . . . .**145** B4
Newton CO10 . . . .**92** D3
North Lopham IP22 . . . . . .**19** A5
Old Newton with Dagworth
  IP14 . . . .**51** F1
Otley IP6 . . . .**69** C1
Pettaugh IP14 . . . .**68** B4
Playford IP6 . . . .**137** B5
Redlingfield IP23 . . . .**38** C1
Rushbrooke with Rougham
  IP30 . . . .**49** C1
Shelfanger IP22 . . . .**20** B6
Snape IP17 . . . .**72** D5
Stambourne CO9 . . . .**89** B1
Stowmarket IP14 . . . . . .**124** D4
Stowupland IP14 . . . .**67** B7
Stutton IP9 . . . .**105** D5
Sudbury CO10 . . . .**148** E4
Sutton IP12 . . . .**85** A1
Tattingstone IP9 . . . .**105** B7
Theberton IP16 . . . .**58** B4
Thistley Green IP28 . . . . . .**29** F6
6 Thorpeness IP16 . . . . . .**73** F6
Thurston IP31 . . . .**49** E4
Tostock IP30 . . . .**50** B2
Uggeshall NR34 . . . .**26** A3
Weybread IP21 . . . .**22** D2
Wheatacre NR34 . . . .**2** A1
Wicken CB7 . . . .**28** B1
Wilby IP21 . . . .**39** C3
Wingfield IP21 . . . .**39** A7
Worlingworth IP13 . . . . . .**54** E7
Wortham IP22 . . . .**19** F1
Wrabness CO11 . . . .**105** F2
Church Rd N IP21 . . . . . .**21** F3
Church Row
  Framsden IP14 . . . .**69** C6
Church Sq 4 CO8 . . . . .**101** C4
Church St 2 Ashley CB8 . .**60** F8
Belchamp Otten CO10 . . . .**90** D5
1 Boxford CO10 . . . .**93** C3
Boxted CO4 . . . .**103** A4
5 Chelmondiston IP9 . . .**106** C8
6 Clare CO10 . . . .**90** A8
Diss IP22 . . . .**20** C2
Exning CB8 . . . .**120** C8
Eye IP23 . . . .**117** D2
Fordham CB7 . . . .**29** A4
Framlingham IP13 . . . . . .**126** D3
2 Fressingfield IP21 . . . . .**39** E8
Gestingthorpe CO9 . . . . . .**90** F1
Groton CO10 . . . .**93** C5
1 Hadleigh IP7 . . . .**149** D5
23 Harleston IP20 . . . . . .**22** D6
5 Harwich CO12 . . . . . .**107** C3
Hundon CO10 . . . .**75** D3
10 Isleham CB7 . . . .**29** C5
Lavenham CO10 . . . .**78** E4
Orford IP12 . . . .**131** C2
Peasenhall IP17 . . . .**56** F8
Saxmundham IP17 . . . . . .**128** D3
12 Southwold IP18 . . . . .**119** D5
Steeple Bumpstead CB9 . . .**88** D4
Stoke-by-Nayland CO6 . . .**102** E6

Church St continued
Stradbroke IP21 . . . .**39** B4
Sudbury CO10 . . . .**148** B4
Wangford NR34 . . . .**26** B2
Wetherden IP14 . . . .**51** A1
Wetheringsett-cum-Brockford
  IP14 . . . .**53** A6
Withersfield CB9 . . . .**74** A3
Woodbridge IP12 . . . . . .**147** A5
Worlingworth IP13 . . . . . .**54** F7
Church Terr IP13 . . . . .**127** C6
Church View
  Halesworth IP19 . . . . . .**118** E4
  Harleston IP20 . . . .**22** E6
  1 Haughley IP14 . . . . . .**51** C1
  Leiston IP16 . . . .**129** B6
  Stowlangtoft IP31 . . . . . .**50** B7
  Wyverstone IP14 . . . .**51** E6
Church View Cl IP12 . . .**147** C7
Church Walks IP33 . . . .**154** C1
Church Wlk
  Aldeburgh IP15 . . . .**130** E4
  Hadleigh IP7 . . . .**149** C5
  3 Laxfield IP13 . . . .**40** B3
  Long Melford CO10 . . . . .**77** E1
  Mildenhall IP28 . . . .**116** B4
  Shelfanger IP22 . . . .**20** B6
  Stowmarket IP14 . . . . . .**124** D6
  Sturmer CB9 . . . .**133** C2
  2 Sudbury CO10 . . . . . .**148** C5
Church Wood IP19 . . . .**118** E4
Churchfields Dr 1 CB9 . . .**88** D3
Churchgate CO10 . . . . . .**77** B3
Churchgate St
  Bury St Edmunds IP33 . . .**154** B2
  15 Soham CB7 . . . .**28** D4
Churchill Ave
  Hadleigh IP7 . . . .**149** D7
  Haverhill CB9 . . . .**132** F7
  Ipswich IP4 . . . .**140** B5
  Newmarket CB8 . . . .**120** D5
Churchill Cl
  3 Lawshall IP29 . . . .**63** D1
  Lowestoft NR32 . . . .**113** C4
  7 Woodbridge IP12 . . . .**146** E4
Churchill Cres IP13 . . . .**127** C7
Churchill Ct CB8 . . . . . .**120** F3
Churchill Dr
  Mildenhall IP28 . . . .**116** B5
  Sudbury CO10 . . . .**148** C8
Churchill Rd
  Halesworth IP19 . . . . . .**118** B5
  6 Southwold IP18 . . . . .**119** C8
  Thetford IP24 . . . .**16** C6
Churchman Cl IP12 . . . .**147** B8
Churchway 3 IP22 . . . . .**36** A8
Churchyard IP14 . . . . . .**154** C2
Churchyard The IP28 . . .**116** B4
Cinnabar Cl 11 IP8 . . . .**142** E8
Civic Dr IP1 . . . .**155** A2
Clacton Rd CO11 . . . . .**104** E1
Clapgate La IP3 . . . . . .**140** A1
Clapham Rd Central 3
  NR32 . . . .**113** D1
Clapham Rd S NR32 . . .**113** D1
Clare Ancient House Mus★
  CO10 . . . .**90** A8
Clare Ave IP12 . . . .**146** E4
Clare Castle (remains of)★
  CO10 . . . .**90** A8
Clare Castle Ctry Pk★
  CO10 . . . .**90** B8
Clare Cl
  2 Bury St Edmunds IP33 .**122** D4
  Mildenhall IP28 . . . .**116** B3
  Stowmarket IP14 . . . . . .**124** E3
Clare Cty Prim Sch
  CO10 . . . .**90** A8
Clare Mid Sch CO10 . . . . .**90** B8
Clare Pl CB8 . . . .**121** B7
Clare Rd Hundon CO10 . . .**75** E2
  Ipswich IP4 . . . .**139** F8
  2 Kessingland NR33 . . . .**11** C1
  Poslingford CO10 . . . .**76** A2
  3 Tattingstone IP9 . . . .**105** B8
Clarence Rd
  7 Clare CO10 . . . .**76** A1
  Ipswich IP3 . . . .**140** B1
  1 Lowestoft NR32 . . . .**113** D2
  Sudbury CO10 . . . .**148** C6
Clarendale Est CB9 . . . . .**74** C7
Clarendon Rd CB9 . . . . .**132** D5
Clark Rd NR35 . . . .**110** C7
Clark Wlk IP32 . . . .**122** D5
Clark's Dro CB7 . . . .**28** B4
Clarke Cl IP22 . . . .**20** C1
Clarke's La NR34 . . . .**8** F3
Clarke's Rd 3 CO12 . . . .**106** F2
Clarkes La NR34 . . . . . .**114** C6
Clarkson Rd NR32 . . . . .**112** D1
Clarkson St IP1 . . . . . .**155** A3
Claude Oliver Cl CO11 . .**104** D1
Claude St IP1 . . . .**155** B3
Claudian Cl CB9 . . . . . .**133** B5
Claverton Way IP4 . . . .**140** D5
Clay Hill Dennington IP13 . .**55** F5
  Hintlesham IP8 . . . .**95** B5
  Monks Eleigh IP7 . . . .**79** D2
  Ubbeston IP19 . . . .**40** E3
Clay La Bacton IP14 . . . . .**51** F6
  Hadleigh IP7 . . . .**94** F4
  Henley IP6 . . . .**82** E7
  Hepworth IP22 . . . .**35** B5
  Ixworth IP31 . . . .**34** A2
  Lavenham CO10 . . . .**78** E4
  Stoke Ash IP23 . . . .**37** B1
Clay Rd
  20 Bury St Edmunds IP32 . .**48** C5

Clay Rd continued
  Bury St Edmunds IP32 . . .**122** E8
  Fornham All Saints IP32 . . .**48** B5
Clay St Soham CB7 . . . . .**28** D4
  Thornham Magna IP23 . . . .**36** F1
Claydon Dr NR32 . . . . .**112** F3
Claydon High Sch IP6 . . .**134** C8
Claydon Prim Sch IP6 . . . .**82** B5
Clayhall La CO10 . . . .**92** C7
Clayhall Pl CO10 . . . .**92** C7
Clayhill La Hitcham IP7 . . .**79** F6
  Wattisham IP7 . . . .**80** A6
Clayhill Rd IP17 . . . . . .**128** E5
Clayhills 8 IP19 . . . . . .**118** A3
Clayhive Dr 4 CB9 . . . . .**132** D5
Claypits Ave 1 CO8 . . . .**101** D4
Claypits La CO10 . . . .**91** B7
Clayton Ct IP12 . . . . . .**146** D3
Clayton Rd 2 CO12 . . . .**106** E1
Clearwing Cl 15 IP8 . . . .**142** E8
Clematis Cl 4 IP28 . . . . .**30** B1
Clemence St NR32 . . . . .**113** C1
Clement Prim Sch
  CB9 . . . .**132** D5
Clement Rd NR33 . . . . .**115** B6
Clement Sq NR33 . . . . .**115** B6
Clement's Way 11 IP28 . . .**30** B4
Clementine Gdns IP4 . . .**140** A5
Clements Cl
  3 Haverhill CB9 . . . . . .**132** D5
  2 Scole IP21 . . . .**20** F1
Clements Dr 2 CB9 . . . .**132** D5
Clements La CO10 . . . . .**132** D5
Clements Rd 4 IP12 . . . .**84** C6
Clench Cl IP4 . . . .**155** C3
Clench La IP9 . . . .**105** E6
Clerk's Piece NR34 . . . . .**111** D3
Clermont Ave CO10 . . . .**148** C8
Cleveland Rd NR33 . . . .**115** C7
Cleves Rd CO10 . . . .**132** B4
Cley Ct 1 CB9 . . . .**132** A7
Clicket Hill CO8 . . . . . .**101** D4
Cliff Farm La NR33 . . . . .**11** B4
Cliff La
  Great Yarmouth NR31 . . . . .**3** E3
  Ipswich IP3 . . . .**139** E3
Cliff La Prim Sch IP3 . . . .**139** E3
Cliff Quay IP3 . . . .**139** D2
Cliff Rd
  Felixstowe IP11 . . . .**153** D6
  Harwich CO12 . . . .**107** B2
  Ipswich IP3 . . . .**139** E3
  Lowestoft NR33 . . . .**115** C6
  Waldringfield IP12 . . . . . .**98** C7
Clifford Dr NR33 . . . . . .**114** C5
Clifford Rd IP4 . . . .**139** F5
Clifford Rd Air Raid Shelter
  Mus★ IP4 . . . .**139** F5
Clifford Rd Prim Sch
  IP4 . . . .**139** F6
Cliffs The NR33 . . . . . .**115** B2
Clifton Rd NR33 . . . . . .**115** C7
Clifton Way IP7 . . . .**149** E4
Clifton Wood 2 IP9 . . . .**105** E7
Cliftonville NR33 . . . . . .**115** B2
Cliftonville Rd NR33 . . . .**115** B3
Clink The IP19 . . . .**41** C5
Clint Hill IP31 . . . .**33** F6
Clint Rd IP23 . . . .**37** D1
Clive Ave IP1 . . . .**135** B2
Clockhall La CO10 . . . . . .**75** D3
Clockhouse La IP14 . . . . .**67** F7
Cloncurry Gdns IP11 . . .**152** D3
Clopton Dr 2 CO10 . . . . .**91** E7
Clopton Gdns IP7 . . . . .**149** E4
Clopton Pk CB8 . . . .**62** A3
Clopton Rd IP6 . . . .**136** C7
Close The Corton NR32 . . . .**3** B4
  9 Harwich CO12 . . . . . .**107** A2
  Kennett CB8 . . . .**45** F7
  North Lopham IP22 . . . . . .**19** A6
Clough Dr 10 IP26 . . . .**4** E5
Cloutings Cl IP17 . . . . . .**128** C6
Clovelly Cl IP4 . . . .**140** F4
Clovelly Rise NR32 . . . .**113** B3
Clover Cl Ipswich IP2 . . .**138** F4
  Needham Market IP6 . . . .**125** D3
Clover Field CB9 . . . . . .**132** B6
Clover Way
  Lowestoft NR32 . . . .**113** C5
  1 Red Lodge IP28 . . . . . .**30** C1
Cloverfields Dr CB7 . . . . .**28** C5
Cloverfields 2 IP31 . . . . .**49** E4
Clovers IP14 . . . .**124** C6
Clowes Ct NR34 . . . . . .**111** B5
Clowes's Cnr IP14 . . . . . .**54** D2
Cluanie Orch CO10 . . . . .**76** F1
Clumps The IP12 . . . . . .**86** A4
Coach La CB8 . . . .**60** E7
Coachman's Paddock 3
  IP9 . . . .**105** E7
Coachmans Ct IP1 . . . . .**155** B2
Coakers La IP13 . . . .**70** A1
Coalpit La IP29 . . . .**46** F4
Coast Guards The 8
  IP16 . . . .**73** F6
Coast Rd IP16 . . . .**3** C5
Coastguard La 22 NR33 . .**11** C1
Coates Dro 1 CB7 . . . . . .**29** C5
Cobbler's Cnr IP8 . . . . . .**95** B5
Cobbold Cl IP14 . . . .**66** C1
Cobbold Mews IP4 . . . . .**155** C3
Cobbold Rd
  Felixstowe IP11 . . . .**153** A4
  Woodbridge IP12 . . . . . .**146** E7
Cobbold St Diss IP22 . . . .**20** B2

Cobbold St continued
  Ipswich IP4 . . . .**155** C3
Cobden Pl IP4 . . . .**155** C3
Cobham Rd IP3 . . . .**140** C2
Coblers Way 3 CO10 . . . .**92** B7
Cock La CO10 . . . .**78** F2
Cock Rd IP14 . . . .**52** A6
Cock's Rd IP23 . . . .**117** F1
Cockfield CE Prim Sch
  IP30 . . . .**64** C1
Cockfield Hall La IP6 . . . .**135** F2
Cockfield Rd IP30 . . . . . .**65** A3
Cockpen Rd CB7 . . . .**28** F1
Cockrell's Rd CO6 . . . . .**102** A2
Cocks Gn La IP30 . . . . . .**64** A5
Coddenham Rd IP6 . . . . .**67** E1
Coddington Way 8 IP31 . . .**34** B1
Codling Rd IP32 . . . . . .**123** E6
Cody Rd IP3 . . . .**140** C4
Coggeshall Rd
  Dedham CO7 . . . .**104** A2
  Foxash Estate CO7 . . . . .**103** F1
Colbeck Rd CB9 . . . . . .**132** C8
Colchester Cl 4 IP27 . . . .**13** F2
Colchester Rd
  Bures CO8 . . . .**101** C4
  Dedham CO7 . . . .**103** C2
  Ipswich IP4 . . . .**135** F1
  10 Manningtree CO11 . . .**104** C2
  Wormingford CO6 . . . . . .**102** A1
Cold Store Rd IP11 . . . . .**152** B2
Coldfair Cl IP17 . . . .**129** B3
Coldfair Gn Prim Sch
  IP17 . . . .**129** B2
Coldham La IP23 . . . .**36** D2
Cole Ness Rd IP3 . . . . . .**144** A8
Cole St IP21 . . . .**39** B2
Coleman Cl IP22 . . . .**20** C1
Coleridge Rd IP1 . . . . . .**134** F3
Coles Croft IP19 . . . .**42** C6
Coles Hill IP19 . . . .**42** C7
Coles Oak La CO7 . . . . .**103** E3
Coles View IP19 . . . .**42** C6
Colethorpe La IP29 . . . . .**46** F3
College Cl 8 IP29 . . . . . .**63** A8
College Gn IP11 . . . .**153** C5
College Heath Mid Sch
  IP28 . . . .**116** C6
College Heath Rd
  IP28 . . . .**116** D6
College La
  Bury St Edmunds IP33 . . .**154** B1
  Worlingham NR34 . . . . . .**111** F2
College Meadows 2
  NR32 . . . .**113** A3
College Rd
  Framlingham IP13 . . . . . .**126** C4
  Hockwold cum Wilton IP26 . .**4** F3
  Lowestoft NR33 . . . .**115** C6
  2 Soham CB7 . . . .**28** D3
College St
  Bury St Edmunds IP33 . . .**154** B1
  Ipswich IP3 . . . .**155** B2
Collett's Wlk IP12 . . . . .**146** E5
Colletts Chase CO6 . . . .**101** F2
Collimer Cl 2 IP9 . . . . . .**106** C8
Collin's Hill CB7 . . . .**29** B1
Collings Pl CB8 . . . .**120** D5
Collingwood Ave 6 IP3 .**140** B3
Collingwood Fields
  CO7 . . . .**151** B6
Collingwood Rd IP12 . . .**146** F7
Collins Cl IP17 . . . .**128** B3
Collinson's IP2 . . . .**138** D5
Colman Rd 4 NR32 . . . . . .**3** D4
Colne Rd CO8 . . . .**101** C4
Colne Springs CO9 . . . . .**89** D4
Colne Valley Rd CB9 . . .**132** E5
Colne Rd IP11 . . . .**153** B6
Colneis Jun Sch IP11 . . .**153** B6
Colneys Cl CO10 . . . . . .**148** B7
Colsterdale NR33 . . . . . .**114** D3
Coltsfoot Cl
  1 Ixworth IP31 . . . .**34** B1
  8 Lowestoft NR33 . . . . .**114** F4
  7 Wickhambrook CB8 . . .**61** E2
Coltsfoot Cnr IP22 . . . . .**123** F5
Coltsfoot Rd IP2 . . . . . .**138** E4
Columbia Cl IP5 . . . . . .**141** A7
Columbine Cl 7 NR33 . . .**114** F4
Columbine Gdns IP2 . . .**138** E4
Columbine Way 3 IP23 . .**36** D2
Columbines The CO10 . . .**76** F1
Columbyne Cl IP14 . . . . .**67** A7
Colville Rd NR33 . . . . . .**114** E6
Colville Way NR33 . . . . .**114** C3
Comber Cl IP21 . . . .**21** A2
Combs Cl NR33 . . . .**114** F2
Combs Ford Prim Sch
  IP14 . . . .**124** E4
Combs Gn IP14 . . . .**66** D2
Combs La IP14 . . . .**124** D4
Combs Wood Dr IP14 . . .**124** D3
Combs Wood Nature
  Reserve★ IP14 . . . .**124** E2
Comet Way IP28 . . . . . .**116** B5
Comfrey Way IP24 . . . . . .**16** D6
Commerce Way 3
  CO11 . . . .**104** E3
Commercial Rd
  Ipswich IP1 . . . .**155** A1
  Lowestoft NR32 . . . .**115** C8
Commister La 14 IP31 . . . .**34** B1
Commodore Rd NR33 . . .**114** D6
Common Gate Dro CB7 . . .**29** A5

Common La
  Beccles NR34 . . . .**111** C5
  Bromeswell IP12 . . . . . .**147** C7
  Syleham IP21 . . . .**22** A2
  Troston IP31 . . . .**33** E3
Common La Ind Est
  NR34 . . . .**111** C6
Common La N NR34 . . . .**111** B6
Common Rd
  Aldeby NR34 . . . .**10** B7
  Botesdale IP22 . . . .**36** B5
  Bressingham IP22 . . . . . .**19** F4
  Hopton IP22 . . . .**18** C2
  St James, South Elmham
  IP19 . . . .**23** D4
  Scole IP21 . . . .**21** B4
  Shelfanger IP22 . . . .**19** F7
Common St 3 CO10 . . . . .**90** A8
Common The
  Beccles NR34 . . . .**111** E5
  Claydon IP6 . . . .**134** A6
  1 Harleston IP20 . . . .**22** D5
  Knodishall Common
  IP17 . . . .**129** A1
  Leiston IP16 . . . .**129** F7
  Southwold IP18 . . . .**119** C5
Compass Cl IP27 . . . . . .**109** D4
Compass St NR32 . . . . .**113** C2
Compiegne Way IP33 . . .**154** B3
Conach Rd IP12 . . . . . .**146** E5
Coney Cl IP24 . . . .**16** A6
Coney Hill NR34 . . . . . .**111** D3
Coney Weston Rd
  Coney Weston IP31 . . . . . .**34** D8
  Fakenham Magna IP31 . . . .**33** F6
  Sapiston IP31 . . . .**34** A6
Congreve Rd IP1 . . . . . .**135** A3
Coniston Cl IP11 . . . . . .**153** E7
Coniston Rd IP3 . . . . . .**140** B2
Coniston Sq E IP3 . . . . .**140** B2
Coniston Sq W IP3 . . . . .**140** B2
Connaught Rd
  Haverhill CB9 . . . .**132** C5
  Ipswich IP5 . . . .**134** D2
Conrad Cl NR33 . . . .**114** D6
Conrad Rd NR33 . . . . . .**114** D6
Consent Ln IP7 . . . .**79** E4
Constable Cl
  Halesworth IP19 . . . . . .**118** A2
  Lowestoft NR32 . . . .**112** F1
  3 Manningtree CO11 . . .**104** C3
  Nayland-with-Wissington
  CO6 . . . .**102** A5
Constable Ct 15 IP20 . . . .**22** D6
Constable Rd
  Bury St Edmunds IP33 . . .**122** E4
  Felixstowe IP11 . . . .**153** B4
  Haverhill CB9 . . . .**132** B7
  Ipswich IP4 . . . .**155** C4
  Sudbury CO10 . . . .**148** C6
Constable Way IP14 . . . .**124** B7
Constantine Rd IP1 . . . .**155** A2
Constitution Hill
  Ipswich IP1 . . . .**139** B8
  2 Needham Market IP6 . .**125** D5
  Southwold IP18 . . . .**119** D4
  Sudbury CO10 . . . .**148** D6
Convalescent Hill
  IP11 . . . .**153** A3
Conway Cl
  Felixstowe IP11 . . . .**153** C7
  4 Haverhill CB9 . . . . . .**132** C6
  Ipswich IP2 . . . .**139** B2
Conway Rd 2 IP32 . . . . . .**48** C3
Conyers Way IP31 . . . . . .**49** A6
Cook's Dro IP28 . . . .**12** D2
Cook's La
  Hawkedon IP29 . . . .**62** C5
  Wortwell IP20 . . . .**22** F6
Cooke Cl NR33 . . . .**114** F2
Cooke Rd NR33 . . . .**114** F2
Cookley & Walpole CE Prim
  Sch IP19 . . . .**41** B5
Cookley La CO10 . . . .**75** D4
Cookley Rd Cookley IP19 . .**41** B5
  Eye IP23 . . . .**38** A5
Cooks Cl IP5 . . . .**141** E8
Cooks Hill Boxted CO4 . . .**103** A4
  Letheringham IP13 . . . . . .**70** C4
Cooks Rd IP30 . . . .**50** E2
Coombers IP9 . . . .**150** D3
Cooper Cl 2 IP17 . . . . . .**128** C4
Cooper La IP29 . . . .**63** E8
Cooper Rd IP6 . . . .**68** C1
Cooper's Cl CB8 . . . .**60** A5
Cooper's La CO7 . . . . . .**103** F3
Cooper's Rd IP6 . . . .**82** C6
Coopers Cl IP6 . . . .**83** A6
Coopers La NR33 . . . . . .**11** B1
Coopers Dr 27 NR33 . . . .**11** C1
Coopers Rd 30 IP5 . . . . .**98** A8
Coopers Way 4 IP6 . . . . .**82** A5
Coopersfield 6 IP12 . . . .**53** F2
Copdock Intc IP8 . . . . . .**138** B2
Copdock Prim Sch IP8 . . . .**95** F4
Copellis Cl CB9 . . . .**132** C8
Copeman Rd 3 IP22 . . . . .**20** A3
Copland Way NR34 . . . . .**10** A3
Copleston High Sch
  IP4 . . . .**140** A5
Copleston Rd IP4 . . . . . .**140** B5
Coplow Dale 2 NR33 . . . .**114** C3
Copper Beech Dr 5
  NR33 . . . .**114** D6
Copper Gr 14 IP8 . . . . . .**142** E8
Copperfield Rd IP2 . . . . .**138** C5
Copperfield Way 11 CB5 . .**44** B5
Coppers Cl IP33 . . . .**154** C1

Copperwheat Ave
  IP18 . . . .**119** B8
Coppice Cl IP12 . . . . . .**147** A6
Coppice Ct NR33 . . . . .**115** A6
Coppice The IP31 . . . . .**49** A6
Copplestone Cl **12** NR34 . . . .**9** F4
Coprolite St IP3 . . . . . .**139** E5
Copse Cl IP33 . . . .**123** B1
Copswood Cl IP5 . . . . . .**141** F7
Copy Hill CB9 . . . .**132** C1
Coral Dr IP7 . . . .**134** D1
Coram St IP7 . . . .**149** A6
Cordell Pl CO10 . . . .**91** E8
Cordell Rd CO10 . . . . . .**91** E8
Corder Rd IP4 . . . .**139** D8
Cordwinders CO7 . . . . .**151** F3
Cordy's La IP11 . . . .**152** B6
Coriander Dr IP24 . . . . . .**16** D6
Corks La IP7 . . . .**149** C6
Corkway Dro IP26 . . . . . .**4** A4
Cormorant Dr IP14 . . . .**124** F5
Corn Craft (Craft Centre)★
  IP7 . . . .**79** D2
Corn Hatches La IP7 . . . .**80** E1
Cornard Rd CO10 . . . . .**148** D5
Cornerth Cres CO10 . . . .**148** F4
Cornfield Ave IP27 . . . .**109** D7
Cornfield Cres **5** NR32 . . . .**3** D4
Cornfield Rd IP33 . . . . .**154** A3
Cornfields IP21 . . . .**21** B5
Cornflower Cl IP2 . . . . .**138** E3
Cornford Way **13** CO11 . .**104** D2
Cornhill
  Bury St Edmunds IP33 . .**154** B2
  Ipswich IP1 . . . .**155** B3
Cornhill Wlk Sh Ctr
  IP33 . . . .**154** B2
Cornish Hall End Rd
  CO9 . . . .**89** A1
Cornish Wlk IP33 . . . . .**122** E8
Cornmill Gn **9** IP30 . . . . .**50** D1
Cornmills Rd CB7 . . . . . .**28** E2
Cornwall Cl **25** CO11 . . . .**104** D2
Cornwall Rd IP11 . . . . .**152** F5
Cornwallis Cl IP28 . . . . .**32** C1
Cornwallis Ct IP33 . . . .**154** C1
Cornwallis Rd CB9 . . . .**132** D4
Cornwell Cl CB7 . . . .**29** B4
Coronation Ave IP12 . . . .**99** D6
Coronation Dr IP12 . . . .**152** D3
Coronation Rd IP4 . . . .**140** B5
Coronation Rise **1** CO10 . .**92** C6
Corporation Ave IP1 . . .**139** B1
Corsbie Cl IP33 . . . .**154** B3
Corsican Pine Cl CB8 . .**120** F5
Corton CE VC Prim Sch
  NR32 . . . .**3** D4
Corton Long La NR32 . .**113** B8
Corton Rd Ipswich IP3 . .**140** B1
  Lowestoft NR32 . . . . . .**113** D6
Cosford Rd IP7 . . . .**94** C7
Cotes The CB7 . . . .**28** B6
Cotman Ave **8** CO11 . . . .**104** D2
Cotman Cl **3** NR32 . . . .**113** B6
Cotman Rd IP3 . . . .**140** A1
Cotmer Rd NR33 . . . . . .**114** D7
Cotswold Ave IP1 . . . . .**135** B1
Cotswold Dr **1** CO10 . . . .**91** E7
Cotswold Way NR32 . . .**112** E2
Cottesford Cl IP7 . . . . .**149** E5
Cottingham Rd IP8 . . . .**138** B2
Cotton End Rd CB8 . . . .**120** C8
Cotton La
  Bury St Edmunds IP33 . .**154** C3
  Cotton IP14 . . . .**52** A6
Cotton La Flats IP33 . . .**154** C3
Coucy Cl IP13 . . . .**126** C4
Coulson La IP27 . . . .**5** F1
Coupals Cl CB9 . . . .**133** A4
Coupals Prim Sch
  CB9 . . . .**133** B5
Coupals Rd CB9 . . . . . .**133** C4
Courier Cl IP28 . . . .**116** B5
Court Knoll (Earthworks)★
  CO6 . . . .**102** A4
Court St CO6 . . . .**102** D5
Courtenay Cl CO10 . . . .**148** B8
Courts The
  Felixstowe IP11 . . . . . .**153** B4
  Playford IP6 . . . .**137** B4
Covehite Ct **4** CB9 . . . . .**132** C4
Covell Cl IP33 . . . .**122** C4
Coverdale **6** NR33 . . . . .**114** E3
Covert Cl IP12 . . . .**132** E7
Covert Rd IP18 . . . .**119** C8
Covert Sycamore **5**
  IP24 . . . .**16** D6
Covey Dr IP27 . . . .**109** E6
Covey Way IP27 . . . . . .**109** E6
Cow and Sheep Dro
  IP28 . . . .**29** E7
Cow Fair **7** IP30 . . . .**50** D1
Cowell St IP7 . . . .**139** C3
Cowle's Dro IP26 . . . .**4** D1
Cowley Rd IP11 . . . . . .**153** A4
Cowper St IP4 . . . .**140** B6
Cowslip Cl
  Bury St Edmunds IP32 . .**123** F5
  Ipswich IP2 . . . .**138** E4
Cowslip Cres NR33 . . . .**114** C5
Cowslip Way IP6 . . . . . .**125** D3
Cox Cl IP5 . . . .**141** B6
Cox Hill CO10 . . . .**93** C3
Cox La Great Barton IP31 . .**49** B6
Cox's Cl NR34 . . . .**111** C3
Cox's Hill CO11 . . . . . .**104** D2
Cox's La IP18 . . . .**119** C8

Coxhall Rd IP9 . . . .**142** E1
Coxs Cl CB9 . . . .**132** A5
Coytes Gdns IP1 . . . . . .**155** B2
Crabbe St
  Aldeburgh IP15 . . . . . .**130** F4
  Ipswich IP4 . . . .**140** A6
Crabbe's Cl **8** IP26 . . . . . .**4** E5
Crabtree Cl IP19 . . . . . .**118** B2
Crabtree La Aldeby NR34 . . .**9** F8
  Little Horkesley CO6 . . .**102** B1
Crabtree Meadow **5**
  IP30 . . . .**50** F2
Crabtree Rise IP21 . . . . .**21** F2
Cracks La CO10 . . . .**77** C1
Crag Farm Rd IP12 . . . .**131** E7
Crag Path IP15 . . . .**130** F3
Craig Cl **7** IP11 . . . .**107** D8
Craig's La CO8 . . . .**101** B3
Cramswell Cl NR34 . . . .**132** B4
Cranberry Sq **2** IP3 . . . .**144** C7
Cranborne Chase **1**
  IP4 . . . .**136** A1
Cranbrook La CO10 . . . .**77** C1
Crane Cl IP12 . . . .**146** D3
Crane Hill London Rd
  IP2 . . . .**138** E4
Cranes Meadow **31** IP20 . .**22** D6
Cranesbill Dr IP32 . . . .**123** E5
Cranesbill Rd NR33 . . . .**114** F3
Cranfield Cl **4** NR33 . . . .**115** A3
Cranfield Pk IP8 . . . .**95** D7
Cranleigh Rd NR33 . . . .**114** F3
Cranley Gn Rd IP12 . . . .**117** D2
Cranley La IP23 . . . .**117** F1
Cranmoregreen La
  CO10 . . . .**77** C1
Cranwell Cres IP3 . . . . .**140** C1
Cranwell St **5** IP1 . . . . .**141** C7
Cranworth Gdns **1**
  NR32 . . . .**112** F4
Cranworth Rd IP7 . . . . .**149** E4
Cratfield La IP19 . . . . . .**40** C4
Cratfield Rd
  Bury St Edmunds IP32 . .**123** E4
  Fressingfield IP21 . . . . .**39** F8
  Huntingfield IP19 . . . . .**40** E5
Craven Way CB8 . . . . . .**120** E6
Crawford Ave IP14 . . . . .**66** D8
Crawford Cl **5** IP14 . . . . .**51** A1
Crawford La **2** IP5 . . . . .**141** C7
Crayford Rd CO10 . . . . .**148** B8
Creed Wlk IP32 . . . .**122** D7
Creeting Hills IP6 . . . . .**125** F6
Creeting La IP14 . . . .**67** B7
Creeting Rd IP14 . . . . . .**124** E6
Creeting St Mary Prim Sch
  IP6 . . . .**125** F8
Crepping Hall Dr IP9 . . .**105** C5
Crescent Rd
  Aldeburgh IP15 . . . . . .**130** E4
  Felixstowe IP11 . . . . . .**153** A4
  Ipswich IP1 . . . .**155** A3
Crescent The
  Dullingham CB8 . . . . . .**59** D5
  East Harling NR16 . . . . .**18** C8
  Great Horkesley CO6 . . .**102** D1
  6 Soham CB7 . . . .**28** D3
  Stowmarket IP14 . . . . .**124** D4
  7 Thurston IP31 . . . . . .**49** D4
  Wicken CB7 . . . .**28** A1
  Wickham Market IP13 . .**127** B6
Crescents The IP18 . . . .**119** B8
Cresmedow Way IP30 . . .**50** F2
Crespigny Rd IP15 . . . . .**130** E3
Cresslands La IP29 . . . . .**76** D8
Crestland Bsns Pk
  CO10 . . . .**92** A8
Crestview Dr NR32 . . . .**113** A4
Crick's Rd
  Beck Row, Holywell Row
    & Kenny Hill IP28 . . . .**30** A6
  Thistley Green IP28 . . . .**29** F6
Cricket Field Rd CB8 . . .**121** B2
Cricket Hill Rd IP11 . . . .**152** D5
Cricketers Cl CO10 . . . .**148** C4
Crimbold's La IP30 . . . . .**64** D1
Crimp Cramp La NR34 . . .**11** B8
Crisp Cl **3** NR32 . . . . . .**113** B4
Crisp Rd NR35 . . . .**8** E7
Crispin Cl CB9 . . . .**132** B5
Crockatt Rd IP7 . . . .**149** E8
Crockfords Rd CB9 . . . .**121** A1
Crocus Cl IP2 . . . .**138** E4
Croft Cl Beccles NR34 . . . .**111** E4
  Diss IP22 . . . .**20** C2
  10 Harleston IP20 . . . . .**22** D6
  3 Wickhambrook CB8 . . .**61** E2
Croft Ct **13** CO10 . . . . . .**148** C5
Croft La Diss IP22 . . . . . .**20** C2
  Haverhill CB9 . . . .**132** C4
  Trimley St Martin IP10 . . .**98** C2
Croft Lea CO10 . . . .**92** E8
Croft Pl IP28 . . . .**30** A6
Croft Rd **15** Isleham CB7 . . .**29** C5
  Newmarket CB8 . . . . . .**120** F5
  Sudbury CO10 . . . .**148** C6
Croft Rise IP33 . . . .**123** B1
Croft St **2** IP2 . . . .**139** C3
Croft The **6** Bures CO8 . .**101** C5
  1 Glemsford CO10 . . . . .**77** A2
  Great Yeldham CO9 . . . . .**90** A1
  1 Lowestoft NR32 . . . . .**113** C1
  2 Sudbury CO10 . . . . . .**148** B8
Crofton Rd IP4 . . . .**140** B7
Cromarty Rd IP4 . . . . . .**140** B8
Crome Wlk NR32 . . . . . .**113** B6
Cromer Rd IP1 . . . .**134** F1

Crompton Rd
  Ipswich IP2 . . . .**138** F7
  Lowestoft NR33 . . . . . .**114** E7
Cromwell Ave NR34 . . . .**111** B3
Cromwell Cl IP13 . . . . .**127** B6
Cromwell Ct NR33 . . . .**114** D2
Cromwell Rd
  Ringsfield NR34 . . . .**9** C2
  Weeting IP27 . . . .**5** E4
  Weston NR34 . . . .**111** B1
Cromwell Sq IP1 . . . . . .**155** B2
Crooked House Gall The★
  CO10 . . . .**78** D4
Cropley Ct IP32 . . . .**123** E4
Cross Cl CB9 . . . .**132** E7
Cross Field Way CO4 . . .**103** A3
Cross La CI IP27 . . . . . .**109** D6
Cross Rd IP20 . . . .**22** C6
Cross St **1** Bungay NR35 . .**110** B4
  Drinkstone IP30 . . . .**65** C7
  Elmswell IP30 . . . .**50** E2
  Eye IP23 . . . .**117** C2
  Felixstowe IP11 . . . . . .**152** E6
  Hoxne IP21 . . . .**38** C7
  Leiston IP16 . . . .**129** C5
  Sudbury CO10 . . . .**148** B4
Cross The IP23 . . . .**117** C2
Cross Ways IP30 . . . .**50** E2
Crossfields CO6 . . . . . .**102** E7
Crossgate Field **3** IP11 .**152** E5
Crossing Rd IP22 . . . . . .**20** C1
Crossley Gdns IP1 . . . . .**134** C2
Crotchets Cl **2** IP9 . . . .**150** E3
Croutel Rd IP11 . . . . . .**153** D5
Crow La IP14 . . . .**124** D5
Crow St IP31 . . . .**34** D8
Crowbrook Pl IP30 . . . . .**78** C8
Crowhurst Cl **4** NR33 . .**114** D4
Crowland Cl **1** IP2 . . . . .**139** A2
Crowland Rd CB9 . . . . .**132** D6
Crowley Rd IP6 . . . .**125** D4
Crown Cl **10** IP12 . . . . . .**84** A1
Crown Cnr IP6 . . . .**68** B1
Crown Cres **15** IP31 . . . .**34** B1
Crown Gn IP22 . . . .**20** E6
Crown La
  Coney Weston IP31 . . . . .**17** E1
  Ixworth IP31 . . . .**34** B1
  Orford IP12 . . . .**131** C2
  Wickham Market IP13 . .**127** C6
Crown Meadow Wlk **3**
  NR32 . . . .**113** C2
Crown Mill **3** IP30 . . . . .**50** F2
Crown Pl IP14 . . . .**147** A4
Crown Rd IP26 . . . .**6** B8
Crown St Brandon IP27 . . .**14** E3
  Bury St Edmunds IP33 . .**154** C1
  Dedham CO7 . . . .**103** F3
  Felixstowe IP11 . . . . . .**152** E5
  Ipswich IP1 . . . .**155** B3
  Leiston IP16 . . . .**129** C5
  Needham Market IP6 . . .**125** D5
  Stowmarket IP14 . . . . .**124** D7
Crown St E **5** NR32 . . . .**113** E2
Crown St W NR32 . . . . .**113** D2
Crown Swimming Pool
  IP1 . . . .**155** B3
Crown Wlk CB8 . . . .**121** A4
Crownfield Rd **8** CO10 . . .**77** A3
Crownfields **2** IP13 . . . .**84** F7
Crownland Rd IP31 . . . . .**35** C1
Crowswell Ct **6** IP11 . . .**107** D8
Croxton Cl IP30 . . . .**98** E2
Croxton Rd IP24 . . . .**16** C7
Crunch Croft CB9 . . . . .**133** C3
Cryspen Ct IP33 . . . . . .**154** B3
Cuckfield Ave IP3 . . . . .**140** E3
Cuckoo Hill (Tumulus)★
  IP28 . . . .**47** C8
Cuckoo Hill CO8 . . . . . .**101** C5
Cuckoo La IP20 . . . .**22** F6
Cucumber La NR34 . . . .**111** D1
Culford Rd
  Bury St Edmunds IP28 . . .**48** C6
  Ingham IP31 . . . .**32** F1
Culford St CB8 . . . .**32** D1
Culford Terr IP33 . . . . .**154** A1
Culford Wlk IP11 . . . . .**152** C3
Culley Way **2** NR31 . . . . .**3** C4
Cullingham Rd IP1 . . . .**139** A6
Cullum Rd IP33 . . . .**154** B1
Culvers Meadow **4** IP31 .**34** E4
Culzean Gdns **1** NR32 . .**113** A4
Cumberland Cl
  4 Felixstowe IP11 . . . .**153** D6
  5 Southwold IP18 . . . .**119** D5
Cumberland Mews
  IP12 . . . .**147** A4
Cumberland Pl **13** NR32 . .113 E2
Cumberland Rd IP18 . . .**119** D5
Cumberland St
  Ipswich IP1 . . . .**155** A4
  Woodbridge IP12 . . . . .**147** A4
Cundle La IP17 . . . .**72** C5
Cundys Marsh **5** IP15 . .**130** E5
Cunningham Way
  NR33 . . . .**115** B3
Curlew Cl IP27 . . . .**109** D5
Curlew Gn NR32 . . . . . .**112** C1
Curlew Rd IP2 . . . .**138** D4

Curlews The IP33 . . . . .**123** C1
Curriers' La IP1 . . . .**155** A2
Curtis Cl IP3 . . . .**138** C1
Curtis Dr **1** IP26 . . . .**4** D5
Curtis Way IP5 . . . .**141** D7
Curwen Rd IP14 . . . . . .**124** C6
Curzon Rd IP3 . . . .**140** A5
Cuthbert Cl **2** IP24 . . . . .**16** D6
Cutler Rd **5** NR32 . . . . .**112** D2
Cutler St IP1 . . . .**155** B2
Cutler's La IP14 . . . .**66** A6
Cutlers Cl CO7 . . . .**151** D7
Cutter's La IP31 . . . .**49** E8
Cutting's Rd IP21 . . . . . .**21** E4
Cypress Way **4** NR33 . .**114** F7

D

Daffodil Cl IP2 . . . .**138** E3
Daffodil Wlk IP2 . . . . . .**114** C5
Dagworth La IP14 . . . . . .**66** D8
Daimler Rd IP1 . . . .**134** C2
Dains Pl IP11 . . . .**152** C7
Daires La IP12 . . . .**147** C7
Dairy Dr **4** IP28 . . . .**48** B6
Dairy Hill IP19 . . . .**118** B4
Dairy La Ipswich IP31 . . . .**34** A2
  Mutford NR34 . . . .**10** C3
Dairy Rd IP7 . . . .**80** A1
Daisy Ave IP32 . . . .**123** F5
Daisy Gn La IP23 . . . . . .**52** D3
Daisy Hill IP21 . . . .**39** F8
Daking Ave CO10 . . . . . .**93** B3
Daking's Drift **6** IP19 . . .**118** A3
Dakota **6** IP28 . . . .**30** A8
Dale End NR33 . . . .**114** E2
Dale Hall La IP1 . . . . . .**135** B1
Dale Hall Prim Sch
  IP1 . . . .**135** B2
Dale Haven NR33 . . . . .**114** D3
Dale Hill IP14 . . . .**53** A6
Dale Rd
  Fressingfield IP21 . . . . .**22** D1
  Stanton IP31 . . . .**34** E5
Dale Tree Rd **11** IP29 . . .**47** A2
Dales Rd IP1 . . . .**135** A1
Dales View IP8 . . . .**95** F4
Dales View Rd IP1 . . . . .**135** A1
Dalham Pl CB9 . . . .**132** F6
Dalham Rd Ashley CB8 . . .**61** B8
  Moulton CB8 . . . .**45** F2
Dallinghoo Rd IP13 . . . .**127** A6
Dalton Rd IP1 . . . .**155** A3
Dam La Burgate IP22 . . . .**36** E7
  Kessingland IP32 . . . . . .**11** A1
Damask Cl **5** NR33 . . . .**114** E4
Damselfly Rd **5** IP3 . . . .**144** C8
Dandalan Cl IP1 . . . . . .**138** E8
Dane Cl CB9 . . . .**133** E8
Dane Comm CB9 . . . . .**133** D8
Dane Hill Rd CB8 . . . . . .**45** E7
Danes Cl IP14 . . . .**124** C5
Danes Ct CO10 . . . .**148** F2
Danescourt Ave IP14 . . .**124** C5
Daneway Gdns IP16 . . .**129** C4
Danforth Cl IP13 . . . . . .**126** B4
Daniel Gdns IP3 . . . . . .**117** C3
Daniels Cl **8** CO10 . . . . .**92** B7
Daphne Rd IP12 . . . . . .**131** C2
Darby Cl IP32 . . . .**123** F6
Darby Rd NR34 . . . .**111** B3
Darcy Cl IP12 . . . .**123** E4
Dark La
  Dickleburgh & Rushall
    IP21 . . . .**20** E2
  Easton IP13 . . . .**70** E7
Darkings La IP30 . . . . . .**64** F2
Darrell Rd **1** IP11 . . . . .**153** H11
Darrow Gn Rd IP20 . . . . .**7** A4
Darrow Wood La IP22 . . .**20** A5
Darsham Cl **1** IP11 . . . .**152** D5
Darsham Marshes Nature
  Reserve★ IP17 . . . .**57** F8
Darsham Rd IP17 . . . . . .**58** B8
Darsham Sta IP17 . . . . . .**57** E8
Darsham Vale **8** NR32 . .**112** F4
Darter Cl **4** IP3 . . . .**144** C8
Darwin Cl IP28 . . . .**116** C6
Darwin Pl CB8 . . . .**121** B1
Darwin Rd IP4 . . . .**139** F5
Dash End CB9 . . . .**133** F8
Dash End La CB9 . . . . . .**133** F8
Dashwood Cl IP8 . . . . . .**138** C1
Daundy Cl IP2 . . . .**138** D5
Davall Cl **16** CO12 . . . . .**106** E1
Davey Cl Bungay NR35 . .**110** E4
  Ipswich IP3 . . . .**139** F1
Davey La IP13 . . . .**70** B4
Davey's La IP31 . . . .**34** C4
Davidson Cl CO10 . . . . . .**92** B2
Davoren Wlk IP32 . . . . .**122** D7
Daw St CO9 . . . .**89** A3
Dawes Cl IP9 . . . .**150** D4
Dawson Dr **1** IP5 . . . . .**141** C7
Dawson Mews NR32 . . .**113** A6
Day's La IP31 . . . .**34** E8
Days Gn IP9 . . . .**150** D3
Days Rd IP9 . . . .**150** D3
Dazeley's La CO7 . . . . .**151** F2
De Burgh Rd **2** CO10 . . .**76** A1
De Greys Cl **8** CO10 . . . .**92** B3
De Havilland Ct **7** IP28 .**116** B5
De Vere Cl IP13 . . . .**126** C3
Deacon Ct **8** IP11 . . . . .**153** D6
Deacon's Cl **2** CO10 . . . .**78** D4
Dead La Ardleigh CO7 . . .**103** E1

Dead La continued
  Bures St Mary CO8 . . . .**101** F5
  Lawford CO11 . . . .**104** E1
Deadman's La
  Benhall IP17 . . . .**128** A2
  Combs IP14 . . . .**66** E1
  Rendham IP17 . . . .**57** A3
  Stoke Ash IP23 . . . .**53** A8
  Woolpit IP30 . . . .**50** C1
Deane's Cl **1** CO12 . . . .**107** A1
Deans Cl CB9 . . . .**132** E7
Deben Ave Ipswich IP5 . .**141** F8
  Martlesham IP5 . . . . . .**137** F5
Deben Dr CO10 . . . .**148** E6
Deben High Sch IP11 . . .**152** F4
Deben La
  Waldringfield IP12 . . . . .**98** E7
  6 Woodbridge Airfield
    IP12 . . . .**85** B3
Deben Mill Bsns Ctr
  IP12 . . . .**147** B6
Deben Pool IP12 . . . . . .**147** A4
Deben Rd Haverhill CB9 . .**132** F6
  Ipswich IP1 . . . .**134** F1
  Saxmundham IP17 . . . .**128** C4
  Woodbridge IP12 . . . . .**147** B5
Deben Rise IP14 . . . .**53** F1
Deben Valley Dr IP5 . . . .**141** C7
Deben Way IP11 . . . . . .**152** E3
Debenham CE High Sch
  IP14 . . . .**53** E3
Debenham Rd
  Crowfield IP6 . . . .**68** E5
  Winston IP14 . . . .**53** F1
Debenham Sports Ctr
  IP14 . . . .**53** E2
Debenside The IP12 . . . .**147** C7
Deck Wlk IP32 . . . .**122** C4
Decoy Rd IP27 . . . .**12** F8
Dedham Dr **4** NR32 . . . .**112** F3
Dedham Meade CO7 . . .**103** F2
Dedham Rd
  Ardleigh CO7 . . . .**103** E1
  Boxted CO4 . . . .**103** A3
  Lawford CO11 . . . .**104** C2
Deepdale NR33 . . . .**114** E2
Deepdale Rd **6** CO12 . . .**107** A2
Deer Row NR35 . . . .**8** D5
Defoe Rd IP1 . . . .**135** A4
Degas Gdns **1** NR32 . . .**113** B6
Delbrig Dro CB7 . . . .**29** A5
Delf Cl IP7 . . . .**149** E7
Delius Way
  Lowestoft NR33 . . . . . .**115** A6
  1 Stowmarket IP14 . . . .**124** C7
Dell Ct NR33 . . . .**114** E7
Dell Prim Sch NR33 . . .**114** E7
Dell Rd NR33 . . . .**114** E7
Dell Rd E NR33 . . . .**114** F7
Dellview IP11 . . . .**153** B5
Dellwood Ave IP11 . . . .**153** B5
Delph Dro IP28 . . . .**12** D1
Delph Rd IP27 . . . .**109** D7
Demesne Gdns **6** IP5 . . .**98** A8
Dene Rd NR32 . . . .**113** D4
Denes High Sch The
  NR32 . . . .**113** D4
Denham Cl IP33 . . . . . .**122** D5
Denham Cnr IP22 . . . . . .**38** D3
Denham La IP29 . . . .**47** A2
Denham Low Rd IP21 . . .**38** C5
Denham Rd Dalham CB8 . .**61** C8
  Denham IP29 . . . .**47** A1
  Hoxne IP21 . . . .**38** D6
Denmark Gdns **1** IP9 . .**105** E7
Denmark Hill IP22 . . . . .**20** C2
Denmark La IP22 . . . . . .**20** B2
Denmark Rd
  Beccles NR34 . . . .**111** B6
  9 Lowestoft NR33 . . . .**115** D8
Denmark Rise IP22 . . . . .**20** C2
Denmark St IP22 . . . . . .**20** C2
Denney's La IP17 . . . . . .**128** D7
Dennington CE Prim Sch
  IP13 . . . .**55** D6
Dennington Rd
  Dennington IP13 . . . . . .**55** F8
  Framlingham IP13 . . . . .**126** B5
  Laxfield IP13 . . . .**40** B1
Denny Ave IP14 . . . .**66** D8
Denny's Hill IP20 . . . . . .**23** A6
Denton Cl IP2 . . . .**138** D1
Denton Dr NR33 . . . . . .**114** F5
Denton Rd IP20 . . . .**7** C2
Depden La IP29 . . . .**62** C5
Depot Rd CB8 . . . .**120** E6
Derby Cl IP4 . . . .**140** A5
Derby Pl **8** IP31 . . . .**49** A5
Derby Rd IP3 . . . .**140** A4
Derby Way CB8 . . . .**120** D5
Dereham Ave IP3 . . . . .**139** F3
Dereham La **17** IP22 . . . .**20** B2
Derry Brook La **1** IP14 . .**53** F7
Derwent Gdns **5** NR32 . .**113** A4
Derwent Rd
  15 Bury St Edmunds IP32 . .**48** C5
  Ipswich IP3 . . . .**139** F3
Desmond Cl **9** NR32 . . .**112** D2
Dettingen Way IP33 . . . .**122** D5
Devereaux Ct IP7 . . . . .**155** C3
Devil's La IP17 . . . .**42** C1
Devils Dyke Nature Reserve★
  CB5 . . . .**44** A3
Devlin Rd IP8 . . . .**138** B1
Devon Cl IP32 . . . .**122** E8

Devon Rd
Felixstowe IP11 . . . . . . **152** F5
7 Stowupland IP14 . . . . . **67** A4
Devon Way 10 CO12 . . . **106** E1
Devonshire Rd IP3 . . . . **139** F5
Dewar La IP5 . . . . **141** C7
Dewarrene Dr IP27 . . . . . **5** E3
Dhobi Pl IP3 . . . . **138** F7
Dial La IP1 . . . . **155** B3
Diamond Cl IP1 . . . . . . **134** D1
Dickens Ct 6 NR32 . . . . . **3** A4
Dickens Rd IP2 . . . . . . **138** E6
Dickinson Terr 8 IP5 . **141** D7
Dickleburgh Prim Sch
IP21 . . . . **21** B5
Dickleburgh Rd IP21 . . . **21** A5
Dicks Mount NR34 . . . . **10** D7
Dicky Hill IP20 . . . . **22** D7
Didsbury Cl IP2 . . . . . . **138** D2
Digby Cl 5 IP5 . . . . **98** A7
Digby Rd IP4 . . . . **140** C7
Dillistone Ct CB8 . . . . **133** C3
Dillwyn St W IP1 . . . . . **155** A3
Dinsdale Rd IP16 . . . . . **129** C6
Diomed Dr IP31 . . . . . . **49** A5
Dip The CB8 . . . . **121** D2
Diprose Dr NR32 . . . . . **113** A6
Dirty La IP21 . . . . **21** F7
Diss Church Jun Sch
IP22 . . . . **20** C3
Diss High Sch IP22 . . . . **20** D3
Diss Inf Sch IP22 . . . . . **20** D2
Diss Mus★ IP22 . . . . . . **20** C3
Diss Rd
Burston & Shimpling IP22 . **20** E5
Garboldisham IP22 . . . . . **18** D4
3 Scole IP21 . . . . **20** F1
South Lopham IP22 . . . . **19** C4
Wattisfield IP22 . . . . **35** D5
Diss Sta IP22 . . . . **20** D2
Ditchingham Dam
NR35 . . . . **110** B5
Ditchingham Gr IP4 . . . **140** F6
Ditton Cl CB8 . . . . **121** A1
Ditton Gn CB8 . . . . **60** B5
Ditton Lodge Fst Sch
CB8 . . . . **121** B2
Dixon Cl 11 CO11 . . . . **104** D2
Dixon Dr NR33 . . . . . . **114** E2
Dobbs Drift IP5 . . . . . . **141** F7
Dobbs La IP5 . . . . **137** E1
Dobson Way NR34 . . . . **111** C5
Dock La IP12 . . . . **147** C7
Dock Rd
Felixstowe IP11 . . . . . . **152** C1
Ramsholt IP12 . . . . **99** B4
Dock St IP2 . . . . **155** B1
Dockfield Ave 5 CO12 . **106** F2
Dockings La 11 CB7 . . . . **29** C5
Doctor Watson's La
IP5 . . . . **137** A1
Doctor's La Ashen CO10 . **89** E5
Orford IP12 . . . . **131** C3
Pulham St Mary IP21 . . . . **22** A4
Doctors La IP21 . . . . . . **39** B4
Dodmans IP9 . . . . **150** E3
Dodson Vale IP5 . . . . . **141** C7
Does Field IP14 . . . . . . **68** C6
Dog La Shelfanger IP22 . . **20** A8
Tannington IP13 . . . . **55** A4
Dogs Head St IP4 . . . . **155** B2
Dogs La NR34 . . . . **9** C7
Dogwood Cl IP3 . . . . . **140** D2
Dogwood Wlk 31 IP27 . . **13** F2
Doit La IP22 . . . . **20** A3
Doit The IP22 . . . . **19** F2
Dolphin Cl 3 NR33 . . . **115** B4
Dombey Rd IP2 . . . . . . **138** E5
Dome Leisure Ctr
IP28 . . . . **116** E4
Donegal Rd IP1 . . . . . . **134** D2
Donkey La
Bradfield Combust with
Stanningfield IP29 . . . . . **63** F2
Friston IP17 . . . . **72** F7
Dooley Rd IP11 . . . . . . **152** C3
Dorchester Rd
Bury St Edmunds IP33 . . **122** D3
Ipswich IP3 . . . . **140** D1
Doric Pl IP12 . . . . **147** A4
Doris St CB8 . . . . **120** F3
Dorking Rd NR32 . . . . . . **3** A6
Dorley Dale IP14 . . . . . **114** E3
Dorothy Hodgkin Ct
NR34 . . . . **111** B4
Dorset Cl IP4 . . . . **135** F1
Double St IP13 . . . . . . **126** D3
Doubleday Cl IP22 . . . . **20** C2
Doug Smith Cl CB8 . . . **120** F6
Doughty Wylie Cres
IP16 . . . . **58** B4
Douglas La
Halesworth IP19 . . . . . . **118** C5
Lowestoft NR33 . . . . . . **114** D3
Douglas Rd 11 CO12 . . **107** A2
Doune Way 9 IP20 . . . . **22** D6
Dove Cl 15 Debenham IP14 **53** F2
9 Harleston IP20 . . . . . **22** D5
Saxmundham IP17 . . . . **128** C4
Dove Cres 9 CO12 . . . . **106** E1
Dove Gdns 2 IP14 . . . . **67** A5
Dove House Rd CB9 . . . **132** E4
Dove La IP23 . . . . **117** D2
Dove Rd IP18 . . . . **119** B7
Dove St Ipswich IP4 . . . **139** E5

Dove St *continued*
Lowestoft NR32 . . . . **113** D2
Dovedale
Felixstowe IP11 . . . . . . **152** D3
2 Lowestoft NR33 . . . . **114** F3
Dovehouse Hill IP29 . . . **77** D7
Dover Rd IP3 . . . . **140** B4
Dovercourt Sta CO12 . . **107** B2
Dovercourt Swimming Pool
CO12 . . . . **107** B1
Dowes Hill Cl NR34 . . . **111** B2
Dowling Rd CO8 . . . . . **101** C2
Downham Bvd IP3 . . . . **144** C7
Downham Way IP27 . . . . **6** A1
Downing Cl
Bury St Edmunds IP32 . . **123** E5
Ipswich IP3 . . . . **138** F2
Mildenhall IP28 . . . . . . **116** D5
Newmarket CB8 . . . . . . **121** B2
2 Woodbridge IP12 . . . **146** E4
Downing Dr 4 IP31 . . . . **49** A6
Downing Prim Sch
IP2 . . . . **138** F2
Downlands 5 IP7 . . . . . **80** F1
Downs Cres CB9 . . . . . **132** D6
Downs Farm La IP20 . . . **23** B7
Downs Pl CB9 . . . . **132** D6
Downs The
Felixstowe IP11 . . . . . . **152** D5
Rushbrooke with Rougham
IP30 . . . . **49** C2
Downside IP14 . . . . . . **124** B6
Downside Cl IP2 . . . . . **142** F8
Downton Dr CB9 . . . . . **132** C6
Dowson Dr 2 NR33 . . . . **11** B1
Drab's La IP13 . . . . **83** E7
Drake Cl IP14 . . . . **124** A6
Drake Inf Sch 3 IP24 . . **16** C7
Drake Rd CO10 . . . . . . **148** E7
Drake Sq S IP3 . . . . . . **140** B2
Drake's Heath NR32 . . . **113** B2
Drapers Cl 1 IP7 . . . . . **149** E6
Drapers Hill IP31 . . . . . **39** B5
Drapers La
Ditchingham NR35 . . . . . . **8** A7
Helions Bumpstead CB9 . . **88** A5
Drapery Comm 3 CO10 . **77** A2
Draymans Way IP3 . . . . **139** E3
Drays The CO10 . . . . . . **91** D7
Drift Ct IP6 . . . . **125** D4
Drift Rd IP27 . . . . **109** C8
Drift The Botesdale IP22 . **36** A7
2 East Bergholt CO11 . . **104** E5
Exning IP28 . . . . **120** A8
Fornham St Martin IP31 . . **48** D5
Holbrook IP9 . . . . **105** E5
Ipswich IP3 . . . . **140** C1
Ipswich IP4 . . . . **140** A6
Levington IP10 . . . . **145** E3
24 Martlesham Heath IP5 . **98** A8
Middleton IP17 . . . . **58** B6
Polstead CO6 . . . . **93** D2
Sudbury CO10 . . . . **92** B3
Tostock IP30 . . . . **50** B2
Wickham Market IP13 . . . **127** D8
Driftway The
16 Grundisburgh IP13 . . . **83** E5
Ipswich IP4 . . . . **140** A6
Drinkstone Gn Cl IP30 . . **65** B7
Drinkstone Mills★
IP30 . . . . **50** C1
Drinkstone Rd
Beyton IP30 . . . . **49** F2
Gedding IP30 . . . . **65** B5
Drinkwater Cl CB8 . . . . **120** E4
Drive The
Harwich CO12 . . . . **107** A1
Heveningham IP19 . . . . . **41** B3
Hitcham IP7 . . . . **80** A8
Lowestoft NR32 . . . . . . **112** F2
Martlesham Heath IP5 . . . **98** B8
Rushbrooke with Rougham
IP30 . . . . **64** B8
Southwold IP18 . . . . . . **119** B7
Drout's La IP31 . . . . . . **34** E7
Drove La IP14 . . . . **51** A3
Drove The IP27 . . . . . . **14** D8
Drover's Ct IP11 . . . . . **152** B8
Drovers Ave NR32 . . . . **123** F5
Druids IP22 . . . . **20** B6
Druids' La IP22 . . . . . . **20** A7
Drum Field 5 CO7 . . . . **103** D5
Drummond Ct IP33 . . . . **154** A1
Drury Cl 19 NR33 . . . . . **11** C1
Drury Dr CO10 . . . . . . **148** D8
Drury La Milden IP7 . . . . **79** B1
Ridgewell CO9 . . . . **89** D3
Wicken CB7 . . . . **28** B1
Drury Pk IP17 . . . . **72** D5
Drury Rd IP6 . . . . **134** C2
Drybridge Hill IP12 . . . **146** E4
Dryden Rd IP1 . . . . **135** A3
Dublin Rd IP23 . . . . . . **53** E8
Duchess Dr
Newmarket CB8 . . . . . . **121** D2
Woodditton CB8 . . . . . . **60** C8
Duck Dro CB7 . . . . **12** A6
Duckamere IP8 . . . . . . **134** A1
Ducks La CB8 . . . . **120** C7
Ducksen Rd IP14 . . . . . **52** E4
Duddery Hill CB9 . . . . . **132** D5
Duddery Rd CB9 . . . . . **132** E5
Dudley St IP27 . . . . . . **109** F1
Duffs Hill CO10 . . . . . . **77** A4
Duke St Beccles NR34 . . **111** D3
4 Bildeston IP7 . . . . . . **79** F4
Hadleigh IP7 . . . . **149** D5
Haughley IP14 . . . . **51** C1

Duke St *continued*
Hintlesham IP8 . . . . **95** C5
Ipswich IP3 . . . . **139** E4
7 Stanton IP31 . . . . . . **34** E4
Duke's Dr IP19 . . . . . . **118** A2
Duke's Meadow IP12 . . **146** D3
Duke's Pk IP12 . . . . . . **146** D3
Duke's Rd NR35 . . . . . . **110** C2
Dukes Cl IP11 . . . . **153** D6
Dukes Head St 6 NR32 . **113** E2
Dukes Meadow
1 Beccles NR34 . . . . . . **111** C4
Cockfield IP30 . . . . **64** D3
Dukesway 1 NR35 . . . . . **7** F4
Dulgate Rd NR35 . . . . . . **7** B7
Dullingham Rd
Newmarket CB8 . . . . . . **120** F1
Woodditton CB8 . . . . . . **59** F7
Dullingham Sta CB8 . . . **59** D5
Dumbarton Rd 3 IP4 . . **136** C1
Dumfries Rd 2 IP4 . . . **136** C1
Dumplingbridge La
IP27 . . . . **109** C6
Dun Cow Rd NR34 . . . . **10** B8
Dunburgh Rd NR34 . . . . **9** A6
Duncan Rise CO9 . . . . . **89** F1
Dunche's La IP6 . . . . . . **67** E4
Dunhill La IP22 . . . . . . **35** B5
Dunlin Rd IP2 . . . . **138** E2
Dunlop Rd IP2 . . . . **138** F6
Dunn Cl IP7 . . . . **149** E5
Dunnoch Cl 18 IP14 . . . **67** A5
Dunsey Wood Cl CB9 . . **132** C7
Dunstall Gn Rd CB8 . . . **61** B6
Dunster Dr 16 CB9 . . . **132** C6
Dunston Dr NR32 . . . . . **112** E4
Dunston's Cnr IP6 . . . . **82** B8
Dunton Gr IP7 . . . . **149** E4
Dunwich Ct 5 CB9 . . . **132** A6
Dunwich Heath Nature
Reserve★ IP17 . . . . . . **58** F7
Dunwich La IP17 . . . . . **41** A2
Dunwich Mus★ IP17 . . **43** B1
Dunwich Pl 2 IP31 . . . . **49** A5
Dunwich Rd
Blythburgh IP19 . . . . . . **42** F5
4 Southwold IP18 . . . . **119** D5
Westleton IP17 . . . . **58** D8
Dunwich Underwater
Exploration Ex★
IP12 . . . . **131** B3
Dunwich Way 11 NR32 . **112** F4
Durban Cl IP31 . . . . . . **118** B2
Durban Rd NR33 . . . . . **115** B7
Durbar Terr IP33 . . . . . **154** A3
Durbidge's Hill IP22 . . . **20** E5
Durham Ct 22 IP32 . . . . **48** C5
Durham Rd 2 IP27 . . . . **14** A3
Durham Way CB8 . . . . . **120** C5
Durrant Rd IP7 . . . . . . **149** D7
Durrant View IP25 . . . . **141** E7
Durrant's Cl 8 NR33 . . . **11** C1
Dutchman St NR33 . . . . **114** D7
Dux St IP7 . . . . **65** B1
Dyer Ct IP7 . . . . **149** F5
Dyers La CO10 . . . . **92** E2
Dyers Rd CO9 . . . . **89** C1
Dyke St IP1 . . . . **155** B3
Dyson's Dro CB5 . . . . . **44** A7

E

Eades Wlk NR33 . . . . . **114** C5
Eagle Cl NR34 . . . . **26** E5
Eagle Dr IP15 . . . . **130** C6
Eagle La CB8 . . . . **59** E5
Eagle St IP4 . . . . **155** C2
Eagle Way IP5 . . . . **98** A4
Eagle Wlk IP32 . . . . . . **122** E8
Eagles Cl IP11 . . . . . . **152** F4
Earl Soham Prim Sch
IP13 . . . . **54** F2
Earl's Cl IP19 . . . . **118** A2
Earls Cl IP11 . . . . **153** D6
Earls Gn 6 CB9 . . . . . **132** A6
Earlsbrook IP14 . . . . . . **51** E6
Earlsfield IP27 . . . . **13** F2
Earlsford Rd Mellis IP23 . **36** F5
Thornham Parva IP23 . . . . **37** A4
Earsham CE VA Fst Sch
NR35 . . . . **7** F4
Earsham Dam NR35 . . . **110** A4
Earsham Rd NR35 . . . . . **7** F6
Earsham St NR35 . . . . . **110** A4
Earth La NR32 . . . . **2** F5
Easdale NR33 . . . . **114** E2
Easlea Rd IP32 . . . . . . **123** C4
East Anglia Transport Mus★
NR33 . . . . **114** A3
East Barton Rd IP31 . . . **49** B5
East Bergholt CE Prim Sch
CO7 . . . . **151** B5
East Bergholt High Sch
CO7 . . . . **151** D6
East Church St NR16 . . . **19** B8
East Cl IP33 . . . . **123** C6
East Cliff IP18 . . . . . . **119** E5
East Dock Rd CO12 . . . **106** F3
East End La CO7 . . . . . **104** E6
East End Rd
East Bergholt CO7 . . . . . **151** F4
Stonham Aspal IP14 . . . . **68** C6
East Fen Dro CB7 . . . . . **28** E4
East Fen Rd CB7 . . . . . **29** D5
East Gn IP18 . . . . **119** D5
East Harling Rd NR16 . . **18** F8
East La Bawdsey IP12 . . . **99** F2

East La *continued*
Dedham CO7 . . . . **104** A2
Middleton IP17 . . . . **58** B6
Ufford IP13 . . . . **85** A7
East Lawn IP4 . . . . **140** C8
East Mill Gn IP9 . . . . . **104** F7
East Point Pavillion Visitor
Ctr★ NR33 . . . . **115** D8
East Rd CB7 . . . . **29** C5
East Side CO4 . . . . **103** A2
East St 6 Harwich CO12 . **107** B2
Southwold IP18 . . . . . . **119** D5
Sudbury CO10 . . . . **148** D5
East View Carlton IP17 . **128** E3
Freckenham IP28 . . . . . . **29** E3
Eastcliff IP11 . . . . **153** E7
Eastern Ave
Haverhill CB9 . . . . **132** D6
18 Soham CB7 . . . . . . **28** D4
Eastern Cl IP4 . . . . **140** C4
Eastern Way
Bury St Edmunds IP32 . . **123** C6
Elmswell IP30 . . . . **50** F2
Lowestoft NR32 . . . . . . **113** B1
Eastfen Dro IP26 . . . . . . **5** B2
Eastfield Gdns 3 NR33 . **114** E4
Eastgate Sh Ctr IP33 . . **155** C3
Eastgate St IP33 . . . . . **154** C2
Eastland Ct IP11 . . . . . **152** D7
Eastlands IP21 . . . . **39** B4
Eastlands La IP23 . . . . . **52** B8
Eastlands Rd IP16 . . . . **129** C6
Eastlow Hill (Tumulus)★
IP30 . . . . **64** C8
Eastlowhill Rd IP30 . . . . **64** B8
Easton Farm Pk★ IP13 . **70** D5
Easton La
Hacheston IP13 . . . . **70** F5
Reydon IP18 . . . . **27** A1
Easton Prim Sch IP13 . . **70** E5
Easton Rd
Hacheston IP13 . . . . **71** A4
Woodbridge Airfield IP12 . **85** B3
Eastward Ho IP16 . . . . **129** C5
Eastward Pl IP14 . . . . . **124** C7
Eastwood Ave NR33 . . . **114** F6
Eaton Cl IP11 . . . . **152** C7
Eaton Gdns IP11 . . . . . **152** C7
Eccles Rd IP2 . . . . **138** D2
Economy Rd NR33 . . . . **115** C7
Eddies The NR33 . . . . . **114** E4
Eddowes Rd 6 IP6 . . . . **82** B5
Edelweiss Cl 1 NR33 . . **114** C4
Eden Rd 5 Haverhill CB9 **132** E5
Ipswich IP4 . . . . **140** B5
Edendale NR32 . . . . . . **112** D2
Edes Paddock 9 IP31 . . **49** A6
Edgar Sewter Prim Sch
IP19 . . . . **118** B5
Edgeborough Cl CB8 . . . **46** A3
Edgecomb Rd IP14 . . . . **124** D3
Edgefield Ave 15 CO11 . **104** D2
Edgerton Rd NR32 . . . . **115** A7
Edgworth Rd CO10 . . . . **148** C4
Edies La CO6 . . . . **102** B7
Edinburgh Cl
6 Barnham IP24 . . . . . . **16** C2
Stowmarket IP14 . . . . . . **124** E6
Edinburgh Gdns IP6 . . . **82** B5
Edinburgh Rd
Lowestoft NR32 . . . . . . **113** D3
Newmarket CB8 . . . . . . **120** E4
Edith Cavell Way CB9 . . **88** E3
Edmonton Cl IP5 . . . . . **141** A7
Edmonton Rd IP5 . . . . **141** A7
Edmund Cl CB9 . . . . . . **132** D6
Edmund Moundford Rd **11**
IP26 . . . . **4** E5
Edmunds Rd IP27 . . . . . **14** D8
Edmunds Rd IP14 . . . . . **65** F4
Edward Cl IP1 . . . . **138** F8
Edward Fitzgerald Ct
IP12 . . . . **146** E6
Edward St 6 CO12 . . . . **106** F3
Edwards La IP19 . . . . . . **41** F5
Edwin Ave IP12 . . . . . . **146** F7
Edwin Terr IP12 . . . . . . **146** F6
Egglestone Cl IP2 . . . . **138** F1
Eggshell La CO9 . . . . . . **88** F1
Eglantine Way 2 CO6 . . **102** A7
Egremont St CO10 . . . . **77** A2
Ehringshausen Way
CB9 . . . . **132** F5
El Alamein Way IP12 . . **146** E6
Elder Crescen 2 IP7 . . . **80** D6
Elders The IP27 . . . . . **109** E5
Elderstub La IP30 . . . . . **49** B1
Eldith Ave CB7 . . . . . . **29** C1
Eldo Gdns 8 IP28 . . . . . **29** F6
Eldo Rd IP28 . . . . **29** F6
Eldon La IP28 . . . . **30** D7
Eldred Cl
Bury St Edmunds IP32 . . **123** E4
Westbourne IP1 . . . . . . **138** D8
Eldred Dr CO10 . . . . . . **92** B2
Eleanor Pl 6 IP31 . . . . . **49** A6
Eley's Cnr IP7 . . . . **94** E8
Elgar Cl IP3 . . . . **115** A6
Elim Terr 11 NR32 . . . . **113** D2
Eliot Way 4 IP14 . . . . . **124** B8
Elizabeth Ave CB8 . . . . **120** C5
Elizabeth Bonhote Cl 3
NR35 . . . . **110** C2
Elizabeth Cl NR32 . . . . **113** A3
Elizabeth Ct 8 CO10 . . **148** D6
Elizabeth Dr IP29 . . . . . **62** D5

Elizabeth Par CB8 . . . . **120** E5
Elizabeth Rd
Brandon IP27 . . . . **5** F1
15 Harwich CO12 . . . . . **107** A2
Elizabeth Way
Burrough Green CB8 . . . . **59** F2
Eye IP23 . . . . **117** C3
Felixstowe IP11 . . . . . . **152** D3
Stowmarket IP14 . . . . . . **124** E6
Sudbury CO10 . . . . **148** A3
Elizabeth Wlk 7 IP20 . . **22** D6
Ellenbrook Gn IP2 . . . . **138** D1
Ellenbrook Rd
Ipswich IP2 . . . . **138** D1
Pinewood IP9 . . . . **142** E8
Ellingham VC Prim Sch
NR35 . . . . **8** D7
Ellington Rd 1 IP24 . . . **16** C5
Elliott Ave IP18 . . . . . . **119** C8
Elliott St IP1 . . . . **139** A6
Ellis Rd CO4 . . . . **102** F2
Elliston Cl 3 CO10 . . . . **93** C3
Ellough Ind Est NR34 . . **10** A3
Ellough Rd
Beccles NR34 . . . . **111** D4
Worlingham NR34 . . . . . **111** F2
Ellwood Cl NR34 . . . . . **111** B7
Ellwoods Cl 2 CB7 . . . . **29** C5
Elm Cl
10 Bentwaters Airfield IP12 **85** E8
6 Brantham CO11 . . . . **104** E5
Dullingham CB8 . . . . . . **59** E5
Haverhill CB9 . . . . **132** D6
Lakenheath IP27 . . . . . . **109** C7
Lowestoft NR33 . . . . . . **114** C3
Elm Coppice 6 NR33 . . **114** E4
Elm Ct CB9 . . . . **133** C3
Elm Dr IP30 . . . . **49** F1
Elm Est CO7 . . . . **151** C5
Elm Gdns IP11 . . . . . . **152** C7
Elm Gr
Garboldisham IP22 . . . . . **18** D4
5 Nayland CO6 . . . . . . **102** C5
Elm La
Capel St Mary IP9 . . . . . **150** E3
Copdock & Washbrook
IP8 . . . . **95** F4
Elm Lodge Rd 7 IP13 . . **40** C3
Elm M
East Bergholt CO7 . . . . . **151** B5
Ipswich IP5 . . . . **140** F7
Stowmarket IP14 . . . . . . **124** C6
Sudbury CO10 . . . . **148** B5
Thetford IP24 . . . . **16** B4
Wickham Market IP13 . . . **127** B6
Elm St IP1 . . . . **155** B3
Elm Tree Cl 1 IP14 . . . . **51** E1
Elm Tree La 5 CO6 . . . **102** A7
Elm Tree Mid Sch
NR33 . . . . **114** E5
Elm Tree Prim Sch
NR33 . . . . **114** E5
Elm Tree Rd NR33 . . . . **114** E5
Elm Tree Rd W NR33 . . **114** E5
Elm Way IP11 . . . . **51** F6
Elm Wlk 30 IP27 . . . . . . **13** F2
Elmcroft La IP28 . . . . . . **30** A8
Elmcroft La IP11 . . . . . **153** C7
Elmcroft Rd IP1 . . . . . . **135** A2
Elmdale Dr
Lowestoft NR33 . . . . . . **114** D4
29 Mistley CO11 . . . . . **104** E5
Elmdon Pl CB9 . . . . . . **132** F6
Elmers La IP5 . . . . **141** D7
Elmham Dr IP10 . . . . . **145** B8
Elmhurst Ave NR32 . . . **112** C1
Elmhurst Cl CB9 . . . . . **132** F5
Elmhurst Dr IP3 . . . . . . **139** F3
Elmhurst Rd 17 CO12 . . **107** B2
Elms Cl 5 Earsham NR35 . **7** F4
Great Barton IP31 . . . . . . **49** B6
Elms La NR34 . . . . **26** B2
Elms Rd Cowlinge CB8 . . **75** B7
Freckenham IP28 . . . . . . **29** F2
Elms The
Framlingham IP6 . . . . . . **126** C4
4 Horringer IP29 . . . . . . **63** A8
Elmsett CE Prim Sch
IP7 . . . . **80** F1
Elmsett Cl IP14 . . . . . . **124** F3
Elmsett Rd IP8 . . . . **81** B3
Elmsley Way IP17 . . . . . **57** C8
Elmswell Prim Sch
IP30 . . . . **50** F2
Elmswell Rd
Great Ashfield IP31 . . . . . **50** F6
Wetherden IP14 . . . . **51** A1
Elmswell Sta IP30 . . . . . **50** E3
Elmtree Bsns Pk IP30 . . **50** E3
Elsey's Yd IP33 . . . . . . **154** B3
Elsmere Rd IP1 . . . . . . **139** C8
Elton Pk IP2 . . . . **138** D6
Elveden CE Prim Sch
IP24 . . . . **15** C2
Elveden Rd IP24 . . . . . . **15** F2
Elvedon Way CB8 . . . . . **120** C5
Ely Cl IP33 . . . . **123** B3
Ely Rd 5 Claydon IP6 . . . **82** B5
Ipswich IP4 . . . . **135** F1
Soham CB7 . . . . **28** B4
Embry Cres 10 IP7 . . . . **80** D6
Emerald Cl IP5 . . . . . . **141** C8
Emily Frost Cl 4 CB8 . . **61** E2
Emlen St IP1 . . . . **155** A3
Emmanuel Cl
Ipswich IP2 . . . . **138** F2

Emmanuel Cl *continued*
Mildenhall IP28 . . . . **116** D5
Emmerson Way IP7 . . **149** D7
Emperor Circ IP3 . . . . **144** C8
Emsworth Cl 2 IP32 . . **123** D6
Endway The CB9 . . . . **88** E4
Engine Rd CB7 . . . . **28** B5
Ennerdale Cl 2 IP11 . . **153** D6
Ensign Way IP22 . . . . . . **20** E2
Enstone Rd IP33 . . . . . **115** B6
Enterprise Bsns Pk
IP33 . . . . **154** C4
Entry The IP23 . . . . **52** D8
Epsom Dr IP1 . . . . **135** A4
Erbury Pl CO10 . . . . **90** A8
Eriswell Dr IP27 . . . . . . **109** D5
Eriswell Rd
Beck Row, Holywell Row
& Kenny Hill IP28 . . . . . **13** C1
Haverhill CB9 . . . . **132** F6
Lakenheath IP27 . . . . . . **109** D4
Ernleigh Rd IP4 . . . . . . **140** B6
Erratts Hill CB8 . . . . **61** B1
Errington Way IP30 . . . . **50** B2
Erskine Rd 14 CO11 . . . **104** E2
Erwarton Wlk IP9 . . . . . **106** E6
Eskdale Way NR32 . . . . **113** A4
Esplanade NR33 . . . . . . **115** D7
Essex Ave CO10 . . . . . . **148** D7
Essex Rd NR32 . . . . . . **113** B1
Essex Way IP3 . . . . **140** E1
Estuary Cres 5 IP9 . . . **107** A4
Estuary Dr IP11 . . . . . . **153** D7
Estuary Rd 7 IP9 . . . . **107** A4
Ethel Mann Rd 5 NR35 **110** C2
Ethel Rd NR32 . . . . **113** D1
Ethelreda Dr 1 IP24 . . . **16** D7
Etna Rd IP33 . . . . **154** B4
Euro Ret Pk IP3 . . . . . . **140** E1
Europa Rd NR32 . . . . . **113** C4
Europa Way
9 Harwich CO12 . . . . **106** F2
Ipswich IP1 . . . . **138** D8
Euroscope★ NR32 . . . . **113** E2
Eustace Rd IP1 . . . . . . **138** E8
Euston Ave IP4 . . . . . . **140** F6
Euston Cl IP33 . . . . . . **154** A1
Euston Ct 4 IP11 . . . . **152** C4
Euston Hall★ IP24 . . . . . **16** E1
Evans Cl IP18 . . . . **119** C7
Evans Dr NR32 . . . . . . **113** B2
Evans' Heath CO10 . . . . . **93** F4
Eve Balfour Way IP14 . . **66** D8
Evelyn Cl IP21 . . . . **38** C7
Everard Cl 5 IP32 . . . . **122** E8
Evergreen La CB8 . . . . . **74** C8
Evergreen Rd NR32 . . . **113** B2
Everitt Rd NR33 . . . . . . **114** D8
Everton Cres IP1 . . . . . **134** F1
Eves Ct 12 CO12 . . . . . **106** E1
Evesham Cl 7 IP2 . . . . **138** F4
Exchange Sq 6 NR34 . . **111** B5
Exchange St 32 IP11 . . . **22** D6
Exeter Cres IP27 . . . . . **109** F1
Exeter Ct 6 CB9 . . . . . **132** C4
Exeter Rd 9 Claydon IP6 **82** B5
Felixstowe IP11 . . . . . . **152** F5
Ipswich IP3 . . . . **140** B4
Newmarket CB8 . . . . . . **121** A4
Exeter Way IP24 . . . . . . **16** A6
Exmoor Rd IP11 . . . . . **152** F6
Exning Prim Sch CB8 . . **120** B8
Exning Rd CB8 . . . . . . **120** D6
Eye Airfield Ind Est
IP23 . . . . **117** A6
Eye Castle★ IP23 . . . . . **117** D2
Eye Hill Dro CB7 . . . . . . **28** B7
Eye Rd Brome IP23 . . . . **117** B7
Yaxley IP23 . . . . **37** C5
Eyke CE Prim Sch IP12 . **85** B6
Eyke Rd IP12 . . . . **85** A5
Eyre Cl IP33 . . . . **154** B1

F

Factory La
Brantham CO11 . . . . . . **104** E4
Chevington IP29 . . . . . . **62** C5
Diss IP22 . . . . **20** B3
Factory St NR32 . . . . . **113** D2
Fagbury Rd IP11 . . . . . **152** A4
Faiers Cl IP33 . . . . **123** B2
Fair Cl Beccles NR34 . . **111** B5
14 Feltwell IP26 . . . . **4** E5
Fair View Rd IP19 . . . . . **118** C5
Fairey Fox Dr 2 IP28 . . **116** B6
Fairfax Ct NR34 . . . . . . **111** B3
Fairfax Dr IP27 . . . . **5** E4
Fairfax Gdns IP6 . . . . . **125** E4
Fairfield Ave IP11 . . . . **153** A5
Fairfield Cres IP13 . . . **126** D3
Fairfield Dr
Lowestoft NR33 . . . . . . **114** D6
Saxmundham IP17 . . . . **128** C3
Fairfield Hill IP14 . . . . **124** D6
Fairfield House Gdns
IP17 . . . . **128** C3
Fairfield Inf Sch IP11 . . **153** A5
Fairfield Rd
Aldeburgh IP15 . . . . . . **130** D5
Bungay NR35 . . . . **110** C2
Ipswich IP3 . . . . **140** A2
Lowestoft NR33 . . . . . . **114** D6
Reydon IP18 . . . . **119** C8
Saxmundham IP17 . . . . **128** C3

Fairfield Way 12 IP26 . . . **4** E5
Fairfields IP24 . . . . **16** C7
Fairhaven Way CB8 . . . **120** E5
Fairhead Loke NR33 . . **114** B1
Fairlawns Rd CB8 . . . . **120** F2
Fairlight Cl 2 IP4 . . . . **136** A1
Fairmead IP30 . . . . **50** F3
Fairmile Rd 2 NR34 . . **111** F4
Fairway The
Aldeburgh IP15 . . . . . . **130** C6
1 Great Yarmouth NR31 . . **3** B8
Lowestoft NR33 . . . . . . **114** F5
Fairways The IP4 . . . . . **140** E5
Fakenham Hill IP31 . . . . **33** F5
Falcon Ave IP22 . . . . . . **20** D3
Falcon Cl CB9 . . . . **133** A6
Falcon Dr IP27 . . . . **6** A1
Falcon Inn Rd NR34 . . . **26** C7
Falcon La NR35 . . . . . . **110** B5
Falcon Rd 15 IP26 . . . . . **4** E5
Falcon St
Felixstowe IP11 . . . . . . **152** E6
Ipswich IP1 . . . . **155** B2
Falcon Way IP28 . . . . . . **13** B1
Falconer Ave 3 IP14 . . . **51** E1
Falconer Rd CB9 . . . . . **133** A3
Falkenham Rd IP10 . . . . **98** E2
Falklands Dr 21 CO11 . . **104** E2
Falklands Rd CB9 . . . . . **132** E7
Fallowfield IP30 . . . . **49** F2
Fallowfield Ct 10 CB9 . . **132** C5
Fallowfield Wlk IP33 . . **123** B1
Fallowfields NR32 . . . . **112** F5
Falmouth Ave CB8 . . . . **120** F3
Falmouth Cl IP5 . . . . . **141** B6
Falmouth Gdns CB8 . . . **121** A4
Falmouth St CB8 . . . . . **120** F3
Famona Rd NR33 . . . . **114** C2
Faraday Rd IP3 . . . . . . **139** F5
Farford Field 5 CO10 . . . **92** B3
Farina Cl IP1 . . . . **138** F7
Farlingaye High Sch
IP12 . . . . **146** E6
Farlingayes IP12 . . . . . **146** F7
Farm Cl Bungay NR35 . . **110** D3
Bury St Edmunds IP33 . . **123** B1
5 Lowestoft NR33 . . . . **114** D5
Wissett IP19 . . . . **24** E2
Farm Ct St IP20 . . . . . . **23** A5
Farmerie Rd CO10 . . . . . **75** D3
Farmland Cl IP33 . . . . . **118** B8
Farnham Cl 5 NR32 . . . **112** F4
Farnham Rd
Blaxhall IP12 . . . . **71** F5
Snape NR31 . . . . **72** D6
Farrier's Rd IP14 . . . . . **124** C3
Farriers Cl
15 Martlesham Heath IP5 **98** A8
Stradbroke IP21 . . . . **39** B4
Farriers Went IP11 . . . . **152** D7
Farrow Cl IP16 . . . . **129** B6
Farthing Dro
Beck Row, Holywell Row
& Kenny Hill IP27 . . . . . **12** E6
Lakenheath IP27 . . . . **13** A6
Farthing Rd Ind Est
IP1 . . . . **138** C7
Farthings The IP28 . . . . **31** D3
Farthings Went IP9 . . . **150** F4
Fastnet Cl CB9 . . . . . . **133** B6
Fastolf Cl 4 IP32 . . . . . **113** A3
Faulkeners Way IP11 . . **152** C7
Faversham Ct NR33 . . . **115** A4
Fawcett Rd IP15 . . . . . **130** E4
Fawley Cl IP4 . . . . **140** C7
Fayrefield Rd IP12 . . . . **147** B7
Feast Cl 7 CB7 . . . . **29** A1
Featherbroom Gdns
IP13 . . . . **127** C5
Feathers Field 3 IP11 . . **152** D5
Feilden Way CB8 . . . . . **120** E5
Felaw St IP2 . . . . **155** C1
Felix Cl IP5 . . . . **141** B7
Felix Rd
Felixstowe IP11 . . . . . . **153** B4
Ipswich IP3 . . . . **140** C2
5 Stowupland IP14 . . . . **67** A4
Felixstowe General Hospl
IP11 . . . . **153** B4
Felixstowe Leisure Ctr
IP11 . . . . **152** F3
Felixstowe Mus★
IP11 . . . . **107** E2
Felixstowe Rd
Ipswich IP3 . . . . **139** A4
8 Martlesham IP5 . . . . . **98** A8
Felixstowe Sta IP11 . . . . **153** A5
Fell Rd CO9 . . . . **89** A4
Fellbrigg Ave IP5 . . . . **140** F6
Fellows Cl IP21 . . . . **21** A1
Felnor Wlk IP11 . . . . . . **153** B3
Felsham Chase CB5 . . . **44** B5
Felsham Ct IP14 . . . . . **124** F3
Felsham Rd
Bradfield St Clare IP30 . . **64** D4
Rattlesden IP30 . . . . **65** C5
Felsham Rise IP17 . . . . **128** C3
Felton Wlk IP32 . . . . . . **122** D8
Feltons 6 CB7 . . . . **29** A1
Feltwell Elementary Sch
IP26 . . . . **4** E6
Feltwell Pl CB9 . . . . . . **132** F6
Feltwell Prim Sch IP26 . . . **4** D5
Feltwell Rd IP26 . . . . **4** F3

Fen Alder Carr Nature
Reserve★ IP6 . . . . . **125** D8
Fen Bank CB7 . . . . **29** C6
Fen Ct NR33 . . . . **115** A6
Fen La Ardleigh CO7 . . . **103** E1
Beck Row, Holywell Row
& Kenny Hill IP28 . . . . . **13** D1
Braiseworth IP23 . . . . . . **37** D3
Creeting St Peter or
West Creeting IP6 . . . . **125** D8
Ditchingham NR35 . . . . . . **7** E7
Garboldisham IP22 . . . . . **18** D3
Hitcham IP7 . . . . **51** C1
Rickinghall Inferior IP22 . . **36** A6
Roydon IP22 . . . . **19** F3
Stonham Earl IP6 . . . . . . **67** D4
Thelnetham IP22 . . . . . . **18** E1
Fen Meadow IP11 . . . . **152** C8
Fen Pk Prim Sch
NR33 . . . . **115** B6
Fen Rd Blo' Norton IP22 . . **18** F2
Pakenham IP31 . . . . **49** F6
Fen St Boxford CO10 . . . **93** C3
Hinderclay IP22 . . . . **18** F1
Nayland CO6 . . . . **102** D5
Fen View
Copdock & Washbrook
IP8 . . . . **95** F4
Thornden IP23 . . . . **53** B8
Fen Way IP33 . . . . **154** A4
Fen Wlk IP12 . . . . **146** F4
Fenbridge La CO7 . . . . **151** B3
Fengate Dro IP27 . . . . . . **5** E2
Fenlands Cres NR33 . . **114** F6
Fenn Cl
Halesworth IP19 . . . . . . **118** A5
Stowmarket IP14 . . . . . **124** D3
Fenn La IP12 . . . . **98** D6
Fenstreet Rd IP17 . . . . . **58** A7
Fenton Rd CB9 . . . . . . **132** F6
Fentons Way IP5 . . . . . **141** C7
Fern Ave NR32 . . . . . . **112** D2
Fern Gn Cl 1 NR32 . . . **112** E4
Fern Gr CB9 . . . . **132** C6
Fernhill Cl IP12 . . . . . . **147** A7
Ferndale Ave NR32 . . . **113** B3
Ferndale Cl CB8 . . . . . **121** B6
Ferndown Rd 3 IP11 . . **153** C6
Ferneley Cres CB8 . . . **121** A4
Fernhayes Cl IP2 . . . . **139** A3
Fernhill Cl IP12 . . . . . . **147** A7
Ferniere Rd 4 CO12 . . **107** B3
Ferry La
Beck Row, Holywell Row
& Kenny Hill IP28 . . . . . **29** F5
Felixstowe IP11 . . . . . . **152** C3
Southwold IP18 . . . . . . **119** C3
Sudbury CO10 . . . . **131** C6
Walberswick IP18 . . . . . **119** B2
Ferry Quay IP12 . . . . . **147** A4
Ferry Rd Bawdsey IP12 . . **99** D1
Felixstowe IP11 . . . . . . **153** D7
Southwold IP18 . . . . . . **119** C3
Sudbury CO10 . . . . **131** C6
Walberswick IP18 . . . . . **119** B2
Fersfield Rd IP22 . . . . . . **19** D5
Festival Cl 4 IP17 . . . . . **72** C8
Festival Rd 14 CB7 . . . . **29** C5
Feveryears Yd 4 IP21 . . **39** D8
Fiddler's La IP23 . . . . . **117** F2
Fiddlers La CO7 . . . . . . **151** C5
Field Cl 3 IP30 . . . . **49** F2
Field Fuller's IP6 . . . . **135** E4
Field Grange NR32 . . . **112** F5
Field House Gdns IP22 . . **20** D2
Field La NR33 . . . . **11** B1
Field Rd IP28 . . . . **116** C5
Field Stile Rd 2 IP18 . . **119** D5
Field Terr Rd CB8 . . . . **120** F5
Field View
Bucklesham IP10 . . . . . . **98** A4
8 Thurstow IP31 . . . . . . **49** E4
Field View Gdns NR34 . . **111** D3
Field Way
Debenham IP14 . . . . **53** F1
18 Stanton IP31 . . . . **34** E4
Field Wlk IP28 . . . . **116** C5
Fields View CO10 . . . . **148** D6
Fieldview Cl IP18 . . . . . **119** B8
Fieldview Dr NR32 . . . . **113** A1
Fife Rd IP4 . . . . **136** B1
Finbars Wlk IP4 . . . . . . **139** F5
Finborough Cl IP4 . . . . **140** F6
Finborough Rd IP14 . . **124** B6
Finborough Sch IP14 . . . **66** B5
Finch Cl 7 IP14 . . . . **67** A5
Finch Wlk CO10 . . . . . . **91** D4
Fincham Rd IP28 . . . . . **116** B5
Finchingfield Rd
Stambourne CO9 . . . . . . **89** B1
Steeple Bumpstead CB9 . . **88** E3
Finchley Ave IP28 . . . . **116** B6
Finchley Rd IP4 . . . . . **139** E6
Fingal St IP13 . . . . **39** A1
Finney's Drift IP10 . . . **145** C5
Finningham Rd
Gislingham IP23 . . . . **36** D1
Old Newton with Dagworth
IP14 . . . . **51** F2
Rickinghall Superior IP22 . **35** A2
Walsham le Willows IP31 . . **35** D2
Finsbury Pl IP33 . . . . . **154** B1
Finsbury Sq IP33 . . . . **154** C1
Fir Cl Barnby NR34 . . . . **10** C4
Mundford IP26 . . . . **6** B8
Wickham Market IP13 . . **127** C6
Fir La NR32 . . . . **113** A2
Fir Rd IP24 . . . . **16** B4

Fir Tree Cl IP21 . . . . . . **22** D2
Fir Tree Hill IP9 . . . . . **105** F7
Fir Tree La IP17 . . . . . . **51** C3
Fir Tree Rise IP8 . . . . **138** C2
Fir Wlk 29 IP27 . . . . **13** F2
Fircroft Rd IP1 . . . . **135** A2
Firebrass La IP12 . . . . . **85** C2
Firebronds Rd 7 IP9 . . **105** F4
Firecrest Dr 2 IP14 . . . **124** F7
Firefly Way 1 NR34 . . . **144** B8
Firfield Cl NR34 . . . . . . **111** B3
Firmin Cl IP1 . . . . **139** A6
Firs The Beccles NR34 . . **111** F4
Lakenheath IP27 . . . . . . **109** E6
Lowestoft NR33 . . . . . . **114** C3
Southwold IP18 . . . . . . **119** B8
First Ave
4 Glemsford CO10 . . . . **77** B3
Sudbury CO10 . . . . **148** E2
First Dro Burwell CB5 . . . **44** B8
Lakenheath IP27 . . . . . . **109** A8
Firtree Cl IP32 . . . . . . **122** D7
Fish Pond Hill IP9 . . . . . **106** B6
Fishbane Cl 9 IP3 . . . . **144** A8
Fisher Cl Haverhill CB9 . . **133** B5
2 Saxmundham IP17 . . **128** C2
Fisher Rd IP22 . . . . **20** D2
Fisher Row
Carlton Colville NR32 . . **114** B8
Lowestoft NR32 . . . . . . **112** B1
Fisher's Dro IP28 . . . . . **12** D3
Fisher's La
East Bergholt CO7 . . . . **104** E6
Hoxne IP21 . . . . **38** C8
Fisherman's Way 13
NR33 . . . . **11** C1
Fishers The IP5 . . . . . **141** C7
Fishpond Rd IP12 . . . . . **98** D7
Fishponds La IP9 . . . . . **105** F7
Fishponds Way IP14 . . . **66** C8
Fiske Cl IP32 . . . . **123** E6
Fison Way IP24 . . . . . . **16** B7
Fitches La IP16 . . . . . . **129** C1
Fitches The IP17 . . . . . **129** A2
Fitzgerald Cl 4 CO11 . . **104** C2
Fitzgerald Rd
Bramford IP8 . . . . **134** A1
Woodbridge IP12 . . . . . **147** A6
Fitzgerald Wlk IP33 . . . **122** A6
Fitzmaurice Rd IP3 . . . **140** B3
Fitzroy St Ipswich IP1 . . **155** B3
Newmarket CB8 . . . . . . **121** A1
Fitzwilliam Cl
6 Woodbridge IP12 . . . **146** E4
Ipswich IP2 . . . . **138** F2
Five Acre La NR35 . . . . . **7** E3
Five Acres 12 IP9 . . . . **105** E7
Five Cross Ways
Butley IP12 . . . . **86** B4
Sudbourne IP12 . . . . . **131** B6
Wetheringsett-cum-Brockford
IP23 . . . . **53** A7
Fiveways IP28 . . . . **116** F3
Flatford La IP14 . . . . . **124** E3
Flatford La CO7 . . . . . . **151** D1
Flatford Mill★ CO7 . . . . **151** D1
Flatford Rd
East Bergholt CO7 . . . . **151** D2
Haverhill CB9 . . . . **132** A6
Flatts La IP30 . . . . **50** B2
Flavian Cl IP33 . . . . . . **133** B5
Flax La CO10 . . . . **77** B2
Fleet Dyke Dr NR33 . . . **114** E5
Fleetwood Ave IP11 . . . **153** B5
Fleetwood Rd IP11 . . . . **153** B6
Fleming Ave IP33 . . . . **116** C5
Flempton Rd IP28 . . . . . **47** D5
Flemyng Rd IP33 . . . . . **122** C5
Fletcher Cl 3 IP6 . . . . . **82** A5
Fletcher Rd IP3 . . . . . . **140** A1
Fletcher's La IP17 . . . . . **58** B6
Fletchers La IP5 . . . . . **141** E8
Flindell Dr IP8 . . . . . . **134** A2
Flint Cl IP2 . . . . **139** B2
Flixton Marsh La
NR32 . . . . **112** B6
Flixton Rd
Blundeston NR32 . . . . . **112** C8
Bungay NR35 . . . . **110** A1
Flixton NR35 . . . . **7** E2
St Mary, South Elmham
otherwise Homersfield
IP20 . . . . **23** B8
Somerleyton, Ashby &
Herringfleet NR32 . . . . . **2** F4
Flora Rd NR33 . . . . **115** A3
Flordon Rd IP6 . . . . . . **125** E6
Florence Rd NR33 . . . . **115** B3
Florence Way NR35 . . . . **8** D7
Flowerday Cl 4 NR31 . . . **3** B7
Flowton Rd Elmsett IP7 . . **81** A1
Flowton IP8 . . . . **95** B8
Somersham IP8 . . . . **81** C3
Floyd Rd IP32 . . . . **122** D8
Foal's Gn Rd IP21 . . . . **39** D2
Fodderfen Dro
Beck Row, Holywell Row
& Kenny Hill IP28 . . . . . **12** C1
Feltwell PE38 . . . . **4** A3
Foden Ave IP1 . . . . . . **134** C2
Folly End IP15 . . . . . . **130** C6
Folly La
Bressingham IP22 . . . . . **19** F4
Copdock & Washbrook
IP8 . . . . **95** E2
Lawshall IP29 . . . . **63** C3

Folly Rd
Great Waldingfield CO10 . . **92** C6
Hundon CO10 . . . . **75** F3
Mildenhall IP28 . . . . . . **116** A7
Folly The Harleston IP14 . **66** C8
Haughley IP14 . . . . **51** C1
Fonnereau Rd IP1 . . . . **155** B3
Forbes Dr NR34 . . . . . **111** B3
Ford Cl
Beck Row, Holywell Row
& Kenny Hill IP28 . . . . . **29** F7
Stowmarket IP14 . . . . . **124** E4
Ford Hill IP12 . . . . **99** B7
Ford Rd IP3 . . . . **71** C5
Ford View Rd IP14 . . . . **124** E4
Fordham Moor CB7 . . . . **29** A3
Fordham Pl
4 Ipswich IP4 . . . . **140** F5
24 Ixworth IP31 . . . . **34** C1
Fordham Rd
Fordham CB8 . . . . **44** F7
Freckenham IP28 . . . . . . **29** D2
Mount Bures CO6 . . . . . **101** C1
Newmarket CB8 . . . . . . **120** F7
Snailwell CB8 . . . . **45** A7
Soham CB7 . . . . **28** F2
7 Soham CB7 . . . . **28** D3
Wormingford CO6 . . . . . **101** E2
Fordhams Cl 21 IP31 . . . **34** E4
Fordley Rd IP17 . . . . **57** F6
Fordson Way NR33 . . . **114** C3
Fore Hamlet IP3 . . . . . **139** E5
Fore St
Framlingham IP13 . . . . **126** D3
Ipswich IP4 . . . . **155** C2
Forest End CB8 . . . . **46** A7
Forest Gdns 9 IP12 . . . . **85** B8
Forest Glade CB9 . . . . **132** D8
Forest La 3 IP5 . . . . **98** A7
Forest Mount NR31 . . . . . **2** B7
Forest Prim Sch The
IP27 . . . . **5** F1
Forest Rd IP14 . . . . **66** B6
Forest Ret Pk IP24 . . . . . **16** A5
Forest Way IP28 . . . . . **116** E4
Forester Cl IP8 . . . . . . **142** E8
Foresters Wlk 6 IP6 . . . **82** A5
Forfar Cl 2 Ipswich IP4 **136** B1
Ipswich IP4 . . . . **140** B8
Forge Cl 2 Benhall IP17 . . **72** C8
Bucklenham IP10 . . . . . . **98** A4
Palgrave IP22 . . . . **20** C1
Forge End IP28 . . . . **48** B6
Forge Gr NR34 . . . . **9** B6
Forge St CO7 . . . . **104** A3
Forge Way IP22 . . . . . . **18** D4
Fornham La IP33 . . . . . **122** A7
Fornham Rd
Bury St Edmunds IP32 . . **154** B4
Fornham St Martin IP31 . . **48** D5
Great Barton IP31 . . . . . **49** A5
Forties Cl IP28 . . . . . . **133** B6
Fortress Rd NR33 . . . . **114** E3
Foster Cl IP18 . . . . **119** D6
Foster Rd 2 CO12 . . . . **106** F3
Foundation St IP4 . . . . **155** B2
Foundry La IP1 . . . . . . **155** B2
Fountain La CB7 . . . . . . **28** D4
Fountain Rd 4 IP12 . . . . **85** D8
Fountain Way IP18 . . . . **119** C8
Fountain's La NR34 . . . . **10** C4
Fountains Rd
Bury St Edmunds IP33 . . **122** D2
Ipswich IP2 . . . . **139** A1
Four Ash Hill CO9 . . . . . **89** C4
Four Elms Residential Sch
IP14 . . . . **68** A8
Four Wheel Dr IP30 . . . **49** B2
Fourth Ave 5 CO10 . . . . **77** A3
Fowe's La CO10 . . . . . . **90** D4
Fowler's Cres 2 NR32 . . . **3** D4
Fox And Pin La IP29 . . . **63** E8
Fox Ct IP14 . . . . **124** D6
Fox Gn CB8 . . . . **74** C8
Fox Hill Hollesley IP12 . . . **99** C7
St Cross, South Elmham
IP20 . . . . **23** C7
Fox La IP17 . . . . **42** B1
Fox Lea IP5 . . . . **141** E8
Fox Wood N 2 CB7 . . . . **28** D5
Fox Wood S 11 CB7 . . . **28** D5
Fox Yd IP18 . . . . **119** D5
Foxborough Mid Sch
NR32 . . . . **113** A5
Foxborough Rd NR32 . . **113** A4
Foxburrow Cl CB9 . . . . **132** D7
Foxburrow Farm Nature
Reserve★ IP12 . . . . . . **84** D6
Foxburrow Hill NR32 . . **113** A6
Foxburrow Rd IP3 . . . . **140** F1
Foxburrow Wood Nature
Reserve★ NR32 . . . . . **113** B6
Foxes La Ashen CO10 . . . **89** C4
Mendham IP20 . . . . **23** B4
Foxes Rd CO10 . . . . **89** C5
Foxes Wlk NR32 . . . . . **113** A6
Foxglade NR32 . . . . . . **112** C2
Foxglove Ave IP6 . . . . . **125** D3
Foxglove Cl
Lowestoft NR33 . . . . . . **115** A2
1 Worlingham NR34 . . . **111** E3
Foxglove Cres IP3 . . . . **140** E1
Foxglove Rd IP24 . . . . . **16** D6
Foxglove Gdns IP11 . . . **153** C5
Foxgrove La IP11 . . . . . **153** C5

Foxhall Cl CO7 ....151 C6
Foxhall Fields CO7 ...151 C5
Foxhall Rd Foxhall IP10 ..98 A6
  Ipswich IP3 ....139 F5
Foxhall Stadium IP4 .141 A5
Foxtail Rd IP3 ....144 D8
Foxwood Cl CO11 .....104 B1
Foxwood Cres IP4 ....140 F5
Framfield Rd NR33 ...114 C4
Framlingham Cl 4 IP12 .85 B3
Framlingham Coll
  IP13 ....126 C4
Framlingham Mere Nature
  Reserve★ IP13 ....126 C4
Framlingham Rd
  Dennington IP13 ....39 F2
  Easton IP13 ....70 E5
  Laxfield IP13 ....40 A2
Framlington Castle (remains
  of)★ IP13 ....126 C4
Framlinham Coll Prep Sch
  IP13 ....70 A7
Frampton Rd IP3 .....144 A8
Framsden Rd IP14 ....69 E7
Framsden Windmill★
  IP14 ....69 B6
Francis Cl
  Haverhill CB9 ....132 D6
  Ipswich IP5 ....141 E8
Francis Rd
  16 Kessingland NR33 ....11 B1
  8 Sudbury CO10 ....148 C5
Franciscan Way IP1 ..155 C2
Frank Bridges Cl 4 CB7 .28 D3
Franklin Cl IP15 .....130 D5
Franklin Rd
  Aldeburgh IP15 ....130 C5
  Ipswich IP3 ....140 B2
Fraser Rd
  Bramford IP8 ....134 B2
  Ipswich IP1 ....138 F7
Freckenham Rd
  Freckenham CB7 ....29 E2
  Worlington IP28 ....30 A3
Fred Archer Way CB8 .121 C4
Fred Dannatt Rd IP28 .116 A6
Frederick Talbot Cl 14
  CB7 ....28 D4
Frederick's Rd 3 NR34 .111 C4
Free La NR35 ....110 A8
Freehold Rd
  Ipswich IP4 ....140 A6
  Needham Market IP6 ...125 C6
Freelands IP14 ....52 E4
Freeman Ave 4 IP6 ...82 D6
Freeman Cl IP7 ......149 D7
Freeman Prim Sch The
  IP14 ....67 B7
Freewood St IP30 ....64 D6
Freezes Barns CB9 ...88 D4
Frenze Hall La IP22 ..20 D3
Frenze Rd IP22 ......20 D2
Frere Cnr 7 IP22 ....20 A3
Frere Rd 30 IP20 ....22 C6
Freshfields
  17 Harwich CO12 .....106 F1
  Newmarket CB8 ....120 F4
Fressingfield CE Prim Sch
  IP21 ....39 D8
Fressingfield Rd IP20 .23 C1
Freston Hill IP9 .....143 E4
Freston St IP9 ....143 D3
Freston Twr★ IP9 .....143 F4
Friar Cl IP33 ....154 B1
Friar's La IP4 ....140 A5
Friars IP9 ....150 F2
Friars Bridge Rd IP1 .155 A2
Friars Cl
  Bury St Edmunds IP33 ..154 B1
  7 Felixstowe IP11 ....153 D6
Friars Croft IP21 ....22 D3
Friars Cl Melton IP12 .147 C7
  Sudbury CO10 ....148 C5
Friars Meadow IP21 ..22 D3
Friars Rd IP7 ....149 C6
Friars St Ipswich IP1 .155 B2
  Sudbury CO10 ....148 C5
Friary Meadow IP28 ..48 D5
Friday St
  Beck Row, Holywell Row
  & Kenny Hill IP28 .....29 F6
  Rendlesham IP12 ....85 D7
Friday St Farm Maize Maze★
  IP17 ....72 B7
Friday's Orch IP16 ..129 C5
Friends Field IP7 CO8 .101 C5
Friends Wlk IP5 .....141 D8
Friston Rd IP12 .....85 C2
Fristonmoor La
  Knodishall IP17 ....57 E1
  Sternfield IP17 ....72 E8
Fritillary Cl IP8 ....142 E8
Fritton Cl Ipswich IP2 .139 A1
  12 Oulton NR32 ....112 F4
Fritton Ct 5 CB9 ....132 C4
Fritton Lake Ctry World★
  NR31 ....2 C6
Frobisher Rd
  21 Harwich CO12 ......106 F1
  Ipswich IP3 ....139 E1
Frog Hall La IP7 .....149 F6
Frogmore CB8 ....120 B7
Frogs Alley IP9 ......106 F6

Frogs Alley Vineyard★
  IP9 ....106 F7
Frogs Hall Rd CO10 ...78 D5
Frogs Hole NR32 .....2 C5
Fronk's Ave 3 CO12 ..107 B1
Fronk's Rd CO12 .....107 A1
Front Rd IP3 ....144 D8
Front St
  Mendlesham IP14 ....52 E4
  Orford IP12 ....131 B3
  Ousden CB8 ....61 E6
Frostenden Cres 1
  NR32 ....113 B4
Frowd Cl CO7 ....29 B1
Fryatt Ave 7 CO12 ..107 A2
Fryth Cl CB9 ....132 E7
Fuchsia La IP4 ......140 A5
Fulcher Cl IP33 .....123 D2
Fulchers Field IP13 ..126 B4
Fulford Cl 8 IP28 ....48 C6
Fuller Rd IP20 ....22 D5
Fullers Cl 2 IP7 .....149 E6
Fullers Teasle NR33 ..114 A3
Fulmar Way NR33 ....114 D5
Fulmerston Rd IP24 ..16 B5
Furness Cl IP12 .....142 F8
Further St CO10 .....92 E2
Furthest Dro IP27 ...4 D1
Furze Cl 4 IP31 ......49 C4
Furze Way IP22 .....36 D5
Fyffe Way 12 NR33 ..115 D8
Fynn La IP6 ....136 C5
Fynn Rd IP12 ....146 D3

G

Gables The CB9 ......133 D3
Gaell Cres 5 IP7 ....149 D5
Gage Cl IP32 ....154 A4
Gage's Rd CO10 .....90 C4
Gainsborough Ctr IP3 .144 B8
Gainsborough Dr
  Halesworth IP19 ......118 A2
  Lowestoft NR32 ....113 B6
  Manningtree CO11 ......104 D2
Gainsborough La IP3 ..143 F6
Gainsborough Rd
  Bury St Edmunds IP33 ..122 D5
  Felixstowe IP11 ....153 A4
  Haverhill CB9 ....132 B7
  Ipswich IP4 ....155 C4
  Stowmarket IP14 ......124 B6
  Sudbury CO10 ....148 C5
Gainsborough St
  CO10 ....148 C5
Gainsborough's House★ wo
  CO10 ....148 C5
Galley Cl NR33 ......114 B4
Galley Rd CO10 .....75 D3
Gallow La IP30 ......78 C7
Gallows Hill IP7 .....149 B7
Gallows La IP14 .....66 C7
Galway Ave IP1 .....134 E1
Gandish Cl CO7 .....151 D3
Gandish Rd CO7 .....151 E4
Ganges Rd 1 IP9 ....107 A4
Gannet Cl CB9 ......133 A6
Gannet Rd IP2 ......138 E3
Ganwick Cl CB9 .....132 D8
Gaol La Beccles NR34 .111 B5
  Sudbury CO10 ....148 C5
Gap The NR33 ......114 F6
Garboldisham Rd
  Harling NR16 ....18 C5
  Kenninghall NR16 ......18 F7
Garboldisham VC Prim Sch
  IP22 ....18 D4
Garden Cl
  Bungay NR35 ....110 C3
  5 Great Barton IP31 ...49 A6
  Normanston NR32 ......113 B2
  Shotley IP9 ....106 F6
Garden Ct 2 CB5 ....44 B6
Garden Field 2 IP11 ..152 E5
Garden Fields IP31 ...33 D3
Garden House La IP30 .65 C6
Garden La
  Beccles NR34 ....111 F4
  Westley IP33 ....122 A5
Garden Pl CO10 .....148 B5
Garden Sq IP12 .....85 D8
Gardeners La 21 CB7 .28 D4
Gardeners Rd IP14 ...53 F1
Gardeners Wlk IP30 ..50 E2
Gardenhouse La IP22 ..36 A6
Gardens The
  4 Beyton IP30 ....49 F2
  Lowestoft NR33 ....114 C2
Gardiner Cl IP33 ....122 C4
Gardner Rd IP18 ....119 D5
Garfield Cl IP11 .....152 F3
Garfield Rd IP11 .....152 F3
Garland Rd 6 CO12 ..106 F3
Garland St IP33 .....154 B3
Garlic St IP21 ....22 A6
Garnons Chase 3 CO6 .101 F2
Garrard Pl 12 IP31 ...34 B1
Garrards Rd 3 IP7 ...80 C7
Garrett Cl IP17 ......72 D5
Garrett Cres IP16 ...129 C5
Garrick Way IP1 ....135 A3
Garrison La
  Felixstowe IP11 ....153 C5
  5 Great Waldingfield CO10 .92 C6
Garrod App IP12 ....84 E7
Garrods IP9 ....150 F3
Garrods End IP29 ...62 C5

Gas Works Rd NR32 ..113 E2
Gascoigne Dr 3 IP6 ..82 D6
Gashouse Dro IP27 ...5 F1
Gaston End CO7 .....151 C5
Gaston St CO7 ......151 C4
Gatacre Rd IP1 ......139 A7
Gate Farm Rd 2 IP9 ..107 A5
Gatesbury's La IP29 ..62 C2
Gateway The IP33 ...123 C3
Gavell St IP19 ....24 D5
Gawdy Cl 2 IP20 ....22 D6
Gaye Cres IP23 .....117 B3
Gaye St IP1 ....155 A3
Gayfer Ave IP5 .....141 F8
Gayford Sq IP7 .....80 C5
Gaymers La IP11 ....152 B8
Gazeley Rd Ashley CB8 .46 A1
  Kentford CB8 ....46 A5
Gdn Room The★ IP6 ..125 D5
Gedding Hill IP30 ....65 B4
Gedding Rd IP30 ....65 B7
Gedge Cl IP33 ......122 C4
Gedgrave Rd IP12 ...131 A1
Geldeston Hill NR34 ..8 F6
Geldeston Rd
  Ellingham NR35 ....8 D6
  Geldeston NR34 ....9 B5
General Castle Way
  IP30 ....49 B2
Generals Mews 12 IP11 .152 D5
Genesta Dr 2 IP31 ...49 D4
Geneva Gdns 4 NR31 ..3 C6
Geneva Rd IP1 ......155 A4
Gentle Ct 3 IP27 ....5 F1
Gents La IP29 ....77 F7
George Baldry Way 2
  NR35 ....110 C2
George Brown Way
  NR34 ....111 C3
George Cl IP32 ......112 E1
George Frost Cl IP4 ..155 C4
George Gent Cl 2 CB9 .88 D3
George Gibson Cl
  CB8 ....120 C8
George Hill IP31 .....34 E4
George La 3 CO10 ...77 B2
George Lambpton Ave
  CB8 ....120 F5
George Rd 3 IP24 ...16 D6
George St Brandon IP27 .5 F1
  Hadleigh IP7 ....149 E6
  2 Harwich CO12 .....107 B3
  Hintlesham IP8 ....95 C4
George Westwood Way
  NR34 ....111 C6
Geralds Ave IP4 .....140 A5
Gestingthorpe Rd CO10 .90 F2
Gibbon Cl IP32 ......123 E5
Gibraltar Cl IP33 ....122 C6
Gibraltar Rd IP6 .....69 B1
Gifford Cl 6 IP9 .....105 E7
Gilbert Cl IP6 ....125 C5
Gilbert Rd 2 CO10 ...90 A8
Giles Way Risby IP28 ..47 E5
  4 Witnesham IP6 .....83 A5
Gillingham Rd NR34 ..9 A6
Gillingham Dam NR34 ..111 A7
Gilpin Rd IP12 ......112 D1
Gilray Rd IP22 ......20 D2
Gilstrap Rd IP31 ....48 D5
Gimbert Rd 7 CB7 ...28 D4
Gin La IP13 ....40 C2
Gippeswyk Ave IP2 ..139 A4
Gippeswyk Rd IP2 ...155 A1
Gipping Cl CB9 ......132 C4
Gipping Pl IP14 .....124 D7
Gipping Rd Claydon IP6 .82 A5
  Stowupland IP14 ....67 A7
Gipping Way
  Bramford IP8 ....134 B4
  Sproughton IP8 ....138 B6
  Stowmarket IP14 ......124 D7
Gippingstone Rd IP8 .134 A1
Gipsy La
  Aldringham cum Thorpe
  IP16 ....129 D1
  Frostenden NR34 ......26 D4
Girling St CO10 .....148 C6
Girton Cl
  Mildenhall IP28 ....116 C6
  Woodbridge IP12 ......146 D4
  Woodditton CB8 ....121 B1
Girton Way IP2 ......138 F1
Gisleham Mid Sch
  NR33 ....114 C1
Gisleham Rd NR33 ..114 B1
Gislingham CE Prim Sch
  IP23 ....36 C2
Gislingham Rd IP14 ..36 C1
Gissing Rd IP22 .....20 F6
Glade Prim Sch The
  IP27 ....5 F1
Glade The IP24 .....16 C7
Glades The NR32 ...112 D2
Gladstone Rd
  1 Corton NR32 ....3 C4
  Ipswich IP3 ....139 F5
  6 Woodbridge IP12 ...147 A5
Glamis Cl CB9 ......132 B6
Glamis Ct 26 IP20 ...22 D6
Glamorgan Rd IP2 ...139 B1
Glanely Gdns CB8 ...120 C8
Glanfield Wlk IP33 ..122 C4
Glanville Pl IP5 .....141 B6
Glanville Rd IP7 .....149 E4

Glassfield Rd IP31 ...34 D4
Glastonbury Cl IP2 ..138 F1
Glastonbury Rd IP33 .122 C6
Glebe Cl
  Baylham IP6 ....81 E6
  Horringer IP29 ....63 A7
  Ingham IP31 ....32 F1
  Lowestoft NR32 ....113 C6
  Sproughton IP8 ....138 B6
  1 Tattingstone IP9 ...105 B8
Glebe End IP9 ......150 F4
Glebe La IP9 ....144 B1
Glebe Meadow IP13 ..54 F2
Glebe Rd Bredfield IP13 .84 C7
  Gissing IP21 ....21 A8
  Weeting IP27 ....5 E3
Glebe Rd E 15 NR33 ..11 C1
Glebe Rd W 18 NR33 ..11 B1
Glebe The
  Haverhill CB9 ....132 E7
  Lavenham CO10 ....78 D3
Glebe View NR34 ....111 C3
Glebe Way 1 Claydon IP6 .82 B5
  Mendlesham IP14 ....52 E4
Glebes The IP17 .....72 D5
Glemham Dr IP4 .....140 F4
Glemham Hall★ IP13 ..71 E6
Glemham Rd IP17 ...56 E2
Glemsford Cl IP11 ..152 D3
Glemsford Com Prim Sch
  CO10 ....77 A3
Glemsford Pl 7 CB9 ..132 F6
Glemsford Rd
  Lowestoft NR32 ....112 F4
  Stowmarket IP14 ......124 E4
Glenavon Rd IP4 ....140 D7
Glenbourne Wlk 2
  NR33 ....114 C3
Glencoe Rd IP4 .....136 C1
Gleneagles Cl
  4 Bury St Edmunds IP28 .48 C6
  1 Felixstowe IP11 ....153 C6
Gleneagles Dr IP4 ...140 D5
Glenfield Ave IP11 ..153 A6
Glenhurst Ave IP4 ...140 B8
Glenside CO10 ......148 E4
Glenwood Ct CB8 ...120 F3
Glenwood Dr NR34 ..111 E4
Globe Yd 3 CO10 ....148 C6
Gloster Rd IP5 ......98 A8
Gloucester Ave NR32 .112 F3
Gloucester Pl 4 CO10 .76 A1
Gloucester Rd
  4 Bury St Edmunds IP32 .122 E8
  Haverhill CB9 ....132 D5
  Ipswich IP3 ....140 A2
Gloucester Way CO10 .148 B8
Go Ape★ IP27 ....15 C8
Gobbets La IP22 ....35 E7
Gobbett's Rd IP22 ...35 E7
Gobbitts Yd IP12 ...147 A4
Godbold Cl 3 IP5 ....141 D7
Goddard Pl IP14 .....66 B7
Goddard Rd IP1 .....134 C3
Goddard Rd E IP1 ...134 D3
Godetia Ct 6 NR32 ..113 B4
Godfrey's Cl IP14 ...66 B7
Godfrey's Hill IP19 ..40 F8
Godfrey's Wood IP12 .147 A7
Godolphin Cl IP33 ...122 C6
Godyll Rd IP18 ......119 C5
Goldcrest Rd IP2 ....138 C3
Golden La IP29 ......63 C2
Golden Lion La 5 CO12 .107 B3
Golden Miller Cl CB8 .120 D7
Goldenlond CO6 .....102 E7
Golding Way 1 CO10 ..77 A2
Golding's La IP16 ...129 C4
Goldings Cl CB9 .....132 E8
Goldsmith Cl IP32 ...122 D7
Goldsmith Way IP21 ..21 F8
Golf La IP15 ....130 C6
Golf Links Rd
  Barton Mills IP28 ......30 C3
  Worlington IP28 ....116 A1
Golf Rd IP11 ....153 D5
Gondree NR33 ......114 E3
Gonville Cl
  Mildenhall IP28 ....116 D6
  1 Woodbridge IP12 ...146 E4
Goodall Terr IP11 ...141 E8
Goodchilds Gdns 8 CB7 .29 C5
Goodlake Cl 9 CO12 ..106 F1
Goodman Gr IP5 ....141 E7
Goose Gn E NR34 ....111 C5
Goose Gn W NR34 ...111 C5
Gorams Mill La IP13 ..40 B3
Gordon Rd
  California IP4 ....140 A6
  5 Harwich CO12 .....107 A1
  Ipswich IP4 ....140 A7
  Lowestoft NR33 ....113 D1
Gordon Richards Cl
  CB8 ....120 F6
Goring Rd IP4 ......140 C6
Gorleston Rd
  Blundeston NR32 ......112 F8
  Corton NR32 ....3 B4
Gorse Cl
  Lakenheath IP27 ......109 E4
  8 Red Lodge IP28 ....30 C1
Gorse Gn NR32 .....113 B3
Gorse Ind Est IP24 ..16 A3
Gorse La IP11 ......119 C7
Gorse Rd Ipswich IP3 .140 B2
  Southwold IP18 ....119 C6
Gorse View IP17 ....58 C8

Gorsehayes IP2 .....139 B3
Gorseland Prim Sch
  IP5 ....141 F8
Gorselands IP12 ....99 F7
Gorst Cl 7 IP32 .....122 E8
Gosford Cl 4 CO10 ...90 A8
Gosford Rd NR34 ....111 C5
Gosford Way IP11 ...153 C6
Gostling Cl 2 IP22 ...20 B2
Gostling Pl IP5 ......141 E8
Gothic Cl 1 IP20 ....22 D5
Gotsfield Cl 1 CO10 ..92 B7
Gough Pl 9 IP31 ....34 B1
Governors Mews IP33 ..123 C2
Gower St IP2 ....155 B1
Gowers Cl IP5 ......141 E7
Gowers End 6 CO10 ..77 B3
Gowle Rd IP14 ......124 C8
Goyfield Ave IP11 ...152 F4
Gracechurch St IP14 ..53 E2
Graften Way IP11 ...155 A2
Grafton Cl IP33 .....122 D5
Grafton Rd 2 CO12 ..107 B2
Grafton Way IP1 ....155 B2
Graham Ave IP1 ....139 B8
Graham Rd
  Felixstowe IP11 ....152 F5
  Ipswich IP1 ....155 A4
Grainge Way 3 IP14 ..51 C1
Grainger Cl IP32 ....123 F5
Grammar Sch Pl 11
  CO10 ....148 C5
Grampian Way NR32 ..112 D2
Granaries The IP6 ....136 C6
Granary Rd CB8 .....121 B2
Granary The Clare CO10 .90 A7
  Hadleigh IP7 ....149 C5
Granby St CB8 ......121 B3
Grand Ave NR33 ....115 B3
Grange Cl
  Felixstowe IP11 ....152 E5
  Ipswich IP5 ....141 F8
Grange Ct IP12 .....147 B6
Grange Farm Ave
  IP11 ....152 D5
Grange La
  Barton Mills IP28 ......116 D2
  Ipswich IP5 ....141 E8
Grange Mill 3 IP29 ..62 C6
Grange Prim Sch
  IP11 ....152 D5
Grange Rd
  Beccles NR34 ....111 C5
  Felixstowe IP11 ....152 D3
  Flixton NR35 ....23 E8
  16 Harwich CO12 ....107 A2
  Ipswich IP4 ....139 E6
  Lawford CO11 ....104 C1
  Lowestoft NR32 ....112 D2
  Wickham Skeith IP23 ..52 D7
Grange View IP17 ...58 B7
Grange Wlk IP33 ....123 A2
Grantchester Pl IP5 ..141 A8
Grantchester Rise CB5 ..44 A7
Grantham Cres IP2 ..155 A1
Granville Gdns 3 IP28 .116 A4
Granville Rd IP11 ...152 F3
Granville St IP1 .....155 A3
Granworth Cl IP13 ..83 E6
Grasmere Ave 5 IP11 .153 D6
Gratton Dale NR33 ..114 E2
Gravel Dam NR32 ...112 B2
Gravel Dro IP28 .....29 E6
Gravel Hill CO6 .....102 D5
Gravel Hill Way CO12 .106 F1
Gravel Pit La CO11 ..104 F5
Gray's La IP19 ......24 C4
Grayling Rd IP8 .....142 E8
Graylings The 10 NR33 .114 C4
Grays Rd NR34 .....10 C7
Grayson Ave NR33 ..115 A3
Grayson Dr NR33 ...115 A2
Great Back La 4 IP14 ..53 F2
Great Barton Prim Sch
  IP31 ....49 B6
Great Colman St IP4 .155 C3
Great Comm La NR34 ..8 E1
Great Cornard Ctry Pk★
  CO10 ....92 B2
Great Cornard Mid Sch
  CO10 ....92 B2
Great Cornard Sports Ctr
  CO10 ....148 F2
Great Cornard Upper Sch
  CO10 ....148 F2
Great Dro CB7 ....28 A4
Great Eastern Rd
  CO10 ....148 D5
Great Eastern Sq
  IP11 ....153 A5
Great Fen Rd CB7 ...28 D8
Great Field IP11 ....152 C8
Great Finborough Prim Sch
  IP14 ....66 A4
Great Gipping St IP1 .155 C2
Great Harlings IP9 ..107 A4
Great Heath Prim Sch
  IP28 ....116 D6
Great Oak Ct CO9 ...90 A1
Great Tufts IP9 .....150 F3
Great Waldingfield VCE Prim
  Sch CO10 ....92 C6
Great Whelnetham CE Prim
  Sch IP30 ....63 F6
Great Whip St IP2 ...155 B2
Grebe Cl Ipswich IP2 .138 C2
  Mildenhall IP28 ....116 D3

Grebe Cl continued
Stowmarket IP14 . . . . .124 A6
Green Acre **2** CO10 . . . . . .92 C6
Green Cres IP10 . . . . .98 A4
Green Dr NR33 . . . . .115 A4
Green Farm La **5** IP29 . . .47 A2
Green Fleet Dr NR32 . . . . .112 E4
Green Hill IP16 . . . . .68 B1
Green La Boxted CO4 . . . .102 E3
Burgh St Peter NR34 . . . . .10 C8
Cockfield IP30 . . . . .64 D2
Creeting St Mary IP14 . . . .67 F5
Ditchingham NR35 . . . . . .110 C7
6 Feltwell IP26 . . . . .4 E5
Frostenden NR34 . . . . . . .26 C4
Great Barton IP31 . . . . . . .49 B5
Hundon CO10 . . . . .75 D2
Kessingland NR33 . . . . . . .11 C1
3 Mettlesham IP12 . . . .84 A1
Pettistree IP13 . . . . .127 D5
Redenhall with Harleston
IP20 . . . . .22 E6
Reydon IP18 . . . . .26 E1
Shipmeadow NR34 . . . . . . .8 F5
Somerleyton, Ashby &
Herringfleet NR32 . . . . . .2 E4
Southwold IP18 . . . . .119 B8
Starston IP20 . . . . .22 D8
Stratford St Mary CO7 . . .103 E6
Syleham IP21 . . . . .38 E8
2 Tattingstone IP9 . . . . .105 B8
Thelnetham IP22 . . . . .35 C6
Thetford IP24 . . . . .16 C6
Thrandeston IP21 . . . . . . .37 B6
Troston IP31 . . . . .33 C5
Tuddenham St Martin
IP6 . . . . .136 C4
Wetheringsett-cum-Brockford
IP14 . . . . .53 A6
Green La Cl IP18 . . . . . . .119 B8
Green Man Pl IP12 . . . . . .71 F2
Green Man Way IP12 . . . .147 B6
Green Oak Glade IP8 . . . .142 D8
Green Pk Brinkley CB8 . . . .59 E1
42 Harleston IP20 . . . . .22 D6
Green Rd Brandon IP27 . . . .6 A1
Newmarket CB8 . . . . .121 A2
Thorpe Morieux IP30 . . . . .64 F1
Woolpit IP30 . . . . .50 D1
Green St IP21 . . . . .38 C8
Green The **4** Ashley CB8 . .60 F8
Beck Row, Holywell Row
& Kenny Hill IP28 . . . . .29 E7
Chedburgh IP29 . . . . .62 C4
8 Earsham NR35 . . . . .7 F4
Fornham All Saints IP26 . . .48 B6
1 Grundisburgh IP13 . . . .83 E5
Hessett IP30 . . . . .64 F8
Kersey IP7 . . . . .94 A7
Kirtling CB8 . . . . .60 E3
Lound NR32 . . . . .2 F6
Lowestoft NR33 . . . . .114 F6
Mendlesham IP14 . . . . . . .52 D2
2 Mistley CO11 . . . . . . .104 E3
North Lopham IP22 . . . . . .19 A6
Snailwell CB8 . . . . .45 A6
Walberswick IP18 . . . . . . .119 B2
Green Willows CO10 . . . .78 C2
Greenacre Cres **1**
NR32 . . . . .113 B2
Greenacres IP14 . . . . .51 F1
Greenbank IP19 . . . . .118 C5
Greene King Brewing Mus★
IP33 . . . . .154 C1
Greene Rd IP33 . . . . .122 C6
Greenfield Rd NR33 . . . . .114 F5
Greenfields CB8 . . . . .121 C3
Greenfields Way CB9 . . . .132 C5
Greenfinch Ave IP2 . . . . .138 D3
Greenhills CB7 . . . . .28 E3
Greens The
Aldeburgh IP15 . . . . .130 C6
Ipswich IP4 . . . . .140 F4
Greensmill **2** CO11 . . . .104 E3
Greenspire Gr IP8 . . . . . .138 B2
Greenview IP29 . . . . .77 B7
Greenway **4** IP31 . . . . . . .49 A5
Greenway The NR34 . . . .111 B4
Greenways IP12 . . . . .85 C2
Greenways Cl IP1 . . . . . . .139 B8
Greenways Cres IP23 . . .123 D6
Greenwich Bsns Pk
IP3 . . . . .139 E2
Greenwich Cl IP3 . . . . . . .139 E2
Greenwich Rd IP3 . . . . . .139 D2
Greenwood Cl CB9 . . . . . .132 C5
Greenwood Way **1**
NR32 . . . . .113 A6
Greenwoods The IP31 . . .49 E6
Gregory Rd IP28 . . . . .116 A6
Gregory St CO10 . . . . . . .148 C5
Grenadier Rd CB9 . . . . . .132 A6
Grenville Rd CO10 . . . . . .148 D8
Gresham Ave NR32 . . . . .112 F2
Gresham Cl NR32 . . . . . . .112 F2
Gresham Rd NR34 . . . . . .111 C6
Gresley Gdns **3** IP2 . . . .139 E3
Gretna Gdns **1** IP4 . . . . .136 B1
Greville Starkey Ave
CB8 . . . . .121 A5
Grey Friars Rd IP1 . . . . . .155 B2
Greyfriars★
Dunwich IP17 . . . . .43 B1
Ipswich IP1 . . . . .155 A2
Woodbridge IP12 . . . . . .146 D4
Greyfriars Rd IP32 . . . . . .123 E4
Greyhound Hill CO4 . . . .103 C2

Greyhound La IP22 . . . . . .18 B1
Greyhound Rd **7** CO10 . .77 A2
Greys Cl **5** CO10 . . . . . . .76 E1
Greys La CB9 . . . . .75 A3
Grice Cl **3** NR33 . . . . .11 C1
Griffith Cl **4** NR33 . . . . . .11 C1
Grime's Graves (Flint
Mines)★ 6 C4
Grimsey Rd IP16 . . . . .129 D5
Grimsey's La IP16 . . . . . . .129 E5
Grimston La IP11 . . . . . . .107 C8
Grimwade Cl **9** CO11 . . .104 E4
Grimwade St IP4 . . . . .155 C2
Grinder's La IP21 . . . . .22 D4
Grindle Gdns IP33 . . . . . .123 B3
Grindle The IP8 . . . . .95 B4
Grinstead Gdns IP6 . . . . .125 E3
Grinstead Hill IP6 . . . . . . .125 E3
Gromford La IP17 . . . . .72 C5
Groomes Cl **5** NR31 . . . . . .3 B7
Grosvenor Cl IP4 . . . . .139 E5
Grosvenor Gdns IP13 . . .122 F3
Grosvenor House Ct **9**
IP28 . . . . .116 B5
Grosvenor Rd
Lowestoft NR33 . . . . .115 C7
Sudbury CO10 . . . . .148 B8
Grosvenor Yd CB8 . . . . . .121 A3
Groton St CO10 . . . . .93 B5
Groton Wood Nature
Reserve★ CO10 . . . . .93 D6
Grove Ave CO10 . . . . .92 C6
Grove Cty Prim Sch
NR33 . . . . .114 C4
Grove End IP21 . . . . .39 B5
Grove Gdns
Carlton Colville NR33 . . .114 C4
Fordham CB7 . . . . .29 A2
Woodbridge IP12 . . . . . .146 E6
Grove Hill Belstead IP8 . .142 C7
Dedham CO7 . . . . .103 E2
Langham CO4 . . . . .103 C3
Grove La
Ashfield cum Thorpe IP14 . .54 C2
Elmswell IP30 . . . . .51 A3
Harkstead IP9 . . . . .106 C4
Ipswich IP4 . . . . .139 E5
Mendham IP20 . . . . .23 A2
Stanton IP31 . . . . .34 F4
Thetford IP24 . . . . .16 C6
Grove Mews **4** NR34 . . .111 C4
Grove Pk
Bury St Edmunds IP33 . .154 A3
Fordham CB7 . . . . .29 A2
5 Walsham le Willows
IP31 . . . . .35 C2
Grove Rd Beccles NR34 . .111 B5
2 Brantham CO11 . . . . .104 E4
Brockdish IP21 . . . . .21 F3
Bury St Edmunds IP33 . .154 A3
Felixstowe IP11 . . . . .153 A6
Gissing IP21 . . . . .21 A8
Knodishall IP17 . . . . .72 F7
Lowestoft NR33 . . . . .114 C4
Pettistree IP13 . . . . .127 A4
Starston IP20 . . . . .22 C6
Walsham le Willows IP31 . .35 C2
Woodbridge IP13 . . . . . . .146 E6
Grove Rd N NR33 . . . . . . .114 D5
Grove The
Great Glemham IP17 . . . . .56 F1
12 Martlesham Heath IP5 . .98 A8
Mildenhall IP28 . . . . .29 F8
Stowmarket IP14 . . . . . . .124 E5
5 Woodbridge IP12 . . . .147 B6
Grove Wlk IP8 . . . . .142 D8
Grove; Henley Rd The
IP1 . . . . .135 C2
Grub La IP19 . . . . .24 E5
Grundisburgh Cty Prim Sch
IP13 . . . . .83 E5
Grundisburgh Rd
Clopton IP13 . . . . .83 D8
Great Bealings IP13 . . . . .137 C6
Tuddenham St Martin IP6 . .136 D6
Grundle Cl **6** IP31 . . . . . . .34 E4
Guildhall Feoffment Cty Prim
Sch IP33 . . . . .154 C1
Guildhall La IP14 . . . . .26 D1
Guildhall of Corpus Christi
The★ CO10 . . . . .78 D4
Guildhall St IP33 . . . . .154 B2
Guineas Cl CB8 . . . . .120 E6
Gules Gn IP21 . . . . .22 F1
Gull Hill IP19 . . . . .25 C3
Gull La
Grundisburgh IP13 . . . . . . .83 D6
Thornham Magna IP23 . . .37 A2
Gull Rd IP17 . . . . .128 B3
Gull The IP13 . . . . .70 C2
Gull's La CO7 . . . . .104 A2
Gulpher Bsns Pk IP11 . . .152 E5
Gulpher Rd IP11 . . . . .152 E6
Gun Hill Dedham CO7 . . .103 D4
Southwold IP18 . . . . .119 D4
Gun La NR32 . . . . .113 E2
Gunton Ave NR32 . . . . . . .113 A7
Gunton Church La
NR32 . . . . .113 C5
Gunton Cliff NR32 . . . . . .113 D5
Gunton Com Prim Sch
NR32 . . . . .113 C6
Gunton Dr NR32 . . . . .113 D5
Gunton St Peter's Ave
NR32 . . . . .113 C5
Gunton Warren Nature
Reserve★ NR32 . . . . . . .113 D6

Guntons Cl **12** CB7 . . . . . .28 D4
Gurdon Rd **5** IP13 . . . . . .83 E5
Gurlings Cl CO10 . . . . .132 E8
Guscot Cl NR32 . . . . .113 A6
Gusford Prim Sch IP2 . . .138 D1
Guston Gdns IP10 . . . . . . .98 E2
Guthrum Rd IP7 . . . . .149 D6
Guy Cook Cl CO10 . . . . . . .92 B2
Guyatt Ct **6** CB5 . . . . .44 A5
Gwendoline Rd IP4 . . . . . .140 E4
Gwynne Rd **4** CO12 . . . .107 A2
Gymnasium St IP1 . . . . . .155 A3

H

Hacheston Rd IP13 . . . . . .70 F5
Hackney Rd
Peasenhall IP17 . . . . .56 E8
Woodbridge IP12 . . . . . .147 B6
Hackney Terr IP12 . . . . . .147 B6
Hackney's Cnr IP6 . . . . . . .81 F5
Haddiscoe Sta NR31 . . . . . .2 A5
Hadenham Rd IP11 . . . . . .114 F1
Hadleigh Bsns Pk IP7 . . . .94 E4
Hadleigh Dr NR32 . . . . . .112 F3
Hadleigh Guildhall★
IP7 . . . . .149 D5
Hadleigh High Sch
IP7 . . . . .149 F5
Hadleigh Prim Sch
IP7 . . . . .149 D5
Hadleigh Railway Walk★
IP7 . . . . .94 E3
Hadleigh Rd Aldham IP7 . .94 E8
Bildeston IP7 . . . . .79 F3
Boxford CO6 . . . . .93 D2
East Bergholt CO7 . . . . . .151 B4
Elmsett IP7 . . . . .80 F1
Higham CO7 . . . . .103 D7
Ipswich IP2 . . . . .138 E6
Hadleigh Rd Ind Est
IP2 . . . . .138 F7
Hadleigh Swimming Pool
IP7 . . . . .149 D6
Hadrian Cl CB9 . . . . .133 B5
Haggars Mead IP14 . . . . . .67 D7
Hague Cl NR33 . . . . .114 C6
Halcyon Cres NR32 . . . . .113 C1
Hale Cl IP7 . . . . .138 D2
Halesowen Cl IP2 . . . . . . .142 F8
Halesworth & District Mus★
IP19 . . . . .118 B4
Halesworth (Holton) Airfield
Mus★ IP19 . . . . .118 D6
Halesworth Gall★
IP19 . . . . .118 B3
Halesworth Mid Sch
IP19 . . . . .118 C5
Halesworth Rd
Brampton with Stoven
IP19 . . . . .25 E3
Heveningham IP19 . . . . . . .40 F3
Linstead Parva IP19 . . . . . .40 F8
Reydon IP18 . . . . .119 B7
St Andrew, Ilketshall
NR34 . . . . .25 A6
St Lawrence, Ilketshall
NR34 . . . . .24 E8
Sibton IP17 . . . . .41 B1
Uggeshall NR34 . . . . .25 F3
Walpole IP19 . . . . .41 C5
Wenhaston with Mells Hamlet
IP19 . . . . .41 F6
Halesworth Sta IP19 . . . .118 B4
Half Moon La
6 Grundisburgh IP13 . . . .83 E5
Redgrave IP22 . . . . .36 A8
Half Moon St IP30 . . . . . . .65 D5
Halfar **8** IP31 . . . . .33 D5
Halfmoon La IP27 . . . . . . .109 C2
Halford La IP22 . . . . .19 D3
Halifax Prim Sch IP2 . . . .139 A2
Halifax Rd Ipswich IP2 . . .139 B2
9 Mildenhall IP28 . . . . .30 A8
Halifax St IP27 . . . . .109 F1
Halifax Way CB8 . . . . .120 E5
Haling Way IP24 . . . . .16 A6
Hall Barn Rd CB7 . . . . .29 B5
Hall Cl IP29 . . . . .62 B4
Hall Cl The IP28 . . . . .31 D4
Hall Dr **17** Feltwell IP26 . . .4 E5
Lakenheath IP27 . . . . . . .109 C2
Lowestoft NR32 . . . . .112 C1
Santon Downham IP27 . . . .6 C2
Hall Farm Cl IP12 . . . . . . .147 B8
Hall Farm La NR34 . . . . . . .10 E1
Hall Farm Rd
Boot Street IP13 . . . . . . .137 E6
Woodbridge IP12 . . . . . .147 B8
Hall Field **1** IP11 . . . . . .152 E5
Hall La Blundeston NR32 . . .3 A4
Bressingham IP22 . . . . . . .19 D5
Brinkley CB8 . . . . .59 F1
Burston & Shimpling IP22 . .21 A6
Claydon IP6 . . . . .134 E8
Harwich CO12 . . . . .107 A1
Hawkedon CO10 . . . . .76 C7
Otley IP6 . . . . .69 C2
Oulton NR32 . . . . .112 C4
Redgrave IP22 . . . . .36 A8
Ridgewell CO9 . . . . .89 D3
Risby IP28 . . . . .47 D5
Roydon IP22 . . . . .20 A3
Scole IP21 . . . . .21 C4
Shelfanger IP22 . . . . .20 B6

Hall La continued
Somersham IP8 . . . . .81 C3
Spexhall IP19 . . . . .24 C1
Wetheringsett-cum-Brockford
IP14 . . . . .53 B4
3 Witnesham IP6 . . . . . . .83 A5
Yaxley IP23 . . . . .37 B4
Hall Pond Way IP11 . . . . .152 D5
Hall Rd Barnardiston CB8 . .75 B5
Barsham NR34 . . . . .8 F3
Bedingfield IP23 . . . . .54 A7
Bedingham NR35 . . . . .7 C7
Belchamp Walter CO10 . . .91 A3
Blundeston NR32 . . . . . . .112 C8
Borley CO10 . . . . .91 D5
Brent Eleigh CO10 . . . . . . .79 A3
Brockdish IP21 . . . . .21 F3
Burston & Shimpling IP22 . .20 E7
Carlton Colville NR33 . . . .114 B2
Charsfield IP13 . . . . .69 F3
Chelsworth IP7 . . . . .79 C2
Cowlinge CB8 . . . . .75 A7
Earsham NR35 . . . . .7 E4
Ellingham NR35 . . . . .8 C7
Foxhall IP10 . . . . .141 E4
7 Hopton on Sea NR31 . . .3 B7
Hundon CO10 . . . . .75 E4
9 Kessingland NR33 . . . .11 C1
Lavenham CO10 . . . . .78 D4
Little Bealings IP5 . . . . . .137 E4
Lowestoft NR33 . . . . .112 D1
Marlesford IP13 . . . . .71 C1
Mount Bures CO8 . . . . . .101 C3
Parham IP13 . . . . .71 B7
Pulham St Mary IP21 . . . . .22 A8
Stowmarket IP14 . . . . . . .124 B8
Thorndon IP23 . . . . .53 C7
Wenhaston with Mells Hamlet
IP19 . . . . .42 D5
Hall Rise CO10 . . . . .148 A3
Hall St
Long Melford CO10 . . . . . .91 E8
Soham CB7 . . . . .28 D4
Hall Wlk IP8 . . . . .81 F1
Hall's La IP31 . . . . .50 B5
Hallfields IP27 . . . . .109 C7
Hallifax Pl IP29 . . . . .77 F7
Halliwell Rd IP4 . . . . .140 B6
Halls Drift IP5 . . . . .141 B6
Hallwong La IP20 . . . . .22 D7
Hallwyck Gdns CB8 . . . . .120 F2
Halton Cres IP3 . . . . .140 C1
Hamblin Rd IP12 . . . . .147 A5
Hamblin Wlk IP12 . . . . . . .147 A5
Hambling's Piece NR16 . .18 C8
Hambrook Cl IP30 . . . . . . .63 F7
Hambros The **3** IP31 . . . .49 D4
Hamilton Ct CB8 . . . . .120 E2
Hamilton Gdns IP11 . . . . .153 A3
Hamilton Rd
Felixstowe IP11 . . . . .153 A4
Ipswich IP3 . . . . .140 B3
Lowestoft NR32 . . . . .113 E1
Newmarket CB8 . . . . .120 D5
7 Sudbury CO10 . . . . . .148 C5
Hamilton St
6 Felixstowe IP11 . . . . .152 E5
4 Harwich CO12 . . . . . .106 F3
Hamilton Way
Ditchingham NR35 . . . . . .110 C8
Stowmarket IP14 . . . . . . .124 D7
Hamiltons The CB8 . . . . .120 F2
Hamlet Ct **2** CO8 . . . . . . .101 C4
Hamlet Rd CB9 . . . . .132 F5
Hammond Cl CB8 . . . . . . .120 E6
Hammond's Cnr IP14 . . . .67 C6
Hammonds Wlk IP19 . . . . .42 C6
Hampstead Ave IP28 . . . .116 B6
Hampton Rd IP1 . . . . .138 F7
Hanchet End CB9 . . . . .74 A1
Hanchett End CB9 . . . . . .132 A6
Hancocks Cl IP16 . . . . . . .129 D5
Handford Cut IP1 . . . . . . .139 A6
Handford Hall Prim Sch
IP1 . . . . .139 A6
Handford Rd IP1 . . . . .155 A3
Hankin Ave **13** CO12 . . . .106 E1
Hanmer Ave IP28 . . . . . . .116 C5
Hanmer Wlk IP33 . . . . . . .122 B6
Hanover Cl
5 Bury St Edmunds IP32 . .123 A8
Exning CB8 . . . . .120 E8
Oulton Broad NR33 . . . . .114 F5
Hanover Ct **11** 148 B4
Ha'penny Field **8** IP9 . . .105 E7
Ha'penny Pier Visitor Ctr★
CO12 . . . . .107 B3
Harbour Cres **7** CO12 . . .107 C3
Harbour La IP22 . . . . .18 D3
Harbour Rd NR32 . . . . . . .112 E1
Harbourage The NR34 . . .116 F1
Harcourt Ave **1** CO12 . . .107 A2
Harding's La IP31 . . . . .50 E4
Hardwick Cl IP4 . . . . .140 E4
Hardwick La IP33 . . . . . . .122 C4
Hardwick Mid Sch
IP33 . . . . .123 B1
Hardwick Pk Gdns
IP33 . . . . .123 A1
Hardwick Prim Sch
IP33 . . . . .123 B2
Hardwick Rd
Haverhill CB9 . . . . .132 F6
Starston IP20 . . . . .22 C7
Hardy Cl
8 Brantham CO11 . . . . .104 E4
Lowestoft NR33 . . . . .115 A7
Hardy Cres IP1 . . . . .134 F4

Gre - Hat **169**

Hardy Ct **1** CO10 . . . . . . .148 D8
Hare & Hounds Cnr
IP6 . . . . .82 F8
Harebell Rd
Ipswich IP2 . . . . .138 F4
Red Lodge IP28 . . . . .30 C1
Harebell Way NR33 . . . . .114 C5
Harefield CO10 . . . . .77 E1
Hares La IP19 . . . . .25 B4
Hares Rd IP7 . . . . .65 D1
Hares Wlk **1** CO10 . . . . . .148 D6
Harewood Terr **7** CB9 . .132 C5
Hargrave Ave IP6 . . . . . . .125 D3
Hargrave Rd IP29 . . . . .62 B6
Harkstead La
Freston IP9 . . . . .105 F8
Woolverstone IP9 . . . . . . .144 A1
Harkstead Rd **3** IP9 . . . .106 A5
Harland St IP7 . . . . .139 C3
Harleston Hill IP21 . . . . . . .39 E8
Harleston Mus★ IP21 . . . .22 D6
Harleston Prim Sch
IP20 . . . . .22 D6
Harleston Rd
Metfield IP20 . . . . .23 B3
Pulham Market IP21 . . . . . .21 E8
Scole IP21 . . . . .21 D5
Weybread IP21 . . . . .22 D4
Harling Dro IP27 . . . . .6 E3
Harling Rd
Garboldisham IP22 . . . . . .18 C6
North Lopham IP22 . . . . . .19 A6
Harling Way IP16 . . . . . . .129 B6
Harman's La IP20 . . . . .22 C5
Harold Rd NR33 . . . . .115 C6
Harp's Cl Rd NR32 . . . . . .113 B3
Harpclose Rd **2** CO10 . . .148 D6
Harper's Est **9** CO6 . . . .102 C5
Harper's Hill CO6 . . . . . . .102 C5
Harpers La IP17 . . . . .128 D3
Harpur's Rd **2** CO10 . . . . .77 A2
Harrier Cl IP3 . . . . .140 B1
Harrier Way IP14 . . . . .67 A5
Harriers Wlk IP13 . . . . .70 E5
Harrington Ave NR32 . . . .113 C6
Harrington Cl IP33 . . . . . .154 C1
Harris Ave NR32 . . . . .113 C4
Harris Ct **12** IP14 . . . . .53 C2
Harris Mid Sch NR32 . . . .113 D3
Harrison Gn **3** IP18 . . . . .119 C8
Harrison Gr IP5 . . . . .141 C8
Harrison Rd NR32 . . . . . . .112 E1
Harrison Way IP26 . . . . .4 F3
Harrisons La IP19 . . . . . . .118 C5
Harrod Cl NR33 . . . . .115 C5
Harrop Dale **10** NR33 . . . .114 C3
Harrow Gn **2** IP33 . . . . . .122 B6
Harrow Gn **2** IP31 . . . . . . .63 D1
Harrow La Benhall IP17 . . .72 A7
Theberton IP16 . . . . .129 A8
Harrow Rd
Haverhill CB9 . . . . .132 C5
Troston IP31 . . . . .33 D4
Harrow St CO6 . . . . .102 B8
Harry Palmer Cl **1** CB7 . .29 A1
Hart Cl CB9 . . . . .132 D8
Hart's La CO7 . . . . .103 E1
Hartest Hill IP29 . . . . .77 C6
Hartest La IP29 . . . . .63 C1
Hartest Prim Sch IP29 . . .77 A7
Hartest Rd IP29 . . . . .63 A1
Hartest Way
Stowmarket IP14 . . . . . . .124 F3
Sudbury CO10 . . . . .148 F4
Hartfield Rd CB8 . . . . .59 F2
Hartington Rd IP15 . . . . . .130 E3
Hartismere High Sch
IP23 . . . . .117 B3
Hartismere Hospl
IP23 . . . . .117 C3
Hartley St IP2 . . . . .155 B1
Hartree Way IP5 . . . . .141 E7
Harvard Rd **6** IP26 . . . . . . .4 D5
Harvest Cl IP14 . . . . .51 D1
Harvest Dr NR33 . . . . .114 C2
Harvesters Way
Martlesham IP5 . . . . .141 F6
2 Martlesham Heath IP5 . .98 A7
Harvey Cl **7** CO11 . . . . . .104 E3
Harvey La IP21 . . . . .21 C5
Harvey's La IP6 . . . . .82 C6
Harwich Int Port CO12 . . .106 A5
Harwich Rd
Foxash Estate CO11 . . . . .104 A4
Mistley CO11 . . . . .105 A2
Ramsey & Parkeston
CO11 . . . . .106 A1
Wrabness CO11 . . . . .105 F1
Harwich Town Sta
CO12 . . . . .107 B3
Harwood Ave IP24 . . . . . . .16 C7
Hascot Hill Barking IP6 . .125 A1
Battisford IP14 . . . . .81 A8
Haselmere Cl **5** IP32 . . .123 D8
Hasketon Rd Burgh IP13 . .83 F6
Woodbridge IP12 . . . . . .146 E6
Haskins Wlk IP5 . . . . .141 E7
Haslemere Dr IP4 . . . . . . .139 E7
Hasse Rd CB7 . . . . .28 E8
Hasted Cl IP33 . . . . .122 C4
Hatchley Cl IP12 . . . . .85 C3
Hatfield Rd IP3 . . . . .140 A3
Hatley Dr CB5 . . . . .44 A6
Hatter St IP33 . . . . .154 B2

Haugh La
Great Ashfield IP31 . . . .**50** F5
Haughley IP14 . . . .**51** D1
Woodbridge IP12 . . . .**146** F6
Haughgate Cl IP12 . . . .**146** F6
Haughley Crawfords CE Prim
Sch IP14 . . . .**51** C1
Haughley Dr IP4 . . . .**140** F6
Haughley Pk★ IP14 . . . . .**51** A1
Haughley Rd IP14 . . . .**66** B7
Hauliers Rd IP11 . . . .**152** D2
Haven Ave NR32 . . . .**113** B3
Haven Cl IP11 . . . .**152** D4
Haven Nature Reserve The★
IP16 . . . .**130** F6
Haven Rd IP16 . . . .**129** D5
Haven The IP16 . . . .**73** F6
Havens The IP10 . . . .**144** E7
Havergate Island National
Nature Reserve★
IP12 . . . .**86** F2
Havergate Rd ⬛ IP3 . . . .**144** D8
Haverhill & District Local
History Ctr★ CB9 . . . .**132** E5
CB9 . . . .**132** E5
Haverhill Arts Ctr★
CB9 . . . .**132** E5
Haverhill Bsns Pk CB9 .**132** F3
Haverhill Leisure Ctr
CB9 . . . .**132** F6
Haverhill Railway Walks
Nature Reserve★
CB9 . . . .**133** B4
Haverhill Rd
Haverhill CB9 . . . .**132** F8
Helions Bumpstead CB9 . .**88** B5
Kedington CB9 . . . .**133** E8
Steeple Bumpstead CB9 . .**88** D5
Haverhill Trade Pk
CB9 . . . .**132** F3
Haward St NR32 . . . .**113** C1
Hawbridge IP9 . . . .**150** E4
Hawe's La Norton IP31 . .**50** B4
Wicken CB7 . . . .**28** A2
Hawes St IP2 . . . .**155** C1
Hawk End La IP30 . . . .**50** E2
Hawk's La IP29 . . . .**63** A2
Hawke Rd IP3 . . . .**139** E1
Hawker Dr IP5 . . . .**98** A8
Hawkes La IP11 . . . .**152** D6
Hawkins Ct ⬛ CO10 . . . .**148** D8
Hawkins Rd CO10 . . . . . .**148** E8
Hawks Mill St IP6 . . . . . .**125** D5
Hawstead La IP29 . . . .**63** E6
Hawthorn Ave NR33 . . . .**115** A7
Hawthorn Cl
Beccles NR34 . . . .**111** E4
Bury St Edmunds IP32 . . .**122** D8
Knodishall IP17 . . . .**129** B2
⬛ Stowupland IP14 . . . . . .**67** A6
Hawthorn Dr
⬛ Horringer IP29 . . . .**63** A8
Ipswich IP2 . . . .**138** D2
Hawthorn La ⬛ IP27 . . . .**13** F2
Hawthorn Pl IP12 . . . . . .**146** E6
Hawthorn Rd
Haverhill CB9 . . . .**132** B7
Middleton IP17 . . . .**58** A5
Sudbury CO10 . . . .**148** F5
Theberton IP16 . . . .**57** F4
Hawthorn Way CB5 . . . . . .**44** B6
Hawthorn Wlk ⬛ IP28 . . .**30** B8
Hawthorns The ⬛ IP31 . . .**49** D4
Hay Barn Meadow ⬛
IP30 . . . .**50** D1
Haycocks Rd CB9 . . . . . .**132** A7
Haygate IP23 . . . .**117** C3
Hayhill Rd IP14 . . . .**139** E7
Hayland Dro IP28 . . . .**29** D7
Haylings Gr IP16 . . . .**129** C4
Haylings Rd IP16 . . . .**129** C4
Hayman Rd IP3 . . . .**139** F1
Haynings Mill IP13 . . . . .**126** D4
Haysborder Rd IP29 . . . . .**46** F3
Haythill La IP26 . . . .**4** D6
Hayward Cl IP23 . . . .**117** C2
Haywards Fields IP5 . . . .**141** D8
Hazel Cl
⬛ Bentwaters Airfield IP12 **85** E8
Haverhill CB9 . . . .**132** C5
Mildenhall IP28 . . . .**116** E4
Hazel Covert ⬛ IP24 . . . .**16** D6
Hazel Ct ⬛ CO10 . . . .**148** D6
Hazel Dr
⬛ Horringer IP29 . . . .**63** A8
Ipswich IP3 . . . .**140** E1
Hazel Rise IP6 . . . .**134** C8
Hazelcroft Rd IP1 . . . . . .**135** B2
Hazels La IP17 . . . .**42** D5
Hazelville Cl ⬛ CO12 . . .**106** F1
Hazelwood ⬛ IP7 . . . .**80** F1
Hazelwood Rd ⬛ IP31 . . .**49** D4
Hazelwood Marshes Nature
Reserve★ IP15 . . . .**73** B4
Hazelwood St IP17 . . . . .**130** A7
Hazlitt Rd ⬛ IP1 . . . .**135** A3
Head La CO10 . . . .**148** F2
Headingham CE ⬛⬛ IP2 .**139** A2
Headland Ave CB8 . . . . . .**132** C5
Headland Dro IP26 . . . .**4** A1
Healey Cl NR32 . . . .**113** A5
Heasman Cl CB8 . . . .**120** F5
Heath Cl
East Bergholt CO7 . . . . . .**151** D5
Hessett IP30 . . . .**64** F8
Polstead CO6 . . . .**93** F3

Heath Ct ⬛ IP11 . . . .**107** D8
Heath Dr IP12 . . . .**99** C7
Heath Farm Rd IP28 . . . . .**30** B1
Heath La Blundeston NR32 . .**3** A4
Ipswich IP4 . . . .**140** C5
Pakenham IP31 . . . .**49** D8
Heath Prim Sch IP5 . . . .**141** B7
Heath Rd Burwell CB5 . . . .**44** C2
East Bergholt CO7 . . . . . .**151** D5
Exning CB8 . . . .**120** A4
Fritton & St Olaves NR31 . . .**2** B5
Geldeston NR34 . . . .**9** A7
Hessett IP30 . . . .**64** F8
Ipswich IP4 . . . .**140** C7
Ixworth IP31 . . . .**33** E2
Kenninghall NR16 . . . .**19** A7
Lowestoft NR33 . . . .**114** F8
Mildenhall IP28 . . . .**116** E5
Mistley CO11 . . . .**105** A2
Newmarket CB8 . . . .**121** C3
Norton IP31 . . . .**50** B4
Polstead CO6 . . . .**93** F2
Sapiston IP31 . . . .**34** B7
Swaffham Prior CB5 . . . . . .**44** A1
Thurston IP31 . . . .**49** D4
Troston IP31 . . . .**33** D4
Wenhaston with Mells Hamlet
IP19 . . . .**42** B7
Woolpit IP30 . . . .**50** D1
Heath The
Dedham CO7 . . . .**104** A2
Great Waldingfield CO10 . .**92** C6
Woolpit IP30 . . . .**65** F8
Heath View
Ipswich IP5 . . . .**141** A6
Leiston IP16 . . . .**129** E5
Heath Way CO10 . . . .**92** C6
Heath Wlk IP12 . . . .**72** A4
Heathbell Rd CB8 . . . . . .**121** C3
Heather Ave IP3 . . . .**140** C2
Heather Cl
⬛ Great Barton IP31 . . . . .**49** D4
Martlesham Heath IP5 . . .**141** F6
Heather Rd NR32 . . . .**113** D4
Heather Way
Brandon IP27 . . . .**6** A1
Worlingham NR34 . . . .**111** F3
Heathercroft Rd IP1 . . . .**135** A3
Heatherhayes IP2 . . . . . .**139** A3
Heatherset Way IP28 . . . .**30** C1
Heathfield IP5 . . . .**141** F6
Heathfield Mews IP5 . . .**141** F6
Heathfield Rd ⬛ IP9 . . . .**105** E7
Heathfields IP11 . . . .**98** D1
Heathgate Piece IP11 . .**152** E2
Heathlands Pk IP4 . . . . .**140** E4
Heathside Specl Sch
IP4 . . . .**140** E4
Hedley La NR33 . . . .**114** A3
Heigham Dr NR33 . . . . . .**114** F5
Heights The NR34 . . . . . .**111** C4
Heldhaw Rd NR32 . . . . . .**123** E5
Helena Rd IP3 . . . .**139** E4
Helens Cl ⬛ IP22 . . . .**36** A8
Helions Bumpstead Rd
CB9 . . . .**132** D3
Helions Pk Ave CB9 . . . .**132** E5
Helions Pk Gdns ⬛ CB9 .**132** E5
Helions Pk Rd ⬛ CB9 . . .**132** E5
Helions Rd CB9 . . . .**88** C4
Helions Service Rd ⬛
CB9 . . . .**132** E5
Helions Wlk CB9 . . . .**132** E5
Helmingham Hall & Gdns★
IP14 . . . .**69** A4
Helmingham Prim Sch
IP14 . . . .**69** B6
Helmingham Rd IP6 . . . . .**69** C2
Helston Cl IP5 . . . .**141** B7
Hemmant Way NR34 . . . . . .**9** B7
Hemplands The ⬛
NR32 . . . .**113** D2
Hempnall Rd NR35 . . . .**7** A8
Hempstead Rd CB9 . . . .**132** A7
Hen Reed Bed Nature
Reserve★ IP18 . . . .**43** B8
Hencote La
Horringer IP29 . . . .**63** C8
Nowton IP33 . . . .**123** A7
Henderson Cl
Bramford IP8 . . . .**134** A1
Haverhill CB9 . . . .**132** A7
Hengrave Cl ⬛ IP2 . . . . .**139** A2
Hengrave Hall★ IP28 . . . .**47** A7
Hengrave Rd NR28 . . . . . .**48** B6
Henham Rd NR32 . . . .**113** A5
Henley Ave IP1 . . . .**135** B3
Henley Cl IP17 . . . .**128** C3
Henley Prim Sch IP6 . . . . .**82** E6
Henley Rd Henley IP6 . . . .**82** D5
Ipswich IP1 . . . .**155** B4
Henniker Rd
⬛ Debenham IP14 . . . .**53** F2
Ipswich IP1 . . . .**138** C8
Henny Rd CO8 . . . .**101** A7
Henry Cl CB9 . . . .**132** B4
Henry Rd IP3 . . . .**140** B1
Henry St IP4 . . . .**155** B3
Henry Ward Rd ⬛ IP20 . .**22** D6
Henry Watson's Potteries★
IP22 . . . .**35** D5
Henslow Rd IP4 . . . .**140** B5
Henstead Gdns IP3 . . . . .**140** A2
Hepworth Ave IP33 . . . . .**122** D5
Hepworth Rd
Barningham IP31 . . . .**34** F7
Hepworth IP22 . . . .**35** A7
Stanton IP31 . . . .**34** B7

Thelnetham IP22 . . . .**35** B7
Herbert Cl CO10 . . . .**148** E8
Herbert Human Cl ⬛
CB7 . . . .**28** D4
Herbert Rd IP5 . . . .**141** E8
Hereford Dr ⬛ IP6 . . . . . .**82** B5
Hereward Ave NR28 . . . .**116** C5
Hereward Way
⬛ Feltwell IP26 . . . .**4** D5
Littleport CB7 . . . .**12** B7
Weeting-with-Broomhill
IP27 . . . .**5** E3
Heritage Gn ⬛ NR33 . . . . .**11** B1
Heritage Workshop Ctr★
NR32 . . . .**113** E3
Herivan Cl NR32 . . . .**112** E4
Herivan Gdns ⬛ NR32 . .**112** E4
Hermitage Ct IP13 . . . . .**126** B3
Hermitage Meadows
CO10 . . . .**76** B1
Herolf Way ⬛ IP20 . . . . . .**22** D6
Heron Cl
⬛ Mildenhall IP28 . . . .**13** B1
Stowmarket IP14 . . . .**124** A6
Heron Ct CB7 . . . .**28** C5
Heron Hill IP14 . . . .**66** C6
Heron Rd
Bury St Edmunds IP33 . . .**123** B2
Ipswich IP2 . . . .**138** E3
Saxmundham IP17 . . . . . .**128** B3
Herons Cl NR32 . . . .**112** D2
Herring Fishery Score ⬛
NR32 . . . .**113** E1
Herring Mkt ⬛ NR32 . . . .**115** D8
Herringfleet Drainage Mill★
NR32 . . . .**2** B4
Herringfleet Rd NR31 . . . . .**2** B5
Herringswell Rd
Herringswell IP28 . . . .**30** D2
Kentford CB8 . . . .**46** A6
Hertford Cl ⬛ IP32 . . . . . .**48** C5
Hertford Pl IP15 . . . .**130** E3
Hertford Rd ⬛ CO10 . . . .**76** A1
Hertfords Pl IP12 . . . .**86** D7
Hervey Cl ⬛ IP9 . . . .**107** A5
Hervey Rd IP33 . . . .**122** E3
Hervey St Ipswich IP4 . . .**155** C4
Lowestoft NR32 . . . .**115** C8
Hessett Cl IP14 . . . .**124** F3
Hethersett Cl CB8 . . . . . .**120** E8
Heveningham Long La
IP17 . . . .**41** A1
Heveningham Rd IP19 . . .**40** C5
Hewitt Rd
⬛ Harwich CO12 . . . .**106** E1
⬛ Ramsey CO12 . . . .**106** E1
Hexham Cl ⬛ IP2 . . . .**139** A2
Heycroft Way ⬛ CO6 . . .**102** C5
Heyford Ct ⬛ IP28 . . . . . .**116** B5
Heyford Rd ⬛ IP31 . . . . . .**33** D5
Heywood Ave IP22 . . . . . .**20** C3
Heywood Cl IP2 . . . .**138** D1
Heywood Rd IP22 . . . .**20** C4
Hibbard Rd IP8 . . . .**134** C2
Hickford Hill CO10 . . . . . .**90** B7
Hickling Dr IP33 . . . .**123** B1
Hicks Way IP32 . . . .**133** C3
High Baxter St IP33 . . . .**154** B2
High Beach IP11 . . . .**153** C4
High Beech NR32 . . . .**113** B2
High Comm Rd IP22 . . . . .**18** F5
High Ct IP20 . . . .**22** E6
High Gn IP16 . . . .**129** C6
High Hall Cl ⬛ IP11 . . . .**107** D8
High House Farm Rd
IP12 . . . .**131** D8
High House La IP7 . . . . . .**79** B5
High La IP14 . . . .**53** B6
High Leas NR34 . . . .**111** C3
High Leas Cl ⬛ NR34 . . .**111** C3
High Lighthouse Wireless
Mus★ CO12 . . . .**107** C3
High Lodge Visitor Ctr
Thetford Forest Pk★
IP27 . . . .**15** C7
High London La IP22 . . . .**20** A8
High Rd Badingham IP13 . .**56** C6
Bressingham IP22 . . . .**19** F4
Felixstowe IP11 . . . .**152** B8
Great Finborough IP14 . . .**66** A2
Kettleburgh IP13 . . . .**55** B2
Leavenheath CO6 . . . . . .**102** A7
Needham IP20 . . . .**22** B3
Roydon IP22 . . . .**20** A3
Swilland IP6 . . . .**83** A7
Trimley St Martin IP11 . . . .**98** C1
Wortwell IP20 . . . .**23** A7
High Rd E IP11 . . . .**153** B5
High Rd W IP11 . . . .**152** F5
High Row Field IP11 . . . .**153** C5
High St Acton CO10 . . . . . .**92** B7
Aldeburgh IP15 . . . .**130** E3
Ashley CB8 . . . .**60** F8
Brandon IP27 . . . .**5** F1
Brinkley CB8 . . . .**59** F1
⬛ Bures CO8 . . . .**101** C5
Burwell CB5 . . . .**44** A5
Cavendish CO10 . . . .**76** C1
Cheveley CB8 . . . .**60** E8
Chippenham CB7 . . . .**45** C8
Clare CO10 . . . .**90** A8
Debenham IP14 . . . .**53** F2
Dedham CO7 . . . .**103** F3
Dunwich IP17 . . . .**43** B1
Felixstowe IP11 . . . .**152** E6
Feltwell IP26 . . . .**4** E5
Flowton IP8 . . . .**81** C1

High St continued
Gislingham IP23 . . . .**36** D2
Great Yeldham CO9 . . . . . .**90** A1
Hadleigh IP7 . . . .**149** D6
Harwich CO12 . . . .**107** B2
Haverhill CB9 . . . .**132** E5
Hemingstone IP6 . . . .**68** C1
Hitcham IP7 . . . .**79** F4
Hopton IP22 . . . .**18** C2
Ipswich IP1 . . . .**155** B3
Ixworth IP31 . . . .**34** B1
Kessingland IP33 . . . .**11** B1
Kirkley Heath IP27 . . . . . .**109** C6
Langham CO4 . . . .**103** B2
Lavenham CO10 . . . .**78** D4
Laxfield IP13 . . . .**40** B3
Leiston IP16 . . . .**129** C6
Long Melford CO10 . . . .**77** E1
⬛ Lowestoft NR32 . . . . . .**113** E2
Manningtree CO11 . . . . . .**104** E2
Mildenhall IP28 . . . .**116** C4
Nayland CO6 . . . .**102** D5
Needham Market IP6 . . . .**125** D5
Newmarket CB8 . . . .**120** F2
Orford IP12 . . . .**131** C2
Pettistree IP13 . . . .**127** C5
Rattlesden IP30 . . . .**65** D6
St Margaret, Ilketshall
NR35 . . . .**24** D7
Saxmundham IP17 . . . . . .**128** D3
Soham CB7 . . . .**28** D4
Southwold IP18 . . . .**119** D5
Sproughton IP8 . . . .**138** A6
Stansfield CO10 . . . .**76** C6
Stetchworth CB8 . . . .**60** A5
Thelnetham IP22 . . . .**18** E1
Thorndon IP23 . . . .**53** C8
Tuddenham IP28 . . . .**30** F2
Tuddenham St Martin
IP6 . . . .**136** B5
Wangford with Henham
NR34 . . . .**26** B2
Wicken CB7 . . . .**28** A1
Wickham Market IP13 . . . .**127** C7
Wrentham NR34 . . . .**26** E5
Yoxford IP17 . . . .**57** D8
High St Ex Gall★ IP1 . . .**155** B3
High View Rd NR31 . . . . .**134** D1
Higham Hill IP7 . . . .**103** D8
Higham Race Course
CO7 . . . .**103** D7
Higham Rd
Higham CO7 . . . .**103** D6
Tuddenham IP28 . . . .**31** A1
Highbridge Gravel Dro
IP27 . . . .**109** B7
Highbury Cres IP33 . . . .**122** E5
Highbury Rd IP33 . . . . . .**122** E5
Highbury Way CO10 . . . .**148** F4
Highclere Cl CB8 . . . .**120** D8
Higher Dr NR32 . . . .**112** F2
Highfield
Blythburgh IP19 . . . .**42** F6
Clare CO10 . . . .**90** B8
Eye IP23 . . . .**117** C3
Highfield App ⬛ IP1 . . . .**134** F1
Highfield Ave CO12 . . . . .**107** A2
Highfield Cl NR33 . . . . . .**114** B1
Highfield Dr IP6 . . . .**134** D8
Highfield Rd
Felixstowe IP11 . . . .**153** A4
Halesworth IP19 . . . .**118** B2
Ipswich IP1 . . . .**134** F2
⬛ Stowupland IP14 . . . . . .**67** A6
Sudbury CO10 . . . .**148** E7
Highfields Bentley IP9 . .**104** F7
Great Yeldham CO9 . . . . . .**90** A1
Lakenheath IP27 . . . .**109** E6
Highfields Dr IP27 . . . . .**109** D6
Highgate La IP13 . . . .**70** B2
Highgrove Cl NR32 . . . . .**113** A3
Highland Dr NR34 . . . . . .**111** E4
Highland Way NR33 . . . .**114** F6
Highlands IP27 . . . .**109** E6
Highlands Cl IP25 . . . . . .**125** C5
Highlands Rd
Hadleigh IP7 . . . .**149** E5
Monks Eleigh IP7 . . . .**79** C4
Highlands The CB8 . . . .**120** D8
Highview Cl CO10 . . . . . .**148** C8
Highwood Cres CB8 . . . . .**46** B2
Highwood La CO10 . . . . . .**92** E5
Highwood Rd CB8 . . . .**46** B2
Hildesley Ct NR33 . . . . .**115** B4
Hill Cl
⬛ Long Melford CO10 . . . .**91** B8
Newmarket CB8 . . . .**120** E3
Hill Cres CB9 . . . .**132** E7
Hill Farm La ⬛ IP9 . . . . .**106** C8
Hill Farm Rd
Grundisburgh IP13 . . . .**83** D6
Halesworth IP19 . . . .**118** C3
Playford IP6 . . . .**137** B4
Rendham IP17 . . . .**56** E4
Hill House Gdns NR33 . .**115** C5
Hill House La IP7 . . . . . .**125** C6
Hill House Rd IP4 . . . . . .**139** E5
Hill La CB3 . . . .**33** D1
Hill of Health (Tumulus)★
IP28 . . . .**32** D2
Hill Rd Lowestoft NR32 . .**113** C1
Southwold IP18 . . . .**119** C6
Wangford with Henham
NR34 . . . .**26** B1
Westley IP33 . . . .**122** A5
Hill Rise IP14 . . . .**124** D3
Hill St ⬛ IP26 . . . .**4** E5
Hill The North Cove NR34 . .**10** C4

Hill The continued
Shipmeadow NR34 . . . .**8** F4
Tuddenham St Martin
IP6 . . . .**136** C5
Westleton IP17 . . . .**58** C8
Hill Top IP31 . . . .**34** E5
Hill View CB8 . . . .**61** C4
Hill View Bsns Pk IP6 . .**134** D6
Hillary Cl IP14 . . . .**140** A5
Hillcrest IP17 . . . .**129** A3
Hillcrest App IP8 . . . .**134** B8
Hillcrest Cl ⬛ NR34 . . . .**111** E3
Hillcrest Dr NR32 . . . . . .**113** B4
Hillcrest Gdns NR32 . . .**113** B3
Hillcrest Rd
Beccles NR34 . . . .**111** B3
Sudbury CO10 . . . .**148** E5
Hillcroft Prep Sch IP14 . .**51** D2
Hillrise Brandon IP27 . . . . .**14** D8
Stowmarket IP14 . . . .**124** D3
Hillside Ave IP14 . . . .**111** E4
Hillside Com Prim Sch
IP2 . . . .**139** C3
Hillside Cres ⬛ IP3 . . . .**140** B3
Hillside Ct ⬛ NR35 . . . . .**110** C2
Hillside Meadow CB7 . . . .**29** B1
Hillside Rd
Southwold IP18 . . . .**119** C7
Sudbury CO10 . . . .**148** E5
Hillside Rd E NR35 . . . . .**110** D3
Hillside Rd W NR35 . . . .**110** B2
Hillside Specl Sch
CO10 . . . .**148** D7
Hillside Way IP19 . . . . . .**118** B5
Hilltop Gn NR32 . . . .**113** A4
Hilltop Rise ⬛ NR34 . . . .**111** B3
Hilltop Way IP31 . . . .**34** E5
Hilly Cl IP31 . . . .**33** F5
Hilly Fields IP12 . . . .**146** E4
Hilton Cl ⬛ CO11 . . . . . .**104** E2
Hilton Rd Ipswich IP3 . . .**140** C1
Martlesham Heath IP5 . . . .**98** A8
Hinderclay La IP22 . . . . . .**18** E1
Hinderclay Rd
Redgrave IP22 . . . .**19** A1
Rickinghall Inferior IP22 . . .**35** F6
Hines Rd IP3 . . . .**140** A4
Hintesham Cl ⬛ IP4 . . . .**140** F5
Hintlesham & Chattisham CE
VCP Sch IP8 . . . .**95** C3
Hintlesham Cl ⬛ IP3 . . .**124** E3
Hintlesham Dr IP11 . . . .**152** D2
Histon Cl IP3 . . . .**140** F7
Hitcham Cswy IP7 . . . . . .**79** E6
Hitcham Rd
⬛ Debenham IP14 . . . . . .**53** F2
Wattisham IP7 . . . .**80** B6
Hitcham's La NR34 . . . . . .**26** E4
Hitchcock Pl CO10 . . . . .**148** C7
HMS Ganges Mus★
IP9 . . . .**107** B4
Hobart Cl NR32 . . . .**112** E3
Hobart Way NR32 . . . . . .**112** E3
Hobbies La IP14 . . . .**52** D4
Hobbs Dr CO4 . . . .**103** A3
Hobbs La CO10 . . . .**77** B2
Hobland Rd
Belton with Browston NR31 . .**2** F8
Bradwell NR31 . . . .**3** A8
Hocket Cres IP12 . . . .**71** F2
Hockey Hill IP14 . . . .**53** A5
Hockney Gdns IP3 . . . . .**144** A3
Hockwold Prim Sch
IP26 . . . .**5** A2
Hodgkinson Rd IP11 . . . .**152** D2
Hodson Cl ⬛ IP32 . . . . . .**122** E4
Hoe La CO10 . . . .**90** F2
Hog La
St Lawrence, Ilketshall
NR34 . . . .**24** F6
Wenhaston with Mells Hamlet
IP19 . . . .**42** C5
Westhall NR34 . . . .**25** A6
Hogarth Rd IP3 . . . .**139** F1
Hogarth Sq IP3 . . . .**140** A1
Hogarth Wlk NR32 . . . . .**113** B3
Hogg La
Bury St Edmunds IP33 . . .**154** B1
Earsham NR35 . . . .**7** C5
Hoggars Rd IP14 . . . .**52** C4
Hogsty La IP21 . . . .**22** A5
Holbecks La IP7 . . . .**149** C4
Holbein Way ⬛ IP3 . . . . .**113** B6
Holborn Ave IP28 . . . . . .**116** D4
Holbrook Barn Rd ⬛
CO10 . . . .**93** C3
Holbrook Cl ⬛ CO10 . . . .**92** C6
Holbrook Cres IP11 . . . .**152** D2
Holbrook High Sch
IP9 . . . .**105** E8
Holbrook Prim Sch
IP9 . . . .**105** E7
Holbrook Rd
Haverhill CB9 . . . .**132** C5
Holbrook IP9 . . . .**106** A5
Ipswich IP3 . . . .**139** F1
Lowestoft NR32 . . . .**112** F4
Stutton IP9 . . . .**105** D5
Holcombe Cres IP2 . . . .**138** D2
Holdans La IP17 . . . .**56** D2
Holdans Meadow IP17 . . .**56** E2
Holden Cl Ipswich IP2 . . .**139** D3
Lowestoft NR32 . . . .**112** C1
Holden Rd IP28 . . . .**31** F1
Holderness Rd IP32 . . . .**123** C7
Holeywall La IP31 . . . .**35** A1
Holfen Cl IP12 . . . .**84** B1

Holkham Cl **7** IP4 . . . . . .**140** F5
Holkham Mead **1** CB5 . . .**44** B5
Holland Pk CB8 . . . .**60** E8
Holland Rd
  Felixstowe IP11 . . . .**152** F3
  Ipswich IP4 . . . .**139** F6
Holland Rise IP19 . . . .**41** A4
Holland's La NR35 . . . .**7** C7
Hollands Bsns Ctr The
  CB9 . . . .**132** E4
Hollands Rd CB9 . . . .**132** E4
Hollands Rd Ind Est
  CB9 . . . .**132** E4
Hollesley Ave CB9 . . . . . .**132** A6
Hollesley Prim Sch
  IP12 . . . .**99** F7
Hollesley Rd
  Hollesley IP12 . . . .**99** D7
  Rendlesham IP12 . . . .**85** D7
Holliday Cl IP32 . . . .**123** F7
Hollingsworth Rd
  Lowestoft NR32 . . . .**113** C3
  3 Stowmarket IP14 . . . . .**124** E5
Hollow Gr Way CB9 . . . . .**114** C4
Hollow Hill CB9 . . . .**74** A2
Hollow Hill Rd NR35 . . . .**110** B7
Hollow La
  Badingham IP13 . . . .**56** C6
  Barningham IP31 . . . .**34** F8
  Bures St Mary CO8 . . . . .**101** C6
  Carlton Colville NR33 . . . .**114** C4
  6 Chelmondiston IP9 . .**106** C8
  Coney Weston IP31 . . . . . .**18** A1
  Earl Soham IP13 . . . .**54** F3
  Mendham IP20 . . . .**23** A4
  Thurston IP31 . . . .**49** F3
  Tostock IP30 . . . .**50** A2
Hollow Rd Ashen CO10 . . .**89** F6
  Bury St Edmunds IP32 . . .**123** C6
  Copdock & Washbrook
    IP8 . . . .**95** E4
Hollow Way Hill NR34 . . . .**9** D8
Hollowell Cl **3** NR32 . . . .**112** E4
Hollows The IP6 . . . .**67** F2
Holly Blue Cl IP8 . . . . . .**142** E8
Holly Bush Cnr CO7 . . . .**103** E7
Holly Cl Beccles NR34 . . .**111** E3
  5 Horringer IP29 . . . .**63** A8
  Little Bealings IP13 . . . . .**137** D5
  6 Red Lodge IP28 . . . .**30** B1
  Warren Heath IP3 . . . . . .**140** F1
Holly Ct **34** IP20 . . . .**22** D6
Holly End IP5 . . . .**141** F6
Holly Gr NR34 . . . .**111** C4
Holly Hill NR32 . . . .**112** C3
Holly La Belstead IP8 . . . .**142** C7
  Great Horkesley CO6 . . . .**102** E2
  Lakenheath IP27 . . . .**109** D5
  Little Bealings IP13 . . . . .**137** D5
  Mutford NR34 . . . .**10** E3
  Rushmere St Andrew
    IP5 . . . .**136** E2
  Stutton IP9 . . . .**105** C6
Holly Oaks **2** CO6 . . . . .**101** C7
Holly Rd
  4 Great Bricett IP7 . . . . . .**80** D6
  Ipswich IP1 . . . .**155** A4
  Lowestoft NR32 . . . .**112** E1
  Willisham IP8 . . . .**81** A5
Holly Wlk **8** IP20 . . . . . .**30** B8
Hollybush Dr IP11 . . . . . .**153** D7
Hollybush La IP30 . . . . . .**64** D6
Hollycroft Cl **5** IP1 . . . . .**135** A3
Hollydene Cl **4** NR32 . . . .**112** D2
Holm Cl **4** NR34 . . . .**9** F4
Holme Cl IP22 . . . .**18** C2
Holme's Hill IP17 . . . .**41** A1
Holmere Dr IP19 . . . .**118** A3
Holmes La **5** CB7 . . . . . .**28** D5
Holmsey Gn
  Beck Row, Holywell Row
   & Kenny Hill IP28 . . . . .**13** C1
  Mildenhall IP28 . . . .**30** B8
Holmsey Gn Gdns **7**
  IP28 . . . .**30** B8
Holst Cl NR33 . . . .**115** A4
Holst Mead IP14 . . . .**124** C8
Holt Rd CO6 . . . .**93** E2
Holt's La IP6 . . . .**125** F6
Holt's Rd CO6 . . . .**102** A2
Holton Ave NR32 . . . .**112** F4
Holton Rd IP19 . . . .**118** C3
Holton St Peter Postmill★
  IP19 . . . .**118** E3
Holton St Peter Prim Sch
  IP19 . . . .**118** E4
Holton Terr IP19 . . . .**118** C4
Holy Wells Rd IP3 . . . . . .**139** E4
Holyhouse Drift **1** IP31 . .**49** A6
Holyrood **4** CO12 . . . . . .**106** F1
Holyrood Cl IP2 . . . .**138** F1
Holywell Dro **13** C2
Holywells Cl IP3 . . . .**139** E4
Holywells High Sch
  IP3 . . . .**140** C1
Home Cl CB9 . . . .**88** E4
Home Farm La IP33 . . . . .**123** B1
Home Farm Rd NR35 . . . . .**8** C7
Home Meadow **4** IP13 . . .**40** B3
Home Piece IP22 . . . .**35** A8
Homefield Boxford CO10 . . .**93** F3
  Capel St Mary IP9 . . . . . .**150** F3
Homefield Ave
  5 Beccles NR34 . . . . . .**111** B5
  Lowestoft NR33 . . . .**114** F6
Homefield Paddock
  NR34 . . . .**111** B5

Homefield Rd CB9 . . . . . .**132** C4
Homefield Rd Ind Est
  CB9 . . . .**132** D4
Homeport NR32 . . . .**113** E3
Homer Cl IP1 . . . .**134** F4
Homestall Cres CB9 . . . . .**74** A2
Homestead Dr **2** IP28 . . .**30** B8
Homestead The NR33 . . . .**114** B3
Homey Bridge Rd CO6 . . . .**93** E1
Honey Hill IP33 . . . .**154** C1
Honey La CO6 . . . .**102** B6
Honeymeade Ct **28** IP31 . .**34** E4
Honeypot La
  Kelsale cum Carlton IP17 . . .**57** E4
  Mendham IP20 . . . .**23** C4
  Monewden IP13 . . . .**69** F4
  Wattisfield IP22 . . . .**35** D4
Honeypot Meadow **2**
  NR35 . . . .**110** B3
Honeysuckle Cl
  8 Haverhill CB9 . . . . . .**132** C7
  Lowestoft NR33 . . . .**115** A3
  1 Red Lodge IP28 . . . . . .**46** A8
  3 Soham CB7 . . . .**28** D4
Honeysuckle Gdns
  IP2 . . . .**138** E4
Honeysuckle Way **4**
  IP32 . . . .**123** E6
Honington CE VC Prim Sch
  IP31 . . . .**33** F5
Honington Rise IP31 . . . . .**33** F5
Hoo La IP12 . . . .**71** E4
Hood Dr IP6 . . . .**81** F5
Hood Rd IP3 . . . .**139** E1
Hood's La NR34 . . . .**25** F4
Hook La IP7 . . . .**149** F4
Hooper Sq IP33 . . . .**122** C6
Hop Meadow CO7 . . . . . .**151** B4
Hope Cres IP12 . . . .**147** A6
Hopelyn Cl **4** NR32 . . . . .**113** B4
Hopper Way IP22 . . . .**20** C4
Hopton CE VC Prim Sch
  IP22 . . . .**18** C1
Hopton Fst Sch NR31 . . . . .**3** C6
Hopton Gdns NR31 . . . .**3** B7
Hopton Rd
  Barningham IP31 . . . .**34** F8
  Thelnetham IP22 . . . .**18** C1
Hopton Rise CB9 . . . .**132** A6
Horham IP21 . . . .**38** E1
Horkesley Hill CO6 . . . . .**102** D4
Horkesley Rd CO6 . . . . . .**102** B4
Horn Hill NR33 . . . .**115** C7
Horn La CB9 . . . .**60** D3
Hornbeam Cl
  Beccles NR34 . . . .**111** E4
  Rosedale Park NR33 . . . .**114** F4
Hornbeam Dr NR29 . . . . . .**63** A8
Hornbeam Rd
  Mildenhall IP28 . . . .**116** E5
  2 Stowupland IP14 . . . . .**67** A6
Horringer Ct Mid Sch
  IP33 . . . .**122** D3
Horringer Rd IP29 . . . . . .**122** D2
Horsecroft IP29 . . . .**122** E1
Horsecroft Rd
  Bury St Edmunds IP33 . . .**122** F2
  Horringer IP29 . . . .**63** C8
Horsefair IP30 . . . .**50** D1
Horsefair Cl IP14 . . . .**52** E4
Horseheath Rd CB9 . . . . .**74** A2
Horseshoe Dr IP28 . . . . . .**30** C1
Horseshoe La CB9 . . . . . .**132** C5
Horsham Ave IP3 . . . .**140** D4
Horsham Cl CB9 . . . .**132** A7
Hospital Rd
  Bury St Edmunds IP33 . . .**154** A1
  Orford IP12 . . . .**131** B6
Hossack Rd IP3 . . . .**144** A8
Hotson Rd IP18 . . . .**119** C6
Houghton Dr
  Hopton on Sea NR31 . . . . .**3** B6
  Oulton NR32 . . . .**112** E4
Houghton Pl **5** IP4 . . . . .**140** F5
Houghtons La CB7 . . . . . .**29** D5
Houldsworth Terr CB8 . . .**120** F5
Houldsworth Valley Prim Sch
  CB8 . . . .**120** E8
How Hill (Tumulus)★
  IP27 . . . .**31** B7
Howard Cl
  6 Framlingham IP13 . . . .**126** C3
  Harleston IP20 . . . .**22** E6
  Haverhill CB9 . . . .**132** B5
Howard Com Prim Sch
  IP32 . . . .**122** E8
Howard de Walden Way
  CB8 . . . .**121** A4
Howard Mid Sch
  Bury St Edmunds IP32 . . . .**48** B5
  Fornham All Saints IP28 . .**122** D8
Howard Rd **1** NR35 . . . . .**110** B4
Howard St IP4 . . . .**140** B7
Howards Way IP5 . . . . . .**141** D8
Howe Ave IP3 . . . .**140** C3
Howe La Cockfield IP30 . . . .**64** C1
  Thornham Parva IP23 . . . .**37** A3
Howe Rd IP3 . . . .**132** D7
Howes Ave IP31 . . . .**49** D4
Howlett Cl IP5 . . . .**141** E7
Howlett Way IP24 . . . .**16** B7
Howley Gdns NR32 . . . . .**113** A6
Hoxne Cl **5** IP14 . . . .**124** E3
Hoxne Rd Eye IP23 . . . . . .**117** E2
  Hoxne IP21 . . . .**38** D3
  Syleham IP21 . . . .**21** F1
  Upper Weybread IP21 . . . .**22** B2
Hoxter Way CO10 . . . . . .**148** C8

Hoylake Cl **6** IP28 . . . . . .**48** C6
Hubbard's Ave **2** NR32 . .**113** C6
Hubbard's Hill IP17 . . . . .**41** B1
Hubbard's La IP30 . . . . . .**64** F8
Hubbard's Loke NR32 . . . .**113** C6
Hubbards Cl IP17 . . . . . .**128** B4
Hudson Cl
  10 Harwich CO12 . . . . .**107** A1
  Haverhill CB9 . . . .**133** A4
Hudson Way **6** IP29 . . . . .**47** A4
Hudsons La CO6 . . . .**103** A7
Huggins La IP23 . . . .**37** B1
Hugh Ager Cl **5** IP14 . . . .**124** D3
Hughes Cnr CO7 . . . .**151** A6
Hughes Rd CO7 . . . .**151** B6
Hull St IP7 . . . .**109** F1
Hulver La IP17 . . . .**72** C6
Hulver Rd NR34 . . . .**9** F2
Humber Doucy La IP4 . . . .**140** D7
Humber Doucy Sports Ctr
  IP4 . . . .**140** D7
Hummingbird Cl IP32 . . . .**49** A3
Humphry Rd CO10 . . . . . .**148** C6
Hundon Cl CB8 . . . .**75** B6
Hundon Pl **6** CB9 . . . . . .**132** F6
Hundon Prim Sch
  CO10 . . . .**75** D3
Hundon Rd
  Hundon CO10 . . . .**75** B1
  Kedington CB9 . . . .**133** F8
Hundred La
  Boxted CO4 . . . .**103** B2
  Old Newton with Dagworth
    IP14 . . . .**51** F3
Hungate NR34 . . . .**111** B5
Hungate Ct NR34 . . . .**111** B5
Hungate La NR34 . . . .**111** B5
Hungerdown La CO11 . . . .**104** B1
Hunston Rd IP31 . . . .**50** E7
Hunt Cl
  5 Redenhall with Harleston
    IP20 . . . .**22** D6
  Stowmarket IP14 . . . . . .**124** D3
Hunter Dr
  19 Manningtree CO11 . . .**104** D2
  18 Thurstow IP31 . . . .**49** D4
Hunter Rd
  Bury St Edmunds IP32 . . .**122** D8
  Honington IP31 . . . .**33** D5
  2 Ipswich IP3 . . . .**144** C8
Hunter's Chase CO7 . . . . .**151** F7
Hunter's La IP20 . . . .**23** A3
Hunters End IP11 . . . .**152** C7
Hunters La IP20 . . . .**23** B2
Hunters Ride **21** IP5 . . . . .**98** A8
Huntingdon Cl **9** NR33 . .**115** A3
Huntingfield Rd
  Bury St Edmunds IP33 . . .**122** C4
  Cratfield IP19 . . . .**40** D5
  Leiston IP16 . . . .**129** C5
Huntley Cres IP19 . . . . . .**118** C5
Hunts Hill CO10 . . . .**77** A2
Hurdle Dro IP28 . . . .**29** F8
Hurdle Makers Hill IP8 . . . .**95** F6
Hurn Crag Rd IP18 . . . . . .**119** C7
Hurricane Pl IP3 . . . .**140** B1
Hurstlea Ct IP6 . . . .**125** D5
Hurstlea Rd IP6 . . . .**125** C5
Hurth Way IP24 . . . .**16** C6
Hurts Croft **3** CB7 . . . . . .**29** A1
Hut Hill (Tumulus)★
  IP31 . . . .**17** E3
Hutland Rd IP4 . . . .**139** F7
Hutton Ct IP23 . . . .**117** D3
Hyam's La IP9 . . . .**105** C5
Hyams La IP9 . . . .**105** C5
Hyde Rd CO10 . . . .**148** C5
Hydewood Rd CO9 . . . . . .**90** A2
Hyem's La IP11 . . . .**153** B7
Hyntle Cl IP2 . . . .**138** E5
Hyperion Way CB8 . . . . . .**120** D8
Hythe Cl **9** CB5 . . . .**44** A6
Hythe La CB5 . . . .**44** A6
Hythe Rd IP26 . . . .**4** E7

Inkerman Row **4** CO10 . .**148** C6
Inkerman Terr **3** IP7 . . . .**149** D6
Innes End **4** IP4 . . . .**138** C2
Inverness Rd IP4 . . . .**136** C4
Inworth La CO6 . . . .**101** B1
Ion Rd **1** IP32 . . . .**122** E8
Ipswich Ave **3** IP2 . . . . . .**85** B3
Ipswich Cl **1** IP12 . . . .**85** B3
Ipswich Ct IP3 . . . .**154** B3
Ipswich High Sch IP4 . . . .**144** C2
Ipswich Hospl IP4 . . . . . .**140** C7
Ipswich Mus★ IP1 . . . . . .**155** B3
Ipswich Pre Prep Sch
  IP14 . . . .**68** B6
Ipswich Prep Sch IP1 . . . .**155** B4
Ipswich Rd
  Brantham CO11 . . . .**104** E5
  Charsfield IP13 . . . .**70** B2
  Claydon IP6 . . . .**134** C8
  Dedham CO4 . . . .**103** D3
  East Bergholt CO7 . . . . .**151** A6
  Elmsett IP7 . . . .**95** A8
  Grundisburgh IP13 . . . . . .**83** E5
  Hadleigh IP7 . . . .**149** F7
  Harkstead IP9 . . . .**106** A6
  Holbrook IP9 . . . .**105** E8
  Lowestoft NR32 . . . .**113** D3
  Nacton IP10 . . . .**145** A5
  Nedging-with-Naughton
    IP7 . . . .**80** C4
  Needham Market IP6 . . . .**125** E4
  Newbourne IP12 . . . .**98** A4
  Orford IP12 . . . .**131** B4
  Otley IP6 . . . .**69** B2
  2 Scole IP21 . . . .**20** C1
  Scole NR15 . . . .**21** C1
  Stowmarket IP14 . . . . . .**124** E4
  Stratford St Mary CO7 . . .**103** C4
  Tattingstone White House
    IP9 . . . .**142** D1
  Waldringfield IP12 . . . . . .**98** D7
  Willisham IP8 . . . .**81** A4
  Winston IP14 . . . .**53** F1
  Witnesham IP6 . . . .**136** A8
  Woodbridge IP12 . . . . . .**146** E3
  Yaxley IP23 . . . .**37** B4
Ipswich Sch IP1 . . . .**155** B4
Ipswich St
  Bury St Edmunds IP33 . . .**154** B3
  Lakenheath IP27 . . . . . .**109** F1
  Stowmarket IP14 . . . . . .**124** D6
Ipswich Sta IP2 . . . .**155** A1
Ipswich Transport Mus★
  IP3 . . . .**140** C2
Ipswich Way IP14 . . . .**68** E6
Ireland Rd IP3 . . . .**139** F1
Irex Rd IP33 . . . .**115** B3
Iris Cl IP2 . . . .**138** F5
Irlam Rd IP2 . . . .**138** D2
Isaacson Rd CB5 . . . .**44** B4
Isinglass Cl CB8 . . . .**121** E2
Isleham Cl CB7 . . . .**29** C2
Ivry St IP1 . . . .**155** A4
Ivy Cl IP13 . . . .**54** E7
Ivy La NR33 . . . .**114** C7
Ivy Lodge Rd IP12 . . . . . .**71** D1
Ivytree La IP7 . . . .**94** C2
Ixer La IP30 . . . .**64** B5
Ixworth Abbey IP31 . . . . .**34** A1
Ixworth CE Prim Sch
  IP31 . . . .**34** B1
Ixworth Mid Sch IP31 . . . .**34** B1
Ixworth Rd
  Haverhill CB9 . . . .**132** C4
  Honington IP31 . . . .**33** F5
  Stowlangtoft IP31 . . . . . .**50** B6
  Troston IP31 . . . .**33** A6
  Walsham le Willows IP31 . . .**35** A1

I

Ice House Quay NR32 . .**114** E8
Iceni Way CB8 . . . .**120** B8
Icepits Cl IP31 . . . .**49** C6
Icewell Hill CB8 . . . .**121** A4
Ickleton Rd **9** CB9 . . . . .**132** F6
Icklingham Rd IP28 . . . . . .**32** B2
Icknield Cl **3** CB8 . . . .**60** E7
Icknield Way IP24 . . . .**16** B5
Ickworth Cres IP4 . . . . . .**140** F5
Ickworth Ct **2** IP11 . . . . .**152** C3
Ickworth Dr IP33 . . . .**154** A1
Ickworth House Pk & Gdn★
  IP29 . . . .**62** F8
Ickworth Pk Prim Sch
  IP29 . . . .**63** A8
Ickworth Vineyard★
  IP29 . . . .**62** E8
Ilex Cl IP33 . . . .**123** A3
Iliffe Way IP14 . . . .**124** D6
Imperial Mews NR31 . . . . . .**3** B6
Impson Way IP26 . . . .**6** A8
Ingestre St **1** CO12 . . . . .**107** B2
Ingham Rd
  Haverhill CB9 . . . .**132** E6
  West Stow IP28 . . . .**32** C1
Ingram's Rd IP21 . . . .**21** F3
Ingram's Well Rd
  CO10 . . . .**148** D5
Inkerman Cl **4** IP7 . . . . .**149** D6

J

Jack Jarvis Cl **5** CB8 . .**121** A3
Jack's Gn Rd IP6 . . . . . .**125** E6
Jack's La IP14 . . . .**124** A2
Jacks Gn IP6 . . . .**125** E7
Jackson Cl IP5 . . . .**141** F7
Jackson Rd IP12 . . . .**98** C5
Jackson Way IP6 . . . . . .**125** D4
Jacob Way **11** IP12 . . . . .**147** A5
Jacobs Cl **14** IP31 . . . . . .**34** E4
Jacobs Meadow IP30 . . . . .**65** D5
Jacobs St **7** NR32 . . . . . .**113** B6
Jacqueline Cl
  Bury St Edmunds IP33 . . .**154** A1
  7 Grundisburgh IP13 . . . .**83** E5
James Boden Cl **7**
  IP11 . . . .**152** E5
James Carter Rd IP28 . . . .**116** A6
Jameson Pl **6** CO10 . . . . .**148** C6
Janet Hadenham Cl **11**
  NR34 . . . .**9** F4
Janus Cl CB9 . . . .**133** B4
Jaques Cl **3** CO10 . . . . . .**77** B3
Jarman Cl IP33 . . . .**123** C3
Jarman's La IP28 . . . .**29** F7
Jarrold Cl **1** IP31 . . . .**34** F7
Jarvis Way CB8 . . . .**120** E5
Jasmine Cl
  9 Felixstowe IP11 . . . . .**107** D8
  Ipswich IP2 . . . .**138** F3
Jasmine Gn IP2 . . . .**138** F3
Jasmine Rd CB9 . . . .**133** C2
Java Lodge Rd IP13 . . . . .**127** C2
Jay Cl CB9 . . . .**133** A5
Jay La NR32 . . . .**3** A6
Jay's Gn IP20 . . . .**22** D6
Jay's Hill Rd
  Ellough NR34 . . . .**10** B2

Jay's Hill Rd continued
  Willingham St Mary NR34 . . .**26** A8
Jays Croft Rd **2** IP12 . . . .**85** E8
Jaywick Rd **2** CB9 . . . . .**132** E6
Jeaffresons Well IP6 . . . .★
Jeannie Mann Ct
  NR32 . . . .**113** B3
Jeavons La IP5 . . . .**141** E7
Jefferies Rd IP4 . . . .**139** E6
Jellicoe Ave NR33 . . . . . .**114** D6
Jenkins Gn NR32 . . . .**113** A5
Jenkinsons Pightle
  NR35 . . . .**7** B8
Jenner Cl NR35 . . . .**110** C2
Jenners Cl **1** IP12 . . . . . .**147** B6
Jennings Way IP22 . . . . . .**20** C3
Jermyn Ave IP32 . . . .**123** F5
Jermyn Way IP19 . . . . . .**118** A2
Jermyns Cl IP9 . . . .**150** F4
Jermyns Rd IP18 . . . .**119** B8
Jervis Rd **10** IP9 . . . .**105** E7
Jewell View IP5 . . . .**141** D8
Jim Mollison Ct **5** IP28 .**116** B5
Jimmy's Farm★ IP9 . . . . .**142** F5
Jimmy's La CO11 . . . .**104** F5
Jocelyn Cl **16** IP32 . . . . . .**48** C5
Jockey's La Combs IP14 . . .**66** C2
  Framsden IP14 . . . .**69** B7
Joes Rd CO10 . . . .**92** C3
John Childs Way
  NR35 . . . .**110** C2
John Lawrence Cl
  NR34 . . . .**111** B2
John Russell Gall★
  IP3 . . . .**155** C2
John Shepherd Rd **1**
  IP21 . . . .**39** D8
John St Leiston IP16 . . . . .**129** C5
  Lowestoft NR33 . . . .**115** C7
  Rose Hill IP3 . . . .**139** E4
John Swain Cl IP6 . . . . . .**125** C5
John Tibauld Ct **4** CB9 . . .**88** D3
Johnson Cl **5** IP2 . . . . . .**139** C3
Johnson Rd **7** IP29 . . . . . .**47** A2
Johnson Way NR32 . . . . .**113** A5
Jolly's Way IP31 . . . .**35** C1
Jones Rd CO10 . . . .**76** C3
Jordan Cl IP6 . . . .**125** E7
Jordayn Rise IP7 . . . .**149** E6
Joshua Ct **5** NR31 . . . .**3** B8
Josselyns The IP11 . . . . .**152** B8
Jovian Way IP1 . . . .**138** E8
Joyce Rd NR35 . . . .**110** D3
Jubilee Ave IP14 . . . .**124** D4
Jubilee Cl **11** Claydon IP6 .**82** B5
  11 Felixstowe IP11 . . . . .**107** D8
  10 Harwich CO12 . . . . . .**106** F1
  13 Isleham CB7 . . . .**29** C5
  2 Laxfield IP13 . . . .**40** B3
  4 Thetford IP24 . . . .**16** B5
  Weeting IP27 . . . .**5** E3
Jubilee Cres IP14 . . . .**67** A7
Jubilee Ctr CB8 . . . .**60** A5
Jubilee Ctr IP28 . . . .**116** C3
Jubilee End **5** CO11 . . . .**104** E3
Jubilee Rd
  Bungay NR35 . . . .**110** B9
  Lakenheath IP27 . . . . . .**109** C8
  Lowestoft NR33 . . . .**114** F6
  Sudbury CO10 . . . .**148** D6
Jubilee Terr **10** IP30 . . . . .**50** F2
Jubilee Way
  Lowestoft NR32 . . . .**113** E2
  Mildenhall IP28 . . . .**116** C4
Jubilee Wlk CB9 . . . .**132** E6
Judas La IP23 . . . .**37** B5
Judith Ave IP17 . . . .**129** E2
Julian Cl CB9 . . . .**133** B5
Julian Way **12** NR31 . . . . . .**3** B7
Julius Martin La CB7 . . . . .**28** C4
Junction Rd IP28 . . . .**116** B5
June Ave Ipswich IP1 . . . .**135** D2
  Lowestoft NR32 . . . .**113** B3
Juniper Cl IP28 . . . .**116** E5
Juniper Rd IP28 . . . .**30** C1
Jupe's Hill CO6 . . . .**101** B1
Jupes Hill CO7 . . . .**104** B3
Jupiter Cl CB9 . . . .**133** B4
Jupiter Rd IP4 . . . .**140** B4
Justinian Cl CB9 . . . .**133** B4

K

Karen Cl Ipswich IP1 . . .**135** B1
  4 Scole IP21 . . . .**20** F1
Kate's La IP14 . . . .**51** A1
Katwijk Way **2** NR32 . . . .**115** D8
Keating Cl **2** CO11 . . . . .**104** D2
Keats Cl IP17 . . . .**128** B4
Keats Cres IP1 . . . .**134** F3
Kebbles **9** CO10 . . . .**77** A3
Kedington Hill CO10 . . . . .**92** A1
Kedington Prim Sch
  CB9 . . . .**133** E8
Kedington Rd CB9 . . . . . .**133** D3
Keebles Yd **9** CB9 . . . . .**132** E6
Keel Cl NR33 . . . .**114** B4
Keens La IP18 . . . .**119** B7
Keep Rise **6** NR35 . . . . . .**110** B4
Keeper's La
  Marlesford IP13 . . . .**71** D5
  Stoke-by-Nayland CO6 . . .**102** C8
  Trimley St Mary IP11 . . . .**152** A7
Keightley Way IP6 . . . . . .**136** B5

Kell's Acres NR34 ....8 F7
Kell's Way NR34 ....8 F6
Kelly Rd IP2 ....138 E5
Kelly-Pain Cl NR32 ....113 D3
Kelsale CE VCP Sch
IP17 ....128 C5
Kelso Rd IP33 ....122 F2
Kelvedon Dr IP4 ....140 F5
Kelvin Pl IP4 ....16 A4
Kelvin Rd IP1 ....134 F1
Kemball St IP4 ....140 A5
Kembold Cl IP32 ....123 E5
Kemps La NR34 ....111 B3
Kempshorne Cl NR32 ..112 E4
Kempson Dr 7 CO10 ...92 B3
Kempson Way IP30 ...123 F4
Kempsters The IP11 ..152 D7
Kempton Cl 4 IP1 ....135 A3
Kempton Cross NR34 ..111 C4
Kempton Rd IP1 ....135 A3
Kemsley Rd IP11 ......152 F5
Kendal Gn IP13 ....153 D7
Kendal Rd NR33 ....115 B6
Kennedy Ave IP19 ....118 A1
Kennedy Cl
Halesworth IP19 ....118 B1
Ipswich IP4 ....140 A6
Kennedy Rd 9 CB7 ....29 C5
Kennedy St IP27 ....109 E1
Kennel Loke NR31 ....3 B8
Kennels La IP13 ....146 C8
Kennels Rd
Brightwell IP10 ....98 A6
Foxhall IP10 ....141 F2
Kennetside CB8 ....61 B1
Kennett Prim Sch CB8 ..45 F6
Kennett Rd or Moulton
CB8 ....45 F3
Kennett Sta CB8 ....45 F6
Kenney Cl IP8 ....95 D7
Kenninghall Prim Sch
NR16 ....19 A8
Kenninghall Rd NR16 ..19 A7
Kennyhill Dro IP28 .....13 A3
Kensington Rd
Ipswich IP1 ....139 A4
Lowestoft NR33 ....115 C5
Stowmarket IP14 ......124 D5
Kent Rd Lackford IP28 ..31 F1
Lowestoft NR32 ....113 B1
Stowmarket IP14 ......124 C7
Kentford Rd 5 IP11 ...152 C4
Kenton Rd IP14 ....53 F2
Kents La Bungay NR35 ..110 D3
Soham CB7 ....28 D4
Kentwell Cl IP4 ....140 F4
Kentwell Hall ★ CO10 ..77 E2
Kentwell Pl 3 CB5 .....44 B5
Kenyon Cl 7 CO7 ......103 C5
Kenyon Dr 9 CO10 .....92 C6
Kenyon Row NR34 ....9 B6
Kenyon St IP2 ....155 B1
Kerridge Way 29 IP20 ..22 D6
Kerridge's Cut 15 CO11 ..105 A2
Kerridges NR16 ....18 C8
Kerrison Con Ctr IP23 ..37 D1
Kerrison Rd NR35 .....110 D2
Kerry Ave IP1 ....134 F4
Kerrys Farm La IP14 ...51 F4
Kersey Ave CO10 ....148 F4
Kersey CE Prim Sch
IP7 ....94 A6
Kersey Cl IP14 ....124 E3
Kersey Pottery ★ IP7 ..94 A7
Kersey Rd IP11 ....152 D4
Kersley Hall La IP21 ...39 A3
Kesgrave Dr NR32 .....112 F2
Kesgrave High Sch
IP5 ....141 C8
Kessingland CE VCP Sch
NR33 ....11 C2
Kesteven Rd IP2 ....155 A1
Kestrel Cl
1 Beck Row, Holywell
Row & Kenny Hill IP28 ..13 B1
Thetford IP24 ....16 C4
Kestrel Dr IP14 ....67 A5
Kestrel Gn NR33 ....114 C6
Kestrel Rd
Bury St Edmunds IP33 ..133 A5
Haverhill CB9 ....133 A5
Ipswich IP2 ....138 D3
Keswick Cl IP11 ....153 C6
Kettle La IP6 ....67 E1
Kettlebaston Way 3
IP1 ....135 D1
Kettleborrow Cl 21 IP31 ..34 B1
Kettleburgh Rd IP13 ..126 C1
Kettlefields CB8 ....59 F5
Kettlefields CP Sch
CB8 ....59 F5
Kevington Dr NR32 ...112 C2
Key St IP3 ....155 C2
Keynes Way 18 CO12 ..107 B2
Khartoum Rd IP4 ......139 F7
Kidz Kingdom ★ IP5 ....98 A8
Kilbourn Rd 6 NR33 ..115 A3
Kilbrack NR34 ....111 C5
Kilbrack Gdns NR34 ...111 C5
Kildare Ave IP4 ....134 D2
Kilmaine Rd 22 CO12 ..106 F1
Kiln Bottom IP7 ....149 E6
Kiln Cotts IP14 ....124 C5
Kiln Dr CO10 ....148 E4
Kiln Farm La IP22 ....35 F5

Kiln Field 1 IP11 ......152 D5
Kiln La Benhall IP17 ..128 C1
Boot Street IP13 ....137 E6
Buxhall IP14 ....65 F3
Dickleburgh & Rushall
IP21 ....21 C2
Elmswell IP30 ....50 E1
Friston IP17 ....72 D7
1 Mistley CO11 ....104 F2
Needham IP20 ....22 A4
Rede IP29 ....62 E4
Stowlangtoft IP31 ......34 E1
Kiln La NR34 ....26 C3
Kilverstone Rd IP24 ....17 A6
Kimberley Rd NR33 ...115 A7
Kimms Belt IP24 ....16 B5
King Edward Ave
IP13 ....127 C7
King Edward Rd
Ipswich IP3 ....140 B3
Leiston IP16 ....129 C6
King Edward VI Sch
IP33 ....154 A3
King Edward VII Dr
IP9 ....107 A4
King Edward VII Rd
CB8 ....120 E5
King George Ave CB8 ..120 B8
King George's Ave
3 Harwich CO12 .....107 A2
Leiston IP16 ....129 E6
King St Aldeburgh IP15 ..130 E3
Felixstowe IP11 ....152 E6
Ipswich IP1 ....155 B3
1 Mildenhall IP28 ....116 C4
Sudbury CO10 ....148 C5
Weybread IP21 ....22 D3
King William St 3 IP6 ..125 D5
King's Ave IP13 ....126 B5
King's Dam NR34 ....9 B6
King's Head St 2 CO12 ..107 C3
King's Hill CB9 ....133 E7
King's La Blyford IP19 ..42 C8
Gosbeck IP6 ....68 D3
Long Melford CO10 .....92 A7
Sotherton NR34 ....25 D2
Tannington IP13 ....55 B7
Walsham le Willows IP31 ..35 C3
Weston NR34 ....9 D1
King's Rd
Bury St Edmunds IP33 ..154 A2
Harwich CO12 ....107 A2
Topcroft NR35 ....7 A8
King's Theatre CB8 ...120 F3
King's Way IP3 ....140 B2
Kingfisher Ave IP2 ....138 D3
Kingfisher Cl CB9 .....133 A6
Kingfisher Cres IP18 ..119 A7
Kingfisher Ct NR33 ...114 C6
Kingfisher Dr
6 Burwell CB5 ....44 A4
Claydon IP6 ....81 F5
18 Harwich CO12 .....106 F1
Kingfisher Leisure Ctr
CO10 ....148 D4
Kingfisher Rd IP32 ....123 F4
Kingfisher Rise IP17 ..128 C4
Kingfisher Way
6 Mildenhall IP28 ....116 D4
Stowmarket IP14 ....67 A5
Kings Ave IP4 ....139 E5
Kings Cl 7 Acton CO10 ..92 B7
1 Manningtree CO11 ..104 E2
Mildenhall IP28 ....116 D5
Woodbridge IP12 ......146 A6
Kings Dr CB8 ....121 B1
Kings Fleet Prim Sch
IP11 ....153 D6
Kings Fleet Rd IP11 ...153 E3
Kings Head La IP22 ...19 A6
Kings Hill CO10 ....148 E4
Kings Mead CB8 ....60 E8
Kings Meadow
Great Cornard CO10 ..148 E4
Kedington CB9 ....133 E7
Kings Parade CB7 ......28 D3
Kings Pk IP29 ....62 D5
Kings Rd Bungay NR35 ..110 C2
Glemsford CO10 ....77 A3
Leiston IP16 ....129 C5
Kingsbury Rd IP11 ....152 C7
Kingsfield Ave IP1 ....139 D8
Kingsgate Dr IP4 ......139 F8
Kingshall St IP30 ....64 D8
Kingsland IP9 ....106 F5
Kingsland La 3 CO6 ..102 A7
Kingsley Cl 8 IP1 .....135 A3
Kingsmead Cl 3 IP14 ..124 C7
Kingsmead Rd IP14 ..124 C7
Kingston Cl NR34 .....115 A3
Kingston Ct NR34 .....111 D5
Kingston Dr NR34 .....111 C5
Kingston Farm Rd
IP12 ....147 A4
Kingston Pas 3 CB8 ..121 A3
Kingston Rd
Ipswich IP1 ....138 F8
Woodbridge IP12 ......147 A4
Kingsway 4 Earsham NR35 ..7 F4
9 Harwich CO12 ......107 B2
Mildenhall IP28 ....116 C4
Newmarket CB8 ....120 F4
Woodbridge IP12 ......147 B5
Kingswood Ave NR34 ..114 D4
Kingsworth Rd IP32 ..123 D6
Kinross Rd IP4 ....136 B1
Kipling Cl 5 NR32 .....11 C1
Kipling Rd IP1 ....134 F3

Kipling Way IP14 ......124 B8
Kirby Cane Wlk NR32 ..113 A3
Kirby St IP4 ....140 A7
Kirby St IP4 ....140 A7
Kirkdale Ct 4 IP32 ...115 B4
Kirkley Cliff Rd NR33 ..115 C5
Kirkley Gdns NR33 ...115 B6
Kirkley High Sch
NR33 ....115 A6
Kirkley Mid Sch NR33 ..115 B7
Kirkley Pk Rd NR33 ...115 B6
Kirkley Run NR33 .....115 A7
Kirkley Sports & Fitness Ctr
NR33 ....115 B6
Kirkley St NR33 ....115 B6
Kirkstead Rd IP33 ....122 D3
Kirkstone Way 4 NR32 ..113 A4
Kirkton Cl IP2 ....107 A5
Kirkwood Dr 1 NR33 ..114 C3
Kirtling Pl 3 CB9 .....132 F6
Kirtling Rd CB8 ....60 E5
Kirton Rd IP11 ....107 D8
Kitchen Hill CO10 ....91 D4
Kitchener Rd
Ipswich IP11 ....138 F8
Leiston IP16 ....129 C6
Kitchener Way 5 IP9 ..107 A5
Kitson Meadows IP33 ..122 A5
Kittiwake Cl
Ipswich IP2 ....138 E3
Lowestoft NR33 ....114 D5
Klondyke IP32 ....122 F8
Knaves Acre Dro CB7 ..29 B6
Knettishall Heath Ctry Pk ★
IP31 ....17 E3
Knight Rd IP12 ....85 D8
Knights Cl
7 Debenham IP14 ......53 F2
6 Felixstowe IP11 ....153 D6
6 Manningtree CO11 ..104 E2
4 Old Newton with Dagworth
IP14 ....51 E1
Knights Ct
19 Haverhill CB9 ......132 C5
Roman Hill NR32 ....113 C1
Knights La 5 IP5 ......141 D7
Knights Yd NR34 ......111 B6
Knightsdale Rd IP1 ...135 A1
Knightswood 3 NR32 ..113 B5
Knoll The IP13 ....126 D3
Knowle The 17 IP31 ...34 E4
Knox La IP31 ....34 C4
Knutsford Cl NR32 ...138 C1
Kreswell Gr 7 CO12 ..107 A1
Kylborne IP33 ....122 C4
Kyson Hill ★ IP12 ....146 E4
Kyson Prim Sch IP12 ..146 D4

L

La Salle Cl IP2 ....139 B3
Laburnum Ave IP28 ...116 E5
Laburnum Cl
3 Ipswich IP8 ....138 C2
Ipswich IP3 ....140 D2
Red Lodge IP28 ....30 B1
Worlingworth IP13 .....54 E7
Laburnum Dr IP4 ....80 C8
Laburnum Gdns IP5 ..136 E1
Laburnum La 11 CB5 ..44 A6
Laburnum Rd 3 NR35 ..110 B3
Laburnum Way 2 CO6 ..102 C5
Lacewing Cl 13 IP8 ...142 E8
Lacey St IP4 ....139 E6
Lacey's La 5 CB8 .....120 B7
Lachlan Gn IP12 ....146 F7
Lackford La IP28 ....47 D6
Lackford Pl 7 IP3 .....144 C8
Lackford Wildfowl Nature
Reserve ★ IP31 ....31 F1
Lacon Rd 2 IP8 ....134 A2
Ladbrook Cl IP7 ....80 C1
Lady La Hadleigh IP7 ..149 E7
Ipswich IP1 ....155 A3
Lady La Ind Est IP7 ...149 E7
Lady Margaret Gdns
IP12 ....146 D4
Lady St 18 CO10 ....78 D4
Lady's La IP22 ....19 F5
Lady's Meadow NR34 ..111 B6
Ladyfield IP14 ....66 D8
Ladygate 1 CB9 ....132 C4
Ladywell Rd IP14 ....51 F7
Ladywood Rd IP4 .....140 C7
Lagonda Dr IP1 ....134 C1
Lake IP32 ....48 C5
Lake Side IP14 ....124 C6
Lake View Rd NR33 ...114 E8
Lakeland 3 IP26 ....5 A3
Lakeland Dr NR32 .....112 F1
Lakenheath Airfield
IP27 ....14 B5
Lakenheath American High
Sch IP27 ....109 F1
Lakenheath Fen Nature
Reserve ★ IP27 ....4 F1
Lakenheath Mid Sch
IP26 ....4 D5
Lakenheath Prim Sch
IP27 ....109 D6
Lakenheath Sta IP27 ...4 F1
Lakeside Ave IP16 .....73 E6
Lakeside Cl IP18 ......119 B7
Lakeside Pk Dr IP18 ..119 B6
Lakeside Rd IP32 ......138 E2
Lakeside Rise NR32 ...112 C8

Lakforth 4 CO10 ....91 E8
Lamarsh Hill CO8 ......101 C5
Lamarsh Rd CO8 ......101 A6
Lamb Ct IP28 ....116 D2
Lambert Cl
Halesworth IP19 ......118 B3
Weeting IP27 ....9 A2
Lambert Dr CO10 ....92 B7
Lambert's La
Mendlesham IP14 .....52 C3
Sudbourne IP12 ....73 B1
Lambert's Way NR35 ..110 C6
Lamberts Cl IP32 .....136 D2
Lamberts La IP5 ....136 E2
Lambeth Cl 1 IP1 .....139 A7
Lambeth Way IP14 .....67 F7
Lamble Cl IP28 ....30 B8
Lambourne Cl 3 IP32 ..123 E6
Lambourne Rd IP1 ...135 B4
Lambs La IP29 ....63 D1
Lambsale Meadow
IP17 ....128 D4
Lambseth St IP27 .....117 C3
Lamdin Rd IP32 ....48 C5
Lammas Cl IP31 ....34 C4
Lanark Rd IP4 ....136 B1
Lancaster Ave IP32 ...122 F8
Lancaster Cl IP28 ......62 C4
Lancaster Dr 8 IP5 ....98 A7
Lancaster Rd
5 Feltwell IP26 ....4 E5
Ipswich IP4 ....139 E6
5 Mildenhall IP28 ......30 A8
Sudbury CO10 ....148 B8
Lancaster Way
10 Claydon IP6 ....82 B5
Stradishall CB8 ....75 C7
Lancers The IP12 .....146 E3
Lancewood Wlk 27 IP27 ..13 F2
Lancing Ave IP4 ....140 A8
Landguard Fort ★
IP11 ....107 F2
Landguard Nature Reserve ★
IP11 ....107 E2
Landguard Rd IP11 ...153 I11
Landsdown Rd CO10 ..148 E7
Landseer Cl IP3 ....140 A1
Landseer Ct 1 CB9 ..132 D4
Landseer Rd IP3 ......139 E2
Landspring La NR33 ..114 E6
Landwade Rd CB8 .....44 D6
Lane The
Creeting St Peter or West
Creeting IP6 ....67 B5
3 Mistley CO11 ....104 F2
Wrentham NR34 ....26 E5
Yoxford IP17 ....57 C8
Lanercost Way IP2 ...139 A1
Lang Gate Way NR35 ..7 D6
Langdale Cl 3 IP11 ...153 D6
Langdale Pk IP32 .....113 A4
Langer Prim Sch IP11 ..152 E2
Langford Cl IP14 ......124 B8
Langham La CO4 ......103 B1
Langham Rd
Blaxhall IP12 ....72 B4
Boxted CO4 ....102 F1
Langham Way CB9 .....74 A1
Langley Ave IP14 .....152 E4
Langley Cl IP11 ....152 E5
Langley Gdns NR33 ..114 F5
Langley Hill CO8 ......101 B6
Langmere Rd IP21 .....21 C4
Langridge The IP31 ....34 B2
Langstons IP11 ....152 D7
Langton Rd 4 IP33 ...122 D4
Lanman Mus ★ IP13 ..126 D4
Lansbury Rd IP19 .....118 B3
Lansdowne Rd
Felixstowe IP11 ....153 B6
Ipswich IP4 ....140 A5
Lowestoft NR33 ....114 F3
Lapwing Cl 17 IP31 ...49 D8
Lapwing Ct 4 IP28 ...116 D4
Lapwing Rd IP2 ....138 D3
Lapwing Way CB7 ......28 C5
Larch Cl IP27 ....109 D7
Larch Gr 6 CO6 ....102 C5
Larchcroft Cl IP1 .....135 B2
Larchcroft Rd IP1 ....135 A2
Larches The NR34 .....26 E5
Larchwood Cl IP8 .....138 C5
Largent Gr IP5 ....141 E8
Lark Cl
4 Stowmarket IP14 ...67 A5
Worlington IP28 ....30 B4
Lark Hill CB8 ....45 F3
Lark Rd IP28 ....116 D4
Lark Rise
23 Martlesham Heath IP5 ..98 A8
Sudbury CO10 ....148 B3
Lark Valley Dr 9 IP28 ..48 C6
Larkhall Rd CB7 ....28 F1
Larkhall Rise IP4 ......140 E5
Larkhill Way 9 IP11 ..152 D5
Larks Cl CB9 ....133 A5
Larks Gate IP28 ....48 C6
Larks Rise IP19 ....118 C3
Larksfield Cres 5 CO12 ..107 A2
Larksfield Rd IP9 .....105 D5
Larkspur Cl
Corton NR32 ....113 B8
1 Red Lodge IP28 ......30 B1
Larkspur Rd IP2 ....138 F3
Larksway IP11 ....152 D5

Larters La IP14 ....67 D8
Lathbury Ct IP33 ......154 B3
Lattens Sq 4 NR32 ...113 C2
Lattice Ave IP4 ....140 C6
Laud Mews IP3 ....140 A2
Laud's Cl IP11 ....152 B8
Laundry La
Bury St Edmunds IP33 ..123 B3
Huntingfield IP19 ......41 A4
Laureate Com Prim Sch
CB8 ....120 E6
Laureate Gdns CB8 ..120 E6
Laureate Paddocks
CB8 ....120 E6
Laureate Sch Rd CB8 ..120 E6
Laurel Ave
1 Harwich CO12 .....106 F1
Ipswich IP5 ....141 A7
Laurel Cl Haverhill CB9 ..132 B7
7 Red Lodge IP28 ......30 C1
19 Thurston IP31 ......49 D4
Laurel Ct 9 IP30 ....50 F2
Laurel Dr 13 Claydon IP6 ..82 A5
8 Long Melford CO10 ..91 E8
Laurel Rd NR33 ....115 B6
Laurel Way 5 IP6 .....134 C8
Laurels The
8 Hopton on Sea NR31 ..3 B7
Worlingham NR34 .....111 F3
Lavender Cl 3 IP28 ....30 B1
Lavender Hill IP2 .....138 F4
Lavenham Guildhall of
Corpus Christi ★ CO10 ..78 E4
Lavenham Prim Sch
CO10 ....78 D4
Lavenham Rd
Great Waldingfield CO10 ..78 D1
Ipswich IP2 ....138 E5
Lavenham Way
5 Lowestoft NR32 ...112 F3
4 Stowmarket IP14 ..124 E3
Law's Drift IP10 ....98 C2
Lawn Gr NR32 ....112 F5
Lawn Way IP11 ....152 E5
Lawns The IP4 ....140 C8
Lawrence Dr NR32 ...113 B6
Lawrence Rd 2 IP24 ..16 D7
Lawshall Rd
Hartest IP29 ....77 B8
Hawstead IP29 ....63 D4
Lawshall Row IP29 ....63 D4
Lawson Ct 2 NR33 ...115 C7
Lawson Pl IP32 ....123 E5
Lawson Rd NR33 .....115 C7
Laxfield & District Mus ★
IP13 ....40 B3
Laxfield Rd
Badingham IP13 ....56 B8
Dennington IP13 ....55 E6
Fressingfield IP21 .....39 F7
Laxfield IP13 ....40 C1
Stradbroke IP21 ....39 E4
Laxfield Way NR33 ...114 F4
Layer Rd NR33 ....132 C5
Layham Dr 4 IP32 ....123 A8
Layham Gdns IP14 ...124 F3
Layham Rd IP7 ....149 D4
Layhill Cl IP32 ....123 D5
Laywood Cl 1 IP32 ..123 D6
Layzell Croft CO10 ....92 B2
Le Grice Wlk IP32 ....122 F2
Lea IP18 ....119 B2
Lea's Drift 1 NR33 ...114 C4
Leabrook Cl IP32 .....123 E6
Leader's Way CB8 ....120 E4
Leas The NR32 ....112 F5
Leather La
Great Yeldham CO9 ...90 A1
Haverhill CB9 ....132 C5
Leathes Cl NR32 ......112 F1
Leathes Ham Nature
Reserve ★ NR32 ......113 A1
Lee Cl IP4 ....132 D8
Lee Rd Aldeburgh IP15 ..130 E3
Harwich CO12 ....107 B2
Ipswich IP3 ....139 F3
Leech Wlk IP32 ....122 E8
Leeks Cl IP7 ....149 D7
Leeks Hill IP12 ....147 A7
Leggatt Dr IP8 ....134 A2
Leicester Cl IP2 ....138 F1
Leighton Rd IP3 ......144 A8
Leighton Sq 8 IP3 ...144 A8
Leiston Abbey ★ IP16 ..58 C3
Leiston High Sch IP16 ..129 C6
Leiston Leisure Ctr
IP16 ....129 C6
Leiston Mid Sch IP16 ..129 C6
Leiston Prim Sch
IP16 ....129 C6
Leiston Rd
Aldeburgh IP15 ....130 D3
Coldfair Green IP17 ...129 B3
Haverhill IP33 ....132 C5
4 Lowestoft NR32 ...113 C1
Theberton IP16 ....58 B5
Leisure Way NR32 ....113 B7
Lely Rd IP3 ....143 F8
Lemons Hill IP9 ....105 B8
Lentins The IP14 ....68 E4
Leona Cres IP14 ......114 C2
Leonard Dr 2 NR32 ..113 A6
Leonard's La IP26 ......4 D5
Leopold Gdns IP4 ....140 B8
Leopold Rd
Felixstowe IP11 ....153 A3
Ipswich IP4 ....140 B7

Leslie Rd IP3 ....140 C1
Lester Piggott Way
  CB8 ....120 F6
Letton Cl IP9 ....150 E3
Leverett's La IP18 ....119 B2
Levington Ct NR33 ....115 D8
Levington La IP10 ....98 A3
Levington Rd
  Felixstowe IP11 ......152 E1
  Ipswich IP3 ....140 A4
  Nacton IP10 ....145 C4
Lewes Cl IP3 ....140 E3
Lewis Cl
  Ditchingham NR35 ...110 C8
  Hopton IP22 ....18 C2
Lewis La IP9 ....105 B5
Ley Rd Barrow IP29 ...47 A2
  Stetchworth CB8 .....60 A5
Leys La IP23 ....37 B5
Leys Rd IP30 ....50 B2
Leyton Ave IP28 ......116 B6
Liberty Cl IP32 ....123 F6
Liberty Intermediate Sch
  IP27 ....14 A3
Lidgate Ct **1** IP11 ....152 C4
Lidgate Rd CB8 ......61 C8
Lighthouse Score **2**
  NR32 ....113 E3
Lilac Cl IP27 ....14 D8
Lilac Dr
  Lakenheath IP27 .....109 D6
  Lowestoft NR32 ......113 B3
Lilac Wlk IP6 ....125 D3
Lilley Cl IP33 ....122 C3
Lily La NR34 ....10 A7
Lily Way NR33 ....114 C5
Lime Ave
  Harwich CO12 ....107 A2
  Lowestoft NR32 ......112 D2
Lime Cl Burwell CB5 ...44 B5
  7 Harleston IP20 ....22 B5
  Lakenheath IP27 .....109 D5
  Mildenhall IP28 .....116 E5
  6 Ufford IP13 ......84 F7
  Wickham Market IP13 .127 B6
Lime Gr CO10 ....148 A3
Lime Kiln Quay IP12 ..147 B5
Lime Kiln Quay Rd
  IP12 ....147 B5
Lime Tree Ave IP16 ...129 C5
Lime Tree Cl **3** IP30 ..64 F8
Lime Tree Pl IP30 ....124 C5
Lime Wlk IP30 ....65 A3
Limecroft IP1 **1** 135 A3
Limekiln Cl **7** IP6 ....134 C8
Limerick Cl IP1 ......134 E2
Limes Ave IP8 ....134 C2
Limes The
  Framlingham IP6 .....126 B4
  Halesworth IP19 .....118 A3
  6 Horringer IP29 ....63 A8
  Long Melford CO10 ...91 E8
  Rushmere St Andrew
    IP5 ....136 D1
Limestone Cl **12** CB7 ..29 C5
Limetree Cl IP6 ......125 E4
Limetree Dr IP3 ......140 D2
Limmer Rd IP21 ......25 C5
Lincoln Ave IP17 .....128 B4
Lincoln Cl IP1 ....135 B3
Lincoln Cl **11** NR33 ...11 B1
Lincoln Gdns **8** IP6 ...82 B5
Lincoln Gn IP33 .....123 B2
Lincoln La CO6 ......102 E1
Lincoln Rd **10** IP28 ...30 A8
Lincoln Terr IP11 .....152 F3
Linda Cl **11** IP4 ......3 D4
Lindbergh Rd IP3 .....140 C1
Linden Cl
  Aldeburgh IP15 ......130 D6
  20 Manningtree CO11 .104 D2
Linden Rd IP15 ......130 C5
Linden Wlk **11** IP28 ...13 B1
Lindisfarne Cl IP2 ....139 A1
Lindisfarne Rd IP33 ..122 D2
Lindsey Ave CO10 ....148 F4
Lindsey Rd IP4 ......140 C7
Lindsey Way IP14 ....124 E3
Ling Rd Palgrave IP22 .20 B2
  Wortham IP22 ....19 F2
Ling's La IP9 ....106 B7
Lingfield Rd IP1 ......135 B4
Lingheath Rd IP27 ....6 A1
Lings Field IP13 ......70 C7
Lingside **1** IP5 ......98 A7
Link La IP9 ....104 E7
Link Rd
  Capel St Mary IP9 ...150 E3
  7 Shotley Gate IP9 ..107 A5
Link The IP9 ....104 E7
Links Ave IP11 ......153 B6
Links Cl
  Bury St Edmunds IP33 .123 B1
  Lowestoft NR33 ......114 F5
  Worlington IP28 .....30 B4
Links Rd
  Great Yarmouth NR31 ...3 B8
  Lowestoft NR32 ......113 D5
Links The Flempton IP28 .32 B1
  Woodditton CB8 .....59 E8
Links View CO10 .....92 D3
Linksfield IP5 ....140 E7
Linksfield Gdns IP5 ...140 E7
Linkwood Rd IP30 ....64 B7
Linnet Dr **14** IP14 ....67 A5
Linnet Pl IP33 ....154 C1
Linnet Rd
  Bury St Edmunds IP33 .122 E4

Linnet Rd continued
  Ipswich IP2 ....138 D4
Linnetts La CB9 ......133 E2
Linstead Rd IP19 .....40 F5
Linton Cl IP28 ....120 F5
Linton Gdns IP33 ....120 E3
Linton Pl **2** IP13 .....132 F6
Linx The **6** IP13 .....40 B3
Lion La IP6 ....125 E3
Lion Meadow CB9 ....88 D4
Lion Rd Glemsford CO10 ..77 A3
  Palgrave IP22 ....20 B1
  Wortham IP22 ....36 F8
Lion St IP1 ....155 B3
Lionel Hurst Cl **15** CO10 ..92 B3
Lisburn Rd CB8 ......121 B3
Lister Rd Hadleigh IP7 ..149 F5
  Ipswich IP1 ....134 F1
Liston La CO10 ......91 D7
Lithgo Paddock **8** IP31 ..49 A6
Little Back La **8** IP14 ..53 F2
Little Fen Dro CB5 ....44 A7
Little Gipping St IP1 ..155 A3
Little Gn Cheveley CB8 ..60 E6
  Earl Soham IP13 .....54 F1
  Elmswell IP30 ....50 E2
Little Gn Cl IP23 ....36 C3
Little Gr IP9 ....150 E2
Little Gulls IP9 ......150 E3
Little Hall* IP9 ....78 E4
Little Hasse Dro CB7 ..28 E6
Little Horkesley Rd
  CO6 ....102 A2
Little Hyde Cl CO9 ...90 A1
Little Hyde Rd CO9 ...90 A1
Little London Hill IP14 ..53 E3
Little London La CB7 ..29 B5
Little Lumpkid IP7 ....149 E8
Little Meadows Dr IP6 ..69 C2
Little Mill La IP29 ....47 A2
Little Oulsham Dro IP26 ..4 B6
Little St* IP7 ....57 C8
Little St John's St **8**
  IP12 ....147 A5
Little St Mary's CO10 ..91 E7
Little Tufts IP9 ......150 F3
Little Whip St IP2 ....155 B1
Little Yeldham Rd CO9 ..90 B2
Little's Cres IP2 .....155 B1
Littlemoor Rd IP17 ...57 F8
Livermere Drift IP31 ..48 E6
Livermere Rd
  Great Barton IP31 ....49 A6
  Troston IP31 ....33 D2
Llewellyn Drift **8** IP5 ..141 C7
Lloyd Rd **3** IP9 ......107 A4
Lloyds Ave Ipswich IP1 ..155 B3
  15 Kessingland NR33 ..11 B1
Lloyds The IP5 ......141 C7
Loam Pit La IP19 ....118 C4
Locarno Rd **1** IP3 ....140 B3
Loch Rannoch Cl IP30 ..50 E2
Lock Cl **14** IP14 ......53 F2
Lock's La
  6 Leavenheath CO6 ..102 A7
  Shipmeadow NR34 ....8 F5
  Wrentham NR34 .....26 F6
Lock's The IP4 ......25 C5
Lockhart Rd NR35 ....8 D7
Lockington Cl **4** IP14 ..124 E5
Lockington Cres IP14 .124 D5
Lockington Rd IP14 ..124 D5
Lockington Wlk IP14 .124 D5
Lockwood Cl **1** IP12 ..147 A5
Loddon Rd
  Ditchingham NR35 ...110 C7
  Gillingham NR34 .....9 B6
  Kirby Cane NR35 .....8 C8
Lode Cl CB7 ....28 D3
Lode La CB7 ....28 A1
Lodge Cl IP14 ....51 D1
Lodge Farm Dr IP11 ..153 C5
Lodge Farm La
  Barsham NR34 ....9 B4
  8 Melton IP12 ......84 E6
Lodge Farm Rd CO10 ..77 B1
Lodge La Claydon IP6 ..134 A8
  Riddlesworth IP22 ....18 A3
  Shelfanger IP22 .....20 B5
Lodge Rd Feltwell IP26 ..4 F6
  Great Bealings IP13 ..137 E5
  Hollesley IP12 ....99 D7
  Holton IP19 ....118 E5
  St John, Ilketshall
    NR35 ....110 F2
  1 Ufford IP13 ......84 F7
  Walberswick IP18 ....119 A2
Lodge Way IP24 .....16 B7
Lofft Cl **11** IP31 .....34 E4
Loftus Ave IP14 .....119 C7
Loganberry Rd **4** IP3 ..144 C7
Loggers La IP22 .....18 E1
Loke The
  Blundeston NR32 .....3 A4
  Ditchingham NR35 ...110 B7
Lombardy Rd CO10 ..148 B8
Lonbarn Hill CO11 ...105 D1
London City Rd IP21 ..39 C3
London La
  Harleston IP14 ......66 C7
  4 Mundford IP26 ....6 B8
London Rd
  Beccles NR34 ....111 B2
  Blythburgh IP19 .....42 E5
  Brampton with Stoven
    NR34 ....25 E6
  Brandon IP27 ....14 E8
  Capel St Mary IP9 ...150 F2

London Rd continued
  Copdock & Washbrook
    ....138 A1
  Elveden IP24 ....15 C2
  Halesworth IP19 .....118 A2
  Harleston IP20 ......22 D5
  Icklingham IP27 .....31 E8
  Ipswich IP1 ....155 A3
  Kessingland NR33 ....11 B2
  Lowestoft NR33 ......115 A2
  Pinewood IP8 ....138 B2
  Thetford IP24 ....16 A5
  Westley Waterless CB8 ..59 A4
  Weston NR34 ....9 D2
  Wrentham NR34 .....26 E4
London Rd N NR32 ...113 D1
London Rd Pakefield
  NR33 ....115 A2
London Rd S NR33 ...115 C5
Lone Barn Ct IP1 ....138 D8
Lonely Rd IP21 ......21 C6
Long Acre
  Lowestoft NR33 ......115 A3
  Southwold IP18 ......119 B7
Long Ave IP17 ....128 B4
Long Brackland IP33 ..154 B3
Long Dolver Dro CB7 ..28 D6
Long Field IP17 ......56 C1
Long La Bawdsey IP12 ..99 E3
  Burston & Shimpling IP22 ..20 E8
  Feltwell IP26 ....4 D5
Long Marsh Cl IP18 ..119 C7
Long Meadow Wlk
  NR33 ....114 D5
Long Meadows **2** CO12 ..106 F1
Long Melford CE Prim Sch
  CO10 ....91 E8
Long Pastures **2** CO10 ..77 B2
Long Perry IP9 ......150 F3
Long Rd
  Lowestoft NR33 ......114 E3
  Manningtree CO11 ...104 D1
Long Rd E CO7 ......104 A2
Long Rd W CO7 .....103 F2
Long Row IP16 ......129 D6
Long Shop Mus★
  IP16 ....129 C6
Long St IP3 ....139 E5
Long Thurlow Rd IP31 ..51 A7
Longacre Gdns IP33 ..122 E3
Longbeach Dr NR33 ..114 D3
Longcroft IP11 ......152 E6
Longden Ave NR32 ...112 F2
Longfield Rd IP9 .....150 E4
Longfield Way **6** NR32 ..112 D2
Longfulans La NR31 ...3 B6
Longmeadow IP33 ...122 E3
Longmere La CB7 ....28 C5
Longnor Rd NR35 ....110 C7
Lonsdale Cl IP4 .....139 F7
Looe Rd IP11 ....153 C5
Looms La IP33 ......154 B2
Lopham Rd NR16 ....18 D8
Lophams CB9 ....132 D8
Loraine Way IP8 ....134 A1
Lord's Croft La CB9 ..132 C5
Lord's Highway The
  IP14 ....67 E5
Lord's La CB8 ....61 E5
Lord's Wlk IP27 .....13 F2
Lorne Pk Rd NR33 ...115 C6
Lorne Rd
  Lowestoft NR33 ......115 C6
  Southwold IP18 ......119 D5
Lothing St NR32 .....112 F1
Lothingland Mid Sch
  NR32 ....3 A5
Lotus Cl IP1 ....134 C1
Loudham Hall Rd
  IP13 ....127 D3
Loudham La IP13 ....85 A7
Louie's La IP22 .....20 C3
Lound Dam NR14 ....2 A3
Lound Rd
  Belton with Browston NR31 ..2 E8
  Blundeston NR32 ....3 A4
Louse La Brandeston CO7 ..83 D2
  Rattlesden IP30 .....65 D3
Louvain St IP14 .....107 A1
Lovat Cl IP13 ....22 E6
Love La Lowestoft NR33 ..114 F4
  Thornton IP23 ......53 B8
  Westleton IP17 .....58 C7
Lover's La IP16 .....129 E4
Lover's La IP9 ......106 B6
Lovetofts Dr IP1 ....134 D1
Lovewell Rd NR33 ...115 C6
Low Comm IP22 ....19 B3
Low Comm La NR34 ..2 A1
Low Comm Rd IP22 ..19 B3
Low Farm Dr NR33 ..114 C3
Low La Brandeston IP13 ..70 A7
  Creeting St Mary IP6 ..125 E8
Low Lighthouse Maritime
  Mus★ CO12 ....107 C3
Low Rd Alburgh IP20 ..7 A1
  Bramfield IP19 ......42 A5

Low Rd continued
  Debenham IP14 ......53 E1
  Denham IP21 ....38 C2
  Denton IP20 ....7 B1
  1 Dickleburgh & Rushall
    IP21 ....20 F2
  Earl Soham IP13 ....54 E2
  Eyke IP12 ....85 B7
  1 Fressingfield IP21 ..39 E8
  Friston IP17 ....72 F6
  Great Glemham IP17 ..56 C1
  Harwich CO12 ......106 F1
  Hasketon IP13 ......146 B8
  Hedenham IP13 .....7 D8
  Marlesford IP13 .....71 C5
  Mettingham NR35 ...110 F5
  Monk Soham IP13 ...54 D3
  Redenhall with Harleston
    IP20 ....22 F5
  St John, Ilketshall NR34 ..8 D2
  Starston IP20 ....22 C7
  Stratford St Andrew IP17 ..71 F7
  Swefling IP17 ....56 E3
  Ubbeston IP19 ....40 D3
  Wenhaston with Mells Hamlet
    IP19 ....42 C7
  Wortham IP22 ....19 E2
  Wortwell IP20 ......23 A7
Low St Badingham IP13 ..56 A7
  Bardwell IP31 ......34 C3
  Glemsford CO10 ....77 B3
  Hoxne IP21 ....38 B8
  Kettleburgh IP13 ....70 F2
  St Margaret, Ilketshall
    NR35 ....24 B8
Low Wr La IP22 .....20 A1
Low's La IP22 ....20 C1
Lower Barn Rd IP8 ...95 D5
Lower Baxter St IP33 ..154 B2
Lower Brook St IP4 ..155 B2
Lower Broom Rd NR32 ..50 C1
Lower Byfield IP7 ....79 C2
Lower Coney Gr IP8 ..81 A4
Lower Cres IP6 ......82 A6
Lower Dales View Rd
  IP1 ....139 A8
Lower Downs Slade **5**
  CB9 ....132 E6
Lower Drag Way IP22 ..19 A4
Lower Farm Rd
  Boxted CO4 ....103 A4
  Ringshall IP7 ....80 C6
Lower Harlings **4** IP9 ..107 A4
Lower House La IP12 ..84 F6
Lower Houses Rd IP9 ..106 B5
Lower Marine Par
  CO12 ....107 B1
Lower N St CO10 ....75 D3
Lower Oakley IP21 ...37 F8
Lower Olland St NR35 ..110 B4
Lower Orwell St **4** ...155 C2
Lower Pk Wlk IP19 ..118 E4
Lower Rd Borley CO10 ..91 D6
  Coddenham IP6 .....68 B3
  Falkenham IP10 ....98 F1
  Glemsford CO10 ....77 B3
  Grundisburgh IP13 ..83 E5
  Hemingstone IP6 ....68 C1
  Hundon CO10 ......75 D3
  Lavenham CO10 ....78 D4
  Little Blakenham IP8 ..81 D3
  Melton IP13 ....84 F6
  Mount Bures CO8 ...101 D3
  Onehouse IP14 .....66 B5
  Westerfield IP6 .....135 D4
  Wicken CB7 ....28 D4
Lower Rose La IP21 ..20 D1
Lower St Baylham IP6 ..81 E7
  Cavendish CO10 ....76 E1
  Great Bealings IP13 ..137 E6
  Rattlesden IP30 ....65 D6
  Sproughton IP8 .....138 A6
  Stansfield CO10 ....76 C6
  Stanstead CO10 ....77 C3
  Stratford St Mary CO7 ..103 E5
  Stutton IP9 ....105 D5
  Ufford IP13 ....85 A6
  Wickham Market IP13 ..127 C7
Lower Ufford La IP13 ..127 C8
Lower Ufford Rd IP13 ..127 C1
Lowes Hill IP7 ......128 E2
Lowestoft & E Suffolk
  Maritime Mus★
  NR32 ....113 E3
Lowestoft Coll NR32 ..113 C2
Lowestoft Hospl
  NR33 ....113 D1
Lowestoft Mus★
  NR33 ....114 D8
Lowestoft Porcelain★
  NR32 ....113 E3
Lowestoft Rd
  Beccles NR34 ....111 E4
  Blundeston NR32 ...112 E8
  Hopton on Sea NR31 ..3 B6
  Lowestoft NR33 .....114 D3
  Reydon IP18 ....119 C8
  Worlingham NR34 ...10 A4
Lowestoft Sta NR32 ..115 D4
Lowestoft War Meml
  Musuem★ NR33 .....113 E3
Lowgate St IP23 ....117 D2
Lowlands Cl **17** NR33 ..11 C1
Lowry Cl CB9 ....132 B7
Lowry Gdns **6** IP3 ...144 C3
Lowry Way
  Lowestoft NR32 .....113 C5
  Stowmarket IP14 ...124 F2
Lowther St CB8 .....120 F3

Loxley Rd NR33 .....114 E6
Lucas Rd CO10 ......148 D5
Lucena Ct IP14 .....124 C6
Lucerne Cl
  Lowestoft NR33 .....114 C5
  5 Red Lodge IP28 ...30 B1
Ludbrook Cl IP6 .....125 C5
Ludgate Cswy IP23 ..117 E2
Ludlow Cl IP1 ....135 B4
Luff Meadow IP6 ....125 C5
Lugano Ave IP12 ....98 B8
Lulworth Ave IP3 ...140 C5
Lulworth Dr **14** CB9 ..132 C6
Lulworth Pk **8** NR32 ..113 A4
Lummis Vale IP5 ....141 C7
Lundy Cl IP9 ....133 B5
Lunnish Hill CO12 ...106 C2
Lupin Cl IP18 ....119 B6
Lupin Rd IP2 ....138 E4
Lupin Way IP6 ......125 D3
Lushington Rd **5** CO11 ..104 E2
Luther Rd IP2 ......155 B1
Lutus Cl IP3 ....90 A7
Lydgate Cl
  11 Bury St Edmunds IP32 ..48 C5
  14 Lawford CO11 ....104 D2
Lydgate Rd IP14 ....124 C7
Lyle Cl IP5 ....141 E7
Lymingster Cl **6** IP32 ..123 D6
Lymm Rd NR32 .....113 B5
Lyncroft Rd NR33 ...115 B3
Lyndhurst Ave IP4 ...140 C5
Lyndhurst Rd NR32 ..113 C4
Lyng La IP22 ....18 F5
Lyngate Ave NR33 ..114 F5
Lynn's Hall Cl CO10 ..92 C6
Lynnbrook Cl IP2 ...138 E1
Lynton Gdns NR32 ..113 C3
Lynwood Ave IP11 ..153 B5
Lynx Bsns Pk CB8 ...44 F7
Lyon Cl IP23 ....37 C4
Lysander Dr **3** IP3 ..144 C8

M

MacAulay Rd IP1 ....134 F3
MacKenzie Dr IP5 ...141 B8
MacKenzie Pl IP30 ..78 C8
MacKenzie Rd IP24 ..16 A5
Maconochie Way
  NR33 ....115 C7
MacPherson Robertson Way
  3 IP28 ....116 B5
Mafeking Rd IP16 ...129 D6
Magdalen Cl **3** NR32 ..113 A3
Magdalen Ct IP23 ...117 C2
Magdalen Dr IP12 ...149 D6
Magdalen Rd IP7 ....149 D6
Magdalen St IP23 ...117 C2
Magdalene Cl IP2 ...138 F2
Magingley Cres IP4 ..140 F6
Magnolia Cl
  9 Beck Row, Holywell
    Row & Kenny Hill IP28 ..13 B1
  2 Red Lodge IP28 ...30 C1
Magnolia Ct **3** NR32 ..113 B2
Magnolia Dr **7** IP12 ..85 D8
Magpie Cl
  8 Ipswich IP8 ....138 C2
  Ramsey CO12 ......106 F1
Magpie Ct **33** IP20 ...22 D6
Magpie Hill IP22 ....19 E1
Maid Marion Ct IP33 ..122 F3
Maiden Way IP7 ....149 D6
Maidenhall App IP2 ..139 B2
Maidenhall Sports Ctr
  IP2 ....139 C2
Maids Cross Hill IP27 ..109 E6
Maids Cross Way
  IP27 ....109 D6
Maidscross Hill Nature
  Reserve★ IP27 ......109 F5
Maidstone Cty Inf Sch
  IP11 ....152 E5
Maidstone Rd
  Felixstowe IP11 .....152 E5
  Lowestoft NR32 .....113 C1
Main Rd Benhall IP17 ..72 C8
  Bucklesham IP10 ....141 F1
  Chelmondiston IP9 ..106 B8
  Darsham IP17 ......42 A1
  Hacheston IP13 ....127 C6
  Harwich CO12 ......106 F1
  Henley IP6 ....82 D6
  Ipswich IP5 ....141 A8
  Kelsale cum Carlton
    IP17 ....128 C8
  Marlesford IP13 ....71 D4
  Martlesham IP12 ...146 C1
  Parham IP13 ....70 F8
  Pettistree IP13 .....127 B3
  3 Ramsey & Parkeston
    CO12 ....106 D1
  Somersham IP8 ....81 C3
  Tuddenham St Martin
    IP6 ....136 B4
  Woolverstone IP9 ...143 D1
  Wormingford CO6 ...101 C7
Main St
  Hockwold cum Wilton IP26 ..4 F3
  Leiston IP16 ....129 C6
Maine Cl **4** IP24 .....16 A5
Maisie's Meadow IP13 ..54 D7
Maitland Rd IP6 ....125 E3

Major La IP23 ....37 A2
Major's Cl IP29 ....62 C6
Makins Rd 2 CO12 ...106 F3
Malcolm Way CB8 .....121 A5
Maldon Ct CO10 ....148 F5
Malin Cl CB9 ....133 B5
Mallard Rd IP18 ......119 B7
Mallard Way
Brandon IP27 ....6 A1
Hollesley IP12 ....99 F7
Ipswich IP2 ....138 F3
Stowmarket IP14 ......124 A6
Sudbury CO10 ....92 B3
Mallards The IP27 ....109 D5
Mallets La IP12 ......131 C2
Mallow Rd 1 IP24 .....16 D6
Mallow Way NR33 .....114 C4
Mallow Wlk 4 CB9 ....132 A6
Mallowhayes IP12 ....139 B3
Malmesbury IP2 ......139 A2
Malt Cl 5 Laxfield IP13 ...40 B3
Newmarket CB8 ....121 B3
Malt Office Ave IP19 ...24 B4
Malt Office La IP19 ....24 A4
Malt's La IP26 ....4 A2
Malthouse Ct 24 IP20 ...22 D6
Malthouse La
Bury St Edmunds IP32 ..154 B4
Gissing IP22 ....20 F8
Malthouse Rd 22 CO11 ...104 E2
Malting Cotts CB9 ....133 D2
Malting End CB8 ......60 E2
Malting Farm La CO7 ..103 E3
Malting La 10 Clare CO10 .90 A8
Isleham CB7 ....29 C5
Malting Row IP31 .....33 F5
Maltings IP14 ....52 D3
Maltings Cl
2 Bures Hamlet CO8 ...101 C5
1 Chevington IP29 .....62 C6
Halesworth IP19 ......118 B4
Moulton CB8 ....45 F3
Maltings Dr 6 IP20 ....22 D6
Maltings Garth 9 IP31 ..24 B7
Maltings La IP31 ......32 F1
Maltings Mews IP7 ...149 D5
Maltings The
Beccles NR34 ....111 B7
Bungay NR35 ....110 C4
Maltsters' Way NR32 ..114 D8
Maltsters Wlk IP14 ...124 C3
Maltward Ave IP33 ....122 C5
Malvern Cl Ipswich IP3 .140 B3
Newmarket CB8 ....121 B2
Malvern Rd IP33 ......122 D3
Malvern Rise NR32 ....113 B3
Malyon Rd IP7 ....149 E8
Manchester Rd IP2 ....138 D2
Manderston Rd CB8 ...120 E3
Manderville Rd IP33 ..122 E4
Mandeville 14 CB5 .....44 A5
Mandy Cl IP4 ....140 A6
Mannall Wlk IP5 ......141 E8
Manners Rd IP31 ......48 D5
Manning Rd
Bury St Edmunds IP32 ..123 F7
Felixstowe IP11 ......152 E2
Manning's La IP22 .....35 D5
Mannings La IP9 ......144 A2
Mannington Cl 3 IP4 ..140 F5
Manningtree High Sch
CO11 ....104 D2
Manningtree Mus★
CO11 ....104 E2
Manningtree Rd
Dedham CO7 ....104 A3
East Bergholt CO7 ....151 A4
Stutton IP9 ....105 C5
Manningtree Sports Ctr
CO11 ....104 D2
Manningtree Sta
CO11 ....104 D3
Manor Ash Dr IP32 ....123 E6
Manor Cl 9 Beccles NR34 .9 F4
3 Cavendish CO10 .....76 E1
Walbersick IP18 ......119 A2
Worlingham NR34 ....9 F4
Manor Farm Cl
Haverhill CB9 ....132 F5
11 Southwold IP18 ...119 D5
Manor Farm Rd
St John, Ilketshall NR34 ..8 D3
1 Thistley Green IP28 ..29 F6
Manor Garth IP31 .....49 E6
Manor Gdns
7 Hopton on Sea NR31 ...3 C6
Saxmundham IP17 .....128 E2
Manor House Mus★
IP33 ....154 C1
Manor La Gosbeck IP6 ..68 D2
14 Harwich CO12 .....107 A2
Horringer IP29 ....122 B1
Stutton IP9 ....105 C5
Manor Pk Rd
Corton NR32 ....3 C4
9 Southwold IP18 ....119 D5
Manor Rd 10 Bildeston IP7 .79 F4
Brandon IP27 ....5 E1
Bungay NR35 ....110 B2
Clopton IP13 ....69 E1
Elmsett IP7 ....80 F2
Felixstowe IP11 ......152 B8
Harwich CO12 ....107 A2
Hasketon IP13 ....146 D6
Haverhill CB9 ....132 F5

Manor Rd continued
Hessett IP30 ....64 F7
Hopton on Sea NR31 ....3 B6
Ipswich IP4 ....139 D8
11 Martlesham Heath IP5 .98 A8
Mildenhall IP28 ......116 B4
Roydon IP22 ....20 B3
Sudbury CO10 ....148 C7
Trimley St Martin IP11 .153 I11
Manor Terr IP11 .....107 F3
Manor View IP28 ....116 D2
Manor Wlk 20 NR33 ...11 B1
Manorhouse La 8
NR34 ....111 B6
Mansbrook Bvd 5 IP3 .144 C7
Manse La IP19 ....40 C6
Mansfield Ave IP1 ...134 E2
Manthorp Cl IP12 ....147 B8
Manwick Rd IP11 ....152 E2
Maple Cl
6 Great Brickett IP7 ...80 D6
Ipswich IP2 ....139 A3
12 Lakenheath IP27 ...13 F2
Rendlesham IP12 ......85 D8
Yaxley IP23 ....37 B5
Maple Covert 5 NR32 .112 F5
Maple Gn IP31 ....49 A6
Maple Gr IP7 ....82 A6
Maple Hill CO10 ......75 E1
Maple Rd
5 Lowestoft NR33 ....114 F7
Stowupland IP14 ......67 A6
Sudbury CO10 ....148 F3
Maple Way
Beccles NR34 ....111 C5
Eye IP23 ....117 D3
Leavenheath CO6 ....102 B7
Maples The IP5 ......140 E8
Marbella Gn NR33 ...114 F4
Marbled White Dr IP9 .142 E8
March Pl 2 CO10 ......76 A1
Marcus Cl CB9 ....133 B5
Marcus Rd IP11 .....153 D5
Mardle La Reydon NR34 .43 B8
Wangford with Henham
NR34 ....26 C1
Mardle The NR33 ....114 C2
Mare Hill CO10 ....75 D3
Margaret Rd 2 IP14 ..124 C7
Margaret St IP33 ....152 E5
Margate Rd IP3 ......140 B3
Marham Rd 4 NR32 ..113 B2
Maria St 7 CO12 ....107 B3
Marigold Ct IP2 .....138 E3
Marigold Dr 3 IP28 ...46 A8
Marina 6 NR32 ....113 E1
Marina Gdns IP11 ...152 E2
Marina Theatre 11
NR32 ....113 D1
Marine Cl 3 NR31 .....3 B8
Marine Par
12 Harwich CO12 .....107 B2
Lowestoft NR33 ......115 D7
Mariner's Cl 2 NR31 ...3 B8
Mariners Pk Cl 11 NR31 .3 B7
Mariners St NR32 ....113 E2
Mariners Way IP15 ..130 D5
Marion Cl 5 NR34 ...111 C3
Mark Jennings La
IP33 ....154 C3
Mark La IP27 ....6 C2
Markant Cl IP2 ......123 E6
Market Cross Pl IP15 .130 F4
Market Gr CO9 ....90 A1
Market Hill 8 Clare CO10 .90 A8
Clopton IP13 ....83 D8
Framlingham IP13 ....126 C3
Haverhill CB9 ....132 E6
Orford IP12 ....131 C2
6 Sudbury CO10 .....148 C5
Market La
Blundeston NR32 ....3 B4
Burston & Shimpling IP22 .20 E5
Somerleyton, Ashby &
Herringfleet NR32 ....2 D6
Market Pl 17 Bildeston IP7 .79 F4
Hadleigh IP7 ....149 D5
2 Halesworth IP19 ...118 A3
22 Harleston IP20 .....22 D6
6 Kessingland NR33 ..11 B1
11 Lavenham CO10 ....78 D4
Saxmundham IP17 ....128 D3
Southwold IP18 ......119 D5
Stowmarket IP14 .....124 D6
Market Row NR34 ....111 B6
Market Sq CB8 ......121 A3
Market St
1 Beccles NR34 ......111 B5
Fordham CB7 ....29 A1
3 Harwich CO12 .....107 C3
Laxfield IP13 ....40 B3
3 Mildenhall IP28 ...116 C4
2 Newmarket CB8 ...121 A3
16 Soham CB7 ....28 C4
Market Thoroughfare
IP33 ....154 B2
Market Weston Rd
IP22 ....35 A7
Markhams Cl CB9 ....132 D7
Marlborough Ct
4 Haverhill CB9 .....132 C5
Lowestoft NR32 ......112 F1
Marlborough Dr 4
CO10 ....148 D6
Marlborough Rd
Ipswich IP4 ....140 A5
Lowestoft NR32 ......112 F1
Saxtead IP13 ....55 A4

Marlborough Rd continued
Southwold IP18 ......119 D6
Marlesford Rd IP13 ...71 B5
Marlow Rd IP1 ......134 D1
Marriott's Wlk 5 IP14 .124 D5
Marsden Cl NR33 ....115 A3
Marsh La Aldeby NR34 ..2 A2
Carlton Colville NR33 .114 A4
3 Earsham NR35 ....7 F4
Felixstowe IP11 .....153 C8
28 Kessingland NR33 ..11 C1
Kessingland NR33 .....27 C8
North Cove NR34 .....10 B5
Reydon IP18 ....26 D2
Somerleyton, Ashby &
Herringfleet NR32 ....2 C4
Worlingham NR34 ......9 F5
Wortham IP22 ....20 A1
Marsh Rd Boxford CO10 .93 C3
Fritton & St Olaves NR31 ..2 B7
Lowestoft NR33 ......114 D7
Stoke-by-Nayland CO6 .103 C7
Marsh View NR34 ....111 D5
Marsh Way IP33 ....154 A4
Marshall Cl IP5 .....141 C8
Marshalls Meadow 3
IP14 ....67 A6
Marshams Piece 4
NR33 ....114 C5
Marshy La CO10 ......90 B4
Martello La IP11 ....153 D5
Martello Rd NR32 ...113 B4
Marten's La CO6 ....102 F8
Martin Cl Brandon IP27 ..6 A1
Lowestoft NR33 ......114 D3
Mildenhall IP28 ......116 D3
8 Soham CB7 ....28 D3
Martin Rd 16 Burwell CB5 .44 A6
Harleston IP20 ....22 E6
Ipswich IP2 ....155 B1
Martin's Ave NR33 ...115 B6
Martin's Meadow Nature
Reserve★ IP13 ....69 E4
Martinet Gn IP3 .....140 C1
Martins La IP13 ......69 F2
Martins Meadow 6 IP23 .36 D2
Martins Mews 2 CB9 .132 A7
Martins Rd CO10 ....148 F7
Martinsyde 9 IP5 .....98 A8
Martlesham Beacon Hill Prim
Sch IP12 ....84 A1
Martlesham Heath Control
Twr Mus★ 31 IP5 ....98 A8
Martlesham Rd IP13 .137 F3
Martyns Rise 5 CO10 ..91 E7
Mary La CO10 ....75 C3
Mary's La IP19 ....40 E6
Maryday Cl IP6 ....68 B1
Maryon Rd IP3 ......140 B1
Masefield Rd Diss IP22 .20 D2
Stowmarket IP14 ....124 B8
Mashay Rd CO9 ......90 B3
Maskell's La IP7 ......80 E4
Mason Ct 1 IP6 ......82 A5
Mason Gdns 2 IP28 ...29 F6
Mason Rd CB5 ....44 A7
Mason's La 5 IP30 ....50 D1
Masons Cl IP4 ....139 F6
Mast Cl NR33 ....114 B4
Masterlord Ind Est
IP16 ....129 B6
Masterson Gr IP5 ...141 C6
Mat Dawson Cl CB8 ..120 F6
Mather La IP20 ....22 B5
Mather Way IP2 ....155 C1
Matlock Cl 13 IP8 ...138 C2
Matlock Dale 11 NR33 .114 E3
Matson Rd IP1 ......138 F8
Matthews La CB8 .....74 C7
Maude St IP3 ....139 E4
Maudslay Rd IP1 ....134 C2
Maulkin Cl IP32 .....123 F7
Mautby Way NR33 ..114 F5
May Rd Ipswich IP3 ..140 C2
Lowestoft NR32 ......113 C1
May's La CO7 ....103 F2
Maybury Rd IP3 .....140 B1
Maybush La IP11 ....153 C5
Maycroft Cl 2 IP1 ...135 A3
Mayes La CO12 ......106 D1
Mayfair Rd NR35 ....110 C3
Mayfield CO6 ....102 B7
Mayfield Ave 12 NR33 ..11 C1
Mayfield La 7 IP5 .....98 A7
Mayfield Rd
Bury St Edmunds IP33 .123 B1
Ipswich IP4 ....140 C7
Lowestoft NR33 ......114 C4
Mayfield Way IP14 ...52 E5
Mayfields
Lakenheath IP27 .....109 C7
6 Martlesham Heath IP5 .98 A7
Mayflower Ave
8 Harwich CO12 .....107 C3
Saxmundham IP17 ....128 B2
Mayflower Way
14 Harleston IP20 ....22 D5
Sudbury CO10 ....148 B8
Mayfly Cl 12 IP8 ....142 E8
Mayhem Adventure Play
Area★ NR33 ....115 E8
Maynewater La NR33 .154 C1
Maynewater Sq NR33 .154 C1
Maypole La CB8 ......60 C6
McCalmont Way CB8 .121 C2
McIntyre Wlk IP32 ...122 E7
McLaren Ct 9 NR34 ..111 C3
McLean Dr 16 NR33 ..11 B1

Mead Dr IP5 ....141 C7
Mead The CO10 .....148 F2
Mead Way IP14 ......52 E5
Meadow Barn IP14 ...66 C2
Meadow Cl
Bury St Edmunds IP33 .122 E3
8 Felixstowe IP11 ...107 D8
Felsham IP30 ....65 A4
Lavenham CO10 ....78 D3
8 Soham CB7 ....28 D3
Westhall IP19 ....25 B4
Meadow Cres IP3 ...140 F1
Meadow Ct
4 Great Yarmouth NR31 ..3 B8
16 Stanton IP31 ......34 C4
Meadow Dr
Horringer IP29 ....63 A8
Lakenheath IP27 .....109 D7
Meadow Gdns NR33 .111 A3
Meadow La
Newmarket CB8 ......121 D1
Sudbury CO10 ....148 C4
Thurston IP31 ....49 E4
Meadow Prim Sch
NR33 ....115 B6
Meadow Rd
8 Barrow IP29 ....47 A2
Bungay NR35 ....110 D2
Lowestoft NR33 ......112 F4
Woolpit IP30 ....65 E8
Meadow Rise IP16 ..129 D2
Meadow Sh Ctr The
IP14 ....124 D6
Meadow Valley IP7 ...80 D5
Meadow View
Needham Market IP6 .125 C5
Woolpit IP30 ....65 E8
Meadow View Rd
CO10 ....148 B4
Meadow Way
Assington CO10 ....92 F1
Lowestoft NR33 ......114 C2
Meadow Wlk 3 IP12 ...72 C8
Meadowlands
1 Blundeston NR32 ....3 A4
11 Burwell CB5 ....44 A5
Kirton IP10 ....98 D2
4 Woolpit IP30 ....50 D1
Meadowlands Cl IP17 ..57 C8
Meadows The
Drinkstone IP30 ......65 B7
Worlington IP28 ......30 B4
Meadows Way IP7 ...149 D6
Meadowside
Blo' Norton IP22 ......18 E2
Wickham Market IP13 .127 C7
Meadowside Gdns
IP4 ....140 E8
Meadowsweet Cl
Haverhill CB9 ....132 C7
3 Lowestoft NR33 ...114 D5
Meadowvale Cl
Beccles NR34 ....111 B2
Ipswich IP4 ....139 F8
Meads The NR32 ....113 C3
Medway 22 CO11 ....104 D2
Mear Cl IP12 ....85 C2
Mechanical Music Mus &
Bygones★ IP14 ......52 A6
Medway Rd IP3 ......139 F2
Meekings Rd CO10 ..148 F6
Meeting Field 10 CO10 .91 E8
Meeting La
Grundisburgh IP13 ....83 E5
Ridgewell CO9 ....89 D4
Meeting Wlk CB9 ....132 F5
Melbourne Dr CB8 ..116 B5
Melbourne Rd
Ipswich IP4 ....140 D7
Lowestoft NR33 ......113 C3
Melford Cl 2 Burwell CB5 .44 A5
8 Ipswich IP4 ....140 F5
Melford Hall★ IP10 ...77 E1
Melford Rd Acton CO10 .92 A8
Cavendish CO10 ......76 F1
Lavenham CO10 ....78 C3
Lawshall IP29 ....63 D1
Stowmarket IP14 ....124 F4
Sudbury CO10 ....148 B7
Melford Way IP11 ...152 C3
Mellis Cl CB9 ....74 A1
Mellis Ct 18 IP11 ...152 D5
Mellis Rd
Gislingham IP23 ......36 D3
Thrandeston IP21 .....37 B6
Wortham IP22 ....36 E7
Yaxley IP23 ....37 B5
Mellisash Rd IP23 ....36 F5
Melplash Cl IP3 .....140 E4
Melplash Rd IP3 ....140 E4
Melrose Cl NR32 ....112 F5
Melrose Gdns
Ipswich IP4 ....140 B8
Newmarket CB8 ......120 E4
Melton Cl CB8 ....121 B2
Melton CP Sch IP12 .147 C2
Melton Grange Rd
IP12 ....147 A6
Melton Hill IP12 ....147 B6
Melton Meadow Rd 4
IP12 ....147 B6
Melton Rd
Hollesley IP12 ....99 F8
Woodbridge IP12 ....147 B6
Melton Sta IP12 ....147 D7
Melville Rd IP4 .....139 F5
Mendham Cl 36 IP20 ..22 D6
Mendham La
38 Harleston IP20 ....22 D6

Mendham La continued
St Cross, South Elmham
IP20 ....23 C6
Mendham Prim Sch
IP20 ....23 A6
Mendham Rd IP20 ...23 A4
Mendip Dr IP5 ......140 F6
Mendip Rd NR32 ...112 E2
Mendlesham Prim Sch
IP14 ....52 D4
Mendlesham Rd IP14 ..52 B5
Mercers Rd NR32 ...123 D7
Mere Cl IP31 ....49 C6
Mere Gdns IP4 ......140 F4
Mere La IP28 ....48 A6
Mere Manor Ct IP22 ..20 C2
Mere Side IP26 ......28 C4
Meredith Rd IP1 ....134 E2
Meriton Rise IP7 ....149 F4
Merivale Rd 17 CO11 .104 D2
Merlewood IP21 .....21 C5
Merlin Rd IP2 ....138 C3
Mermaid Cl IP2 .....123 A8
Merriam Cl 5 CO11 ..104 E4
Merrifield Rd NR33 ..114 F3
Merrion Cl 12 IP8 ...138 C2
Merrylees NR34 .....111 C4
Mersey Rd IP3 ......139 F2
Merville 9 NR33 ....114 E3
Messenger Cl NR35 ..110 B2
Metfield Rd IP20 .....23 D3
Metfield St IP20 .....23 C3
Methersgate Hall Dr
IP12 ....84 E1
Meynell Gdns CB8 ...121 A3
Micawber Mews 4 IP8 ..3 A4
Michaelhouse Way 12
IP31 ....34 C4
Michaels Mount IP13 .137 D5
Michaelstowe Cl 1
CO12 ....106 E1
Michigan Cl IP5 .....141 B7
Mickfield Mews 16
IP11 ....152 D5
Micklegate Rd IP11 ..152 E2
Micklesmere Dr 23 IP31 .34 B1
Mid Suffolk Leisure Ctr
IP14 ....124 B7
Middle Dro CB7 ......28 B4
Middle Gn CO6 ......101 B3
Middle La NR34 ......10 D3
Middle Rd
Blo' Norton IP22 ......18 D3
Earsham IP20 ....7 C4
Middle Way CO10 ....91 E8
Middle Wlk NR32 ...113 C5
Middlefield Dr 3 IP14 ..66 B4
Middlefield Rd 10 CO11 .105 A2
Middleton Cl IP2 ....138 D2
Middleton Prim Sch
IP17 ....58 B6
Middleton Rd
Sudbury CO10 ....148 B4
Yoxford IP17 ....57 E7
Midhurst Cl 3 IP32 ..123 D6
Midmeadow 4 NR34 .111 B5
Mid-Suffolk Light Rly Mus
The★ IP14 ....53 B4
Mights Rd IP18 .....119 C6
Milano Ave IP32 .....98 B8
Milburn Dro CB8 .....45 F3
Milden Cl 6 IP14 ...124 C1
Milden Rd
Brent Eleigh CO10 .....79 C4
Ipswich IP2 ....138 F5
Mildenhall Airfield
IP28 ....30 D7
Mildenhall Coll of Tech
IP28 ....116 B4
Mildenhall Dro IP28 ..12 F3
Mildenhall Ind Est
IP28 ....116 B6
Mildenhall Mus★
IP28 ....116 C4
Mildenhall Pl 1 CB9 .132 F6
Mildenhall Rd
Barton Mills IP28 ....116 C2
Beck Row, Holywell
Row & Kenny Hill IP28 .116 C8
2 Bury St Edmunds IP32 .123 A8
Fordham CB7 ....29 C1
Icklingham IP28 ......31 A5
Littleport CB7 ....12 A3
Mildenhall Stadium
IP28 ....29 D3
Mildmay Rd IP3 .....140 B1
Mile End IP27 ....14 E8
Mile End Rd CB7 .....12 A7
Miles Hawk Way IP28 .116 A5
Miles Paddock IP14 ..52 A6
Military Rd CB7 ......28 E2
Military Way 5 CO12 .106 E1
Mill Bank 1 NR32 ...112 F2
Mill Broadway IP12 ..131 C4
Mill Chase CB7 ......88 E3
Mill Cl 6 Burwell CB5 ..44 B5
Capel St Mary IP9 ...150 C3
Exning CB8 ....120 B8
Felixstowe IP11 .....152 D3
Kirby Row NR35 ....8 E2
1 Walsham le Willows
IP31 ....35 C2
Mill Cnr CB8 ....28 C5
Mill Croft 9 CB7 .....28 C3
Mill Drift IP26 ....5 A3
Mill Dro CB7 ....28 C3
Mill End La IP14 .....67 C7

Mill Field
- 3 Aldeburgh IP15 .....130 E5
- Bramford IP8 ....134 B2
- Pettaugh IP14 ....68 E6

Mill Fields IP14 .....51 D1

Mill Gdns
- Bedingham NR35 ....7 B8
- Elmswell IP30 ....50 F2

Mill Hill (Tumulus)★
- NR31 ....2 C8

Mill Hill Burgh IP13 ..83 F6
- Capel St Mary IP9 ...150 C3
- Cotton IP14 ....52 A6
- Earl Soham IP13 ......54 E1
- Hadleigh IP7 ....94 B7
- Haverhill CB9 ....132 D5
- Lawford CO11 ....104 B2
- Leiston IP16 ....129 C2
- Manningtree CO11 ....104 E2
- Mettingham NR35 ......8 D5
- Newmarket CB8 ....121 A4
- Peasenhall IP17 ......56 F8
- Rattlesden IP30 ......65 D6
- Sudbury CO10 ....148 B5
- Wormingford CO6 ....101 F3

Mill Hill Dr IP19 ...118 A4
Mill Hill Est IP16 ..129 C2
Mill Hoo IP12 ....99 E4

Mill La
- All Saints & St Nicholas, South Elmham IP20 ..23 E5
- Barnham IP24 ....16 B2
- Barrow IP29 ....47 A2
- Baylham IP6 ....81 F7
- Benhall IP17 ....72 C8
- Boyton IP12 ....86 B2
- Bradfield CO11 ......105 B1
- Bramford IP8 ....134 B1
- Brandeston IP13 ......70 A7
- Bruisyard IP17 ....56 C5
- 7 Burwell CB5 ....44 B5
- Butley IP12 ....86 B6
- Campsey Ash IP13 ...127 F6
- Cavendish CO10 ....90 D8
- Chelmondiston IP9 ..106 B8
- Coddenham IP6 ....68 B1
- Combs IP14 ....124 B1
- Copdock & Washbrook IP8 ....138 A1
- Corton NR32 ....3 D4
- Cowlinge CB8 ....75 B8
- Creeting St Peter or West Creeting IP6 .125 D8
- Dedham CO7 ....103 F4
- Dennington IP13 ......55 D5
- Ellingham NR35 ....8 E7
- Exning CB8 ....120 B8
- Fordham CB7 ....29 B1
- Felixstowe IP11 .....152 F4
- Garboldisham IP22 ....18 D3
- 9 Great Blakenham IP6 ..82 A5
- Great Yeldham CO9 ....90 A2
- Hasketon IP13 ....146 A7
- Henley IP6 ....82 D6
- Hockwold cum Wilton IP26 ..5 A3
- Hoo IP13 ....70 C6
- Hopton IP22 ....18 C3
- Hundon CO10 ....75 D3
- Kersey IP7 ....94 A7
- Layham IP7 ....149 E2
- Leiston IP16 ....129 C2
- 18 Manningtree CO11 ...104 E2
- Marlesford IP13 ......71 C5
- Metfield IP20 ....23 C3
- North Cove NR34 ......10 C4
- Polstead IP7 ....102 E8
- Pulham St Mary IP21 ..21 F8
- 4 Redgrave IP22 ......36 A8
- St John, Iketshall NR34 ..8 E2
- Shadingfield NR34 ....25 D7
- Somersham IP8 ....81 C3
- Southwold IP18 ......119 D5
- Stetchworth CB8 ......59 F5
- Stoke Ash IP23 ....52 F8
- Stonham Earl IP14 ....67 D5
- Stradbroke IP21 ......39 C5
- Sudbury CO10 ....148 B5
- Thetford IP24 ....16 B5
- Thurston IP31 ....49 D5
- Tunstall IP12 ....72 B1
- Weybread IP21 ....22 C3
- Wickham Market IP13 .127 C6
- 2 Witnesham IP6 ......83 A5
- Woodbridge IP12 ....147 A5
- Woolpit IP30 ....50 D1
- Wrentham NR34 ....26 F5

Mill Piece IP10 .....145 C6
Mill Pool La NR35 .....8 D6
Mill Pouch IP11 .....152 C8
Mill Rd (South) IP33 ..154 A1

Mill Rd
- Aldeby/Wheatacre/Burgh St Peter NR34 ....10 B8
- Ashley CB8 ....45 F1
- Badingham IP13 ....56 A7
- Barningham IP31 ......34 E7
- Battisford IP14 ......80 B8
- Beccles NR34 ....111 C2
- Birdbrook CO9 ....89 C5
- Botesdale IP22 ....36 B6
- Boxted CO4 ....102 E8
- Brockdish IP21 ....21 E3
- Burston & Shimpling IP22 ..20 E6
- Bury St Edmunds IP33 .154 A2
- Buxhall IP14 ....65 F4
- Chevington IP29 ......62 C6
- Clare CO10 ....90 B8

Mill Rd continued
- Coldfair Green IP17 .129 A2
- Cotton IP14 ....52 A6
- East Bergholt CO7 ...151 E4
- Ellingham NR35 ....8 D7
- Foxearth CO10 ....91 B7
- Friston IP17 ....72 E6
- Gazeley CB8 ....46 B3
- Great Barton IP31 ....49 A6
- Halesworth IP19 .....118 E3
- Haverhill CB9 ....132 E5
- Hemley IP12 ....98 E5
- Hengrave IP28 ....48 A7
- Honington IP31 ....33 F5
- Hundon CO10 ....75 D4
- Ipswich IP3 ....140 F1
- Kedington CB9 ......133 E8
- Kirtling CB8 ....60 F3
- Lakenheath IP27 .....109 D6
- Laxfield IP13 ....40 B2
- Lowestoft NR33 ......115 C7
- Mendlesham IP14 ......52 D4
- Moulton CB8 ....46 A1
- Mutford NR34 ....10 D3
- Newbourne IP12 ....98 D5
- Occold IP23 ....37 F1
- Peasenhall IP17 ......56 E8
- Redlingfield IP23 ....38 C2
- Ridgewell CO9 ....89 D3
- Rumburgh IP19 ....24 B4
- Saxmundham IP17 ....128 C3
- Stambourne CO9 ....89 B2
- Swefling IP17 ....56 E3
- Thelnetham IP22 ......18 E1
- Westleton IP17 ....58 C7
- Weybread IP21 ....22 C4
- Winfarthing IP22 .....20 B8
- Wissett IP19 ....118 A5
- Worlingworth IP13 ....54 D7
- Wyverstone IP14 ......51 D6

Mill Rd S IP22 ....36 B4
Mill Reef Cl CB8 ....120 D7
Mill Rise 11 Holbrook IP9 ..105 E7
- Saxmundham IP17 ....128 C3

Mill St Gislingham IP23 ..36 B2
- Isleham CB7 ....29 C5
- Middleton IP17 ....58 A6
- Mildenhall IP28 .....116 B3
- Nayland CO6 ....102 D5
- Stowupland IP14 ......67 A6
- Westleton IP17 ....58 C7

Mill Tye CO10 ....148 E2
Mill View IP8 ....46 B3
Mill View IP12 ......146 E5
Millbank CB8 ....120 F4

Millennium Grandstand CB8 ....120 C1

Millennium Way
- Kesgrave IP5 ....141 E7
- Lowestoft NR32 .....113 A4

Miller Cl Elmswell IP30 ..50 F2
- Lowestoft NR33 .....115 B5

Millers Cl Bungay NR35 .110 C3
- Hadleigh IP7 ....149 E6
- Stowmarket IP14 ....124 C3

Millers Ct 5 IP6 .....82 A5
Millers Dr IP21 ......21 B5
Millers Gn 44 IP20 ...22 D6
Millers View IP1 ....138 F7
Millfield IP23 ......117 B3
Millfield Ave IP14 ..124 C5

Millfield Cl
- Ditchingham NR35 ...110 C8
- 1 Saxmundham IP17 .128 C2

Millfield Dr IP14 ....65 F4
Millfield Gdns IP4 ..140 A7

Millfield Rd
- 2 Barningham IP31 ...34 F7
- Walberswick IP18 ...119 A2

Millfields
- 2 Peasenhall IP17 ...56 F8
- Wangford NR34 ....26 B2

Millfields Way CB9 ..132 F6
Millmarsh Dro IP27 ..109 A7
Mills Dr NR32 ....3 D4
Mills La CO10 ....91 E6
Mills Meadow IP13 ..126 D3
Mills Rd CO10 ....148 E6

Mills The
- Framlingham IP13 ...126 C3
- Ipswich IP4 ....140 E8

Millside IP13 ....37 C4
Millway NR34 ....10 C4
Millway Ave IP22 ....20 C3

Millway La
- Palgrave IP22 ....20 A1
- Wortham IP22 ....19 F1

Millwood Rd CO6 .....94 A3
Milner Cl Chilton CO10 ..92 B4
- Sudbury CO10 ....148 F6

Milner St IP4 ....139 E6
Milnes Way NR33 ....114 B3
Milnrow 10 IP6 ......138 C2
Milton Cl IP17 ......128 B4
Milton Rd CO11 .....104 D1

Milton Rd E
- Lowestoft NR32 .....113 D1
- Stowmarket IP14 ....124 E6

Milton Rd N 4 IP14 .124 D6
Milton Rd S IP14 ...124 E6
Milton Rd W NR32 ...113 D1
Milton St IP14 ......140 B7
Mimosa Wlk NR32 ....113 B2

Mincarlo Trawler★ NR33 ....115 D8

Minden Cl IP33 .....154 C2

Minden Dr
- Bury St Edmunds IP33 ..122 D5

Minden Dr continued
- Leiston IP16 ....129 D5

Minden Rd
- Lowestoft NR32 .....113 C2
- Sudbury CO10 ....148 D5

Minerva Cl CB9 .....133 B4
Minos Rd NR32 ......113 C4
Minos Way IP1 ......138 D8

Minsmere House Hospl IP4 ....140 C6

Minsmere Nature Reserve★ IP17 ....58 E6

Minsmere Rd IP17 ....58 F8
Minsmere Rise IP17 ..58 A6
Minsmere Way CO10 ..92 B3
Minster Rd IP3 .....132 D7
Minton Ent Pk CB8 ..120 E7
Mirbeck's Cl 6 NR34 ..9 F4
Misburgh Way NR31 ...3 C6
Mission La CO7 .....104 C6
Mission Rd IP22 .....20 D2
Mistley Sta CO11 ...104 F2
Mistley Way IP12 ...146 F6
Mitchell Ave IP32 ...48 C5
Mitchery La IP14 ....65 E4
Mitford Cl IP1 .....135 A4
Mitford Rd IP17 .....72 B8
Mitre Way IP3 ......139 E4
Mitre Cl 6 IP30 .....50 D1

Moat Cl
- Alphamstone CO8 ...101 A6
- Rushbrooke with Rougham IP30 ....49 D1

Moat Rd Birdbrook CO9 ..89 B4
- Theberton IP16 ......57 F4

Moat Wlk 2 CB9 ....132 C6
Mobbs Way NR32 ....112 E3

Mockbeggars Hall★ IP8 ....134 C6

Moffat Ave IP4 .....136 B1
Moles La NR34 ....8 D1
Moll's La NR34 ......25 D5
Monarch Cl CB9 ....132 A6

Monarch Way
- Carlton Colville NR33 .114 A3
- Pinewood IP8 ....142 D8

Monastery Ct IP7 ..149 E7
Monastery Hill IP17 ..43 B1
Monckton Ave NR32 .112 F2
Monckton Cres NR32 .112 F2
Monet Sq NR32 .....113 B5
Monewden Rd IP13 ...70 A3
Moneyhole Cnr CO10 .78 E5
Moneypiece Cl IP3 ..132 D7
Moneypot La IP22 ....19 B1
Monk's La CO7 ......103 E2
Monks Cl IP11 .....153 D6

Monks Eleigh CE VC Prim Sch IP7 ....79 B2

Monks Gate IP8 ....138 A6
Monksgate IP24 .....16 B6
Monkshood Cl NR33 .114 F2
Monmouth Cl IP2 ...139 B1
Montagu Dr IP27 .....5 E4
Montague Rd IP11 ..153 A4
Montana Rd IP5 ....141 A7

Montessori Sch The IP7 ....94 E6

Montfort Cl CB5 .....44 B6
Montfort Cl 11 CB9 .132 D5

Montgomery Ave NR32 ....113 B4

Montgomery Rd IP2 .139 B1
Monton Rise IP2 ....138 D2
Montpelier Dr 1 IP24 .16 A5

Monument Farm La IP10 ....141 C3

Monument Farm Rd IP10 ....141 B4

Moo Play Farm★ NR34 .25 C5
Moon Hall La CB9 ..132 E3

Moor Rd
- Burston & Shimpling IP21 ..21 B6
- Langham CO4 ....103 B2
- Middleton IP17 ......57 F6

Moor's Way IP12 ...146 E5
Moorbridge La IP14 ..66 B8
Moore Rd Ipswich IP4 .134 F3
- Rushbrooke with Rougham IP30 ....49 B2

Moore's Cl 17 IP14 ..53 F2
Mooreland Dr IP31 ..49 C6
Moorfield Rd IP12 ..146 E5
Moorhall Cswy IP23 .117 C1
Moorsfield CO10 ....148 F2

Moreton Hall Prep Sch IP32 ....123 D5

Morgan Ct 3 IP6 ...134 C1
Morgan Dr IP1 .....134 C1
Morgan Meadow IP14 .124 C2

Morland Prim Sch IP3 ....144 A8

Morland Rd 1 IP3 ..144 A8
Morley Ave IP12 ...146 F4
Morley Cl 3 IP28 ....30 B8
Morleys La IP23 .....36 D2
Mormor La IP21 .....21 F4
Mornington Ave 2 IP1 .134 F1
Morris Way IP6 ....125 D4
Mors End 2 CO7 ...103 E5
Morston Hall Rd IP11 .98 B1
Mortimer La IP28 ....29 E3
Mortimer Pl 3 CO10 ..76 A1
Morton Peto Cl NR32 ..2 D3
Morton Rd NR33 ...115 B4
Moss La IP6 ....135 F4
Mother Quy's IP24 ..15 C5

Mottram Cl 14 IP8 ..138 C2
Moulton Ave CB8 ....46 A5

Moulton CE Prim Sch CB8 ....45 F3

Moulton Cl 5 IP30 ...64 F8

Moulton Packhorse Bridge★ CB8 ....45 F3

Moulton Paddocks CB8 ....121 F7

Moulton Rd
- Cheveley CB8 ....121 D4
- Gazeley CB8 ....46 B3
- Kentford CB8 ....46 A5
- Moulton CB8 ....45 F1

Mount Cl 5 IP30 .....64 F8
Mount Dr IP3 ....140 F1

Mount Pleasant
- Framlingham IP13 ...126 B4
- Halesworth IP19 ....118 B5
- Lowestoft NR32 .....113 C3
- 1 Peasenhall IP17 ...56 F8
- Southwold IP18 ....119 C8

Mount Rd
- Bury St Edmunds IP32 .123 D6
- Haverhill CB9 ....132 E5
- Rushbrooke with Rougham IP30 ....49 A3

Mount St IP22 ....20 C3
Mountbatten Cl IP30 .148 D8
Mountbatten Ct IP1 .139 A7

Mountbatten Rd
- Bungay NR35 ....110 B2
- Lowestoft NR32 .....113 B4
- Sudbury CO10 ....148 D8

Mounts The IP17 ....56 F8
Mouse La IP30 ....49 C2
Moverley Way 1 IP15 .130 E5
Mow Hill IP6 ....83 A5
Mowbrays The IP13 .126 D3
Mowlands IP9 ......150 F3
Mowness Hall La IP14 .68 A6
Moyes Rd NR32 .....112 D1
Moyse Ave 4 IP18 ..119 C8

Moyse's Hall Mus★ IP33 ....154 B2

Mulberry Cl
- Beccles NR34 ......111 C5
- 18 Feltwell IP26 .....4 E5
- Mildenhall IP28 ....116 E4

Mulberry Gdns 11 IP6 .82 A5
Mulberry Rd 3 IP3 .144 C7
Mumford Rd IP1 ...138 E8
Munday's La IP12 ..131 B3

Mundford Prim Sch IP26 ....6 A8

Mundford Rd
- Brandon IP27 ....5 F2
- Thetford IP24 ....16 B7
- Weeting-with-Broomhill IP27 ....6 A4

Mundy's Rd IP20 ....23 A5

Munnings Cl
- Haverhill CB9 ......132 B7
- 3 Lowestoft NR33 ..114 C3
- Newmarket CB8 .....121 A5

Munnings Way CO11 .104 D3
Munson's La IP26 ....4 E6
Munson's Pl IP26 ....4 E6
Murfitt's La CB7 .....29 A2
Muriel Cl 4 IP7 ....149 E6
Murillo Dr 1 NR32 ..113 C6
Murray Rd IP3 .....140 A3

Murrayfield Prim Sch IP3 ....140 A3

Murrills Rd IP3 ....140 E1
Murton Cl 10 CB5 ...44 B4

Museum of E Anglian Life★ IP14 ....124 D5

Museum St IP1 .....155 B3
Musgrave Rd IP22 ..106 F1
Mustards Gapp CB9 .133 A5
Mustow St IP33 ....154 C2
Mutford Cl NR32 ...112 F1
Mutford Gn IP27 ...109 C2
Mutford Wood NR33 .10 D4

Mutfordwood La NR33 ....114 A2

Mutton La IP13 .....70 A8
Mylford Cl IP32 ....123 D4
Mylodon Rd NR32 ..113 C4

Myrtle Cl
- Bury St Edmunds IP33 .154 A3
- 26 Eriswell IP27 ....13 F2
- Lowestoft NR33 ....113 B2

Myrtle Rd IP3 ......139 E4

N

Nacton CE VC Prim Sch

Nacton Cl 5 IP12 ...85 B3
Nacton Cres IP3 ...140 B2
Nacton La 2 IP31 ...49 A6

Nacton Rd
- Felixstowe IP11 ...152 E1
- Ipswich IP10 ....144 D7
- Levington IP10 ....145 E3

Nan Hazle's La IP22 .36 B4
Nansen Rd IP3 ....140 B2
Napier Pl IP24 .....16 B5
Naples Cl 5 NR31 ...3 C6
Narrow Way IP19 ..42 C6
Nash Cl CO11 .....104 D3
Nash Gdns 2 IP3 ..144 B8
Nat Flatman St CB8 .121 B3

National Horseracing Mus★ CB8 ....121 A3

Mil – New 175

National Stud★ CB8 ..59 B8
Nato Pl IP27 ....109 F1
Naughton Gdns 8 IP14 .124 E3
Naughton Rd IP7 ....80 C1
Naunton Rd IP7 ....146 E5
Navarre St IP1 .....155 B3

Naverne Meadow IP12 ....147 A5

Nayland Prim Sch CO6 ....102 D5

Nayland Rd
- Bures St Mary CO8 .101 D4
- 1 Felixstowe IP11 ..152 C3
- Great Horkesley CO6 .102 D2
- Haverhill CB9 ....132 C4
- Little Horkesley CO6 .102 C3

Naylor Ct IP14 .....124 B7
Neale Cl IP16 ......129 B6
Neale St IP1 ....155 B3
Neath Dr IP2 ......139 A1
Neaves La IP21 .....39 B4
Nedging Rd IP7 .....79 B3
Needham La IP7 .....79 F4

Needham Lake Nature Reserve & Visitor Ctr★ IP6 ....125 E4

Needham Mkt Mid Sch IP6 ....125 E4

Needham Mkt Sta IP6 .125 E4

Needham Rd
- Coddenham IP6 ......67 F1
- Needham IP20 ....22 C5
- Stowmarket IP14 ...124 E4

Needham Rd W IP14 .124 F4
Needle Cnr IP9 ....106 B5
Nelson Cnr IP7 .....83 A8
Nelson Cres 2 IP24 ..16 B5

Nelson Rd
- Bury St Edmunds IP33 .154 A2
- Ipswich IP3 ....140 A4
- 1 Lowestoft NR33 ..115 A3
- Sudbury CO10 ......148 E7

Nelson Way
- Beccles NR34 ......111 A4
- Woodbridge IP12 ..146 F4

Nelson Wharf NR33 .114 F7
Nene Dr IP3 ....144 D7
Neptune Quay IP4 .155 C2
Neptune Sq IP3 ....155 C2
Neptune St NR32 ..115 C8
Ness Rd Arwarton IP9 .106 D5
- Burwell CB5 ....44 B4

Nether Hall Mus & Gall★ CO10 ....76 E2

Nether Hill CO9 .....90 E2
Nether Rd 2 CO10 ..76 E1

Nethergate St
- Bungay NR35 ....110 A5
- Clare CO10 ....90 A2
- Hopton IP22 ....18 B2

Netherhall Cl IP2 ...52 A1
Netley Cl IP2 ......142 F8
Netley Rd IP33 ....122 D3
Nettlestead Rd IP8 ..81 D4
Neve Gdns IP28 .....30 A6

New Cangle Com Prim Sch CB9 ....132 B2

New Cardinal St IP1 .155 A2
New Cheveley Rd CB8 .121 C3
New Comm Rd IP22 ..35 B8
New Cut 5 Bures CO8 .101 C4
- 8 Glemsford CO10 ..77 A2
- Hadleigh IP7 ....149 E6
- Halesworth IP19 ...118 B4
- Newmarket CB8 .....121 A4
- Saxmundham IP17 ..128 D3

New Cut E IP3 .....155 C1
New Cut W IP2 ....155 C1

New Dro
- Beck Row, Holywell Row & Kenny Hill IP28 ..12 E1
- Soham CB7 ....28 A4

New England Way 2 IP24 ....16 A5

New Gn Ave 15 IP31 ..49 E4

New Hampshire Way 5 IP24 ....16 A5

New House La CO10 ..76 B3
New La IP9 ....105 F6
New Mkt NR34 ......111 B5
New Path 4 CB7 .....29 A1
New Quay Ct IP12 .147 B5
New Quay La IP12 .147 B6
New Quay Terr IP12 .147 B6
New Queens Rd CO10 .148 C7

New Rd Ampton IP31 ..33 A1
- Aspall IP14 ....53 E4
- Badingham IP13 .....56 B8
- Barnby NR34 ....10 C4
- Barrow IP29 ....47 B3
- Beccles NR34 ......111 B7
- Brettenham IP24 ....17 B6
- 5 Burwell CB5 ......44 A6
- Chevington IP29 ....62 C7
- Dickleburgh & Rushall IP21 ....21 A4
- Elmswell IP30 ....50 E2
- Exning CB8 ....120 B8
- Felixstowe IP11 ...152 C7
- Framlingham IP13 ..126 C5
- Fritton & St Olaves NR31 ..2 D1
- Gissing IP22 ....20 F8
- Great Glemham IP17 .71 E8
- Helmingham IP14 ...69 A5
- 19 Ixworth IP31 .....34 B1

New Rd continued
Little Livermere IP31 ......**33** A2
Long Melford CO10 ....**91** D8
Manningtree CO11 ......**104** E2
Marlesford IP13 ....**71** C6
Melton IP12 ....**84** D6
Mettingham NR35 ......**110** F2
Nedging-with-Naughton
IP7 ....**80** C3
Rumburgh IP19 ....**24** C4
Rushbrooke with Rougham
IP30 ....**49** D1
St Cross, South Elmham
IP20 ....**23** D5
Sibton IP17 ....**41** D1
Thelnetham IP22 ......**35** B7
Thrandeston IP21 .....**37** C8
Timworth IP31 ....**48** E8
Tivetshall St Mary NR15 ..**21** B8
Tostock IP30 ....**50** B2
Troston IP31 ....**33** D4
Worlingworth IP13 .....**54** F8
New River Gn CB8 .....**120** B8
New St Chippenham CB7 ..**29** E1
Framlingham IP13 ....**126** A4
Fressingfield IP21 ......**39** D8
Glemsford CO10 ....**77** A3
4 Mildenhall IP28 .....**116** C4
Sudbury CO10 ....**148** C6
9 Woodbridge IP12 ....**147** A5
New St Cl IP21 ....**39** A4
New Way IP7 ....**138** F6
New Wolsey Theatre★
IP1 ....**155** A3
Newall Rd 2 IP24 ......**16** C2
Newark Cl IP2 ....**138** F1
Newark Rd
3 Lakenheath IP27 ....**13** F2
Lowestoft NR33 ......**115** B6
Newberry Rd 7 IP7 .....**79** F4
Newburn Rd IP10 ......**98** C4
Newbourne Gdns
IP11 ....**152** D3
Newbourne Rd
Brightwell IP10 ....**98** A6
Martlesham IP12 ......**84** B1
Waldringfield IP12 .....**98** C7
Newbourne Springs Nature
Reserve★ IP12 ......**98** D6
Newbury Rd IP4 ......**140** C6
Newby Cl IP4 ....**118** A3
Newby Dr IP4 ....**140** F5
Newcastle Cl 6 IP27 ...**13** F2
Newcombe Dr 16 IP26 ...**4** E5
Newcombe Rd NR32 ....**113** C1
Newdelight Rd IP22 ....**35** F2
Newell Rise IP6 ......**134** C8
Newfen Gravel Dro
IP27 ....**109** A8
Newgate Beccles NR34 ...**111** B5
Kirby Row NR35 ....**8** E7
Newgate La NR35 ......**8** E7
Newhaven Way IP7 ....**149** E7
Newland Ave NR34 .....**111** E4
Newlands 2 Elmsett IP7 ..**80** F1
Otley IP6 ....**69** D2
Newlands Cl
46 Harleston IP20 ......**22** D6
Lowestoft NR33 ......**114** F3
Newlands La CO6 ......**102** D5
Newman's Rd CO10 ....**148** C6
Newmarket Coll CB8 ...**120** F4
Newmarket Com Hospl
CB8 ....**120** F5
Newmarket Lawn Tennis
Club CB8 ....**120** E3
Newmarket Leisure Ctr
CB8 ....**120** F4
Newmarket Racecourse
CB8 ....**120** B1
Newmarket Rd
1 Ashley CB8 ....**60** F8
Barton Mills IP28 .....**116** D1
Burwell CB5 ....**44** B5
Bury St Edmunds IP33 ..**122** D6
Cowlinge CB8 ....**61** B2
Fordham CB7 ....**44** E8
Moulton CB8 ....**45** F3
Newmarket CB8 ......**121** B8
Red Lodge IP28 ......**30** C2
Risby IP28 ....**47** C5
Snailwell CB8 ....**45** A5
Newmarket Sports Ctr
CB8 ....**121** A4
Newmarket Sta CB8 ...**121** A2
Newmarket Swimming Pool
CB8 ....**120** F3
Newmarket Upper Sch
CB8 ....**120** F4
Newmill La CO11 ......**105** A5
Newnham Ave IP12 ....**146** A4
Newnham Cl IP28 .....**116** D5
Newnham Ct IP2 ......**138** E1
Newnham Dro CB5 .....**44** A6
Newnham La 14 CB5 ....**44** A6
Newport Ave CB7 ......**29** C1
Newport Cl 7 IP27 .....**13** F2
Newquay Cl IP5 ......**140** F6
Newry Ave IP11 ......**152** C4
Newson Ave NR34 .....**10** C3
Newson St IP1 ....**155** A4
Newson's Meadow 1
NR32 ....**113** C2
Newthorpe IP30 ......**49** C1

Newton Croft CO10 ....**148** E5
Newton Pl 4 CB9 ......**132** F6
Newton Rd
17 Harwich CO12 ......**107** A2
Ipswich IP3 ....**140** A4
Stowupland IP14 .....**124** D8
Sudbury CO10 ....**148** D5
Newton St IP4 ....**155** C3
Nicholas Dr IP18 .....**119** C7
Nicholas Everitt Pk
NR33 ....**114** D8
Nicholas Rd IP11 .....**152** C4
Nicholas's St IP22 .....**20** C3
Nicholls Cl 7 IP13 .....**84** F7
Nichols Cl 24 CO11 ....**104** D2
Nicholson Dr NR34 ....**111** C2
Nicholson Sq 2 NR32 ...**113** C2
Nicholsons Ct CO10 ....**92** D3
Nick's La IP23 ....**117** B6
Nidderdale 8 NR33 ....**114** E3
Nightall Rd 5 CB7 .....**28** D4
Nightingale Ave IP18 ...**119** B7
Nightingale Cl
Bury St Edmunds IP33 ..**154** A1
19 Harwich CO12 ......**106** F1
5 Mildenhall IP28 ....**116** D4
5 Stowmarket IP14 ....**67** A5
Nightingale Hill CO4 ...**103** C3
Nightingale La 9 IP26 ...**4** E5
Nightingale Piece
IP12 ....**131** C3
Nightingale Rd
Ipswich IP3 ....**144** A8
Lowestoft NR33 ......**115** B3
Nightingale Sq 5 IP3 ...**144** A8
Nimbus Way CB8 .....**120** E8
Nine Acres IP2 ......**138** D6
Ninfield Cl NR33 ......**11** B1
No Man's Meadow★
IP33 ....**123** C4
Noahs Ark Pl CO10 ....**148** B5
Noahs Dr 5 NR33 .....**11** B1
Noaks Rd IP7 ....**94** F1
Nock Gdns IP5 ......**141** C6
Noel Cl NR31 ....**3** B7
Noel Murless Dr CB8 ...**120** F6
Noel Rd NR32 ......**112** C1
Noel's Wlk NR34 .....**111** B6
Noller's La IP19 ......**24** F4
Nonsuch Meadow 2
CO10 ....**148** C5
Norbury Rd IP4 ......**140** B7
Nordalls The 16 NR33 ...**11** C1
Norfolk & Suffolk Aviation
Mus★ NR35 ....**7** D2
Norfolk Ave CB8 .....**120** E5
Norfolk Cres 1 IP13 ...**126** C3
Norfolk Rd
Bury St Edmunds IP32 ..**123** A8
9 Honington IP31 .....**33** D5
Ipswich IP4 ....**155** C3
Thetford IP24 ....**16** C6
Wangford NR34 ......**26** B2
Norfolk St NR32 ......**113** B1
Norgate La IP21 ......**21** B2
Norman Cl
Felixstowe IP11 ......**153** D6
Woodbridge IP12 .....**147** A2
Norman Cres IP3 .....**140** A2
Norman Rd
6 Bury St Edmunds IP32 .**48** C5
Bury St Edmunds IP32 ..**122** F8
23 Manningtree CO11 ..**104** E2
Norman Way 1 CO10 ...**78** D4
Normandie Way 8 CO8 ..**101** C4
Normandy Cl IP14 ....**124** D3
Normandy Rd NR32 ...**113** B4
Normanhurst Cl NR32 ..**113** A4
Normanston Dr 5 NR32 .**113** B2
Nornea La CB7 ....**28** A8
Norse Ave IP29 ......**64** A3
North Acres IP8 ......**81** A6
North Ave CB9 ......**132** C6
North Cl Bacton IP14 ...**51** F6
Ipswich IP4 ....**135** E1
9 Stanton IP31 ....**34** E4
North Cres CB9 ......**88** D4
North Dr
Newmarket CB8 ......**120** F5
1 Soham CB7 ....**28** D5
North End CB8 ......**120** B8
North End Ave IP16 ...**73** F6
North End Rd CO9 ....**90** C2
North Entrance IP17 ...**128** D3
North Field Cl 3 NR32 ..**112** F5
North Gn IP18 ....**119** D6
North Gn Rd
Cratfield IP19 ....**40** C7
Pulham St Mary IP21 ...**22** A8
North Hill IP12 ......**146** F6
North Hill Gdns IP4 ...**139** E6
North Hill Rd IP4 ....**139** E6
North Lawn IP4 ......**140** D3
North Lopham Rd
NR16 ....**19** A7
North Par Gdns IP18 ...**119** E6
North Parade
Lowestoft NR32 ......**113** D4
Southwold IP18 ......**119** E5
North Pl IP28 ....**116** C4
North Rd
Great Yeldham CO9 ....**90** A1
Lakenheath IP27 .....**109** E4
Southwold IP18 ......**119** D6
North Rise CO10 .....**148** E4
North St Burwell CB5 ...**44** A6
Freckenham IP28 .....**29** E3
Hundon CO10 ....**75** D4

North St continued
11 Manningtree CO11 ...**104** E2
Steeple Bumpstead CB9 ..**88** D4
Sudbury CO10 ....**148** C6
Wicken CB7 ....**28** A1
North St Parade 5
CO10 ....**148** C5
North Terr IP28 ......**116** C5
North Warren IP15 ...**130** C8
North Warren Nature
Reserve★ IP15 ......**73** D6
Northacre 12 NR33 ....**11** B1
Northcroft 1 CO10 ....**148** C5
Northern Rd CO10 ....**148** F7
Northern Rose Cl
IP32 ....**123** F7
Northern Way IP32 ....**48** C5
Northfield Ct IP15 ....**130** E5
Northfield La IP15 ....**130** E5
Northfield Pk CB7 .....**28** C5
Northfield Rd
Onehouse IP14 ....**66** C6
Soham CB7 ....**28** C5
Northfield St Nicholas CP
Prim Sch NR32 .....**113** C3
Northgate
Beccles NR34 ....**111** B6
11 Harleston IP20 .....**22** D5
Lowestoft NR32 ......**113** B2
Northgate Ave IP32 ...**154** B4
Northgate Cty High Sch
IP4 ....**136** A1
Northgate Lodge IP32 ..**154** B3
Northgate Sports Ctr
IP4 ....**136** A2
Northgate St Bsns Pk
IP33 ....**154** C3
Northgate St Bury St Edmunds IP33 ..**154** C3
Ipswich IP4 ....**155** B3
Northgate St Bsns Pk
IP33 ....**154** C3
Northumberland Ave
IP32 ....**122** E8
Northwood Cl NR34 ...**114** F6
Norton CE Prim Sch
IP31 ....**50** B5
Norton Rd
Haverhill CB9 ....**132** C4
Hunston IP31 ....**50** E5
11 Thurstow IP31 .....**49** D4
Tostock IP30 ....**50** B2
Norway Cres 2 CO12 ...**106** F2
Norwich La
Bardwell IP31 ....**34** C8
Coney Weston IP31 ....**17** E2
Norwich Rd Barham IP6 ..**82** A6
Claydon IP6 ....**134** C8
Denton IP21 ....**7** B3
5 Dicklingburgh & Rushall
IP21 ....**20** F1
Ditchingham NR35 ....**110** A8
Earsham NR35 ....**7** E5
Gillingham NR34 .....**111** A8
Halesworth IP19 .....**118** C5
Ipswich IP1 ....**155** A3
5 Lakenheath IP27 ....**13** F2
Lakenheath IP27 .....**109** F1
Lowestoft NR32 ......**113** C1
Newmarket CB8 ......**121** D6
Pulham St Mary IP21 ...**21** F8
Scole IP21 ....**21** B5
Stockton NR34 ....**9** A8
Thetford IP24 ....**16** C6
Norwich Rd Sch IP24 ..**16** C6
Norwood Rd IP27 .....**14** E8
Notcutts CO7 ....**151** E3
Notley Dr CB9 ......**132** A7
Notley Ent Pk CO7 ....**95** A2
Notley Rd NR33 .....**115** A7
Nottidge Rd IP4 ......**139** E6
Nova Scotia La IP7 ....**79** B4
Nowton Ctry Pk★ IP33 ..**63** E8
Nowton Pk IP29 .....**123** D1
Nowton Rd
Bury St Edmunds IP33 ..**123** C1
Nowton IP29 ....**63** E8
Noyes Ave IP13 .....**40** B3
Nuffield Hospl (Private)
IP33 ....**154** C1
Nunn Cl 1 IP12 ......**84** A1
Nunn Sq IP32 ....**122** D8
Nunn's Hill IP19 .....**24** C3
Nunn's La IP19 ......**23** E1
Nunnery Gn 2 CB8 ....**61** E2
Nuns' Bridges Rd IP24 ..**16** B5
Nuns Wlk CO10 .....**89** F1
Nursery Cl Isleham CB7 ..**29** B4
Mildenhall IP28 ......**116** D4
Nursery La IP26 ......**5** A2
Nursery Rd CO10 ....**148** F2
Nursery Wlk IP11 ....**152** F4
Nursey Cl NR35 ......**8** D7
Nuttery Vale IP23 ....**38** B6

O

Oak Ave NR34 ....**111** F5
Oak Cl
Bury St Edmunds IP28 ..**48** C6
Felixstowe IP11 ......**152** E4
4 Great Finborough IP14 .**66** B4
Oak Cres IP23 ......**117** C3
Oak Dr Diss IP22 .....**20** E2
6 Mildenhall IP28 ....**30** B8
Oak Eggar Chase IP8 ..**142** D8
Oak Farm La IP14 ....**52** D6
Oak Gn IP19 ....**118** B2

Oak Gr
Fornham St Martin IP31 ..**48** D5
Sproughton IP8 ......**138** A6
Oak Hill Cl NR34 ......**26** E5
Oak Hill La IP2 ......**139** B3
Oak La Beccles NR34 ...**111** D2
Cheveley CB8 ....**60** E6
Elmswell IP30 ....**50** F3
Ipswich IP1 ....**155** A4
Rushbrooke with Rougham
IP30 ....**64** D8
Woolpit IP30 ....**65** E8
Oak Meadow Cl IP19 ...**42** C6
Oak Rd 3 Sudbury CO10 ..**92** B3
Sudbury CO10 ......**148** F4
Oak St IP26 ....**4** E5
Oak Tree Way 8 IP20 ...**22** D5
Oak Way IP19 ....**118** A1
Oakdene IP10 ....**98** D2
Oakes Cl IP32 ......**122** E7
Oakes Rd IP32 ......**122** E7
Oakey Field Rd 6 IP31 ..**49** E4
Oakey Ley IP30 ......**64** D6
Oakfield Rd Bacton IP14 .**52** A6
Copdock & Washbrook
IP8 ....**142** A6
Oakfield Wood Nature
Reserve★ CO11 .....**105** E3
Oakland Rd 15 CO12 ...**107** B2
Oaklands CO6 ......**102** B8
Oaklands Dr IP27 .....**14** D8
Oakley Church La IP21 ..**37** F8
Oakley Rd 11 CO12 ...**106** E1
Oakley Sq IP15 ......**130** E4
Oaks Bsns Pk CB8 ....**120** E7
Oaks Com Prim Sch
Chantry IP2 ....**138** E4
Ipswich IP2 ....**138** E3
Oaks Dr IP2 ....**138** E4
Oaks La NR34 ....**2** B1
Oaks The
7 Horringer IP29 .....**63** A8
Martlesham Heath IP5 ..**141** F6
Soham CB7 ....**28** D3
Wattisfield IP22 ......**35** C5
Woolpit IP30 ....**65** F8
Oaksmere Gdns 8 IP2 ..**139** A2
Oakwood Pk IP17 ....**57** D7
Oakwood Rd NR34 ...**114** F6
Oasis Camelid Ctr★
IP19 ....**40** C3
Oast Ct IP33 ....**154** C1
Oatfields IP21 ......**39** D8
Oatlands Cl 4 NR33 ...**114** E4
Oban St IP1 ....**155** A4
Occold Prim Sch IP23 ..**37** F1
Occold Rd IP23 .....**38** B2
O'feld Terr IP11 .....**153** C6
Off Sea View Rd IP18 ..**119** C7
Offton Rd Elmsett IP7 ..**81** A2
Great Bricett IP7 .....**80** F5
Ohio Cl 4 NR33 .....**114** E3
Old Barn Rd CO8 .....**101** C3
Old Barningham Rd 1
IP31 ....**34** E4
Old Barrack Rd IP12 ..**146** E4
Old Brandon Rd IP26 ...**4** F5
Old Brewery Yd IP19 ..**118** A3
Old Buckenham Hall Sch
IP7 ....**79** B7
Old Bungay Rd NR35 ...**8** D8
Old Bury Rd
Alpheton CO10 ....**78** A6
Lackford IP28 ....**31** F1
Palgrave IP22 ....**37** A8
Stanton IP31 ....**34** E4
Stuston IP21 ....**20** D1
Wortham IP22 ....**36** F8
Old Cattle Mkt IP1 ...**155** B2
Old Church La
Bulmer CO10 ....**91** C1
Westley IP33 ....**122** A6
Old Church Rd 1 NR31 ..**3** B6
Old Clements La 5
CB9 ....**132** D5
Old Coll Cl NR34 .....**111** B6
Old Convent Orch
IP33 ....**154** B1
Old Dairy Bsns Pk IP31 ..**49** B5
Old Farm Rd
Beccles NR34 ....**111** C5
4 Lowestoft NR33 ....**114** D5
Old Forge Cl IP22 ....**36** D8
Old Forge Ct IP21 ....**22** A2
Old Foundry Pl IP16 ...**129** C6
Old Foundry Rd IP4 ...**155** C3
Old Gram La NR35 ....**110** B3
Old Hall Cl 3 IP29 ....**62** D6
Old Hall La Bentley IP9 ..**95** F2
Bury St Edmunds IP28 ..**48** D5
Cockfield IP30 ....**64** B3
Westleton IP17 ......**58** B8
Old Hall Meadow IP30 ..**65** D6
Old Hall Rd IP13 .....**56** C8
Old Harleston Rd NR35 ..**7** E3
Old Haverhill Rd CB9 ..**74** F2
Old High Rd
Roydon IP22 ....**20** B3
Yoxford IP17 ....**57** D7
Old Homes Rd 7 IP16 ...**73** F6
Old House La CO4 ....**103** A1
Old House Rd CO6 ....**102** D1
Old Ipswich Rd IP6 ...**134** C7
Old Kirton Rd IP11 ...**107** D8
Old La
Bradfield Combust with
Stanningfield IP29 ....**63** F3

Old La continued
Corton NR32 ....**113** B8
Thelnetham IP22 .....**35** C6
Old London Rd IP9 ...**150** D1
Old Maids' La IP13 ....**70** A7
Old Maltings App
IP12 ....**147** B6
Old Maltings Ct IP12 ..**147** B5
Old Methwold Rd IP26 ..**4** E6
Old Mill Dr IP21 .....**21** F8
Old Mill La
Barton Mills IP28 .....**116** F2
Beccles NR34 ....**111** B4
Old Mill Rd CO4 .....**103** B3
Old Mill Terr 2 NR34 ..**111** B6
Old Mkt 6 NR34 .....**111** B6
Old Mkt Pl
21 Harleston IP20 .....**22** D6
19 Harleston IP20 ....**148** C5
Old Mkt Plain 8 NR32 ..**113** E2
Old Mkt St IP14 .....**52** E4
Old Nelson St 4 NR32 ..**113** C1
Old Newton CE Prim Sch
IP14 ....**52** A1
Old Norwich Rd
Whitton IP1 ....**134** D5
Yaxley IP23 ....**37** C5
Old Orch IP7 ....**149** F1
Old Orch Cl IP19 ....**118** A2
Old Paper Mill La 8
IP6 ....**134** C8
Old Post Office La
Blaxhall IP12 ....**72** A4
Kirby Row NR35 ......**8** E7
Sutton IP12 ....**99** A8
Old Post Office Rd
IP29 ....**62** C6
Old Priory Gdns NR34 ..**2** D6
Old Rd The CO6 .....**102** B8
Old Rectory Cl
2 Claydon IP6 ....**82** B5
6 Roydon IP22 ......**20** A3
Old Rectory Gdns 3
IP23 ....**37** F1
Old Rectory La IP29 ...**77** E6
Old Rectory Rd IP13 ...**56** A6
Old Rectory Sch The
IP7 ....**65** C1
Old Rectory Wlk IP9 ..**150** D3
Old Rly Rd Alburgh IP20 ..**7** B1
Bungay NR35 ....**110** A4
Old Rope Wlk CB9 ...**132** C2
Old Sch Cl
Brampton with Stoven
IP19 ....**25** E5
5 Burwell CB5 ....**44** B6
Leiston IP16 ....**129** C6
4 Soham CB7 ....**28** D5
Old Sch Dr IP28 .....**26** E1
Old Sch Hall The★
IP33 ....**154** B3
Old Sch La CB8 ......**59** F1
Old Sch Rd IP29 .....**63** A5
Old Sch The NR34 ....**10** E1
Old Schools Ct IP30 ...**50** E2
Old St IP1 ....**51** C1
Old St The IP9 ......**150** F3
Old Sta Rd
Ellingham NR35 ......**8** D6
Halesworth IP19 .....**118** B5
Mendlesham IP14 ....**52** E3
Newmarket CB8 ......**121** B4
Old Stores Cl IP13 ....**54** E7
Old Stowmarket Rd
IP30 ....**50** D1
Old Town La IP33 ....**123** C1
Old Vicarage Dr IP31 ..**50** F7
Old Vicarage Rd 13
CO12 ....**107** B2
Oldfield Rd IP8 ......**138** B1
Oldhall Rd IP9 ......**106** F6
Olding Rd IP33 ......**122** D6
Olive Cl 2 IP27 ......**13** F2
Olive Ct NR32 ......**113** B4
Oliver Cl NR33 ......**114** D2
Oliver Ct IP27 ......**5** E4
Oliver Rd IP33 ......**122** C6
Olivers Cl CO10 .....**91** E8
Olland Ct 5 NR35 ....**110** B3
Olle Cl IP33 ....**123** C1
Olympus Cl IP1 .....**134** C2
One Eyed La IP21 ....**22** D3
Onehouse La IP1 ....**135** C1
Onehouse Rd IP14 ...**124** B6
Onner's La IP16 .....**58** C4
Ontario Rd NR33 ....**115** C6
Opal Ave 1 Ipswich IP1 ..**134** D1
Ipswich IP1 ....**138** D8
Orchard Ave NR33 ...**114** E6
Orchard Cl Beyton IP30 ..**49** F1
2 Blundeston NR32 ...**3** A4
Elmswell IP30 ....**50** F3
Great Livermere IP31 ...**33** C2
6 Haverhill CB9 .....**132** D5
Lidgate CB8 ....**61** C4
2 Ramsey & Parkeston
CO12 ....**106** D1
Ridgewell CO9 ....**89** D3
Risby IP28 ....**47** D5
Rushbrooke with Rougham
IP30 ....**64** D8
Woodbridge IP12 ....**147** A5
Orchard Croft 4 NR33 ..**114** E4
Orchard Dr IP14 .....**65** F4
Orchard End 16 IP13 ...**83** E5
Orchard Farm Barns 2
IP29 ....**47** A2

Orchard Farm Bsns Pk
CB7 ....28 C7
Orchard Gate
Ipswich IP2 ....138 C5
1 Needham Market IP6 .125 D5
Orchard Gdn NR33 .....114 E7
Orchard Gr
Claydon IP6 ....134 C7
Ipswich IP5 ....141 A7
Orchard La
3 Blundeston NR32 .....3 A4
Thurston IP31 ....49 E5
Orchard Pl
Sudbury CO10 ....148 B4
Wickham Market IP13 ...127 B6
Orchard Rd
6 Bramford IP8 ....134 A2
Leiston IP16 ....129 C5
Orchard Rise
Badingham IP13 ....56 A7
Beccles NR34 ....111 F4
Orchard Row CB7 ....28 E2
Orchard St
Bury St Edmunds IP33 ..154 B3
Ipswich IP4 ....155 C3
Orchard Terr **4** NR33 ..115 C7
Orchard The
5 Ashley CB8 ....60 F8
Felsham IP30 ....65 A4
Redisham NR34 ....25 B7
Orchard Valley IP19 ...118 D4
Orchard Way
Badwell Ash IP31 ....50 F7
12 Barrow IP29 ....47 A2
4 Burwell CB5 ....44 A6
4 Glemsford CO10 ....77 A2
Scole IP21 ....21 A2
Orchard Way The **2**
IP29 ....63 A8
Orchards The **1** IP13 ..40 B3
Orchid Cl
Halesworth IP19 ......118 C4
Ipswich IP2 ....138 E4
Orchid Way IP6 ....125 D3
Orchids Cl NR35 ......110 D3
Oregon Rd IP5 ....141 A6
Orford Castle Mus & Visitor
Ctr★ IP12 ....131 B2
Orford CE VA Prim Sch
IP12 ....131 B3
Orford Dr IP12 ....112 F3
Orford Ness★ IP12 ....131 C1
Orford Ness National Nature
Reserve★ IP12 ....87 C1
Orford Rd
Bromeswell IP12 ......147 F7
Butley IP12 ....86 A6
Felixstowe IP11 ......152 E1
Haverhill CB9 ....132 D4
Tunstall IP12 ....71 F2
Orford St IP1 ....155 A4
Oriel Cl CO10 ....148 F4
Original Factory Shop The
IP32 ....123 D7
Orkney Cl CB9 ....133 B5
Orkney Rd **4** IP4 ....136 A1
Orttewell Rd IP32 ....123 E6
Orvis La CO7 ....151 E3
Orwell Ave IP17 ......128 C4
Orwell Ct IP12 ....146 E4
Orwell Dr **1** NR32 ...112 F4
Orwell Ctry Pk★ IP3 ..139 F3
Orwell High Sch IP11 .152 E5
Orwell Pk Sch IP10 ...145 B3
Orwell Pl IP4 ....155 C2
Orwell Rd
Felixstowe IP11 ......152 F3
10 Harwich CO12 ....107 B2
Ipswich IP3 ....140 A4
Stowmarket IP14 ......124 D4
Orwell Ret Pk IP2 ....139 A5
Orwell Rise **10** IP9 ..106 C8
Orwell View Rd IP9 ...106 F6
Osborne Rd IP3 ....140 A4
Osborne St **4** NR32 ..113 E3
Osier Cl IP12 ....147 B6
Osier Rd IP33 ....154 B3
Osiers The IP14 ......124 D7
Osmund Wlk IP33 ......122 C4
Osprey Gn NR32 ....114 C6
Osprey Rd CB9 ....133 A5
Oswyn Cl IP32 ....123 D4
Otley Coll IP6 ....69 C1
Rendlesham IP12 ....85 E8
Otley Ct **6** IP11 ....152 D5
Otley Gdns IP9 ....69 C1
Otley Hall★ IP6 ....69 C3
Otley Prim Sch IP6 ....69 C2
Otley Rd IP12 ....85 C2
Otten Rd CO10 ....90 D5
Otter Trust The★ NR35 ..7 E3
Oulton Broad N Sta
NR32 ....112 F1
Oulton Broad Prim Sch
NR32 ....112 C2
Oulton Broad S Sta
NR33 ....113 D7
Oulton Broad Wr Sports Ctr
NR33 ....114 D7
Oulton Cl **6** CO12 ...106 F2
Oulton Ct NR32 ....112 E4
Oulton Ind Est NR32 ..112 F4
Oulton Rd Flixton NR32 .112 F7
Ipswich IP3 ....139 F2
Lowestoft NR32 ....112 E5
Oulton Rd N NR32 .....112 F5
Oulton St NR32 ....112 F4

Ound Farm Nature Reserve★
IP17 ....56 C1
Ousden Rd IP29 ....62 A6
Out Northgate IP33 ...154 B4
Out Risbygate IP33 ...122 E6
Out Westgate IP33 ....154 B1
Outney Meadow Cvn Pk
NR35 ....110 A5
Outney Rd NR35 ......110 A4
Overbury Hall Rd IP7 .149 D1
Ovington Pl **5** CB9 ..132 F6
Owell The IP31 ....49 E6
Oxer Cl IP30 ....50 F2
Oxford Cl
Mildenhall IP28 ......116 A4
Sudbury CO10 ....148 E4
Oxford Dr Hadleigh IP7 .149 D8
Woodbridge IP12 .....146 D3
Oxford Rd **4** Feltwell IP26 ..4 C1
Ipswich IP4 ....139 E5
Lowestoft NR32 ......113 D3
25 Manningtree CO11 ..104 E2
Oxford St CB8 ....120 B8

P

Packard Ave IP3 ......140 B2
Packard Pl IP8 ....134 B2
Packards La
Fordham CO6 ....102 A1
Wormingford CO6 .....101 F1
Packway La IP31 ....50 A5
Packway The IP20 ......23 A7
Paddock Cl IP33 ......122 C5
Paddock Farm IP31 .....34 D8
Paddock Hill **2** NR33 .114 E7
Paddock Rd **13** IP20 ..22 D6
Paddock St CB7 ....28 D4
Paddock The **16** IP31 ..34 B1
Paddock Way
Chedburgh IP29 ....62 C4
Troston IP31 ....33 D3
Paddock Wood Cl **8**
NR33 ....114 C4
Paddocks Cty Prim Sch
CB8 ....120 E4
Paddocks Dr CB8 .....121 A2
Paddocks Gn NR34 ....111 F4
Paddocks The
Ashen CO10 ....89 E5
Badwell Ash IP31 ......50 F7
6 Bures CO8 ....101 C4
12 Burwell CB5 ....44 A5
Halesworth IP19 .....118 C4
3 Martlesham Heath IP5 .98 A8
Tuddenham St Martin
IP6 ....136 B5
Worlington IP28 ....30 A4
Padstow Rd IP5 ......141 A6
Page Gdns IP5 ....141 E8
Page's La IP14 ....124 C6
Pages Hill Rd IP29 ....63 B6
Paget Cl IP6 ....125 C5
Paget Ct CB8 ....121 A6
Paget Rd IP1 ....155 A4
Pains Cl **2** NR34 .....9 F4
Pains Hill IP14 ....67 F6
Pakefield Mid Sch
NR33 ....115 A3
Pakefield Prim Sch
NR33 ....115 A3
Pakefield Rd NR33 ...115 C5
Pakefield St NR33 ...115 B4
Pakenham Pl CB9 ....132 F5
Pakenham Rd IP31 ....49 D6
Pakenham Watermill★
IP31 ....49 F8
Pakenham Windmill★
IP31 ....49 F8
Palace La IP6 ....45 B8
Palace St **4** CB8 ....121 A3
Palfrey Height CO11 ..104 E4
Palgrave VC Prim Sch
IP22 ....20 C1
Palmcroft Cl **10** IP1 .135 A3
Palmcroft Rd IP1 ....135 A3
Palmer Cl NR32 ......113 B6
Palmer Dr IP27 ......109 C7
Palmer St IP31 ....35 C1
Palmer's La IP18 .....119 A2
Palmerston Rd IP4 ...139 E6
Palmerswent Cl CO10 ..91 F8
Pamment's La **5** IP28 .29 F6
Pannels Cl **5** CO10 ...77 A2
Pantile La **12** CB5 ....44 A6
Papeley Meadow IP29 ..47 B2
Paper Mill La IP8 ....134 B4
Parade Dr **6** CO12 ..106 E1
Parade Rd IP4 ....139 F7
Parade Rd N **13** NR33 .115 D8
Parade Rd S NR33 ...115 D7
Parade The CB9 .....133 F8
Paradise Pl IP16 ....129 C5
Pardoe Pl IP4 ....140 E5
Parham Airfield Mus★
IP13 ....71 C7
Parish Bush Dro CB7 ..12 A1
Park Ave
Felixstowe IP11 ......153 B5
3 Fornham St Martin IP28 .34 D8
Newmarket CB8 ......121 B3
Saxmundham IP17 ....128 C3
Park Cl
2 Bentwaters Airfield
IP12 ....85 D8
1 Lowestoft NR33 ....114 D4

Park Cl continued
5 Martlesham Heath IP5 ..98 A8
4 Moulton CB8 ....45 F3
Sudbury CO10 ....148 E6
Park Cotts CB8 ......121 B2
Park Dr NR34 ....111 E4
Park End IP17 ....128 C2
Park Farm Dr
Barton Mills IP28 .....30 C2
Stanton IP31 ....34 E3
Park Farm La
Euston IP24 ....33 E8
Hoxne IP21 ....38 E6
Park Hill IP16 ....129 C6
Park La Aldeburgh IP15 .130 E4
Bulmer CO10 ....91 C2
Charsfield IP13 ....70 C3
Eye IP23 ....117 D1
Glemsford CO10 ....77 B2
Hawstead IP29 ....63 D7
Kirton IP10 ....98 E3
Langham CO4 ....103 C2
Newmarket CB8 ......121 B3
Southwold IP18 ......119 D4
Thornham Parva IP23 ..37 A3
Park Meadows NR32 ..112 F6
Park N IP1 ....139 D8
Park Pl IP17 ....57 D7
Park Rd
Aldeburgh IP15 ......130 D4
Benhall IP17 ....72 A7
Boot Street IP13 ....137 D8
Burwell IP28 ....44 A5
Bury St Edmunds IP33 .122 D4
Cheveley IP31 ....60 D7
Combs IP14 ....124 B2
Diss IP22 ....20 C2
Drinkstone IP30 ....50 B1
East Bergholt CO7 ...104 D5
Great Horkesley CO6 .102 D4
Grundisburgh IP13 ....83 E5
Halesworth IP19 .....118 A5
3 Harwich CO12 ....107 B2
Haverhill CB9 ....132 B7
Ipswich IP1 ....139 C8
Lavenham CO10 ....78 D4
Letheringham IP13 ....70 D4
Lowestoft NR32 ......113 D3
Needham Market IP6 ..125 D4
St Cross, South Elmham
IP20 ....23 C7
Southolt IP23 ....23 A7
Stoke-by-Nayland CO6 .102 F6
Sudbury CO10 ....148 E6
Wetherden IP14 ....51 A1
Park St CO6 ....102 E7
Park The
3 Great Barton IP31 ...49 A5
Tannington CO11 .....104 E2
Park View
Botesdale IP22 ....36 B7
Weeting IP27 ....5 C3
Wetherden IP14 ....51 A1
Park View Rd IP1 ....135 B1
Park Wlk IP19 ....118 E5
Parker Ave IP11 .....152 B4
Parker's Dro **3** IP28 ..29 F6
Parker's Rd IP14 ......52 A5
Parker's Way CO6 ...102 D5
Parkers Pl **1** IP5 ....98 A8
Parkers Wlk CB8 ....120 E8
Parkeston Rd
Felixstowe IP11 ......152 D4
Harwich CO12 ....107 A2
Parkhill NR32 ....112 F5
Parkington Wlk IP32 .122 D7
Parklands **5** IP13 ....84 F7
Parklands Cl **9** CO10 ..77 B3
Parklands Gn **2** IP28 .48 C6
Parklands The NR33 ..114 D4
Parklands Way **41** IP20 .22 D6
Parkside
Chippenham CB7 ......45 C8
Haverhill CB9 ....132 D4
Mildenhall IP28 ....30 C8
3 Stanton IP31 ....34 E4
Parkside Ave IP4 ....155 C4
Parkside Dr NR32 ....113 A2
Parkway
Bury St Edmunds IP33 .154 A2
Wickham Market IP13 .127 C2
Parkway Mid Sch CB9 .132 B6
Parkwood Dr CO10 ..148 C8
Parliament Rd IP4 ...140 B5
Parmenter Dr **13** CO10 .92 B3
Parnell Cl IP1 ....134 F3
Parnell La IP30 ....50 D3
Parnell Rd IP1 ......134 F3
Parnham Pl **2** IP4 ...140 F5
Parr Rd CB9 ....132 B4
Parrington Way **26**
CO11 ....104 D2
Parry Cl IP19 ....118 B5
Parsonage Cl
5 Burwell CB5 ....44 A5
Felixstowe IP11 .....152 D4
Parsonage Farm La
CB8 ....60 C5
Parsonage Gdns **16** CB9 132 C5
Parsonage Gr **7** C08 ..101 C4
Parsonage La
Burwell CB5 ....44 A5
Chelsworth IP7 ....79 E3
Parson's Field CO7 ..104 A3
Parsons Cl IP27 ....5 E3
Parsons Ct IP33 .....122 A6
Parsons Field **4** IP15 .130 E5
Parsons Hill IP12 .....99 F7

Parsons Yd **24** CO11 ..104 E2
Partridge Cl
Boxford CO10 ....93 C4
15 Thurstow IP31 ......49 D4
Partridge Rd IP2 ....138 D3
Pashford Cl IP27 ....109 D6
Pashford Pl **6** IP3 ...144 C8
Paske Ave CB9 ......132 D5
Pastures The
Ipswich IP4 ....140 F5
Oulton NR32 ....112 F6
Patricia Cl NR32 ....112 D2
Patrick Stead Hospl
IP19 ....118 C5
Patten La NR15 ....21 B7
Patterdale Gdns **3**
NR32 ....113 A4
Pattern Bush Cl **4**
CO11 ....104 E4
Patteson Rd IP3 .....139 E4
Patticroft **7** CO10 ...77 A3
Paul's Rd IP2 ....138 F5
Pauline St IP2 ......155 B1
Pavilion Cl IP2 .....132 F5
Paxton Chadwick Cl **1**
IP16 ....129 D5
Payne St NR33 ......115 C7
Payne's La IP26 ....4 A1
Peach Maltings IP33 .154 B4
Peacock Cl
Hockwold cum Wilton IP26 ..4 F3
5 Ipswich IP8 ....138 C2
Lowestoft NR33 .....114 C2
Peacock Rise **18** IP31 ..34 B1
Peacock St IP5 .....141 D6
Peacock's Pyghtle
IP12 ....131 C3
Peacocks Cl **1** CO10 ..76 E1
Peacocks Rd CO10 ...76 E2
Peak Dale NR33 .....114 E3
Pear Cl **2** IP23 ......36 D2
Pearce Rd IP3 ......140 A4
Pearce's Cl **2** IP26 ...5 A3
Pearcroft Rd IP1 ....135 B3
Pearl Cl IP6 ....69 C2
Pearl Rd IP1 ....138 D8
Pearmain Wlk **8** CB9 ..36 A4
Pearse Way IP3 .....140 E1
Pearson Rd IP4 .....140 C5
Pearsons Way IP8 ....95 F5
Peart Gr IP5 ....141 D6
Peartree Cl IP17 ....128 C6
Peartree Hill CO8 ...101 D2
Peasecroft Rd **3** IP31 .34 A1
Peasenhall Cl **2** IP12 .85 B3
Peasenhall Prim Sch
IP17 ....56 E8
Peasenhall Rd IP19 ...41 C3
Peasey Gdns IP5 ....141 C6
Peasey La IP5 ......141 C6
Pebble Cl IP3 ......140 E3
Pebble View Wlk **8** NR31 ..3 C6
Peckham St IP33 ....154 B3
Pecockes Cl **10** CO10 ..92 B3
Peddars Cl **1** IP31 ...34 B1
Peddars La NR34 ....111 B4
Peddars Way IP33 ...113 B4
Peel St IP1 ....155 B3
Peel Yd **2** IP5 ......98 A8
Peewit Hill IP11 ....152 D3
Peewit Rd IP2 ......138 E5
Pegasus Mews **1** NR32 112 D1
Pegg's Hill IP20 ......22 F2
Pelham St **21** CO12 ..106 F1
Pelican Cl IP2 ......138 D3
Pemberton Rd **6** IP20 ..22 D5
Pemberton Wlk IP33 .123 A2
Pembroke Ave IP12 ..146 E4
Pembroke Cl
Ipswich IP3 ....139 B3
Mildenhall IP28 ......116 C5
Newmarket CB8 ......121 B2
Pembroke Pl CO10 ..148 B8
Pembroke Rd
Bury St Edmunds IP33 .122 D3
Framlingham IP13 ....126 B4
Pembrooke Way **1**
NR32 ....113 A3
Pendleton Rd IP2 ...138 D1
Penfold Rd IP11 ....153 C4
Penn Cl IP9 ....150 F4
Pennine Way NR32 ..112 E2
Pennings Nature Reserve
The★ IP23 ....117 E2
Penny La **5** Ipswich IP3 .140 F1
Lowestoft NR32 .....112 E2
Penny Meadow **3** IP9 .150 E3
Pennycress Dr **4** IP24 .16 D7
Pennyfields NR35 ...110 B3
Pennygate Dr NR33 .114 E6
Pennyroyal Gdns IP2 .138 F3
Penryn Rd IP5 ......141 A7
Penshurst Rd IP3 ...140 D4
Pentland Wlk **9** NR32 .113 A4
Pentlow Dr CO10 .....76 C1
Pentlow Hawke Cl
CB9 ....133 A5
Pentlow Hill CO10 ....91 A8
Penzance Rd IP5 ....141 A6
Pepper La IP31 ....49 E3
Pepper Pl IP5 ......141 D6
Pepper's Rd CO4 ....102 F1
Peppercorn Way **2** IP2 139 C3
Peppers Cl IP27 ......5 E3
Peppers Wash IP19 ...30 E4
Pepys Ave **1** NR34 ...9 F4
Percy Ruse Cl CO10 .148 F5
Peregrine Way **18** NR33 .11 C1

Orc - Pip **177**

Periwinkle Cl **8** NR33 .114 C5
Perkins Rd IP30 ......49 B2
Perkins Way
Ipswich IP3 ....139 F1
Tostock IP30 ....50 B3
Perry La CO4 ....103 D2
Perrydown La IP30 ...64 C1
Perryfields CO10 ....148 F2
Persimmon Wlk CB8 .120 E7
Pesthouse La IP6 .....82 A6
Petch CI IP33 ....154 B3
Peter Dr **3** IP24 .....16 D7
Peter's Gr **4** IP9 ...150 E3
Peterhouse Cl
Ipswich IP2 ....138 F2
Mildenhall IP28 ......116 D4
Peterhouse Cres IP12 .146 D4
Peterhouse Dr CB8 ..121 A2
Petingo Cl CB8 .....120 D7
Petit Couronne Way
NR34 ....111 D3
Peto Way NR32 .....113 A1
Pets Cnr NR33 ......114 D7
Pettaugh La IP6 ......68 E2
Petticoat La
9 Barrow IP29 ....47 A2
Bury St Edmunds IP33 .154 A1
Pettits La IP21 ....20 F3
Petunia Way IP27 ....14 E8
Pheasant Cl **14** IP31 ..49 D4
Pheasant Rd IP2 ....138 C3
Pheasant Rise IP8 ....95 F4
Pheasant Way IP27 ...6 A1
Pheasants Wlk NR35 ..7 E4
Philip Ave IP11 .....152 E3
Philip Rd
Bury St Edmunds IP32 .122 F8
Ipswich IP2 ....155 B1
Philipps Cl CB8 .....120 D4
Phillipps Rd **3** IP6 ...82 B5
Phillips Cres IP6 ....125 E4
Phillips Field Rd CO10 .148 E3
Phoenix Day Hospl
IP33 ....154 A1
Phoenix Rd IP4 .....140 A7
Phoenix Way IP14 ...124 F7
Phoenix Yd CB9 .....132 E4
Picketts Rd IP11 ....153 C5
Pickwick Cres IP33 ..154 C3
Pickwick Dr **5** NR32 ...3 A4
Pickwick Rd IP2 ....138 E6
Picton Ave **5** IP1 ...135 D1
Pier Ave IP18 ....119 D6
Pier Terr NR33 .....115 D8
Pig La NR34 ....111 B6
Pigeon La IP28 ....48 B6
Pigeon's La IP8 ....138 A3
Pightle Cl IP30 ....50 E2
Pightle The
Capel St Mary IP9 ...150 F4
Haverhill CB9 ....132 E6
4 Needham Market IP6 .125 D5
North Cove NR34 .....10 B4
Pilgrim's Way **7** IP20 ..22 D6
Pilgrims Way
Bungay NR35 ....110 C3
6 Great Finborough IP14 .66 B4
1 Thorpeness IP16 ....73 F6
Pimpernel Rd IP2 ...138 F3
Pin Mill Cl IP3 .....138 C1
Pin Mill Cliff★ IP9 ..106 D8
Pinbush Cl NR33 ....114 F2
Pinbush Rd NR33 ...114 F2
Pine Ave IP1 ....135 B1
Pine Bank IP5 ......141 F6
Pine Cl
1 Brantham CO11 ....104 E4
Eye IP23 ....117 D3
4 Harleston IP20 .....22 D5
3 Lakenheath IP27 ...13 C7
Rendlesham IP12 .....85 D8
Pine Gr **14** IP13 ....83 E5
Pine Sq IP7 ....80 D6
Pine Tree Cl NR34 ..111 F4
Pine Tree Ct IP22 ...18 C2
Pine Trees Ave IP28 .116 E4
Pine View IP14 ......52 A6
Pine View Rd IP3 ...139 B8
Pinecroft Rd IP1 ....135 A2
Pinecroft Rise CO10 .148 B3
Pinecroft Way IP6 ..125 E4
Pines Ind Est The CB8 ..44 F6
Pines The Claydon IP6 .134 C8
Felixstowe IP11 .....153 E6
Pinetree Cl IP5 .....140 F4
Pinetrees NR31 ......2 B3
Pineview Cl IP14 ...124 D5
Pineway Cl **1** IP29 ...63 A1
Pinewood IP12 .....146 E3
Pinewood Ave NR33 .114 F6
Pinewood Dr IP27 ...14 E8
Pinewood Gdns NR34 ..10 B4
Pinhoe Dr **1** CB9 ...132 A6
Pinkney's La IP18 ..119 D5
Pinkuah La CO10 .....90 F7
Pinmill Rd IP9 ......106 C8
Pinners La IP13 ....146 B2
Pinners Way IP33 ...122 E4
Pintail Cl IP2 ....138 E3
Pintail Rd IP14 ......67 A5
Pinza Cl CB8 ....120 D8
Piperell Way CB9 ...132 C8
Pipers Cl CB9 ......133 A4
Pipers Meadow IP13 .54 E7

Pipers Vale Cl IP3 .....139 E1
Pipers Vale Com Prim Sch
 Gainsborough IP3 ....139 F1
 Ipswich IP3 ....139 F1
Pipers Vale Nature Reserve★
 IP3 ....143 F7
Pipney Hill IP17 ....56 F4
Pipp's La IP6 ....135 E6
Pippin Cl 2 IP2 ....123 E6
Pippin Post Cl CO10 ....76 C6
Pippins The
 Blundeston NR32 ....3 A4
 Glemsford CO10 ....77 B2
Pirnhow St NR35 ....110 D5
Pit Rd NR34 ....10 B8
Pitcairn Rd IP11 ......138 E8
Pitman's Gr IP19 ......42 A4
Pitmire La CO8 ....101 A7
Pits The CB7 ....29 C4
Pitts End CO7 ....151 D5
Place Farm Com Prim Sch
 CB9 ....132 D6
Place for Plants The★
 CO7 ....151 F3
Plampin Cl CO10 ......148 E4
Plantation The IP15 ..130 D5
Plantation Way IP14 ...66 C1
Planters Gr 3 NR33 ...114 F7
Plash Rd IP23 ....53 F7
Plashwood Rd IP14 .....51 B1
Platers Wlk IP16 .....129 C5
Platten Cl IP6 ....125 C5
Platters Cl IP3 ......144 A7
Platters Rd IP11 .....152 E2
Playfield Rd IP9 .....150 F3
Playford La IP13 .....136 E2
Playford Mount IP13 ..137 C6
Playford
 Ipswich IP4 ....140 E8
 Playford IP13 ....137 B2
Pleasant Pl NR34 .....111 B3
Pleasant Row IP4 .....155 C2
Pleasurewood Cl 5
 NR32 ....113 B5
Pleasurewood Hill
 NR32 ....113 A7
Pleasurewood Hills Leisure
 Pk★ NR32 ....113 C8
Plough Hill CO10 ......76 C7
Plough La
 Leavenheath CO6 .....102 B7
 Sudbury CO10 ....148 B5
Plough Rd
 Capel St Mary IP9 ....150 D3
 Woolpit IP30 ....50 D1
Plough St IP3 ....139 E4
Ploughman's Dro IP26 ...4 B5
Plover Cl
 4 Mildenhall IP28 .....13 B1
 11 Stowmarket IP14 ...67 A5
Plover Rd IP2 ....138 E2
Plovers Way
 Bury St Edmunds IP33 .123 C1
 Hockwold cum Wilton IP26 ..4 F3
 Lowestoft NR33 ......114 D5
Plum St CO10 ....77 A3
Plum Tree Rise 3 IP7 ..80 D6
Plummer Cl 22 IP31 ....34 B1
Plummers Dell 10 IP6 ...82 A5
Plumpton Ave IP28 ....116 C5
Plumtrees 8 NR32 ....112 D2
Plymouth Rd
 Felixstowe IP11 ......152 F6
 4 Troston IP31 ....33 D5
Pole Hill (Tumulus)★
 IP10 ....141 F5
Police Sta Rd 5 NR32 .113 D1
Pollard Piece NR33 ...114 C5
Pollards La IP28 ......29 F7
Polls La NR34 ....9 C2
Polstead Cl IP14 .....124 F4
Polstead Hill CO6 .....93 F1
Polstead St CO6 .....102 E7
Pond Cl IP11 ....152 D5
Pond End IP6 ....82 E6
Pond Gn CB7 ....28 A1
Pond Gr Cl IP32 ......123 E6
Pond Hall Rd IP7 .....149 F5
Pond Piece IP13 ....70 A7
Ponds End La IP22 .....35 A8
Poole Cl IP3 ....140 D3
Poole St CO10 ....76 E1
Pooley St IP22 ....19 C3
Pope's Gn La IP7 .....94 B2
Popes Ct CB9 ....133 C2
Poplar Cl 1 Barrow IP29 .47 A2
 4 Claydon IP6 ....134 C8
 Haverhill CB9 ....132 B4
 Mildenhall IP28 .....116 C6
Poplar Farm La IP14 ..124 E4
Poplar Farm Rd IP12 ...73 A2
Poplar Hill IP14 .....124 E4
Poplar La IP8 ....138 B3
Poplar Rd
 Lowestoft NR33 ......114 D3
 Sudbury CO10 ....148 F5
Poplars Cl 3 IP5 .....44 A5
Poplars CP Sch The
 NR32 ....113 D3
Poplars The
 Beck Row, Holywell Row
  & Kenny Hill IP28 ...13 D1
 3 Brantham CO11 ....104 E5
 Spexhall IP19 ....24 F5

Poppy Cl
 Bury St Edmunds IP32 .123 E5
 Ditchingham NR35 ....110 B7
 Ipswich IP2 ....138 F5
 Worlingham NR34 .....111 F3
Poppy Fields 9 CB7 ....28 D5
Popson St NR35 ......110 A4
Port La IP23 ....37 C3
Port of Felixstowe Rd
 IP11 ....152 C3
Portal Ave IP5 ....84 A1
Portal Cl 4 Barnham IP24 ...4 D5
 7 Feltwell IP26 ......4 A5
Porter Rd 3 IP3 ......140 F1
Porthole Cl NR33 .....114 B4
Portland Ave 16 CO12 .107 B2
Portland Cl 18 IP27 ...13 F2
Portland Cres 4 IP12 .146 E4
Portland Gn CB8 .....120 E3
Portland Pl 3 IP24 ....16 A5
Portland Rd CB8 .....120 E3
Portlight Cl 3 CO11 ..105 A2
Portman Rd IP1 ......155 A2
Portman's Wlk IP1 ...139 A5
Portsmouth Cl 19 IP27 ..13 F2
Portsmouth Rd 3 IP31 .33 D5
Post Mill Cl IP4 .....139 F6
Post Mill Cres 12 IP13 .83 E5
Post Mill Gdns 10 IP13 .83 E5
Post Office La
 Glemsford CO10 ......77 A3
 Martlesham IP12 .....146 C1
Post Office Rd IP17 ..129 A3
Posters La IP31 ......35 A2
Posting House Pottery The★
 CO10 ....91 D8
Pot Kiln Chase CO9 ...90 F1
Pot Kiln Prim Sch
 CO10 ....148 E4
Pot Kiln Rd CO10 ....148 F4
Pot Kilns The CO10 ...92 B3
Potash La Bentley IP9 .104 F8
 Eye IP23 ....117 B5
 Polstead CO6 ....93 F4
 Wyverstone IP14 ......51 D7
Potkins La IP12 .....131 B3
Potland La 15 CO10 ...78 D4
Pott Hall Rd IP28 .....30 A6
Potter's La
 Rickinghall Superior IP22 ..36 B5
 Stanton IP31 ....34 E4
Potter's St IP16 .....58 C4
Potters Brook IP6 ...126 B3
Potters Dr NR31 ......3 B7
Potters Vale IP22 .....35 E7
Pouch Mill IP11 .....152 B8
Poulter's La IP29 .....62 F6
Poultry Rd IP27 ......13 A7
Pound Cl 8 Burwell CB5 .44 A5
 Halesworth IP19 .....118 B3
 4 Harleston IP20 ....22 D6
 4 Walsham le Willows
  IP31 ....35 C2
Pound Farm Dr
 8 Harwich CO12 .....107 A2
 Lowestoft NR32 .....112 F4
Pound Farm Parade 7
 NR32 ....112 F4
Pound Fm Nature Reserve★
 IP17 ....56 C1
Pound Gn Rd IP13 .....56 C7
Pound Hill Bacton IP14 .51 F6
 Dallinghoo IP13 ......70 C1
Pound Hill Cl IP14 ....51 F6
Pound La
 Blundeston NR32 ......3 A4
 Bramford IP8 ....81 F3
 Capel St Mary IP9 ...150 D1
 Dallinghoo IP13 ......70 C1
 Ditchingham NR35 .....7 E6
 Hadleigh IP7 ....149 C6
 Isleham CB7 ....29 C5
 Stowmarket IP14 .....124 D7
Pound Meadow 3 IP28 ..48 B6
Pound Pl NR34 ....111 B6
Pound Rd
 3 Beccles NR34 .....111 B4
 Creeting St Peter or West
  Creeting IP6 ....67 B4
 Sotterley NR34 ....26 A7
Pound Wlk NR34 .....111 B6
Pouy St IP17 ....41 B1
Powling Rd IP3 ......140 A2
Powney St IP7 ....93 B8
Pratt St CB7 ....28 D4
Pratt's La IP9 ....144 A2
Prentice Rd IP14 ....124 E6
Prentice St 8 CO10 ...78 D4
Prentices La IP13 ...146 D6
Prescott Dr 11 IP30 ...50 F2
Presland Ct IP27 ....109 B7
Presmere Rd IP13 ....127 A4
Preston Dr IP1 ......134 F2
Preston Rd CO10 ......78 D4
Prestwick Ave 2 IP11 .153 C6
Pretty Dr IP21 ....21 A2
Pretty Rd IP16 ....58 A4
Pretyman Ave IP14 ....51 F6
Pretyman Rd
 Felixstowe IP11 .....152 F6
 Ipswich IP3 ....140 B3
Prevetts Way IP15 ...130 E5
Prickwillow Rd CB7 ....2 E8
Priestly Cl IP14 ....124 B8
Priestly Rd IP6 .....125 D4
Prigg Wlk IP32 ......122 E7
Primes La Blyford IP19 .42 B8

Primes La continued
 Holton IP19 ....118 F5
Primrose Alley IP18 ..119 D4
Primrose La NR33 ....114 F2
Primrose Hill
 Haverhill CB9 ....132 D5
 Ipswich IP2 ....138 F4
Royal Hospital School
 IP9 ....105 E6
Primrose La
 Frostenden NR34 ......26 E4
 Ramsey & Parkeston
  CO11 ....106 A1
 10 Soham CB7 ....28 D5
Primrose Rise NR34 ...111 B3
Primrose Way IP6 ....125 D3
Prince Charles Ave 17
 IP32 ....48 C5
Prince Charles Cl
 CO10 ....148 D6
Prince Cl CB8 ....120 B8
Prince of Wales Cl
 IP33 ....122 E5
Prince of Wales Dr 9
 IP2 ....139 A2
Prince St CO10 ......148 C6
Prince's Rd NR35 ....110 B2
Princedale Cl IP1 ...135 A1
Princel La CO7 ......103 F2
Princes Gdns IP11 ...152 F4
Princes' Gdns 8 IP5 ..81 C3
Princes Gn IP19 .....118 A2
Princes Rd
 Felixstowe IP11 .....152 F4
 13 Harwich CO12 ....107 A2
 Lowestoft NR32 .....113 C2
Princes St
 Bury St Edmunds IP33 .154 A2
 Ipswich IP2 ....155 A1
Princes Wlk NR32 ...113 A2
Princess Rd 2 IP18 ..119 C8
Princess Way
 5 Earsham NR35 ......7 F4
 Haverhill CB9 ....132 B6
 Newmarket CB8 .....120 E4
Princethorpe Rd IP3 .140 C4
Prior Stephen Way
 IP24 ....16 B5
Prior's Ave IP33 ....122 E4
Priors Cl
 Lowestoft NR32 .....113 C5
 Rushbrooke with Rougham
  IP30 ....64 D8
Priors Hill Rd IP15 ..130 D3
Priors Way IP15 .....130 E4
Priory Ave 1 NR32 ...132 D5
Priory Cl 7 Burwell CB5 .44 A5
 Ingham IP31 ....32 F1
 Palgrave IP22 ....20 C1
 St Olaves NR31 ......2 A6
 Stradbroke IP21 .....39 B4
Priory Cres IP21 .....39 D8
Priory Gdns
 Isleham CB7 ....29 C5
 St Olaves NR31 ......2 A6
 Sudbury CO10 ......148 B4
Priory La Bungay NR35 .110 B4
 Carlton Colville NR33 .114 A2
 Darsham IP17 ....42 B1
 Debenham IP14 ......53 F2
Priory Pk IP10 ......144 C6
Priory Rd Beccles NR34 .111 B4
 Blythburgh IP19 ......42 F6
 Felixstowe IP11 .....153 C5
 Fressingfield IP21 ....39 D7
 Fritton & St Olaves NR31 ...2 A6
 Palgrave IP22 ....20 C1
 Snape IP17 ....72 E5
 Sudbury CO10 ......148 B7
 Wrentham NR34 ......26 C5
Priory Specl Sch IP32 .123 C5
Priory Stadium CO10 .148 C4
Prittlewell Cl IP2 ...138 F1
Private Rd Earsham NR35 ..7 D4
 Mutford NR34 ....10 B2
 4 Oulton Broad NR33 .114 E7
Privet Gn NR33 ......115 A7
Progress Way IP23 ...117 B5
Promenade
 Harwich CO12 ....107 A1
 Southwold IP18 .....119 D4
Prospect Hill CO10 ...92 B2
Prospect Pl
 Leiston IP16 ....129 D6
 Lowestoft NR33 .....115 B3
Prospect Rd
 Ipswich IP1 ....139 A6
 Lowestoft NR32 .....112 C1
 Norton IP31 ....50 C4
Prospect Row IP33 ...154 B2
Prospect Terr CB9 ...133 F8
Providence La 5 IP1 .139 A7
Providence Stree IP1 .155 B3
Provost Rd IP11 ......26 D5
Prussia La IP33 .....154 C1
Puddingmoor NR34 ...111 A5
Puddleduck La NR34 .111 F3
Pug St IP21 ....21 A2
Pump Cl IP13 ....84 C7
Pump Ct 9 CO10 ......78 D4
Pump House La IP17 ...57 A8
Pump La IP33 ....154 B2
Pump St
 Needham Market IP6 .125 E4
 Orford IP12 ....131 C2
Punchard Way IP11 ..152 C8
Purcell Rd IP14 .....124 B8

Purdis Ave IP3 ......140 F2
Purdis Farm La
 Foxhall IP10 ....141 C2
 Ipswich IP3 ....140 F2
 Purdis Farm IP10 ...141 B2
Purdis Rd IP10 ......141 D2
Purplett St IP2 .....155 C1
Putney Cl IP27 ......14 E8
Putticks La CO7 .....151 E5
Pyes Meadow 1 IP30 ..50 F2
Pykenham Way IP7 ...149 D6
Pytches Cl 2 IP12 ...147 B6
Pytches Rd IP12 .....147 A6

Q

Quadling St IP1 .....155 B2
Quail Cl IP32 ....123 E6
Quaker La Bardwell IP31 .34 C4
 Beyton IP30 ....49 F1
Quaker's La 2 CB9 ...132 E5
Quakers' Rd IP28 ....116 F5
Quakers Way 3 IP16 ..129 D5
Quantock Cl IP5 ....140 F7
Quantrill Terr IP5 ..141 D6
Quarries Cross IP14 ..66 C8
Quaves La NR35 .....110 B4
Quay La Reydon IP18 ..26 D1
 Sudbury CO10 ......148 C4
Quay Side IP12 .....147 A4
Quay St
 Halesworth IP19 ....118 B4
 13 Manningtree CO11 .104 E2
 Orford IP12 ....131 C2
 Woodbridge IP12 ....147 A4
Quay The 1 CO12 ....107 B3
Quay Theatre The
 CO10 ....148 C4
Quay View NR32 .....113 A1
Quay's Rd IP28 ......47 E5
Quayside Ct IP27 ....109 C7
Quebec Dr IP5 ......141 B8
Queech La IP9 ......105 B4
Queen Edith Dr CB9 ..88 D3
Queen Elizabeth Cl
 IP16 ....129 C4
Queen Elizabeth Dr
 NR34 ....111 D3
Queen St Cowlinge CB8 .61 B1
 Felixstowe IP11 .....152 E5
 6 Hadleigh IP7 .....149 D6
 Haverhill CB9 ....132 E6
 Ipswich IP1 ....155 B2
 Newmarket CB8 .....121 B3
 Southwold IP18 .....119 D5
 Stradbroke IP21 .....39 B5
Queen's Cl IP33 .....122 E5
Queen's Dr IP28 ....116 B4
Queen's Head La IP12 .131 D2
Queen's Head Rd CO4 .102 F1
Queen's Highway
 NR32 ....112 C2
Queen's Rd
 Beccles NR34 ....111 B6
 Bungay NR35 ....110 B2
 Bury St Edmunds IP33 .154 A2
 4 Harwich CO12 ....107 A1
 Lowestoft NR32 .....113 D3
 Southwold IP18 .....119 D4
Queen's Way IP3 ....140 B2
Queens Ave 5 IP12 ..146 E4
Queens Cl Combs IP14 .124 A1
 Halesworth IP19 ....118 A2
 Saxmundham IP17 ...128 C3
 Sudbury CO10 ......148 C6
Queens Ct CB9 ......132 C6
Queens Dr IP19 .....118 A2
Queens La IP29 ......62 D5
Queens Rd Brandon IP27 .14 E8
 1 Southwold IP18 ...119 C4
 Sudbury CO10 ......148 C6
Queens Sq 7 CB9 ....132 E6
Queens St CB9 ......74 B2
Queens View CB8 ...120 A8
Queensberry Rd
 1 Ipswich IP3 ......144 B8
 Newmarket CB8 .....121 A3
Queenscliffe Rd IP2 .139 A3
Queensdale Cl IP1 ..135 B1
Queensdale Rd IP1 ..135 B1
Queensgate Dr IP4 ..139 F8
Queensland IP9 .....106 F5
Queensway 4 Acton CO10 .92 B7
 7 Earsham NR35 .....7 F4
 Exning CB8 ....120 B8
 Haverhill CB9 ....132 C6
 3 Manningtree CO11 .104 E2
 2 Mildenhall IP28 ..116 B4
 8 Soham CB7 ....28 D4
 Thetford IP24 ....16 B5
Queensway Com Jun Sch 7
 IP24 ....16 B5
Queensway Inf Sch
 IP24 ....16 B5
Quendon Pl CB9 .....132 F6
Quentin Cl IP1 .....138 E8
Quilter Dr Ipswich IP8 .138 C1
 Pinewood IP8 ....142 C8
Quilter Rd IP11 .....153 B4
Quince Cl 6 CO11 ...104 E5
Quinnell Way 5 NR32 .113 A6
Quinton Rd IP6 .....125 C4
Quinton's La IP11 ...153 C5
Quintons Cnr CO7 ...151 D6

Quintons Rd CO7 ....151 C5
Quoits Field 2 IP6 ..134 C8
Quoits Meadow IP14 ..68 B6

R

Rackham Cl 1 NR31 ....3 B7
Radcliffe Dr IP2 ....138 D2
Radcliffe Rd 8 IP27 ..14 A2
Radiator Rd CO10 ...148 E3
Radleys La CO6 .....102 B6
Radnor Cl IP32 .....123 E6
Raeburn Rd IP3 .....139 F1
Raeburn Rd S IP3 ...139 E1
Raedwald Dr IP32 ...123 D5
Raedwald Way IP14 ...53 F1
Rag's La IP30 ....50 D1
Raglan Rd 2 NR32 ...113 D1
Raglan St NR32 .....113 D1
Raile Wlk CO10 ......91 E8
Railway App IP11 ...153 A5
Railway Cl CB5 .....44 A4
Railway Hill IP20 ....22 C6
Railway St 19 CO11 ..104 E2
Railway Terr CB9 ...133 E7
Raine Ave CB9 ......132 B6
Rainey Ct 37 IP20 ...22 D6
Raingate St IP33 ...154 C1
Raleigh Cl CO10 ....148 E8
Raleigh Inf Sch 1 IP4 .16 C7
Raleigh Rd CO10 ....148 E8
Ram La NR15 ....21 C8
Rampart Way IP24 ...16 C5
Rampling Cl IP7 ....149 D7
Ramsey Cl IP7 ......139 A1
Ramsey Rd
 Hadleigh IP7 ....149 F7
 Harwich CO12 ......106 D1
Ramsgate Dr IP3 ....140 B3
Randall Cl
 2 Hopton on Sea NR31 ...3 B7
 Ipswich IP5 ....141 C7
Randolph Cl IP4 ....140 B5
Rands Rd IP7 ....149 B1
Rands Way IP3 ......140 B2
Randwell Cl IP4 ....140 B5
Ranelagh Prim Sch
 IP2 ....138 F7
Ranelagh Rd
 Felixstowe IP11 .....153 A5
 Ipswich IP2 ....155 A1
Ransom Rd IP12 .....146 E4
Ransome Ave IP21 ....21 A2
Ransome Cl IP8 .....138 A6
Ransome Cres IP3 ...140 B2
Ransome Rd IP3 ....140 B2
Ransomes Europark
 IP10 ....144 F7
Ransomes Way IP3 ..140 D1
Ranson Rd IP6 .....125 C4
Rant Score NR32 ....113 E2
Ranville NR33 ......114 E3
Ranworth Ave NR33 .114 C5
Raphael Wlk 10 NR32 .113 B6
Rapier St 6 IP2 ....139 C3
Rare Breeds Farm★
 CO7 ....151 A1
Rat Hill IP9 ....106 C5
Rattla Cnr IP16 .....58 C5
Rattler's Rd IP27 ....5 F1
Rattlerow Hill IP21 ..39 B6
Rattlesden CE Prim Sch
 IP30 ....65 D6
Rattlesden Rd 2 IP14 .124 D3
Rattlesden Rd IP30 ..65 D6
Raven Cl
 Mildenhall IP28 .....116 C5
 Stowmarket IP14 ....124 F4
Raven Rd IP33 ......123 C1
Raven Way IP7 .....149 D4
Raveningham Rd NR34 ..9 C8
Ravens La IP8 ......134 A2
Ravens Way 6 IP2 ...84 A1
Ravensfield Rd IP1 ..134 E1
Ravensmere NR34 ...111 B6
Ravensmere Cty Inf Sch
 NR34 ....111 B7
Ravensmere E NR34 .111 B6
Ravenswood Ave IP3 .144 B8
Ravenswood Com Prim Sch
 IP3 ....144 C8
Ravenwood Mews
 NR33 ....115 A5
Ravine NR32 ....113 C6
Rawlings Way 22 IP26 ..4 E5
Ray Ave CO12 ......107 A2
Ray La 8 CO12 .....106 F3
Raydon Croft IP14 ..124 F3
Raydon La IP12 .....131 D3
Raydon Rd CO7 .....150 A4
Raydon Way CO10 ...92 B3
Rayes La CB8 ......121 A4
Rayleigh Rd IP1 ....134 E1
Rayment Drift 5 IP5 .141 C7
Rayner's La NR35 ....8 D3
Raynham Rd IP32 ...154 A4
Raynsford Rd NR30 ..63 F7
Reach Rd CB5 ......44 A5
Reade Rd 5 IP9 ....105 E7
Reading Gn IP21 .....38 C3
Reading Rd IP4 .....140 B7
Reading's La IP31 ....35 A3
Rebow Rd 9 CO12 ...107 A1
Reckford Rd IP17 ....58 B6
Recreation La IP11 ..152 F6
Recreation Rd
 Haverhill CB9 ....132 D5

Recreation Rd *continued*
Stowmarket IP14 ... 124 C6
Recreation Way
Ipswich IP3 ... 140 C2
Mildenhall IP28 ... 116 C4
Recreation Wlk CO10 ... 148 F3
Rectory Cl
Beccles NR34 ... 111 F4
3 Glemsford CO10 ... 77 A3
Ousden CB8 ... 61 E6
Raydon IP7 ... 94 F1
Rectory Field 4 IP9 ... 106 C8
Rectory Gdns IP30 ... 49 F1
Rectory Gn IP19 ... 118 A4
Rectory Gr IP29 ... 63 B5
Rectory Hill
Botesdale IP22 ... 35 F6
East Bergholt CO7 ... 151 C3
Polstead CO6 ... 102 E8
Rickinghall Superior IP22 ... 36 A5
Rectory La Beccles NR34 ... 9 F4
Brantham CO11 ... 104 F5
Hedenham NR35 ... 7 D8
Hintlesham IP8 ... 95 C6
Kettlebaston IP7 ... 79 B5
Kirton IP10 ... 98 D2
Mettingham NR35 ... 110 F3
4 Ramsey & Parkeston CO12 ... 106 D1
Scole IP21 ... 21 C5
Stuston IP21 ... 37 D8
Whatfield IP7 ... 80 C1
3 Woolpit IP30 ... 50 D1
Rectory Meadow 5 IP28 48 B6
Rectory Pk 3 CO10 ... 93 C3
Rectory Pl IP29 ... 47 A1
Rectory Rd
Aldeby/Wheatacre/Burgh St Peter NR34 ... 10 A8
Bacton IP14 ... 51 E5
Blaxhall IP12 ... 71 F4
Brome & Oakley IP23 ... 117 B7
Broome NR35 ... 8 B7
Burston & Shimpling IP22 ... 20 E6
Dickleburgh IP21 ... 21 B5
Gillingham NR34 ... 9 B7
Gissing IP22 ... 20 F8
Great Waldingfield CO10 ... 92 D6
Harkstead IP9 ... 106 B6
Hemingstone IP6 ... 68 C1
Hollesley IP12 ... 99 F7
Ipswich IP2 ... 155 B1
Kedington CB9 ... 133 F8
Langham CO4 ... 103 C3
7 Lowestoft NR33 ... 115 C6
Mellis IP23 ... 36 F5
Middleton CO10 ... 148 C2
Newton CO10 ... 92 D2
Orford IP12 ... 131 C3
Shelfanger IP22 ... 20 B6
Sotterley NR34 ... 26 A7
Tivetshall St Mary NR15 ... 21 C8
Whepstead IP29 ... 63 B4
Wortham IP22 ... 19 F1
Wrabness CO11 ... 106 A2
Wyverstone IP14 ... 51 D6
Rectory St IP19 ... 118 B4
Red Barn Dr 4 CO6 ... 102 A7
Red Barn Piece 11 IP13 ... 83 E5
Red Dock La CB8 ... 61 C1
Red Hall Ct IP11 ... 153 C4
Red Hill IP7 ... 94 D7
Red Hill Rd IP7 ... 149 E8
Red House★ IP15 ... 130 C6
Red House Cl
3 Felixstowe IP11 ... 107 D8
Lowestoft NR32 ... 112 F5
Red House La
Leiston IP16 ... 129 D4
Sudbury CO10 ... 148 E2
Red House Wlk IP10 ... 145 E4
Red La
Capel St Mary IP9 ... 150 E2
Sternfield IP17 ... 72 D8
Red Lion Cl IP21 ... 38 C7
Red Rose Cl IP12 ... 99 E4
Red Sleeve IP9 ... 150 D3
Redan St IP1 ... 155 A4
Redbarn La IP17 ... 72 D7
Redcastle Furze Prim Sch 6 IP24 ... 16 B5
Reddells Cl CO10 ... 148 D5
Rede La IP6 ... 134 F8
Rede Rd IP29 ... 62 F4
Rede Way CO10 ... 92 B3
Rede Wood Nature Reserve★ IP6 ... 82 D5
Redenhall Rd IP20 ... 22 D6
Redgate IP24 ... 16 C6
Redgate La IP9 ... 143 D5
Redgrave & Lopham Fen National Nature Reserve★ IP22 ... 19 C2
Redgrave & Lopham Fen Visitor Ctr★ IP22 ... 19 C3
Redgrave Rd IP22 ... 19 B3
Redhouse Gdns 5 CB7 ... 28 D3
Redhouse La
Bawdsey IP12 ... 99 E3
Boxted CO4 ... 102 E1
9 Sudbury CO10 ... 148 C5
Redhouse Rd IP13 ... 56 B8
Redisham Cl NR32 ... 113 A5
Redisham Rd
Redisham NR34 ... 25 B6
Weston NR34 ... 9 C1
Redlingfield Rd
Horham IP21 ... 38 D2
Redlingfield Rd *continued*
Occold IP23 ... 37 F2
Redshank Cl CB9 ... 133 A5
Redwald Rd IP12 ... 85 E8
Redwing Cl IP2 ... 138 D3
Redwing Rd IP33 ... 123 C1
Redwings Horse Sanctuary (Caldecott)★ NR31 ... 2 C8
Redwings Horse Sanctuary (Stonham)★ IP14 ... 68 C6
Redwold Cl IP12 ... 146 C1
Redwood Gdns IP33 ... 154 C2
Redwood La 23 IP27 ... 13 F2
Reed's Bldgs IP33 ... 154 C3
Reedland Way 4 IP11 ... 152 D5
Reeds La CB9 ... 132 E6
Reeds Way IP14 ... 67 A7
Reet 1 NR32 ... 115 D8
Reeve Cl
12 Bury St Edmunds IP32 ... 48 C5
Scole IP21 ... 21 A2
Reeve Gdns IP5 ... 141 C8
Reeve St NR32 ... 113 D2
Reeve's Cl NR35 ... 110 C3
Reeves La IP26 ... 5 A3
Refinery Rd CO12 ... 106 F3
Regal Dr CB7 ... 28 E3
Regal La CB7 ... 28 E3
Regan Cl NR32 ... 113 A5
Regent Pl 3 CB7 ... 28 D3
Regent Rd NR32 ... 113 D1
Regent St
20 Manningtree CO11 ... 104 E2
Stowmarket IP14 ... 124 D7
Regent Theatre★ IP4 ... 155 C3
Regents Ct 8 CB8 ... 121 A4
Regimental Mus★ IP33 ... 122 E6
Regimental Way
18 Harwich CO12 ... 106 E1
18 Ramsey CO12 ... 106 E1
Regina Cl IP4 ... 140 B5
Reigate Cl IP3 ... 140 B3
Rembrandt Cl 3 NR32 ... 113 C6
Rembrandt Gdns 4 IP33 ... 122 F3
Rembrandt Way IP33 ... 123 A3
Rembrow Rd IP9 ... 150 E3
Rememberance Rd IP16 ... 73 F6
Remercie Rd 7 CO11 ... 105 A2
Rendall La IP14 ... 67 A8
Rendham Hill IP17 ... 56 F7
Rendham Rd
Bruisyard IP17 ... 56 D4
Kelsale cum Carlton IP17 ... 128 A6
Peasenhall IP17 ... 56 F7
Rendlesham Est★ IP12 ... 85 D6
Rendlesham Forest Ctr★ IP12 ... 85 F3
Rendlesham Rd
15 Felixstowe IP11 ... 152 D5
9 Ipswich IP1 ... 139 A7
Renfrew Rd IP4 ... 136 B1
Renoir Pl 2 NR32 ... 113 B5
Renson Cl 6 IP30 ... 64 F8
Reydon Bsns Pk IP18 ... 119 D8
Reydon Cl 2 CB9 ... 132 A6
Reydon La IP18 ... 26 D1
Reydon Mews NR32 ... 113 A6
Reydon Prim Sch IP18 ... 119 C8
Reydon Wood Nature Reserve★ IP34 ... 26 C2
Reynolds Ave 2 IP3 ... 144 A8
Reynolds Ct 10 IP11 ... 152 D5
Reynolds Rd IP3 ... 140 A1
Reynolds Way CO10 ... 148 E8
Reynolds Wlk
Bury St Edmunds IP33 ... 122 B6
Gunton NR32 ... 113 B6
Ribblesdale NR33 ... 114 E3
Riby Rd IP11 ... 152 F3
Richard Burn Way CO10 ... 148 C8
Richard Crampton Rd NR34 ... 111 B3
Richard Easter Rd IP24 ... 16 C7
Richards Dr IP13 ... 137 D5
Richard's Cl NR33 ... 114 E6
Richardson Rd CO7 ... 151 D5
Richardsons La IP9 ... 106 B8
Richer Cl IP31 ... 50 E7
Richer Rd IP31 ... 50 F7
Richmond Cres 8 CO12 107 A1
Richmond Pl 3 NR33 ... 115 C6
Richmond Rd
Brandon IP27 ... 14 E8
Ipswich IP1 ... 138 F7
Lowestoft NR33 ... 115 C6
Riddlesworth Hall Sch IP22 ... 17 F4
Rider Haggard La 7 NR33 ... 11 C1
Rider Haggard Way NR35 ... 110 C7
Ridgeville 9 NR33 ... 114 F3
Ridgeway IP14 ... 124 B6
Ridgeway The 10 CO12 ... 107 A2
Ridgeways The NR33 ... 114 D5
Ridgewell Rd CO10 ... 89 D5
Ridings The
3 Beccles NR34 ... 111 F4
Leavenheath CO6 ... 102 B8
Ridley Rd IP33 ... 122 C6
Rigbourne Hill NR34 ... 111 C3
Rigbourne Hill La 6 NR34 ... 111 C2
Rigby Ave CO11 ... 105 A2
Riley Cl IP1 ... 134 C1
Rimmer Cl CO10 ... 148 E8
Ringham Rd IP4 ... 140 A6
Ringsfield CE VCP Sch NR34 ... 9 B2
Ringsfield Rd
Beccles NR34 ... 111 A4
6 Lowestoft NR32 ... 113 A3
Ringsfield NR34 ... 9 A1
Ringshall Prim Sch IP14 ... 80 E6
Rio Cl 2 NR33 ... 114 C5
Risbridge Dr CB9 ... 133 E8
Risby Barn Antique & Craft Ctr★ IP28 ... 47 D5
Risby CE VC Prim Sch IP28 ... 47 D5
Risby Cl IP4 ... 140 B6
Risbygate St IP33 ... 154 B2
Riseway Cl IP33 ... 123 B1
Rishton Rd 7 NR32 ... 113 D1
Rising Sun Hill IP30 ... 65 D5
Rissemere La E IP18 ... 119 C8
Ritabrook Rd IP2 ... 138 E1
Rivendale 4 NR33 ... 114 D3
River Gdns IP14 ... 124 E4
River Hill IP8 ... 138 C8
River La Fordham CB7 ... 29 A1
Halesworth IP19 ... 118 B3
River View NR34 ... 111 B7
River View Rd 1 IP9 ... 106 A5
Riverbank Cl CO10 ... 90 B8
Rivers St IP4 ... 139 F7
Riverside
4 Framlingham IP13 ... 126 C3
Hasketon IP13 ... 146 A7
Palgrave IP22 ... 20 B2
Riverside Ave E 6 CO11 ... 104 E3
Riverside Ave W 4 CO11 ... 104 E3
Riverside Bsns Ctr NR33 ... 115 C8
Riverside Cl IP28 ... 116 B4
Riverside Ct IP32 ... 123 A8
Riverside Ind Est IP13 ... 127 C7
Riverside Ind Pk IP2 ... 139 D3
Riverside Mid Sch IP28 ... 116 B4
Riverside Rd
Ipswich IP1 ... 138 F7
Lowestoft NR33 ... 115 B8
Riverside Theatre The★ IP12 ... 147 A4
Riverside View IP13 ... 127 C8
Riverside Way IP27 ... 5 F2
Riverview IP12 ... 147 C7
Riverwalk Sch IP33 ... 154 A1
Rivish La CO10 ... 91 E8
Rixon Cres 3 IP12 ... 84 E6
Roamwood Gn La IP14 ... 53 E3
Robeck Rd IP3 ... 139 E1
Robert Boby Way IP33 ... 154 B2
Robert's Hill CO8 ... 101 C2
Roberts Rd IP16 ... 129 D6
Robertsbridge Wlk 6 NR33 ... 114 D4
Robin Cl Haverhill CB9 ... 133 A5
Mildenhall IP28 ... 116 D4
15 Stowmarket IP14 ... 67 A5
12 Thurstow IP31 ... 49 D4
Robin Dr IP2 ... 138 D3
Robin Hill NR32 ... 113 A2
Robin Rd IP33 ... 123 C1
Robin Way CO10 ... 148 A3
Robins Cl 16 CB7 ... 29 C5
Robinson Cl IP33 ... 122 D6
Robinson Rd 7 IP21 ... 20 F1
Robinson Wlk IP32 ... 122 D7
Robletts IP13 ... 84 D7
Robletts Way 1 CO6 ... 101 F2
Rochdale 3 NR33 ... 114 F3
Rochester Rd 1 NR33 ... 115 B4
Rochester Way CO10 ... 148 B8
Rochfort Ave CB8 ... 120 E5
Rock Rd NR32 ... 112 D1
Rockall CB8 ... 61 E6
Rockall Cl CB9 ... 133 B5
Rockalls Rd CO6 ... 93 F1
Rockingham Rd IP33 ... 123 B3
Rockstone La IP19 ... 41 C7
Rodber Way NR32 ... 113 A6
Rodbridge Hill CO10 ... 91 D6
Rodney Ct IP12 ... 146 F7
Roebuck Dr IP27 ... 109 E4
Roebuck The IP27 ... 109 E1
Roger's Cl NR31 ... 3 B7
Roger's La CO10 ... 92 F4
Rogeron Cl CO10 ... 75 D3
Rogers Cl IP11 ... 152 F6
Rogue's La IP13 ... 127 C5
Rokewood Pl IP29 ... 64 A3
Roman Cl 3 CB5 ... 44 A5
Roman Hill Mid Sch NR32 ... 113 C1
Roman Hill Prim Sch NR32 ... 113 C1
Roman Rd NR32 ... 113 C1
Roman Way
Felixstowe IP11 ... 153 D6
Halesworth IP19 ... 118 A3
Haverhill CB9 ... 133 B4
Long Melford CO10 ... 91 E7
Romany La NR33 ... 11 B3
Romany Rd NR32 ... 114 C8
Romany Way IP33 ... 123 D3
Romney Pl 6 NR32 ... 113 B6
Romney Rd IP3 ... 140 A1
Romsey Rd IP33 ... 122 D3
Ronald La IP17 ... 128 D5
Ronden Cl NR34 ... 111 B2
Rook's La 7 NR34 ... 111 B5
Rookery Chase CO7 ... 103 F1
Rookery Cl NR33 ... 114 F7
Rookery Dro 2 IP28 ... 13 B1
Rookery La IP19 ... 23 F4
Rookery Rd Elmsett IP7 ... 80 E2
Monewden IP13 ... 69 F5
Rookery Sh Ctr CB8 ... 121 A4
Rookery The
Brandon IP27 ... 5 D1
Eye IP23 ... 117 D2
4 Manningtree CO11 ... 104 E2
Newmarket CB8 ... 121 B3
Rookery Way IP14 ... 51 F1
Rookery Wlk IP27 ... 109 B7
Rookwood La CO10 ... 78 F6
Rookwood Way CB9 ... 132 E4
Roosevelt Wlk 5 NR33 ... 114 C5
Rope Wlk
Carlton Colville NR33 ... 114 B4
Ipswich IP4 ... 155 C2
Roper's Ct 3 CO10 ... 78 D4
Ropers La CO10 ... 91 D7
Ropes Dr IP5 ... 141 B8
Rosbrook Cl 1 IP33 ... 122 D4
Rose Acre CO7 ... 103 F7
Rose Ave IP22 ... 20 A3
Rose Ct Lowestoft NR32 ... 113 B2
Shotley IP9 ... 106 F6
Rose Gn CO10 ... 101 F8
Rose Gn La 4 IP28 ... 30 B8
Rose Hall Gdns NR35 ... 110 B3
Rose Hill
Grundisburgh IP13 ... 83 E5
Withersfield CB9 ... 74 B3
Witnesham IP6 ... 135 F7
Rose Hill Prim Sch IP3 ... 140 A4
Rose La Botesdale IP22 ... 36 A7
Bungay NR35 ... 110 B3
Diss IP22 ... 20 D1
Elmswell IP30 ... 50 E2
Ipswich IP4 ... 155 B2
Wickham Skeith IP23 ... 52 D8
Rose La Cl IP22 ... 20 C1
Rose Wlk IP6 ... 125 D3
Rosebay Gdns 1 CB7 ... 28 D4
Rosebery Rd
Felixstowe IP11 ... 153 B4
Ipswich IP4 ... 139 F5
Rosebery Way CB8 ... 120 E5
Rosecroft Rd IP1 ... 135 A2
Rosecroft Way IP24 ... 16 D6
Rosedale Gdns 9 NR33 114 E4
Rosefinch Cl CB9 ... 133 A5
Rosehill Cres IP3 ... 139 F4
Rosehill Rd IP3 ... 139 F4
Rosemary Ave IP11 ... 153 B5
Rosemary Cl 4 IP28 ... 30 C1
Rosemary Gdns CO10 ... 148 D8
Rosemary La
Ipswich IP4 ... 155 B2
Kelsale cum Carlton IP17 ... 128 C6
Rosemary Musker Cty High Sch IP24 ... 16 C7
Rosemary Rd 5 IP32 ... 48 C5
Rosery La IP13 ... 137 F6
Rosewood NR33 ... 115 A5
Rosewood Cl 22 IP27 ... 13 F2
Ross Cl CB9 ... 133 B5
Ross Peers Sports Ctr The CB7 ... 28 D3
Ross Rd IP4 ... 136 B1
Rosyth Rd 5 IP31 ... 33 D5
Rotheram Rd 9 IP7 ... 79 F4
Rotten Row CO10 ... 92 D2
Rotterdam Rd NR32 ... 113 B1
Rougham CE Prim Sch IP30 ... 49 D1
Rougham Control Twr Musuem★ IP30 ... 49 B3
Rougham Hill IP33 ... 123 D3
Rougham Ind Est IP30 ... 49 B2
Rougham Rd
Bradfield St George IP30 ... 64 D7
Bury St Edmunds IP33 ... 123 C3
Roughlands IP27 ... 109 D6
Roundridge Rd IP9 ... 150 F4
Roundwood Rd IP4 ... 140 A7
Rous Meml Ct CB8 ... 121 B3
Rous Rd CB8 ... 121 B3
Rousies Cl 6 IP7 ... 149 E6
Routh Ave 4 IP3 ... 140 F1
Row The Bramford IP8 ... 134 A2
Gipsy Row CO7 ... 150 A4
Stratford St Mary CO7 ... 103 E5
Rowan Cl Haverhill CB9 ... 132 C7
Priory Heath IP3 ... 140 D2
Rowan Dr Brandon IP27 ... 14 F8
Bury St Edmunds IP32 ... 123 F6
Rowan Gn 7 IP30 ... 50 F2
Rowan Way
Beccles NR34 ... 111 E3
Lowestoft NR33 ... 114 D6
5 Thurstow IP31 ... 49 D4
Rowan Wlk IP28 ... 116 E5
Rowanhayes Cl IP2 ... 139 B3
Rowans Way 1 CO6 ... 102 A7
Rowarth Ave IP5 ... 141 C7
Rowe's Hill IP13 ... 40 C2
Rowell Cl CB9 ... 132 E8
Rowell's La IP14 ... 51 D4
Rowley Cl 7 CO11 ... 104 E4
Rowley Ct
Newmarket CB8 ... 120 E3
Sturmer CB9 ... 133 C3
Rowley Dr CB8 ... 120 F3
Rowley Hill CB9 ... 133 B3
Rowntree Cl 6 NR32 ... 113 A6
Rows The CB8 ... 120 E3
Roxburgh Rd IP4 ... 136 B1
Roy Ave IP4 ... 140 B5
Roy Cl IP5 ... 141 B7
Royal Ave NR32 ... 113 D3
Royal Hospl Sch IP9 ... 105 E6
Royal Naval Patrol Service Mus★ NR32 ... 113 E3
Royal Pal Cl CB8 ... 120 D7
Royal Plain NR33 ... 115 D8
Royal Terr NR33 ... 115 D7
Roydon Fen IP22 ... 20 B2
Roydon Prim Sch IP22 ... 20 B3
Roydon Rd IP22 ... 20 C3
Roydon Way 10 NR32 ... 112 F4
Roylands La CO10 ... 93 D3
Royston Dr IP2 ... 138 D2
Rozlyne Cl 8 NR33 ... 114 E4
Rubens Rd IP3 ... 140 A1
Rubens Wlk
Gunton NR32 ... 113 B6
Sudbury CO10 ... 148 E8
Ruby Cl 9 NR32 ... 3 D4
Rudlands IP8 ... 138 C1
Rudlands Cl 6 CB7 ... 29 C5
Rue's La IP11 ... 153 C8
Ruffles Rd CB9 ... 133 A5
Rugby Rd CO10 ... 148 F2
Rumburgh La NR35 ... 24 D6
Rumburgh Rd
Lowestoft NR32 ... 113 B5
Rumburgh IP19 ... 24 B3
Run Meadow NR33 ... 114 C6
Run The NR34 ... 26 A7
Runce's La NR33 ... 114 C3
Runnacles Way IP11 ... 152 D5
Runnymede Gn IP33 ... 123 A3
Rush Cl IP4 ... 140 E4
Rushall Rd IP20 ... 22 B6
Rushbrooke La IP33 ... 123 D3
Rushbury Cl IP4 ... 140 B8
Rushford Rd
Coney Weston IP31 ... 17 E1
Euston IP24 ... 16 E2
Rushlake Way 7 NR33 ... 114 D4
Rushmeadow Way 1 IP11 ... 153 D7
Rushmere Hall Prim Sch IP4 ... 136 A1
Rushmere Pl CB9 ... 132 F6
Rushmere Rd
Gisleham NR33 ... 114 B1
Ipswich IP4 ... 140 A7
Rushmere NR33 ... 10 F3
Rushmere St IP5 ... 136 E1
Rushton Dr NR33 ... 114 B3
Ruskin Cl 3 IP14 ... 124 B8
Ruskin Rd IP4 ... 139 F5
Russell Baron Rd IP31 ... 48 D5
Russell Cl IP12 ... 146 E6
Russell Rd
Felixstowe IP11 ... 152 F2
Ipswich IP1 ... 155 A2
Russell's Gn NR34 ... 9 C2
Russet Cl
4 Beccles NR34 ... 111 C3
Great Barton IP32 ... 123 E7
Russett Cl CB9 ... 132 A6
Rutland Ct 15 CB9 ... 132 C5
Rutland Sq IP33 ... 154 C1
Rydal Ave IP11 ... 153 D7
Rydal Cl IP14 ... 124 B6
Rydal Wlk IP3 ... 140 C2
Ryders Way 2 IP22 ... 36 A6
Rye Cl Ipswich IP3 ... 140 D4
3 Lowestoft NR33 ... 114 D4
Rye Ct 8 CB9 ... 132 C5
Ryeburn Cl 1 NR33 ... 11 B1
Ryedale 1 NR33 ... 114 F3
Ryefields 9 IP31 ... 49 E4
Ryes La CO10 ... 91 D1
Ryes Sch The
Bulmer Tye CO10 ... 91 E1
Kesgrave IP5 ... 137 E1
Rylands IP9 ... 150 E4
Rylands Cl 1 IP31 ... 49 E4

S

Sackville St CB8 ... 121 B4
Sackvylle St IP14 ... 53 E1
Saddlemakers La IP12 ... 147 C8
Saddlers Meadow 2 IP13 ... 83 E5
Saddlers Pl 19 IP5 ... 98 A8
Saddlers Yd 17 IP31 ... 34 B1
Saffron Sq NR33 ... 115 A2
Saffrons Cl IP30 ... 50 D1
Sagehayes Cl IP2 ... 139 B3
Sages End Rd CB9 ... 88 A4
St Agnes Way IP5 ... 140 F6
St Alban's Cath High Sch IP4 ... 140 D7
St Albans CB8 ... 121 A6

St Andrew **2** CB8 . . . . . .**121** A4
St Andrew **1** NR31 . . . . . .**3** C7
St Andrew's Church Cl
IP5 . . . .**136** D1
St Andrew's Cl IP12 . . . .**147** D7
St Andrew's Cl **4** IP33 . .**154** B2
St Andrew's Dr **3** IP9 .**106** C8
St Andrew's Pl IP12 . . . .**147** D8
St Andrew's Rd
  Beccles NR34 . . . .**111** C2
  Coldfair Green IP17 . . . .**129** B2
  Felixstowe IP11 . . . .**153** A5
St Andrew's St IP28 . . . .**116** C4
St Andrew's St N IP33 . .**154** B1
St Andrew's St S IP33 . .**154** B2
St Andrews CE VA Prim Sch
IP22 . . . .**19** A5
St Andrews Cl
  2 Barningham IP31 . . . . .**34** E7
  2 Great Finborough IP14 . .**66** B4
  Ipswich IP4 . . . .**140** D5
  3 Isleham CB7 . . . .**29** C5
St Andrews Dr **7** IP28 . .**48** C6
St Andrews Mead IP14 . . .**68** B8
St Andrews Rd
  Scole IP21 . . . .**21** A1
  Sudbury CO10 . . . .**148** E4
St Anne's Cl NR34 . . . . . .**111** C4
St Anne's Dr IP28 . . . . . .**116** B4
St Anne's Rd NR34 . . . . .**111** C4
St Annes Cl IP12 . . . .**146** D3
St Anthony **3** CB8 . . . . . .**121** A4
St Anthonys Cres IP4 . . . .**139** F6
St Aubyn's Rd **6** NR33 . .**115** C6
St Aubyns Rd IP4 . . . . . .**140** A5
St Audrys Pk Rd **5** IP12 .**84** E6
St Audrys Rd IP12 . . . . . .**84** E6
St Augustine Rd IP3 . . . .**140** D4
St Augustine's Gdns
IP3 . . . .**140** C3
St Austell Cl IP5 . . . .**141** A6
St Austin's La **1** CO12 . .**107** C3
St Barbara's Ct **18** CO10 . **148** C5
St Bartholomews La
CO10 . . . .**148** B7
St Benedict's Rd NR34 . .**111** B6
St Benedicts Cath Sch
IP32 . . . .**122** F8
St Benedicts Rd IP27 . . . .**6** A1
St Benet's Dr NR34 . . . . .**111** C3
St Benet's RC Minst
NR34 . . . .**111** A4
St Benets RC Prim Sch
NR34 . . . .**111** A5
St Botolph's La CO13 . . . .**36** C1
St Botolph's Way CB9 . . .**132** D6
St Botolphs CE VC Prim Sch
IP22 . . . .**36** B7
St Botolphs Pl **13** CB9 . .**132** D5
St Catherine's Cl
NR33 . . . .**114** E4
St Catherine's Ct IP22 . .**138** E1
St Catherine's Rd **11**
CO10 . . . .**91** E8
St Catherines CE IP28 . . .**116** D6
St Clare Ct **15** NR31 . . . . .**3** B7
St Clement Mews **13** NR31 .**3** B7
St Clement's Hospl
IP3 . . . .**140** C4
St Clements Church La
IP4 . . . .**155** C2
St Cross Rd IP20 . . . .**23** B8
St David **4** CB8 . . . .**121** A4
St David's Cl **5** NR34 . . .**111** C2
St David's Rd **7** IP3 . . . .**140** B3
St Denis Cl **11** CO12 . . . .**107** A1
St Denys **5** CB8 . . . .**121** A4
St Domonic's Dr IP27 . . . .**6** A1
St Edmund Cl **8** IP31 . . . .**34** B1
St Edmund Rd IP27 . . . . .**5** E4
St Edmund's Cl **1** IP21 . .**85** A5
St Edmund's Dr IP30 . . . .**50** F3
St Edmund's Hill CO10 . .**101** B7
St Edmund's Pl IP1 . . . . .**139** C8
St Edmund's Rd
  Felixstowe IP11 . . . .**152** E2
  Ipswich IP1 . . . .**139** B8
  Southwold IP18 . . . .**119** D6
St Edmunds Cl
  2 Beccles NR34 . . . . . .**111** C2
  12 Harwich CO12 . . . . .**107** A1
  Stowmarket IP14 . . . . . .**124** C8
  3 Woodbridge IP12 . . . .**146** E4
St Edmunds Cres **1**
NR33 . . . .**11** C1
St Edmunds Gate **11**
IP31 . . . .**33** D5
St Edmunds La CO8 . . . .**101** D5
St Edmunds Pl IP33 . . . .**154** B3
St Edmunds Prim Sch
IP21 . . . .**38** C6
St Edmunds RC Prim Sch
NR35 . . . .**110** B4
St Edmunds RC VA Prim Sch
IP33 . . . .**154** B1
St Edmunds Rd IP14 . . . .**124** C7
St Edmunds Sq **10** IP31 . .**33** D5
St Edmundsbury Cath *
IP33 . . . .**154** C2
St Edmundsbury CE VA Prim
Sch IP33 . . . .**154** B3
St Edmundsbury Mews
IP33 . . . .**154** B1
St Edmundsbury Ret Pk
IP32 . . . .**123** E4

St Etienne IP14 . . . .**69** B6
St Fabians Cl CB8 . . . . .**120** F5
St Fabians CE Sch CB8 . .**120** E5
St Felix CE VE Mid Sch
CB8 . . . .**120** F6
St Felix Cl **2** CB7 . . . .**28** D5
St Felix RC Prim Sch
CB9 . . . .**132** B5
St Felix St IP18 . . . .**119** A6
St George **1** CB8 . . . . . .**121** A4
St George's Ave **2**
CO12 . . . .**107** B3
St George's Rd
  Beccles NR34 . . . .**111** B4
  Felixstowe IP11 . . . .**153** C6
  Lowestoft NR33 . . . .**115** B4
  Stowlangtoft IP31 . . . . . .**50** B7
St George's St IP1 . . . . . .**155** B3
St Georges St **17** IP18 . .**119** A7
St Gotthards Ave IP12 . . . .**98** B8
St Gregory Ct CO10 . . . .**148** B6
St Gregorys CE VC Prim Sch
CO10 . . . .**148** B5
St Gregorys Cl **1** IP12 . . .**85** E8
St Helena Wlk IP28 . . . . .**116** C6
St Helen's St **1** IP28 . . . .**155** C3
St Helens Prim Sch
IP4 . . . .**139** E6
St Helens Way IP24 . . . . .**16** B7
St Isidores IP5 . . . .**141** E7
St Ives Cl IP5 . . . .**141** A6
St James **6** CB8 . . . .**121** A4
St James Cl **3** CB9 . . . . .**132** C6
St James' Gn **7** IP18 . . . .**119** D5
St James La IP33 . . . .**154** A2
St James' La
  Chediston IP19 . . . .**24** A3
  St James, South Elmham
  IP19 . . . .**23** F4
St James Mid Sch
IP33 . . . .**123** C7
St James Rd
  All Saints & St Nicholas,
  South Elmham IP19 . . . .**24** A4
  St James, South Elmham
  IP19 . . . .**23** F4
St James's St IP1 . . . .**43** B1
St John's Cl IP28 . . . . . .**116** D6
St John's Hill
  Bungay NR35 . . . .**110** C2
  4 Woodbridge IP12 . . . .**147** A5
St John's Pl IP33 . . . .**154** B3
St John's Rd
  Bungay NR35 . . . .**110** B3
  Ipswich IP4 . . . .**140** A7
  Lowestoft NR33 . . . .**115** D7
  Saxmundham IP17 . . . . .**128** C3
St John's St
  Beck Row, Holywell Row
  & Kenny Hill IP28 . . . . . .**30** C8
  Bury St Edmunds IP33 . .**154** B3
  Woodbridge IP12 . . . . . .**147** A5
St John's Terr **5** IP12 . . .**147** A5
St John's Way
  16 Feltwell IP26 . . . .**4** C5
  Thetford IP24 . . . .**16** A5
St Johns Ave CB8 . . . . . .**121** A1
St Johns CE Prim Sch
IP4 . . . .**140** A7
St Johns Ct IP11 . . . .**153** A4
St Johns Meadow IP2 . . .**139** A3
St Josephs Coll IP12 . . . .**139** A3
St Josephs RC Prim Sch
CO10 . . . .**148** B6
St Lawrence Cl NR34 . . .**111** C2
St Lawrence Gn IP5 . . . .**141** A7
St Lawrence Prim Sch
NR34 . . . .**24** F6
St Lawrence St IP1 . . . . .**155** B3
St Lawrence Way IP5 . . .**141** B6
St Leonard's Rd **1**
NR33 . . . .**115** C7
St Leonards Cl IP21 . . . . .**21** A1
St Leonards Hospl
CO10 . . . .**148** B5
St Leonards Rd **2** IP30 .**140** B3
St Leonards St IP26 . . . . . .**6** B1
St Louis Cath Mid Sch
IP33 . . . .**154** B1
St Louis RC Prim Sch
CB8 . . . .**121** A4
St Margaret's Cres
  Leiston IP16 . . . .**129** B6
  3 Thetford IP24 . . . .**16** B5
St Margaret's Gn IP4 . . .**155** C3
St Margaret's Pl CB8 . . . .**75** E7
St Margaret's Rd
  Bungay NR35 . . . .**110** B1
  3 Lowestoft NR32 . . . .**113** E3
St Margaret's St IP4 . . . .**155** C3
St Margaret's Way **3**
NR31 . . . .**3** B7
St Margarets CE VA Prim Sch
IP4 . . . .**155** C3
St Margarets Com Prim Sch
NR32 . . . .**113** C3
St Margarets Plain
IP4 . . . .**155** B3
St Marks RC Prim Sch
IP2 . . . .**138** F3
St Martin's Cl CB8 . . . . .**120** C7
St Martin's La IP24 . . . . . .**16** B2
St Martin's St IP33 . . . . .**154** B3
St Martin's Way IP33 . . . .**16** B5
St Martins Ct IP5 . . . .**141** E7
St Martins Gn **14** IP11 . .**107** D8
St Mary's Ave **13** IP14 . .**51** C1
St Mary's Cl **1** Bacton IP14 .**51** F6

St Mary's Cl continued
  Bramford IP8 . . . .**134** B1
  Felixstowe IP11 . . . .**152** B7
  Flixton NR35 . . . .**7** E1
  Harleston IP20 . . . .**22** E6
  Horham IP21 . . . .**38** F3
  Mildenhall IP28 . . . .**116** C3
  Sudbury CO10 . . . .**148** F8
St Mary's Cres
  Badwell Ash IP31 . . . . . .**50** E7
  Felixstowe IP11 . . . .**152** F9
St Mary's Gdns IP6 . . . .**125** E6
St Mary's Rd
  Aldeby NR34 . . . .**10** A7
  Beccles NR34 . . . .**111** A5
  Creeting St Mary IP6 . . .**125** E5
  Stowmarket IP14 . . . . . .**124** B7
St Mary's Sq IP33 . . . . . .**154** C1
St Mary's St **2** NR35 . . .**110** B4
St Mary's Wlk **2** CB9 . . .**88** D3
St Marys Cath Prim Sch
IP4 . . . .**139** F6
St Marys CE Aided Prim Sch
IP12 . . . .**146** E5
St Marys CE VA Prim Sch
IP28 . . . .**116** C5
St Marys Cl **1** IP23 . . . . .**36** D2
St Marys Pk IP10 . . . .**98** A4
St Marys Prim Sch
IP7 . . . .**149** E6
St Marys RC Prim Sch
NR33 . . . .**115** C5
St Marys Rd IP4 . . . .**139** F6
St Marys Sq **9** CB8 . . . .**121** A4
St Marys View IP31 . . . . .**49** E6
St Marys Way IP6 . . . . . .**135** F4
St Mathew's St Service Rd
IP1 . . . .**155** A3
St Matthew's Ave **3**
NR34 . . . .**111** C2
St Matthew's CE VA Prim Sch
IP1 . . . .**155** A3
St Matthew's St IP1 . . . .**155** A3
St Michael's Cl
  1 Beccles NR34 . . . . . .**111** C2
  Ipswich IP5 . . . .**141** A6
  Lowestoft NR32 . . . .**112** C1
St Michael's Rd **4** CO12 .**107** B1
St Michael's Way IP19 . . . .**42** C6
St Michaels CE VA Prim Sch
NR34 . . . .**9** B6
St Michaels Cl IP6 . . . . .**126** C4
St Michaels Ct **18** CO11 .**104** E2
St Nicholas Cl
  Bury St Edmunds IP32 . .**123** C4
  Rattlesden IP30 . . . .**65** D5
St Nicholas Ct IP1 . . . . .**155** B2
St Nicholas Dr **23** IP26 . . .**4** E5
St Nicholas St **1** IP1 . . .**155** B2
St Olaves Prec IP32 . . . .**122** D8
St Olaves Precinct
IP32 . . . .**122** E8
St Olaves Rd
  Bury St Edmunds IP32 . .**122** E8
  Herring Fleet NR32 . . . . . .**2** D4
  Ipswich IP5 . . . .**141** C8
St Osyth Cl IP2 . . . .**142** F8
St Pancras Cath Prim Sch
IP1 . . . .**134** F2
St Patrick **7** CB8 . . . . . .**121** A4
St Paul's Cl
  4 Beccles NR34 . . . . . .**111** C2
  Brockdish IP21 . . . .**21** F7
St Pauls Cl IP15 . . . .**130** E5
St Peter & Paul CE VA Prim
Sch IP23 . . . .**117** D2
St Peter's Ave **1** IP6 . . .**134** C4
St Peter's Brewery & Visitor
Ctr * NR35 . . . .**24** A8
St Peter's Cl
  Brockdish IP21 . . . .**21** F7
  8 Claydon IP6 . . . .**82** A5
  Stowmarket IP14 . . . . . .**124** B7
  Woodbridge IP12 . . . . . .**146** D4
St Peter's Ct **16** CO10 . .**148** C5
St Peter's Hall * NR35 . .**24** A8
St Peter's Rd
  Lowestoft NR33 . . . .**115** C6
  Stowmarket IP14 . . . . . .**124** B6
St Peter's St
  Ipswich IP1 . . . .**155** B2
  4 Lowestoft NR32 . . . .**113** D2
St Peter's Wlk IP26 . . . . . .**4** F3
St Peters Ave CB8 . . . . . .**45** F2
St Peters Cl
  Charsfield IP13 . . . .**70** B3
  6 Moulton CB8 . . . . . .**45** F3
St Peters Ct IP33 . . . . . .**154** B1
St Peters Path IP19 . . . . .**118** E4
St Peters Pl CB7 . . . .**29** B1
St Peters Rd
  Aldeburgh IP15 . . . .**130** E5
  Lowestoft NR33 . . . .**114** C3
St Peters Way **11** IP31 . .**49** E4
St Philips Rd CB8 . . . . . .**120** F5
St Quinton's Ct NR33 . . .**115** B5
St Stephens Ct IP33 . . . .**123** C6
St Stephens La IP1 . . . . .**155** B2
St Vincent Wlk **14** NR31 . .**3** B7
St Wendred's Way
CB8 . . . .**120** B7
Salehurst Rd IP3 . . . .**140** E3
Salisbury Ct **12** CB9 . . . .**132** D5
Salisbury Gn IP33 . . . . . .**123** B3
Salisbury Rd
  Ipswich IP3 . . . .**140** A3
  Lowestoft NR33 . . . .**115** C7
  1 Southwold IP18 . . . .**119** D5

Salisbury Terr **1** CO10 . .**148** C6
Sallows Cl IP1 . . . .**138** F7
Sally Wood's La IP6 . . . .**125** F6
Salmet Cl IP2 . . . .**139** A3
Salmon Wlk IP32 . . . . . .**122** D7
Salmond Dr **5** IP24 . . . . .**16** C2
Salter Cl IP32 . . . .**123** E4
Salters Gdns **4** IP13 . . . .**83** E5
Salters Hall Mews
CO10 . . . .**148** B5
Saltgate **5** NR34 . . . . . .**111** B6
Salthouse La IP4 . . . .**155** C2
Saltwater Way NR33 . . . .**114** E8
Samford Cl IP9 . . . .**105** E8
Samford Ct **5** NR34 . . . .**111** F4
Samford Pl IP8 . . . .**138** B6
Sampson Dr **5** CO10 . . . .**91** E8
Samson Cl **14** IP32 . . . . .**48** C5
Samson's La IP22 . . . .**19** F4
Samuel Cl IP4 . . . .**155** C3
Samuel St Wlk IP33 . . . .**123** A2
Samuel Vince Rd **2**
IP21 . . . .**39** D8
Samuel Ward Arts & Tech
Coll CB9 . . . .**132** F7
San Francisco Wlk **3**
NR33 . . . .**114** C5
Sancroft Way
  5 Fressingfield IP21 . . . .**39** D8
  Wortwell IP20 . . . .**23** A7
Sancroft Wlk IP33 . . . . . .**122** B6
Sanctuary Gdns **4**
NR32 . . . .**112** F5
Sanctuary The IP16 . . . . .**73** F6
Sanctuary Way **9** NR33 . .**11** B1
Sand Acre Cl IP28 . . . . . .**116** D5
Sand Hill CO10 . . . .**93** C3
Sand St IP7 . . . .**28** D3
Sandbank Rd **1** NR33 . .**114** E4
Sandbanks Ct IP7 . . . .**28** D3
Sanderling Cl **3** IP28 . . .**116** D4
Sanders Cl **2** NR32 . . . .**112** F4
Sandford Rd IP14 . . . .**52** A1
Sandgalls Rd IP27 . . . . . .**109** D6
Sandholme Cl IP33 . . . . .**123** B2
Sandhurst Ave IP3 . . . . . .**139** F4
Sandling Cres IP4 . . . . . .**140** E5
Sandlings Prim Sch
IP12 . . . .**85** C7
Sandlings The
  Aldeburgh IP15 . . . .**130** C6
  Ipswich IP3 . . . .**140** D1
Sandown Cl **3** IP1 . . . . .**135** A3
Sandown Rd IP1 . . . .**135** A3
Sandpath **5** IP21 . . . .**39** E8
Sandpiper Cl CB9 . . . . . .**133** A6
Sandpiper Rd
  Bury St Edmunds IP33 . .**123** C2
  Ipswich IP2 . . . .**138** E2
  1 Stowmarket IP14 . . . .**124** F7
Sandpit Cl IP4 . . . .**140** F5
Sandpit Dr **3** IP31 . . . . . .**49** E4
Sandpit Hill IP20 . . . .**23** B3
Sandpit La
  Thurston IP31 . . . .**49** E4
  Worlingham NR34 . . . .**9** F4
Sandringham Cl IP2 . . . .**138** F2
Sandringham Rd
NR32 . . . .**113** C1
Sands Cl **9** NR31 . . . .**3** D4
Sands La NR32 . . . .**112** D2
Sandy Cl **5** IP11 . . . .**107** D8
Sandy Dro IP28 . . . .**30** F3
Sandy Hill Barham IP6 . . .**82** B7
  Wormingford CO6 . . . . . .**101** E3
Sandy La Barham IP6 . . . .**82** A6
  Barningham IP31 . . . .**34** E8
  Barsham NR34 . . . .**9** A4
  2 Bromeswell IP12 . . . . .**85** A5
  Bulmer CO10 . . . .**91** D3
  Diss IP22 . . . .**20** D2
  Gisleham NR33 . . . .**11** A1
  Holton IP19 . . . .**118** E4
  Hoo IP13 . . . .**70** B4
  Iken IP12 . . . .**72** F2
  Little Bealings IP13 . . . . .**137** D4
  Marlesford IP13 . . . .**71** C5
  Rendham IP17 . . . .**56** F3
  Ringshall IP14 . . . .**80** D3
  St Mary, South Elmham
    otherwise Homersfield
    IP20 . . . .**23** B7
  Sternfield IP17 . . . .**72** C8
  Stowlangtoft IP31 . . . . . .**50** A7
  Sudbury CO10 . . . .**148** A4
  Sutton IP12 . . . .**99** B8
  Waldringfield IP12 . . . . . .**98** E8
  Westerfield IP6 . . . .**135** E5
  Wickham Market IP13 . . .**127** D5
  Witnesham IP6 . . . .**136** B8
  Woodbridge IP12 . . . . . .**146** D2
Sandyhill La IP3 . . . .**139** E1
Sapiston Rd IP31 . . . .**33** F5
Sapling Pl IP4 . . . .**140** F5
Saracens House Bsns Ctr
IP4 . . . .**155** C3
Sarah Ct CB9 . . . .**132** E3
Sarsen Cl IP19 . . . .**118** C4
Sascombe Vineyard *
CB8 . . . .**60** F2
Saturn Cl NR32 . . . .**113** D4
Sawmill La IP10 . . . .**145** B6
Sawmills Rd IP22 . . . .**20** E2
Sawston Cl **10** IP2 . . . . .**139** A2
Sawyers IP7 . . . .**80** F1
Sawyers Cl IP9 . . . .**150** E2
Saxham Bsns Pk IP29 . . . .**47** E4

Saxmundham Mid Sch
IP17 . . . .**128** C2
Saxmundham Mus *
IP17 . . . .**128** D3
Saxmundham Prim Sch
IP17 . . . .**128** C3
Saxmundham Rd
  Aldeburgh IP15 . . . .**130** C5
  Framlingham IP13 . . . . .**126** E3
  Friston IP17 . . . .**72** F7
  Knodishall IP17 . . . .**57** F1
  Theberton IP16 . . . .**58** A2
Saxmundham Sports Club
IP17 . . . .**128** C4
Saxmundham Sta
IP17 . . . .**128** C3
Saxon Cl Exning CB8 . . .**120** D8
  11 Felixstowe IP11 . . . .**153** D6
Saxon Cres **7** IP31 . . . . . .**33** D5
Saxon Dr **9** CB5 . . . .**44** A5
Saxon La IP8 . . . .**95** E4
Saxon Pl **1** Thetford IP24 .**16** B5
  Weeting IP27 . . . .**5** E3
Saxon Rd
  Lowestoft NR33 . . . .**115** B3
  Saxmundham IP17 . . . . .**128** B3
Saxon Rise IP33 . . . .**122** E3
Saxon St Rd CB8 . . . .**60** E6
Saxon Way IP12 . . . .**147** A7
Saxon Wlk IP26 . . . .**6** A8
Saxonfields IP17 . . . .**72** D5
Saxons Way IP19 . . . . . .**118** B4
Saxstead Gn Postmill *
IP13 . . . .**55** B3
Saxtead Rd
  Dennington IP13 . . . .**55** D5
  Framlingham IP13 . . . . .**126** A5
Scales St NR35 . . . .**110** A4
Scalesbrook La IP19 . . . .**118** E7
Scaltback Cl CB8 . . . . . .**120** E6
Scaltback Mid Sch
CB8 . . . .**120** E5
Scama La IP22 . . . .**36** C6
Scarlin Rd IP33 . . . .**122** C3
Schneider Rd **3** IP11 . . .**153** H11
Scholars Wlk IP22 . . . . . .**20** C3
School Ave IP30 . . . .**50** E2
School Cl
  1 Capel St Mary IP9 . . .**150** E3
  Cheveley CB8 . . . .**60** E8
  Hadleigh IP7 . . . .**149** B6
  Kenninghall NR16 . . . . . .**19** A8
  North Cove NR34 . . . .**10** C4
  Norton IP31 . . . .**50** B4
  20 Stanton IP31 . . . .**34** E4
School Cres CB9 . . . .**133** E8
School Farm La CO10 . . . .**78** C2
School Hill
  Boxford CO10 . . . .**93** C3
  Copdock & Washbrook
    IP8 . . . .**95** F4
  Kettleburgh IP13 . . . .**70** C7
  Nacton IP10 . . . .**145** B4
School La
  Bardwell IP31 . . . .**34** C4
  Bawdsey IP12 . . . .**99** E2
  Benhall IP17 . . . .**72** C8
  5 Brantham CO11 . . . .**104** E5
  16 Burwell CB5 . . . .**44** A5
  Dedham CO7 . . . .**103** F4
  East Bergholt CO7 . . . . .**151** B5
  Easton IP13 . . . .**70** E5
  Fornham St Martin IP31 . .**48** D4
  Great Barton IP31 . . . . . .**49** B6
  Great Horkesley CO6 . . .**102** C3
  Halesworth IP19 . . . .**118** A4
  17 Harleston IP20 . . . . . .**22** C6
  Haverhill CB9 . . . .**132** B5
  Hollesley IP12 . . . .**99** F7
  Little Horkesley CO6 . . . .**102** B3
  Long Melford CO10 . . . . .**77** E1
  Manningtree CO11 . . . . .**104** D1
  Martlesham IP12 . . . . . .**146** C1
  Metfield IP20 . . . .**23** C3
  4 Mistley CO11 . . . . . .**104** F2
  Reydon IP18 . . . .**26** E1
  Stratford St Mary CO7 . .**103** E5
  Thelnetham IP22 . . . .**18** E1
  7 Thurston IP31 . . . .**49** E4
  Ufford IP13 . . . .**84** F7
School Meadow
  1 Stowmarket IP14 . . . .**124** E3
  4 Wetherden IP14 . . . . .**51** A1
School Rd Alburgh IP20 . . . .**7** A1
  Bedingham NR35 . . . .**7** B7
  Blaxhall IP12 . . . .**72** A3
  Bressingham IP22 . . . .**19** E4
  Coddenham IP6 . . . .**68** B1
  Coldfair Green IP17 . . . . .**129** A3
  Earsham NR35 . . . .**7** F4
  Elmswell IP30 . . . .**50** E2
  Great Ashfield IP31 . . . . . .**50** F6
  Great Barton IP31 . . . . . .**49** B6
  Great Wratting CB9 . . . . .**74** F3
  Hinderclay IP22 . . . .**35** C2
  Hollesley IP12 . . . .**99** F7
  Kedington CB9 . . . .**133** E8
  Kirby Cane NR35 . . . .**8** E8
  Knodishall IP17 . . . .**73** A8
  Langham CO4 . . . .**103** D4
  Little Horkesley CO6 . . . .**102** B2
  Little Yeldham CO9 . . . . . .**90** B2
  Lowestoft NR33 . . . .**114** F8
  Monk Soham IP13 . . . . . .**54** D4
  Pentlow CO10 . . . .**90** F7
  Ringsfield NR34 . . . .**9** D1
  Risby IP28 . . . .**47** E5
  St Andrew, Ilketshall
    NR34 . . . .**8** E2

School Rd continued
9 Shotley Gate IP9 ......107 A4
Sudbourne IP12 ....87 A8
Tattingstone IP9 ....142 D1
Thurstow IP31 ....49 E4
Tunstall IP12 ....71 F2
Waldringfield IP12 ......98 D7
Woodditton CB8 ....60 D6
School St Foxearth CO10 .91 B7
Needham Market IP6 ....125 D4
Stoke-by-Nayland CO6 ..102 E7
Sudbury CO10 ....148 C5
School View NR34 ......24 F5
Schoolhall La IP33 ...154 B3
Schreiber Rd IP4 .....140 B7
Scofield Ct CO10 .....148 E4
Scole Comm IP21 ....20 F3
Scole Comm Rd IP21 ....21 A2
Scole Prim Sch IP21 ...21 A2
Scole Rd IP21 ....21 F2
Sconch Beck Rd IP20 ..23 A4
Scopes Rd IP5 ....141 C8
Scotland End CB7 ......29 E1
Scotland St CO6 ......103 A7
Scott Ave CO10 ....116 C5
Scott La 2 IP12 ....84 E6
Scott Rd Ipswich IP3 .140 B1
13 Ixworth IP31 ....34 B1
Scott's Hill IP14 .....68 B6
Scott's La IP13 ....84 C7
Scotts Cl 14 NR33 .....11 B1
Scrivener Dr IP8 .....138 B2
Scudamore Pl NR35 ....110 B7
Scuffin's La IP14 .....52 A6
Sea Lake Rd NR32 .....114 E8
Sea Rd IP11 ....152 F2
Sea View NR33 ....11 C1
Sea View Rise NR31 .....3 C6
Sea View Wlk NR33 ....115 B4
Seabreeze Rd IP14 ....124 D5
Seafield Ave 5 CO10 ..105 A2
Seafield Rd 6 CO12 ...107 A1
Seafields Dr 3 NR31 ...3 B6
Seago St NR32 ....113 D1
Sealodes Rd CB7 ....28 A5
Seaman Ave IP17 ......128 B2
Seaton Cl 18 CO11 ....104 D2
Seaton Rd IP11 ....152 E5
Seavert Cl 3 NR33 ....114 E3
Seaview Rd IP18 ....119 C7
Seaward Ave 2 IP16 ...129 D5
Sebert Rd IP32 ....123 E5
Sebert Wood Cty Prim Sch
IP32 ....123 D5
Seckford Almshouses
IP12 ....146 F5
Seckford Cl 1 IP4 ....140 F5
Seckford Hall Rd
IP12 ....146 D3
Seckford St IP12 .....146 F5
Second Ave
Felixstowe IP11 ....152 B7
2 Glemsford CO10 ....77 B3
Sudbury CO10 ....148 E2
Second Dro IP27 ....13 C7
Sedan Wlk IP1 ....155 A2
Sedge Way IP3 ....154 A4
Sedgefen Rd IP27 ......12 F7
Sedlescombe Rd 8
NR33 ....114 D5
Sefton Way CB8 ....120 D5
Selby St NR32 ....113 C1
Self's La IP22 ....18 F3
Selkirk Rd IP4 ....136 C1
Selvale Way IP11 .....152 E4
Selwyn Cl Ipswich IP2 .155 B1
Mildenhall IP28 ....116 C6
Newmarket CB8 ....121 A1
Semer Cl IP14 ....124 E3
Semere Gn La IP21 .....21 D6
Semere La IP21 ....21 D8
Sergeants Wlk IP33 ...154 B3
Serpentine Rd IP3 ....140 B2
Seven Acres NR33 .....115 C4
Seven Cotts La IP5 ...136 C1
Seven Gdns Rd IP13 ....83 F6
Seven Hills (Barrow
Cemetery)★
Brettenham IP24 ....16 F4
Little Livermere IP31 ...33 A4
Sevenhills La IP31 ....33 A4
Several Rd IP13 ....55 B3
Severalls La IP13 .....55 D6
Severals The CB8 .....121 B4
Severn Rd
Bury St Edmunds IP32 ...48 C5
Ipswich IP3 ....139 F3
Sewell Wontner Cl
IP5 ....141 D8
Sewell's La CO10 ......90 D5
Sewells IP7 ....79 E6
Sewells The IP33 .....123 A2
Sexton Rd NR35 ....7 D6
Sextons Manor Prim Sch
IP33 ....122 C6
Sextons Mdw IP33 .....123 B3
Sextons Meadow IP33 ..123 B3
Sextons Mews IP33 ....154 C1
Seymore Dr CB9 ....132 B5
Seymour Ave IP27 ......14 D8
Seymour Cl CB8 ....121 C4
Seymour Rd IP2 ....155 B1
Shackleton Cl 20 CO12 .140 E3
Shackleton Rd IP3 ....140 E3
Shackleton Sq 3 IP3 ..140 E3
Shaddick Rd IP18 .....119 B8
Shade The CB7 ....28 C5

Shadingfield Cl NR33 .113 A5
Shadowbush Cl CB9 ....132 D7
Shadwell Cl IP27 ....5 E3
Shadwell Wlk IP33 ....122 B6
Shaftesbury Ave 4
CO12 ....107 A2
Shaftesbury Sq IP4 ...155 C2
Shafto Rd IP14 ....134 E1
Shaker's La IP33 .....123 C5
Shaker's Rd IP29 ......47 B4
Shakers' Rd
Brandon IP27 ....15 A5
Wangford IP27 ....14 E4
Shakespeare Rd
Ipswich IP1 ....134 E3
Stowmarket IP14 ....124 B8
Shamrock Ave IP2 .....138 E4
Shannon Cl CB9 ....133 B5
Shannon Rd 4 IP3 .....144 A8
Shardlow Cl CB9 ......132 A7
Sharman's Rd CB7 ......29 A1
Sharon Dr NR32 ....113 B3
Sharon Rd IP33 ....122 D5
Sharp Rd IP33 ....122 F2
Sharp's Gn 11 IP29 ....63 A8
Sharpe's Hill IP29 ....47 B2
Sharpe's La IP29 ......63 A7
Sharpe's Row IP30 .....65 E8
Sharper's Cnr IP27 ...109 B8
Sharpes Cnr IP27 .....109 C7
Shaw Ave NR33 ....114 D3
Shaw Rd CO10 ....91 E8
Shaw Valley Rd 7 IP3 ..84 A1
Shawlands Ave CO10 ...148 F5
Shawsgate Vineyard★
........................126 F6
Shearman Rd IP7 ......149 F5
Sheepdrift Rd IP12 ....85 B5
Sheepgate NR34 ....111 B5
Sheepgate La
Badwell Ash IP31 ....51 B4
Falkenham IP10 ....98 F1
Sheepshead Hill 2 CO10 92 B3
Sheepwash La IP17 .....58 E6
Sheerwater 9 IP14 .....67 A5
Sheerwater Cl IP30 ...123 F6
Shelbourne Cl 7 IP5 ..141 D7
Sheldrake Dr IP2 .....138 E1
Sheldrick's Rd CB7 ....29 D5
Shelley Ave CO10 .....148 F4
Shelley Cl IP14 ......124 F3
Shelley Rd
3 Bury St Edmunds IP32 ..48 C5
Layham IP7 ....149 E1
Shelley St IP2 ....155 B1
Shelley Way
Bacton IP14 ....51 E5
Thetford IP24 ....16 C7
Shelterhouse Cnr IP24 .32 C8
Shelton Hill IP21 .....39 B5
Shelton Rd 4 NR33 ....114 F3
Shenley Rd IP3 ....140 B1
Shenstone Dr IP1 .....135 A3
Shepherd Dr IP8 ......138 C2
Shepherds Cl IP3 .....132 C5
Shepherds Dr 1 IP29 ...63 D1
Shepherds Gr Ind Est
IP22 ....35 B4
Shepherds La
Burgate IP22 ....36 D7
Glemsford CO10 ....77 A3
Onehouse IP14 ....124 A8
Sheppards Way 6 IP5 ..141 D7
Sherborne Ave IP4 ....136 A2
Sherborne Rd IP33 ....122 D3
Sherbourne St CO10 ....93 B4
Sheridan Cl IP14 .....124 A8
Sheridan Wlk NR34 ....111 E4
Sheriffs Ct CB8 ....59 F2
Sherrington Rd IP1 ...139 A8
Sherwood Fields 4 IP5 141 C7
Shetland Cl
5 Ipswich IP4 ....136 A1
Ipswich IP4 ....140 A8
Shetland Rd CB9 ......133 B5
Shetlands 13 IP31 ......34 E4
Shickle Pl IP22 ....18 C2
Shilling St 14 CO10 ....78 D4
Shillitoe Cl IP33 ....154 A2
Shimpling Cl 7 IP14 ..124 E3
Shimpling Rd IP21 .....21 B5
Shingle Hill IP21 .....38 C4
Ship Gdns IP28 ....116 B3
Ship La Bradfield CO11 105 C2
Bramford IP8 ....134 B1
Ship Launch Rd IP3 ...139 E3
Ship Rd NR33 ....115 A3
Shippea Hill Sta CB7 ...12 C7
Shire Ct 11 CB9 ......132 C5
Shire Hall Yd IP4 ....155 C2
Shires The NR32 ......113 B4
Shirley Cl 9 IP1 .....135 A3
Shoals Wlk NR33 ......114 E6
Shoe Devil La NR35 ....24 C3
Shoebridge's Hill CO7 .103 F3
Shop Hill CB8 ....61 D1
Shop La IP13 ....71 E5
Shop Rd IP13 ....69 E1
Shop St IP13 ....54 D7
Shore La
Bradfield CO11 ....105 C2
Harkstead IP9 ....106 A5
Nacton IP10 ....145 B3
Shores Ct IP28 ....29 E2
Short Beck 19 IP26 .....4 E5
Short Brackland IP33 ..154 B2
Short La Feltwell IP26 ..4 D5
Lowestoft NR33 ....114 C2

Short La continued
Walberswick IP18 ....43 C5
Short Rd
Belton with Browston NR31 .2 D1
Blundeston NR32 ....3 A4
Snailwell CB8 ....45 A5
Short St 2 NR33 ......115 B4
Shortlands IP33 ......138 D1
Shotford Rd IP20 ......22 D5
Shotley Cl
Felixstowe IP11 ....152 D4
Ipswich IP8 ....138 C2
Shotley Mews 8 IP12 ...85 B3
Shotley Prim Sch IP9 ..106 F5
Shotley Wlk IP9 ......106 E7
Shrimpling Rd IP29 ....77 C6
Shrub House Cl 1 IP28 .30 B8
Shrubberies The CB8 ..121 D1
Shrubbery Cl IP11 ....152 F4
Shrubbery Rd IP13 ....146 B7
Shrubland Ave IP1 ....134 E1
Shrubland Dr IP4 .....140 F5
Shrubland Pk Gdns★
IP6 ....82 A6
Shrubland Rd 11 CO11 .105 A2
Shrublands IP28 ......116 C4
Siam Pl 4 CO10 ....148 C5
Siamhall La CO10 ......92 F3
Sicklesmere Rd
Bury St Edmunds IP33 ..123 D2
Nowton IP30 ....63 E8
Sidegate Ave IP4 .....140 A8
Sidegate La IP4 ......136 A1
Sidegate La W IP4 ....135 F1
Sidegate Prim Sch
IP4 ....140 A8
Sidegate Rd NR31 ....3 A8
Siding Rd NR34 ....10 C5
Silent St IP4 ....155 B2
Silhalls Cl 7 CB8 .....60 F8
Silk Mill Cl IP7 .....149 D5
Silver Dr IP15 ....130 C6
Silver Hill IP8 ....95 D6
Silver Leys IP9 ......104 F7
Silver St Burwell CB5 ..44 A6
Kedington CB9 ....133 F7
Old Newton with Dagworth
IP14 ....51 E2
South Lopham IP22 ......19 C3
Withersfield CB9 ....74 A2
Silverdale Ave IP14 ..124 C7
Silverdale Cl IP1 ....135 A1
Silverley Way 6 CB8 ...60 F8
Sim's La CB9 ....133 F7
Simon's Cross IP13 ...127 B7
Simons Rd IP12 ....147 A7
Simpers Drift IP17 ....56 D1
Simpson Cl IP3 ....139 F1
Sinclair Dr IP2 ......139 C3
Singleton Ct CO10 ....148 E3
Sir Alf Ramsey Way
IP4 ....155 A4
Sir John Leman High Sch
NR34 ....111 A4
Sir John Leman Rd
NR34 ....111 D2
Sir Robert Hitcham CE VA
Prim Sch IP14 ....53 E2
Sir Robert Hitchams CE VAP
Sch IP12 ....84 A6
Sirdar Rd IP1 ....139 A6
Siskin Gn 1 NR33 .....114 F3
Sitwell Cl 12 CO11 ...104 D2
Sitwell Rd 3 IP33 ....126 C3
Sizewell Belts Nature
Reserve★ IP16 ....58 E2
Sizewell Gap IP16 .....58 F1
Sizewell Power Sta
IP16 ....58 F2
Sizewell Rd IP16 .....129 D5
Sizewell Visitor Ctr★
IP16 ....58 F2
Skamacre Cres NR32 ...113 B2
Skate's Hill CO10 .....77 A2
Skeaping Cl CB8 ......121 A5
Skelton Cl 9 CO11 ....104 E2
Skelton Rd IP22 ....20 D2
Skelton's Dro IP28 ....13 A2
Skilman Hill IP18 ....119 D4
Skinner St IP33 ......154 B2
Skinner's La
Metfield IP20 ....23 C3
Starston IP20 ....22 B8
Skipper Cl IP8 ....142 E8
Skipper Rd IP2 ....138 D1
Skipper's La CB9 ......74 A3
Skoulding Cl 11 NR33 .114 F7
Sky Hall Hill CO4 ....103 B4
Skylark Cl IP32 ....49 A4
Skylark La IP8 ....138 C2
Slade Cl IP22 ....19 E2
Slade St IP4 ....155 C2
Slade The IP6 ....134 D8
Slades Cl 7 CO10 ......77 B3
Slaters Dr CB9 ....132 C8
Slaughden Rd IP15 ....130 E2
Sleaford Cl IP2 ......139 A3
Sloe La IP17 ....129 A2
Slough Hill IP29 ......77 E7
Slough Rd
Botesdale IP22 ....36 C5
Brantham CO11 ....104 E5
Slugs La NR32 ....2 C4
Sluice Dro IP26 ....4 E3
Slushy La IP9 ....106 A6

Smaley La 1 CO10 ......91 E8
Smallbridge Entry
CO8 ....101 E4
Smallbridge Hall★
CO8 ....101 E4
Smallworth La IP22 ....18 E3
Smart St IP4 ....155 C2
Smear La IP18 ....26 D2
Smear La E IP18 ....26 F1
Smeetham Hall La
CO10 ....91 C3
Smith Cres 17 NR33 ....11 B1
Smith Wlk IP33 ....123 D2
Smith's Wlk NR33 .....114 C6
Smithbrook La IP29 ....77 A8
Smithers Cl 9 IP9 ....150 E3
Smithfield IP12 ......147 B6
Smiths Cl IP14 ....54 E7
Smiths Dr IP21 ....21 B5
Smiths Pl 9 IP5 ......141 D7
Smithy Cl
Bradfield Combust with
Stanningfield IP29 .....64 A3
Rushbrooke with Rougham
IP30 ....64 D8
Smock Meadow 8 IP7 ...79 F4
Snab Hill NR33 ....11 A1
Snailwell Rd
Fordham CB8 ....44 F7
Newmarket CB8 ....121 B7
Snailwell Short Rd CB8 .44 F5
Snake's La Lound NR32 ..2 F6
Topcroft NR35 ....7 A8
Snape Com Prim Sch
IP17 ....72 D5
Snape Dr NR32 ....113 A4
Snape Hill IP22 ....35 F6
Snape Maltings★ IP17 ...72 F6
Snape Rd Friston IP17 .129 A2
Sudbourne IP12 ....131 A7
Tunstall IP12 ....72 A7
Snare Dro IP28 ....12 E3
Snipe Farm Rd IP13 ....69 E1
Snow Hill CO10 ....76 A1
Snow Hill La CO6 .....103 B7
Snowberry Way 6 CB7 ..28 D5
Snowcroft IP9 ....150 E3
Snowdon Cl 7 CB9 ....132 C4
Snowdon Hill IP33 ....127 C6
Snowdon Rd IP2 ....139 B2
Snowdrop Cl IP32 .....123 F5
Soames Cl IP14 ....124 C7
Soane St IP4 ....155 C3
Soft Rd CO10 ....90 F3
Soham Cl CB7 ....28 A8
Soham Town Cnr IP13 ...54 F3
Solace Cl NR35 ....35 D3
Solomon Rd 10 NR33 ...11 C1
Somerleyton Hall & Gdns★
NR32 ....2 E4
Somerleyton Prim Sch
NR32 ....2 D4
Somerset Ct 12 CB9 ...132 C5
Somerset Rd IP4 ......139 F8
Somersham Prim Sch
IP8 ....81 C3
Somersham Rd IP8 ......81 F2
Somerton Ave NR32 ....113 C3
Somerton Rd IP27 ......77 A8
Somerville Lea 2 IP15 .130 C5
Sorrel Cl IP2 ....138 F3
Sorrel Wlk CB9 ....132 B7
Sorrell Gn IP14 ....51 D6
Sorrell Wlk IP5 ......141 F7
Sotterley Cl 7 NR32 ..113 A6
Sotterley Rd
6 Lowestoft NR32 ......112 F4
Sotterley NR34 ....10 C1
Willingham St Mary NR34 .25 F7
Sound The NR34 ....114 E5
South Cl Beccles NR34 .111 A3
Bury St Edmunds IP33 ..154 A1
Ipswich IP4 ....139 E8
Leiston IP16 ....129 D5
9 Melton IP12 ....84 E6
South Coast National Nature
Reserve★ IP17 ....43 B4
South Dr IP33 ....120 C4
South Elham Hall★
IP20 ....23 A4
South Elmham Terr
NR33 ....114 E8
South Entrance IP17 ..128 D2
South Gn IP19 ....119 D4
South Hill IP17 ......152 F3
South Lee Sch IP33 ....123 C2
South Leet Cl 4 NR32 .112 E4
South Lodge Dr 1 IP28 .48 C6
South Lowestoft Ind Est
NR33 ....114 E4
South Pk IP27 ....5 E3
South Rd Beccles NR34 .111 A3
Lakenheath IP27 ....109 E3
South St
Hockwold cum Wilton IP26 .4 F2
Ipswich IP1 ....155 A4
12 Manningtree CO11 ...104 E2
Risby IP28 ....47 D4
South Strand 1 CO11 ..104 E2
South View Cl 3 NR32 .113 B2
South View Gn IP17 ...128 D2
Southend Rd 4 NR35 ..110 B3
Southern Belle Cl
IP32 ....123 F7
Southern La IP22 ......19 A1

Southery Rd IP26 ....4 B6
Southfield Dr IP16 ...129 C5
Southfield Gdns NR33 .114 F6
Southfields CO7 ......103 F3
Southfields Cl CB8 ...120 E4
Southgate 12 IP20 .....22 D5
Southgate Ave IP28 ...116 B7
Southgate Gdns
Bury St Edmunds IP33 ..123 C3
3 Long Melford CO10 ....91 E7
Southgate Rd IP8 .....138 B1
Southgate St
Bury St Edmunds IP33 ..154 C1
4 Long Melford CO10 ....91 E7
Southolt Rd
Athelington IP21 ....38 F1
Bedfield IP13 ....54 D6
Southwell La NR34 .....26 A6
Southwell Rd IP33 ....115 B7
Southwold & District Hospl
IP18 ....119 D6
Southwold Lighthouse★
IP18 ....119 D5
Southwold Maze★
IP18 ....43 C7
Southwold Mus★
IP18 ....119 D5
Southwold Pier★
IP18 ....119 E6
Southwold Prim Sch
IP18 ....119 D5
Southwold Rd
Blyford IP19 ....42 B8
Brampton with Stoven
NR34 ....25 E5
Holton IP19 ....118 F3
Wrentham NR34 ....26 E5
Southwold Sailors Reading
Rm★ IP18 ....119 D5
Southwood Cl IP17 ....128 D2
Spalding's Chair Hill
IP17 ....17 B3
Spanbies Rd 3 CO7 ....103 E5
Sparhawk St IP33 .....154 C1
Sparkes Cl 5 CB7 ......29 C5
Sparks La CO9 ....89 D3
Sparrow Ct 11 IP14 ....53 F2
Sparrow Rd CO10 ......148 C5
Sparrowhawk Rd
IP19 ....118 C7
Sparrows Croft Rd 5
IP12 ....85 E8
Spartan Cl 3 CB9 .....132 A6
Spashett Rd 2 NR32 ..113 B4
Speckled Wood Cl
IP6 ....142 D8
Speed La CB7 ....28 D4
Speedwell Cl 7 NR33 .115 A3
Speedwell Rd IP2 .....138 F2
Speedwell Way 18 IP20 .22 D5
Spencer Dr NR32 ......113 B6
Spencer Dro CB7 ....28 C4
Spencer Rd 4 IP12 .....85 E8
Spencer Way IP14 .....124 B7
Spenser Rd IP1 ....134 E3
Sperling Dr CB9 ......132 C8
Spexhall Way NR32 ....113 B5
Spicers La 2 CO10 .....91 E8
Spiers Way 1 IP22 .....20 B2
Spike's La IP14 ....66 E7
Spindle Rd CB9 ....132 B7
Spindler Cl IP5 ....141 D7
Spinks' La NR35 ....7 D6
Spinnel's Hill CO11 ..105 D1
Spinnel's La CO11 ....105 E1
Spinner Cl IP1 ....138 D8
Spinners La 3 IP18 ...119 D5
Spinney Cl NR34 ....10 B4
Spinney Gdns NR33 ....114 C4
Spinney Hill IP7 ....81 A1
Spinney Rd IP31 ....33 B3
Spinney The
Beccles NR34 ....111 D4
Ipswich IP4 ....140 F4
Spinning Cl IP17 .....128 D5
Spire Chase CO10 .....148 E8
Spirkett's La IP20 .....22 D5
Spitfire Cl IP3 ....140 B1
Spong Cl IP30 ....50 E2
Spong The IP20 ....23 C3
Spooner's La NR34 .....26 A1
Spooners Cl CB8 ....59 F4
Spooners La 5 IP7 ....149 D6
Spout La CO10 ....101 B8
Spring Cl
3 Bentwaters Airfield
IP12 ....85 E8
Burwell CB5 ....44 A5
Spring La
Bury St Edmunds IP33 ..154 A3
Crowfield IP6 ....68 B3
Dennington IP13 ....55 B5
5 Lavenham CO10 ....78 D4
Polstead CO6 ....93 D2
Ufford IP13 ....127 B1
Wickham Market IP13 ...127 D7
Spring Meadow
10 Glemsford CO10 ......77 A3
Playford IP6 ....137 B4
Spring Pk IP6 ....69 C2
Spring Rd Bardwell IP31 .34 C3
Copdock & Washbrook
IP8 ....95 E5
Ipswich IP4 ....139 F6
Spring Row IP14 ......124 D7

Spring St **6** CO10 . . . . . .78 D4
Spring Wood Nature
Reserve★ IP9 . . . . .142 E7
Springbank Ave **16**
CO11 . . . . .104 D2
Springett's Hill CO8 . . . .101 B5
Springfield IP18 . . . . .119 A7
Springfield Ave
Bury St Edmunds IP33 . . . .154 A3
Felixstowe IP11 . . . . .153 A5
Springfield Dr IP27 . . . . .109 D6
Springfield Gdns
NR33 . . . . .114 F5
Springfield Inf Sch
IP1 . . . . .138 F8
Springfield Jun Sch
IP1 . . . . .138 F8
Springfield La IP1 . . . . . .138 F8
Springfield Rd
Aldeburgh IP15 . . . . .130 C5
Bury St Edmunds IP33 . . . .154 A3
4 Somersham IP8 . . . . . .81 C3
Sudbury CO10 . . . . .148 C7
Springhurst Cl IP4 . . . . . .139 F6
Springland Cl IP4 . . . . . .140 A6
Springlands Way
CO10 . . . . .148 D8
Springtail Rd IP8 . . . . . . .142 E8
Sprites End IP11 . . . . . . .152 D7
Sprites La IP2 . . . . .138 C1
Sprites Prim Sch IP2 . . . .138 C2
Spriteshall La IP11 . . . . . .152 D7
Sproughton Bsns Pk
IP1 . . . . .138 D7
Sproughton CE Prim Sch
IP8 . . . . .138 B6
Sproughton Cl IP8 . . . . . .138 A6
Sproughton Rd IP1 . . . . . .138 C7
Spruce Cl **14** IP27 . . . . . .13 F2
Spruce Ct NR32 . . . . . . .113 C3
Spruce Dr IP27 . . . . .5 F1
Spur End IP12 . . . . .147 C7
Spurgeon Score **12**
NR32 . . . . .113 E2
Spurling Cl **2** CB8 . . . . . .60 E7
Square The IP2 . . . . .124 E4
Squires Ct **21** CB9 . . . . . .132 C5
Squires La **4** IP5 . . . . . . .98 A8
Squires Wlk NR32 . . . . . .113 C5
Squirrels Mill Rd **3** IP7 . .79 F4
Squirrels The IP9 . . . . . . .150 E4
Stackwood Rd CO6 . . . . . .93 F3
Stafford Cl NR32 . . . . . . .112 E4
Staithe Cl **4** NR35 . . . . . .110 B4
Staithe Rd
Bungay NR35 . . . . .110 B4
Burgh St Peter NR34 . . . . .10 C7
Staithe The NR33 . . . . . .114 E6
Stambourne Rd CO9 . . . . .89 E2
Stamford Cl IP2 . . . . .142 F8
Stamford Ct **3** IP33 . . . . .122 F3
Stamford St CB8 . . . . . . .121 B2
Stammers Pl IP5 . . . . . . .141 E8
Stanford St **3** NR32 . . . . .113 C1
Stanhope Cl IP17 . . . . . . .72 D5
Stanley Ave IP3 . . . . .140 A4
Stanley Drapkin Prim Sch **8**
CB9 . . . . .88 D3
Stanley Rd Diss IP22 . . . . .20 B2
Felixstowe IP11 . . . . .153 A3
Lowestoft NR33 . . . . .114 E7
Newmarket CB8 . . . . .121 C3
Sudbury CO10 . . . . .148 C6
Stanley St NR32 . . . . . . .113 D1
Stanley Wood Ave
CO10 . . . . .148 D7
Stannard Way CO10 . . . . .148 E4
Stanningfield Rd IP30 . . . .63 F5
Stansfield Cl NR33 . . . . . .114 E6
Stanton Cl
Beccles NR34 . . . . .111 C3
Lowestoft NR32 . . . . .113 C5
Stanton Com Prim Sch
IP31 . . . . .34 E4
Stanton Hughes Way **10**
CO11 . . . . .104 D2
Stanton Pl **12** CB9★ 132 F6
Stanton Postmill★
IP31 . . . . .34 F4
Stanton Rd IP31 . . . . .34 C4
Stanway Cl CO10 . . . . . . .77 B3
Staple Cl IP31 . . . . .35 C1
Staplehurst Cl **7** NR33 . .114 C4
Staples La CB7 . . . . .28 D3
Star And Garter La CB8 . . .60 E8
Star La IP4 . . . . .155 C2
Starfield Cl IP4 . . . . .140 B6
Starhouse La IP14 . . . . . . .66 C5
Starre Rd IP33 . . . . .122 C5
Starston La IP20 . . . . .22 C5
Station App
Newmarket CB8 . . . . .121 A2
Saxmundham IP17 . . . . . .128 D3
Station Gate CB5 . . . . . . .44 A4
Station Hill
1 Bures CO8 . . . . .101 C4
Bury St Edmunds IP33 . . . .154 B4
Harleston IP20 . . . . .22 D6
Little Whelnetham IP30 . . . .64 B4
Thurstow IP31 . . . . .49 D4
Station La IP14 . . . . .107 B2
Station Rd Alburgh IP20 . . . .7 A1
Bacton IP14 . . . . .52 A6
Barnham IP24 . . . . .16 B2
Beccles NR34 . . . . .111 B5

Station Rd continued
Bentley IP9 . . . . .104 E7
Birdbrook CO9 . . . . .89 B4
Blaxhall IP12 . . . . .71 E3
Bradfield CO11 . . . . .105 B2
Brampton with Stoven
NR34 . . . . .25 C5
Burston & Shimpling IP21 . .20 F6
Clare CO10 . . . . .90 B8
Claydon IP6 . . . . .134 B8
8 Corton NR32 . . . . .3 D4
Corton NR32 . . . . .113 C8
Diss IP22 . . . . .20 D2
Ditchingham NR35 . . . . . .110 C6
Dullingham CB8 . . . . .59 E5
2 Earsham NR35 . . . . . . .7 F4
Ellingham NR35 . . . . .8 D7
Elmswell IP30 . . . . .50 F2
Felixstowe IP11 . . . . .152 C7
Fordham CB7 . . . . .29 A1
Framlingham IP13 . . . . . . .126 C2
Geldeston NR34 . . . . .8 F6
Haddiscoe NR31 . . . . .2 A5
Hadleigh IP7 . . . . .149 E5
Halesworth IP19 . . . . .118 B4
Harleston IP20 . . . . .22 D6
1 Harwich CO12 . . . . . .106 F3
Haughley IP14 . . . . .51 D1
4 Haverhill CB9 . . . . . . .132 E6
Hopton on Sea NR31 . . . . . .3 B6
Isleham CB7 . . . . .29 C4
Kennett CB8 . . . . .45 F7
Lakenheath IP27 . . . . .109 C7
Laxfield IP13 . . . . .39 F4
Leiston IP16 . . . . .129 C6
Long Melford CO10 . . . . . .91 E7
Lowestoft NR32 . . . . .113 D4
Manningtree CO11 . . . . . .104 E3
Mildenhall IP28 . . . . .116 B3
Pulham Market IP21 . . . . . .21 E8
Pulham St Mary IP21 . . . . .22 A8
Ramsey & Parkeston
CO12 . . . . .106 F3
Soham CB7 . . . . .28 C4
Somerleyton, Ashby &
Herringfleet NR32 . . . . . . .2 C3
Southwold IP18 . . . . .119 C6
Sudbury CO10 . . . . .148 C5
Tattingstone IP9 . . . . .105 A7
Thetford IP24 . . . . .16 B6
Wetheringsett-cum-Brockford
IP14 . . . . .53 B4
Woodbridge IP12 . . . . . . .147 A4
Wrabness CO11 . . . . .105 F2
Station Rd E IP14 . . . . . .124 E6
Station Rd W IP14 . . . . . .124 D6
Station Sq **11** NR32 . . . . .115 D8
Station St IP7 . . . . .139 C3
Station Terr IP13 . . . . . . .126 C2
Station Yd
Hadleigh IP7 . . . . .149 E5
Mildenhall IP28 . . . . .116 B3
Needham Market IP6 . . . . .125 E4
Staverton Cl IP12 . . . . . . .85 B6
Stayngate Wlk **4** NR32 . .112 E4
Stearn Dr IP14 . . . . .66 C6
Stearn's La IP14 . . . . .67 E7
Stebbings La IP12 . . . . . . .99 E7
Stedman Terr IP18 . . . . . .119 C8
Steeds Meadow **7** CO10 . .91 E4
Steeles Rd IP30 . . . . .50 D1
Steeple Bumpstead Pottery★
CB9 . . . . .88 B4
Steeple Bumpstead Rd
CB9 . . . . .88 B4
Steeple End IP19 . . . . . . .118 B3
Steeplechase CO10 . . . . . .75 C4
Steggall Cl IP6 . . . . .125 C6
Stella Maris IP2 . . . . .138 D5
Stennetts Cl IP11 . . . . . . .152 B8
Stephen Cl
Haverhill CB9 . . . . .132 D6
Long Melford CO10 . . . . . .91 D7
Stephen Rd IP5 . . . . .141 E8
Stephen's Ct IP14 . . . . . . .140 B6
Stephenson Way IP24 . . . .16 A4
Stephensons Wlk
NR32 . . . . .113 D4
Stepping Hill **3** NR34 . . . .111 B5
Stetchworth Rd
Dullingham CB8 . . . . .59 F4
Stetchworth CB8 . . . . .60 B4
Stevens Cl NR32 . . . . . . .113 C1
Stevenson Rd IP1 . . . . . . .155 A3
Steward Rd IP7 . . . . .123 C2
Stewards Field CB7 . . . . . .29 A1
Stewart Young Gr
IP5 . . . . .141 D7
Stimpson Cl **3** NR32 . . . .113 A6
Stirling Cl
Lowestoft NR32 . . . . .112 F4
7 Thistley Green IP28 . . .29 F6
Stirling Dr **13** CB9 . . . . . .132 C6
Stirling Gdns CO10 . . . . . .120 E4
Stirling Rd **3** IP26 . . . . . . .4 E5
Stirrups La NR32 . . . . .3 C5
Stobart Cl NR34 . . . . .111 D3
Stockley Cl CB9 . . . . .133 A5
Stockmers End **8** IP9 . . .150 E3
Stocks La IP18 . . . . .119 A2
Stockton Cl IP7 . . . . .149 F4
Stockton Rd NR34 . . . . . . .9 A7
Stoke Ash Prim Sch
IP23 . . . . .52 F8
Stoke Coll CO10 . . . . .89 E6
Stoke Hall★ IP2 . . . . .155 B1
Stoke Hall Rd IP2 . . . . . .155 B1
Stoke High Sch IP2 . . . . .139 C3

Stoke Pk Dr IP2 . . . . .139 A1
Stoke Quay IP2 . . . . .155 C1
Stoke Rd Clare CO10 . . . . .90 A7
Layham IP7 . . . . .149 D1
Leavenheath CO6 . . . . . . .102 B8
Nayland-with-Wissington
CO6 . . . . .102 D5
Stoke Ash IP23 . . . . .37 C1
Stoke-by-Clare CO10 . . . . .89 F7
Stoke St IP2 . . . . .155 B1
Stoke-by-Nayland CE VC
Prim Sch CO6 . . . . .102 E7
Stoke-by-Nayland Mid Sch
CO6 . . . . .102 D7
Stollery Cl IP5 . . . . .141 B7
Stonalls IP30 . . . . .50 C1
Stone Hall Rd IP23 . . . . . .36 A2
Stone La
Bressingham IP22 . . . . . . .19 F6
Wrabness CO11 . . . . .105 F5
Stone Lodge La IP2 . . . . .139 A3
Stone Lodge La W
IP2 . . . . .138 F3
Stone Lodge Wlk IP2 . . . .139 B3
Stone St Boxford CO6 . . . .93 C3
Crowfield IP6 . . . . .68 C3
Hadleigh IP7 . . . . .149 B8
Spexhall IP19 . . . . .118 C8
Stone St Rd **2** CO10 . . . .93 C3
Stonebridge Ave IP33 . . . .122 F3
Stonebridge La IP14 . . . . .67 A8
Stonechat Rd IP2 . . . . . . .138 C3
Stonegrove Rd IP11 . . . . .152 D1
Stonehouse Rd IP7 . . . . . .149 D6
Stonewell Hill IP6 . . . . . . .68 D1
Stoney La Barrow IP29 . . . .47 B2
Thurston IP31 . . . . .49 F4
Stoney Rd IP13 . . . . .83 D6
Stonham Aspal CE Prim Sch
IP14 . . . . .68 B6
Stonham Barns Leisure
Complex★ IP14 . . . . . . .68 C6
Stonham Rd IP14 . . . . . . .52 B4
Stony La
2 Aldringham cum Thorpe
IP16 . . . . .73 F6
Debenham IP14 . . . . .53 D2
Wortwell IP20 . . . . .22 F8
Stopford Ct **8** IP1 . . . . . .139 A7
Store St IP22 . . . . .20 C3
Stour Ave IP11 . . . . .152 E3
Stour Cl Glemsford CO10 . .77 B1
4 Harwich CO12 . . . . . .106 E1
Saxmundham IP17 . . . . . .128 C4
Stour Gdns CO10 . . . . . . .148 E2
Stour Rd CO12 . . . . .107 B3
Stour St Cavendish CO10 . .90 D8
17 Manningtree CO11 . . .104 E2
Sudbury CO10 . . . . .148 B5
Stour Vale CO9 . . . . .89 B5
Stour Valley Rd CB9 . . . . .132 F5
Stour Wood Nature
Reserve★ CO12 . . . . . . .106 B2
Stourdale Cl **27** CO10 . . .104 D2
Stourmead Cl CB9 . . . . . .133 E8
Stourside IP9 . . . . .107 A4
Stourview Ave **4** CO11 . .105 A2
Stourview Cl **6** CO11 . . .105 A2
Stoven Cl NR32 . . . . .113 B5
Stoven Rd NR34 . . . . .25 C5
Stow La IP31 . . . . .50 A8
Stow Rd IP31 . . . . .34 B1
Stowmarket High Sch
IP14 . . . . .124 B7
Stowmarket Mid Sch
IP14 . . . . .124 C6
Stowmarket Rd
Badley IP14 . . . . .125 A8
Great Blakenham IP6 . . . . .81 C4
Old Newton with Dagworth
IP14 . . . . .51 E1
Rattlesden IP30 . . . . .65 E6
Stonham Aspal IP14 . . . . . .68 A6
Wetherden IP14 . . . . .51 A1
Stowmarket Sta IP14 . . . .124 E6
Stowupland High Sch
IP14 . . . . .67 A7
Stowupland Rd IP14 . . . . .124 F7
Stowupland St IP14 . . . . .124 D6
Stradbroke CE Prim Sch
IP21 . . . . .39 A5
Stradbroke High Sch
IP21 . . . . .39 B4
Stradbroke Rd
Fressingfield IP21 . . . . . . .39 D7
Ipswich IP4 . . . . .140 A7
Lowestoft NR33 . . . . .115 A4
Southwold IP18 . . . . .119 D5
Stradishall Rd CO10 . . . . .75 E5
Straight La IP20 . . . . .22 B6
Straight Rd
Battisford IP14 . . . . .66 D1
Boxted CO4 . . . . .102 F1
Bradfield CO11 . . . . .105 B1
Foxhall IP10 . . . . .141 C1
Polstead CO6 . . . . .93 F3
Whepstead IP29 . . . . .63 C4
Strand The IP2 . . . . .143 C8
Strasbourg Sq **11** CB9 . .132 F6
Stratford Rd
Dedham CO7 . . . . .103 E4
Ipswich IP1 . . . . .134 D7
Stratford St Mary Prim Sch
CO7 . . . . .103 E3
Strattonhall Drift
IP10 . . . . .145 F2
Straw La CO10 . . . . .148 B5

Strawberry Fields
CB9 . . . . .132 B5
Strawberry La IP19 . . . . . .25 D3
Street Farm La **4** IP31 . . .34 B1
Street Farm Rd IP17 . . . .128 D3
Street The Aldeby NR34 . . . .9 F8
Alderton IP12 . . . . .99 E3
Aldham IP7 . . . . .94 E8
Ashen CO10 . . . . .89 E5
Ashfield cum Thorpe IP14 . .54 C1
Bacton IP14 . . . . .51 E5
Barnham IP24 . . . . .16 B2
Barrow IP29 . . . . .47 A2
Barton Mills IP28 . . . . . . .116 E2
Bawdsey IP12 . . . . .99 E3
Beck Row, Holywell Row
& Kenny Hill IP28 . . . . . . .30 C8
Belchamp Otten CO10 . . . .90 E4
Belstead IP8 . . . . .142 C6
Benacre NR34 . . . . .27 A7
Birdbrook CO9 . . . . .89 A3
Blo' Norton IP22 . . . . .18 E2
Blundeston NR32 . . . . .3 A4
Botesdale IP22 . . . . .36 A6
Boxted IP29 . . . . .77 A6
Bradfield CO11 . . . . .105 C1
Bradfield Combust with
Stanningfield IP30 . . . . . . .64 B4
Bramfield IP19 . . . . .41 F5
Bramford IP8 . . . . .134 A2
Brampton with Stoven
NR34 . . . . .25 E4
Brandon IP27 . . . . .5 E1
Brantham CO11 . . . . .105 A5
Bredfield IP13 . . . . .84 C8
Bressingham IP22 . . . . . . .19 D6
Brettenham IP7 . . . . .65 C1
Bridgham NR16 . . . . .17 E8
Brockdish IP21 . . . . .21 E2
Brome & Oakley IP23 . . . .117 D8
Bruisyard IP17 . . . . .56 D4
Brundish IP13 . . . . .39 D1
Bulmer CO10 . . . . .91 C3
Burrough Green CB8 . . . . .59 E3
12 Bury St Edmunds IP28 . .48 C6
Butley IP12 . . . . .86 A6
Capel St Mary IP9 . . . . . .150 D3
Cavenham IP28 . . . . .47 A8
Charsfield IP13 . . . . .70 B3
Chattisham IP8 . . . . .95 C4
Chedburgh IP29 . . . . .62 C4
Chelsworth IP7 . . . . .79 D3
Coney Weston IP31 . . . . . .17 E1
Copdock & Washbrook
IP8 . . . . .95 F5
Corton NR32 . . . . .3 D4
Cratfield IP19 . . . . .40 D5
Cretingham IP13 . . . . .69 E7
Culford IP28 . . . . .48 B8
Dalham CB8 . . . . .61 B8
Darsham IP17 . . . . .42 B1
Dennington IP13 . . . . .55 E6
Dickleburgh IP21 . . . . .21 B5
Drinkstone IP30 . . . . .65 B8
Earl Soham IP13 . . . . .54 F2
Earsham NR35 . . . . .7 F4
East Bergholt CO7 . . . . . .151 B4
Easton IP13 . . . . .70 E5
Elmsett IP7 . . . . .80 F1
Eriswell IP27 . . . . .13 C1
Eye IP21 . . . . .38 B4
Eyke IP12 . . . . .85 B6
Farnham IP17 . . . . .72 A7
Flixton NR35 . . . . .7 E2
Foxearth CO10 . . . . .91 B7
Framsden IP14 . . . . .69 B6
Freckenham IP28 . . . . .29 E3
Gazeley CB8 . . . . .46 B3
Geldeston NR34 . . . . .9 A7
Great Barton IP31 . . . . . . .49 B5
Great Bricett IP7 . . . . .80 D5
Great Livermere IP31 . . . . .33 C2
Great Waldingfield CO10 . . .92 D6
Great Wratting CB9 . . . . . .74 F3
Grundisburgh IP13 . . . . . . .83 E5
Hacheston IP13 . . . . .71 A6
Halesworth IP19 . . . . .118 E3
Harkstead IP9 . . . . .106 A5
45 Harleston IP20 . . . . . .22 D6
Hessett IP30 . . . . .64 F8
Hinderclay IP22 . . . . .35 E7
Holbrook IP9 . . . . .105 E7
Hollesley IP12 . . . . .99 F7
Horham IP21 . . . . .38 E3
Horringer IP29 . . . . .122 B1
Huntingfield IP19 . . . . .41 A4
Icklingham IP28 . . . . .31 D4
Kersey IP7 . . . . .93 F7
Kettleburgh IP13 . . . . .70 C7
Kirtling CB8 . . . . .60 E3
Lawshall IP29 . . . . .63 E1
Layham IP7 . . . . .149 E2
Letheringham IP13 . . . . . . .70 D4
Lidgate CB8 . . . . .61 B4
Little Bealings IP13 . . . . . .137 D4
Little Thurlow CB9 . . . . . . .74 D5
Little Waldingfield CO10 . . .92 E8
Lound NR32 . . . . .2 F6
Lowestoft NR33 . . . . .114 C2
Market Weston IP22 . . . . . .35 A8
Martlesham IP12 . . . . .146 C1
Middleton CO10 . . . . .148 C1
Mildenhall IP28 . . . . .30 B8
Monks Eleigh IP7 . . . . . . .79 C2
Moulton CB8 . . . . .45 F3
Nacton IP10 . . . . .145 C5

Street The continued
Newbourne IP12 . . . . .98 D6
North Cove NR34 . . . . .10 B4
North Lopham IP22 . . . . . .19 A6
Norton IP31 . . . . .50 B4
Occold IP23 . . . . .37 F1
Pakenham IP31 . . . . .49 E6
Parham IP13 . . . . .71 A7
Peasenhall IP17 . . . . .56 F8
Pettistree IP13 . . . . .127 C4
Poslingford CO10 . . . . .76 A3
Preston St Mary CO10 . . . .79 A5
Ramsey & Parkeston
CO12 . . . . .106 D1
Raydon IP7 . . . . .94 E1
Redenhall with Harleston
1 Redgrave IP22 . . . . . .36 A8
Riddlesworth IP22 . . . . . . .18 A3
Rumburgh IP19 . . . . .24 C4
Rushmere NR33 . . . . .10 C1
St James, South Elmham
IP19 . . . . .23 F4
Shotley IP9 . . . . .106 F6
Shottisham IP12 . . . . .99 B7
Snailwell CB8 . . . . .45 A6
Somerleyton, Ashby &
Herringfleet NR32 . . . . . . .2 D4
South Lopham IP22 . . . . . .19 B4
Southolt IP23 . . . . .54 B7
Stanton IP31 . . . . .34 E4
Starston IP20 . . . . .22 C7
Sternfield IP17 . . . . .72 D8
Stoke Ash IP23 . . . . .52 F8
Stoke-by-Clare CO10 . . . . .89 D6
Stonham Aspal IP14 . . . . . .68 B6
Stowlangtoft IP31 . . . . . . .50 B6
Stradishall CB8 . . . . .75 E6
Stratford St Mary CO7 . . .103 E4
Sturmer CB9 . . . . .133 D3
Thorndon IP23 . . . . .53 B8
Thornham Magna IP23 . . . .37 A2
Troston IP31 . . . . .33 D3
Tuddenham St Martin
IP6 . . . . .136 C5
Ubbeston IP19 . . . . .40 F3
Walberswick IP18 . . . . . . .119 A2
Wattisfield IP22 . . . . .35 C4
Wenhaston IP19 . . . . .42 C6
Westleton IP17 . . . . .58 C7
Wetheringsett-cum-Brockford
IP14 . . . . .52 F4
Weybread IP21 . . . . .22 D2
Whatfield IP7 . . . . .80 C1
Wherstead IP9 . . . . .143 A6
Winfarthing IP22 . . . . .20 B8
Wissett IP19 . . . . .24 D2
Witnesham IP6 . . . . .136 A8
Woodbridge IP12 . . . . . . .147 C2
Wooddition CB8 . . . . .60 D5
Woolpit IP30 . . . . .50 D1
Worlington IP28 . . . . .30 B4
Streetfield Cl IP29 . . . . . . .77 F7
Stretham Rd CB7 . . . . .28 A2
Stretton Ave CB8 . . . . . . .121 B2
Strickland Manor Hill
IP17 . . . . .57 C8
Strickland Pl **18** IP18 . . . .119 D5
Stricklands Rd **1** IP14 . . .124 E5
Strickmere CO7 . . . . .103 E5
Strollers Way CB8 . . . . . . .60 A5
Strowger's Way **6** NR33 . .11 C1
Struggler's La IP6 . . . . . . .136 A8
Stuart Cl
5 Felixstowe IP11 . . . . .153 C2
Ipswich IP4 . . . . .139 F7
Stuart Dr NR34 . . . . .111 C4
Stubbin's La CB8 . . . . .46 B3
Stubbing's La IP21 . . . . . . .22 E3
Stubbs Cl Ipswich IP3 . . . .140 E1
9 Manningtree CO11 . . . .104 D2
Stubbs Wood NR32 . . . . . .113 B6
Studio Cl IP17 . . . . .58 C8
Studlands Pk Ave
CB8 . . . . .120 D6
Stump St IP13 . . . . .127 A3
Stump's Cross CO9 . . . . . .89 D1
Sturdee Ave IP3 . . . . .140 B3
Sturgeon Way **22** IP31 . . .34 C4
Sturmer End Ind Est
CB9 . . . . .133 A3
Sturmer Rd CB9 . . . . .133 D5
Sturston Cl IP24 . . . . .16 C7
Stuston La IP21 . . . . .117 D3
Stuston Rd IP21 . . . . .20 D1
Stutton CE Prim Sch
IP9 . . . . .105 D5
Stutton Cl IP9 . . . . .105 D5
Stutton Gn IP9 . . . . .105 E5
Stutton La IP9 . . . . .105 B7
Stutton Rd CO11 . . . . . . .105 A5
Sub-station Rd IP11 . . . . .152 D2
Sucklings Yd CB9 . . . . . . .88 E4
Sudbourne Rd
14 Felixstowe IP11 . . . . .152 D5
Orford IP12 . . . . .131 B2
Sudbury Arts Ctr
CO10 . . . . .148 D7
Sudbury Common Lands
Nature Reserve★
CO10 . . . . .148 B6
Sudbury Rd Acton CO10 . . .92 B7
Bulmer CO10 . . . . .91 C3
Bures St Mary CO8 . . . . . .101 C5
3 Felixstowe IP11 . . . . .152 C4
Gestingthorpe CO9 . . . . . .90 F1
Great Whelnetham IP30 . . . .64 A6
Lavenham CO10 . . . . .78 D3

Sudbury Rd continued
Long Melford CO10 . . . . . . .91 D6
Newton CO10 . . . . .92 C4
Stoke-by-Nayland CO6 . . .102 D7
Sudbury Ret Pk CO10 . . .148 F6
Sudbury Sports Ctr
CO10 . . . . .148 D7
Sudbury Sta CO10 . . . . .148 D5
Sudbury Upper Sch & Arts
Ctr CO10 . . . . .148 D7
Sue Ryder Foundation Mus★
CO10 . . . . .76 E1
Suffolk Ave IP31 . . . . . . .33 D5
Suffolk Bsns Pk IP30 . . .123 F4
Suffolk Coast National
Nature Reserve★
IP19 . . . . .43 A5
Suffolk Coll IP4 . . . . . .139 E5
Suffolk Ct 2 IP27 . . . . . .5 F1
Suffolk Dr IP12 . . . . . . .85 D8
Suffolk Horse Mus★
IP12 . . . . .147 A5
Suffolk Nuffield Hospl The
IP10 . . . . .141 B4
Suffolk Odyssey Llamas★
IP19 . . . . .41 D5
Suffolk Owl Sanctuary★
IP14 . . . . .68 C6
Suffolk Pl IP12 . . . . . . .147 B5
Suffolk Rd
2 Bury St Edmunds IP32 .122 E8
Ipswich IP4 . . . . .155 C4
Lowestoft NR32 . . . . . . .115 D8
Sudbury CO10 . . . . .148 C6
Suffolk Ret Pk IP1 . . . . .139 A6
Suffolk Ski Ctr★ IP2 . . .143 B7
Suffolk Sq 5 CO10 . . . .148 C6
Suffolk Way CB8 . . . . . .120 E5
Suffolk Wildlife Pk★
NR33 . . . . .11 B1
Suffolk Wr Pk★ IP8 . . .134 A5
Sulleys Hill IP7 . . . . . . .103 D8
Sullivan Pl IP12 . . . . . . .98 D7
Summer La IP12 . . . . . . .85 A6
Summer Rd 8 NR32 . . . .113 D1
Summerfield Cl IP4 . . . .140 D8
Summerfield Gdns
NR33 . . . . .115 A6
Summerhill Sch IP16 . . .129 C7
Summers Rd IP32 . . . . .122 E8
Summit Bsns Pk IP11 . . .152 E1
Sumner Rd IP22 . . . . . . .35 B4
Sun La Newmarket CB8 . .121 A3
Woodbridge IP12 . . . . . .147 A5
Sun Rd NR35 . . . . .110 D8
Sun St 4 CB7 . . . . .29 C5
Sunbeam Cl NR33 . . . . .114 A3
Sunderland Rd 2
IP11 . . . . .153 H11
Sunfield Cl IP4 . . . . . . .140 B6
Sunley Cl NR35 . . . . . . .110 E8
Sunningdale Ave
Ipswich IP4 . . . . .140 D5
Lowestoft NR33 . . . . . . .115 A4
Mildenhall IP28 . . . . .30 A8
Sunningdale Dr IP11 . . .153 B6
Sunnyfields NR33 . . . . .115 A7
Sunnyhill IP12 . . . . .98 D7
Sunnyside
Bedingham NR35 . . . . . . .7 C8
Diss IP22 . . . . .20 C3
Sunray Ave IP11 . . . . . .153 B6
Surbiton Rd IP1 . . . . . . .138 F7
Surrey Cl 8 IP13 . . . . . .126 C3
Surrey Rd
Felixstowe IP11 . . . . . . .152 F4
Ipswich IP1 . . . . .139 A6
Surrey St
6 Lowestoft NR32 . . . . .113 D1
4 Lowestoft NR32 . . . . .115 D8
Sussex Crof 9 IP12 . . . . .85 B3
Sussex Rd NR32 . . . . . . .113 B5
Sutherland Dr NR32 . . . .113 B5
Sutton Cl
Bury St Edmunds IP32 . . .123 E5
Woodbridge IP12 . . . . . .147 B5
Sutton Hoo★ IP12 . . . .147 D5
Sutton Hoo Maze Adventure
Pk★ IP12 . . . . .146 D5
Sutton Rd IP12 . . . . . . .147 F5
Suttons Rd 10 NR34 . . . . .9 F4
Swaffham Heath Rd
CB8 . . . . .59 A7
Swaffham Rd
Burwell CB5 . . . . .44 A3
Mundford IP26 . . . . .6 B8
Swainston Way IP13 . . . .55 D5
Swallow Cl
Felixstowe IP11 . . . . . . .153 C7
12 Harwich CO12 . . . . . .106 F1
Swallow Dr Brandon IP27 . .6 A1
3 Stowmarket IP14 . . . . . .67 A5
Swallow Rd IP2 . . . . . . .138 C3
Swallowfields NR33 . . . .114 D3
Swallowtail Cl IP8 . . . . .142 E8
Swamp La IP22 . . . . .20 A3
Swan Cl
Halesworth IP19 . . . . . . .118 B3
29 Martlesham Heath IP5 . .98 A8
Stowmarket IP14 . . . . . .124 A6
Swan Ct 12 CO11 . . . . . .105 A2
Swan Gn La IP19 . . . . . . .40 C5
Swan Gr CB8 . . . . .120 B8
Swan Hill IP8 . . . . .138 A2
Swan La
Bury St Edmunds IP33 . . .154 C1
Coney Weston IP31 . . . . . .34 D8
Cretingham IP13 . . . . .69 E8

Swan La continued
Exning CB8 . . . . .120 B8
Halesworth IP19 . . . . . . .118 B3
Haverhill CB9 . . . . .132 E6
9 Long Melford CO10 . . . .91 E8
North Cove NR34 . . . . . . .10 C4
Redenhall with Harleston
IP20 . . . . .22 D6
Westerfield IP6 . . . . .135 E4
Swan Meadow CO7 . . . .103 E5
Swan Rd IP13 . . . . .54 E7
Swan St CO10 . . . . .93 B3
Swanfield CO10 . . . . . . .91 E8
Swansea Ave IP2 . . . . . .139 B1
Swatchway Cl 3 IP3 . . . .144 B8
Swaynes IP7 . . . . .103 E5
Sweden Cl 1 CO12 . . . . .106 F2
Swift Cl NR33 . . . . .114 D3
Swift Dr IP14 . . . . .67 A5
Swilltub La IP14 . . . . .52 A4
Swinburne Rd IP1 . . . . .134 E3
Swine's Gn NR34 . . . . . .111 C4
Swingleton Hill IP7 . . . . .79 C2
Swinton Cl IP2 . . . . . . .138 D1
Swonnell's Wlk 2 NR32 .112 D1
Swonnells Ct NR32 . . . .114 D8
Sycamore Ave NR33 . . . .114 D7
Sycamore Cl
Beccles NR34 . . . . .111 E3
7 Great Bricett IP7 . . . . .80 D6
Ipswich IP8 . . . . .138 C1
Leiston IP16 . . . . .129 C5
Sycamore Dr
8 Beck Row, Holywell
Row & Kenny Hill IP28 . .13 B1
5 Mildenhall IP28 . . . . . .30 A8
Rendlesham IP12 . . . . . . .85 D8
Sycamore Rd
Stowupland IP14 . . . . .67 A6
Sudbury CO10 . . . . .148 F4
Sycamore Way
Brantham CO11 . . . . . . .104 E5
Diss IP22 . . . . .20 D3
Sycamore Wlk 20 IP27 . . .13 F7
Syleham Hall La IP21 . . . .22 C1
Syleham Rd
Brockdish IP21 . . . . .22 A2
Syleham IP21 . . . . .38 D8
Sylvester Rd IP16 . . . . . .129 D5
Symonds Rd IP33 . . . . . .123 C1

T

Tacket St IP4 . . . . .155 C2
Tacon Cl IP23 . . . . .117 C2
Tacon Rd IP11 . . . . .152 E1
Takers La IP14 . . . . .124 E4
Talbot Rd CO10 . . . . . . .148 D7
Tallboys Cl IP5 . . . . . . .141 C8
Tallyho Cnr 8 CO7 . . . . .103 E5
Talmash Gdns IP2 . . . . .139 A4
Tamage Rd CO10 . . . . . . .92 B7
Tan House La CB5 . . . . . . .44 A4
Tan Office La
Chevington IP29 . . . . .62 C5
Mendlesham IP14 . . . . . . .52 E1
Tanners La CB7 . . . . .28 D3
Tanners View IP1 . . . . . .138 F7
Tannersfield Way CB8 . . .120 F4
Tannery Bsns Ctr The
IP14 . . . . .66 E2
Tannery Dr IP33 . . . . . . .123 B3
Tannery Rd IP14 . . . . . . .124 C1
Tannington Long Rd
IP13 . . . . .39 D1
Tanns La IP22 . . . . .19 A6
Tansy Cl 5 NR33 . . . . . . .114 F3
Tansy Meadow 3 IP21 . . .39 D8
Target Hill IP20 . . . . .23 B6
Tarn Hows Cl 1 IP11 . . . .153 D6
Tasman Rd CB9 . . . . .133 A5
Tasmania Rd IP4 . . . . . . .140 D6
Tassel Rd IP22 . . . . .123 F6
Tattingstone CE Prim Sch
IP9 . . . . .105 B8
Taunton Cl IP1 . . . . .135 B4
Taunton Rd IP11 . . . . . . .152 F5
Tavern La IP33 . . . . .154 B2
Tavern St Ipswich IP1 . . . .155 B3
Stowmarket IP14 . . . . . .124 D6
Tawneys Ride 2 CO8 . . . .101 D4
Tayberry Pl IP3 . . . . . . .144 C7
Tayfen Rd IP33 . . . . .154 B3
Tayfen Terr IP33 . . . . . . .154 B3
Tayler Cl 4 IP7 . . . . .149 D5
Tayler Rd IP7 . . . . .149 E5
Taylor Dr 8 CO11 . . . . . .104 E2
Taylor Rd 8 IP22 . . . . . . .20 B2
Taylors Farm IP14 . . . . . . .66 C1
Taylors Farm Rd CB9 . . . .75 A2
Taylors Field CB8 . . . . . .59 F4
Tea Kettle La CB8 . . . . . .59 F5
Teal Ave CB7 . . . . .28 C5
Teal Cl IP2 . . . . .138 D3
Teal Wlk IP27 . . . . .6 A1
Teasel Cl CB9 . . . . .132 B7
Tedder Cl 3 IP24 . . . . . . .16 C2
Tedder Rd NR32 . . . . . . .113 B4
Teesdale NR33 . . . . .114 E3
Telesia St NR32 . . . . . . .113 B4
Temperance Pl 8 NR34 . .111 B5
Templars Ct 20 CB9 . . . .132 C5
Temple Cl IP28 . . . . .31 C4
Temple End CB9 . . . . .74 C5
Temple Pattle 11 CO11 . .104 E4
Temple Rd Ipswich IP3 . . .140 C4
Isleham CB7 . . . . .29 B4

Temple Rd continued
Stowmarket IP14 . . . . . .124 D5
Ten Bell La 10 CB7 . . . . . .28 D4
Tenby Rd IP2 . . . . .139 B1
Tennyson Cl IP12 . . . . . .146 E6
Tennyson Rd
13 Bury St Edmunds IP32 . .48 C5
Lowestoft NR32 . . . . . . .113 D2
Saxmundham IP17 . . . . .128 B4
Tennyson Way IP24 . . . . .16 C7
Tenter Field 4 CO7 . . . .103 E5
Tenter Piece 5 CO10 . . . .78 D4
Tenterden Cl 6 NR33 . . .114 D5
Tenth Rd IP10 . . . . .98 A3
Tentree Rd CO10 . . . . . . .92 C7
Terence Airey Ct 25 IP20 .22 D6
Tern Cl CB9 . . . . .133 A5
Tern Rd Ipswich IP2 . . . .138 E2
Stowmarket IP14 . . . . . .124 F6
Terr The
Aldeburgh IP15 . . . . . . .130 E4
Newmarket CB8 . . . . . . .121 A5
Snape IP17 . . . . .72 D5
Terry Gdns IP5 . . . . .141 E7
Tewkesbury Pl 7 IP31 . . . .49 A5
Thackeray Gr IP14 . . . . .124 B7
Thackeray Rd IP1 . . . . . .134 E3
Thanet Rd IP4 . . . . .140 B6
Tharp Way CB7 . . . . .29 E1
Thatchers Wlk 4 IP14 . . .124 D3
Theatre Royal★ IP33 . . .154 C1
Theatre St IP12 . . . . . . .146 F5
Theberton Rd IP16 . . . . .130 B1
Thedwastre Cl 8 IP30 . . . .50 F2
Thedwastre Rd IP31 . . . . .49 E3
Theinetham Fen Nature
Reserve★ IP22 . . . . . . .18 E1
Thellusson Rd 3 IP12 . . . .85 E8
Thelnetham Rd IP22 . . . . .18 E2
Thelnetham Windmill★
IP22 . . . . .18 E1
Theobald Cl 7 IP6 . . . . .125 D4
Thetford Adult Ed Ctr 5
IP24 . . . . .16 B5
Thetford Cl 16 IP27 . . . . .13 F7
Thetford Cottage Hospl
IP24 . . . . .16 C6
Thetford Gram Sch
IP24 . . . . .16 B6
Thetford Heath National
Nature Reserve★
IP24 . . . . .16 A3
Thetford Mus★ IP24 . . .16 C6
Thetford Rd Brandon IP27 . .5 F1
Coney Weston IP31 . . . . . .34 D8
Euston IP24 . . . . .16 E2
Fakenham Magna IP24 . . . .33 E8
Fornham St Martin IP31 . . .48 D5
Garboldisham IP22 . . . . . . .18 C4
2 Ipswich IP1 . . . . .139 A7
Ixworth IP31 . . . . .34 A2
Ixworth Thorpe IP31 . . . . . .33 F3
Mildenhall IP28 . . . . . . .116 E4
Santon Downham IP27 . . . . .6 B1
South Lopham IP22 . . . . . .19 A4
Thetford Sta IP24 . . . . . .16 B6
Thieves La IP31 . . . . .49 F8
Thingoe Hill IP32 . . . . . .154 B4
Third Ave CO10 . . . . .77 B3
Thirlmere Ct IP11 . . . . . .153 D6
Thirlmere Dr IP14 . . . . . .124 B6
Thirlmere Wlk NR32 . . . .113 A4
Thirlwall Dr CB7 . . . . . . .29 C1
Thistle Cl IP2 . . . . .138 F4
Thistledown NR33 . . . . .114 D4
Thistledown Dr IP31 . . . . .34 B2
Thixendale NR33 . . . . . . .114 E2
Thomas Arne Cl IP14 . . .124 C4
Thomas Ave IP11 . . . . . .152 C8
Thomas Bardwell Dr 4
NR35 . . . . .110 C2
Thomas Bole Cl IP22 . . . .18 D4
Thomas Cl 20 IP31 . . . . . .34 B1
Thomas La IP33 . . . . . . .154 B1
Thomas Mills High Sch
IP13 . . . . .126 A5
Thomas Walls Cl 3 IP13 . .83 E5
Thomas Wolsey Specl Sch
IP1 . . . . .134 E3
Thomas Young Cl 3
IP14 . . . . .124 D3
Thompson Cl IP14 . . . . . .51 D1
Thompson Rd IP11 . . . . .138 F8
Thompson Wlk IP32 . . . .122 D7
Thomsons La IP6 . . . . . . .69 A2
Thong Hall Rd IP13 . . . . .127 A5
Thorington Rd IP19 . . . . . .42 A5
Thorn Cl CB7 . . . . .28 C5
Thorn Way IP11 . . . . . . .152 E4
Thorn Wlk IP12 . . . . .85 C2
Thornbush La IP8 . . . . . .138 A8
Thorndon CE Prim Sch
IP23 . . . . .53 B8
Thorney Gn Rd IP14 . . . . .67 A6
Thorney Hall Cl IP14 . . . .124 E6
Thorney Rd IP9 . . . . .150 D4
Thornham Cl 5 NR33 . . . .114 F4
Thornham Rd IP23 . . . . . .36 D2
Thornham Walled Gdn★
IP23 . . . . .37 A2
Thornhayes Cl IP2 . . . . . .139 A3
Thornhill Rd IP6 . . . . .82 B5
Thornley Dr IP4 . . . . . . .140 C8
Thornley Rd IP11 . . . . . . .153 C4
Thorns Cl 6 CB8 . . . . .61 E4
Thornton Cl 15 IP27 . . . . .13 F2
Thornton Rd IP33 . . . . . .122 E2

Thornycroft Gdns
NR33 . . . . .114 A3
Thoroughfare IP19 . . . . .118 B3
Thoroughfare The
Brundish IP13 . . . . .55 C8
Harleston IP20 . . . . .22 D6
Wilby IP21 . . . . .39 D1
10 Woodbridge IP12 . . . .147 A5
Thorpe Abbots Rd
IP21 . . . . .21 D4
Thorpe Hall Rd IP21 . . . . .38 F4
Thorpe La
Ashfield cum Thorpe IP14 . . .69 C8
Debenham IP14 . . . . .53 F1
Trimley St Martin IP11 . . .107 C8
Thorpe Rd
Aldeburgh IP16 . . . . . . .130 F6
Aldringham IP16 . . . . . . .129 D2
Thorpe's Hill IP15 . . . . . .95 E6
Thorpeness Windmill★
IP16 . . . . .73 E6
Thrandeston Rd IP23 . . .117 F7
Threadneedle St
Dedham CO7 . . . . .103 F4
1 Hadleigh IP7 . . . . . . .149 D6
Three Marsh La IP18 . . . .119 B6
Throckmorton Rd
NR35 . . . . .110 D3
Through Duncans
IP12 . . . . .146 E3
Through Jollys IP5 . . . . .141 D8
Thunderbird Way
IP27 . . . . .109 F1
Thurleston High Sch
IP1 . . . . .135 A4
Thurleston La IP1 . . . . . .134 F5
Thurlow CE Prim Sch
CB9 . . . . .74 D6
Thurlow Cl IP17 . . . . . . .128 B3
Thurlow Ct 2 IP14 . . . . .124 D6
Thurlow Pl 13 CB9 . . . . .132 F6
Thurlow Rd CB9 . . . . .74 D7
Thurmans La IP11 . . . . . .152 B8
Thurne Rd NR33 . . . . . . .114 F5
Thurston CE Prim Sch
IP31 . . . . .49 E4
Thurston Com Coll
IP31 . . . . .49 D4
Thurston Ct 6 IP11 . . . . .152 C4
Thurston La CO10 . . . . . . .76 C7
Thurston Rd
1 Beyton IP30 . . . . .49 F2
Lowestoft NR32 . . . . . . .113 D2
Thurston IP31 . . . . .49 E3
Thurston Sta IP31 . . . . . .49 D3
Thwaite Rd
Ditchingham NR35 . . . . .110 C7
Thorndon IP23 . . . . .53 B8
Wickham Skeith IP23 . . . . .52 D7
Tibbenham's Score 6
NR32 . . . . .3 D4
Tiberius Cl CB9 . . . . .133 B5
Tide Mill★ IP12 . . . . . . .147 B4
Tide Mill Way IP12 . . . . .147 A4
Tideway NR32 . . . . .114 E8
Tidys Ct IP33 . . . . .154 B3
Tiger Hill Nature Reserve★
CO8 . . . . .101 E6
Tiggins La IP17 . . . . .128 D8
Tilbury Rd
Great Yeldham CO9 . . . . . .90 A2
Ridgewell CO9 . . . . .89 E4
Tile Barn La CO11 . . . . . .104 B1
Tillbrooks Hill CB8 . . . . . .61 B1
Timperley Cl IP7 . . . . . . .149 D7
Timperley Rd IP7 . . . . . .149 E7
Timperleys IP8 . . . . .95 C6
Tinabrook Cl IP2 . . . . . . .138 E1
Tinker Brook IP13 . . . . . . .71 F5
Tinker St CO12 . . . . .106 C1
Tinker's La
Hadleigh IP7 . . . . .149 D5
Tivetshall St Mary NR15 . . .21 C8
Tinkers La NR34 . . . . .10 D1
Tintern Cl 5 IP2 . . . . . . .139 A4
Tippet Ave IP14 . . . . . . .124 C8
Titchwell Dr 2 IP3 . . . . .144 D8
Tithe Ave IP28 . . . . .30 B8
Tithe Cl CB8 . . . . .46 C3
Title Rd IP17 . . . . .58 A6
Titlow Rd 28 IP20 . . . . . .22 D6
Toad Row NR34 . . . . .10 F1
Todhunter Ave NR34 . . . . .9 B6
Tog La CO6 . . . . .102 D2
Tokio Rd IP4 . . . . .140 A6
Toll Gate Rd 6 IP9 . . . . .150 E3
Tollemache Bsns Pk
IP7 . . . . .80 E4
Toller Cl IP12 . . . . .131 C4
Toller Rd IP3 . . . . .139 E3
Tolley Cobbold St 3
IP28 . . . . .30 A8
Tollgate La 3 IP32 . . . . .123 A8
Tollgate Prim Sch
IP32 . . . . .122 F8
Tolworth Rd IP4 . . . . . . .140 A6
Tom Jennings Cl CB8 . . . .120 F5
Tomline Ct IP10 . . . . . . .145 C5
Tomline Rd
Felixstowe IP11 . . . . . . .153 A3
Ipswich IP3 . . . . .140 A5
Tomline Wlk IP32 . . . . . .122 B6
Tommy Flowers Dr
IP5 . . . . .141 E7
Tomo Bsns Pk IP14 . . . . .124 F6
Tomo Ind Est IP14 . . . . .124 E6
Tomtit's La IP14 . . . . .51 B2
Tonning St NR32 . . . . . . .113 C1

Tooks Comm La NR34 . . . .8 F1
Top Rd Hasketon IP13 . . .146 B8
Rattlesden IP30 . . . . .65 D5
St Andrew, Ilketshall
NR34 . . . . .8 E1
Wingfield IP21 . . . . .39 A7
Top St IP12 . . . . .146 C2
Toper La IP33 . . . . .154 C1
Toppesfield Cl 3 IP7 . . . .149 D5
Toppesfield Gdns IP7 . . .149 D5
Tortoiseshell Cl IP9 . . . .142 E8
Tostock Rd IP30 . . . . .49 F2
Tot Hill IP14 . . . . .66 C8
Tottington La IP22 . . . . . .20 B2
Tovell's Rd IP4 . . . . .139 F6
Tovells 4 IP13 . . . . .84 F7
Tower Field Rd IP12 . . . . .85 D7
Tower Hill NR34 . . . . . . .111 C4
Tower Mill La IP7 . . . . . .149 E6
Tower Mill Rd
Bungay NR35 . . . . .110 B3
Ipswich IP1 . . . . .138 F7
Tower Ramparts IP1 . . . .155 B3
Tower Ramparts Sh Ctr
IP1 . . . . .155 B3
Tower Rd
Felixstowe IP11 . . . . . . .152 F4
Lowestoft NR33 . . . . . . .115 A2
Tower St IP1 . . . . .155 B3
Town End Cl CB9 . . . . . .132 D7
Town Farm Cl IP20 . . . . . .23 C3
Town Farm Est IP12 . . . .131 B3
Town Gn IP14 . . . . .124 C4
Town Hall Galleries★
IP1 . . . . .155 B3
Town House Cnr IP14 . . . .68 F7
Town House La IP22 . . . . .35 D6
Town La IP14 . . . . .53 A3
Town Stps IP15 . . . . .130 E4
Townhouse Rd IP31 . . . . . .35 C1
Townlands Dr NR34 . . . . .111 B3
Townlane Rd IP23 . . . . . .123 B1
Townsend CB7 . . . . .28 C5
Townsend Way NR32 . . . .113 A6
Toyse Cl 1 CB5 . . . . .44 B6
Toyse La CB5 . . . . .44 A6
Trafalgar Cl IP12 . . . . . .139 F6
Trafalgar Rd CO10 . . . . .148 E7
Trafalgar St
4 Lowestoft NR32 . . . . .113 C1
Lowestoft NR32 . . . . . . .115 C8
Trafford Cl 3 IP14 . . . . . .51 E1
Tranmere Gr IP1 . . . . . . .134 F2
Traveller's Hill (Tumuli)★
IP28 . . . . .32 E5
Travellers Rd IP13 . . . . . .69 E5
Traverse The IP33 . . . . . .154 B2
Treetops IP11 . . . . .152 E7
Treeview IP14 . . . . .124 B6
Trefoil Cl IP2 . . . . .138 F4
Tremlett La IP5 . . . . .141 F7
Trenchard Sq 8 IP26 . . . . .4 D5
Trent Rd
1 Bury St Edmunds IP32 . .48 C5
Ipswich IP3 . . . . .139 F2
Trevethan Cl IP22 . . . . . .122 E7
Triangle Yd 9 NR32 . . . . .113 E2
Trimley Marshes Nature
Reserve★ IP11 . . . . . . .107 B6
Trimley St Martin Prim Sch
IP11 . . . . .98 D1
Trimley St Mary Prim Sch
IP11 . . . . .152 C8
Trimley Sta IP11 . . . . . . .152 C7
Trinity Ave
Felixstowe IP11 . . . . . . .152 B3
Mildenhall IP28 . . . . . . .116 C5
Trinity Cl Fordham CB7 . . .29 B1
Ipswich IP5 . . . . .140 F7
28 Manningtree CO11 . . .104 E2
16 Southwold IP18 . . . . .119 D5
Woodbridge IP12 . . . . . .146 D3
Trinity Distribution Pk
IP11 . . . . .152 B4
Trinity Dr CB8 . . . . .121 B2
Trinity Gdns 3 NR35 . . . .110 B4
Trinity Gild 7 CO10 . . . . .78 D4
Trinity Link CB9 . . . . . . .132 E7
Trinity Mews NR33 . . . . .154 A3
Trinity Rd
Lowestoft NR32 . . . . . . .113 E1
Manningtree CO11 . . . . .104 E2
Trinity St Bungay NR35 . . .110 B4
Rose Hill IP3 . . . . .139 E4
15 Southwold IP18 . . . . .119 D5
Trinity Wlk IP14 . . . . .67 A7
Triple Plea La NR35 . . . . . .7 B8
Triple Plea Rd NR35 . . . . . .7 B8
Troon Ct 5 IP28 . . . . .48 C6
Troon Gdns 8 IP4 . . . . . .136 B1
Trossachs The 1 NR32 . . .112 D2
Troston Mount (Tumulus)★
IP31 . . . . .33 D5
Troston Rd IP31 . . . . .33 E5
Trott's La CO10 . . . . .92 F3
Trotting Horse La CB8 . . . .75 A8
Trunch Hill IP20 . . . . .7 A3
Trunch Rd IP20 . . . . .7 B2
Trundley Cl IP27 . . . . . . .132 D7
Tuddenham Ave IP4 . . . .139 E7
Tuddenham CE Prim Sch
IP28 . . . . .30 F2
Tuddenham Cnr IP28 . . . .46 E6

Tuddenham La IP5 . . . .**136** B2
Tuddenham Rd
Barton Mills IP28 . . . .**116** F2
Ipswich IP4 . . . .**155** C4
Westerfield IP4 . . . .**136** A3
Tudor Ave IP22 . . . .**20** B3
Tudor CE VC Prim Sch
CO10 . . . .**148** C7
Tudor Cl
Chedburgh IP29 . . . .**62** D5
9 Framlingham IP13 . . .**126** C3
3 Shotley Gate IP9 . . . .**107** A5
Sudbury CO10 . . . .**148** C7
Tudor Ct Ipswich IP4 . . .**155** C3
1 Occold IP23 . . . .**37** F1
Westhorpe IP14 . . . .**51** E7
Tudor Gn CO10 . . . .**148** C8
Tudor Rd CO10 . . . .**148** C7
Tudor Wlk
8 Honington IP31 . . . .**33** D5
11 Lowestoft NR33 . . . . .**114** E4
Tuffen La IP22 . . . .**35** D8
Tuffields Rd IP29 . . . .**63** B3
Tuffs Rd IP23 . . . .**117** D4
Tumbril La IP21 . . . .**22** A3
Tunbeck Cl IP20 . . . .**23** A7
Tunbeck Rd IP20 . . . .**23** A8
Tunbridge Cl 4 CB5 . . . . . .**44** A5
Tunneys La NR35 . . . .**110** C8
Tuns La IP33 . . . .**154** C1
Tunstall Dr NR32 . . . .**112** F4
Tunstall Gn IP12 . . . .**71** F2
Turin St IP2 . . . .**155** B1
Turin Way 2 NR31 . . . .**3** C6
Turino Ave IP12 . . . .**98** B8
Turkentine Cl 14 CO10 . . . .**92** B3
Turkeyhall La IP14 . . . .**51** F6
Turn La IP12 . . . .**147** A4
Turnberry Cl 3 NR33 . . . . .**114** F4
Turnberry Dr 11 IP28 . . . . .**48** C6
Turnbull Cl IP5 . . . .**141** E7
Turner Ave 1 CO11 . . . . . .**104** D2
Turner Cl
Ditchingham NR35 . . . . . .**110** C7
Haverhill CB9 . . . .**132** B7
4 Lowestoft NR32 . . . . .**113** C6
Sudbury CO10 . . . .**148** E8
Turner Gdns IP12 . . . .**146** D3
Turner Gr IP5 . . . .**141** D8
Turner La 4 IP14 . . . .**51** C1
Turner Rd Ipswich IP3 . . .**144** A8
Stowmarket IP14 . . . .**124** B7
Turnpike Hill CB9 . . . .**74** B2
Turnpike Rd
Chippenham CB8 . . . .**45** F8
Red Lodge IP28 . . . .**30** B1
Woodbridge IP12 . . . .**147** B6
Turnstile Cl 7 NR35 . . . . .**110** B4
Turnstone Cl 2 IP28 . . . . .**116** D4
Turnstone Dr IP32 . . . .**49** A3
Turret La IP4 . . . .**155** B2
Tut Hill IP28 . . . .**48** B5
Tutelina Rd IP30 . . . .**64** A6
Tutt Hill (Tumulus) ★
IP24 . . . .**16** D4
Tuyar Wlk CB8 . . . .**120** E8
Tweed Cl CB8 . . . .**45** F3
Twelve Acre App IP5 . . . .**141** B7
Twin Oak Dr IP13 . . . .**56** B7
Twinnings The IP14 . . . . . .**124** C3
Twiss Cl 5 IP22 . . . .**20** A3
Two Acres IP9 . . . .**150** F4
Two House Cl IP13 . . . . . .**127** C7
Two Pole Dro CB7 . . . .**28** A7
Tydemans Ct 1 IP14 . . . .**124** D6
Tye Gn CO10 . . . .**77** A3
Tye La IP8 . . . .**81** D2
Tyler St 3 Harwich CO12 .**106** F3
Ipswich IP1 . . . .**155** B1
Tylers Gn IP11 . . . .**152** C7
Tylers Way 1 IP14 . . . . . .**124** D3
Tymmes Pl IP13 . . . .**146** C8
Tyrone Cl IP1 . . . .**134** D2

U

Ubbeston Way NR33 . . .**114** F4
Ufford Pl
10 Haverhill CB9 . . . .**132** F6
8 Ufford IP13 . . . .**84** F7
Ufford Rd Bredfield IP13 .**84** D7
Eyke IP12 . . . .**85** B6
Uggeshall Cl NR32 . . . . . .**113** A5
Ullswater NR33 . . . .**114** D2
Ullswater Ave 4 IP11 . . . .**153** D7
Ullswater Rd IP12 . . . .**71** C2
Ulster Ave IP1 . . . .**134** D1
Una Rd CO10 . . . .**106** F2
Uncle's La IP19 . . . .**24** B6
Undercliff Rd E IP11 . . . . .**153** C4
Undercliff Rd W IP11 . . . .**153** A3
Underhill IP14 . . . .**124** C5
Underwood Cl NR32 . . . . .**114** A4
Undley IP27 . . . .**109** B5
Undley Rd IP27 . . . .**109** B4
Unicorn Pl IP33 . . . .**123** C6
Union Hill IP7 . . . .**94** A8
Union La
Lowestoft NR32 . . . .**112** F5
Wortham IP22 . . . .**20** A1
Union Pl 3 NR33 . . . .**115** C7
Union Rd
Lowestoft NR32 . . . .**113** C1
Onehouse IP14 . . . .**66** C6

Union Rd continued
Stowmarket IP14 . . . .**124** A7
Union St IP4 . . . .**155** C3
Union St E IP14 . . . .**124** D6
Union St W IP14 . . . .**124** D6
Unitarian Meeting House ★
IP1 . . . .**155** B2
Unitarian Meeting House
The ★ IP33 . . . .**154** B2
Unity Rd IP14 . . . .**124** D5
Unity St IP3 . . . .**139** E4
Up St IP31 . . . .**34** C4
Upland Rd IP4 . . . .**140** A6
Uplands Cl NR33 . . . .**114** D4
Uplands Cres CO10 . . . . .**148** C7
Uplands Mid Sch
CO10 . . . .**148** D7
Uplands Rd
3 Aldringham cum Thorpe
IP16 . . . .**73** F6
Sudbury CO10 . . . .**148** C7
Uplands Rd N NR33 . . . . .**114** D5
Uplands Rd S NR33 . . . . .**114** C3
Uplands The
Aldringham cum Thorpe
IP16 . . . .**73** E6
Beccles NR34 . . . .**111** D4
Halesworth IP19 . . . .**118** B5
Upper Ave IP19 . . . .**118** B5
Upper Barclay St IP4 . . . .**155** C2
Upper Brook La IP20 . . . . .**22** B4
Upper Brook St IP4 . . . . .**155** B3
Upper Burnthouse La
IP20 . . . .**22** A5
Upper Cavendish St
IP3 . . . .**140** A5
Upper E St CO10 . . . .**148** D6
Upper Farm Rd CO10 . . . .**89** E4
Upper Grange Rd
NR34 . . . .**111** A4
Upper Harmans La
IP20 . . . .**22** B3
Upper High St IP1 . . . . . .**155** B4
Upper Melton Terr 10
IP12 . . . .**84** E6
Upper Moorfield Rd
IP12 . . . .**146** F6
Upper Oakley IP23 . . . . . .**117** F8
Upper Olland St NR35 . . .**110** B3
Upper Orwell St IP4 . . . . .**155** C2
Upper Rd CO10 . . . .**101** C8
Upper Rose La IP22 . . . . . .**20** C1
Upper St
Brome Street IP23 . . . . . .**117** F8
Gissing IP22 . . . .**20** F8
Layham IP7 . . . .**149** F1
Stansfield CO10 . . . .**76** C6
Stanstead CO10 . . . .**77** C4
Stratford St Mary CO7 . . .**103** E5
Upper Tumbril La IP20 . . .**22** A4
Upperfield Dr IP11 . . . . . .**153** C6
Upsons Way IP5 . . . .**141** E8
Upthorpe Rd IP31 . . . .**34** F4
Upton Cl IP4 . . . .**139** E6
Upton Pl IP16 . . . .**129** C5
Urban Rd IP16 . . . .**129** D6
Uvedale Gdns IP6 . . . . . .**125** E4
Uxbridge Cres IP3 . . . . . .**140** C1

V

Vale Ct IP27 . . . .**5** E4
Vale La
Bury St Edmunds IP33 . . .**123** C3
Kersey IP7 . . . .**94** A6
Stutton IP9 . . . .**105** A6
Valentine Way IP30 . . . . . .**64** F7
Valerian Rise 7 IP24 . . . . .**16** D6
Valiant Rd IP31 . . . .**33** D4
Valiant St 6 IP28 . . . .**13** B1
Valley Cl
4 Brantham CO11 . . . . .**104** E5
Halesworth IP19 . . . .**118** E4
Ipswich IP1 . . . .**135** C1
Valley Farm Camargue
Horses ★ IP13 . . . .**127** A8
Valley Farm La IP7 . . . .**94** E5
Valley Farm Rd IP12 . . . .**147** B8
Valley La Battisford IP14 . .**80** F8
Buxhall IP14 . . . .**65** F3
Wherstead IP9 . . . .**143** A3
Valley Rd Battisford IP14 . .**66** E1
Chilton CO10 . . . .**92** C5
Great Bricett IP7 . . . .**80** D6
Harwich CO12 . . . .**106** E1
Ipswich IP1 . . . .**135** B1
Leiston IP16 . . . .**129** E6
Little Blakenham IP8 . . . . .**81** E4
Valley View CO10 . . . .**77** C4
Valley Wash CO10 . . . .**75** D4
Valley Way CB8 . . . .**120** E3
Valley Wlk IP11 . . . .**152** F5
Valleyview Dr IP4 . . . .**140** F4
Vallibus Cl 5 NR32 . . . . . .**112** E4
Van Dyck Cl 9 NR32 . . . . .**113** B6
Vandyck Rd 7 IP3 . . . . . .**144** A8
Vanners Rd CB9 . . . .**132** E5
Vaughan St IP2 . . . .**155** B1
Vaunce's La IP21 . . . .**21** C4
Vaunces La IP21 . . . .**21** C4
Vaux Ave 15 CO12 . . . . . .**106** F1
Velda Cl NR33 . . . .**114** F4
Ventris Cl IP2 . . . .**138** D5
Verdons La IP21 . . . .**39** E4
Verdure Cl 2 NR32 . . . . . .**112** F5
Vere Gdns IP1 . . . .**135** C2

Vermeer Cl 5 NR32 . . . . .**113** B6
Vermont Cres IP4 . . . .**155** C4
Vermont Rd IP4 . . . .**155** C4
Verneuil Ave IP14 . . . .**124** D3
Vernon St IP2 . . . .**155** B1
Vetch Wlk CB9 . . . .**132** B7
Veyses End 6 CO7 . . . .**103** E5
Viburnum Gn NR32 . . . . .**113** C2
Vicarage Cl CB8 . . . .**59** E5
Vicarage Field CO10 . . . .**148** F3
Vicarage Gdns
16 Debenham IP14 . . . . .**53** F2
4 Mildenhall IP28 . . . . .**116** B4
Vicarage Hill 7 IP12 . . . .**147** A5
Vicarage La Acton CO10 . .**92** A6
Bramford IP8 . . . .**134** B1
Bungay NR35 . . . .**110** B3
Wherstead IP9 . . . .**143** B5
Woodditton CB8 . . . .**60** B6
Vicarage Rd
Belchamp St Paul CO10 . . .**90** D5
Felixstowe IP11 . . . .**152** M5
Laxfield IP13 . . . .**40** B3
Newmarket CB8 . . . .**121** B3
Thetford IP24 . . . .**16** C6
Wingfield IP21 . . . .**39** A8
Winston IP14 . . . .**54** A1
Victor Charles Cl IP27 . . . .**5** E3
Victor Rd IP31 . . . .**33** D4
Victoria Cl 5 IP31 . . . .**49** E4
Victoria Cres 2 CO11 . . . .**104** E2
Victoria Hill IP23 . . . .**117** C4
Victoria Mill Rd IP13 . . . .**126** B2
Victoria Rd
Aldeburgh IP15 . . . .**130** E4
Diss IP22 . . . .**20** D2
Felixstowe IP11 . . . .**152** F3
Haverhill CB9 . . . .**132** B5
1 Lowestoft NR33 . . . . .**114** E7
Stowmarket IP14 . . . .**124** E7
Woodbridge IP12 . . . .**147** A5
Victoria St
Bury St Edmunds IP33 . . .**154** A2
Felixstowe IP11 . . . .**153** A4
7 Harwich CO12 . . . . . .**107** B2
Ipswich IP1 . . . .**139** A6
13 Southwold IP18 . . . .**119** D5
Victoria Terr
3 Fressingfield IP21 . . . .**39** E8
Lowestoft NR33 . . . .**115** D7
Victoria Way CB8 . . . .**120** E7
Victory Cl IP33 . . . .**123** C2
Victory Ct IP14 . . . .**124** D4
Victory Rd Ipswich IP4 . . .**140** A7
Leiston IP16 . . . .**129** C5
View Point Rd IP11 . . . . . .**153** H10
Viking Cl IP12 . . . .**84** B1
Viking Hts IP12 . . . .**84** B1
Viking Rd IP14 . . . .**124** C5
Villa Hill IP12 . . . .**99** B7
Village Way
Lowestoft NR32 . . . .**113** B5
Waldringfield IP12 . . . .**98** D7
Vince's Rd IP22 . . . .**20** D2
Vincent Cl Exning CB8 . . .**120** E7
7 Feltwell IP26 . . . .**4** E5
Ipswich IP1 . . . .**138** E8
Vincent Drift IP5 . . . .**141** F7
Vine Cl IP31 . . . .**17** E1
Vine Rd IP6 . . . .**69** C2
Vine Wlk IP9 . . . .**150** E3
Vinefields The IP33 . . . . .**154** C2
Vinery Cl IP13 . . . .**127** C6
Vinery Rd IP33 . . . .**122** F3
Vines The IP17 . . . .**128** D7
Vinesse Rd CO6 . . . .**102** B2
Vineway The 2 CO12 . . . .**107** A2
Violet Cl
Bury St Edmunds IP32 . . .**123** F5
Ipswich IP2 . . . .**138** E4
Violet Hill Rd IP14 . . . . . .**124** C7
Virginia Rd 11 IP28 . . . . . .**30** A8
Viscount Cl IP22 . . . .**20** E2
Vyces Rd IP13 . . . .**126** B3

W

Wacker Field Rd 8 IP12 . .**85** E8
Wadd La IP17 . . . .**72** C6
Waddesdon Rd SCO12 . . .**107** B2
Waddlegoose La IP14 . . . .**54** D2
Waddling La NR32 . . . . . .**112** A7
Wade Cres CO10 . . . .**92** E8
Wade's La Raydon IP7 . . . .**94** E1
Shotley IP9 . . . .**106** E2
Wadehall La NR34 . . . .**10** B5
Wades Gr IP5 . . . .**141** E7
Wades Wood 1 IP30 . . . . .**50** D1
Wadgate Rd IP11 . . . .**152** E6
Wadhurst Rd IP3 . . . .**140** D3
Waggoners Ct IP12 . . . . .**146** F5
Wagtail Dr IP32 . . . .**123** F7
Wainford Cl 5 NR34 . . . . . .**9** F4
Wainford Rd NR35 . . . . . .**110** E5
Wainwright Cl 4 NR32 . . .**113** A6
Wainwright Gdns IP6 . . . . .**81** F5
Wainwright Way IP5 . . . . .**141** D8
Wake Ave IP28 . . . .**116** C5
Wakeshall La CO10 . . . . . .**90** B4
Walberswick Visitor Ctr ★
IP18 . . . .**119** B2
Walberswick Way 8
NR33 . . . .**113** A3
Walcot Rd IP22 . . . .**20** D3
Walcot Rise IP22 . . . .**20** D3
Walcott Wlk NR33 . . . .**115** B5
Waldegrave Cl 23 CO11 . .**104** D2

Waldegrave Rd CO11 . . . .**104** D2
Waldingfield Rd
10 Acton CO10 . . . .**92** B3
Chilton CO10 . . . .**148** F8
Waldringfield Prim Sch
IP12 . . . .**98** D7
Waldringfield Rd 11 IP12 . .**84** C1
Walk The Bacton IP14 . . . .**51** D5
Beccles NR34 . . . .**111** B6
Ipswich IP1 . . . .**155** B3
Walton IP11 . . . .**152** E6
Walker Chase IP5 . . . .**141** C6
Walker Cl 4 IP11 . . . .**140** C5
Walker Gdns NR34 . . . . . .**26** E5
Walks The NR34 . . . .**10** A8
Wall La CO11 . . . .**105** C2
Wallace Rd IP1 . . . .**138** E8
Walled Gdn The ★ IP17 . .**72** B8
Waller's Gr IP2 . . . .**138** F4
Wallow La IP7 . . . .**80** D4
Walls The CO11 . . . .**104** E2
Walmer Cl NR33 . . . .**115** A5
Walmer Rd NR33 . . . .**115** A5
Walnut Cl Acton CO10 . . . .**92** B8
Felixstowe IP11 . . . .**153** D7
Hopton IP22 . . . .**18** C1
13 Lakenheath IP27 . . . .**13** F2
Walnut Gr IP28 . . . .**30** A8
Walnut Tree Ave IP12 . . . .**85** D8
Walnut Tree Cl 4 IP8 . . . .**134** A2
Walnut Tree La
2 Harkstead IP9 . . . . . .**106** A5
Sudbury CO10 . . . .**148** B5
Walnut Tree Meadow
IP14 . . . .**68** B6
Walnut Tree Wlk IP14 . . . .**124** C6
Walnut Way IP13 . . . .**127** B5
Walnuts The
Beccles NR34 . . . .**111** E4
3 Ufford IP13 . . . .**84** F7
Walnuttree Hospl
CO10 . . . .**148** B5
Walpole Cl NR35 . . . .**110** D7
Walpole La IP19 . . . .**41** D5
Walpole Rd
Bramfield IP19 . . . .**41** E4
Halesworth IP19 . . . .**118** A4
Walsham Le Willows CE VC
Prim Sch IP31 . . . .**35** C2
Walsham Rd
Finningham IP14 . . . .**36** A1
6 Ixworth IP31 . . . .**34** B1
Wattisfield IP22 . . . .**35** C3
Walsingham Cl 11 CO10 . . .**92** B3
Walsingham Rd IP33 . . . .**122** D3
Walters Cl 9 NR31 . . . .**3** B7
Waltham Cl IP2 . . . .**139** A2
Walton Ave IP11 . . . .**152** E6
Walton Cl 5 Fordham CB7 .**29** A1
1 Stowmarket IP14 . . . .**124** B8
Walton Rd NR32 . . . .**113** D1
Wamil Rd IP28 . . . .**30** B5
Wamil Way IP28 . . . .**116** B4
Wangford Rd
Lakenheath IP27 . . . .**13** F7
Reydon IP18 . . . .**26** D1
Southwold IP18 . . . .**119** B8
Uggeshall NR34 . . . .**26** A3
Westhall IP19 . . . .**25** B4
Wannock Cl NR33 . . . .**114** D4
Wantisden Cnr IP12 . . . . . .**86** A6
Ward Cl IP7 . . . .**149** D8
Ward Rd IP8 . . . .**138** B2
Ward's View IP5 . . . .**141** E8
Wardlaw Ct 10 IP14 . . . . . .**53** F2
Wardley Cl IP2 . . . .**138** D1
Wardley Hill Rd NR35 . . . . .**8** B8
Ware Rd IP7 . . . .**80** B6
Wareham Ave IP3 . . . .**140** D3
Warene Cl 3 IP13 . . . .**126** C3
Warham Rd CO12 . . . .**106** F1
Warner Way CO10 . . . . . .**148** E6
Warren Chase IP5 . . . .**141** E7
Warren Cl Elmswell IP30 . . .**50** E2
Lakenheath IP27 . . . .**109** D5
Warren Ct 14 CB9 . . . .**132** C5
Warren Heath Ave
IP3 . . . .**140** D2
Warren Heath Rd IP3 . . . .**140** D2
Warren Hill La IP15 . . . . .**130** D7
Warren Hill Rd IP12 . . . . .**146** E4
Warren La
Arwarton IP9 . . . .**106** D6
Elmswell IP30 . . . .**50** E2
27 Martlesham Heath IP5 . .**98** A8
Woolpit IP30 . . . .**50** F1
Warren Loke NR31 . . . .**2** B7
Warren Rd
Great Yarmouth NR31 . . . . .**3** B8
Herringswell IP28 . . . .**46** A8
Hopton on Sea NR31 . . . . .**3** C7
Lowestoft NR32 . . . .**113** D4
Red Lodge IP28 . . . .**30** C1
Warren Sch NR33 . . . . . .**114** C6
Warren The IP18 . . . .**119** E8
Warren's La NR34 . . . .**10** A2
Warrington Rd IP1 . . . . . .**155** A4
Warrington St CB8 . . . . . .**121** A2
Warwick Ave
Halesworth IP19 . . . .**118** C5
Woodbridge IP12 . . . .**146** F6
Warwick Ct 10 CB9 . . . . . .**132** C6
Warwick Rd IP4 . . . .**139** E6
Wash La Beccles NR34 . . .**111** B2
Boxford CO6 . . . .**93** D2
Burgh St Peter NR34 . . . . .**10** C8
Dennington IP13 . . . .**55** E6
Frostenden NR34 . . . .**26** C3

Wash La continued
Great Finborough IP14 . . .**124** A5
Hinderclay IP22 . . . .**35** E8
Kessingland NR33 . . . .**11** C1
Mendlesham IP14 . . . .**52** E3
Redgrave IP22 . . . .**19** D1
Reydon IP18 . . . .**26** D2
St Peter, South Elmham
NR35 . . . .**23** F7
Shelfanger IP22 . . . .**20** B6
Spexhall IP19 . . . .**118** A7
Stanton IP31 . . . .**34** F3
Topcroft NR35 . . . .**7** A8
Wenhaston with Mells Hamlet
IP19 . . . .**118** E1
Westleton IP17 . . . .**58** B8
Witnesham IP6 . . . .**83** A6
Washington St 4 IP28 . . . .**30** A8
Wassicks La IP14 . . . .**51** E3
Watch House Hill
NR35 . . . .**110** E4
Water Farm Dr IP7 . . . .**94** E1
Water La
Athelington IP21 . . . .**38** F1
Barnardiston CB9 . . . .**75** B4
Barnham IP24 . . . .**16** C2
Botesdale IP22 . . . .**35** F5
3 Bures CO8 . . . .**101** C5
Cavendish CO10 . . . .**76** E1
Debenham IP14 . . . .**53** F2
Denston CB8 . . . .**75** F7
Garboldisham IP22 . . . .**18** D4
Great Bradley CB8 . . . .**74** C8
Great Horkesley CO6 . . . .**102** C4
Great Whelnetham IP30 . . .**64** A6
Helions Bumpstead CB9 . . .**88** B4
Kersey IP7 . . . .**94** A6
Layham IP7 . . . .**149** E1
Lowestoft NR32 . . . .**113** C2
Polstead CO6 . . . .**102** F8
Steeple Bumpstead CB9 . . .**88** D3
Sturmer CB9 . . . .**133** D3
Thelnetham IP22 . . . .**18** E1
Thornham Magna IP23 . . . .**37** A1
Weybread IP21 . . . .**22** D4
Worlingworth IP13 . . . .**54** D8
Water Mill La IP21 . . . .**38** C8
Water Run The IP7 . . . .**79** F7
Water Street CO10 . . . .**78** D4
Watercourse The CB8 . . . .**121** A4
Waterford Rd IP12 . . . . . .**134** D2
Waterhead La IP12 . . . . . .**147** D6
Watering Cl 1 IP8 . . . .**81** C3
Watering La IP17 . . . .**72** C7
Watering Rd IP21 . . . .**38** D5
Waterloo Ave
Leiston IP16 . . . .**129** B6
4 Roydon IP22 . . . .**20** A3
Waterloo Cl CB8 . . . .**120** D8
Waterloo Rd
4 Ipswich IP1 . . . .**139** A7
Lowestoft NR33 . . . .**115** D7
Sotterley NR34 . . . .**26** A7
Watermill Cl IP7 . . . .**149** E2
Watermill Rd IP12 . . . .**98** C5
Waters Ave NR33 . . . .**114** C3
Waterside CB7 . . . .**29** C5
Waterworks Rd 12 IP28 . . .**30** A8
Waterworks St IP4 . . . . . .**155** C3
Watery La IP13 . . . .**146** A8
Watson Cl IP33 . . . .**123** B2
Watson Way IP12 . . . .**99** E4
Watson's Hill IP7 . . . .**79** F1
Watsons Cl 3 NR31 . . . .**3** C6
Watt Cl IP12 . . . .**99** E4
Wattisfield Rd IP31 . . . . . .**35** C2
Wattisham Airfield ★
IP7 . . . .**80** C6
Wattisham Airfield Mus ★
IP7 . . . .**80** C6
Wattisham Rd IP7 . . . .**79** F4
Waveney Cl 3 IP17 . . . . . .**128** C4
Waveney Cres NR33 . . . . .**115** B7
Waveney Dr NR33 . . . .**115** A7
Waveney Hill
Carlton Colville NR32 . . . .**114** B8
Lowestoft NR32 . . . .**112** B1
Waveney Hts IP21 . . . .**21** F2
Waveney Rd
Beccles NR34 . . . .**111** B4
Bungay NR35 . . . .**110** D3
10 Bury St Edmunds IP32 . .**48** C5
Ditchingham NR35 . . . . . .**110** D3
Felixstowe IP11 . . . .**152** E3
Ipswich IP1 . . . .**138** E4
10 Lowestoft NR32 . . . . .**115** D8
Waveney Sports & Leisure
Ctr NR32 . . . .**113** C2
Waveney Terr 4 CB9 . . . . .**132** E5
Waveney Valley Swimming
Pool NR33 . . . .**110** D2
Way Bank La CO9 . . . .**89** C7
Wayne Cl NR32 . . . .**113** B5
Wayside Cl IP14 . . . .**124** D3
Weald The NR32 . . . .**112** B4
Weatheralls Cl 9 CB7 . . . . .**28** D4
Weaver Cl IP1 . . . .**138** D8
Weavers Cl
2 Hadleigh IP7 . . . .**149** D6
4 Lavenham CO10 . . . . .**78** D4
Stowmarket IP14 . . . .**124** C3
Weavers Croft 8 IP20 . . . .**22** D6
Weavers Ct 12 CO10 . . . .**148** C5
Weavers Dr 6 CO10 . . . . .**77** A2
Weavers La CO10 . . . .**148** C5
Weavers Marsh La
IP17 . . . .**41** E2
Weavers Way 2 IP6 . . . . . .**82** A5
Webb Rd IP14 . . . .**124** D3

Webb St **1** IP2 .....139 C3
Webb's Cl IP14 .....124 C1
Webbs Ct IP5 .....141 C7
Webster St NR35 .....110 A4
Weddell Rd CB9 .....133 A4
Weeting Castle★ IP27 ..5 E4
Weeting Heath Nature
  Reserve★ IP27 .....5 C3
Weeting Heath Visitor Ctr★
  IP27 .....6 C4
Weeting Prim Sch IP27 ..5 E3
Weir Pl IP10 .....98 D2
Weirs Dro CB5 .....44 A6
Welbeck Cl
  Felixstowe IP11 .....152 C7
  North Grove NR34 .....10 C4
Welbourne Way NR34 ..10 C4
Welch Cl NR34 .....10 D3
Welham La IP28 .....47 D5
Well Bottom CB8 .....45 C4
Well La **9** CO10 .....90 A8
Well St IP33 .....154 B2
Wellesley Rd
  Ipswich IP3 .....139 F5
  Troston IP31 .....33 D4
Wellington Cl
  Hadleigh IP7 .....149 D7
  Thistley Green IP28 .....30 B4
Wellington Espl NR33 .115 C6
Wellington Rd
  Eye IP23 .....117 D3
  4 Feltwell IP26 .....4 E5
  6 Harwich CO12 .....107 C3
  2 Lowestoft NR33 .....115 A3
  8 Mildenhall IP28 .....30 A8
  13 Troston IP31 .....33 D5
Wellington St
  7 Ipswich IP1 .....139 A7
  1 Newmarket CB8 .....121 A3
Wellington Terr **5** CB9 .132 C5
Wells Cl IP4 .....139 E6
Wells Cnr IP13 .....39 F2
Wells Ct IP28 .....116 B5
Wells Hall Com Prim Sch
  CO10 .....148 F2
Wells Hall Rd CO10 ...148 F3
Wells' La IP20 .....22 D5
Wells Rd IP20 .....22 C5
Wells Way IP14 .....53 F1
Wellum Cl **13** CB9 .....132 C5
Wembley Ave NR34 ....111 B4
Wendy Cl **7** IP9 .....106 C6
Wenham La
  East Bergholt CO7 .....151 D8
  Wenham Magna CO7 ...150 A2
Wenham Rd IP8 .....150 E8
Wenhaston La IP19 .....42 D5
Wenhaston Prim Sch
  IP19 .....42 C6
Wenhaston Rd IP19 .....42 B5
Wenhaston Way **2**
  NR32 .....112 F3
Wensleydale **5** NR33 ..144 E5
Wensum Gdns NR32 ...113 C3
Wentford Ct **7** CB9 ....132 A6
Wentford View **1** CO10 .76 A1
Wentworth Cl
  14 Fornham All Saints IP28 48 C6
  Hadleigh IP7 .....149 F5
  Weeting IP27 .....5 E4
Wentworth Dr
  Felixstowe IP11 .....153 C6
  7 Ipswich IP8 .....138 C2
  10 Mildenhall IP28 .....116 B5
Wentworth Rd IP15 .....130 E3
Wentworth Terr **5** CB9 .132 C6
Wentworth Way **2**
  NR33 .....114 F4
Wesel Ave IP11 .....152 D3
Wesley Cl NR34 .....111 B2
Wesley End Rd CO9 ....89 B2
Wesley Way IP11 .....138 F8
West Dock Rd CO12 ...106 F3
West Dr
  Mildenhall IP28 .....116 B4
  Soham CB7 .....28 C4
West Dr Cres CB7 .....28 C4
West Dr Gdns CB7 .....28 C4
West End CB8 .....60 B5
West End La
  Great Thurlow CB9 .....74 B4
  16 Harwich CO12 .....107 A1
West End Rd IP1 .....155 A2
West Gr NR33 .....115 A3
West Hall Dr IP26 .....6 A8
West Hall Rd
  1 Mundford IP26 .....6 B8
  Walsham le Willows IP22 .35 F3
West Harling Rd NR16 ..18 B8
West Herne La IP22 .....19 A1
West Hill IP16 .....129 C2
West La IP15 .....130 E3
West Lawn IP4 .....140 C8
West Meadows IP1 ....134 C4
West Mill Gn IP9 .....104 F7
West Row
  Bury St Edmunds IP33 ..122 E4
  Ipswich IP3 .....140 E1
West Row Prim Sch
  IP28 .....29 E7
West Row Rd IP28 .....116 A5
West Side CB7 .....113 C5
West St Harwich CO12 ..107 B3
  Feltwell IP26 .....31 C4
  Isleham CB7 .....29 D5
  Rickinghall Inferior IP22 .35 E3

West Stow Anglo-Saxon
  Village★ IP28 .....31 F2
West Stow Ctry Pk★
  IP28 .....31 F2
West Stow Rd IP28 .....32 B1
West Suffolk Coll
  IP33 .....122 E6
West Suffolk Hospl The
  IP33 .....123 A2
West Tofts Rd IP26 .....6 D7
West View Burstall IP8 ..95 F7
  Carlton IP17 .....128 D6
  Stowmarket IP14 .....124 B6
West View Gdns **4** IP23 .36 D2
West Wood **9** IP31 .....49 A5
Westbourne Ct **6** CB9 .132 E6
Westbourne High Sch
  IP1 .....134 E1
Westbourne Rd IP1 ....134 F1
Westbury Ave IP33 ....122 D5
Westbury Rd IP4 .....140 B8
Westend La CB9 .....133 F8
Westerfield La IP6 .....136 A5
Westerfield Rd
  Ipswich IP1 .....155 C4
  Westerfield IP6 .....135 E4
Westerfield Sta IP6 ....135 E3
Western Ave
  Felixstowe IP11 .....153 D6
  Haverhill CB9 .....132 C7
Western Cl **4** Feltwell IP26 4 D5
  Ipswich IP4 .....140 F4
Western Way IP33 .....122 D6
Western's End **6** CO11 .104 E4
Westfield CO10 .....90 A7
Westfield Com Prim Sch
  CB9 .....132 F5
Westgarth Gdns IP33 ..122 E3
Westgate **8** IP16 .....73 F6
Westgate Prim Sch
  IP33 .....154 A1
Westgate St
  Bury St Edmunds IP33 ..154 C1
  Ipswich IP1 .....155 B3
  Long Melford CO10 .....77 E1
Westgate St Service Rd
  IP1 .....155 B3
Westhall IP19 .....39 B5
Westhall Rd NR32 .....113 B5
Westholme Cl IP12 .....146 F4
Westholme Rd IP1 .....135 A1
Westhorpe **3** CB5 .....44 A6
Westhorpe Rd
  Finningham IP14 .....52 A8
  Wyverstone IP14 .....51 E6
Westland **20** IP5 .....98 A8
Westland Rd NR33 .....114 E6
Westleton Heath National
  Nature Reserve★
  IP17 .....58 E8
Westleton Rd IP17 .....57 E8
Westleton Rd **17** IP11 ..152 D5
Westley Bottom Rd
  CB8 .....59 A4
Westley Mid Sch IP33 .122 C5
Westley Rd IP33 .....122 D5
Westley Way IP31 .....50 E7
Westminster Cl IP4 ....140 B5
Westminster Dr IP33 ..122 D3
Westmorland Cl **8**
  CO11 .....105 A2
Westmorland Rd IP11 .153 D7
Weston Colville Rd
  CB8 .....59 E1
Weston Rd NR32 .....113 B5
Weston Way CB8 .....120 F6
Westropps **6** CO10 .....91 E7
Westward Deals CB9 ..133 F8
Westward Ho IP16 .....129 C6
Westwood Ave
  Ipswich IP1 .....139 A8
  Lowestoft NR33 .....114 E6
Wet La CO4 .....102 F3
Wetherby Cl IP1 .....135 B3
Wetherden Rd
  Elmswell IP30 .....50 F2
  Great Ashfield IP31 .....51 B6
Wetheringsett CE Prim Sch
  IP14 .....53 A5
Wexford Rd IP1 .....134 D2
Weyland Rd IP6 .....83 A6
Weylands Cl IP14 .....67 D7
Whalebone Cnr CO4 ..103 C4
Whapload Rd NR32 ....113 E1
Wharf La **3** CO8 .....101 C4
Wharfedale NR33 .....114 F3
Wharfedale Rd IP1 ....135 A1
Wharton St NR35 .....110 B4
Whatfield CE Prim Sch
  IP7 .....80 C1
Whatfield Rd
  Aldham IP7 .....94 C7
  Elmsett IP7 .....80 F1
Whatfield Way IP14 ...124 E3
Wheatacre Dr **3** NR32 ..3 C4
Wheatfield Rd NR33 ..114 D4
Wheatfields
  3 Botesdale IP22 .....36 A6
  4 Thurston IP31 .....49 E4
Wheatsheaf Cl CO11 ..105 E2
Wheatsheaf La CO11 ..105 E2
Wheelbarrow La IP20 ..23 F5
Wheeler's La IP31 .....51 A5
Wheelwright Cl IP30 ...49 C2

Wheelwrights The
  IP11 .....152 C8
Whepstead Rd
  Hawstead IP29 .....63 B7
  Horringer IP29 .....122 D1
Wherry La IP4 .....155 C2
Wherry Quay IP4 .....155 C2
Wherry Rd
  3 Bungay NR35 .....110 D3
  3 Dunnis Hill NR35 .....110 D3
Wherstead Rd IP2 .....155 B1
Whights Cnr IP8 .....138 A1
Whin Marsh **6** IP15 ....130 E5
Whinchat IP7 .....138 D3
Whinfield **13** IP5 .....98 A8
Whinfield Ave **28** CO12 .106 F1
Whinfield Cl IP5 .....98 A8
Whinneys The IP5 .....141 B6
Whinyard Way **3** IP11 .153 D7
Whiskin Cl **7** NR32 ....112 D2
Whistle Dr IP28 .....12 D5
Whitby Rd
  Bury St Edmunds IP33 ..122 D3
  Ipswich IP4 .....139 F8
White Elm Rd IP30 .....50 C1
White Elm St IP3 .....139 E4
White Foot La IP13 .....83 E6
White Hall Cl CO10 .....92 C5
White Hart La **20** CB7 ..28 D4
White Horse Cl **4** IP11 .153 C6
White Horse Hill IP9 ...142 D1
White Horse La IP30 ...64 D7
White Horse Rd
  Capel St Mary IP9 .....150 F3
  East Bergholt CO7 .....151 D3
  Kedington CB9 .....133 E8
White Horse St **4** NR32 113 E2
White House Farm La
  IP21 .....22 B6
White House Gdns
  NR34 .....111 A4
White House Rd IP14 ..134 D2
White Lion Ct IP7 .....149 D5
White Lion Rd NR34 ....10 B8
White Meadow **3** IP4 ..51 A1
White Womans La IP12 .85 B7
White's La NR33 .....11 B1
Whitedike Dro IP26 .....4 B4
Whitegates CB8 .....121 B3
Whitehall Rd IP14 .....51 F1
Whitehouse Com Inf Sch
  IP1 .....134 E1
Whitehouse Ind Est
  IP1 .....134 C3
Whitehouse Jun Sch
  IP1 .....134 D3
Whitehouse La
  Belchamp Otten CO10 ...90 D5
  Earsham NR35 .....7 C5
  Stowupland IP14 .....67 D8
Whitepost Cnr IP14 ....54 C1
Whites Cl IP21 .....39 B4
Whites Field CO7 .....151 B5
Whitethorn Rd IP3 ....140 F1
Whitewood Wlk **8** IP27 .13 F2
Whithersfield Rd CB9 .132 C8
Whiting Rd NR32 .....112 C2
Whiting St IP33 .....154 B1
Whitland Cl IP2 .....143 A8
Whitlands **5** CO10 .....77 A3
Whitlock Dr CO9 .....89 F1
Whittle Rd IP2 .....138 F6
Whitton Church La
  IP1 .....134 F4
Whitton Cl IP33 .....114 E6
Whitton Com Prim Sch
  IP1 .....134 F5
Whitton Ct NR33 .....115 A3
Whitton Gn Prim Sch
  NR33 .....114 F5
Whitton La IP1 .....134 C4
Whitton Leyer IP6 .....134 C2
Whitton Sports Ctr IP1 .134 E4
Whitworth Cl IP2 .....138 D2
Whyteway IP19 .....24 B4
Wick La CO12 .....107 A1
Wick Rd Langham CO4 .103 C2
  Stoke-by-Nayland CO6 ..103 A6
Wicken Rd CB7 .....28 D1
Wickham Com Prim Sch
  IP13 .....127 B6
Wickham La IP14 .....52 A6
Wickham Mkt Sta IP12 .71 C2
Wickham Rd IP23 .....52 F7
Wickhambrook Ct **2**
  IP11 .....152 C4
Wickhambrook Prim Sch
  CB8 .....61 E2
Wickhambrook Rd IP29 .62 A5
Wicklow Rd IP1 .....134 D2
Wicks La IP14 .....67 D7
Widgeon Cl IP2 .....138 F3
Wigg's Way **3** NR32 .....3 A8
Wiggin Cl IP28 .....116 D2
Wiggs Acre NR34 .....10 C4
Wigmore Cl
  Ipswich IP2 .....138 F1
  Stoke Park IP2 .....139 A1
Wignall St CO11 .....104 C2
Wigston Rd IP33 .....122 C3
Wigwam Hill IP22 .....19 F1
Wilby CE Prim Sch
  IP21 .....39 B2
Wilby La IP13 .....39 A4
Wilby Rd IP21 .....39 A4
Wilbye CO7 .....123 E4
Wild Acres **13** CB5 .....44 A5

Wild Tracks Offroad Activity
  Pk★ CB7 .....45 E7
Wild St Est IP28 .....13 D1
Wilderness Cl **3** IP20 ...22 D5
Wilderness Hill IP8 .....95 B6
Wilderness La
  Harleston IP20 .....22 D6
  Woodbridge IP12 .....147 A6
Wildes St NR32 .....113 E2
Wildflower Way NR35 ..110 B7
Wilding Dr IP5 .....141 D7
Wilding Rd IP8 .....138 C1
Wildmere La IP28 .....13 D1
Wilford Bridge Rd
  IP12 .....147 D7
Wilford Bridge Spur
  IP12 .....147 C7
Wilfred Hurry Cl IP8 ...134 A1
Wilfred Sherman Cl
  CB8 .....121 A4
Wilkes Cl IP5 .....141 E7
Wilkes Way IP14 .....124 C6
Wilkinson Dr IP5 .....141 C6
Wilkinson Way IP12 ...147 A6
Wilks Rd IP33 .....123 B2
Willbye Ave IP22 .....20 D3
Willcox Ave IP33 .....122 C6
William Armstrong Cl **6**
  IP30 .....50 F2
William Blake Ct CB9 .132 C7
William Booth Way **11**
  IP11 .....152 D5
William Groom Ave **2**
  CO12 .....107 A1
William St IP1 .....155 B3
William's Way **4** IP28 ..29 F6
Williamsport Way IP6 .125 F3
Willie Snaith Rd CB8 ..120 F6
Willoughby Cl IP13 .....71 A7
Willoughby Rd IP2 ....155 A1
Willow Cl
  Badwell Ash IP31 .....50 F8
  6 Claydon IP6 .....134 C8
  Haverhill CB9 .....132 B7
  Stradbroke IP21 .....39 B5
  1 Sudbury CO10 .....148 C4
  Worlingham NR34 .....111 F3
  Wortwell IP20 .....23 A8
Willow Cres CB8 .....121 B2
Willow Gr IP13 .....54 E7
Willow Gr **3** CO6 .....102 C5
Willow La
  Bedingham NR35 .....7 B7
  Broome NR35 .....8 C7
  Cotton IP14 .....52 B6
Willow Marsh La
  Darsham IP17 .....42 A1
  Yoxford IP17 .....41 F2
Willow Rd IP33 .....115 A2
Willow Tree Cl IP13 ...127 B6
Willow Way
  Bury St Edmunds IP33 ..154 A3
  9 Great Bricett IP7 .....80 C6
  3 Harwich CO12 .....106 F1
  8 Rendlesham IP12 .....85 D8
Willow Wlk
  5 Harleston IP20 .....22 D5
  Needham Market IP6 ...125 D6
Willowbrook Cl IP33 ..114 A3
Willowcroft Rd IP1 .....135 A2
Willowvale NR32 .....112 F6
Willrede Cl NR34 .....111 B3
Wilmslow Ave IP12 ...146 E5
Wilmslow Dr IP8 .....138 C2
Wilson Rd Hadleigh IP7 .149 E5
  Ipswich IP8 .....138 B1
  Lowestoft NR33 .....115 C5
Wilton Rd IP26 .....4 E5
Wimbledon Ave IP27 ..14 E8
Wimborne Ave IP3 ....140 D4
Wimpole Cl IP5 .....140 F6
Wincanton Cl IP4 .....136 A1
Winchester Cl IP14 ...124 B6
Winchester Gdns **4** IP6 .82 B5
Winchester Rd IP33 ...122 D4
Winchester Way IP2 ..142 F8
Windermere Cl IP3 ....144 B8
Windermere Pk NR32 .113 A4
Windermere Rd
  6 Felixstowe IP11 .....153 D7
  Stowmarket IP14 .....124 C6
  Sudbury CO10 .....148 E6
Windgap La IP14 .....51 D1
Windham Rd CO10 ....148 B6
Winding Piece **5** IP9 ..150 E3
Windings Rd **4** IP7 .....80 F1
Windmill Ave IP30 .....50 C1
Windmill Cl
  Boxted CO4 .....102 F2
  Ramsey & Parkeston
  CO12 .....106 C1
  Soham CB7 .....28 E2
  3 Somersham IP8 .....81 C3
Windmill Gn
  Ditchingham NR35 ....110 C2
  19 Stanton IP31 .....34 E4
Windmill Hill
  Capel St Mary IP9 .....150 C3
  Exning CB8 .....120 C8
  Long Melford CO10 .....77 D1
Windmill La IP21 .....38 F8
Windmill Rd IP26 .....23 A7
Windmill Rise
  Bury St Edmunds IP33 ..154 A1
  Hundon CO10 .....75 D4
  1 Wetherden IP14 .....51 A1
Windmill Row **5** CO10 ..77 B3
Windrush Rd IP5 .....141 C8

Windsor Circ
  1 Lakenheath IP27 .....14 A3
  Lakenheath IP27 .....109 F1
Windsor Cl
  7 Barnham IP24 .....16 C2
  Lawshall IP29 .....63 D2
Windsor Pl CO10 .....148 E5
Windsor Rd
  Felixstowe IP11 .....152 E5
  Ipswich IP1 .....138 F7
  Lowestoft NR33 .....115 C7
  Newmarket CB8 .....120 E4
  Southwold IP18 .....119 B8
Windsor Terr **12** CB9 ..132 C6
Windward Way NR33 ..114 E5
Windyridge Rd CO10 ...65 D5
Winfarthing Rd IP22 ...20 B6
Winfrith Rd IP3 .....140 D4
Wingfield Ave IP27 ....109 D7
Wingfield Meadows
  IP14 .....68 B6
Wingfield Old Coll & Gdns★
  IP21 .....39 A7
Wingfield Rd
  Lakenheath IP27 .....109 D7
  Syleham IP21 .....21 F1
  Weybread IP21 .....22 C2
Wingfield St
  Bungay NR35 .....110 B3
  Ipswich IP4 .....155 C2
Wings Rd IP27 .....109 D6
Wings Rd Cl IP27 .....109 D6
Winnipeg Rd NR32 ....113 D2
Winsford Rd IP32 .....123 E6
Winston Ave
  Ipswich IP4 .....140 C8
  Lowestoft NR33 .....114 E7
Winston Cl
  5 Felixstowe IP11 .....152 D5
  11 Kessingland NR33 ...11 C1
Winston Rd
  Southwold IP18 .....119 C7
  Winston IP14 .....53 F1
Winthrop Rd IP33 .....122 D4
Winthrops The CO10 ...93 B4
Wissett Cl IP19 .....118 B4
Wissett Rd
  Chediston IP19 .....41 B8
  Halesworth IP19 .....118 A5
  Wissett IP19 .....24 D1
Wissett Way NR32 .....113 B4
Wissey View **2** IP26 .....6 B8
Wissington Uplands
  CO6 .....102 A5
Wiston Rd CO6 .....102 B4
Withers Pl **2** CB7 .....29 A1
Withersdale Rd
  Mendham IP20 .....23 A5
  Weybread IP21 .....22 D4
Withersfield Rd
  Haverhill CB9 .....132 C4
  Withersfield CB9 .....74 C4
Withingdale Gall The★
  CO10 .....91 D7
Withipoll St IP4 .....155 C3
Witnesham Church La
  IP6 .....82 F5
Witnesham La IP6 .....136 C7
Witnesham Prim Sch
  IP6 .....83 A7
Witney Gn NR33 .....115 A3
Witney Rd **3** NR33 .....115 A3
Wittons La IP21 .....38 C7
Wix Rd CO12 .....106 C1
Wollaston Cl IP32 .....122 D8
Wollaston Rd NR32 ....113 D1
Wolsey Art Gall★ IP1 ..155 C4
Wolsey Cl IP33 .....153 A3
Wolsey Ct **4** IP14 .....124 C7
Wolsey St IP1 .....155 B2
Wolton Rd IP5 .....141 C7
Wolves Farm La IP7 ....94 E6
Wolves Wood Nature
  Reserve★ IP7 .....94 F6
Wood Cl
  1 Bentwaters Airfield
  IP12 .....85 D8
  Kenninghall NR16 .....19 A8
  Tostock IP30 .....50 B3
Wood Farm La IP18 .....26 C2
Wood Farm Rd IP13 ....83 C5
Wood Hall La IP23 .....37 B1
Wood La Bedingham NR35 .7 A2
  Bressingham IP22 .....19 A6
  Dallingho IP13 .....70 B1
  Dickleburgh & Rushall
  IP21 .....21 C2
  Fressingfield IP21 .....40 A8
  Henstead with Hulver Street
  NR34 .....26 E7
  Hepworth IP22 .....35 A6
  Oulton NR32 .....112 C3
  Reydon IP18 .....26 C1
  Scole IP21 .....21 C4
  Thelnetham IP22 .....35 C6
Wood Rd
  Badingham IP13 .....56 B6
  Woolpit IP30 .....65 F8
Wood Side IP14 .....124 B5
Wood View **4** IP17 .....56 F8
Woodbridge Gall★
  IP12 .....146 F5
Woodbridge Mus The★
  IP12 .....147 A5

Woodbridge Prim Sch **15**
 IP12 ....**147** A5
Woodbridge Rd
 Alderton IP12 ....**99** D5
 Bredfield IP13 ....**84** C7
 Butley IP12 ....**86** A5
 Framlingham IP13 ......**126** C1
 Grundisburgh IP13 ......**83** E6
 Ipswich IP4 ....**155** C3
 Sutton IP12 ....**85** A1
 Tunstall IP12 ....**71** E1
 Waldringfield IP12 ......**98** D6
 Wantisden IP12 ....**85** E5
Woodbridge Rd E IP4 .**140** C7
Woodbridge Sch IP12 .**146** F5
Woodbridge Sta **147** B4
Woodchurch Ave 6
 NR33 ....**114** C4
Woodcock Cl CB9 ....**133** A5
Woodcock Rd IP2 ....**138** E2
Woodcock Rise IP26 ....**6** A1
Woodcote IP14 ......**124** B6
Woodcrofts Cl 2 IP29 ..**63** A1
Woodcutters Way
 IP27 ....**109** D7
Woodditton Rd
 Kirtling CB8 ....**60** D3
 Newmarket CB8 ....**121** A1
 Woodditton CB8 ....**60** B6
Woodfield Cl NR34 ....**25** E7
Woodfield Dr IP14 ...**124** E5
Woodfield La
 Stowmarket IP14 ......**124** D4
 Stutton IP9 ....**105** C5
Woodfields IP21 ....**39** A4
Woodgates Rd CO7 ..**151** D7
Woodhall Bsns Pk
 CO10 ....**148** D8
Woodhall Cl CO10 ....**148** C7
Woodhall Com Prim Sch **3**
 CO10 ....**148** D8
Woodhall Rd CO10 ...**148** C7
Woodhouse La IP10 ..**141** C2
Woodhouse Sq IP4 ...**155** C2
Woodland Ave NR34 ..**111** F4
Woodland Cl
 Onehouse IP14 ....**66** C6
 Risby IP28 ....**47** D5
 Thurston IP31 ....**49** E3
Woodland Dr
 Bungay NR35 ....**110** B1
 Ellingham NR35 ....**8** E7
Woodland Pl 7 IP31 ...**49** A6

Woodlands
 1 Chelmondiston IP9 ...**106** C8
 Hadleigh IP7 ....**149** B7
 35 Harleston IP20 ......**22** D6
 Lakenheath IP27 ......**109** D8
 Leiston IP16 ....**129** C4
Woodlands Ave 4
 NR33 ....**114** C3
Woodlands Bsns Pk
 IP30 ....**49** B3
Woodlands Dr IP24 ....**16** C7
Woodlands Rd
 Holbrook IP9 ....**105** E8
 Raydon IP7 ....**94** F2
 Rushbrooke with Rougham
  IP30 ....**49** B3
Woodlands Rise IP27 ..**14** D8
Woodlands The NR32 .**113** B8
Woodlands Way
 Bramford IP8 ....**134** C4
 Mildenhall IP28 ....**116** F5
Woodlane Rd IP23 .....**38** C1
Woodlark Cl IP2 ......**138** E1
Woodlark Dr 4 IP14 ..**124** F7
Woodley Com Sch
 IP14 ....**124** B7
Woodleys Yd IP18 ....**119** D5
Woodpecker Ave 2
 NR33 ....**114** D5
Woodpecker Cl 16 IP14 .**67** A5
Woodpecker Rd IP2 ..**138** D3
Woodrush Rd IP3 .....**140** E2
Woods Cl
 Ditchingham NR35 .....**110** B7
 Sturmer CB9 ....**133** C3
Woods La IP12 ....**147** B7
Woods Loke E NR32 ..**113** A3
Woods Loke Prim Sch
 NR32 ....**112** F3
Woods Loke W NR32 .**112** F3
Woodside
 Beccles NR34 ....**111** D3
 Brampton with Stoven
  NR34 ....**25** E5
 Martlesham Heath IP5 ...**98** B8
Woodside Bsns Pk
 IP31 ....**32** F2
Woodside Cl
 Bury St Edmunds IP33 ..**123** B1
 Lowestoft NR33 ....**114** C3
Woodspring Cl 12 IP2 .**139** A2
Woodstone Ave IP1 ..**135** C1
Woodthorpe Cl IP7 ...**149** F5
Woodthorpe Rd IP7 ..**149** E5
Woodville Rd IP4 ....**139** F5
Woodward Ave IP14 ...**51** F6

Woodward Cl IP2 .....**138** D5
Woolhall St 2 IP33 ...**154** B2
Woollards Cl IP1 .....**139** A6
Woollards Gdns 3 CO10 .**91** E8
Woolmers Cl IP14 ....**124** D4
Woolner Cl
 7 Claydon IP6 ....**82** A5
 5 Hadleigh IP7 ....**149** E6
Woolnough Cl 6 CB9 ...**88** D3
Woolnough Rd IP12 ..**146** F6
Woolnoughs The 2
 IP5 ....**141** D7
Woolpit & District Musuem★
 IP30 ....**50** D1
Woolpit Prim Sch IP30 .**50** D1
Woolpit Rd IP31 ......**34** C2
Woolverstone Cl IP2 .**138** D1
Worcester Cl 6 IP32 ..**123** E6
Worcester Rd IP3 ....**144** A8
Wordsworth Cl IP17 ..**128** B4
Wordsworth Cres IP1 .**134** E3
Wordsworth Rd
 4 Bury St Edmunds IP32 ..**48** C5
 2 Stowmarket IP14 ....**124** B8
Worell Dr NR34 ......**111** E4
Workhouse Hill
 Boxted CO4 ....**102** F3
 Hartest IP29 ....**77** B8
Workhouse La IP17 ...**57** E2
Workhouse Rd
 Little Horkesley CO6 ..**102** B2
 Thornham Magna IP23 ...**37** A1
Workshop La IP10 ...**145** C5
World's End La IP14 ...**65** F2
World's End Rd IP13 ..**55** B4
Worlingham Mid Sch
 NR34 ....**111** F3
Worlingham Prim Sch
 NR34 ....**9** F5
Worlingham Way
 NR32 ....**113** A4
Worlington Rd
 Barton Mills IP28 ....**30** E3
 Worlington IP28 ......**116** A3
Worlingworth CE Prim Sch
 IP13 ....**54** D7
Worlingworth Rd IP21 .**38** F3
Wortham Ling Nature
 Reserve★ IP22 ....**19** F2
Wortham Pl 1 CB9 ...**132** E6
Wortham Prim Sch
 IP22 ....**36** E7
Worthing Rd NR32 ...**113** D3
Wrabness Local Nature
 Reserve★ IP9 ....**105** E2
Wrabness Rd 1 CO12 .**106** D1

Wrabness Sta CO11 ...**106** A2
Wragg Dr CB8 ....**121** A6
Wratting Rd
 Great Thurlow CB9 .....**74** D5
 Haverhill CB9 ....**132** E7
Wren Ave IP2 ....**138** D3
Wren Cl
 Bury St Edmunds IP32 ...**49** A4
 Mildenhall IP28 ....**116** D4
 1 Stowmarket IP14 ....**67** A5
 13 Thurstow IP31 ....**49** D4
Wrens Pk 2 IP11 ....**153** D7
Wriggle St IP13 ......**70** A7
Wright Cl IP14 ......**124** D3
Wright La IP5 ....**141** D8
Wright Rd IP3 ......**140** C2
Wrights Way
 Leavenheath CO6 .....**102** A7
 Woolpit IP30 ....**50** C1
Wroxham Rd IP3 ....**139** F3
Wyatt Cl IP30 ....**50** F3
Wyatt Way IP24 ......**16** B7
Wyatts La CO10 .....**101** B8
Wyken Rd IP31 ......**34** D3
Wyken Vineyard & Gdns★
 IP31 ....**34** E2
Wykes Bishop St IP3 .**139** E4
Wymering Rd 10 IP18 .**119** D5
Wyncoll's La IP7 ......**94** B2
Wyndham Way CB8 ..**121** A6
Wynterton Cl IP3 ....**140** B1
Wynton Rise IP14 ...**124** E4
Wyvern Rd IP3 ......**140** C1
Wytchwoods The IP14 ..**68** E6
Wyverstone Rd
 Badwell Ash IP31 ....**51** B7
 Wyverstone Green IP14 ..**51** E6

Y

Yale Bsns Pk IP3 .....**144** F8
Yarmouth Pl 3 CB9 ..**132** E6
Yarmouth Rd
 Corton NR32 ....**113** A8
 Ditchingham NR35 ....**110** D7
 Geldeston NR34 ....**9** A7
 Ipswich IP1 ....**139** A6
 Kirby Cane NR35 ....**8** E7
 Lound NR32 ....**2** F7
 Lowestoft NR32 ....**113** B5
 Melton IP12 ....**84** B8
 Ufford IP13 ....**127** B1
 Woodbridge IP12 .....**147** C8
Yarrow Dr NR33 .....**114** C4

Yaxley Hall La IP23 ...**37** C4
Yaxley Rd IP23 ......**37** C3
Yeldham Pl CB9 .....**132** E6
Yeoman Cres IP7 ...**149** E5
Yeoman Rd IP11 ....**152** D3
Yeoman Way IP7 ...**149** E5
Yeoman's Cl NR35 ...**110** C3
Yeomanry Yd IP33 ..**154** A2
Yeovil Rd NR32 ......**113** C2
Yerril Gdn CB9 ......**132** C5
Yew Cl 1 IP27 ....**13** F2
Yew Ct IP2 ....**139** A3
Yew Tree Ct 1 IP33 ..**122** F3
Yew Tree Rise IP13 ..**127** C2
Yewdale NR33 ......**114** D2
Yewlands Gr IP30 ....**65** A4
Yewtree Gr IP5 .....**140** F7
Yewtree Rise IP8 ...**138** C1
York Cl
 Bury St Edmunds IP33 .**122** E5
 1 Mildenhall IP28 .....**30** A8
 Sudbury CO10 ....**148** C7
York Cres 12 Claydon IP6 .**82** B5
 Claydon IP6 ....**134** C8
York Rd
 Bury St Edmunds IP33 .**154** A2
 Felixstowe IP11 ......**153** A4
 Foxhall IP5 ....**98** A7
 Haverhill CB9 ....**132** C5
 Ipswich IP3 ....**140** A4
 Lowestoft NR32 ......**113** C1
 Southwold IP18 ......**119** B5
 Sudbury CO10 ....**148** C6
York Terr IP33 ......**154** A2
Yoxford Gdns★ IP17 ...**57** C8
Yoxford Mews 7 IP12 ..**85** B3
Yoxford Prim Sch IP17 .**57** D8
Yoxford Rd
 Middleton IP17 ....**57** F6
 Sibton IP17 ....**57** A8

Z

Zanetta Ct NR32 ....**113** C1
Zurich Cl 3 NR31 .....**3** C6

Name and Address	Telephone	Page	Grid reference

Addresses

Name and Address	Telephone	Page	Grid reference

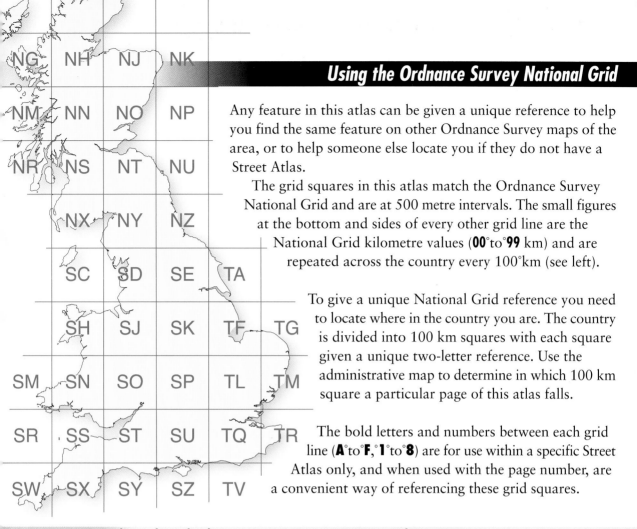

Any feature in this atlas can be given a unique reference to help you find the same feature on other Ordnance Survey maps of the area, or to help someone else locate you if they do not have a Street Atlas.

The grid squares in this atlas match the Ordnance Survey National Grid and are at 500 metre intervals. The small figures at the bottom and sides of every other grid line are the National Grid kilometre values (**00** to **99** km) and are repeated across the country every 100 km (see left).

To give a unique National Grid reference you need to locate where in the country you are. The country is divided into 100 km squares with each square given a unique two-letter reference. Use the administrative map to determine in which 100 km square a particular page of this atlas falls.

The bold letters and numbers between each grid line (**A** to **F**, **1** to **8**) are for use within a specific Street Atlas only, and when used with the page number, are a convenient way of referencing these grid squares.

Example   The railway bridge over DARLEY GREEN RD in grid square B1

Step 1: Identify the two-letter reference, in this example the page is in **SP**

Step 2: Identify the 1 km square in which the railway bridge falls. Use the figures in the southwest corner of this square: Eastings **17**, Northings **74**. This gives a unique reference: **SP 17 74**, accurate to 1 km.

Step 3: To give a more precise reference accurate to 100 m you need to estimate how many tenths along and how many tenths up this 1 km square the feature is (to help with this the 1 km square is divided into four 500 m squares). This makes the bridge about **8** tenths along and about **1** tenth up from the southwest corner.

This gives a unique reference: **SP 178 741**, accurate to 100 m.

Eastings (read from left to right along the bottom) come before Northings (read from bottom to top). If you have trouble remembering say to yourself Along the hall, THEN up the stairs !

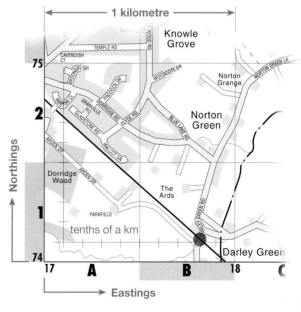

PHILIP'S MAPS

the Gold Standard for drivers

◆ **Philip's street atlases cover every county in England, Wales, Northern Ireland and much of Scotland**

◆ Every named street is shown, including alleys, lanes and walkways

◆ Thousands of additional features marked: stations, public buildings, car parks, places of interest

◆ Route-planning maps to get you close to your destination

◆ Postcodes on the maps and in the index

◆ Widely used by the emergency services, transport companies and local authorities

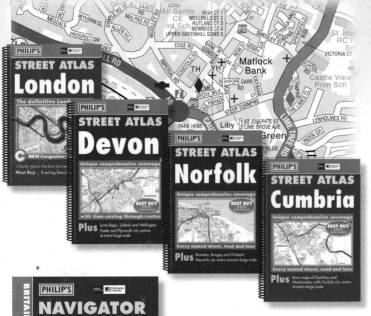

For national mapping, choose
Philip's Navigator Britain
the most detailed road atlas available of England, Wales and Scotland. Hailed by Auto Express as 'the ultimate road atlas', this is the only one-volume atlas to show every road and lane in Britain.

Street atlases currently available

England
Bedfordshire
Berkshire
Birmingham and West Midlands
Bristol and Bath
Buckinghamshire
Cambridgeshire
Cheshire
Cornwall
Cumbria
Derbyshire
Devon
Dorset
County Durham and Teesside
Essex
North Essex
South Essex
Gloucestershire
Hampshire
North Hampshire
South Hampshire
Herefordshire Monmouthshire
Hertfordshire
Isle of Wight
Kent
East Kent
West Kent
Lancashire
Leicestershire and Rutland
Lincolnshire
London
Greater Manchester
Merseyside
Norfolk
Northamptonshire
Northumberland
Nottinghamshire
Oxfordshire
Shropshire
Somerset
Staffordshire
Suffolk
Surrey

East Sussex
West Sussex
Tyne and Wear
Warwickshire
Birmingham and West Midlands
Wiltshire and Swindon
Worcestershire
East Yorkshire Northern Lincolnshire
North Yorkshire
South Yorkshire
West Yorkshire

Wales
Anglesey, Conwy and Gwynedd
Cardiff, Swansea and The Valleys
Carmarthenshire, Pembrokeshire and Swansea
Ceredigion and South Gwynedd
Denbighshire, Flintshire, Wrexham
Herefordshire Monmouthshire
Powys

Scotland
Aberdeenshire
Ayrshire
Dumfries and Galloway
Edinburgh and East Central Scotland
Fife and Tayside
Glasgow and West Central Scotland
Inverness and Moray
Lanarkshire
Scottish Borders

Northern Ireland
County Antrim and County Londonderry
County Armagh and County Down
Belfast
County Tyrone and County Fermanagh

How to order Philip's maps and atlases are available from bookshops, motorway services and petrol stations. You can order direct from the publisher by phoning **01903 828503** or online at **www.philips-maps.co.uk** For bulk orders only, phone 020 7644 6940